The Illustrated Companion to South Indian Classical Music

The Illustrated Companion to South Indian Classical Music

Ludwig Pesch

OXFORD
UNIVERSITY PRESS

OXFORD
UNIVERSITY PRESS

YMCA Library Building, Jai Singh Road, New Delhi 110 001

Oxford University Press is a department of the University of Oxford. It furthers the University's objective of excellence in research, scholarship, and education by publishing worldwide in

Oxford New York

Athens Auckland Bangkok Bogota Buenos Aires Cape Town Chennai Dar es Salaam Delhi Florence Hong Kong Istanbul Karachi Kolkata Kuala Lumpur Madrid Melbourne Mexico City Mumbai Nairobi Paris São Paulo Shanghai Singapore Taipei Tokyo Toronto Warsaw

with associated companies in Berlin Ibadan

Published in India
By Oxford University Press, New Delhi

First published 1999
Fourth Impression 2001

ISBN 019 564382 8

Typeset by Guru Typograph Technology, New Delhi 110 045
Printed in India by Paul's Press, New Delhi 110 020
Published by Manzar Khan, Oxford University Press
YMCA Library Building, Jai Singh Road, New Delhi 110 001

Dedicated to the memory of my Guru

Venugāna Siromaṇi

Sri H. Rāmachandra Shāstry (1906–92)

Is there any bliss greater than this—
To deem it sufficient to dance, to sing divine music,
To pray for His presence and to be in
communion with Him in mind—

And to become one with Him—
And to realize at the time of worship and meditation
That He is the whole universe
And this is admitted by all the good souls.

From a song by Tyāgarāja—Intakanna yānanda mēmi,
O Rāma (rāga Bilahari, rūpaka tāla)

(Translation by C. Rāmānujāchari,
The Spiritual Heritage of Tyāgarāja)

Contents

Acknowledgements

The author wishes to express his gratitude for all the assistance, advice, criticism, and encouragement graciously extended by many, including his family and personal friends.

Without the help of the following persons and institutions, this book could not have been completed in its present shape:

Anandhi Ramachandran, K.P. Anil Kumar, K. Chandra, T.N. Chitra, Dr S.A.K. Durga, Max Mueller Bhavan (Goethe-Institute, Chennai), Mrinalini Nair, Dr Feridun Rahimi-Laridjani, N. Rajagopalan, S. Rajam, S. Rajaram (Director, Kalākshētra Foundation), Rajeswari Padmanabhan, T.K. Ramakrishnan, Pakala Ramdas, Sampradāya Centre (Chennai), S. Sarada, L. Saravanan, T. Sashidhar, P. Seralathan, S. Seshadri, Dr Sylvia Stark, Dr K.S. Subramanian (Bṛhaddhvani Centre, Chennai), V. Swaminathan, and Vidya Shankar.

Professor S.A. Srinivasan (Hamburg University) and Dr Pia Srinivasan (Reinbek).

Anuradha Roy and Atanu Raychaudhuri, Oxford University Press, and Ranjini Rajagopal (New Delhi).

Mieke Beumer (University Library, Amsterdam); Annemette Karpen (Copenhagen).

All sections pertaining to tāla, rhythm, and percussion

T.R. Sundaresan, Kalākshētra College of Fine Arts (Chennai)

Art work and photo credits

S. Rajam: Modern portraits of Karnatic composers
V.C. Arun: Illustrations based on photos and traditional iconography
Photographs and technical illustrations by the author

List of Figures, Plates, Tables and Staves

Figures

Plates (between pages 206 and 207)

Tables

Staves

Guide to Pronunciation and Transliteration

The Anglicized expression 'Karnatic' or 'Carnatic' music signifies 'South Indian classical music' (Sanskrit *Karnāṭaka saṅgīta*, Tamil சங்கீதம், *saṅgīdam*). Both spellings are widely used, but the first variant has been given preference for the sake of consistency. In transliterations, the letter 'c' is thus reserved for the unaspirated consonant, e.g. Cakravāka, *Cōla*, and the letter combination 'ch' for the aspirated consonant 'ch' e.g. Chāyānāṭa.

To enable non-Indian readers to pronounce the names of musicians correctly, diacritics have often been added. Because the names of living persons should remain recognizable even if these diacritics are deleted, some exceptions have been made which reflect the apparent preferences of the persons concerned, e.g. Shankar, Śaṅkar. The names of places that are prefixed to personal names have similarly been diacriticized while others reflect contemporary or official usage, e.g. Chidambaram.

Titles of works, technical terms and personal names are sometimes split if this facilitates reading and pronunciation; yet both words remain a single unit from a grammatical point of view, e.g. *Saṅgīta Ratnākara*.

Many Sanskrit words have been assimilated and modified in South Indian languages (e.g. Sanskrit *mātrā* = Tamil மாத்திரை, *mättirai*, 'unit of time, small measure'; Sanskrit *vīṇā* = Tamil வீணை, *vīṇai*, lute). The instrument widely known as *nāgasvaram* is also being referred to as *nādasvaram* (நாதஸ்வரம்) in Tamil.

To facilitate pronunciation, diacritics for many words of Sanskrit origin are adapted to reflect actual usage in South India (e.g. தேவதாசி, *dēvadāsi*, formerly a 'female dancer attached to a temple'). Many Sanskrit words that end on a long vowel, e.g. 'ī' are similarly rendered with a short final vowel appropriate to Dravidian languages, e.g. rāga Nāgānandini.

A popular form of Tamil–English transliteration, namely the insertion of '-h' in dental 'd' and 't' (i.e. 'th' and 'dh'), is *not* being followed here except for some personal names, e.g. Dhandapani, Muraḷīdharaṉ.

The pan-Indian variants of those words that end on '-m' in Tamil and Malayālam are generally retained wherever this is conducive to comprehension and easy reading: *rāga* (Tamil ராகம், *rāgam*), *tāla* (Tamil தாளம், *tāḷam*), and *svara* (Tamil ஸ்வரம், *svaram*). While in Kannaḍa (Canarese), the original Sanskrit terms are being preferred, the same words would end on '-mu' in Telugu, another important Dravidian language (i.e. *rāgamu*, *tālamu*, *svaramu*).

The names of many rāgas and *mēḷakartā rāgas* do not follow any particular convention regarding endings in the aforementioned languages, e.g. Sāma, Takka, Kharaharapriya; but Hindōḷam, Supradīpam, Dhīraśaṅkarābharaṇam, etc.

For the benefit of most readers, those words that contain the Tamil characters for 'k' (க்), 'c' (ச்), 'ṭ' (ட்), 't' (த்), and 'p' (ப்) are transliterated in accordance with their actual pronunciation. This means, depending on its position in a word or expression, the Tamil character 'k' (க்) is transliterated and pronounced either as 'k' (e.g. கொலு, *kolu*) or 'g' (ராகம், *rāgam*); on similar lines, the Tamil character 'c' (ச்) is either transliterated as 'c' (e.g. சோழன், 'a *Cōla* king') or 's' (e.g. சங்கீதம், *saṅgīdam* = *saṅgītam*); 'ṭ' (ட்) as 'ṭ' or 'ḍ' (e.g. கடம், *kaḍam* = *ghaṭam*); 't' (த்) as 't' (e.g. தம்பூரா, *tambūrā*) or 'd' (e.g. நாதஸ்வரம் , *nādasvaram* = *nāgasvaram*); and 'p' (ப்) as 'p' (e.g. பிடில், *piḍil* = fiddle, violin) or 'b' (e.g. தம்பூரா, *tambūrā*).

The word 'Tamiḻ' (தமிழ்) is rendered without diacritics throughout the book.

Table 1: Guide to pronunciation

a	*but*	**ṅ**	lo*ng*
ā	f*a*ther	**ñ**	*new*
ai	k*i*te	**ṇ**	(nasal 'n' with the tip of the tongue turned far back)
au	c*ow*	**ṉ**	ear*n*
bh	clu*bh*ouse	**o**	t*o*p; short in Tamil and Telugu; always long in Sanskrit (= 'ō'; e.g. *yoga*)
c	*ch*ain	**ō**	n*o*ble (the plain long 'o' in Tamil and Telugu)
ch	bea*ch-h*oliday	**ph**	u*ph*ill
ḍ	(cerebral 'd'; i.e. dull and deep 'd' with the tongue kept back)	**ṛ**	[Sanskrit] *r*ing (rolled 'r'; e.g. 'Kṛṣna')
ḍh	(ḍ + h; aspirated 'ḍ')	**ṟ**	[Tamil] single like 'r' in 'd*r*aw' when doubled ('rr'), like '*tr*' in true or '*dr*' in *dr*aw
d	*d*isc	**s**	*s*it
dh	win*d-h*ose	**ṣ**	par*ti*al
e	m*e*dal; short in Tamil and Telugu; always long in Sanskrit (= 'ē'; e.g. *Veda*)	**ś**	*sh*e
ē	r*eig*n (the plain long 'e' in Tamil and Telugu)	**ṭ**	(cerebral 't'; i.e. dull and deep 't' with the tongue kept back)
g	le*g*	**ṭh**	(ṭ + h; aspirated 'ṭ')
gh	do*g-h*ouse	**t**	*t*ill
i	s*i*ng	**th**	an*th*ill
ī	fl*ee*t	**u**	p*u*t
j	*j*ump	**ū**	m*oo*d
jh	he*dgeh*og	**v**	*v*ast
kh	in*kh*orn	**y**	*y*oung
ḷ	wor*l*d		
ḻ	[Tamil] as American 'r' (e.g. squi*rr*el); common Indian transliteration: 'zh' (e.g. 'yazh' = *yāḻ*)		

Table 2: Transliteration of Tamil and Grantha characters

Vowels and diphthongs	அ	ஆ	இ	ஈ	உ	ஊ	எ	ஏ	ஐ	ஒ	ஓ	ஔ
Transliteration	a	ā	i	ī	u	ū	e	ē	ai	o	ō	au
Consonants	க்	ங்	ச்	ஞ்	ட்	ண்	த்	ந்	ப்	ம்	ய்	ர்
Transliteration	k, g	ṅ	c, s	ñ	ṭ, ḍ	ṇ	t, d	n	p, b	m	y	r
Consonants	ல்	வ்	ழ்	ள்	ற்	ன்						
Transliteration	l	v	ḻ	ḷ	ṟ	ṉ						
Grantha characters	ஸ்	ஜ்	ஶ்	ஹ்	ஷ்	க்ஷ்	ஸ்ரீ					
Transliteration	s	j	ś	h	ṣ	kṣ	Śrī					

1

Conventions

Note: For conventions pertaining to spelling and transliteration, see Guide to Pronunciation.

The basic pitch (ṣaḍja, sa)

A musician is free to choose a basic note (*ādhāra ṣaḍja*) corresponding to the 'tonic' of Western music. This note should correspond to the pitch which suits the natural range of his or her voice or melody instrument.

All the instruments used in a performance are tuned to a common basic note. To accompany a male voice or a long bass flute, low-pitched types of drone (*tambūrā*) and drum (*mṛdaṅgam*) are used. Conversely, to accompany a female voice or treble flute, high-pitched types of *tambūrā* and *mṛdaṅgam* are chosen.

Transposition of music examples rendered in staff notation

All music examples rendered in staff notation can be transposed from key signature 'C' to any convenient key signature (e.g. 'G'). However, none of the rāgas performed in classical South Indian music corresponds to the Western *scale of equal*

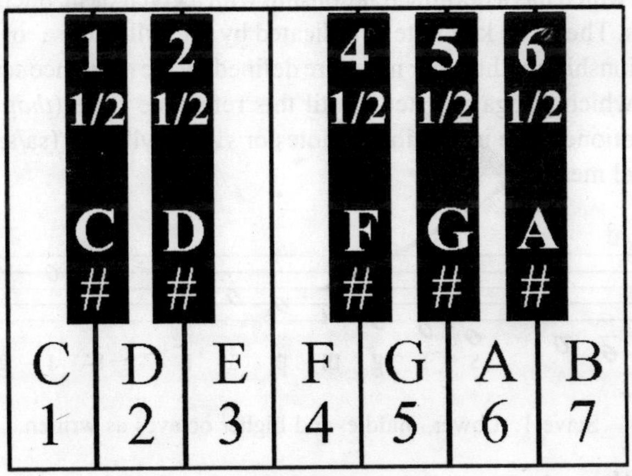

Fig. 1: Modern reference pitch for any type of voice or instrument ('C' = 1 '*śruti*'; 'C' sharp = '1 1/2 *śruti*', etc.).

temperament. In practice, rāga Śaṅkarābharaṇam sounds quite different from the major scale while it appears to be similar when rendered in staff notation. The *tempered scale* of Western music contains no pure interval other than the octave. Conversely, the *sa-pa* (*ṣaḍja-pañcama*) interval found in most Karnatic rāgas denotes a natural or pure fifth interval. Similarly, the interval pairs *ri-dha* (*ṛṣabha-dhaivata*) and *dha-ga* (*dhaivata-gāndhāra*), for instance in rāga Mōhanam, denote natural or pure fifth intervals in acoustical terms. In the absence of musical chords, the simultaneous sounding of three or more notes which is characteristic of classical European music, the concept of *equal temperament* has no meaning and even obstructs the perception of harmonious notes (*saṁvādin*) and dissonant notes (*vivādin*) applicable in Karnatic music. Although a piano, harmonium or synthesizer can convey an approximate idea of the interval patterns underlying a scale or rāga, the instruments cannot do justice to the more differentiated intervals on which all classical Indian music is based.

Pitch

In modern times, South Indian musicians and instrument makers have adopted Western 'middle C' with a frequency of 261.6 vibrations per second as reference pitch (*ādhāra ṣaḍja*) (Fig. 1). With the help of a tuning pipe, a soloist can accurately communicate the basic pitch and tonal range required for accompaniment.

In popular usage, 'one *śruti*' refers to a basic note corresponding to Western 'C' on a harmonium keyboard irrespective of the octave it belongs to. In the same manner, 'two *śruti*' refers to 'D', and 'seven *śruti*' to 'B natural'. The intermediary black keys on the keyboard of a harmonium are reckoned as 'half *śruti*'. Thus '1$^1/_2$ *śruti*' denotes a pitch located a semitone above 'C' or 'C sharp'; '6$^1/_2$ *śruti*' to 'A sharp' (= 'B flat') and so forth. This usage of the term *śruti* has, however, nothing in common with the concept of microtone or 22 subdivisions of the octaves.

In the context of Indian music, therefore, the indication of a musical note (*svara*) refers to a 'relative pitch'. In practice, each scale degree is based on a particular interval which has a definite relationship with a given basic pitch and its neighbouring notes. The basic key note is indicated by the syllable 'sa' or letter 's'. The interval-relationships of the other notes are defined by the reference scale (*mēḷakartā rāga*) under which a rāga is listed. Until this reference scale (*ṭhāṭ* in Hindustānī music) is mentioned, the indication of notes or *svara* syllables (sa/s, ri/r, ga/g . . .) has no musical meaning.

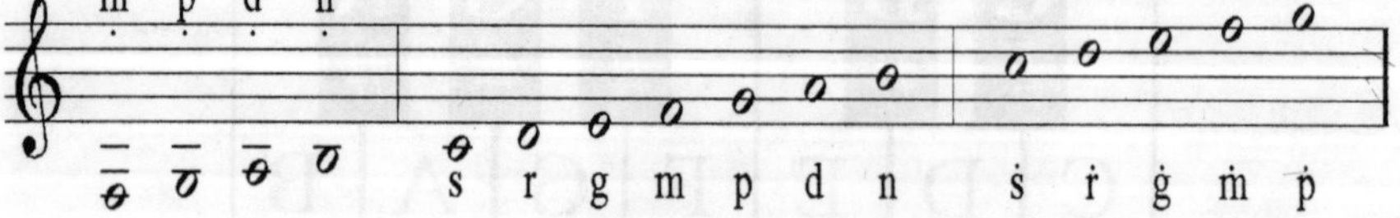

Stave 1: Lower, middle, and higher octaves as written.

Indicating the octave

In order to indicate that a note belongs to the lower octave (*mandra sthāyī*), a dot is placed under a letter (s for *ṣaḍja*, r for *ṛṣabha*, etc.). Conversely, a dot above a letter indicates that a note belongs to the higher octave (*tāra sthāyī*). In the absence of a dot, a note belongs to the middle octave (*madhya sthāyī*). It is not useful to write out each note as '*ṣaḍja*', '*ṛṣabha*', etc. nor is the writing of syllables, such as 'sa', 'ri', etc. useful for the sketching of a melody.

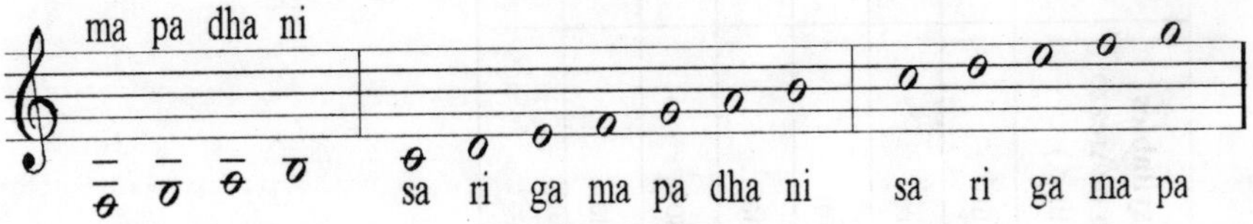

Stave 2: Lower, middle, and higher octaves as sung.

Staff notation of scale and rāga patterns

Irrespective of actual pitch or interval, the notes of a rāga are articulated with the help of syllables (*sa, ri, ga, ma, pa, dha*, and *ni*). All variants of the 2nd scale degree (*ṛṣabha*) are sung as '*ri*': minor 2nd (*śuddha ṛṣabha*), major 2nd (*catuḥśruti ri*), augmented 2nd (*ṣaṭśruti ṛṣabha*). The 3rd, 4th, 6th, and 7th tonal steps are similarly variable but always sung as '*ga*', '*ma*', '*dha*' and '*ni*' respectively.

Range

The melodic range required for singing or playing South Indian music is slightly more than two octaves. A much wider tonal range is available to the *vīṇā, gōṭṭuvādyam* (*citravīṇā*) and the violin. Some flautists use two complementary flutes, one for the normal vocal range, and a second one to cover the lower octave more effectively.

This range is divided into three regions (*sthāyī*), a full middle octave (*madhyama sthāyī*), half an upper octave including the high 5th (*tāra sthāyī pañcama*), and a lower octave including the lower 4th (*mandra sthāyī madhyama*).

Although there is no absolute pitch in Indian music, most male vocalists today prefer Western 'C' as their basic note from which they are expected to reach another half an octave below and one and a half octaves above.

Before the introduction of amplification a few decades ago, 'F' or 'G' (Tamil *heccu*) was regarded as the ideal basic pitch for a cultured male voice because a high-pitched voice reaches a large audience more effortlessly than a lower voice (Tamil *taggu*). The same applies to wind instruments. In this century, the basic pitch of bamboo flutes and oboes (*nāgasvaram*) has been lowered considerably which means that the dimensions of these instruments (length and diameter) have increased correspondingly.

Scale division of the octave

For practising musicians the division of the octave (*sthāyī*) into seven main notes (*saptasvara*) is the fundamental order from which all other divisions are derivable (Table 3).

Table 3: The seven notes within an octave

The seven notes short solfa names as sung (*sargam*)	**Written** (in any script)	**Full technical names** (*svara*)	**Tonic SOL-FA** Western syllables (as sung today)	**Latin syllables** of Guido d'Arezzo (11th c.)	**Steps**
sa	s	*ṣaḍja*	do	ut	1st (tonic)
ri	r	*ṛṣabha*	re	re	2nd
ga	g	*gāndhāra*	mi	mi	3rd
ma	m	*madhyama*	fa	fa	4th
pa	p	*pañcama*	so	sol	5th
dha	d	*dhaivata*	la	la	6th
ni	n	*niṣāda*	ti	–	7th

The approximate intervals of what is known as a diatonic scale (*mēḷakartā rāga*) were arrived at by way of dividing the octave into twelve half-tone steps (*svarasthāna*). While the tonic and the fifth have been kept unchangeable (*avikṛta*) or devoid of variants, all the remaining five notes were made variable (*vikṛta*) in the new system of scales used since the seventeenth century. While the natural fourth has a tritone (sharp or augmented fourth) as its sole variant, the other four tonal steps have a lower or higher variant with regard to their basic note as well as a third variant. This third variant has its equivalent in the concept of enharmonic change of Western music. It means that twelve actual half-tone steps are given sixteen different names out of which four are identical with four others: the *augmented second* equals the *minor third* (4th semitone, 'D sharp' or 'E flat'); and the *diminished seventh* equals the *major sixth* (10th semitone, 'A natural'). The difference between the 'enharmonic' variants lies therefore in the names applicable in a particular context, not in pitch. These names must, of course, correspond to the notes belonging to a chosen rāga. This system is unique to the southern branch of classical Indian music and has yielded the 72 scales (*mēḷakartā rāga*) that have acquired musical respectability in the last two centuries. True to their enharmonic character and as can be seen in Table 4, the 16 notes underlying all these scales can in fact be represented as 12 chromatic half-tone steps. Each among these 16 notes has its own mnemonic syllable distinguishable from all the other 15 notes: different vowels ('a', 'i' and 'u') are attached to them.

Solfa notation (solmization)

For the purpose of singing, seven different syllables (*sargam*) represent the element-ary notes of a rāga. This practice resembles the modern English *Tonic Sol-fa* system used since the nineteenth century. Singing *Tonic Sol-fa* means to use a simple device, namely remembering and pronouncing seven syllabic names for seven tonal steps ('solmization'). We can assume, for the sake of simplicity, that the Western note 'C' stands for the basic note *sa* (*ādhāra ṣaḍja*). Its actual pitch, however, can be freely chosen to match one's voice or any melody instrument. In the context of improvisation, this method is known as *svaram* or *svara kalpana*. As part of a Karnatic composition, the same procedure is called *ciṭṭasvaram* if the song belongs to the *kṛti* or *kīrtana* form; and *ettugaḍa svara* if the song belongs to the *varṇam* form.

For the purpose of simplifying staff notation and making it readable, the rule 'C' = *sa,* 'D' = *ri*, etc. is upheld. The advantage is that a given note set on a particular line or between two lines is instantly recognized as a form of *ri* (*ṛṣabha*), *ga* (*gāndhāra*), etc. Variants (*svarasthāna*) other than 'natural' notes are marked by the symbol '*b*' for a flat note, '*bb*' for a diminished note (double flat), and '#' for a sharp or augmented note.

This inclusion of *enharmonic* intervals is alien to Hindustānī music where only lower (*komal*) and higher (*tīvra*) variants occur. But *enharmonic* intervals are equally important in both Western and South Indian classical music where they fulfil the practical function of widening the scope of tonal relationships.

Table 4: Semitone steps

Semitone step (1–12)	**Interval** from tonic	**Mnemonic svara name** semitone (*svarasthāna*) *[= enharmonic equivalent]	**Svara name** sargam-syllable (as sung)	**Full technical name** (*svarasthāna*)
1	(tonic or first note)	sa	sa	*ṣaḍja*
2	minor 2nd	ra	ri	*śuddha ṛṣabha*
3	major 2nd	ri [= ga]*	ri	*catuḥśruti ṛṣabha*
4	augmented 2nd	ru [= gi]*	ri	*ṣaṭśruti ṛṣabha*
3	diminished 3rd	ga [= ri]*	ga	*śuddha gāndhāra*
4	minor 3rd	gi [= ru]*	ga	*sādhāraṇa gāndhāra*
5	major 3rd	gu	ga	*antara gāndhāra*
6	perfect 4th	ma	ma	*śuddha madhyama*
7	augmented 4th (tritone)	mi	ma	*prati madhyama*
8	perfect 5th	pa	pa	*pañcama*
9	minor 6th	dha	dha	*śuddha dhaivata*
10	major 6th	dhi [= na]*	dha	*catuḥśruti dhaivata*
11	augmented 6th	dhu [= ni]*	dha	*ṣaṭśruti dhaivata*
10	diminished 7th	na [= dhi]*	ni	*śuddha niṣāda*
11	minor 7th	ni [= dhu]*	ni	*kaiśikī niṣāda*
12	major 7th	nu	ni	*kākalī niṣāda*

Scales and rāgas

To remember a melody or composition based on a particular rāga, a traditional musician merely needed to write down the regular occurrence or omission of several notes as an aid to memory. But this is a method which needs to be supplemented by personalized guidance and exposure to a good musical rendition of a rāga. The common way of describing a scale or rāga is to indicate a series of seven notes (*svara*) or approximate intervals (*svarasthāna*) which are derived from twelve semitones. This outline does not yet reveal the finer intonation required to bring out the character of a particular rāga. There is, for that matter, no recognized method of fixing all the intervals used in Karnatic music.

The ascending series of notes (*ārohaṇa*) and its descending counterpart (*avarohaṇa*) form the barest outline associated with every scale and rāga. In addition there is a repertoire of typical phrases (*sañcāra* or *prayoga*) and extraordinary phrases (*viśeṣa sañcāra*) which provide guidance concerning the application of those additional notes (*anyasvara*) and rare notes (*alpa svara*) that are not furnished by the *ārohaṇa-avarohaṇa* series of notes. To keep track of such complexities, many musicians maintain notebooks (*kaṭakam*) or phrase books (*tāna pustaka*).

Staff notation of symmetrical scale patterns

It is customary to define a scale or rāga by giving its ascending (*ārohaṇa*) and descending (*avarohaṇa*) scale pattern. But in those instances where the descending scale pattern follows the same course as the ascending one, in a reversed order like a mirror image, staff notation delineates only the ascending sequence. This saves space and helps the reader to identify such symmetries among less regular examples of rāgas.

Additional notes (anyasvara)

The presence of 'foreign' or 'alien' notes (*anyasvara*) is characteristic of a large group of rāgas (*bhāṣāṅga rāgas*) with regard to their 'parental' or reference scale (*mēḷakartā rāga*). Such notes are often rendered within the regular ascending and descending pattern of a particular rāga (e.g. Bhairavi); otherwise, *anyasvaras* are also conveyed by special phrases (*viśeṣa sañcāra*) to specify the context within which they may occur. Such notes and phrases are printed alongside the regular scale pattern of the *janya rāga* in question (e.g. rāgas Byāg and Khamās).

In a few cases, one or several additional or 'alien' notes (*anyasvara*) are also printed alongside some of the 72 *mēḷakartā rāgas* (e.g. Hanumatōḍi, the 8th *mēḷakartā rāga*). There are comparatively few scales where 'alien' notes have been introduced for the purpose of deriving particular rāgas (*janya rāga*). Additional notes of this kind are confined to specific rāgas and by definition do not belong to the respective scale itself.

Grace notes (anusvara)

In Staves 7 and 27 small note symbols are used to indicate the occurrence of auxiliary or intermediary notes (*anusvara*). These grace notes precede or follow the main note (*svara*). An *anusvara* is either attached to a single note, or it helps to join two notes in a pleasing manner. In Karnatic music, several types of embellishments and grace notes (*gamaka*) are best described as combinations of auxiliary notes.

In traditional syllabic notation, these grace notes are never indicated. The duration of an *anusvara* depends on its immediate context, especially the rāga wherein it occurs, and the tempo (*kāla*) in which a song or rāga exposition (*ālāpana*, *tānam*) is performed. The emphasis of a given phrase (*sañcāra*), and the emotive quality of the underlying lyrics (*sāhitya*) further determine the precise duration allocated to an *anusvara* or a group of *anusvaras*.

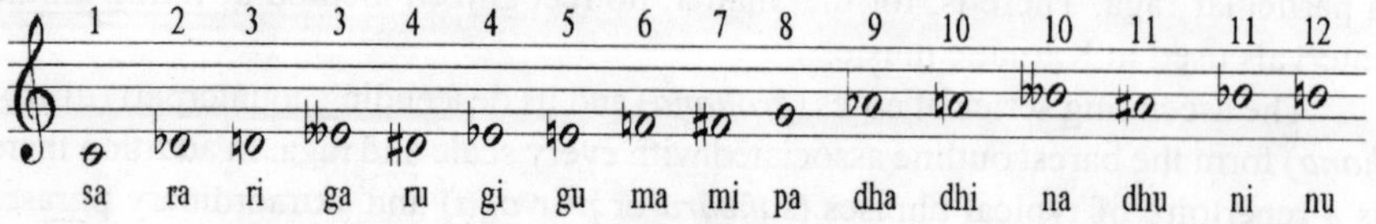

Stave 3: Semitones

Semitones (chromatic progression)

Chromatic progression, a series of two or more half-tone (semitone) intervals, is admissible in theory but mostly avoided in practice. There are indeed a few prominent rāgas which admit some chromatic progressions. Varāḷi offers a typical example of a rāga characterized by five half-tone steps.

The treatment of 'dissonant' scale patterns

In compositions based on older rāgas, the dissonant effect of some notes (*vivādin*) is often tempered. A common method for achieving a mellow rather than sharp-edged impression consists in avoiding one of the adjoining notes concerned either in the ascending or in the descending course of the melody. Another effective means is the introduction of a 'zig-zag' pattern (*vakra prayoga*), for instance in the ascending course of melody (e.g. rāga Varāḷi).

There are several old rāgas which were originally based on *vakra* patterns but re-defined as regular heptatonic scales (*mēlakartā rāga*) by later theorists who filled in those notes that used to be deleted (*varja*) originally. In this manner, the number of scales has grown from about twenty used three centuries ago to 72 used today. The number of rāgas derived from these scales has grown into several hundred. Less than a hundred rāgas, however, have sufficient appeal for elaboration beyond a single song (*ekaika kṛti rāga*).

2

Graceful Dialogues

Fig. 2: The *Tiger Cave*. This ancient concert shell is carved of the living rock (8th c., ascribed to the reign of Narasiṁha Varman II).

The *Pallava* dynasty was deeply involved in all the arts. Mahendravarman Pallava (7th c.) was himself a great musician and poet whose comedies (*prahasana*) still convey a delightful blend of humour, social criticism and artistic sophistication. This platform has room for several persons and possesses excellent acoustic properties. It is therefore unlikely to have served any other purpose than that of a concert shell in an ideal setting for enjoying music and poetry. Its decoration includes life-size elephant heads to its left, perhaps an allusion to the elephant motive recommended by Bharata (2nd c. BC–2nd c. AD) for the decoration of a theatre. The head of a mythical animal (*yāḷi*), a chimerical creature with feline traits, is a decorative design found on the ancient Indian harp (*yāḻ*) as well as its modern successor, the *Sarasvati Vīṇā*. The stylized head of a lion (*siṁha*) is also the symbol of the *Pallava* dynasty.

Music has always played a major role in the social and spiritual life of India. Although there were, and still are, specialized forms and techniques for specific occasions and situations, music has generally been an open platform where a broad range of ideas and concepts could be explored. The association of Indian music with dance, drama, rituals, sacrifice and poetry of every kind is too well known; but an inner circle of musicians, priests and scholars had begun early to investigate the very nature of sound (*nāda*), rhythm (*laya*), and emotion (*bhāva*) in a more systematic manner. Numerous treatises are the outcome of these efforts. Like their counterparts in ancient Europe and China, Indian scholars (particularly those of the *Tantra* school) have always believed in the magic power of music. Some forms of music are shrouded in secrecy, just as the prevalence of unwritten performing conventions (*pāṭhāntara*) can no longer be taken for granted. For these and similar reasons, the terminology and concepts outlined in many ancient and medieval treatises are no more intelligible to modern performers. Indian musicians of the remote past were just as keen on absorbing new ideas as their successors are today.

Archaeology, epigraphy, iconography, literature, musical treatises and even the lyrics of many songs make up a colourful mosaic which conveys an impression of the musical practices of various regions and epochs. Viewed in a larger context it seems evident that the Indian musician, like musicians elsewhere in the world, sought to make his art interesting by way of innovation. Originality has thus been as important as authenticity at most times. Most professional artists did, after all, depend on influential patrons or affluent temples. In the absence of other sources of income, it was in their own interest not only to excel but also to increase the appeal of their art by any available means. The result is a music system which still provides musicians with room to continually update their repertoire without destroying the foundations of their art.

South Indian music has a long history of interaction with the music traditions of other cultures. Before the British colonial period and the gradual decline of the Mughal dynasty, there was the *Renaissance* which engulfed the entire known world with its attending quest for new horizons. It brought Europeans again in direct contact with India although Columbus missed India, his declared target, by 180 degrees. Trade links between South India and the Mediterranean world had been maintained by Arab seafarers ever since antiquity. This was partly due to the fact that, since the time of the Greek expansion, *Hellenistic* civilization had built bridges between different peoples, creeds, languages and cultures. Indeed, all the countries touched by it were involved in an amazing process of international give and take.

Raṅgarāmānuja Ayyaṅgār, a well-known author and musician, proudly states: 'The eclecticism of Tamil culture has given it endurance and vitality. Ethnically, it is among the oldest in the whole world. It has always been quick to profit by outside contacts.' He pictures the early cultural exchange between Europeans (*yavana*, from 'Ionian', i.e. Greek) in the following words: 'Maritime activity linked South India with distant Greece. Greek wine flowed in goblets of gold in the royal household in Tamil Nad. The Makara Yazh came from Greece and joined the others here.' This large harp or *yāḻ* is said to have been used until the tenth century and described as having the shape of a fish-like chimera with the head of an alligator and the body of a dog. At the same time, the author warns against the 'Back to the Yazh slogan',

Fig. 3: The temple at Bēlūr (*Hoysala*, early 12th c.). Dance as a part of temple ceremony has been banned since the early part of the 20th century.

thereby making 'a fetish of the past and not a source of inspiration for incentive and progress'. He dismisses the 'persistent clamour to bring the Yazh back to life and dethrone the *vīṇā*', his favourite instrument, because 'a harp-like Yazh is too poor a vehicle for the high standard of music revealed in the literature of the period, especially Silappadikaram'. Before the *vīṇā* could gradually attain its present perfection, it is believed to have met with formidable resistence: 'In the early centuries of the Christian era, Buddhist priests identified themselves with the masses and strengthened their hold on them by encouraging the use of the Yazh in preference to the Veena. With the decline of Buddhism from the seventh century and the revival of Hinduism and Sanskrit, Matanga's Brihaddesi popularized the old Sanskrit terminology and the fretted Veena. The Yazh lingered for a while and disappeared ultimately.'

Quotations from *History of South Indian (Carnatic) Music*, pp. 48–50.

In the year 1945, literary evidence of an ancient and extensive Indian trade network was corroborated by Sir Mortimer Wheeler's excavations. More recent archaeological finds have added to our insights into this interesting chapter of two great civilizations. Numerous hoards of Roman gold and silver coins, issued by Augustus, Tiberius, and Trajan, were found in the area of modern Andhra Pradesh, Karnataka, Kerala, and Tamil Nadu. The most important foreign settlement so far discovered is the Roman *emporium* at Arikkamēṭṭu village near Pondicherry (from Tamil *puduccēri*, 'new quarter'). This trading post has been identified as the *Poduke* mentioned in the *Periplus*, a Greek seaman's guide written towards the end of the first century AD. Excavations at the Arikkamēṭṭu site yielded fragments of pottery, glass objects, lamps, and wine amphorae belonging to the same period.

Early Greek sources inform us that the *aulos*, their most prominent wind instrument, was of Eastern origin. Double-reed instruments, which belong to the same family as the European oboe, are found in most music cultures of Europe and Asia. Hereditary musicians claim to have used several such instruments (i.e. *nāgasvaram* or *nādasvaram, timiri,* and *kuḻal*) since time immemorial. Although their sound, which is considered to be auspicious, has become an indispensable part of temple and marriage functions as well as popular drama, it remains uncertain where and when double-reed instruments were first introduced in South India. On the other hand, the key role played by the ancestor of the modern *mṛdaṅgam* (*muḻavu*) and various other drums (*kiṇai, paṟai, taṭāri*) is quite well documented by early Tamil literature.

The duty of professional bards (*pāṇaṉ*, 'the singers of the *paṇ* modes') and drummers (*kiṇaiyaṉ*) consisted mainly in entertaining a king in return for gifts, or awakening him with the sounds of the sacred *muracu* drum. The duty of a bard's wife, known as *viṟali* (from *viṟal*, 'victory'), was to accompany his music by her dancing. Such ancient customs remind us of a custom which still prevails in South Indian temples, namely the awakening of the presiding deity with auspicious songs. In addition to such duties, ancient musicians were also expected to contribute to victory in battle, and to protect a wounded hero by singing while holding his sword and shield (*The Poems of Ancient Tamil* by George L. Hart, p. 138).

The long coastline of Kerala, situated in the south-west of India, has been the natural choice for conducting intercontinental trade ever since antiquity. This region possesses an extraordinary array of musical instruments which are played during temple festivals (*utsava*) and amidst breathtaking parades of beautifully caparisoned elephants. These ritual performances of large instrumental ensembles (*pañcavādya*) evoke immensely powerful sounds and rhythms that might well resemble those heard by Alexander's troops in 326 BC.

In the fifth century AD, a part of North-Western India, known as Sind (now in modern Pakistan), was annexed by Persia. Persian records belonging to the pre-Islāmic period of the Sāsānid dynasty (AD 224–*circa* 650) refer to the migration of about 3000 Indian musicians to Iran. They are described as having a dark complexion, and their exotic appearance and manners provided Persian poets with an interesting literary subject. They are therefore likely to have made a profound impact on Persian music. For this reason, Persian court music is believed to be a synthesis of indigenous traditions and elements that were absorbed during several centuries of political and cultural ties with ancient Greece, Western and Central Asia, and India. The introduction of the lute (Sanskrit *vīṇā*, Persian *setār*) in Persian music is traceable to the Sāsānid period.

For centuries, South India maintained contact with Chinese Buddhists, the countries of South-East Asia up to Vietnam, and the Roman Empire. In the absence of detailed records or iconographic evidence, it is difficult to determine the ultimate source of any particular theoretical concept or musical instrument which is still in

Fig. 4: *Pañcavādya*—percussion and wind instruments played during a temple festival in Kerala (seen in the photo: *kuḻal*, a double-reed instrument; *ceṇḍa*, a double-faced drum).

use today. Music and poetry are the 'light baggage' which cannot be stolen from travellers, censored by authorities, or levied at every border.

It is not surprising, therefore, to find some striking resemblances between a contemporary description of courtly music (Minnesang), prevalent in medieval Europe, and some practices which have not merely survived in South Indian classical music, but have further evolved into the improvisational techniques (*manodharma saṅgīta*), compositional forms (*kalpita saṅgīta*), ornamentation (*gamaka*), phrases (*prayoga*) of a *rāga ālāpana*, and the beginning (*graha*) and ending notes (*nyāsa*) of these phrases. Similarly, the modern concert format (*paddhati*)—an opening *tāṉa-varṇam*, some small *kṛtis*, *ālāpana*, *tāṉam*, a major *kṛti*, *pallavi, niraval*, *svara kalpana*, some 'lighter' devotional pieces, and love songs—may not have appeared 'alien' to a skilled musician traversing Europe some eight centuries ago. On the contrary, it would have provided the basis for creative exchanges similar to those taking place as part of today's 'World Music' movement.

Gottfried's *Tristan* contains several scenes in which Minnesang is performed, and by combining these scenes we can obtain a picture of a typical performance. First the performer had to 'warm up' . . . He played some preliminary snatches of melody . . . Then he played a few more preliminary pieces . . . and only then did he play the song he intended to perform . . .

His fingers were very nimble as he played . . . [*walgende*] 'rolling, rotating, moving around' and also 'swarming, teeming.' . . . At the appropriate place the minstrel began to sing . . .

Beginnings and endings of musical phrases were particularly important and had to be managed well . . . And in general, a good musician produces the notes correctly and is able to understand the song and interpret it with fingers and voice . . .

We can approach the true understanding of these songs only through performance. They constituted a living tradition for generations of performers before they were written down and their form was fixed for posterity, but our modern reverence for the written text leads us to overloook the importance of performance.

Quoted from *The Music of Early Minnesang* by James V. McMahon, pp. 71–3.

Long before art objects and wares were buried or submerged for later archaeologists to unearth, ideas were traded for very practical reasons. Knowledge, information, social skills, poetic and artistic sense were always in high demand because they opened the doors to a better life wherever a traveller went. The strain and anxiety suffered during long journeys, the pain due to separation from beloved ones and the sheer boredom of long nights and winters in far-off places could solely be overcome by way of sharpening one's wits. Along the trade and military routes, human beings were dependent on one another. Finely tuned sensibilities and attention to detail were prerequisites for their safety and the success of their missions. Already in antiquity, music was regarded as the key to acquiring these qualities. This explains why in India and Europe alike music was held in high esteem by the elite and practised by all classes with such unrelenting zeal.

When native and foreign traders, sailors, missionaries and adventurers found their way in and out of India, Indian artists and craftsmen knew how to harness every source of inspiration. They did this with great felicity and ingenuity. For this reason it is often impossible to identify the sources of their inspiration. Each part of the subcontinent has a cultural identity of its own. In fact the cultural diversity among the peoples of India has always been such that the grade of distinctiveness from European culture during the colonial period almost pales into insignificance.

The Āḻvār and Nāyanmār saints of the Tamil-speaking South laid the foundations for poetical mysticism (*bhakti*). This joyful form of devotion took the form of total surrender to a universal, compassionate, indescribable but approachable Being. Soon all of India came under the influence of the *bhakti* movement.

From the twelfth century, the *Gītagovinda* of Jayadeva, had emerged as the most popular work of Sanskrit poetry. From Bengal and Orissa, the fame of the *Gītagovinda* rapidly spread throughout the country and reached a wider public through the media of music, dance, and miniature painting. Countless works, written in various Indian languages, were inspired by it.

Throughout the middle ages, peoples of Arabic and Central Asian origin continued to invade India. They often tried, although hampered by internal strife and therefore with varying success, to place their stamp on most parts of India. Among them there was a versatile and celebrated *Sūfi*, Amir Khusro (Khusrau, *circa* 1253–1325). Being a scholar, poet, composer and a musician in his own right, he warmly responded to the music he encountered in India and asserted that he was under its spell although he was rooted in the Turkish culture of Central Asia. He blended

Persian and Indian classical music of his time, and he is even credited with several innovations that are now considered to be an integral part of the music of northern India (Hindustānī music).

Life in the South of the Indian subcontinent was generally less affected by the expansion of Islāmic culture until Malik Kafur raided Śrīraṅgam around AD 1327. But the ensuing shifts of strategic realities in many parts of India contributed to the spread of reform movements that sought to renew the cultural and social foundations of Hinduism. Ancient traditions were either revived, re-invented or often complemented by new practices. 'In Tāyumāṉavar, an eighteenth-century poet, the three main tendencies—philosophical, mystical and eclectic—confluence. Though the origins of the mystic poetry could be traced to the lives of the Hindu saints, its flowering might have taken place under the influence of Sufism, the Islamic mysticism. Kuṇaṅkuṭi Mastāṉ was a famous Sufi. Several poems of these two look almost alike. Tāyumāṉavar's poems spring from his mystic experience, kindled by philosophical study and intense bhakti' (p. 85, vol. I, *Encyclopedia of Tamil Literature*).

Idries Shah, the renowned writer on *Sūfism*, even believes that the *Sūfi* teachers 'were responsible in great measure for the establishing of what became known as great Hindu schools of mysticism'. His understanding of the origins of the *Vedānta* system is that of a revival based upon the ancient Hindu scriptures interpreted over a thousand years after their composition by Śaṅkara (788–820) which 'covers the ground introduced by Ghazali, Ibn El-Arabi and Rumi, following the Sufi ancients'. To support his conviction, he quotes a passage from the *Cultural History of India* by Dr Tara Chand stating that 'certain other characteristics of South Indian thought from the ninth century onward, however, strongly point to Islamic influence. There is the increasing emphasis on monotheism, emotional worship, self-surrender (parpatti) and adoration of the teacher (guru bhakti) and, in addition to them, laxity in the rigors of the caste system and indifference to mere ritual . . . absorption in God, through devotion to a teacher . . . The Sufi conception of the deified teacher was incorporated into medieval Hinduism.' Yet Idries Shah emphasizes that the significant points listed by Dr Chand are, 'in their grouping and emphasis, Sufic rather than directly Islamic in the usual sense . . . as understood by the Moslem clergy.'

Quotations from *The Sufis* by Idries Shah, p. 356.

The profound changes that took place in the realm of Indian music were symptoms of far-reaching political developments. The present concept of *rāga* evolved at a time when the fretted lute (*vīṇā*) displaced the older harps (*yāḻ*). The drone was initially a small, single-stringed instrument (*ektār*), consisting of a gut or wire tied to a bamboo stick and attached to a resonator made of a hollow gourd. Under the influence of West Asian lutes, it was refined and became the wonderful instrument which is today known as the *tambūrā*. Thus equipped with better tools, musicians again acted as popular communicators of ideas and values.

South Indian culture and spirituality were re-invigorated by the mystic movement whose members were known as *Haridāsa* ('God's servant'). It left a permanent stamp on Karnatic music because music was viewed as a means of communicating with the Divine, and was therefore taught and practised in a systematic manner. The Haridāsa movement sought to liberate the individual by way of devotion to Kṛṣṇa or Rāma, both described as incarnations of Viṣṇu. Saintly preacher-musicians (*bhāgavatar*), recognizable from afar by their characteristic attire, further equipped themselves with castanets (*cipla*), a pair of small cymbals (*jālrā*), and small bells attached to their feet, and moved from place to place, delighting their audiences with entertaining discourses (*kālakṣepam*) on God (*Hari*). The art of storytelling was developed and practised by them in a dramatic form known as *harikathā kālakṣepam*, which requires a good knowledge of popular religious lore (*Purāṇa*), the epics (*Rāmāyaṇa, Mahābhārata*), and a wide musical repertoire. It is performed by way of singing and dancing, sometimes accompanied by percussionists and other singers and instrumentalists. As a source of education and entertainment, this art is still held in high esteem in parts of rural Karṇāṭaka. Unlike the members of some earlier sects or schools of philosophy, the Haridāsas experience God as a loving Being. Believed to be directly involved with mankind, God is seen as someone who is always ready to communicate with every human being who is prepared to make a beginning.

Lofty philosophy and abstract ethical teachings were replaced by emotional involvement and the ecstasy of a personal rapport with divine incarnations of righteousness, grace, and compassion. Purandara Dāsa and other leaders of this movement refined, propagated and employed the medium of music as a quicker means to spread these tenets and to cut across all social barriers. This personalized form of religion sought to liberate the individual from dependence on expensive sacrifice, fear, superstition, and reliance on obscure magical practices. The *bhakti* movement rapidly spread across many regions of India. Due to its diversification and adaptation to different cultural environments, it cannot be reduced to a single theological doctrine. Through its interaction with the *Sūfi* movement, it reached the Middle East, Central Asia and even Europe.

Khwaja Salahudin of Bokhara is quoted by Idries Shah as stating: 'All religious presentations are varieties of one truth, more or less distorted. This truth manifests itself in various peoples, who become jealous of it, not realizing that its manifestation accords with their needs. It cannot be passed on in the same form because of the difference in the minds of different communities. It cannot be reinterpreted because it must grow afresh. It is presented afresh only by those who can actually experience it in every form, religious and otherwise, of man.'

Quotations from *The Way of the Sufi* by Idries Shah, p. 264.

Subrahmaṇya Bhārati, popularly known as Bhāratiyar (1882–1921), contributed to the liberation struggle which ultimately led to independence from colonial rule in 1947. His poem Viḍutalai ('Freedom') challenges every form of oppression, whether imposed from outside or from within:

> There shall be none of low degree,
> And none shall be oppressed:

Born in India, all are of noble birth.
In man and woman alike,
No more of subordination.

Quoted from 'Music as a Mode of Transcendence' by G.N.S. Raghavan, p. 35, *Indian Horizons* (vol. XXXIV N. 3–4, 1985).

Bhāratiyar's patriotic songs were preceded by those of Bankim Chandra Chatterjī (1838–94) who composed the song *Vande Mātaram* which almost became India's national anthem. Their soul-stirring lyrics, composed with musical sense, were combined and focused to awaken their compatriots. With the experience of countless centuries behind them, they created many songs that served as an effective tool for a type of communication which could neither be suppressed nor appropriated by anybody.

The present interaction between Karnatic musicians and fellow musicians from all over the world has gained momentum in the context of World Music, a kind of movement which defies definition. Its protagonists take advantage of modern mass media and fast travel. Some governments, local administrations and organizations have adopted policies, intended to foster 'cultural diversity', from which Indian music stands to gain. The Festivals of India, initiated by the Government of India in the 1980s, left a profound impact among sophisticated audiences abroad from which many Indian performing artists continue to benefit.

The unprecedented cultural exchanges of recent decades have, superficially seen, affected Karnatic music. A perusal of the history of Indian music will reveal, however, that there is nothing intrinsically novel or problematic about the adoption of a foreign instrument. Accomplished Indian musicians who handle unconventional instruments such as the saxophone (Kadri Gōpālnāth), the electric mandolin (U. Śrīnivās), and the occasional electronic keyboard have a *tradition of innovation* behind them which favours eclecticism.

The introduction of the European violin is the most spectacular success story which dispels any doubt about the integrity of most Karnatic musicians. Its widespread use rests solely on its perfection as an instrument. Musicians from different cultures have adapted this instrument without having to compromise in terms of stylistic or aesthetic integrity.

Several royal patrons proudly imported European instruments to adorn their palaces. They often enlisted the services of music teachers or even players to put these instruments to good use. Many regional potentates maintained music ensembles; some even had small orchestras and marching bands of European origin for which local talent was recruited. Most of these musicians lost their livelihood when India became independent. But in all cities and many towns we still find colourful brass bands that add a festive atmosphere to marriage processions and other spectacular events.

There are examples of great musicians who knew how to put their experience in a hybrid musical sphere to good use. Palace musicians in Mysore drew inspiration from the sounds of the piano. Their musicianship transformed this experience in a manner which is so characteristic of the charming Mysore style of *vīṇa* playing, if

Fig. 5: A Karnatic ensemble. H. Ramachandra Shastry (the author's *guru*) playing the bamboo flute accompanied by a violin. The violin has for nearly two centuries played an important role in South Indian music for melodic accompaniment as well as solo performance. The other instruments are a long-necked lute (*tambūrā*), the Jew's harp (*mōrsiṅg*), a double-faced drum (*mṛdaṅgam*), and a tambourine (*kañjīrā*).
Photo: from the family album of R. Vaidyanathan, Madras (1937).

not of Karnatic music as a whole. On similar lines, Dwāram Veṅkaṭasvāmi Naidu was a great Karnatic violinist from Andhra Pradesh who taught and influenced other musicians. He played on an excellent violin from the former palace ensemble and remained an ardent admirer of Western music and a collector of classical Western violin records throughout his life.

The portable harmonium has a small keyboard arranged like that of a piano. After being introduced by missionaries, it gained popularity among Hindustānī musicians. In North India, the harmonium is still widely used for the melodic accompaniment of singers. In spite of efforts to brand it as a symbol of all that is bad about foreign culture and unsuitable for refined Indian tastes, it has been popular with musicians and audiences all over India. Subrahmaṇya Bhārati is known to have opposed the use of the harmonium, presumably because for him it symbolized the very insensitivity of colonial rule which he sought to counter through his patriotic songs and literary work. For some time it was even banned from national broadcasting studios.

In South Indian music, the harmonium also enjoyed some temporary popularity in the early decades of this century. Because it cannot produce all the embellishments (*gamaka*), an important element in South Indian music, it has since disappeared from classical concerts. In view of the high standard and popularity of the violin for accompaniment and solo performances, nobody seems to have any regrets. In rural Tamil drama (*kūṭṭu*), the harmonium continues to be an important instrument, and it is played along with a smaller, high-pitched variant of the *nāgasvaram*, also known as the *mukhavīṇā*.

The *jalataraṅgam* is a rare instrument consisting of an array of finely tuned water-bowls. It may have been introduced from China either directly or via North India. There were contacts between China and South India in or before the period of the *Pallava* dynasty (*circa* 7th c.). In the past the *jalataraṅgam* had outstanding exponents like Āvuḍaiyārkōvil Harihara Bhāgavatar and Aṉayampaṭṭi S. Daṇḍapāṇi, but it never played a major role in classical South Indian music. In spite of some limitations, especially the lack of melodic continuity, far from having an adverse effect, it has enriched the experience of music with its charming sounds and appearance. Many music lovers would surely welcome its return at the hands of young musicians capable of treating it with skill, feeling, and taste.

Leading musicians have experimented with hybrid forms and styles for several centuries. Muttusvāmi Dīkṣitar studied at Benares (Vārāṇasī) and incorporated some elements of Hindustānī music into his compositions. Tyāgarāja often employed a peculiar type of ādi tāla in his compositions (*kṛti*, *kīrtana*) which is believed to be his own idea but could also have been inspired by the devotional songs of the mendicant singers (*bhāgavatar*) who came to the region of Tañjāvūr from Mahārāṣṭra.

Some music forms of South India (e.g. *jāvaḷi* and *tillānā*) evolved from the musical exchange with Hindustānī music which was promoted at different South Indian courts (*ghazal* and *taranā* respectively). Even today, joint performances with

Fig. 6: The harmonium still plays a role in devotional ensembles and popular theatre. This *bhajan* group in Tamil Nadu is also seen using two pairs of cymbals (*tāḷam* or *jālrā*).

Hindustānī musicians (*jugalbandī*) are a common feature of music festivals although they often fail to generate a lasting interest among musicians.

Fortunately, even the least desirable feature of contemporary music practice, the excessive use of amplification, has little bearing on the continuity of outstanding musicianship. This one-sided dependence on volume rather than rapport has been lamented by sensitive critics, listeners as well as exasperated organizers and fellow musicians abroad; and it continues to be an alienating, if not inhibiting, factor as far as interaction on a higher level of musicianship is concerned. But some leading young performers have already recognized that this is a problem to be addressed. A few have accepted the psychological challenge and, in spite of indifferent or insensitive colleagues and organizers, they are geared to build a reputation not with the help of mindless technology but on the strength of their artistic accomplishment.

For over two decades there have been exchanges between South Indian music and styles as diverse as Jazz, Rock and *New Age* music. Some of the best-known exponents of Karnatic music have contributed to numerous recordings and concert tours in these areas. As in the past, exoticism often provides no more than short-lived thrills. Yet classical standards cannot be said to have been undermined or diluted. On the contrary, there is a growing number of young people in India and abroad who cultivate a profound interest in every aspect of South Indian music. As soon as the novelty has worn off, they begin to explore the depth of genuine music. There is, after all, a way of making music which moves an individual on a very personal level, and transcends all conventional barriers—age, race, language, creed, and status.

The present debate on the protection and preservation of any nation's 'cultural identity' or 'heritage' has become politicized as a result of global communications and the increasing commercialization of the electronic media. Yet lovers and practitioners of classical music have no reason to doubt the strength and resilience which India's artistic traditions derive from a constant process of self-rejuvenation. Sir Mortimer Wheeler, in his analysis of Mediterranean trade with South India titled *Rome Beyond the Imperial Frontiers* (1954), came to the conclusion that it 'had no appreciable or durable effect upon the cultures of the peninsula. It left a superficial imprint here and there, sometimes in remarkably remote places, but nowhere south of the Vindhyas was that imprint more than a graffito upon an essentially self-sufficient native fabric'.

Quotation from *Tamil Culture and Civilization*, p. 150.

3

Variety

Of variety . . . all the senses delight in it and equally are averse to sameness. The ear is as much offended with one even continued note . . . as the eye is with being fixed to a point, or to the view of a dead wall.

William Hogarth in *The Analysis of Beauty.*

The English-born artist and theorist William Hogarth (1697–1764) sought to sharpen the sensibilities underlying European aesthetics in the age of *rococo*. His observations probe into the very essence of beauty and his work deals with the manifold ways by which beauty can be expressed most effectively. Thus Hogarth's unconventional ideas are of interest also for our times when all cultures of the world come into contact with one another by necessity if not by choice. Hogarth is not limited to the perspectives of his own age or, for that matter, the purview of European or Western culture. Closer scrutiny is bound to reveal the common ground between the interdisciplinary principles articulated by William Hogarth, their remarkable consequences for the artistic traditions of the West, and the principles underlying the integration of different artistic traditions of India.

It does not appear as if Hogarth was given to conceptual vagueness or an otherworldly outlook in life. Hogarth had a training as an engraver in gold and silver which, above all, requires a commitment to precision and discipline before the question of creative expression even arises. Hogarth was also acutely aware of the social conditions which artists and artisans had to endure and actually contributed to improving their lot by gaining legal protection and preparing the ground for the modern concept of copyright.

Most importantly, Hogarth used his rare combination of talents—critical faculty, imagination and curiosity—to analyse what kindles our sense of beauty. In his main work, *The Analysis of Beauty*, he shares with us his discovery that there are certain common factors which determine the causes for the lasting impact a work of art leaves on the human mind.

Strangely enough, common language could not express his findings. Therefore Hogarth resorted to concepts that had been in circulation since antiquity. He quotes a passage from Milton's *Paradise Lost* (AD 1667), the description of angels dancing about the sacred hill:

Mystical Dance!—
—Mazes intricate,
Eccentric, intervolv'd, yet regular
Then most, when most irregular they seem.

'Dances', Hogarth boldly declares, 'are composed of variety of movements and performed in proper time, but the less they consist of serpentine or waving lines, the lower they are in the estimation of dancing masters: for, as has been shewn [sic] when the form of the body is divested of its serpentine lines it becomes ridiculous as a human figure, so likewise when all movements in such lines are excluded in a dance, it becomes low, grotesque and comical.'

The Analysis of Beauty, p. 158.

'Simplicity, without variety, is wholly insipid, and at best does only not displease; but when variety is join'd to it, then it pleases, because it enhances the pleasure of variety by giving the eye the power of enjoying it with ease. . . . Thus we see simplicity gives beauty even to variety, as it makes it more easily understood, and should be ever studied in the works of art, as it serves to prevent perplexity in forms of elegance . . . Intricacy in form, therefore, I shall define to be that peculiarity in the lines, which compose it, that *leads the eye a wanton kind of chace* [sic], and from the pleasure that gives the mind, intitles [sic] it to the name of beautiful; and it may be justly said, that the idea of grace more immediately resides in this principle. . .'

The Analysis of Beauty, pp. 39–43.

He even states that a fine figure and its parts ought always to have a serpent-like and flaming form and life, so as to resemble the activity of a serpent and of a flame.

Joseph Campbell has aptly summarized the dilemma faced by modern onlookers and listeners, both Indian and 'Western', when first exposed to works which originated in artistic traditions not primarily intended to delight but to transform:

'In India, there are two orders of art: one is esthetic art; the other, temple art, is not esthetic in its aim. Temple art is concerned not with arresting the eye but with affecting a psychic transformation in the artist and the beholder. We're into another kind of art here. The source of the image is vision. Europeans for quite a while had a hard time appreciating Indian art. Indian poetry and philosophy were appreciated, but not the art, until they realized the images weren't representations of things, but tools for psychic transformation.'

Quotation from *Reflections on the Art of Living, A Joseph Campbell Companion*, p. 275.

Depending on the temple art or music tradition we are dealing with, there is, of course, room for debate whether such a distinction between aesthetic and religious art can always be made.

Since ancient times, the snake has been the universal symbol of fertility. In many cultural traditions, it symbolizes our latent potential, our creative as well as destructive urges, the act of healing as well as mortal danger. Thus the snake instils fear and fascination in equal measure—even in its most abstract representation as in the techniques described by Hogarth.

The latent power which is encountered by any human being in search of self-realization and liberation (*mokṣa*) is also symbolized by a serpentine entity in the traditions of *Yoga* and *Tantra*. This untapped source of spiritual power is known as *kuṇḍalinī* (from Sanskrit *kuṇḍalin*, 'circular, spiral, winding, coiling as a serpent'). The awakening of this power is regarded as a precarious process during which the adept is in need of guidance by an experienced master. Breath control (*prāṇāyāma*) is considered to be an indispensable aid in this process. According to this tradition, the inner fire, when kindled by the breath of life, becomes primordial sound.

Tyāgarāja, the great composer, points to this ancient concept already articulated by Śārṅgadēva in his famous music treatise, the *Saṅgīta Ratnākara* (13th c. AD). A composition (*kṛti*) by Tyāgarāja in rāga Sāramati, ādi tāla, provides a good example for the integration of mysticism and art which characterizes many Indian traditions:

'In *Mōkṣamu galadā* the saint asks if there can be liberation for those who have not known release, those who have neither true devotion nor musical wisdom. He explains that through the combination of the life-force or vital breath (*prāṇa*) and fire (*anala*) the vibration of *Om* manifests in the form of the seven tones of music, an idea stated in the *Saṅgīta Ratnākara*.'

Quotation from *Tyāgarāja: Life and Lyrics* by William J. Jackson, p. 122.

In India, the arts are rarely if ever seen as an end in themselves. Instead, they act as catalysts that facilitate our perception of a larger reality. All this eludes, of course, rational analysis but strongly determines the mental make-up of musicians, patrons and audiences alike.

Although Hogarth played an important role in the history of European fine arts and romantic literature, he remains little understood. This is not surprising, considering that his ideas were complex and, as far as his understanding of the interdisciplinary and synaesthetic aspects of the arts is concerned, generations ahead of his contemporaries:

'There is so strict an analogy between shade and sound, that they may well serve to illustrate each other's qualities, for as sounds gradually decreasing and increasing give the the idea of progression from, or to the ear, just so do retiring shades shew [sic] progression, by figuring it to the eye.'

The Analysis of Beauty, p. 110.

In our age, his ideas seem almost modern and are certainly relevant for widening our perceptions about world art and music. He repeatedly uses three words, *graceful, elegant, and genteel*, which he associates with the beautiful. For Hogarth, *grace* embraces beauty but is of a superior order. Most strikingly, the *line of beauty* is described as being serpentine in two dimensions, and the superior *line of grace* waves in three dimensions.

We may infer that two-dimensional beauty connotes glamour. Its superficiality results in an aesthetic experience that is at best shallow or short-lived. Conversely, what we should expect of a work or performance of art is a degree of depth that amounts to the experience of grace.

Indian thinkers would not hesitate to speak of the experience of a sublime quality and ultimate satisfaction by which we are made aware of the divine nature we are born with. To experience this ultimate dimension of art we need to make an effort ourselves. We have to become sensitive to *grace* and find the right kind of guidance. This quest underlies the *Sūfi* parables of *The Conference of the Birds* by Farid Ud-din Attar (b. 1120), the legends, precepts and myths of medieval India's *Purāṇas* and epics as well as Hermann Hesse's *Journey to the East* (*Die Morgenlandfahrt*, 1932), to name but a few. In spite of their obvious differences, these works share a belief in the need for the individual to chart out his or her own quest, embark on a solitary inner journey with all the attending fear, pain, ridicule, risks, and failures, before attaining something that is infinitely more valuable than any worldly gratification. The ultimate price sought during this quest defies description although it has variously been symbolized by the holy grail and the philosopher's stone in Western literature, and by *nirvāṇa* or *mokṣa* in the Eastern tradition. But most importantly, this price can never be lost again once gained.

Music has always been regarded as India's most efficient vehicle on which to undertake this journey. The *bhakti* movement thought of it as the least difficult but safest path for the common man.

While the artistic and psychological phenomena under consideration are very 'real' and while Hogarth is said to have belonged to the great tradition of English empirical philosophy, his words seem rather to belong to the realm of the ideal and mystical which perhaps explains his influence on Romantic literature. Yet, when we look at medieval Indian sculpture, we instantly recognize that indeed, a *superior line of grace waves in three dimensions* in a dancer's graceful S-shaped *tribhaṅga* (three-bent) pose (Fig. 7). This pose still figures prominently in the performance of any dancer faithful to the precepts of South India's classical traditions. A closer look at these beautiful sculptures reveals that dance and music are indeed perceived as being inseparable (Fig. 8).

It is difficult to ascertain whether Hogarth could have had access to specimens of Indian art and aesthetic literature, nor would it matter in our present context. His vision of grace in art, and the sensation of beauty derived from it, transcend his historical and cultural context. The experiences and ideals conveyed by Hogarth can perhaps help us forge a link between cultures that otherwise seem to be so different from one another. 'Westernized' lifestyles, or plainly consumerism and value-free utilitarianism, increasingly engulf and equalize, if not suffocate the entire globe, Indian culture included. If we fail to genuinely *feel* beauty and recognize it also in the artistic expressions of cultures other than our own, little diversity shall be left to be enjoyed by ourselves and by future generations. After all, Western arts are themselves amalgams of many traditions, and if we are to believe Greek sources, not just a few of them are of 'oriental' derivation or inspiration.

Growing familiarity with South Indian music will lead us to the wonderful discovery that our ears, far from being offended by one continued note, can enjoy

Fig. 7: The graceful S-shaped (*tribhaṅga*) pose associated with the female (*lāsya*) aspect of Indian dance which is identified with the goddess Pārvatī (Cennakeşava temple at Bēlūr; *Hoysala*, early 12th c.).

this single note in its own right. In Indian music there is beauty and variety even when the basic note is sounded alone and continually. If properly articulated, this basic note (*ādhāra ṣaḍja*, sa) lends luminosity and depth to every other note that

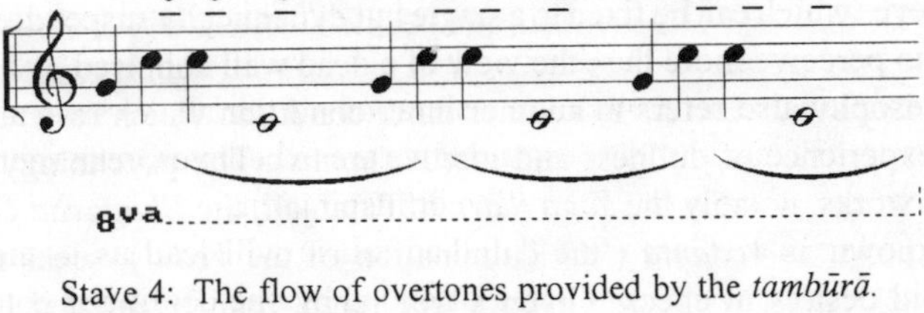

Stave 4: The flow of overtones provided by the *tambūrā*.

Fig. 8: Dance and music combine in this small panel which decorates the temple at Somnāthpur (*Hoysala*, 1238). The dancer playing the flute clearly demonstrates the S-shaped (*tribhaṅga*) pose associated with the graceful, female (*lāsya*) aspect of Indian dance. By contrast, the drummers assume the basic pose of South Indian dance (*bharata nāṭyam*), a pose characterized by the bent knees with the feet pointing outward (*ardhamaṇḍalī*). In accordance with the action of drumming, their movement is depicted in such a way as to indicate the vigorous, male aspect of dance (*tāṇḍava*). The panel depicts musicians who themselves participate in a dance scene. Alternatively, musicians stood behind or moved along with a dancer. This convention prevailed until early in the twentieth century.

follows it or is set against it by way of contrasting melody. For this purpose there is a special drone, the four-stringed lute known as the *tambūrā*.

This reminds us of the foreword to the *Sacred Books of the East* by Max Müller (1823–1900), the great Sanskritist: '. . . onepointedness . . . *ekāgratā* . . . as the Hindus call it, is something to us almost unknown. Our minds are like Kaleidoscopes of thoughts in constant motion; and to shut our inner eyes to everything else, while dwelling on one thought only, has become to most of us as impossible as to appreciate one musical note without harmonies.'

Through meditation, our gaze is trained to probe the inner depths of our own being with eyes which can be fixed to a single but dynamically suspended point. This enables us to perceive more than the view of a dead wall abhorred by Hogarth. Yet Indian philosophy also refers to another inner condition which resembles a 'dead wall', the experience of dullness and inertia (*tamas*). The psychology underlying many great works, notably the *Yoga Sūtra* of Patañjali, the *Bhagavad Gītā*, and the teachings known as *Vedānta* ('the culmination of the *Veda*'), seeks to keep our thoughts and desires in check. Given a free reign, undifferentiated thoughts are

Fig. 9: D. Pasupathi, renowned vocalist and composer, accompanying himself on the *tambūrā* at Kalākshētra.

known to result in mental delusion (*māyā*), and an excessive attachment to worldly affairs (*saṁsāra*). Both conditions are interrelated and eventually push us into the abyss of debauchery, a condition where we find neither fulfilment nor enjoyment. Egotism and ignorance (*avidyā*) would prevent us from perceiving beauty even when surrounded by it.

The Āḻvārs, Tamil saints of the first millennium AD, did not advocate rigidity in order to cope with the problems caused by the fickleness of the human mind. On the contrary, theirs was a dynamic and poetic approach which speaks of great insight into the human psyche. They advise us to move like bees from object to object but ensure that these objects are of a divine rather than a mundane nature. Virtually anything that fills the mind with a sense of beauty, joy and serenity was therefore viewed as conducive to a meaningful life and worthy of our single-minded attention.

According to the Āḻvārs, each human being has to set out to travel on the royal road that leads to one's true inner Self. On this quest we are led to an unobstructed vision of what it means to partake in lasting fulfilment.

4

Child's Play

Indian education is rooted in a tradition of apprenticeship based on respect for elders, self-discipline, service, faith, and trust. Customarily, a pupil (*śiṣya*) was entrusted to the care of a respected exponent in any field of learning, art, and science. In return for providing a novice with a living example to emulate, and with formal teaching or professional guidance, a teacher (*guru*) could expect unconditional obedience and practical help of any kind. Money was rarely transacted except for the parting gift (*gurudakṣiṇa*) which was presented to the teacher when the training was completed to mutual satisfaction. The underlying ideal was that lack of wealth should not prevent a gifted and dedicated youth from realizing his potential. In the absence of worthy disciples, a teacher would have been faced with the decline of his own lineage (*guruśiṣya paramparā*). It was thus mandatory to ensure that sufficient numbers of new entrants were trained in any field.

This practice, whereby a pupil becomes a member of the teacher's household (*gurukula*), is referred to as *gurukulavāsa*. In an urbanized environment, the rural custom of pledging services and bartering goods and foodstuffs is replaced by monetary transactions. Inevitably this entails a devaluation of personal and mutual service over an entire lifetime, not to mention the commitment to personalities belonging to previous or future generations. To fill this gap between rural and urban lifestyles, between past, present and future, and to provide meaningful education irrespective of the wealth and influence of a child's family, Rabīndranāth Tagore (1861–1941) sought to give his vision of a 'World University' concrete shape in the form of Viśva Bhāratī. In 1921, he established this famous and influential institution, which has since been converted into a university, at Śāntinikētan, his father's country retreat. His example was emulated and developed by two other personalities of this century whose influence has spread around the world, Jiddu Krishnamurti, and Rukmini Devi-Arundale. Many other institutions, established in this century and equally dedicated to providing an integrated approach to cultural and ecological education, were inspired by the Indian *gurukula* system where humility, spirituality, service, and accomplishment, not material considerations, are believed to have reigned supreme.

Dance and music have again become respectable in Indian society. Three generations of leading artists owe their professional training and livelihood to the late Rukmini Devi (1904–86) and to Kalākshētra, the institution founded by her in 1936.

Each year a number of children can attend school as well as dance and music classes in Kalākshētra. They grow up in the inspiring surroundings characteristic of this institution. Kalākshētra (Sanskrit Kalākṣetra) literally means a 'sacred place (*kṣetra*) for the arts (*kalā*)'. Outwardly seen, it is a nature sanctuary filled with trees and birds, a park laid out near the seashore in what has since become a southern suburb of metropolitan Madras (now renamed 'Chennai'). Until recently, most classrooms in Kalākshētra were simple bamboo cottages with thatched roofs that offered shade and a cool breeze even in the hottest season.

The splendid sights, sounds and fragrance of a *Sarasvatī pūjā* leave impressions on the minds of children that will never be forgotten in a lifetime (Fig. 10). This is an occasion for holding a special exhibition that lasts ten days. At its centre there is a lovely image of Sarasvatī, considered to be the consort of Brahmā, the deity who, according to ancient lore, created the world. The image of Sarasvatī is set in gold-leaf and painted with lively colours. She personifies the divine nature of the arts and letters, sublime creativity. There are musical instruments, costume parts (such as ornate crowns), and dolls apart from other objects of sentimental value. Prayers from many religions are recited collectively or individually each morning. Sometimes resonant voices recite Sanskrit verses from the sacred scriptures.

The atmosphere is serene and informal. Every child, student and teacher enjoys the auspicious proceedings. On this and similar occasions students learn to cooperate

Fig. 10: The festival in honour of Sarasvatī, divine personification of the letters and the fine arts; an annual display (*kolu*) of musical instruments, dance costume accessories, dolls and devotional objects.

and to share their art with one another rather than pursuing their studies as separate careers. Religion ceases to be a private or sectarian concern, a mere flight from 'real' life. A spiritually sensitive and responsible attitude thus becomes an experience to be cherished, respected, nurtured, and transmitted. It is an experience that contributes to a lasting sense of inner fulfilment. Everyone present is given an opportunity to experience a spiritual dimension of life that is emotionally satisfying and aesthetically stimulating.

In the Indian tradition of spirituality, creation has a playful aspect to it. The themes and conflicts expressed in India's scriptures, treatises, poetry, the great epics, legends, myths and parables, reflect a dynamic relationship between the individual soul (*jīvātma*) and an all-embracing divine reality (*brahman*). At the same time, objective reality is understood to be beyond ordinary human comprehension. After all, human beings are prone to delusion (*māyā*) and superstition with all the folly that inevitably follows from such characteristics. The spectacular adventures narrated in countless stories found in the *Mahābhārata* and *Rāmāyaṇa* serve to illustrate this point and therefore do not limit themselves to an exclusively Indian situation.

From ancient times, the performing arts have served to playfully, that is

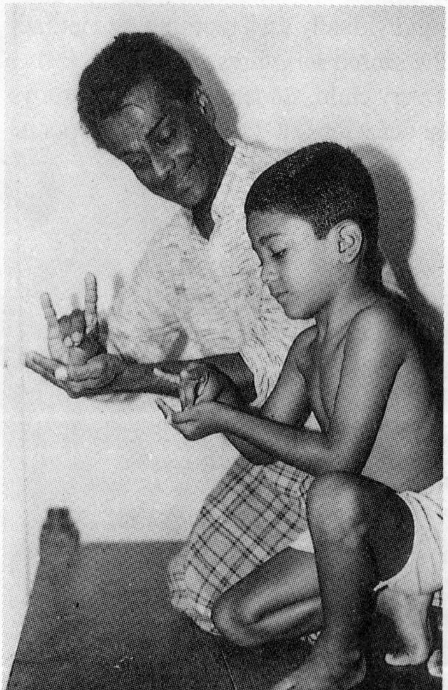

Fig. 11

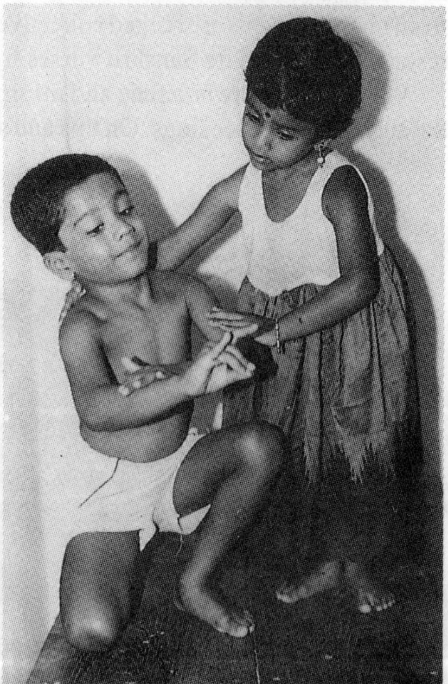

Fig. 12

Fig. 11: Actor-dancer Balagopalan with his son Pranesh (Kalākshētra); the teaching of hand gestures (*mudra*) to depict a deer.

Fig. 12: Pranesh and Pritvija playfully enact the scene describing the golden deer in the *Rāmāyaṇa* epic; hand gestures, posture and facial expression are those which have been used in classical dance and drama for many centuries.

enjoyably, enact every conceivable variation of the dynamic relationship of the Creator of the universe and individualized creation, a cosmic drama as it were. For this reason several types of relationships between a human being and the Creator seem to be conceivable as well as meaningful. The most universal and congenial one, the one that lends itself best to poetic treatment and therefore the one preferred as a theme for dance and music lyrics, is a relationship of intense love and longing (*śṛṅgāra*). But the Divine can also be playfully reproached for failing to come to His devotee's rescue. Popular forms of devotion (*bhakti*) address the Divine as mother, father, child or even lover in either male or female form. What matters are neither the form of devotion nor understanding of Divinity but the devotee's sincerity and faith. A visual representation is understood to be nothing if not an aid to meditation (*dhyāna*).

In an age of relentless internationalization, with consumerism, television, cinema and computer threatening to reign supreme even in India, a few niches remain where childhood and imagination can thrive. Some children are fortunate enough to be encouraged in their explorations of popular mythology. The mysteries behind the colourful images of gods and goddesses lend themselves to being enacted and experienced. For a child, it is not difficult to empathize with a childlike Kṛṣṇa who is admonished by his foster mother for his pranks and apparent recklessness. Youthful Kṛṣṇa is adored but also scolded by the *gopīs* (cowherdesses)—each one wants him for herself while he really is there for every single devotee. In the language of Indian mythology and philosophy, every devotee should imagine himself or herself in the role of a pining *gopī*. These and other fanciful images and stories, first developed in the *Bhāgavata Purāṇa* in or before the tenth century, evoke a spontaneous response not only in children. Behind the veil of childlike myths stands a philosophy that advocates total egoless dedication to a greater purpose in life, a type of fulfilment beyond material gain and gratification of the senses.

There are innumerable joyful songs inspired by such stories. The mythology of India's ancient epics and legends (*Purāṇa*) constitute a teaching method by which illiterate masses could be instructed as to how to cope with life and death and find solace amidst the drudgery of daily life. Even sophisticated adults find relief in these musical expressions of their forefathers which counteract the unprecedented pressures and anxieties of modern life. It is therefore not surprising to see ancient traditions effortlessly coexisting with the trappings of twentieth-century industrial society not just in India but wherever Indians have settled in pursuit of a career.

The most valuable gifts Kalākshētra bestows on its students are self-confidence and creative involvement. This is the ultimate purpose of art education in Kalākshētra because not every student is expected to pursue an artistic career. Many individual teachers who had their training at Kalākshētra, or were inspired by it, are equally committed to a form of art education which sets the students free as artists and responsible members of society.

Indian art education values concentration and cooperation with others. This aim is advanced by the melodies, rhythms, lyrics and movements of traditional songs and choreographies. New songs and dances can thus be created before a background of an ancient tradition without having to violate its aesthetic principles.

At Kalākshētra, a part-time course for young children consists in daily lessons given after regular school hours and in a playful spirit. This is a remarkable experiment which has nurtured the talents of hundreds of children over a period of more than sixty years. The children who attend music and dance classes in Kalākshētra come from diverse backgrounds and from many parts of the world. At an impressionable age they are given an opportunity to interact with professional artists. They benefit from years of exposure to beauty in every conceivable form. Later they can opt for a more intensive form of artistic formation on the level of college education.

Fig. 13: Balagopalan teaching rhythmic dance steps with a wooden stick (*taṭṭuppalakai*) and a block (*taṭṭukali*) to coordinate rhythm and movements.

The rigorous basic training a dancer or musician undergoes as part of a diploma course lasts four and five years respectively. Only a few graduates are admitted to the post-diploma and advanced training course. Besides daily practical lessons and theory classes, students get familiar with subjects outside their area of specialization. A sound knowledge of music is a must for every dance student. Depending on their abilities, students participate in performances or help performers, both students and teachers, with the complex tasks of applying make-up and readying their stage-costumes.

Modern pedagogy has re-discovered the fact that a child's intellect, skills and sensibilities develop better when there is sufficient room for artistic education. Dr Maria Montessori (1870–1952) was intrigued by this phenomenon. During World War II, the great educationist spent several years with the founders of Kalākshētra, and all her life she remained deeply committed to the cause of education on the Indian subcontinent. Having earned a reputation for herself through medical, social and educational work, she became convinced that the cultivation of aesthetic and spiritual sensibility was the key to meaningful personal development. What made her cause so special is the fact that she never allowed herself to be deterred or lured by narrow sectarian considerations. Her approach was thus by no means unfamiliar to educated Indians who willingly extended hospitality and cooperation to Maria Montessori. But ideas of this kind needed re-statement in India just as in the 'developed' countries that have been ravaged by two barbaric wars in this century alone. Maria Montessori returned to Europe after the war. There she continued working for a humane type of education. The movement inspired and guided by her is still growing all over the world. In the meantime Rukmini Devi and other progressive educationists set out to identify and nurture India's indigenous roots from which a meaningful educational system could evolve. This quest involved a painstaking process of locating artistic expertise that had survived an era of unsympathetic attitudes to the arts both among Indians and their colonial oppressors. With the help of senior artists and scholars, she succeeded in harnessing the living traditions that go back to India's early civilizations. Just as in the case of the great institutions founded in Bengal by Rabīndranāth Tagore, Kalākshētra did pioneer work both locally as well as on a national scale. It was a courageous effort to re-kindle public awareness that the arts and crafts, science and education, creativity and spirituality, belong to all and cannot flourish if divorced from one another. If these facets of human endeavour can flourish and rejuvenate themselves, so will civilized society as a whole. To achieve this, they must be combined and enhance one another. Then only does it become possible and desirable for all to live and work together in harmony.

In the face of many adversities, this undertaking grew into an international centre for the performing arts and education. Kalākshētra was recognized as an *Institution of National Importance* by the Government of India in 1993.

For many Indians, it is easy to master several languages. It appears that to Indian children, the memorizing of intricate songs, poems, dance movements, or drama-dialogue, poses fewer problems than to their Western counterparts. Given congenial conditions, such as have been advocated by Maria Montessori, all children can convince us that music, dance, painting, and spiritual discipline are more than just childish or otherworldly pursuits. The practical value of aesthetic discernment rooted in child-like curiosity, a positive attitude to the unknown, and courage must therefore not be underestimated and neglected.

Apart from their aesthetic appeal and spiritual dimension, Indian arts constitute the highly developed language of emotion (*bhāva*). If we are to believe the latest findings of psychological research by Daniel Goleman, it is not intelligence in the conventional sense which determines success in life, but control over one's emotions (emotional intelligence). To learn any one of India's performing arts means not only that one depicts, interprets or expresses individual emotions. Studying the origins of these arts means exploring the very nature of emotion, with regard to human relations, or even their relevance to a benevolent Creator. What seems to be mere child's play, the initial excitement and wonder of getting involved in an art, comes to mean that one is given the skills and tools to effectively enhance the quality of one's own life and thereby to make a contribution to society as a whole.

Every practitioner of dance and music knows that India's performing arts are both stimulating and energizing. Classical dance and music provide us with a positive outlook, the ability to realize and express ourselves, and to share this ability and our delight with one another. The offering of flowers, so characteristic of South Indian culture, symbolizes that it is one's Self which is being offered. This act is done voluntarily and joyfully as it means immersing oneself in something greater than oneself through an inner communion with the Divine. Neither dance performance nor prayer (*pūjā*) would feel complete without the colours and fragrance of flowers. A *rāgamālikā* means that a musician strings melodies together as if they were flowers in a garland.

For the medieval Āḻvār saints, *becoming a flower* was the highest goal of existence, or transforming oneself into *a bird with golden wings*. It is this childlike innocence which can also merge all arts into one subtle language beyond words. This language is understood by all beings and brings home the fact that mankind means more than the sum total of countless individuals.

5

Instrumental Music (Vādya)

In the treatises on the performing arts as well as other literary sources we find evidence that musical instruments played an important role throughout Indian music history. Theorists, educationists, singers and composers have made systematic use of the *tambūrā* and *vīṇā* to explore or describe the laws underlying sound and music. The various branches of vocal and instrumental music, and dance, are listed among the proverbial 64 arts (Sanskrit *catuṣṣaṣṭi kāla*, Tamil *aṟubattu nāṉgu kalaigaḷ*).

All great exponents of South India—instrumentalists and vocalists—have in fact sought to blend the stylistic features of the voice and various instruments. Therefore, an independent instrumental repertoire never seemed appropriate to South Indian music. Even today, a few leading *vīṇā* players (*vaiṇika*) like Rājēswari Padmanābhan often sing along with the *vīṇā*. T. Viswanāthaṉ continues the tradition of his illustrious grandmother, Vīṇā Dhanammāḷ, by interspersing his flute recitals with passages sung by himself. Bālamuraḷī Krishna, the renowned vocalist, composer and viola exponent, has emphatically stated that a singer should also play an instrument. Karnatic music thus fosters a notion of stylistic integrity which requires a vocalist to have some working knowledge of an instrument in order to master the various facets of intonation (*śruti*) and ornamentation (*gamaka*), the chief elements from which music based on rāga derives its melodious quality (*rāga bhāva*). On the other hand, an instrumentalist must strive towards achieving a 'vocal' type of expression (*gānam*); at times, this is also referred to as *gāyakī* (literally denoting a female singer). Every instrument has its own special appeal as well as limitations regarding tonal range, audibility, scope for fast passages, and ornamentation.

A rare exception in this regard is an instrumental piece known as *mallāri* (rāga Gambhīranāṭa, ādi tāla) performed by *nāgasvaram* and *tavil* players at the outset of a procession during the main festival (*brahmōtsavam*) of a temple. The 'English note' (*nōṭṭusvara*) of the twentieth century is a simple piece of salon music which is also devoid of lyrics.

Some compositions are more frequently heard in concerts where the principal performer is an instrumentalist. Compositions with variegated variations (*saṅgati*) are the natural choice for musicians in command of advanced technique. A small composition by Tyāgarāja, 'Ninnuvinā nāmadēndu' (rāga Navarasakannaḍa, rūpaka tāla) is a case in point. This piece has for several generations been a popular composition with flautists and a favourite with their audiences.

The typical classification in Indian music differentiates between wind instruments (*suṣīra vādya*), string instruments (*tata vādya*, i.e. chordophones), and two classes of percussion instrument, namely *ghana vādya* (solid percussion instruments, i.e. idiophones), and *avanaddha vādya* (percussion instruments with a membrane, i.e. membranophones). Other classifications are based on the mode of producing sound (blown, plucked, bowed, and struck).

Although many instruments are found in collections and mentioned in historical accounts, relatively few instruments are regularly used in today's concerts, temple music, and dance performances.

The present format of a classical Karnatic concert evolved with the emergence of music societies (*sabhā*) since 1895. These societies are patronized by an educated middle class and organize regular concerts as well as dance and music conferences in most cities and towns. Previously, public music life was largely confined to temples, royal or princely courts, and performances intended to entertain marriage parties who gather in their home village or town and stay there for several days. Musical discourses (*harikathā kālakṣepam*) and dance-dramas provided an entertaining and educative type of music. The concert format (*kaccēri paddhati*) has gradually changed to suit the tastes of an urban public with less time at its disposal.

The relationship between the different instruments during a concert is guided by conventions that form an unwritten code of conduct (*kaccēri dharma*). It is impracticable to describe all the possible musical situations that are common in South Indian music. The experience and prestige of each performer, whether soloist or accompanist, play a major role. The actual course of a performance depends on circumstances like audience rapport.

Accompaniment

Vocalists like Kāñcīpuram Naina Piḷḷai and his disciple, Chittoor Subramaṇia Piḷḷai, were known for their mastery of the rhythmic aspect of music (*laya*). Therefore they often chose to perform with a type of ensemble known as 'full bench'. It comprises violin, *mṛdaṅgam*, *kañjīrā*, *koṉṉakkōl*, *ghaṭam*, *mōrsiṅg*, and, of course, a *tambūrā*. In a music system where there is room for spontaneity, the success of such an ensemble depends on familiarity with the main performer's repertoire, style, and restraint. An accompanist must anticipate every melodic and rhythmic detail of a composition, and synchronize with the flow of creative musical ideas (*manodharma saṅgīta*).

For a concert which features a vocalist, flautist or violin player as the main performer, the primary accompaniment (*pakkavādya*) comprises a *tambūrā*, violin or a second violin, and *mṛdaṅgam*. This ensemble is often enlarged by one or several instruments belonging to the secondary category of accompaniment (*upapakkavādya*) which comprises the *ghaṭam*, *kañjīrā*, and *mōrsiṅg*. The vocal rendering of rhythmic syllables (*jati*) constitutes the art of solmization (*koṉṉakkōl*) which is, in fact, an art form in its own right although it is rarely heard in modern concerts. Not only does this 'percussive' discipline require aesthetic sense and restraint on the part of its performer in the role of an accompanist; to be accompanied by *konnakkōl* also tests the rhythmic sureness of the main performer, especially if he or she is a vocalist.

Although there are no fixed rules, it can be said that performances featuring a *viṇā* or *gōṭṭuvādyam* (*citraviṇā*) usually have fewer accompanists. Pairs of instrumentalists are always a popular attraction. Here the second instrumentalist sometimes acts as an accompanist; at other times he enhances the effect of a composition by faithfully duplicating the melody and rhythm around which music in a concert develops.

All instruments that take part in a concert have ample scope for solo improvisation. A melody instrument takes up the thread spun by the principal musician. During *ālāpana*, *niraval* and *svara kalpana* improvisations, performers take turns in repeating or varying the melodic improvisation of the previous soloist. Similarly, percussionists participate in a major rhythmic interlude (*taniyāvarttanam*) which is a highlight of every concert.

There are two basic types of melodic accompaniment that are mainly performed by violinists. The first type involves the repetition of a phrase (*sañcāra*), particularly during an improvised exposition of a rāga (*ālāpana*); and the other one is a simultaneous or *unisono* mode of performance. The latter requires considerable experience in order to take the idiosyncrasies of the principal performer into account. For this reason, a violinist has to commit a very large repertoire to memory in order to succeed as a professional performer. In dance music, the flute plays a similar role as the violin in a concert, namely, to accompany the voices and other instruments and to play instrumental interludes in an improvised manner which is similar to *ālāpana* or *niraval*.

An accompanist can also pause, for instance in order to give room for a soloist to perform fast and intricate variations (*briga* or *birkā*). Such passages mark the end of an *ālāpana*. The switching to a lower or higher octave during a *unisono* passage is a common technique which can be freely used by any instrumentalist.

There appear to be two rival schools of thought regarding the principles that guard the relationship of the main performer and the musicians who provide accompaniment in a typical concert. According to one school, endorsed by senior vocalist Semmaṅguḍi Śrīnivāsa Ayyar, a clear division of tasks is preferable whereby the main vocalist (or instrumentalist) concentrates on the melodious aspect of Karnatic music from which listening pleasure (*saukhyam*) is to be derived. Calculated patterns (*kōrvai*) are either avoided or treated with utmost restraint except for the main percussion solo (*taniyāvarttanam*). The other school seeks to structure every minute of a concert, leaving little to chance. Hereby, an audience is offered rare and surprising ideas and challenges that require a high degree of alertness among musicians and listeners alike. Both schools tend, of course, to mingle in most performances and are not as mutually exclusive as it may appear. A good musician knows by experience how to integrate the various aspects of a performance (*kaccēri*)—spontaneity (*manodharma*), meticulous planning, genuine feeling (*bhāva*) and impeccable technique—in such a manner that a listener will forever remember the concert for the aesthetic delight (*rasa*) derived from it.

Tambūrā

Before the subtle facets and moods of music become even perceptible to human ears and minds, a state of tranquillity (*śānta*) needs to be established. For this purpose a drone (i.e. an instrument designed to continuously give a particular base-sound)—mostly the long-necked lute (*tambūrā*)—continually provides the basic key or tonic (*ādhāra ṣaḍja*). More than a mere point of departure, the sounds of a well-tuned *tambūrā* create a pleasant rainbow of harmonics, as it were, which illumines all other notes. Before this background, at once steady and vibrant, every well-chosen note conveys feeling and leads to a whole series of connected notes which ultimately form a melody.

The *tambūrā*, a *tata vādya* (string instrument), serves to set the mood for a performance. It can be described as a long-necked lute similar to a *vīṇā* but without

Fig. 14: The playing position of the *tambūrā* shown by vocalist K. Hariprasad; the straightened forefinger of the right hand presses and releases each string in a gentle and reposeful manner; the left hand is free and keeps musical time (*tāla*).

the frets. Its resonator is generally made of jackwood (Tamil *palāmaram*, Latin *artocarpus integrifolia*). Rosewood can also be used for some parts like the sounding board. Four, five or six strings are played with the middle finger for the first string (*pañcama*), and the index finger for the remaining *ṣadja* strings in the middle and lower octaves. Depending on the vocal or instrumental range of the main performer, one or two strings are sometimes coiled by copper to obtain a lower pitch. Nowadays the *tambūrā* is increasingly being replaced by an electronic device (electronic *tambūrā*).

The same basic pitch is mostly maintained throughout a performance. During a concert, the continuous playing of a *tambūrā* is subject to two occasional changes, namely the omission of the first string to avoid the 5th (*pañcama*) in the event that a rāga without *pañcama* is performed; and the raising of the basic pitch by four steps (*madhyama śruti*) by way of re-tuning the first or *pañcama* string which thus becomes the new *ṣaḍja* string while the other three strings remain tuned as before; three strings are then heard as the *pañcama* (5th) of the first string, the new *ṣaḍja*. After the completion of a piece set to a *madhyama śruti* rāga, the original tuning is restored to the *tambūrā*.

Vīṇā

Indian literature and iconography associates the *vīṇā* mainly with Sarasvatī, the embodiment of wisdom and beauty, and the consort of Brahmā. For this reason, the South Indian *vīṇā* (Tamil *vīṇai*) is also known as the *Sarasvatī vīṇā*.

Its present form is believed to have been perfected by Gōvinda Dīkṣitar, a minister and music scholar, at the court of Raghunātha Nāyak who ruled Tañjāvūr from 1600 to 1634. Gōvinda Dīkṣitar named his new instrument *Raghunātha mēḷa vīṇā* in honour of his royal patron. He also wrote an important music treatise, *Saṅgīta sudhā*, which mentions Raghunātha Nāyak as its author in accordance with prevailing conventions. In this work he proposes a system of 15 reference scales (*mēḷa*

Fig. 15: The South Indian *vīṇā* (*Sarasvatī vīṇā*).

rāga), and credits Vidyāraṇya, the famous sage of Vijayanagar (14th century), with having first introduced it in a work called *Saṅgīta sāra*.

Veṅkaṭamakhi, Gōvinda Dīkṣitar's son, continued to expand the scope of South Indian music by writing his famous work, *Caturdaṇḍī Prakāśikā* (1660), wherein a scheme of 72 reference scales is outlined for the first time, although not yet in the fully-fledged form followed now. Veṅkaṭamakhi thus succeeded in strengthening the bond between the fields of instrumental music, the source of empirical knowledge about scales and their effects, and music theory. At the root of such painstaking and persistent efforts, documented in a series of Sanskrit treatises, lay the determination to guide those practising musicians who were not scholars themselves, with the aim of enabling them to maintain the highest standards in terms of singing and playing technique, coherence of expression, and variety of aesthetic experience. This interdisciplinary approach goes back to the times when the *Nāṭya Śāstra* and the *Cilappatikāram* were written (i.e. the early centuries of our era). The fertile interaction between theory and practice was reasserted in numerous compositions of Muttusvāmi Dīkṣitar, and it continues to live in those *vaiṇika* traditions of our times which represent a combination of scholarship, experimentation, analysis, and faithful transmission of a vast repertoire of compositions. A rival system was soon formulated by Gōvinda, the author of a work entitled *Saṁgraha-Cūḍā-Maṇi*. Tyāgarāja and most later composers have followed Gōvinda's system, which is now associated with the system and nomenclature of 72 *mēḷakartā* scales. Both systems are still being debated by scholars, particularly those attached to the musical lineage of Muttusvāmi Dīkṣitar and Veṅkaṭamakhi, although this discussion seems to have little bearing on contemporary music practice.

The *vīṇā*, *tambūrā* and *gōṭṭuvādyam* (*citravīṇā*) belong to the South Indian family of 'long-necked lutes'. Both the main resonator and the stem of these three types of instrument are generally made of jackwood (*palāmaram*), although rosewood is also used for some parts like the sounding board. The *vīṇā* and the *gōṭṭuvādyam* have a secondary resonator which adds balance visually and physically. Such a resonator is made of a lighter material such as a gourd (calabash), specially grown for this purpose. Subbarāma Ayyar ('Karaikudi Brothers') was one of the last *vīṇā* exponents (*vaiṇika*) who played his instrument by holding it in an upright position.

The modern *vīṇā* has four main or melody strings made of steel, of which two are coiled with copper to produce the lower range of notes. A set of 24 brass frets, so arranged as to facilitate the playing of a chromatic scale extending over two octaves, is mounted on a base of hard wax to which resin and lamp soot have been added. This feature accounts for the characteristic sound of the *vīṇā*. The frets need to be reset from time to time by an expert as a result of the vigorous movements that are performed whenever embellishments of notes are produced on a particular fret, or between two frets.

A *vīṇā* has a tonal range covering $3^1/2$ octaves. Three secondary strings, also made of steel, are fitted on the side. This serves the function of marking the time cycles (*tāla*) of a song, to articulate phrases, and to provide the basic note (drone).

Because of its well-balanced features, the *vīṇā* is traditionally valued as a

Fig. 16: *Vīṇā* held in an upright position.

sarva vādya, an instrument which is so 'complete' or self-sufficient (*sarva*) that it requires no accompaniment.

Most *vīṇās* are decorated with intricate inlay work such as geometric designs (*mandala*) made of stag horn; some older ones have ivory decoration, some parts covered with gold leaf, and have a brightly painted gourd. The stem (*daṇḍi*) ends in a wood carving in the shape of a dragon (*yāḷi*).

Except for the *vīṇā* tradition of Vīṇā Dhanammāḷ, the sound is produced with the help of two or three plectra made from metal wires attached to the forefinger, the middle finger, and the ring-finger. Apart from the strokes employed to form melodic phrases and embellishments, there are frequent strokes by the little finger to mark the basic pattern of a particular tāla. Similar strokes also serve the purpose of providing continuity by way of repetition, thus reviving the sound of a long note before it becomes inaudible. Quite obviously, the very nature of this instrument does not permit the use of sustained notes and phrases in the same manner as the human voice, the flute or the violin.

In a solo performance, the *vīṇā* is sometimes accompanied by a second *vīṇā* and a *tambūrā* but rarely by a violin. Percussion support is provided by a *mṛdaṅgam* and sometimes also a *ghaṭam*.

Some types of grace notes (*gamaka*) commonly sung in Karnatic music have their origin in the advanced playing techniques of the *vīṇā*. Special techniques were developed for the *vīṇā* in order to circumvent the problems that arise from the use of a limited number of frets in a piece of music which has unlimited scope for microtonal differentiation.

Thus two distinct characteristic traits are combined in the *Sarasvatī vīṇā*. On the one hand, playing the *vīṇā* can be said to require rational analytic thinking and well-planned movements on account of its sheer size; on the other hand, the *vīṇā* calls for being played with a gentle, feminine touch in order to make its music come alive. The challenge is to play the *vīṇā* in such a manner as to convey a rāga in a mellifluous manner. Like the violin, the *vīṇā* is mostly tuned to D sharp ('2½ *śruti*') or E ('3 *śruti*') when played as a solo instrument.

Gōṭṭuvādyam

The modern *gōṭṭuvādyam* is a fretless variant of the *Sarasvatī vīṇā*. Like the *vīṇā*, the *gōṭṭuvādyam* is an instrument which is so 'complete' (*sarva vādya*) that it pleases even in the absence of any accompaniment. It is played with the help of a gliding 'stick' from which it derives its name. (Ravi Kiran, a renowned exponent, prefers

Fig. 17: The *gōṭṭuvādyam*, an instrument similar to the *vīṇā;* instead of the fingers pressing the strings onto metal frets as on the *vīṇā*, a sliding stick is used to touch the melody strings at various places to obtain the desired pitch.

the more elegant name *citravīṇā*, which he derives from an instrument mentioned in old Sanskrit texts.) This cylinder of polished hardwood is held by the player's left hand and gently pressed against the open strings to obtain distinct pitches (*svarasthāna*) and subtle embellishments (*gamaka*). In spite of its outward similarity with the *vīṇā*, the *gōṭṭuvādyam* has a special sound of its own which is characterized by continuity and warmth, endowing this instrument with the 'vocal' character which is much sought after in Karnatic music. Like the violin, the *gōṭṭuvādyam* poses some difficulties for a beginner because there is no visual aid in the form of frets to find the positions for various notes. In recent years, a cylinder made of synthetic materials like teflon is also being used due to advantages like greater smoothness and reduction of weight.

As a concert instrument in Karnatic music, the *gōṭṭuvādyam* was introduced by Śrīnivāsa Rao. Like Vīṇā Dhanammāḷ, he preferred to perform without any percussion support. His son, Sakharāma Rao was the first musician to specialize in playing the modern *gōṭṭuvādyam*. Nārāyaṇa Ayyaṅgār, a disciple of Sakharāma Rao, is credited with having introduced an instrument with several sympathetic strings that are placed beneath the melody strings. His grandson, N. Ravikiran, plays an instrument with 21 strings, out of which twelve are sympathetic strings, and three serve the purpose of marking the tāla of a composition.

The *gōṭṭuvādyam* has never had as many exponents as the *vīṇā*, but *gōṭṭuvādyam* exponents like Sakharāma Rao, Nārāyaṇa Ayyaṅgār, Nārāyaṇa Ayyar, and Budalūr Krishnamūrti Śāstrigaḷ are reckoned among the great names of Karnatic concert music.

The traditional ensembles: ci<u>nn</u>a mēḷam and periya mēḷam

A dance ensemble is called *ci<u>nn</u>a mēḷam* (Tamil, 'small ensemble'). Depictions in temples as well as references in literary works suggest that dance ensembles are indeed the oldest type of ensemble found in Indian music.

The work of a *naṭṭuvanar* is simultaneously that of a dance master, choreographer and conductor. Known as *naṭṭuvāṅgam,* this has been a profession in its own right for many centuries. Special rhythmic syllables (*jati*) are recited for South Indian dance (e.g. *bharata nāṭya*) while playing the *tāḷam* cymbals at the same time. In this manner dance movements (*aḍavu*) and music ensemble are perfectly synchronized during a performance.

One or two vocalists, supported by a drone (*tambūrā* or *śruti peṭṭi*), lead the ensemble. A pair of metal discs (*tāḷam*), a bamboo flute (*pullāṅkuḻal*), and a double-faced drum (*mṛdaṅgam*) are the main instruments used for a dance recital. Other drums are sometimes used for greater variety and dramatic effect. A violin and sometimes a *vīṇā* supplement the ensemble. Contemporary dancers and choreographers avail of all conceivable combinations involving traditional as well as unconventional instruments.

Nāgasvaram/Nādasvaram

The *nāgasvaram* enjoys the special status of an 'auspicious' instrument (*maṅgaḷa*

Fig. 18: The *nāgasvaram,* the large double-reed instrument of South India which is played in temples and on the occasion of a marriage; it is mostly accompanied by a small harmonium that serves as a drone (*śruti box*).

vādya). Festive occasions, such as processions during the annual temple festival (*brahmōtsavam*) and marriages, are accompanied by an ensemble known as *periya mēḷam* ('large ensemble'). Today the *periya mēḷam* consists mostly of two double-reed pipes (*nāgasvaram*, *nāyanam*), two drums (*tavil*), a pair of thick brass cymbals (*tāḷam*) for rhythmic coordination, and a drone. The drone was traditionally provided by a type of *nāgasvaram* known as *ottu* which played but one continuous note. Today, a *śruti box* (box-harmonium) is generally used for the same purpose. But this innovation has two marked disadvantages. On the one hand, there are now less opportunities for apprentices to accustom themselves to vigorous blowing under concert conditions. On the other hand, it has been observed that a *śruti box* , unlike the *ottu*, does not adjust itself to the gradual variations of pitch (*śruti*) caused by changes of temperature and moisture.

In this century, the name *nādasvaram* ('sound-note') has also been introduced in Tamil, although there are no references to this name in earlier literature. The absence of ancient literary and iconographic evidence has led some scholars to the conclusion that this type of instrument must have found its way into South Indian music about eight centuries ago. A short, high-pitched variant, known as *mukhavīṇā* (Sanskrit, 'mouth-*vīṇā*'), is referred to in the *Saṅgīta Ratnākara* (13th c.). Short instruments of the same name, also called *ciṉṉa* ('small') *nāgasvaram*, are still played in *Vaiṣṇava* temples and rural drama (*kūttu*). Another high-pitched variant, the *timiṟi*, with a basic pitch corresponding to '5 *śruti*' ('G'), was generally preferred until the longer, low-pitched type gained popularity a few decades ago. This *bāri nāgasvaram* (Tamil *pāri*, 'bulky') has a basic pitch which ranges from '2 *śruti*' ('D') to '3 *śruti*' ('E').

The playing technique of the *nāgasvaram* is similar to that of the bamboo flute (*pullāṅkuḷal*). This is due to the fact that the advanced playing technique, introduced by the legendary blind flautist Śarabha Śāstrigaḷ at the end of the nineteenth century, was derived from that of the *nāgasvaram*. It was also during that period that exponents of both instruments began to establish themselves as concert musicians. Most flutes have eight finger-holes, the *nāgasvaram* only seven. The tube of a *nāgasvaram* is conical, whereas a bamboo flute has a near-cylindrical bore. Five additional holes at the lower end of the *nāgasvaram* facilitate further adjustments of the air-flow. Its mouthpiece consists of a double-reed which is inserted into a metal cylinder. The bore widens out into a bell either made of a hard and dark variety of wood (*āccāmaram*), like the main tube, or of metal.

Tavil

The *tavil* is a type of drum used in the *periya mēḷam* ensemble. It is played with a short stick in one hand. The fingers of the other hand are bandaged with strips of cotton fabric to which rice paste is applied. After this paste has solidified, it greatly increases the volume which can be produced by the player's fingers. The leather membrane is rather rigid, which gives the *tavil* its powerful sound.

Fig. 19: The *tavil*, a double-faced drum which is used as an accompaniment for the *nāgasvaram* in the *periya mēḷam* ensemble.

Bamboo flute

The South Indian transverse flute (*veṇu*, Tamil *pullāṅkuḻal*) consists of a near-cylindrical bamboo tube with eight finger-holes of which seven are mostly used. It has been a popular instrument from early times. Although ancient and medieval texts mention flutes made from other materials such as bronze or rosewood, there is agreement among flute players that bamboo is the best material. Two finger-holes next to the mouth-hole are closed to produce the tonic or keynote (*sadja*). If the 'natural' scale is played by way of fully opening and closing the finger-holes in various combinations, the resulting scale resembles the 28th *mēḻakartā rāga*, known as Harikāmbhōji (i.e. the Western Mixolydian church mode).

For playing South Indian music, several intermediary intervals are also required. Most of these intervals, such as the chromatic variants (*svarasthāna*) of five variable notes (*vikṛta svara*), and even smaller 'microtonal' variants or 'quartertones' (*śruti*), are obtained by closing some finger-holes partially rather than fully. An intricate technique of cross-fingering was introduced by Śarabha Śāstrigal, the blind virtuoso whose performances are said to have, for the first time, raised the status of the flute to that of a concert instrument in its own right.

The natural range of the bamboo flute comprises two octaves and a third. By changing the angle of the instrument and by increasing or decreasing the air pressure, additional notes can be obtained in the upper and lower registers. For the lowest notes, the last finger-hole is also closed. For dance music and 'light' compositions (*tukkaḍā* items) at the end of a concert, several flutes are used in such a manner that their ranges match. A short, high-pitched flute which matches the female vocal range has, for instance, F ('4 *śruti*') as its fundamental note, and its length is about 40 cm. The use of longer flutes also in Karnatic concert music has been pioneered

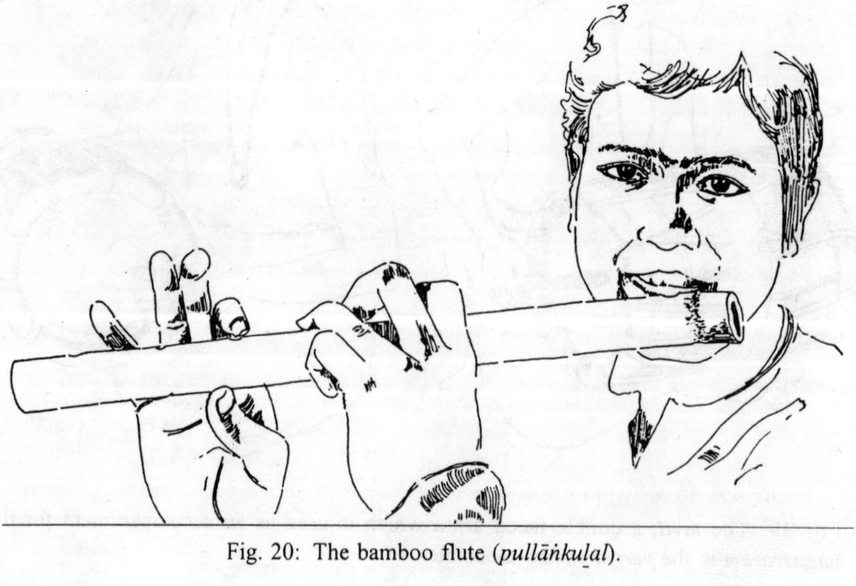

Fig. 20: The bamboo flute (*pullāṅkuḻal*).

by N. Ramani in recent years. In popular dance items, films, poetry, songs, paintings, and sculptures, the flute is mainly associated with Kr̥ṣṇa, the divine cowherd (Venugopal).

Percussion and rhythmic solmization (konnakkōl)

Percussion lends excitement, intellectual stimulation, and a sense of enjoyment to a performance (*kaccēri*) of classical music. During a regular music concert, a South Indian percussionist has always the twin tasks of being an accompanist as well as a soloist. Unlike his North Indian counterpart, he or she is expected to perform an extensive solo (*taniyāvarttanam*). A performance mainly intended to display complex rhythmic patterns (*tālaprastāra*) is sometimes also announced as *laya vinyāsa*.

A percussion solo is more than a mechanical display of virtuosity and clever calculations. Pudukōṭṭai Mānpūṇḍiyā Piḷḷai is credited with laying the foundations for a balanced approach to percussion music as well as raising the *kañjīrā* to the rank of a fully-fledged concert instrument.

A master percussionist's reputation rests on his or her ability to construct an aesthetically satisfying rhythmic edifice during each concert.

Some of the patterns performed by Palghat Maṇi Ayyar as conclusion (*muktāyi*) of a *taniyāvarttanam* now form part of the repertoire of every South Indian percussionist (Table 5).

For many centuries, Indian musicians have been using various kinds of rhythmic and melodic solmization for the purpose of teaching and accompanying dance, and as an aid to memory. Perfect coordination of rhythmic footsteps and movements is indispensable for classical South Indian dance forms such as *bharata nāṭya*. As a result, solmization for the purpose of accompanying dance (*naṭṭuvāṅgam*) is regarded as an art form in its own right.

The recitation of rhythmic syllables (Sanskrit *jati*, Tamil *sorkaṭṭu* or *sollukkaṭṭu*) has become known as *konnakkōl* since Mannārguḍi Pakkiri Piḷḷai (1857–1937) developed it into a musical speciality in its own right. As a consequence, *konnakkōl* (*konugōl*) acquired so much prestige that it continued to play an important role in the concerts of leading musicians until a few decades ago. Nowadays, however, *konnakkōl* is rarely heard as an accompaniment.

The enduring importance of *konnakkōl* lies in the fact that it relates to all the other branches of music, and thus to the ancient convention of regarding all arts and poetry as being allied to music. It is useful for the appreciation of this seemingly minor art to recall here that the earliest Sanskrit texts on music (*saṅgīta*) are all rooted in the tradition of drama as documented in the *Nāṭya Śāstra*. Thus the concept of *saṅgīta* comprises vocal music (*gītam*), instrumental music (*vādyam*), and dance (*nr̥tyam*). On similar lines, the ancient concept of *muttamil* ('threefold Tamil') envisages the three branches literature (*iyal*), music (*isai*) and drama (*kūttu* or *nāṭakam*) as an integrated whole. It is believed that this concept was first outlined in the *agattiyam*, an early grammatical work ascribed to the sage Agattiyar (Agastya *r̥ṣi*) which later writers regarded as the first and prime source (*mudal nūl*) on various subjects.

Table 5: The *muktāyi* of a *taṉiyāvarttaṉam*

I.

6	5	6	5	5	5	= 32
tā - jām - - -	ta ka jām - -	ta ki ṭa jām - -	ta dhi ki na tom	ta dhi ki na tom	ta dhi ki na tom	[tām]

IIA.

8	6	4	8	8
tā - dhī - ta ka di na	dhī - ta ka dhi na	ta ka dhi na	ta dhī - ki na tōm - -	ta dhī - ki na tōm - -

IIB.

6	3	7	7	7	= 64
ta dhī - ki na tom	tām - ku	tā - dhī - ki na tom	tā - dhī - ki na tom	tā - dhī - ki na tom	[tām]

(Courtesy: *Mṛdaṅga Vidvān* T.R. Sundaresan)

Note: Each hyphen (-) corresponds to one syllable or basic unit; syllables extended by one or several hyphens are also marked by a long vowel 'ā' ('tā', 'jām'); both patterns (I and II) can be played for different tālas if the starting point (*eḍuppu*) is carefully calculated; if performed in ādi tāla (32 *mātrā*), their beginning and end coincides with the same *eḍuppu*, and they can be accommodated in one and two tāla cycles (*āvarta*) respectively; the first *muktāyi* (I) is very popular and consists of 32 units (*mātrā*); it is repeated twice (i.e. performed thrice) and thus comprises three tāla cycles (*āvarta*); an additional syllable 'tām' coincides with the starting point (*eḍuppu*) of the theme; from this *eḍuppu* the *taṉiyāvarttaṉam* is taken up; and it is here that it is also concluded (e.g. the *pallavi* of a *kṛti*). The second *muktāyi* (II) comprises 64 units (*mātrā*); although less commonly heard, it is regarded as being more elegant than the first *muktāyi*.

In the context of contemporary concert music, the *tillānā,* a type of composition which contains lively syllabic patterns (*jati*) suggestive of rhythmic movements, is a case in point. Although it belongs to the dance repertoire, the *tillānā* is equally popular in music concerts, and many *tillānās* have been composed even in recent years.

South Indian rhythm displays some strikingly modern qualities on account of its unique combination of spontaneity (*manodharma*) and calculated permutation of patterns (*prastāra*). Simple patterns are recombined and juxtaposed to form more complex ones and in this manner, the various traditional time cycles (*tāla*) yield a wealth of cross-rhythms, a rhythmic counterpoint as it were.

PERCUSSION INSTRUMENTS USED IN TRADITIONAL CONCERTS

Four percussion instruments are currently used in the following order of popularity and status: the double-faced drum (*mr̥daṅgam*); the claypot (*ghaṭam*); the small hand-held drum (*kañjirā*); and the Jew's harp (*mōrsiṅg*).

Mr̥daṅgam

The *mr̥daṅgam* leads the others in a percussion solo. Its modern form is believed to have originated during Marāṭhā rule in Tañjāvūr which had created favourable conditions for the introduction of popular devotional music (*kīrtana*) from Mahārāṣtra and Karṇāṭaka. Tyāgarāja is believed to have been greatly inspired by

Fig. 21: The *mr̥daṅgam*, the most important percussion instrument of South India.

the art practised by learned musicians known as *kirtankār* and *bhāgavatar*. In his composition (*kṛti*) *Sogasugā mṛdaṅga tālamu* (rāga Śrīrañjani, rūpaka tāla), he pays tribute to the expertise of these musicians who blended the various elements of music, dance, poetry, and religious lore into an aesthetically satisfactory performance:

Who is the hero able to melt you
co-ordinating the ensemble
with such elegance of drum rhythm?
. . . .
Is it possible for Tyāgarāja
to worship with *kritis* full
of the nine great emotions
smacking with sweetness of grape nectar,

Is he able to make the rhythmic pauses
in songs of soulful love
with rhymes and in line with all
the rules of prosody

Quotation from *Tyāgarāja, Life and Lyrics* by William Jackson, p. 326.

According to musicologist B.M. Sundaram (*Great Layavaadyakaaraas of Karnatak Music*), the musicians who introduced the *mṛdaṅgam* in the present concert format, which gradually evolved from the eighteenth century, were either hereditary dance musicians (*naṭṭuvanar*), or accompanied the exponents of religious discourses (*bhāgavatar*) who had migrated from Mahārāṣṭra. All the present South Indian styles of playing the *mṛdaṅgam* can thus be traced to experts in rhythm (*layavādyakāra*) who were trained by musicians from these two groups whose joint expertise has been consolidated in the early part of the twentieth century.

Tañjāvūr Nārāyaṇasvāmi Appā, a versatile musician of the nineteenth century, is credited with developing the complex patterns from which the modern playing technique of the *mṛdaṅgam* has evolved. Such rhythmic patterns (Urdu *faran*) were originally practised on a type of drum known as *dōlak* which was played by Nārāyaṇasvāmi Appā and other exponents of Marāṭhi devotional music who were patronized by Śarabhōjī II (Serfōjī, 1798–1832), and Śivājī II (1832–55) at their court in Tañjāvūr.

A *mṛdaṅgam* constitutes a hollow cylinder with unequal diameters at both ends. An instrument of this name, meaning a 'body' (limb, Sanskrit *aṅgam*) made of earth (*mṛd*), is mentioned by early writers. Although its name indicates that the *mṛdaṅgam* was originally made of clay, its body is now made of jackwood (*palāmaram*), like the resonators of most other South Indian instruments. Its length, diameter, wall thickness at various points, and the curvatures of the inner and outer surfaces determine the pitch and tonal quality of each individual instrument.

The larger left-hand side of the instrument (seen from the perspective of a right-handed player) produces a variety of bass sounds, a melody of distinct notes as well as glides between several notes. This difficult technique is known as *gumki* and requires that the wrist of the left hand presses the leather near its outer rim while the tips of one or two fingers—mostly the middle and ring fingers—briefly strike the centre to allow a free vibration of the membrane. To increase its elasticity, the left side is temporarily loaded with a moistened wheat paste. This enables a skilled player to produce five or six different notes (*svara*) covering a range from the tonic *sa* (*ādhāra ṣaḍja*) to *pa* (*pañcama*) or even *dha* (*dhaivata*). Other strokes of the left side prevent the free vibration of the membrane.

The right-hand side of the *mṛdaṅgam* has a smaller diameter and is permanently loaded by a round 'black spot'. For this purpose, many layers of cooked rice paste, mixed with powdered iron oxide or manganese, are slowly applied with the help of a polishing stone and allowed to dry. An expert *mṛdaṅgam* maker takes a number of factors, such as required thickness and diameter, into account, which enables a player to produce a range of distinct sounds. Depending on the intensity of use and force applied by its player, a *mṛdaṅgam* needs to be re-worked in this manner after several months, or sometimes just a few performances.

Larger instruments are suitable for low-pitched voices or instruments, and smaller ones for high-pitched ones. A few 'free' strokes permit the membrane to resonate and thereby produce distinct intervals or notes (*svara*), while most strokes executed by the hands and fingers of the right hand are percussive sounds of indeterminate pitch. The most important 'free' strokes are known as 'din', a sound corresponding to the basic pitch or tonic (*ādhāra ṣaḍja*), produced by the forefinger; and 'dhīm', a stroke of all the four fingers of the right hand which produces the major second (*catuḥśruti ri*).

Both sides consist of several kinds of leather worked into thick rings that can be tightened or loosened to adjust the instrument's pitch. The membranes are connected by a long leather tape which can be adjusted by inserting wooden pegs between several strands.

A combination of rapid strokes, mostly intended to arrest the free vibration of either membrane, yields the intricate tāla patterns which are so characteristic of South Indian music. Most of the syllables (*jati*) that represent particular strokes or drum sounds also apply to other percussion instruments.

Ghaṭam

The *ghaṭam* is a solid instrument (idiophone) without a membrane. Derived from a common water pot, it is now made from special clay to which metal filings are added for additional resonance. The pitch of each *ghaṭam* is predetermined by its shape and size. Its sound can be modulated by skilfully adjusting the distance between the aperture and the player's belly. Special sounds are obtained by striking the aperture with the flat palm.

Polagam Chidambara Ayyar (b. 1841) is believed to have been the first *ghaṭam* exponent in Karnatic music. He is also credited with developing its present playing technique.

Kañjīrā

As an accompanying instrument (*pakkavādya*) in concerts, the *kañjīrā* was introduced by Pudukōṭṭai Mānpūṇḍiyā Piḷḷai, a famous percussionist of the

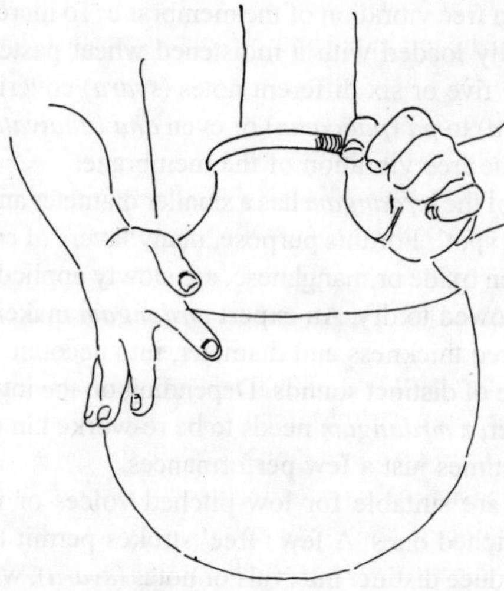

Fig. 22: The *ghaṭam*, an earthen pot used for percussion.

nineteenth century, who is credited with developing its playing technique. Like a European tambourine, it consists of a round wooden frame over which a membrane (mostly lizard skin) is stretched. After applying a few drops of water, this membrane becomes sufficiently elastic to enable a skilled player to produce distinct pitches and continuous glides (*gumki*). One or several pairs of small brass coins or discs produce an additional accent which can be adjusted by changing the playing position.

Mōrsiṅg

The instrument called *mōrsing* in South India is popular in several cultures, e.g. the 'Jew's harp' of the West. It consists of a steel arch in which a bent metal reed is fixed. This reed vibrates between the player's lips and is struck in accordance with the tāla patterns also applicable to other percussion instruments. Various sounds are produced by adjusting one's jaw, tongue, and the roof of the mouth. Additional sound effects are produced by inhalation and exhalation techniques.

According to B.M. Sundaram, the *mōrsing* was introduced in Karnatic music by Adicayapuram Sītarāmayyar, a vocalist (early 20th c.) whose interest in the *mōrsing* was kindled by a Muslim juggler who used it to attract an audience. Since then, it has served as an accompaniment along with the other secondary rhythm instruments (*upapakkavādya*), namely the *kañjīrā* and the *ghaṭam*.

OTHER PERCUSSION INSTRUMENTS

Tāḷam (Jālrā)

The *tāḷam* is a pair of metal discs, a lighter one (made of bell-metal), and a heavier one (made of iron). It is mostly played by the musician or dance master (*naṭṭuvanar*) who leads a performance. Its function is to indicate musical time (*tāla*), or the number of counts per rhythmic cycle (*āvarta*), besides marking rhythmic accents. The heavier disc is held in the left hand, and struck by the other which is held in the right hand.

The *jālrā* resembles the *tāḷam* but is made of thinner bell-metal discs. This results in a more gentle sound which suits the purpose of congregational singing (*bhajana*). It is also used during musical discourses (*harikathā kālakṣepam*), whose performers (*bhāgavatar*) traditionally accompanied their own singing by a small drone (*tambūrā*), with *jālrā*, *cipla*, and small bells (worn on the ankles) for rhythm.

Cipla

The *cipla* is a small rhythm instrument which is used in the context of musical discourses (*harikathā kālakṣepam*). It is traditionally associated with mystic mendicants (*Haridāsa*) and serves to dramatize a recitation or to mark the beginning and end of a lively musical item. It consists of two small wooden planks, each with a metal grip to hold them between the fingers and the thumb of one hand while the other hand is free for gestures or playing a *tambūrā*. Small bell-metal discs give the *cipla* its bright tonal quality.

Taṭṭuppalakai and taṭṭukaḻi

In a dance class, a wooden stick (*taṭṭuppalakai*) and a block (*taṭṭukaḻi*) are used for the purpose of coordinating rhythm (*tāla*), dance poses and movements (*aḍavu*). They serve as a substitute for the *tāḷam* (see Fig. 13).

NON-CONVENTIONAL INSTRUMENTS

Violin

For about two centuries, the violin (Tamil *piḍil*, from 'fiddle') has been adapted for use in classical South Indian music. Bālusvāmi Dīkṣitar, a brother of the famous Muttusvāmi Dīkṣitar, first realized the scope for employing the modern violin in Karnatic music. Other bowed instruments, such as the *rāvaṇahasta*, were, of course, known in different parts of India before the violin was introduced in South India. In view of the chequered history of the subcontinent, not to forget the early and flourishing trade relations between India, the peoples surrounding her, and even more remote centres of civilization, it is impossible to ascertain where a bowed instrument akin to the violin was first invented. Other instruments of the violin family are also found in many countries whose cultures came under the influence of Islām. The origins of the European violin are similarly traced to the Middle East.

Vaḍivēlu, one of the four brothers known as the Tanjore Quartette and a disciple of Muttusvāmi Dīkṣitar, popularized the violin in the nineteenth century all over South India. Its early acceptance and enduring popularity is due to its unmatched resonance, tonal range and flexibility. The violin is equally suited for solo performance and accompaniment. A skilled player can match the expression of any other melody instrument as well as any type of voice. Glides and any other embellishments

Fig. 23: The characteristic way in which the violin is played in Indian music.

(*gamaka*) and fast passages (*briga, birkā*) can be played with great effect. Light weight and compact size are other reasons why musicians, often compelled to travel under difficult circumstances, have taken to the violin. Not surprisingly, the violin has largely replaced the *vīṇā* as an accompanying instrument with the exception of some didactic and dance programmes.

As in the case of other Indian music instruments, the basic playing position for the violin is seated on the floor, with the player's left hand pointing towards the right foot. The South Indian system of tuning gives the freedom of adopting any basic pitch which is convenient for the main performer (e.g. vocalist). This pitch serves as a reference point for the first string to the left (from the player's perspective), which provides the tonic (*ādhāra ṣaḍja* or *sa*) in the lower octave (*mandra sthāyī ṣaḍja*). The second string is tuned to the fifth (*mandra sthāyī pañcama*) above the lower tonic. Similarly, the third and fourth strings are tuned to the tonic note and its fifth in the middle octave (*madhya sthāyī ṣaḍja* and *madhya sthāyī pañcama* respectively).

Like the *vīṇā*, the violin is mostly tuned to D-sharp ('European 2¹/₂ *śruti*') or E ('3 *śruti*') when played as a solo-instrument in Karnatic music. By comparison, the European tuning is based on a series of three fifths (G, D, a and e).

Śruti box

The *śruti box* (Tamil *śruti peṭṭi*) is a simple drone. It has always been popular with flute and *nāgasvaram* players because of its relatively loud and continuous tone, and also because it is easy to travel with. As playing it requires no skill, it has also become common in classrooms. Its name derives from the popular usage of the term *śruti* in the sense of basic pitch (*ādhāra ṣaḍja*). This usage has nothing to do with the concept of 22 micro-intervals (also known as *śruti*). The mechanical (pneumatic) type consists of a small harmonium equipped with a few metal reeds, often attached to a wooden dial or lever system to choose among several pitches, but has no keyboard. Although it lacks the brilliant and soothing sound quality of a well-tuned *tambūrā*, it has served as a handy substitute for about a century. It is operated by an outer and an inner pair of bellows. There is also an inexpensive electronic version of the *śruti peṭṭi* which has become popular because, unlike the pneumatic type, it can be tuned to virtually any pitch.

Jalataraṅgam

The *jalataraṅgam* consists of an assortment of porcelain bowls filled with water. It is played with two sticks which gives this instrument a percussive character. This has always been an exceptional instrument which was mastered by few because it lacks prestige. The best known exponent was the late Anayampatti S. Dhandapani who, like his father, was also a violinist. Not surprisingly, *jalataraṅgam* concerts are often accompanied by a violin, which helps to compensate for its inability to produce long notes.

Saxophone and clarinet

The saxophone is played by Kadri Gōpālnāth and other musicians whose ancestors were temple musicians. The expressive quality of the saxophone brings out the nuances of South Indian music in a modern way. Another reed instrument, the clarinet (clarionet) is used in a similar manner by A.K.C. Naṭarājan.

Mandolin

The mandolin is a fretted instrument with a short neck which lends itself to virtuosity of the kind which is displayed by U. Śrīnivās. Fitted with a pickup like an electric guitar, it has won a large and devoted following among South Indians who are interested in new sounds but prefer classical music to cinematic entertainment. Since the problem of difference in volume among various instruments is overcome by amplification, every conceivable combination has been tried out.

6

The Voice in South Indian Music

The *Nārada Purāṇa* (*circa* 10th c. AD) is a famous Sanskrit compilation which suggests that the seven notes (*saptasvara*) correspond to seven animals (Fig. 24, Table 6).

Table 6: The *saptasvara* corresponding to seven animals

Tonal step	**Animal** (*Sanskrit* name)	**Svara** (syllable to be sung)	**Tonic Sol-Fa** (Italian variant)
1st (tonic)	peacock (*mayūra*)	*ṣaḍja* (sa)	do
2nd	bull (*go*)	*ṛṣabha* (ri)	re
3rd	goat (*aja*)	*gāndhāra* (ga)	mi
4th	heron (*krauñca*)	*madhyama* (ma)	fa
5th	cuckoo 'in spring' (*kokila*)	*pañcama* (pa)	so (sol)
6th	horse (*aśva*)	*dhaivata* (dha)	la
7th	elephant (*kuñjara*)	*niṣāda* (ni)	ti (si)

How can poetic imagery of this type contribute to the effective use of the human voice? In the context of scientific voice culture, the association of musical notes with animals appears a rather outdated, perhaps all too fanciful concept to be of any practical value. But we should try to find out whether there are good reasons why this concept is echoed by many later writers. Perhaps there is common ground for both systems of voice culture, one traditionally practised in India, the other developed for European music.

Could any musician possibly be so naive as to try imitating the sounds made by a peacock, bull, goat, heron, cuckoo, horse, or elephant? Hardly by way of outward vocal mimicry, at least in the course of a recital.

In the best tradition of mnemonics, let us play with these images. They form a 'keyboard', a musical toy which solely exists in our minds to be played for our

Fig. 24: Animal imagery (Drawing by V.C. Arun).

entertainment and self-education. We need not imitate any existing animal sound but instead, we contemplate the beauty of each animal from various angles. For everyone interested in the wealth of India's cultural traditions, not only music and singing, it would be instructive to look beyond the fanciful poetic aspect of imagery. In many cases the various levels of meaning inherent even in common symbols will yield something of practical value if taken seriously.

The music traditions of India evolved over countless generations. A considerable amount of professional experience needs therefore to be taken into account.

The hereditary priests who chant sacred texts (*Veda*) and the singers (*ōduvār*) entrusted with sacred music employ a range of psycho-physiological and mnemonic techniques. Delivering dialogues in drama, reciting poetry and singing dance music have also been important professions since antiquity. The very livelihood of these professionals depended on maintaining high standards of voice production.

Besides the use of fanciful animal imagery, the *Nārada Purāṇa* also suggests the following correlation of areas of the human anatomy and the basic intervals used by a singer:

Table 7: Correlation of areas of human anatomy and basic intervals

Human anatomy	**Musical note (svara)**
throat (*kaṇṭha*)	basic note or tonic (*ṣaḍja*, sa)
head (*śiras*)	second (*ṛṣabha*, ri)
nose (*nāsikā*)	third (*gāndhāra*, ga)
chest (*uras*)	fourth (*madhyama*, ma)
chest & head & throat	fifth (*pañcama*, pa)
forehead	sixth (*dhaivata*, dha)
all of the above combined (*sarva sandhija*)	seventh (*niṣāda*, ni)

Ancient practitioners devised methods which enabled their voices to express any emotion at will. Expressive power had to be combined with the greatest possible clarity of diction. After all, the lyrics of a song, their beauty and meaning, had to be comprehensible both within and outside the premises of a temple. This requirement must have acquired greater urgency in medieval times when religious fervour was awakening on a great scale. Ecstatic movements (*bhakti*) began to sweep the subcontinent for many generations and carried mysticism, sacred lore, and musical knowledge to every corner of the land.

In order to comprehend the concept of animal imagery and also to apply it, we have to remember that the art of singing requires the mobilization of parts of the human anatomy other than the vocal cords proper. In order to produce musical notes, not merely intervals, and even embellishment and microtones, a singer has to manipulate an entire system of muscles and nerves rather than individual muscles. This approach includes an awareness of the areas where the vocal cords and the diaphragm are located (neck and abdominal region respectively) but goes much further. Mere anatomical knowledge is therefore of rather limited use because most muscles involved in the process of singing cannot even be directly activated at will.

The full potential of the voice can only unfold if various emotional states such as joy, anxiety, or surprise are invoked and consciously observed. In this manner a singer can effortlessly activate the relevant muscles in various parts of the body. The concepts of postures (*hathayoga*), breath control (*prāṇāyāma*), and those derived from medicine (*ayurveda*), as well as various philosophical traditions (*Tantra*), have contributed to the terminology of indigenous South Indian voice culture which must be taken into account.

Most languages have expressions such as 'gut feelings' which in the context of voice culture must be regarded as a most appropriate image. It is no secret that the human voice is the mirror of one's emotional state. But it is left to a trained singer or actor to invoke various emotional states (*bhāva*) at will and to kindle the attending feelings (*rasa*) in a listener. In Karnatic music the various emotions are not so much illustrated as suggested in a subtle manner. The feelings thus evoked transcend the corresponding emotions experienced in daily life. In this manner, they are not only refined aesthetically but also begin to relate to a spiritual dimension which is so precious to practitioners and listeners alike.

A closer look at the Indian tradition of dance, drama, and aesthetics leaves no doubt that the psycho-physiological aspects of these arts were well understood and systematically applied over a long period of time. A good command of the relevant techniques of voice culture was a basic requirement for all artists. If there is still a lack of more detailed information about voice production this must be ascribed to the fact that many basic principles were too widely used to require elucidation. The subtleties underlying any field of knowledge, on the other hand, were generally guarded as professional secrets to be shared only with a chosen few. The cryptic, if not enigmatic, nature of most treatises and manuals is certainly due to such considerations.

A look at Western techniques used for voice culture makes it clear, however, that visualization techniques are equally useful in the training of opera and *Lied* singers. There is a common approach in spite of differences in details: professional singers need to learn singing with a minimum of strain on the vocal cords. This is particularly important when a voice is used continuously for an extended period of time. It is not surprising that Indian vocal teachers of the past should have devoted much attention to the problem of how to put a pupil on the right track. The didactic use of animal motifs, far from being a mere distraction, did indeed serve a practical purpose. Apart from training the faculty of empathy, so important in the work of any performing artist, it orchestrated all components of the immensely complex and fragile vocal apparatus into a single organ which is capable of performing wonderful feats. At the same time, this ingenious method was appropriate to its cultural environment. If its utility ceased to be understood by recent generations of music teachers, this must be ascribed to an overall shift from the fanciful and mythical imagery of an ancient society to a more mechanical, albeit less effective method of vocal instruction.

Good voice production, control of pitch, volume, and timbre in all available vocal registers, are more easily achieved when the singer's mind is applied to something outside his or her own body. In view of the Indian propensity for spiritual pursuits (*sādhanā*) it is not surprising that musicians of the past could wholeheartedly submerge themselves in a routine of singing which ultimately produces results that are unsurpassed anywhere in the world.

Feeling (*bhāva*) is conveyed through concentration on an idea or mood which is in harmony with the occasion when music is performed, irrespective of whether this is done for one's own pleasure or for that of others. This fact is even reflected in the compositions of the three composers known as the Trinity—Śyāmā Śāstri, Tyāgarāja, and Muttusvāmi Dīkṣitar, who applied their genius to entirely different themes.

Indian singers of the past were accustomed to singing almost continuously for several hours. Today there are pauses for a singer when the accompanists play their solo parts. There are reliable accounts of public performances when hundreds if not thousands of listeners were spellbound by a singer. Nowadays, due to the introduction of amplification, singers rarely, if ever, reach their audience in a natural way; nor do Indian voices receive a training which is sufficiently systematic to do so.

The most remarkable aspect of the animal imagery in voice production is the fact that the heaviest creatures are those associated with higher notes. Images are combined with the feeling evoked by the respective animal. Behind the more apparent meaning of this imagery there are other layers where each symbol evokes a myth or some virtue which is regarded as being worth attaining by musicians and listeners alike, be they courage (*vīra*), compassion (*karuṇa*), devotion (*bhakti*), or attraction (*śṛṅgāra*). This poetical device has its counterparts in many other disciplines. There can be no doubt that it must have served the purposes of voice culture quite elegantly. It would also have aided the memorization of musical details if applied playfully and gracefully since the classical art of memory uses comparable techniques. The association with a horse (sixth note) and elephant (seventh) prevents the voice from becoming thin and strained particularly in the ascent. This is a very common problem not just for beginners, and difficult to overcome in the absence of imaginative techniques such as the one under discussion.

Many voice trainers in Western music will guide their students in a similar but less poetical fashion. Quite contrary to a lay-person's expectation, the key to successful voice control lies in envisioning antagonistic directions for the muscles involved. Undesirable tendencies of the vocal apparatus are thus counteracted. In this manner the voice begins to relate to the entire body and thereby gains resonance, expressiveness, and carrying power.

Practical experience shows that high notes, not the low ones, stand to gain from an 'earthbound' feeling. This 'low' feeling while singing high notes balances the vocal apparatus. Similarly, a 'high' feeling enhances the quality of the voice in the lower register for the same reason. A 'heavenward' feeling thus liberates the voice from near-inaudibility caused by a faulty placing of notes.

A rising series of seven notes (*saptasvara*) in a slow tempo would then depart from the image of a splendid peacock whose dazzling colours suggest that the tonic or basic note is charged with the qualities of all the other notes which in their totality create a colourful effect. It is not by chance that there is a synaesthetic dimension to Indian music. The notion of 'colour' (and its attending emotion) is all-pervasive in ancient and medieval Indian music terminology. *Rāga* derives from *rañj* (tinge) and even the lyrics often describe colourful attributes associated with divinity. The tonic is constantly reinforced by the use of a *tambūrā*, a lute serving as a drone which, provided it is well tuned, is so rich in overtones that a few notes suffice to establish the feeling associated with a particular *rāga* according to time-honoured tradition. Starting from the basic premises of traditional music theory, some modern composers and performers like Bālamuraḷī Krishna are in the process of probing the verity of these concepts.

There is a beauty about the progression from the splendour of the peacock, via the good-natured Indian cow or buffalo at the second, the self-assured goat at the third note, to the heron, a majestic bird. This series of four notes (tetrachord) leads us to the next which is more than a symmetrical image of the first. The cuckoo evokes romantic memories at the natural fifth, a very stable note. The horse conveys an image of controlled energy and elegance at the sixth note, and the elephant is the very embodiment of strength and intelligence at the seventh note. The choice of the weighty elephant at the last note in this series is quite ingenious. This mental image certainly helps to counteract the tendency of most singers to narrow their vocal apparatus to the point of concealing the beauty of their voice when progressing to the higher octave.

In the context of practical experience, this 'heavier' or 'lighter' feeling in conjunction with 'high' and 'low' notes respectively is therefore most sensible. But as these feelings cannot just be produced at will by a singer, they are induced in a more imaginative and playful, yet equally purposeful manner, with the help of these animal images. The peacock, the heron and the cuckoo are, in a way, quite ideal choices for the first, fourth and fifth notes since these are also the notes that are likely to occur most often in many rāgas. They also tend to be extended for a long time and serve as tonal centres for neighbouring notes. Giving them a more 'airy' quality by associating them with birds almost appears to be natural.

From the above it will be evident that in the proper context, the traditional imagery referring to certain animals is a useful method of practising voice culture. It can even prevent such common vocal problems as tension in the throat area and lack of resonance. The greatest benefit of such fanciful methods is that they have a prophylactic side to them without any need to be constantly self-conscious about certain muscles. Every vocalist or singing teacher knows from experience that thinking about one's own anatomy is quite counterproductive in singing. For this reason the animal imagery of Indian music helps to overcome the problems encountered by every singer.

In South Indian music, the instrument with the greatest range of notes is the lute (*vīṇā*) with three and a half octaves from a very low fifth (*anumandra pañcama)* to the tonic of the very high octave (*atitāra ṣaḍja*). Interestingly, the voice with its fairly large range when properly trained and used, is also referred to as a 'human lute' (*gātravatī vīnā* or *gātra vīnā*) in the *Nārada Purāṇa*. This terminology proves that, contrary to popular notions, vocal and instrumental music were both held in equal esteem from early times.

To cope with the demands of the Karnatic repertoire, commanding a range of two octaves is generally quite sufficient. This is also a range which virtually every healthy voice can master with some regular practice. For musical purposes, these two octaves are re-distributed and arranged in three registers (*tristhāyī*), a middle octave (*madhya*) bracketed between half an octave below (*mandra*), and another four to five notes above it (*tāra*) (Stave 5).

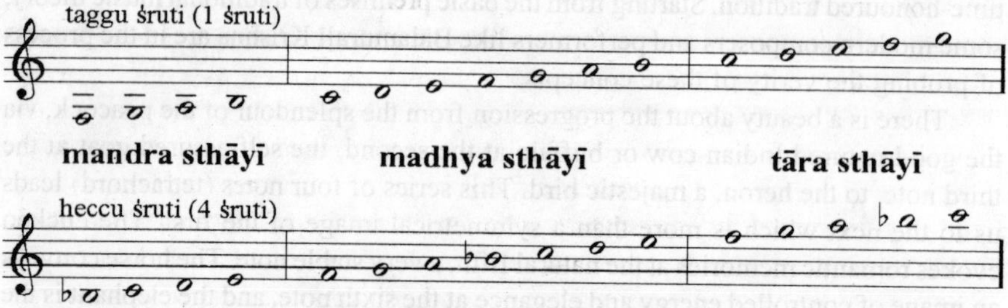

Stave 5: Vocal range.

Mahāvaidyanātha Śivan (1844–93), the great singer and scholarly composer, is said to have commanded a vocal range equal to that of the *vīṇā*.

A juxtaposition of the relevant ideas and syllables will show that imaginative usage and correct guidance of a singer's voice will protect it from several dangers inherent in unguided vocal practice such as mechanical sound production and boredom. Either of these is sufficient to reduce the expressive power of one's voice, and combined they are bound to ruin it. For the purpose of concentration, expressive power and suppleness, past musicians used didactic songs (*gītam*) which evoked familiar images (*rūpa*), colours (*rañj*), and moods (*rasa*) in the mind of a serious practitioner. The melodic form of each rāga was remembered with the help of corresponding attributes which were borrowed from various other disciplines including *Yoga* and *Tantric* philosophy, iconography, and mythology, to name but a few.

A conscientious vocal instructor can be expected to know how to modify conventional methods for the benefit of his pupils, taking their individual abilities and problems into account. Failing to do so, particularly at an early stage of vocal instruction, can even jeopardize their very ability to sing. For these reasons the charmingly simple correlation of musical notes and the images of animals, or the feelings evoked by them, is a very valuable tool from which every singer can benefit. Tyāgarāja was a teacher who took care that various disciples developed their respective faculties in accordance with time-honoured principles as well as his own high standards. In accordance with his own family background and personal disposition, he favoured concepts akin to *Yoga*, based on physiological knowledge. Tyāgarāja's music remains so appealing and lively to the present day because he succeeded in evoking the powerful personages and dramatic events of the *Rāmāyaṇa* not only in his lyrics but also by means of intricate melodic and rhythmic devices.

Table 8: Correlation of animal imagery, areas of human anatomy and basic intervals

Tonal step	Animal	Placement (human anatomy)	Musical note (svara)	Sol-Fa
1st	peacock	throat (*kantha)*	*ṣadja* (sa)	do
2nd	bull	head (*śiras*)	*ṛṣabha* (ri)	re
3rd	goat	nose (*nāsikā*)	*gāndhāra* (ga)	mi
4th	heron	chest (*uras*)	*madhyama* (ma)	fa
5th	cuckoo	chest and head and throat	*pañcama* (pa)	so
6th	horse	forehead	*dhaivata* (dha)	la
7th	elephant	all of the above combined	*niṣāda* (ni)	ti
		(*sarva sandhija*)		

An integration of Indian and Western voice culture

In order to appreciate the scope for cultivating one's voice within the framework of the *Sāmaveda*, *Yoga* techniques, and the music systems associated with these traditions, we should take notice of some specific references made by Tyāgarāja in the lyrics for his *kṛti* Śōbhillusaptasvara (rāga Jaganmōhinī, rūpaka tāla).

Tyāgarāja is revered not only as a poet-composer (*vaggēyakāra*), but is believed to have been an accomplished singer in his own right. His erudition was such that specific instructions for voice production contained in his lyrics must not be dismissed as poetic fancy. On the contrary, it is no exaggeration to observe that 'Sōbhillusaptasvara' contains the key to traditional Indian voice culture and should be taken seriously as a proven method of soulful voice production.

Worship the beautiful goddesses presiding over the seven notes (*saptasvara*), which shine through navel (*nābhi*), heart (*hṛt*), throat (*kaṇṭha*), tongue (*rasanā*), and nose (*nāsā*) . . . through *Ṛg* and *Sāmaveda*, the heart of the *Gāyatrī Mantra* and the minds of gods, holy men and Tyāgarāja.

(Translation by C. Rāmānujāchāri, *The Spiritual Heritage of Tyāgarāja*, p. 596.)

The *mūlādhāra cakra* at the base of the spine is considered as the source of primordial sound as well as of the seven fundamental notes or *saptasvara* (*ṣaḍja, ṛṣabha, gāndhāra, madhyama, pañcama, dhaivata* and *niṣāda*). This implies that, for the purpose of using one's voice effectively, one needs to 'place' all the notes produced not just in one or another register (*sthāyī*) in accordance with its apparent 'high' (*tāra*), 'middle' (*madhya*) or 'low' (*mandra*) position. On the contrary, all notes produced must be rooted in the *mūlādhāra* besides being modulated for the purpose of expressing various aspects of human sentiments or emotions (*bhāva*). The predominant sentiments in Indian music are chiefly described in terms of devotion (*bhakti*) and love (*śṛṅgāra*), and neither is complete without the other. In South Indian music and dance, all the major sentiments (e.g. *karuṇa*) tend to amalgamate with either *bhakti*, or *śṛṅgāra*, or both.

The Indian view of singing does not disagree with the European art of cultivating one's own voice or that of one's students. In either system, music is a reflection of the same basic human condition in which inspiration and creativity are first ignited in the *mūlādhāra cakra* (corresponding to the reproductive centre), but needs to be tempered and guided towards a worthwhile goal. Yet there are known to be dangers that arise if this urge is given free reign. This danger applies to the voice itself, the singer's own psyche, as well as to the welfare of others—the power of music has been known from ancient times and still operates on similar lines today. The inherent danger of realizing this power can be averted by an experienced teacher in order to benefit from the great energizing potential of music in full measure. In the Indian tradition, devotion is the most suitable and enjoyable means for tempering the valuable yet volatile urge of realizing one's enormous potential through music. The compositions of Tyāgarāja, just as those of many others before and after him, provide us with lively glimpses of a philosophy of musical devotion (*nādopāsanā*) which is at once ecstatic and controlled, filled with love for God and mankind, sensuous and sublime. In *Nādopāsanacē* (rāga Bēgaḍa , ādi tāla), Tyāgarāja proclaims that through musical worship (*nādopāsanā*), even the scriptures (*Veda*) are transcended. According to him, the basic elements inherent in music—notes, tunes, and rhythm (*svara*, *rāga*, and *laya* respectively)—are liberating in themselves; they are the very life of sacred syllables (*mantra*), symbols (*yantra*), and rituals (*tantra*). Several other compositions like *Cētulāra śṛṅgāramu* (rāga Naṭhabhairavi, ādi tāla) are addressed to Rāma, his beloved family deity (*iṣṭadevatā*), and through these, he accomplishes the difficult yet characteristic feat of expressing his devotion in a most personal, affectionate manner:

> I shall decorate you with my own hands so beautifully as to elicit the admiration of even Brahmā and other devotees, and enjoy the sight myself. You will have golden anklets, golden clothes, and be decorated with fragrant flowers. I shall kiss your beautiful face . . . I shall hug you the beautiful one . . . your body shall be besmeared with sweet-scented sandal paste. Sarasvatī will come and fan you then. In that exaltation, I shall exclaim 'well done, well done', and cast aside everything else.
>
> (Based on the translation by C. Rāmānujāchāri,
> *The Spiritual Heritage of Tyāgarāja*, pp. 526–7.)

Tyāgarāja is referred to as a *nāda yogi*, a mystic whose quest for self-realization took the shape of sanctified music (*nāda*). In several compositions, he refers to a useful system for the control and refinement of the voice: in 'Svararāgasudhārasa', he states that *nāda* originates in the lower torso (*mūlādhāra*). In 'Śōbhillusaptasvara', he refers to the principal areas of the human anatomy from which the seven notes (*saptasvara*) originate. The seven musical notes are indeed the very foundation not only of Indian music but most advanced music systems of the world. Therefore they are treated with great reverence, in this song even as 'beautiful goddesses'. We should not underestimate the value of these hints, bequeathed by the greatest among the saint-composers of South India. They point the way towards a sensible way of using our voices. They will be found to be more than mere poetic images if properly understood in the light of other traditions of voice culture.

A similar system of voice culture is often used by professional Western singers, whose roles in operas and performances of cycles of songs (German *Lied*) are both psychologically and physically very demanding. As part of their training and regular exercise, many singers associate various places of the human anatomy, comparable to the seven *cakras*, with certain qualities. Some places (hence the term 'placing the tone') serve as focal points for specific sounds as well as qualities: (1) The rootpoint at the lower spine (*mūlādhāra*) is associated with sensuality (*śṛṅgāra*), or creative energy. (2) The navel (*nābhi*) is the place where emotional forces (*bhāva*) can be activated. (3) Control of the diaphragm determines the smooth flow and intensity of breath; thus it concerns the power to radiate sound waves just as ideas or feelings; this is also the place where rhythm is felt most directly, or from where rhythm is conveyed; hence it is best activated by practising laughter, namely by producing a few short bursts of sounds (*staccato*). (4) From the chest, a singer develops resonance. From the type of singing which is located at the heart (*hṛd*), listeners derive reassuring

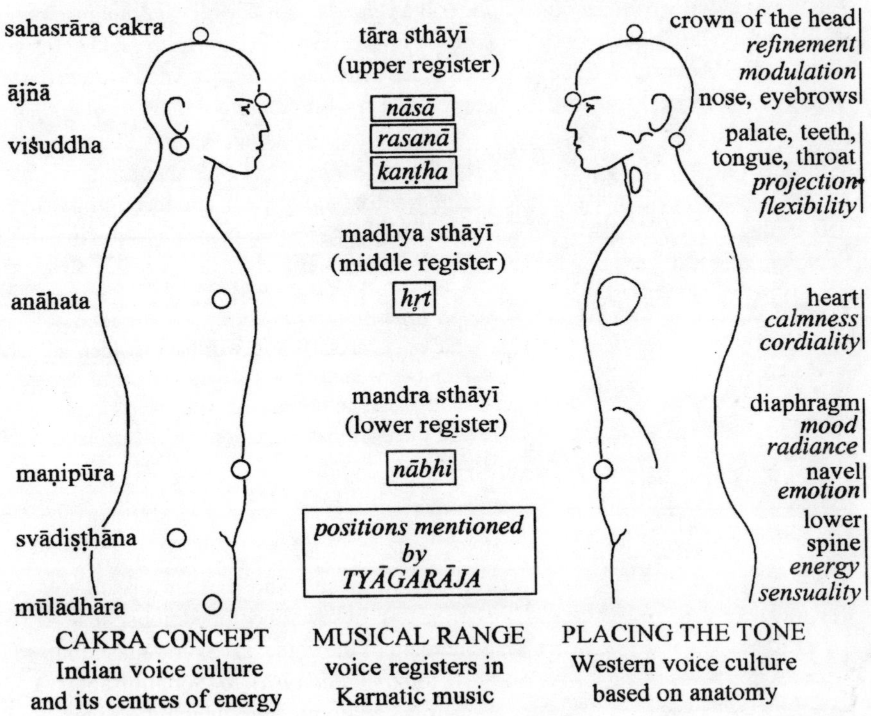

Fig. 25: Diagram of human anatomy.

sensations best described as cordiality and calmness; here, good practice involves the 'placing' of the vowels 'a' and 'o'. (5) The hard and soft palates are associated with the feeling of projecting the voice into space; the soft palate needs to be relaxed in order to avoid obstruction of sound and breath (a precondition for natural audibility); the throat (*kaṇṭha*) is attended to by way of 'placing' the vowels 'o' and 'u' and 'm'; by placing the tone at the 'neck-point', accompanied by a feeling of 'singing into a helmet', an inspired type of singing is facilitated. Placing the tone at the teeth involves the vowels 'i' and 'e'. Similarly, the tongue (*rasanā*) also controls the flexibility of a voice. (6) The nose (*nāsā*) and eyebrows serve as focal points for a type of singing which aims at finer modulation; this is practised by way of 'placing' the vowels 'a' and 'o' at these points; the desired sound is described in terms of a 'velvet-like' quality; it is more easily obtained by singing into an imaginary 'mask'. (7) The crown of the head (*sahasrāra*) is the focus of the vowels 'u' and 'ue' (a diphthong located between 'u' and 'i'); here the singer seeks to obtain the highest degree of vocal refinement.

7

Music for All

Ever since antiquity, music has been both the hobby of cultured rulers and citizens, as well as a professional pursuit. In early Tamil history there were clans of bards (*pāṇar*) who earned their living by singing the praise of their patrons. A similar practice of 'praising mortals' (*narastuti*), although vehemently condemned by religious composers like Tyāgarāja and discouraged by Svāti Tirunāḷ, was still in vogue among court musicians until India became a modern democracy in 1947. Since the middle ages the study and performance of music were usually maintained by hereditary temple singers (*ōduvār*), mystic sects like the Haridāsa as well as noblemen and citizens. A high level of critical faculty has always been regarded as the hallmark of a refined person (*sahṛdaya*). This not only favoured competition and the pursuit of excellence but was equally rife with professional jealousy and possessiveness.

Buddhism and Jainism played a major role in the evolution of Indian art in general and South Indian music and dance in particular. Before the eighth century AD, the major dynasties of South India supported the great monasteries, places of worship and educational institutions established by Jains and Buddhists. These institutions fostered an atmosphere where valuable contributions were made in the fields of traditional art and science. Two early epic poems, the *Cilappatikāram* of a Jain prince, Ilaṅgo Aṭikaḷ, and its sequel entitled *Maṇimēkalai* (a work with a Buddhist theme), are reckoned among the greatest works of Tamil literature ever written. The *Cilappatikāram* contains numerous descriptions of the practice of music and dance in the early centuries of our era, known as the *Saṅgam* age of South India. The contributions made by early followers of these two beliefs have benefited later artists and scholars.

The Gupta period (*circa* 320–540) is known as the 'Golden Age' in which the 'classical' pattern of Indian civilization was established. Samudragupta (*circa* 335–76) ruled a greater part of the Indian subcontinent including the southern peninsula up to Kāñcīpuram. On one of his coins, he is seen playing a stringed instrument (*vīṇā* or *yāḷ*) and thereby sets an example for later rulers who not only patronized the arts but often proved to be competent musicians and music scholars. It is believed that Kālidāsa, India's greatest poet and dramatist, wrote his masterpieces during the reign of Samudragupta's successor, Candra Gupta II (*circa* 376–415). In Kālidāsa's imaginative works, we find references to the profound emotions evoked by music: the symphonies of nature when bamboo is gently blown by mountain wind to accompany the singing of heavenly beings (*Kumārasambhava*, *Meghadūta*); and the inexplicable sadness that befalls Duṣyanta, the young king, when he overhears the sweet strands of a love song in his palace before lost memories begin to surface again and remind him of his true love (Act V, *Abhijñāna Śākuntalam*).

The artistic contributions made with the patronage of more recent dynasties of Tañjāvūr, Mysore and Travancore (Trivandrum) are better preserved, more widely accessible and closer to the aspirations of contemporary man than the intricate symbolism of ancient and medieval India, of which merely a fraction has survived the ravages of war and plunder in the north and central parts, and of climate in the southern peninsula.

Images of great perfection were sculpted for the embellishment of Hindu shrines since the sixth century if not earlier. Such architecture was inextricably linked with a rich iconographic vocabulary inspired by the personages described in the epics

MODERN STATE ■ cultural capital of historical importance
(language used in lyrics) ○ place of importance for music/dance

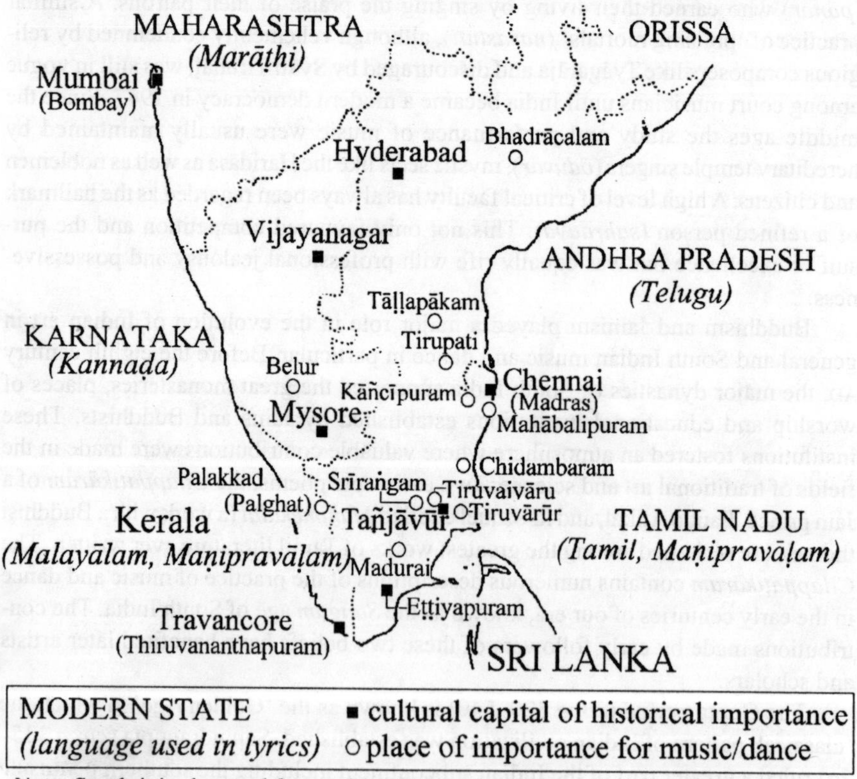

Note: Sanskrit is also used for music lyrics in South India; and Maṇipravāḷam, its hybrid form, mainly in Kerala and Tamil Nadu.

Telugu is widespread in Tamil Nadu; and Marāṭhī was the court language of the Marāṭhā rulers of Tañjāvūr (18th/19th century).

Fig. 26: Map of South India.

(*Rāmāyaṇa* and *Mahābhārata*). The religious and didactic works known as the *Purāṇa*, mostly written from this period onwards, gave free reign to the imagination of sculptors and architects. This delight in sculpted imagery first evolved from Buddhist and Jain models of earlier centuries but soon acquired a character of its own. Gradually these physical expressions of religion were subjected to codification. A body of specialized manuals came into being which comprised texts pertaining to architecture and iconography (*vāstu*), the various crafts (*śilpa śāstra*), and ritualistic practice (*āgama*). Two principal dynasties, the *Pallava* and the *Cāḷukya*, vied with one another. For some time the *Pallava* of Kāñcīpuram and Māmallapuram (Mahābalipuram) continued to patronize Jainism and Buddhism. The *Cāḷukya* of the Western Deccan plateau in Karṇāṭaka (Aihole, Badāmi, Paṭṭadakal) provided the stage on which north and south Indian culture mingled in every conceivable way, most conspicuously in their architecture. Both are credited with carrying sculpture to new heights in their cave shrines and stone temples. From then on, decorative friezes, sculptures and icons depict gods, saints and royal patrons who delight in music and dance. Religious activity was no longer reflected in the arts. The arts themselves became an integral part of religious activity. Participation in the arts, or at least artistic appreciation, began to define the individual's real identity on a metaphysical scale.

In a scenario marked by rapidly changing social and economic conditions, most musicians have become keen to re-establish and preserve their traditions. This has led to a wider availability of specialist information. Rather than guarding information, many musicians readily share their knowledge through interviews, lectures and publications. Musical training is easier to come by and hardly, if ever, denied due to considerations of caste or class. Classical Karnatic music, far from having lost its fascination for younger people, begins to be patronized by modern Indians with a secular rather than sectarian outlook. As the restlessness, uniformity, and shallowness of modern life become increasingly oppressive, this art is re-discovered for its timeless beauty. If much traditional music has not been faithfully preserved in the recent past, this is certainly a deplorable loss. At the same time this poses a challenge to the ingenuity and creativity of new generations of musicians and listeners. This challenge has already been taken up with fervour, talent, and imagination.

8

Intonation (Śruti)

Early writers used the term *śruti* ('heard', 'revealed') for the smallest shift of pitch a listener can discern and appreciate. Most early authorities have agreed that 22 steps or micro-intervals, each equal to one *śruti*, should be accommodated within an octave. Some writers have even proposed including 24 or more *śruti* steps within an octave, albeit in vain. The 22 *śruti* theory is still widely accepted although ancient music theory is likely to have differed from modern practice. Various methods have been proposed by modern theorists for determining the values of musical intervals based on *śruti*. Keyboard instruments are not helpful in this regard as Indian music does not use the so-called scale of *equal temperament* of Western classical music which was introduced over two centuries ago. For practising musicians it matters little if *śruti* values are established by way of the empirical methods described in ancient treatises or based on mathematical calculation.

Several attempts were made to formulate accurate scale and interval systems. A special terminology evolved for the purpose of describing and remembering rāgas (*rāga lakṣaṇa*). This terminology has no value unless it can be translated into musical practice based on experience (*lakṣya*) and knowledge. It is possible to distinguish between those intervals of a rāga that corresponded to a particular reference scale (*mēḷakartā rāga*), and others whose pitches have been reduced or raised. All theoretical methods, however, need to be supplemented by the personal guidance of an experienced teacher, by repeated listening to good renditions of a rāga, or by both.

The 72 scales of Karnatic music are obtained by dividing the octave into twelve semitones (*svarasthāna*). A different set of seven notes (*saptasvara*) is chosen for each scale. All scales share the same tonic (*ṣaḍja*, 'C') and its natural 5th (*pañcama*, 'G'). But by themselves, these seven tonal steps (*svara*) do not reveal the finer nuances of intonation. The nuances that bring out the character (*rūpa*) of each rāga are obtained by further modification of specific notes (*svara kāku*). The actual process of microtonal adjustment is far too intricate to be reduced to formulae and statistics. The individual qualities and problems associated with different voices and instruments also need to be taken into account.

Within the framework of the modern Karnatic rāga system, the 22 microtonal steps within the octave can be distributed in the following manner: two notes, the basic note (*ṣaḍja*) and its natural fifth (*pañcama*), are defined as being fixed in relation to one another and therefore without variants (*avikṛta svara*). The remaining five notes are variable (*vikṛta svara*), and each of these notes has four microtonal variants (5 × 4 = 20; 20 + 2 = 22). This division is based on practical rather than theoretical considerations and should not be equated with ancient theories.

Scale divisions capture melodic features just like a pencil sketch helps to prepare a painting: after several improvements of a sketch, the artist paints the final picture with various natural or imaginary colours and textures. In rāga-based music, 'sketch-like' intervals are combined into phrases (*sañcāra* or *prayoga*). All melodic features can be sung as syllables '*sa*', '*ri*', '*ga*' (*sargam*) and, for the sake of brevity, written as letters '*s*', '*r*', '*g*', '*m*'. These syllables serve as an aid to memory. Over a period of time, such sketches developed into didactic music forms (*abhyāsa gāna*). Some of these forms are entirely based on musical elements (e.g. *saraḷi variśai*, *alaṁkāram*, *svarajati*) and thus concentrate on the feeling conveyed by the treatment of musical notes (*rāga bhāva*). The other forms, namely *gītam* and *tāṉavarṇam*, are combined with lyrics (*sāhitya*) that convey meaning or feeling (*sāhitya bhāva*).

Within a given rāga, the pitches of individual notes tend to be slightly higher in the ascending series (*ārohaṇa*) than in the descending series (*avarohaṇa*). In some rāgas, tonal steps are entirely obscured because certain notes should be executed in the form of oscillating movements between neighbouring notes (*gamaka*).

The subjective perception of pitch and intervals depends on several factors. The most tangible factor that influences our hearing is volume (sound pressure), which nowadays is increased by ubiquitous amplification. Another factor is the difference experienced between the impression caused by pitches that are sounded together, and pitches that are heard in succession. Since the pitch of a voice or wind instrument is subject to constant changes, the *tambūrā* and the *vīṇā* have played a major role

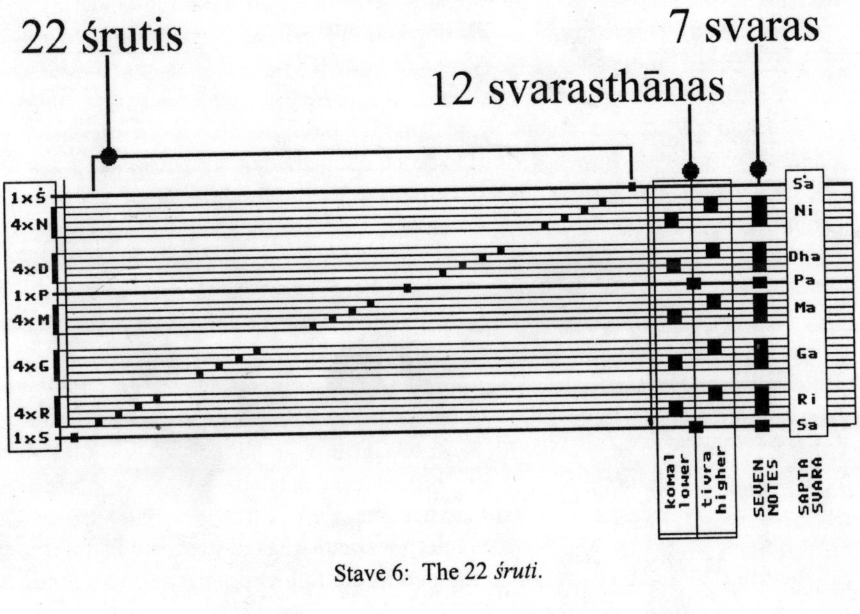

Stave 6: The 22 *śruti*.

in the development of the South Indian rāga system. By tuning several strings on one or two instruments one can establish a wide range of tonal relationships that account for the diversity of rāgas and scales in use today.

Within the framework of the Karnatic rāga system, some notes have little resemblance with the familiar musical notes and semitones found in other music systems including that of North Indian (Hindustānī) music. Individual notes (*svara*) and phrases (*sañcāra*) are subjected to various manipulations (*kāku*) in order to make every conceivable type of melodic music pleasing (*saukhyam*). The dynamics of melody could be likened to the erotic symbolism (*nāyaka nāyikā bhāva*) of South India's devotional (*bhakti)* movements which is the subject dealt with in the lyrics of many songs (*padam*). *Advaita* philosophy, which inspired most composers of South India, speaks of an innate yearning for the union with one's beloved; and lover and beloved are images of the relationship between the divine Absolute (*para-brahman*) and the human soul (*jīvātman*). Applied to the relationship of various musical notes, one could liken the basic note or tonic (*ṣaḍja*) to the immutable Divine aspect of existence while the mutable notes (*vikṛta*) are engaged in a constant quest for harmony by shedding their dissonant properties. The great diversity of notes and interval relationships has yielded a corresponding variety of modulations by which harmony is induced in the minds of listeners. This subject is all the more intriguing as the underlying notes themselves are emanations of various degrees of dissonance. Each degree of dissonance or consonance can be expressed in terms of a mathematical ratio belonging to every interval or pair of pitches. But whether this subject is pursued intuitively or scientifically, it is the lasting aesthetic effect (*rasa*) which the experience of rāga leaves behind that ultimately matters.

9

Embellishment (Gamaka)

An embellishment enhances the experience of beauty (*rasa*) derived from melody. Without grace notes, pure melody would sound static or 'colourless'. Some types of *gamaka* are reminiscent of vocal music (*gāyakī*) even if performed by an instrument. Many others are derived from the playing technique of the *vīṇā*. Most of the *gamaka* variants described here are widely used in several rāgas and are equally applicable in vocal, instrumental, and dance music. A musician needs to adapt embellishment to the possibilities and limitations inherent in different types of voices and musical instruments. Thus there is scope for discretion on the part of a performer. The application of *gamaka* is partly based on aesthetic criteria, partly on technical considerations.

The concept of *gamaka* is difficult to convey in words since the application of some embellishments tends to vary from tradition to tradition. Most contemporary performers habitually employ a multitude of embellishments without referring to any particular system or theory.

To preserve its special appeal, a more conspicuous type of *gamaka* like the slide (*jāru*) is not used routinely but applied with restraint. It is futile to try to determine the precise duration of an ornamental note or phrase unless a specific melodic context is taken into consideration. Where an oscillation occurs within an ascending or descending series of notes (*ārohaṇa-avarohaṇa*), it is important that the notes before and after such a *gamaka* are rendered in a steady and plain manner, on their proper pitch (*svarasthāna*) rather than embellished. The prolonged practice of *alaṅkāra* exercises helps to internalize all applicable combinations of embellished and unembellished notes.

The importance of embellishment

In early treatises like the *Nāṭya Śāstra*, a rāga without subtle ornamental features (*alaṅkāra*) has been compared to a moonless night, a creeper without flowers, a river without water, and a woman without jewellery. At a later stage, all embellishments of melody came to be called *gamaka*—which refers to both, an ornamental note, and a type of short decorative phrase—which has become an integral part of a particular rāga.

Traditional concepts

The concept of 'ten types of gamaka' (*daśavidha gamaka*) evolved from an older, more complex concept. Muttusvāmi Dīkṣitar, in the lyrics of his compositions 'Mīṉākṣīmē' (rāga Pūrvīkalyāṇi, ādi tāla) describes Mīṉākṣi as the goddess who delights in the *daśavidha gamaka*. The famous *tāṉavarṇam Viribōni* (rāga Bhairavi) is regarded as an exemplary demonstration of this concept. Most theorists and musicians habitually refer to it although its terminology is inadequate to explain some aspects of modern performing practice.

Differentiation and diversification of the concept of gamaka

In the course of many centuries, the art of melodic ornamentation has undergone considerable changes. Scale degrees (*svarasthāna*) were systematized with the help of abstract reference scales (*mēḷakartā rāga*). Minute intervals (*śruti*) were sought to be standardized in the concept of 22 *śruti* based on experiments with string instruments (*viṇā*). These efforts yielded the modern concept of rāga. Because each vocal and instrumental tradition (*sampradāya*) has its own stylistic and technical specialities, often jealously guarded by its living exponents, there is a corresponding lack of agreement among experts on how a particular *gamaka* should be called or executed in a performing context.

Types of embellishments

Instrumentalists find it convenient to analyse and explain some forms of *gamaka* in terms of auxiliary notes (*anusvara*). An *anusvara* has no existence of its own but is inevitably tied to another note. Often an *anusvara* has the function of connecting or dividing two notes. In this manner, one or several auxiliary notes produce the ef-fect of a *gamaka* or embellishment. Most important notes of a rāga derive their individuality from the appropriate application of such embellishments.

On the surface, we can distinguish three 'families' of embellishment: those confined to a single note, those involving two or more notes, and a straight slide from one note to another. But a closer look reveals many subtle variants belonging to a particular rāga, technique, or style.

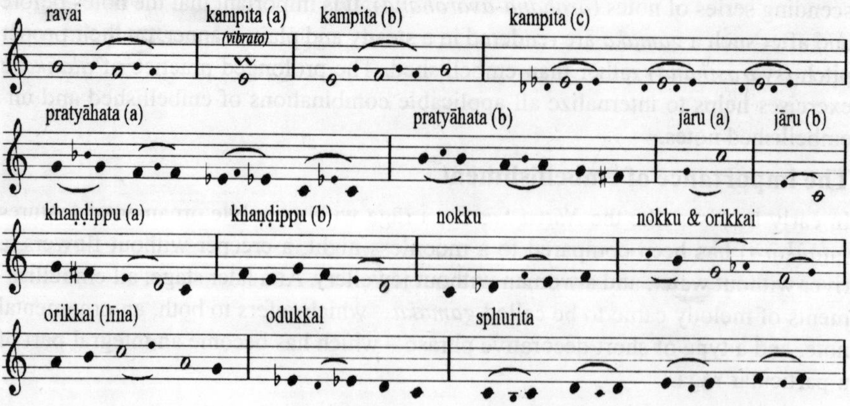

Stave 7: Embellishments (*gamaka*).

The following descriptions and transcriptions are mainly based on the published works as well as personal information graciously furnished by Smt. Vidya Shankar, a senior music scholar and *vaiṇika* of Madras.

Ravai

The *ravai* is a combination of shakes (*kampita*) and involves two pitches. The pitch of the preceding note is first repeated in the form of a short and soft *anusvara*. The *anusvara* leads to a second pitch, the target note, which is followed by another shake.

Kampita

Any pitch variation of a note (*svara*) can be said to constitute a shake (*kampita*). A shake forms the basis for several types of embellishment (e.g. *nokku* and *odukkal*) besides being regarded as a *gamaka* in its own right.

Kampita (a): if a shake is limited, it is heard as a *vibrato* provided the manipulation of an individual note (*svara*) does not touch the realm of a neighbouring note. This means the pitch value (*śruti*) of the embellished note is altered to a small, but audible extent (*svara kāku*) without any 'shade' (*chāyā*) of another note. A typical example is the major 3rd, *antara gāndhāra*, if extended during the special phrase or *viśeṣa sañcāra* '*s r G r*'.

Kampita (b, c): a long shake in the form of an oscillation between two distinct notes, usually starting with the upper note. If these notes are far enough apart, a *kampita* tends to obscure the pitch (*svarasthāna*) of the embellished note. Typical examples are a particular variant of the 4th (*śuddha madhyama*) which occurs in rāga Śaṅkarābharaṇam, and the 3rd (*sādhāraṇa gāndhāra*) of rāga Bhairavi.

The note embellished by a *kampita* is often considered the principal 'life-note' (*jīva svara*), around which an *ālāpana* exposition can be developed, for instance the *sādhāraṇa gāndhāra* ('E flat') in rāga Tōḍi. The *jīva svara* is also described as the most characteristic note (*chāyā svara*) of a rāga.

Pratyāhata

In this type of *gamaka*, the upper adjacent note of the rāga is faintly heard as an auxiliary note (*anusvara*).

Jāru (Glissando)

A *jāru* is an up- or downward movement and elegantly connects any two pitches with one another. It involves a sliding (*glissando*) from an auxiliary note (*anusvara*) to a target note (*svara*).

There are two *jāru* variants: (a) the upward sliding movement from an auxiliary note to its adjacent higher note (*ēṟṟa jāru*); and (b) the downward sliding movement from an auxiliary note to any lower note (*iṟakka jāru*).

The *jāru* is one of the few types of *gamaka* which can be applied to the basic note (*ṣaḍja*) and its natural 5th (*pañcama*), another being the *odukkal gamaka*. While both notes, *ṣaḍja* and *pañcama*, serve as auxiliary notes and thus embellish their adjacent notes, neither should be embellished by a shake or vibrato. The most common form of *jāru* starts from the lower 5th (*mandra sthāyī pañcama*) and lands on the basic note (*madhya sthāyī ṣaḍja*). In a repetition, the starting note of a *jāru* is often altered in order to cover the interval between the last note of the theme with its beginning note.

Khaṇḍippu

The *khaṇḍippu gamaka* involves a sliding movement from a higher note (*anusvara*) to the target note and is preceded by a brief pause. This pause and the brevity of the *anusvara* lends weight to a target note which is already elongated (e.g. the 2nd, *svara catuḥśruti ri*, in the rāgas Kalyāṇi and Surați). Otherwise it resembles the *nokku*.

Nokku

The *nokku* is a short and simple embellishment which resembles the *khaṇḍippu gamaka*. Both involve the descent from an auxiliary note (*anusvara*) to the target note (*svara*). The *nokku* appears to be derived from the playing technique of the *vīṇā*, namely the deflecting of a note by releasing the tension of a string (e.g. *madhyama* preceding *gāndhāra* in rāga Māyāmāḷavagauḷa).

Orikkai

This *gamaka* can be described as a brief 'flash' after which a note or phrase is cut off. A long note (*svara*) is followed by its adjacent higher note in the form of a short *anusvara*. The *orikkai gamaka* lends variety to a phrase by way of reversing the sequential order of notes for a fleeting moment. If the *anusvara* is the extension of a long note (e.g. upper *ṣaḍja* in rāga Śaṅkarābharaṇam), it is believed to be identical with the 'vanishing' (*līnam*) *gamaka*.

Odukkal

The Tamil name of this *gamaka* indicates that a note is 'pushed aside'. It is a form of shake (*kampita*) and emphasizes a note by setting it apart. To emphasize the main note (*svara*), it is preceded by an intermediary note (*anusvara*) in the form of its lower adjacent note which is articulated in a brief but firm manner. A specimen of the *odukkal* is found in the last section of the famous *varṇam* in rāga Bhairavi, aṭa tāla (*Viribōni*) where the second *gāndhāra* is embellished. The *odukkal* is one of the few types of *gamaka* which can be applied to the basic note (*ṣaḍja*) and its natural 5th (*pañcama*), another characteristic one being the *jāru gamaka*.

Sphurita

The Sanskrit name of this *gamaka* indicates a 'throbbing' applied to a pair of notes (*janta svara*). Both notes are usually, but not always, of the same pitch. The second note of the pair is stressed by inserting their lower adjacent note as an auxiliary note (*anusvara*). The *anusvara* is merely hinted at.

Melodious lines of beauty

In South Indian music, lines of beauty and grace permeate the realm of pure melody at every level. Here they take the form of waving phrases (*prayoga*, *sañcāra*) which are so characteristic of most rāgas. The ascending and descending scale patterns (*ārohaṇa-avarohaṇa*) of many rāgas such as Bēgaḍa, Khamās, Mukhāri are embellished by curvatures (*vakra prayoga*) that can be compared to vines that grow on familiar scale patterns. Similarly, a musician always returns to the basic note (*ṣadja*), its 5th (*pañcama*), or octave (*tāra sthāyī ṣadja*) at the conclusion of a theme. This return often follows the most beautiful rather than the shortest course available.

Particularly in rāga Bēgaḍa, we can also discern delicate wave-shaped features in the form of ornamentation applied to two notes, the 4th and the 7th which are not found in any other rāga. Intermediary or auxiliary notes (*anusvara*) connect all notes with one another. Although an *anusvara* or *gamaka* is rarely committed to writing, it plays a major role in distinguishing different rāgas with similar melody patterns. Some notes are not even heard as distinct pitches but merely suggested by an oscillation between their neighbouring notes. Minute melodic details of this kind are treated as part of the art of embellishment. Even before all the admissible notes of a rāga are introduced, an experienced listener recognizes a rāga among numerous similar ones because of its characteristic notes (*aṁśa svara*) and most beautiful phrases (*rañjaka prayoga*). Such features are often associated with a well-known song and remembered along with its text rather than as a rāga in the sense of an abstract melodic entity.

Functional and stylistic aspects of gamaka

The most elementary function of an embellishment is to lend individuality to each note of a rāga. This function can be compared to the lines and curves of a printed letter (*serif*). A letter type with ornate features of the *serif* variety is designed to enable the eye of a reader to distinguish one letter from another even if a text is printed in a very small size. For this reason, most periodicals and dictionaries continue to be printed with *serif* typefaces rather than with modern, plain *sans-serif* typefaces. In a similar manner, a listener easily distinguishes musical notes that are endowed with *gamaka*, no matter how short or softly they are rendered by a musician.

As a case in point we should turn to the musical heritage of Vīṇā Dhanammāḷ who continues to have a large following of admiring musicians and listeners. An uncompromising *vaiṇika* and singer, she was known to equally abhor technical effects and loudness. Instead of exploring the spectacular side of music, her genius gave new life to the essential values and attributes of South Indian music. The enduring appeal of her musical style is traced to a subtle approach to the aspect of rāga which was based on her discerning application of *gamaka*.

On another level, a *gamaka* guides the ear from note to note in a graceful manner. Again, we can compare a text printed with *serif* features with the rāga enriched by *gamaka*. If applied judiciously, both types of features enable the perceiver to follow, absorb, and even enjoy a great amount of information. Similarly, any listener will be spellbound even by a lengthy *rāga ālāpana* if a performer knows how to apply all the varieties of *gamaka* that belong to a major rāga (*naya rāga*). An accomplished musician applies an embellishment so effectively as to induce a profound experience of harmony in any given rāga.

Tempo and gamaka

Far from tiring a listener, a performance that is rich in *gamaka* is most rewarding at a slow pace (*cauka kāla*) and at a medium tempo (*madhya kāla*). Generally speaking, a faster tempo calls for a reduction of *gamaka* to remain pleasing to the ear. But there are a few rāgas that lend themselves to a rich application of *gamaka* even in a faster tempo (e.g. *madhya kāla* or *tānam*). These rāgas are known as *ghana rāga*. There are five well-known rāgas of this type (*ghana rāga pañcaka*). Another set of five rāgas is known as the 'second set of five *ghana rāga*' (*dvitīya ghana rāga pañcaka*). A 'weighty' style of rendering a given rāga in a faster tempo is also referred to as *ghanam*.

Time and melody

Melodic variety springs from a conscious process of withholding, anticipating, omitting, extending or repeating a particular note in the course of time. All these options in the treatment of individual notes and phrases become effective only if they are anchored in a disciplined manner of handling musical time (*kālapramāṇam*) and an appropriate choice of tempo, pulse, accent and metre.

Karnatic music continually intertwines the three aspects by which time is experienced by man, the past, the present, and the future. This is done by skilfully applying auxiliary and ornamental notes, *anusvara*, and *gamaka*. If so desired, a musical note (*svara*) can be enriched with an echo of its predecessor. Alternatively, a hint of the following note can also be imprinted on a given note by means of an appropriate *anusvara* which is embedded in a *gamaka*.

Similar techniques are applied in painting where mixing is done in such a manner as to heighten or subdue the effect of neighbouring shades and forms in accordance with its subject. There are inflections of musical notes that are described in terms of 'shade' (*chāyā*).

Indian theorists of the past introduced 'synaesthetic' terms and concepts because they were aware of the complementary relationship which exists between the ways in which music and painting are perceived by our senses and minds. The physiological and psychological processes behind this wonderful phenomenon are presently being investigated by scientists with the help of modern equipment. But the 'soulful' aspect of music and dance (*bhāva*), and the nature of aesthetic delight (*rasa*), will remain beyond the purview of natural science.

10

Music Education

The training of a musician has undergone major changes in the course of this century. But this does not diminish the role which is still being played by those musicians who devote themselves to teaching without monetary considerations. In any field of learning and the arts, only a preceptor of great authority and integrity is regarded as being a real *guru*. But while the informal yet intensive apprenticeship (*gurukulam*) was the prevailing form of music education until a few decades ago, there is now greater emphasis on a regular course of lessons. The ability to apply grace notes and embellishments (*gamaka*) correctly was mainly acquired in the process of incessant listening to an experienced musician. This time-honoured practice was, and still is, indispensable for the maintenance of an oral tradition or *karṇa parampara* (literally, an 'ear-based' lineage or succession).

As in other countries, the diploma given by a recognized institution after a course of several years has become a necessity for aspiring musicians who seek employment as teachers or as staff artists with the national radio network (All India Radio) and television (Doordarshan).

The syllabus followed in such a course conveys a greater amount of theoretical knowledge and insights into music life than an apprentice of earlier times would have gained in most cases. A learning process which consists in observing and emulating a master musician cannot be substituted by a classroom situation of an institution. But in the past, regular lessons were often unheard of if one's teacher was a busy performer. Even today, most musicians supplement their regular training and performing careers by personal association with a senior master willing to guide them. In the absence of an adequate pension, many senior musicians depend on teaching fees for their living, while those who can avoid teaching for a fee, prefer to follow the example of great masters of the past who taught unconditionally or in return for some form of personal assistance.

It is a well-established practice for an aspiring musician to enrich his musical vocabulary and style by way of emulating a respected master who, with or without his knowledge, is regarded as one's indirect teacher (*mānasa guru* or *mānasika guru*). For instance, Pāpanāsam Śivan̲ is said to have chosen Konērirājāpuram Vaidyanātha Ayyar, a famous musician twelve years his senior, as his *mānasika guru*. In modern times, this concept has acquired a new dimension as repeated listening to recordings of *live* concerts, commercial studio productions, and broadcasts enables a musician to analyse and memorize even complex improvised passages (e.g. *ālāpana*) which earlier could not have been reproduced with similar accuracy.

The first public performance (*araṅgērram*) is the culmination of several years of training which helps the candidate and others to gauge whether or not the requirements for a successful artistic career can be met. Amply equipped with advice by his or her teacher, and assisted by experienced accompanists, a novice is introduced to the public in a full concert programme. For a serious artist, this occasion also provides an opportunity to open a new chapter of advanced studies and specialization.

Scale and tāla exercises

The first set of basic exercises (*saraḷi variśai*) is set to *mēḷakartā rāga* 15 (rāga Māyāmāḷavagauḷa) and a metric cycle of eight beats and 32 sub-units (ādi tāla). Because they are commonly sung *unisono* by mixed groups—children, adults, men, and women—they are confined to the middle octave which makes them suitable for all types of voices. The main purpose of these exercises is to enable a musician to perceive and produce pitches accurately as well as rapidly. Other benefits include training of the voice and, most importantly, familiarity with the seven solfa or *solmization* syllables (*sargam*) which is required by vocalists and instrumentalists alike. For memorization and notation of songs, these solfa syllables can be used in any convenient script. For notation, only the consonants (*s, r, g, m, p, d, n*) are used while for the purpose of teaching and singing, the original vowels need to be remembered (*sa, ri, ga, ma, pa, dha, ni*). Gradually, other important scales are introduced and practised in a similar fashion in order to internalize the basic techniques of singing or playing an instrument. Countless repetitions are the 'secret' to the fluency required to execute the intricate melodic and rhythmic figures underlying a rāga elaboration (*ālāpana*), variations (*saṅgati*), ornamental passages (*ciṭṭasvaram*), and similar challenges to a performer's memory and skills. The following examples of *saraḷi variśai* exercises are representative of a great number of others (Stave 8, p. 81).

All relevant embellishments (*gamaka*) and metric divisions (*tāla*) are also practised with the help of basic scales. The basic set of exercises for the advanced stage of an elementary course of music is known as *alaṅkāra* (Staves 9–15). At this stage of a beginner's training, the relevant embellishments of each *mēḷakartā rāga* are introduced and practised before progressing further. (The examples are given for *mēḷakartā rāga* Dhīraśaṅkarābharaṇam which corresponds to the major scale of Western music; any other *mēḷakartā rāga* can be used; to do so, the key signature is changed correspondingly while syllables, tāla and patterns are retained.) The *alaṅkāra* are exercises that consist of sequences comprising five steps for both, the ascending (*ārohaṇa*) and the descending scale (*avarohaṇa*). Just as the *saraḷi variśai*, they are confined to the middle octave (*madhya sthāyī*). The original set of seven tālas (*sūḷādi sapta tāla*) is used here. Only a few of these tālas are com-monly used in the context of concert or dance music.

Stave 8: Basic exercises (*saraḷi variśai*).

Didactic music forms (abhyāsa gānam)

South Indian music is believed to have been systematized by Purandara Dāsa in the sixteenth century. The elementary course (*abhyāsa gānam*) ascribed to him starts with the singing of basic intervals, the basic note (*sa* or *ṣaḍja*) to the 5th (*pa* or *pañcama*), and the higher octave (*tāra sthāyī ṣaḍja*). The learner is then led to simple melodic exercises (*saraḷi variśai*) and more complex exercises known as *alaṁkāram* which are combinations of rhythm, melody, and embellishment. All

Staves 9–15: Exercises in seven tālas (*alaṅkāra*).

Stave 9

Stave 10

Stave 11

Stave 12

Stave 13

Stave 14

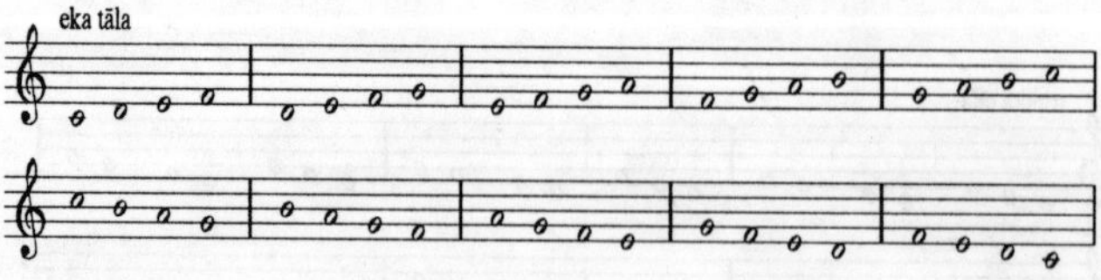

Stave 15

these exercises are to be practised in several scale patterns (*mēḷakartā rāga*) and three degrees of speed (*trikāla*), namely slow (*cauka kāla*), medium (*madhyama kāla*), and fast (*druta kāla*), each being double as fast as the prior one.

Purandara Dāsa is also credited with a number of small didactic songs (*gītam*). Similar songs were composed and widely practised until the early part of this century. In recent years there has been renewed interest in this type of composition. It began to be absorbed even in the dance repertoire, although this is quite unconventional.

From the *gītam* form, a learner is introduced to a more advanced type of technical composition (*tāṉavarṇam*) which furnishes models for the rendering of the rāgas in which they are composed. From this level onwards, the various techniques and stylistic principles of Karnatic music, assimilated with the help of *abhyāsa gāna*, can be applied to other musical forms, whether composed (*kalpita saṅgīta*) or improvised (*manodharma saṅgīta*).

Rhythmic patterns and their syllabic recitation (solmization)

An aspiring percussionist is taught to memorize and practise elaborate patterns with the help of solfa syllables (*jati*) before translating them into the actual drum-beats applicable to any instrument (e.g. *mṛdaṅgam*). This general approach helps a musician to exchange musical ideas with any other musician and to instantly respond to any challenge that may occur during a live concert. A large repertoire of well-structured rhythmic formulae is therefore a basic requirement for any professional percussionist. Pleasing patterns, namely the shorter *tīrmāṇam*, and the more elaborate *kōrvai*, mark the conclusion of any given theme or percussive interlude (*taṉiyāvart-taṉam*). The most conspicuous feature of all these patterns is the occurrence of two repetitions of a basic pattern (i.e. it is performed thrice) before returning to the initial point of departure (*eḍuppu*) of a given theme. A typical example is the following *naḍai* in rūpaka tāla (Table 9):

Table 9: Basic rhythmic sequence (*naḍai*) for a *taṉiyāvarttaṉam* in *rūpaka tāla*

1	2	3	1 (beat)	2 (beat)	3 (wave hand)
(- - - -)	(- - - -)	(- - - -)	ta ka dhi mi	ta ka dhi mi	ta ka dhi mi

I. (repeat I. from beginning; then continue with II.)

tām - ki ta	ta ka dīn -	dīn - nā -			
dīn - ki ta	ta ka dīn -	dīn - nā -			
tām - ki ta	ta ka dīn -	dīn - nā -	tām - - -	- - - -	ta ka dhi na

II. (continue immediately with III.)

tām - ki ta	ta ka dīn -	dīn - nā -	tām - - -	- - - -	ta ka dhi na
dīn - ki ta	ta ka dīn -	dīn - nā -	tām - - -	- - - -	ta ka dhi na

III. (continue immediately with IV.)

tām - ki ta	ta ka dīn -	ta ka dhi na
dīn - ki ta	ta ka dīn -	ta ka dhi na
tām - ki ta	ta ka dīn -	ta ka dhi na

IV. conclusion (*tīrmāṇam*; thrice = repeat twice; conclude with final 'tām' in IV. or repeat from I.)

tām - ta ka	dhi na tām -	ta ka dhi na	tām - - -	- - - -	ta ka dhi na

(Courtesy: *Mṛdaṅga Vidvān* T.K. Ramakrishnan)

11

Rāga

Colours cannot be too brilliant if properly disposed, because the distinction of the parts are thereby made more perfect . . . Rubens boldly, and in a masterly manner, kept his bloom tints bright, separate and distinct . . . what indeed is known to every painter, that had the colours . . . been all smooth'd and absolutely blended together, they would have produced a dirty grey instead of flesh-colour.

William Hogarth in *The Analysis of Beauty.*

The concept of rāga envisages the fashioning of an 'audible image' (*rāga rūpa*) from the continuum of all the available pitches the ear can discern (*śruti*). The term *rāga* is derived from the Sanskrit root *rañj* which has a variety of connotations such as 'colour', 'tinge', 'red', and 'passion'. This concept has several sources, notably the tradition which traces itself to the sacred chants (*Sāma veda*) and other religious scriptures. Most authors of ancient and medieval treatises (*śāstra*) sought sanction from these scriptures and from the commentaries later written on them. On the other hand, there was always a rich store of lively music practised by the different peoples living on the Indian subcontinent. There are numerous ethnic and linguistic groups who proudly maintain their own customs, styles of music, and dance.

The prevailing theory about the origin and nature of music has been wedded to the notion that the art of music is a reflection of an otherwise impenetrable divine will conveyed through primordial sound (*nāda*). While all energy (*śakti*) and even matter manifests itself through some kind of vibration, whether light, heat or sound, music evokes a supreme sense of delight (*ānanda*) in all creatures. In this context music and the allied arts of dance and poetry are understood as being the quintessential expression of a greater dimension natural to all life which cannot be conquered by any other means. Indian mythology is rich in stories with music as its subject and gods (*deva*), demons (*asura*), nymphs (*apsarā*), celestial musicians (*gandharva*), men and beasts playing a variety of roles. There are many stories and instructive passages relating to music in the large body of literature and mythological writing known as the *Purāṇas*. Some texts even contain an element of comic relief when dealing with the serious matter of divine music:

Nārada, the divine singer and perfect devotee of Viṣṇu, attained divine knowledge with the help of Śiva and others. But even before he became the legendary master of music, he was so proud about his greatness as a musician that Viṣṇu decided to put an end to this conceit. In a forest they encountered several women in great agony because their limbs had been cut. They identified themselves as the personifications of rāgas (*rāgiṇī*), mutilated by Nārada's faulty singing. In another episode, Nārada failed to extricate his *vīṇā* from a rock after listening to Hanūmān who had sung so beautifully that the rock on which it was placed had melted. Challenged by Hanūmān to melt the solidified rock again, Nārada also sang, but without any success.

(Based on *Puranic Encyclopaedia* by Vettam Mani, pp. 527–9)

Thus the message can be said to be loud and clear: humility and perseverance are required to master the art and science of music; and there are no shortcuts. The happy outcome of Nārada's perseverance is the fact that he has been credited with several important texts on music. Modern music historians ascribe these texts to different authors whose period cannot be ascertained. In accordance with prevailing pious conventions, they preferred to remain anonymous. Nārada is quoted by Mataṅga, the author of *Bṛhaddeśī*, which is believed not only to be the first independent text on the subject of music (*saṅgīta*), but also the first one to deal with the concept of *rāga*. On similar lines, Tyāgarāja is said to have relied on a rare work titled *Svarārnavam*, ascribed to Nārada, as the source of his musical expertise.

Before the *Bṛhaddeśī*, literature on the subject of music takes the allied arts of dance and theatre into consideration. It is rarely detached from the larger context of philosophical and religious questions that inspired an immense body of literature of every conceivable type. Although literature on music forms but a small fraction of Indian writing and much has been lost in the turbulent history of the subcontinent, there are many technical treatises written since ancient times. Much early literature must, however, be understood in the context of a type of writing based on concise formula (*sūtra*), literally, 'thread' which serves as an aid to memory rather than constituting conventional literature. If written out in the form of a complex document, one's artistic legacy would have been too bulky to carry and difficult to protect from insects, natural decay or the preying eyes of those one regarded as unauthorized. By comparison a form of knowledge which could be memorized faithfully was safe and available at all times anywhere. Mythical authorship, obscure symbolism and codified language were often employed as didactic or mnemonic devices. But the bewilderment caused by these factors, exacerbated by later interpolations and mistakes made by those copyists who were unfamiliar with the subject of these texts, often pose a problem for modern scholars trying to reconstruct ancient music practice.

The arts of poetry (*iyal*), music (*iśai*), and dance (*nāṭakam*) are known as *Muttamiḻ*, the cultural foundations of Tamil, which is believed to be the most ancient living language on the Indian subcontinent. Equipped with the tools provided by the famous manual of total theatre (*Nāṭya Śāstra*), and with psychological insight sharpened by the theories of literary criticism (*rasa* and *dhvani*), musicians, poets and scholars could devote themselves to more differentiated manners of creating melody. As the concept of rāga evolved, music also emerged as an art form in its own right. If earlier music was understood to be inseparable from its sister arts, poetry, dance and drama, there now arose a new awareness that music possesses a dimension all of its own. Just a few notes, carefully selected and endowed with feeling (*bhāva*), would suffice to move a sensitive listener (*rasika*). Ideally, such a person is also a connoisseur of beauty in all fields of the arts and learning, 'an appreciator with critical faculties' (*sahṛdaya*), somebody whose heart (*hṛd*) can be reached by any evolved artist. The key to this new dimension of music-making lay in a musician's ability to extract the essence (*rasa*) of the very experience of sound. Pure melody began to be savoured in the form of rāga.

Although the dividing line between a mere scale and a rāga has been subject to change in the past, it is clear that Indian musicians and listeners associate numerous delicate nuances and the mood evoked by them as the hallmark of a rāga. While there appears to be a subjective or cultural aspect to this question there can be no doubt that the aesthetic experience (*rasa*) associated with a particular rāga is shared by people with different backgrounds. This can be interpreted as a psycho-acoustic basis for the rāga system which has been vigorously explored by musicians and theorists alike. The dislike for plain notes has been shared by all major branches of classical Indian music for at least two millennia and is particularly pronounced in Karnatic music. Vocalists and instrumentalists agree that ornamentation (*gamaka*) cannot be applied mechanically but depends on the rāga to which it belongs. The majority of modulations are derived from the spontaneous adjustments any well-trained voice will apply to intervals as well as groups of notes (*sañcāra*). This vocal approach, known as *gāyakī aṅg* in Hindustānī music, is an ideal which all Indian instrumentalists seek to emulate by way of analysing each note and phrase. Failing to do so will make a rāga rendered on an instrument sound mechanical, devoid of feeling and colour.

Tamilians remember the famous episode involving two musicians of the seventh century. Like the bards of ancient Europe, Tirujñāna Sambandar, a saintly composer and singer, was accompanied on the lute or harp (*yāḻ*). A Tamil poem by Sambandar illustrates how the *yāḻ* was unsuitable to render the intricacies of a particular tune (*yāḻmuri paṇ*). This tune is thought to have corresponded to Nīlāmbari, one of the rāgas whose very life and soul consists of subtle inflections of its notes and cannot be conveyed by words nor captured by musical notation. Tirunīlakaṇṭha Nāyanār, his despairing accompanist, broke his *yāḻ*. An era came to an end, and the *yāḻ*, once the favourite instrument of South India's bards and mystics, was never to play an important role again.

According to R. Raṅgarāmānuja Ayyaṅgār, *yāḻmuri paṇ* corresponds to modern rāga Aṭāṇa, which is characterized by embellishments and phrases that are difficult to reproduce with an instrument like the *yāḻ* (p. 54 of his *History of South Indian* [*Carnatic*] *Music*).

This episode is interpreted as an illustration of increased musical sophistication emerging in the late middle ages. Musicians were no longer bards who recited poetry to the accompaniment of pleasant notes. Their music had to fuse with poetry to the extent that a melodic line or rāga could express any nuance of feeling and evoke a chosen mood at will.

It is a matter of debate whether the open-stringed lyre or harp (*yāḻ*) coexisted

Fig. 27: *Yālmuri paṇ*. Tirunīlakaṇṭha Nāyanār (7th century) despairs of playing his harp (*yāl*) due to its limited ability to express the finer nuances of melody (Copyright: S. Rājam).

with the fretted lute (*vīṇā*) for some time before becoming obsolete and disappearing from Indian soil. The pre-eminence of the human voice has never been challenged although instrumental music (*vādya*) began to command respectability and increased in importance in the centuries when the classical music of South India acquired its present shape. Some string instruments evolved from single-stringed drones (*ektār*). Harps and lutes have sensitized Indian musicians to the finer intervals from which an appealing melody can be formed. Not surprisingly, quite a number of the great composers, vocalists, theoreticians, and teachers are known to have been competent *vīṇā* players (*vaiṇika*); and there is little doubt that their music has also been refined by the inherent quality of that most perfect and complete of South Indian instruments (*sarva vādya*), the *Sarasvatī Vīṇā*. The playing technique of the *vīṇā*, determined by a need for effective phrasing to obtain continuity, and for embellishment to compensate for the rapid decay of individual notes, contributed to the rich store of melody which gives Karnatic music its flavour and buoyancy. Very few notes are left unembellished. But the nature of an embellishment and its applicability varies from rāga to rāga. The treatment of a rāga, its notes, embellishments and phrases may also reflect the idiosyncrasies of a style (*bāṇī*) established by a famous musician which, if exceedingly at variance with time-honoured conventions, is unlikely to remain an acceptable interpretation (*pāṭhāntara*) if adopted by another musician.

From the time of Mataṅga, who wrote a treatise entitled *Bṛhaddeśi* in the fifth century, the word rāga has come to mean 'a pleasing combination of musical notes'.

In the late middle ages various attempts were made to map the musical landscape of India. Sanskrit treatises like the *Saṅgīta Ratnākara* (13th century) sought to categorize musical expression under two broad categories. One category was essentially rooted in the official tradition (*mārga*) and thus sought to conform with norms that had been laid down in ancient times; the other category took care of all music that might have originated in regional traditions (*dēśī*) with or without concern about norms. Although the former was influenced by Sanskrit literature and the latter shaped by different vernacular literatures, there can be no doubt that in an ongoing process of cross-fertilization, both branches have influenced one another from very early times. Today, the distinction between *mārga* and *dēśī* cannot be applied to any branch of music any more.

The confluence of Sanskrit and vernacular languages found its expression in a mixed language called Maṇipravāḷam or 'diamond-coral' (*maṇi*, the 'diamond' of the Sanskrit, and *pravāḷa*, the 'coral' of Tamil).

Compared with literature and the performing arts described by the *Nāṭya Śāstra*, the depiction of musical subjects is a more recent phenomenon. Paintings, friezes and sculptures with musical subjects are rooted in an older, more subtle tradition of inner visualization.

For the purpose of meditation and concentration, Sanskrit verses with visual imagery (*dhyāna śloka*) were composed. Such verses formed an integral part of many schools of Indian philosophy and therefore cover many subjects. A *dhyāna śloka* could personify or deify any rāga or tāla and endow it with colourful attributes to stimulate a musician's imagination and feeling:

In the glow of sunset this esteemed prince makes his presence felt in the temple of music. His face is radiant with the kisses of his queen; his emerald and ruby earrings are as pretty as parrots. He wears a beautiful garland, Māḷavarāga Rājā.

Borne along on the shoulders of six women, he is seated in a swaying palanquin, his lady by his side. A maid in front fans him with a cāmara. He is clad in yellow silk and adorned with flashing ruby earrings. The sacred thread gleams on his shoulder. I worship the lord of Ādi Tāla.

'Meditation on Māḷava Rāga' and 'Meditation on Ādi Tāla', p. 3 in
Shobhillu Saptasvara by Savithri Rajan and Michael Nixon.

The six women are a reference to the more exotic side of Indian music theory which took form during the Mughal period. In accordance with the customs of feudal society, each 'male' rāga had a number of wives (*rāgiṇi*). The *rāgamāla* paintings were charming renderings of such feudal fantasies. South Indian paintings with musical subjects were created in the Nāyak and Marāṭhā courts of Tañjāvūr. They belong to a genre of devotional paintings which are often gilded and studded with precious stones or painted behind glass.

Theorist Prem Lata Sharma summarizes the importance of visual associations in India's music traditions as follows: 'Both modern physics and our tradtional metaphysics of sound uphold that the objects of visual and auditory perception are not basically different, but are mutually convertible. It is common experience that hearing and seeing are not only mutually supplementary or complementary, but are also replacing each other to a considerable extent. The tradtion of *raga-dhyana* was, therefore, nothing far-fetched or fantastic; it was a realistic approach to artistic imagery.'

Quotation from *Sangeet Natak: Silver Jubilee Volume*, pp. 17–18.

12

The System of 72 Scales (Mēḷakartā Rāga)

The aesthetic and acoustic laws underlying the different scales (*mēḷakartā rāga*) and melodic patterns (*rāga*) have been subject to incessant investigation by many generations of Indian scholars, scientists and musicians. The science of acoustics could not, however, develop beyond a certain point until empirical verification of data became possible in recent times. Keeping the great number of variables involved in the acoustics of a musical instrument (e.g. weight, diameter, tension and length of a string), one should not be surprised that early experts had to use procedures that are as difficult to convey through words as they are to apply in practice.

Early Indian music theorists relied on a method based on the shifting of the basic note (*mūrchanā*) which yielded several variants of a given scale. This means that one needed only one basic scale pattern, and others could easily be calibrated with reference to its intervals. In this manner, it was found that different moods could be expressed or evoked with just a few basic intervals, provided one had the understanding of how the key note of a scale needed to be shifted in order to obtain other scales. Such theoretical knowledge was of great practical value for musicians whose tasks included the accompaniment of dance, drama or rituals or the composing of suitable tunes for poetry. This process was also useful to overcome the artistic constraints caused by the limited tonal range of open-stringed instruments that belong to the family of harps and lyres. Many instruments of this type were used in India and other ancient cultures of Asia, Africa, and Europe.

Some types of harps, such as the Greek *lyra*, were made from tortoise shell, and others were elegantly carved from wood and decorated, such as the South-East Asian *harp* (locally known as *saun* and by other names). Except for India, such archaic instruments are still being used today in many parts of Africa and Asia, while the modern concert harp of Western music employs a pedal mechanism to produce all the required combinations of notes, in succession or in combination. All these instruments originated in civilizations where bards played an important role in the social life of the people, be it as chroniclers of heroic deeds of the kings, or for the entertainment of nobles and rich patrons in whose service they were often found.

In the Tamil-speaking South, the saint-poets known as Nāyanmār are known to have been accompanied by an instrument called the *yāḻ*, a simple frame with a resonator with several strings attached to it. It is a matter of dispute whether the ancient *vīṇā* also belonged to this category, since any plucked instrument is referred to as *vīṇā* in Sanskrit literature. A harp or lyre is quite different from the modern fretted *vīṇā* (*Sarasvatī vīṇā*), which belongs to the family of fretted lutes. The *Sarasvatī vīṇā* is an instrument which is believed to have been perfected by Govinda Dīkṣitar, a minister and music scholar in the court of Raghunātha Nāyak (1600–34). In the past, the South Indian *vīṇā* was therefore also called Raghunātha *mēḷa vīṇā* in honour of Govinda Dīkṣitar's royal patron and pupil. The historical importance of the *vīṇā* for the development of the South Indian music system is evident from the fact that Veṅkaṭamakhi, the famous theorist and author of the *Caturdaṇḍī Prakāśikā*, was the son of Govinda Dīkṣitar. In his treatise, he outlined the modern *mēḷakartā rāga* system. There can be little doubt that the straightforward arrangement of frets (*mēḷam*) on the modern *vīṇā*, just as its advanced playing technique, inspired Veṅkaṭamakhi to develop a theoretical pattern of musical intervals and scales. This innovative scale system owes its success to the fact that Veṅkaṭamakhi endowed it with an elegance which comes from simplicity and genuine functionality.

There are six scales which are both useful for the process of modal shift, and also pleasing to hear. These are, quite understandably, the scales that are most widely used in South Indian music: Dhīraśaṅkarābharaṇam (*mēḷa* 29), Kharaharapriya (*mēḷa* 22), Hanumatōḍi (*mēḷa* 8), Mēcakalyāṇi (*mēḷa* 65), Harikāmbhōji (*mēḷa* 28), and Naṭhabhairavi (*mēḷa* 20).

Harikāmbhōji is believed to have been the original scale (*śuddha mēḷa*) of the ancient Tamils and is associated with the greatest number of derivative (*janya*) rāgas.

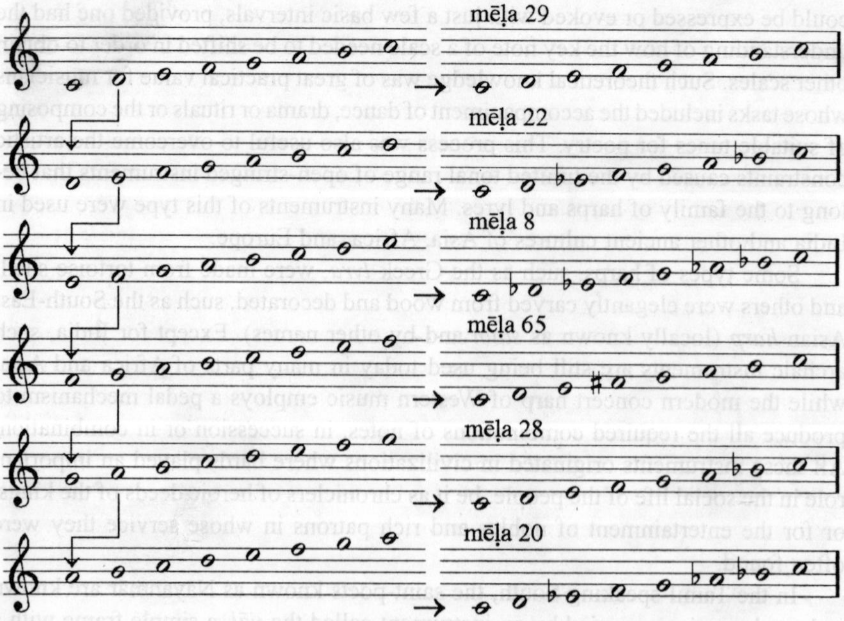

Stave 16: The scales obtained by modal shift.

The scale system of South Indian music (*mēḷakartā paddhati*) is designed to help musicians, composers and musicologists to deal with hundreds of rāgas by distributing them between a certain number of distinct scales. In the present system there are 72 reference scales (*mēḷa* or *mēḷakartā rāga*). Earlier in this century, ten out of these 72 scales were adopted by Hindustānī musicians. Instead of *mēḷakartā rāga*, they call their scales *ṭhāṭ*. The analytic framework of the *mēḷakartā rāga* system focuses on the distinguishing features of rāgas and provides the terminology to describe their attributes. The 72 scales are arranged in twelve recurring patterns or 'wheels' (*cakra*). Each *cakra* contains six scales; and each scale has seven notes (*saptasvara*). These seven notes are selected from twelve semitonal steps (*svarasthāna*). Some scales are therefore comparable to the Western arrangement of major and minor scales (scales 29 and 20 respectively). None of these scales, however, is in complete agreement with the Western system of tuning which is known as equal temperament. Each rāga derives its musical notes from the intervals of a particular scale. Some of these intervals are retained while others are modified further (*svarakāku*). In many rāgas, one or several notes are either deleted or concealed by specific embellishments (*gamaka*).

When a scale is modified to yield a particular rāga, such modification can entail three types of distinguishing features: (1) the deletion of one or several notes (*varja*); rāgas with five notes (*auḍava*), six notes (*ṣāḍava*), or a combination of five, six and seven notes belong to this category; (2) the inclusion of one or several alien notes (*anya svara*); and (3) the presence of 'zigzag' patterns (*vakra prayoga*) in the arrangement of notes.

All rāgas can be described as belonging to one or several of these three categories which are also termed (1) *asampūrṇa*, (2) *bhāṣāṅga*, and (3) *vakra*. If the above modifications of basic scale patterns are absent in a particular rāga, this rāga is labelled *sampūrṇa* or heptatonic, *upāṅga* or unmodified, and *krama* or straight. If any of these features are to be applied sparingly, they are merely regarded as extraordinary but characteristic phrases (*viśeṣa sañcāra*). A rāga is not re-classified due to the occasional occurrence of such a phrase. For instance, rāga Śaṅkarābharaṇam is a krama rāga with an occasional *vakra prayoga*.

The characteristic features of a rāga are contained in concise descriptions (*rāga lakṣaṇa*). Many such descriptions of traditional rāgas are found in musicians' handbooks (*lakṣaṇagrantha*). This practice made it possible to compare the features of one rāga with those of another. A rāga that lacks distinctive features (*rāgarūpa*) is not considered as having an identity or 'personality' of its own; rather than constituting an independent rāga, it is a mere variant of another rāga. For this reason, it is far from easy to create new rāgas.

By themselves, reference scales (*mēḷakartā rāga*) are devoid of musical appeal. The function of a scale is to help a musician to explore the appeal of various intervals and to practise what critics call perfect '*śruti* alignment'. This means that musicians are exhorted to first calibrate the musical notes produced by their voices or any instrument before embellishing any notes or resorting to musical expression.

Each reference scale has a corresponding rāga. Among the 72 *mēḷakartā rāgas* in use today there were several ones that were already known as major rāgas before they were designated as reference scales. A combination of features determines the character of a rāga and the mood it evokes. The most important features consist of modulations of individual notes (*svarakāku*), embellishments (*gamaka*), and intermediary notes (*anusvara*) that connect the main notes with one another in a pleasing or 'vocal' manner (*gāyakī*). It is important to keep in mind that a *mēḷakartā rāga*, in its function as a reference scale, has none of these features. But since theorists, musicians and composers began to work with newly formulated scales some three centuries ago, nuances were added that help to extract the qualities expected of a rāga from every available scale. At the same time, these scales continue to serve as 'parental' or abstract reference scales for numerous *other* rāgas. Many of the derived rāgas (*janya rāga*) belonging to the same reference scale have indeed distinct musical 'personalities' of their own.

It is known that Tyāgarāja, the musician who shaped Karnatic music as perhaps no other composer before or after him, took great interest in this subject. He and his disciples adopted the modern *mēḷakartā rāga* nomenclature introduced by Akalanka, the author of a music treatise entitled *Saṅgītasāra Samgraha*. Akalanka advocated a theory of 24 micro-intervals which did not find lasting acceptance. But his importance lies in the introduction of the requirement of 'fullness' (*sampūrṇa*) for a *mēḷakartā rāga*. This is in fact the main characteristic of a modern scale and means that by definition it has a complete set of seven notes both in the ascending and descending series (*ārohaṇa-avarohaṇa*). In other words, all the 72 scales are 'heptatonic' and free from any irregularities that may characterize a rāga. The *mēḷakartā* system kindled Tyāgarāja's imagination and through him, the floodgates of unprecedented musical innovation were opened. Thanks to his masterly treatment of this subject, his music continues to inspire composers to the present day. In view of its limitless potential, it has been studied by musicians around the world. Exponents of other styles and systems of music such as Jazz and World Music are taking an interest in the treatment of melody found in Karnatic music because of the endless possibilities it offers by intelligent, soulful, and imaginative treatment of every basic element rather than mere quantitative expansion. For this very reason, the music of South India transcends the conventional boundaries of language and culture.

Through his compositions (*kṛti*) Tyāgarāja particularly popularized two rāgas that hitherto had merely been reference scales. These are rāgas Kharaharapriya (*mēḷakartā rāga* 22) and Harikāmbhōji (*mēḷakartā rāga* 28). He not only wrote a great many songs in both these scales/rāgas but also created many derivative (*janya*) rāgas on the basis of their tonal material. There are also compositions in other, less common *mēḷakartā rāgas*. Characteristic examples are *Prāṇanātha*, a *kṛti* describing the irresistible sound of Kṛṣṇa's flute (*mēḷakartā rāga* 35, Śūlini, dēśādi tāla); and *Paramātmuḍu*, a *kṛti* in which Tyāgarāja expresses his wonder at the mystery of God's omnipresence (*mēḷakartā rāga* 34, Vāgadhīśvari, ādi tāla).

There are numerous rāgas for which only one composition exists (*ekaika kṛti rāga*). Tyāgarāja was a composer who often created a special rāga for just one song. Typical examples are *Varasikhivāhana* (rāga Supradīpam, derived from *mēḷa* 17, Sūryakāntam, ādi tāla), *Sarasasāmadāna* (rāga Kāpinārāyaṇi, derived from *mēḷa* 28, Harikāmbhōji, ādi tāla), and *Edārisañcarinturā* (rāga Śrutirañjani, derived from *mēḷa* 61, Kāntāmaṇi, dēśādi tāla). Some rāgas of this category have gained importance because they have been popularized through one devotional song (*kīrtana*) or concert item (*kṛti*). Tyāgarāja's *Nādatanumaniśam* Śaṅkaram (raga Ciṭṭarañjani, ādi tāla, from *mēḷa* 19, Jhaṅkāradhvani) and *Marukēlarā* (rāga Jayantaśrī, ādi tāla, from *mēḷa* 20, Naṭhabhairavi) are typical examples of popular compositions in uncommon rāgas. There are many similar examples of *ekaika kṛti rāgas* by other composers as well. A few minor rāgas like Kadanakutūhalam, first introduced by Paṭṭaṇam Subrahmaṇya Ayyar in his *kṛti Raghuvaṁśa Sudhā* (ādi tāla), are endearing and often heard. In spite of its limitations for rāga exposition (*ālāpana*), this rāga outgrew its *ekaika kṛti rāga* status and has inspired a number of compositions by several renowned composers of the twentieth century.

Several hundred rāgas are thus listed under the 72 *mēḷakartā* headings. For this purpose each rāga is allocated to a 'parent' rāga (*janaka rāga*) or reference scale (*mēḷakartā rāga*). This means that any rāga can be described in terms of being 'born of' (*janya*) the parental rāga, a useful mnemonic device which is supplemented by an ingenious alpha-numerical method. In a historical perspective, however, it is more correct to state that many rāgas have been in use before the *mēḷakartā* scheme (*mēḷa janya paddhati*) was first introduced by Veṅkaṭamakhi around AD 1660 in a treatise entitled *Caturdaṇḍī Prakāśikā*. He derived his reference scales from nineteen existing rāgas but had the vision to expand them to the 72 scales now in use. It took several generations to create soulful music from melodic formulae that seemed at first too complex and diverse to be of practical use. The number of rāgas increased from less than a hundred three centuries ago, to several hundred that are in the modern repertoire. There is a handwritten reference book (*lakṣaṇagrantha*) which lists over two thousand rāgas most of which are rarely if ever heard in concerts and recordings today. In view of this increase it has become all the more useful to organize all rāgas, even those that are based on folk tunes.

Govindācāri, the author of a music treatise entitled *Saṁgraha-Cūḍā-Maṇi* (*circa* 18th century), is credited with combining the traditional 'alpha-numerical system' of mnemonics (*kaṭapayādi saṁkhyā*) with the current nomenclature for the 72 *mēḷakartā* scales.

In Table 10, the serial number of a scale (*mēḷakartā rāga*) is found by first identifying its constituent notes (*svarasthāna* or scale degree). Conversely, the interval pattern can be deduced from the name of a scale with the help of the traditional *kaṭapayādi* formula described below. Once the number is found, it can be used to look up the name of the scale in a written index although traditionally, this number was meant to be used as an aid to memory in the manner described below (see Alpha-numerical mnemonics).

All rāgas (*janya rāga*) are understood to derive their tonal material from one particular *mēḷa*. But those rāgas that have less than seven notes can, of course, be classified under more than one scale. The decision as to which scale should be referred to depends on the source or tradition. In musical practice, such differences hardly matter since the semitones (*svarasthāna*) of the respective rāgas remain the same, no matter which among the applicable scales is chosen as a point of reference.

Table 10: The arrangement of the 72 scales used in South Indian music

	dha, na	**dha, ni**	**dha, nu**	**dhi, ni**	**dhi, nu**	**dhu, nu**	
ra, ga	1/37	2/38	3/39	4/40	5/41	6/42	**2nd b, 3rd bb**
ra, gi	7/43	8/44	9/45	10/46	11/47	12/48	**2nd b, 3rd b**
ra, gu	13/49	14/50	15/51	16/52	17/53	18/54	**2nd b, 3rd**
ri, gi	19/55	20/56	21/57	22/58	23/59	24/60	**2nd, 3rd b**
ri, gu	25/61	26/62	27/63	28/64	29/65	30/66	**2nd, 3rd**
ru, gu	31/67	32/68	33/69	34/70	35/71	36/72	**2nd #, 3rd**
	6th b, 7th bb	**6th b, 7th b**	**6th b, 7th**	**6th, 7th b**	**6th, 7th**	**6th#, 7th**	

2nd = 'ri', 3rd = 'ga', 6th = 'dha', 7th = 'ni'; b = flat; # = sharp/augmented; bb = diminished (an enharmonic variant)

Note: All the numbers before symbol '/' pertain to the first 36 scales (*mēḷakartā rāga*); each of these scales has a natural fourth (*śuddha madhyama*); the 2-digit numbers after symbol '/', on the other hand, pertain to scales numbered 37 to 72; each of these scales has an augmented fourth (*prati madhyama*). In the absence of any symbol (#, *b* or *bb*), a note is 'natural'; i.e. it corresponds to the *mēḷa* Dhīraśaṅkarābharaṇam (29th scale), which is known as Bilāval *ṭhāṭ* in Hindustānī music, and as the major scale of Western music.

Alpha-numerical mnemonics (Kaṭapayādi)

The *kaṭapayādi sūtra* (also termed *kaṭapayādi saṁkhyā*) constitutes an ingenious *mnemonic* device which can also be described in terms of a traditional *alpha-numerical* system. Apart from being used in Karnatic music, this system is also used in other arts, traditional sciences, and astrology. The formula (*saṁkhyā*) underlying this mnemonic device is based on the standardized order of the Sanskrit alphabet.

With the help of the *kaṭapayādi saṁkhyā* (*sūtra*), the serial numbers of specific words, names, or terms, are arranged in a coherent scheme which can be committed to memory. In Karnatic music, the names and interval patterns of the 72 scales (*mēḷa*) are correlated for the same purpose, and each name of an existing rāga is prefixed with a suitable combination of syllables: for instance, 'Hanu' is prefixed to the name of an old rāga, Ṭōḍi; the *mēḷakartā rāga* is henceforth referred to as Hanumatōḍi. In the absence of printed books, this system stimulated the exploration of scales and melodies that were hitherto unknown.

In the initial stages of acceptance, this rāga nomenclature has been deliberately concealed, for instance in the manuscript copies belonging to disciples of Tyāgarāja. These musicians sought to preserve the secret character of the new system of nomenclature. On account of its lucidity, it has become the standard pattern followed by most theorists, composers, and musicians since the nineteenth century. But one should keep in mind that in the tradition of Muttusvāmi Dīkṣitar, a different nomenclature is followed. This older system is based on incomplete scale patterns (*asampūrṇa mēḷa*) rather than complete scale patterns (*sampūrṇa mēḷa*). But even the *asampūrṇa mēḷa* rāgas used by Muttusvāmi Dīkṣitar (e.g. Dhautapañcama; Phenadyuti) have names that match the *kaṭapayādi* formula.

The name of this system (*kaṭapayādi*) derives from the initial letters of each among the four groups of consonants and semivowels. Each letter is normally supplemented by a final vowel 'a' (i.e. *'Ka, Kha, Ga, Gha'*, etc.) for the purpose of easy pronunciation.

Two syllables (*saṁkhyākṣara*) are prefixed to the name of each of the 72 *mēḷakarta* scales. Each syllable corresponds to a number between 1 and 9, or 0 (zero). The two-digit number corresponding to these two syllables must, however, always be reversed to obtain the correct *mēḷa* index number (see examples given below).

A total of 33 Sanskrit letters (consonants and semivowels) figure in the *kaṭapayādi sūtra*. Of these, only 24 actually occur in the present *mēḷakarta* nomenclature, which means that nine Sanskrit letters are never applied for the alpha-numerical codification of scales: 'ṅ', 'ch', 'ñ', 'ḍ', 'ḍh', 'ṇ', 'dh', 'ph', and 'b' (Table 11).

Group 4 consists of semivowels—*palatal* 'ya', *retroflex* 'ra', *dental* 'la' and *labial* 'va'; followed by three *sibilants*: *palatal* 'śa', *retroflex* 'ṣa', *dental* 'sa', and *final* 'ha'.

Some typical examples for the application of this system:

Kanakāngi: K (**Ka-**) = 1 + N + (**-na**) = 0 => **10** (reversed = **01**st *mēḷa*)

Hanumatōḍi: H (**Ha-**) = 8 + N + (**-nu**) = 0 => **80** (reversed = **08**th *mēḷa*)

Table 11: *Kaṭapayādi sūtra*

	1	**2**	**3**	**4**	**5**	**6**	**7**	**8**	**9**	**0**	
kādi-nava	ka	kha	ga	gha	ṅa	ca	cha	ja	jha	ña	1st group
ṭādi-nava	ṭa	ṭha	ḍa	ḍha	ṇa	ta	tha	da	dha	na	2nd group
pādi-pañca	pa	pha	ba-	bha	ma	-	-	-	-	-	3rd group
yādy-aṣṭa	ya	ra	la	va	śa	ṣa	sa	ha	-	-	4th group

(*Nava* = nine, denoting nine letter/number= positions plus a tenth position for zero (0); *pañca* = five; *aṣṭa* = eight.)

Māyāmāḷavagauḷa: M (**Ma-**) = 5 + Y + (**-ya**) = 1 = > **51** (reversed = **15**th *mēḷa*)
Kāmavardhani: K (**Kā-**) = 1 + M + (**-ma**) = 5 + = > **15** (reversed = **51**st *mēḷa*)
Naṭhabhairavi: N (**Na-**) = 0 + ṬH + (**-ṭha**) = 2 + = > **02** (reversed = **20**th *mēḷa*)
Harikāmbhōji: H (**Ha-**) = 8 + R + (**-ri**) = 2 + = > **82** (reversed = **28**th *mēḷa*)
Jhālavarāḷi: JH (**Jha-**) = 9 + L + (**-la**) = 3 + = > **93** (reversed = **39**th *mēḷa*)
Rasikapriya: R (**Ra-**) = 2 + S + (**-si**) = 7 + = > **27** (reversed = **72**nd *mēḷa*)

As a rule, the second letter of a conjunct consonant gives the correct *mēḷa* number. But there are seven exceptions to this rule, namely the names of scales that are believed to have been named in a hurry. The following seven scales are coined with the *kaṭapayādi* number of the first rather than the second letter of the relevant conjunct consonant combination:

Cak*ravākam—the 16th *mēḷa*
Div*yamaṇi— the 48th *mēḷa*
Viś*vambhari— the 54th *mēḷa*
Ś*yāmalāṅgi—the 55th *mēḷa*
Siṁ*hēndramadhyamam—the 57th *mēḷa*
Cit*rāmbari—the 66th *mēḷa*
J*yōtisvarūpiṇi—the 68th *mēḷa*

(To mark the seven letter-combinations that deviate from the standard pattern of alpha-numerical codification, conjunct letters are split by symbol '*'.)

In this manner the underlying interval pattern of a scale is also revealed to a musician familiar with this system.

Numerous 'living' rāgas have been created from seemingly sterile scale material since the *mēḷakartā* system was first proposed in the seventeenth century.

The final breakthrough for the improved system of heptatonic or 'complete scales' (*sampūrṇa*) apparently came with the composition of a 'garland of mēḷakartā rāgas' (*mēḷarāga mālikā cakra*). In this long and intricate composition, entitled

Praṇatārtiharaprabho, the name of each scale (*rāga mudrā*) is introduced by the singer. Its composer, Mahāvaidyanātha Śivan̲ (1844–93), was the first composer who made use of all the 72 scales in accordance with the *kaṭapayādi sūtra*. He sought to demonstrate the potential for aesthetic values and emotional impact among those numerous scales that had not yet been fully absorbed in the music repertoire of his time. This composition, rated as a masterpiece of imagination and intellectual ingenuity, has been recorded by a legendary singer of our times, Smt. M.S. Subbulakshmi.

After Mahāvaidyanātha Śivan̲, several other composers have used the entire gamut of the 72 *mēḷakartā rāgas*. Kōṭīsvara Ayyar (1870–1936) and Smt. D. Paṭṭammāḷ belong to the select group of scholarly musicians who dared to accept this challenge to their creativity.

Scale formation

Each scale comprises an octave, a series of eight notes from middle tonic 'C' (*madhya sthāyī ṣaḍja*) to its equivalent in the higher range, higher 'C' (*tāra sthāyī ṣaḍja*). This octave is divided into two halves ('tetrachords'). The lower tetrachord (*purvāṅga*) comprises *sa* ('C'), *ri* ('D'), *ga* ('E'), and *ma* ('F'); and the higher tetrachord (*uttaraṅga*) comprises middle *pa* ('G'), *dha* ('A'), *ni* ('B'), and upper *sa* ('c'). These are, however, mere indications of tonal steps. 'C' can stand for any chosen pitch, and the actual intervals vary from scale to scale. There are no variations for the basic note nor for its natural fifth. This means that 72 possible combinations of intervals of twelve semitones and another four 'enharmonic' variants, thus sixteen interval combinations, are distributed among the seven available notes or tonal steps. If properly arranged, one set of 36 scales almost forms a mirror image of the other set. There is but one important difference, namely the bifurcation of the fourth interval (*madhyama*). Out of these 72 scales, 36 take the lower variant, the natural fourth (*śuddha madhyama*), and the other 36 scales take the augmented or sharpened variant of the fourth (*prati madhyama*). These two variants of the fourth interval thus form a pivot for the entire arrangement.

This scale system was quite revolutionary when first proposed by Veṅkaṭamakhi in the seventeenth century because it regularized the tritone interval (*prati madhyama*) with regard to the tonic or basic note (*sa*, *ṣaḍja*). Although there existed already some rāgas that contained this interval, its systematic application was another matter. It was likened to the drop of buttermilk which turns the entire milk into curd. The *prati madhyama* interval creates an entirely new auditory impression wherever it is introduced into a familiar melodic context.

There is but a small number of popular rāgas that contain a *prati madhyama* as part of their ascending and descending interval pattern (*ārohaṇa-avarohaṇa*). Notable examples are rāgas Pūrvīkalyāṇi and Varāḷi apart from several major *mēḷakartā rāgas* such as Hēmavati (58), Mēcakalyāṇi (65, = Kalyāṇi), Kāmavardhani (51, = Pantuvarāḷi), Latāṅgi (63), Ṣaṇmukhapriya (56), Simhēndramadhyama (57), Śubhapantuvarāḷi (45), and Vācaspati (64). Other rāgas containing *prati madhyama* are Amṛtavarṣiṇi, Dīpakam, Hamīr Kalyāṇi, Haṁsanādam, Haṁsānandi, Mandāri, Mohana Kalyāṇi, Rañjani, Sarasvati, Śrutirañjani, Vijayavasanta and Yamunā

Kalyāṇi. In addition there are rāgas that have the natural fourth as a regular note with an augmented fourth also introduced as an accidental note (*anya svara*). Such additions are introduced in the course of pleasing phrases (*rañjaka prayoga*). The only common rāgas of this type are Gauḷipantu, Hindustānī Bēhāg (Byāg) and Sindhubhairavi.

The diversity of rāgas is thus based on specific interval combinations. It might be compared to the unlimited variety of images an artist can paint with just a few colours which have been carefully mixed on a palette. A painting depicts its subject and feeling through countless separate patches of pigment, even through colours and shades not seen in the subject they depict; but viewed from a proper distance, it conveys a lifelike impression of plants, animals, a landscape, or human being. The spectator enjoys the total effect but largely remains unaware of the technical, optical and psychological side of painting. In a manner comparable to this impressionist approach to painting, a rāga enables a musician to convey various moods and feelings that are recognized and shared by most human beings. The difference between singing and playing an instrument can be likened to the use of a brush, a pencil, or crayon in the hands of an artist who is at home with different techniques. A few notes, skilfully mixed or contrasted with one another convey an entire 'picture' of pure delight and imagination without the constraints of realism faced by a painter. Perhaps it is this abstract quality which makes the rāga concept so timeless, fresh, and at the same time so conducive to personal feelings. The techniques and theories underlying the concept of rāga have occupied the minds of musicians, musicologists, mystics, and listeners for almost two millennia. For this reason it is unlikely that Indian musicians will dispense with the rāga system or subject it to sudden or radical changes. After all, visual artists have continued to use colours and brushes even in the age of photography, television, and computer graphics.

Staves 17–19 show the 72 scales in staff notation. These scales are arranged in two columns, each column containing 6 groups with 6 scales each. The left column follows the numerical order from 1 to 36, and the right one from 37 to 72. All the scales on the left side use a natural fourth (*śuddha madhyama*), and all those on the right side use an augmented fourth (*prati madhyama*), a tritone if reckoned from the basic note (*ṣaḍjam*). In other words, the scales on the left side (1 to 36) are almost identical with those on the right side (37 to 72), the variants of the fourth note (natural/sharp 'F') being the only difference between both groups.

Stave 17: *Mēḷakartā rāgas* (numbers 1 to 12 & 37 to 48).

Stave 18: *Mēḷakartā rāgas* (numbers 13 to 24 & 49 to 60).

Stave 19: *Mēḷakartā rāgas* (numbers 25 to 36 & 61 to 72).

13

Types of Rāga (Janya Rāga)

Several types of 'derived' rāgas (*janya rāga*) use additional notes that are not found in their 'parental' scale (*janaka rāga*). All the accidental or 'alien' notes (*anya svara*) that may occur in these rāgas are shown alongside the scale from which they are derived in the form of individual notes (separated by a bar line). This does not mean, however, that these additional notes can be used freely. On the contrary, their pleasing and sometimes surprising quality is retained only if excessive dissonance (*vivādī*) can be avoided. This is achieved by way of using these notes sparingly rather than liberally. In other words, such notes either occur in the context of a scale pattern or in special phrases (*viśeṣa sañcāra*) that characterize a particular *janya rāga*.

Some rāgas have been created by individual musicians and composers while others have been distilled from many melodies. A majority of rāgas fall under the heading *janya* ('derived') rāga to indicate that these rāgas differ in one or several respects from the reference scales (*mēḷakartā rāga*) under which they are listed. While some of these scales also have corresponding rāgas (*sampūrṇa* or heptatonic rāgas) which are capable of evoking feelings (*rāgabhāva*), a *janya rāga* is further distinguished from such rāgas.

The Western major scale is a case in point (see Staves 19 and 27). Its Karnatic counterpart is known as rāga Śaṅkarābharaṇam (literally, 'ornaments of Śaṅkara' or Śiva). Like its underlying scale, the 29th *mēḷakartā rāga* Dhīraśaṅkarābharaṇam, it comprises all the seven notes of the diatonic scale. But unlike the scale, it does not afford equal treatment for all the seven notes even in its most basic outline. In a rendition close to the vocal ideal, several notes barely touch their underlying intervals. The most conspicuous feature of Śaṅkarābharaṇam is the discretion accorded to the seventh note, 'B sharp' (*ni*). This note is merely hinted at rather than extended. It is rarely, if ever, used as an ending or 'landing note' (*nyāsa svara*) of a phrase in Śaṅkarābharaṇam. Conversely, the seventh note of Kalyāṇi rāga, also a form of 'B sharp' (*ni*), is often emphasized, dwelt upon and can serve as *nyāsa svara*. One should therefore not be deceived by the fact that in musical notation, both rāgas appear to be near-identical but for the natural fourth ('F') of Śaṅkarābharaṇam, and the tritone ('F-sharp') of Kalyāṇi. In practice, both rāgas are treated in a very different manner. An appropriate choice of micro-intervals, embellishments and phrasing make

Staves 20–26 *Janya rāgas* (see also staves 28 to 35).

Stave 20

it possible to evoke moods that are quite distinct. Countless other examples could be cited for such minute differences between similar rāgas. The description of such features (*rāga lakṣaṇa*) is regarded as the most demanding branch of traditional South Indian musicology.

Stave 21

Other differences between a scale and its *janya rāga* may consist of the deletion or addition of specific notes either as a regular feature (*prayoga*) or as a rare but characteristic occurrence (*viśeṣa sañcāra*). The deletion of a note often induces a feeling of grandeur or tension, while the introduction of additional notes (*anya svara*) tends to soften the effect of some intervals (e.g. rāga Bhairavi) or even to

Stave 22

blur the contours of a rāga (e.g. Hindustānī Kāpi, Dvijāvanti). In some cases, two or more *mēḷakartā rāgas* are associated with a *janya rāga* because several versions or opinions coexist.

Rāgas that are based on just five notes (*auḍava rāga*) are no less appealing than their counterparts based on six notes (*ṣāḍava rāga*) or seven notes (*sampūrṇa*

Stave 23

rāga). It is a remarkable fact that several pentatonic or five-tone rāgas (*auḍava rāga*), notably Ābhōgi, Haṁsadhvani, Hindōḷam, Madhyamāvati and Mōhanam, are loved by musicians and audiences, as they yield the most variegated melodies. Combinations of less than five notes are not accepted as rāgas because they seem to lack aesthetic appeal although some attempts have been made in recent years to introduce such miniature rāgas.

At the other end of the spectrum, there are rāgas like Sindhubhairavi (Stave 34) with a profusion of eight, nine, up to twelve different notes (*bhāṣāṅga rāga*). Music literature describes many such rāgas as regional variants (*dēśya rāga*) related to major rāgas to which 'foreign notes' (*anya svara*) have been added. Byāg (Hindustānī Bēhāg), Hindustānī Kāpi, Kānaḍa, Sindhubhairavi are rāgas whose sentimental appeal never fails. But their place is mostly in the segment devoted to popular or 'light' items (*tukkaḍā*) towards the closing of a Karnatic concert. Here the less unrestricted combination of numerous intervals has a relaxing if not sedative effect on most listeners. As a rāga sheds its own 'colours' and assimilates the

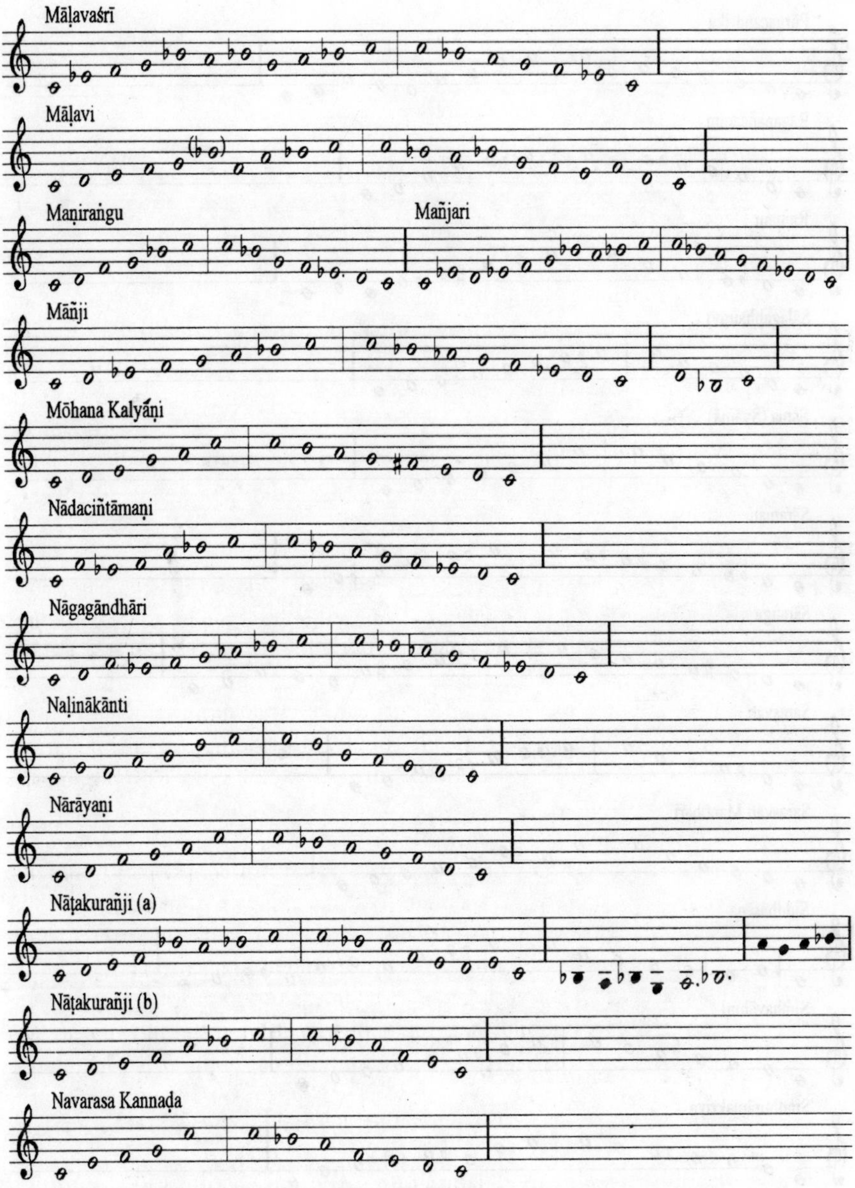

Stave 24

characteristics of other rāgas, the boundaries of a listener's individual consciousness are also blurred. Rāgas Dvijāvanti and Ghaṇṭa are rāgas that belong to this group and are described in terms of being 'tinged' (*chāyālaga*) or 'mixed' (*miśra, saṅkīrṇa*) because they derive their beauty from the suggestion of the colours or graces of other rāgas.

Stave 25

Important rāgas are characterized by the golden mean between two extremes, very few or too many available notes. Some rāgas are described in terms of having a distinct, but 'soft' (*naya*) character of their own. They could be compared to a beautiful face that requires a delicate method of portrayal by a painter in order to appear lifelike. Another descriptive term for a number of established rāgas suggests

Stave 26

a charming or colourful quality (*rakti rāga*) which can be established through a few characteristic phrases. Accidental notes (*anya svara*) should be applied sparingly if admitted at all. Ānandabhairavi is a special rāga of this category, although it is rarely taken up for a detailed rāga *ālāpana*. The same can be said of Yadukulakāmbhōji. Some of the most moving songs have been composed in these rāgas over a period of at least two centuries, for instance Syāmā Sāstri's *O Jagadamba* (Ānandabhairavi, ādi tāla), Tyāgarāja's Ētāvuna Nercitivō Rāma (Yadukulakāmbhōji, ādi tāla). Although other rāgas lend themselves more to an elaborate *rāga ālāpana* than

Stave 27: The melodic curve of rāga Śaṅkarābharaṇam.

Stave 28: *Auḍava rāgas.*

Ānandabhairavi and Yadukulakāmbhōji, few others seem to be as satisfying even when presented in a nutshell.

Typically, a *rakti rāga* is performed in or around the central part of a performance. Both terms, *naya* and *rakti*, imply ample scope for imaginative treatment by a musician as well as enduring appeal even for the most ardent listeners (*rasika*). *Rakti rāgas*, such as Bhairavi, Kalyāṇi, Kāmbhōji, Śaṅkarābharaṇam, and Tōḍi, are regarded as the most prominent rāgas of South Indian music. Among these rāgas, only Bhairavi and Kāmbhōji admit the inclusion of an accidental note (*anya svara*) which needs to be applied sparingly in order to be pleasing. Tōḍi, on the other hand, derives its charm from the intensity of embellishment applied to all notes. Occasionally this ornamentation is contrasted by an extended and unembellished minor third (*sādhāraṇa gāndhāra*).

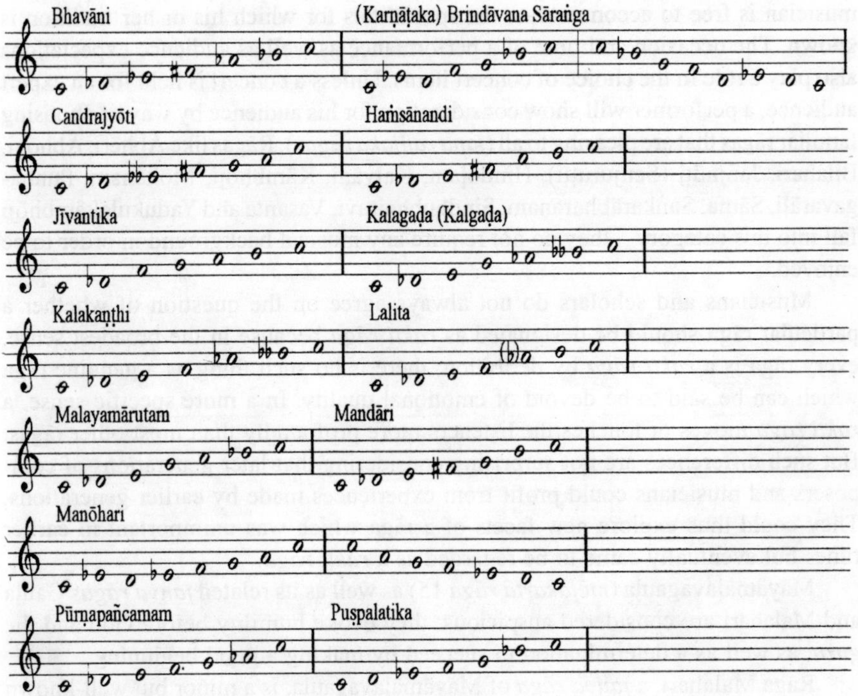

Stave 29: *Ṣāḍava rāgas.*

The choice of rāgas for a concert programme

A concert (*kaccēri*) mostly follows a familiar pattern (*kaccēri paddhati*) which covers a variety of compositions and improvised items. This sequence sometimes corresponds to a traditional categorization of rāgas into *ghana rāga*, *rakti rāga* and *dēśya rāga*. There is room for discretion, personal preferences and spontaneity. A musician is free to accommodate the specialities for which his or her tradition is known. The occasion and time of a performance as well as audience expectations also play a role in the choice of concert items. Unless a concert is held for an expert audience, a performer will show consideration for his audience by way of choosing familiar rāgas that are pleasing to all (*jana rañjaka rāgas*). Rāgas like Ābhēri, Ābhōgi, Bilahari, Jañjhūṭi (Senjuruṭṭi), Hindōḷam, Kalyāṇi, Kāmbhōji, Mōhanam, Punnāgavarāḷi, Sāma, Śaṅkarābharaṇam, Sindhubhairavi, Vasanta and Yadukulakāmbhōji fall into this category—they do not require any musical background in order to be enjoyed.

Musicians and scholars do not always agree on the question of whether a particular rāga should be designated as *rakti rāga* because in the broadest sense, every rāga is a *rakti rāga* by definition; there is no such thing as a genuine rāga which can be said to be devoid of emotional quality. In a more specific sense, a *rakti rāga* moves or touches the listeners more profoundly than most other rāgas. But such differences are not surprising considering that later generations of composers and musicians could profit from experiences made by earlier generations. They could thus explore new facets of a rāga which was unimportant in earlier times but eventually came to be regarded as a *rakti rāga*.

Māyāmāḷavagauḷa (*mēḷakartā rāga* 15) as well as its related *janya rāgas* Gauḷa and Malahari are considered auspicious: they evoke humility before God and the *guru*, as well as a determination to succeed by making a good beginning.

Rāga Malahari, a *janya rāga* of Māyāmāḷavagauḷa, is a minor but well-known rāga. As it is believed to have a purifying effect on the mind, it is still the rāga of the first composition taught to a beginner. The best-known composition in Malahari rāga is the *gītam* 'Śrī Gaṇanatha' of Purandara Dāsa (rūpaka tāla).

Rāga Haṁsadhvani is best known through 'Vātāpigaṇapatim', an invocation of Gaṇeśa (ādi tāla). Like most songs about Gaṇeśa, embodiment of good luck, this *kṛti* is performed at the beginning of a concert. Haṁsadhvani is believed to be a creation of the composer's father, Rāmasvāmi Dīkṣitar, who was himself an important figure in the field of music during the eighteenth century.

There are a number of rāgas like Malahari that practically owe their popularity to a single composition although other compositions are also available. Typical examples are Bahudāri ('Brōvabhāramā' by Tyāgarāja, ādi tāla), Kēdāram ('Rāmanīpai' by Tyāgarāja, ādi tāla), Māñji ('Brōvavamma' by Śyāmā Śāstri, miśra cāpu tāla), and Nāṭakurañji ('Cālamēla', a popular *tānavarṇam* by Mūlaīviṭṭu Raṅgasvāmi, ādi tāla).

A charming example for the popularity of a minor and modern rāga is Kadanakutūhalam, a creation by Paṭṭaṇam Subrahmaṇya Ayyar. This rāga is mostly heard in combination with the *kṛti* 'Raghuvaṁśasudha' (ādi tāla). Its playful quality, numerous variations (*saṅgati*), and the scope it offers for displaying one's virtuosity have ensured that 'Raghuvaṁśasudha' remains a favourite composition of instrumentalists and listeners alike.

There are no rāgas which would be considered as 'inauspicious'. But Varāḷi is an attractive rāga which is difficult to teach because of the close vicinity of its notes.

It has a reputation of causing a rift between teacher and student. Most teachers avoid teaching Varāḷi directly to a student for this reason. Varāḷi is mostly learnt by listening to the renditions of other musicians.

Rāga Madhyamāvati (*auḍava-auḍava*) is reputed to restore the unity and stillness of the mind after a variety of moods have been experienced during the course of a performance. For this reason, the audience is treated to it before returning home. But the emotive potential of Madhyamāvati is by no means exhausted in this context and therefore it appears in a variety of contexts.

Ghana rāga, ghanam

In Sanskrit and Tamil, the word *ghana* means 'heavy'. In Tamil, this word is used when a person is referred to as 'respectable'. In the most narrow sense, *ghana rāga* refers to the five rāgas known as *ghana rāga pañcaka*: Nāṭa, Gauḷa, Ārabhi, Varāḷi and Śrī. This group of five rāgas has found its masterly expression in the five compositions of Tyāgarāja known as *Ghana Rāga Pañcaratna*. There is a second set of five *ghana rāgas* (*dvitīya ghana rāga pañcaka*) which includes Kēdāram, Nārāyaṇagauḷa, Rītigauḷa, Sāraṅganāṭa and Bauḷi.

In the context of contemporary performance practice, a *ghana rāga* can be said to be 'weighty' or substantial enough to provide for creative elaboration in the form of *ālāpana* and *tāṉam*. Sometimes *ghana rāga* is also used to designate those rāgas that lend themselves to elaboration in the *rāgam tāṉam pallavi* format. Taken in this sense, the term *ghana rāga* does not necessarily imply a fast tempo.

Viewed in the light of music history, the term *ghanam* denotes a style of singing which is characterized by *ālāpana* exposition in medium if not fast tempo which is reminiscent of *tāṉam*. Hence the term *ghana tāṉam* applies to *tāṉam* performed in three degrees of speed. Ghanam Kr̥ṣṇa Ayyar was a famous nineteenth-century musician and composer who specialized in the *ghanam* style of singing.

A *ghana rāga* retains its characteristic appeal even when the amount of embellishments (*gamaka*) is reduced in a faster tempo. Such a rāga is therefore less likely to be chosen for a slow *ālāpana* exposition. A *rakti rāga*, on the other hand, will unfold much of its beauty in a slow tempo. A traditional *ghana rāga* is therefore performed at the beginning of a concert or as part of a *rāgamālikā* ('garland of rāgas'). The *rāgamālikā* mostly forms a part of the main item in a concert (e.g. *rāgam tāṉam pallavi*).

Because a *ghana rāga* can be rendered very effectively by the *vīṇā*, an instrument which produces notes of a relatively short duration, it is often chosen for the highlight of a *vīṇā* concert, an elaborate *tāṉam* exposition.

The term *ghanam* also refers to a style of reciting vedic texts which resembles the *tāṉam* form of vocal or instrumental improvisation. Both the *tāṉam* of classical music and the vedic *ghanam* recitation involve methodical repetitions and permutations of syllables and words. The *ghanam* procedure progresses by way of taking up segment after segment of a given text, and each segment is subjected to a specified number of repetitions and permutations based on three notes (*svara*). A *tāṉam* can similarly be described as a procedure which progresses by subjecting a

Stave 30: *Ghana rāga pañcaka* and *dvitīya ghana rāga pañcaka.*

musical phrase or word ('*anaṁta*') to a process of repetition and permutation. In each stage, a *tāṉam* phrase is first confined to three neighbouring notes (*svara*) before covering a wider melodic range in accordance with the ascending and descending patterns (*ārohaṇa-avarohaṇa*) of the chosen rāga.

It may be recalled that Indian music is widely believed to have been inspired by the scriptures (*Veda*) that were perceived (*śruti*) by ancient sages (*ṛṣi*). Particularly that section of the *Ṛgveda* which has later been re-arranged for the purpose of melodious chanting (*Sāma Veda*) is regarded as being the foundation for the early forms of sacred music (*mārga saṅgīta*) from which Indian classical music has evolved in several stages.

In the *ghanam* style of recitation based on the *Ṛgveda*, an 'essential' group of words or syllables (*mūlamantram*) is arranged in a sequential order (*kramam*) and recited five times. Then another group is taken up for similar treatment. Such a recitation involves three notes (*svara*) similar to those found in music based on rāga, namely *udātta* (raised or upper), *anudātta* (secondary or lower) and *svarita* ('articulated note', 'mixed tone'), the middle note to which the other two notes are joined by way of gliding movements. A person trained to recite Sanskrit texts in this manner is called *ghanapāṭhigaḷ*. Although vedic recitation has a purpose which is different from that of art music, it is believed to have created an awareness of distinct pitches from which classical music could gradually develop. For the purpose of chanting the *Sāma Veda*, four other notes were added to the original *udātta, anudātta* and *svarita* to form a complete scale of seven notes. The original scale associated with the *Sāma Veda* is said to correspond to the modern rāga Kharaharapriya, the 22nd *mēḷakartā rāga*. According to this theory, the upper half of this scale, belonging to the middle octave, provides the first four notes of Kharaharapriya (*sa, ri, ga* and *ma*). Correspondingly, the lower half provides the remaining three notes (*pa, dha* and *ni*). From this basic scale, other scale patterns could be derived by way of shifting the basic note from *ṣadja* to another note. On the basis of vedic culture, a system of art music called *gāndharva saṅgīta* was described by Dattila, an ancient writer on music. Various forms of song and dance evolved in different regions of India (*dēśa*) which were termed *dēśī saṅgīta* by early writers. The distinction of *mārga saṅgīta* and *dēśī saṅgīta* became irrelevant after the *Saṅgīta Ratnākara*, an important musical treatise, was written in the thirteenth century. This development preceded the emergence of the two musical systems prevalent in modern India, *Karṇāṭaka Saṅgīta* of South India and *Hindustānī Saṅgīt* of North India.

There is another variant of *ghanam* recitation termed *jata* which similarly involves repetitive patterns. In the *jata* style, each statement is recited thrice instead of five times.

Rakti or naya rāga

Both terms, *rakti* ('pleasing') and *naya* ('soft') are applied to a type of rāga which can be sustained in an exposition (*ālāpana*) of considerable length; it lends itself to slow phrases enriched by a variety of embellishments (*gamaka*). For this reason, a *rakti* or *naya rāga* is considered as the most suitable choice for the main part of a concert. Listeners do not tire of hearing rāgas of this type time and again. A congenial rendition of a *rakti rāga* by way of improvised exposition, especially *ālāpana* and *niraval*, is regarded as the hallmark of a musician. As in the case of other rāgas, the compositions of the Trinity (Śyāmā Śāstri, Tyāgarāja and Muttusvāmi

Dīkṣitar) provide the models for a musician's own creativity and ability to evoke the emotive power of a rāga (*rāga bhāva*). Other sources of inspiration are the numerous technical compositions (*tānavarṇam*) available for any *rakti rāga*. The most important example for rāga Bhairavi is the aṭa tāla *varṇam* 'Viribōni'.

Rakti rāgas mentioned by different authors include: Āhiri, Ānandabhairavi, Aṭāṇa, Bēgaḍa, Bhairavi, Bilahari, Dēvagāndhāri, Ghaṇṭā, Kalyāṇi, Kāmbhōji, Kēdāragauḷa, Kharaharapriya, Madhyamāvati, Mukhāri, Nāyaki, Nīlāmbari, Pantuvarāḷi (Kāmavardhani), Punnāgavarāḷi, Pūrvīkalyāṇi, Śahāna, Śaṅkarābharaṇam, Ṣaṇmukhapriya, Saurāṣṭram, Sāvēri, Tōḍi, Vācaspati and Yadukulakāmbhōji.

Rakti rāgas belong to different types of rāgas, including *mēḷakartā* and *auḍava-auḍava rāgas*. There is but one *niṣādāntya rāga*, Punnāgavarāḷi. No popular *ṣāḍava-ṣāḍava* rāga belongs to this group. Kurañji, an old South Indian rāga, and Nīlāmbari are mostly described as *dēśya rāgas*, but sometimes also listed among the *rakti* group of rāgas.

The term *nayam* is also used to characterize a performer's approach to music,

Staves 31 & 32: *Rakti rāgas.*

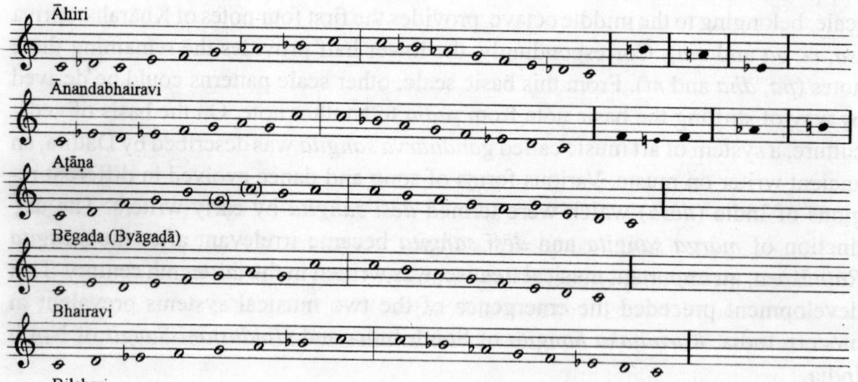

Stave 31

Stave 32

for instance that of Mahāvaidyanātha Śivaṉ ('persuasively soft'). On the other end of the stylistic or temperamental spectrum, we hear of performers like Rāghava Ayyar who publicly challenged Mahāvaidyanātha Śivaṉ in a music contest. His strength lay in the realm of *ghanam*, not *nayam*, meaning that his singing was characterized by vigour and majesty.

Dēśya rāga

A *dēśya* rāga is associated with simple devotional songs and 'light' or 'folk' songs of various kinds (*tukkaḍā*). Many *dēśya rāgas* were adopted from Hindustānī music (e.g. rāga Deś), including the patriotic songs of Subrahmaṇya Bhārati. Although the term *dēśya* has almost become synonymous with a 'rāga of North Indian origin', even those *dēśya rāgas* whose names and structure still betray a Hindustānī origin, are presently rendered in a manner which differs from that which is characteristic of Hindustānī music.

Dēśya rāgas believed to be inspired by the folk music of South India include: Dēśya Tōḍi, Jañjhūṭi, Kurañji, Nādanāmakriya, Navarōj, Nīlāmbari, and Punnāgavarāḷi.

Dēśya rāgas either derived from Hindustānī music or inspired by it are: Bāgēśrī,

Bimplās, Byāg, Brindāvana Sāraṅga, Byāg, Deś, Dhanāśrī, Dīpakam, Durgā, Dvijāvanti, Hamīr Kalyāṇi, Haṁsānandi, Hindustānī Kāpi (Kāfi), Husēni (Usāni, Usēni), Jañjhūṭi (Jhinjōṭī, Senjuruṭṭi), Kānaḍa (Darbāri Kānaḍa), Khamās, Māṇḍ, Pharas (Paraz, Paraju), Pilū, Saurāṣṭram, Sindhubhairavi (Dvādaśi Bhairavi), Tilaṅg, and Yamunā Kalyāṇi.

Staves 33 & 34: *Dēśya rāgas*.

Stave 33

Stave 34

Sampūrṇa and asampūrṇa rāga

One common way of classifying rāgas is based on the number of permissible notes, for instance five, six, seven, or more. If the seven notes of the *mēḷakartā rāga* scale are all present in a rāga, it can be termed *sampūrṇa*; if one or several notes must be avoided to bring out the character of a given rāga, it can be called *asampūrṇa*. More specifically, an *asampūrṇa rāga* is either called *auḍava* (if it has five notes) or *ṣāḍava* (if it has six notes).

The ascending and the descending scale patterns of a *janya rāga* often differ from one another. Bilahari is a case in point: it permits the use of five notes in its ascent and seven notes in its descent (*auḍava-sampūrṇa*).

Bhāṣāṅga rāga

The class of rāgas known as *bhāṣāṅga* rāga refers to an 'alien' note (*anya svara*) that needs to be taken into account (e.g. rāgas Bilahari and Kāmbhōji). There may even be several such *anya svara* (e.g. Ānandabhairavi, Hindustānī Kāpi, the *bhāṣāṅga* type of Kānaḍa). An *anya svara* may be rare (*alpa*) or common (*bahutva*). In some rāgas, as in rāga Bhairavi, the *anya svara* occurs in the basic scale pattern (*catuḥśruti dhaivata* or natural 6th in the ascending scale). The correct usage regarding an *anya svara* is guided through compositions learnt from an experienced teacher.

Pañcamāntya, dhaivatāntya and niṣādāntya rāgas

These are *dēśya* rāgas that are mostly performed towards the end of a concert in the *tukkaḍā* group of items. The terms *pañcamāntya*, *dhaivatāntya* and *niṣādāntya* refer to the fact that these rāgas have a tonal range limited to one octave (*ēkasthāyī rāga*): notes in the upper range (*tāra sthāyī*) are avoided altogether; and the upper limit is defined by the fifth or *pañcama* (*pañcamāntya rāga*), the 6th or *dhaivata* (*dhaivatāntya rāga*), and the 7th *niṣāda* (*niṣādāntya rāga*), respectively.

When rāgas of this group are sung, a *tambūrā* is re-tuned in such a manner that the first string (5th or *pa*) is reduced by one full note. The natural 4th (*śuddha madhyama*) is then heard in the place of the 5th. This string then provides the new tonic (*ṣaḍja*). The result is that the rāga is sung in a key and range which is raised by four notes. The two middle strings which earlier provided the tonic (*ṣaḍja*) are now heard as the 5th (*pañcama*), and the former lower tonic (*mandrasthāyī ṣaḍja*) is heard as the 5th of the lower octave. In view of this predominance of the fifth note, now sounded by three strings, a *tambūrā* player needs to re-modify his playing in order to make the new tonic audible.

Vakra rāga

This classification pertains to a 'zigzag' (*vakra*) pattern either in the ascent (*ārohaṇa*), the descent (*avarohaṇa*), or both. A great number of *janya rāgas* belong to this category: Bēgaḍa, Kēdāram, Mukhāri, Rītigauḷa and Varāḷi, to name but a few.

Pañcama varja rāga

This is a type of rāga in which the 5th note (*pañcama*) must be avoided altogether. The *tambūrā* string tuned to the fifth is generally not played with such a rāga. This produces a striking contrast to other rāgas that have a fifth, generally as an important resting note. The following rāgas of this category are found in the present repertoire: Ābhōgi, Haṁsānandi, Hindōḷam, Jayamanōhari, Lalita, Mēgharañjani, Rañjani, Ravicandrika, Śrīrañjani, Śuddha Tōḍi, and Vasanta. All these rāgas are very pleasing and popular.

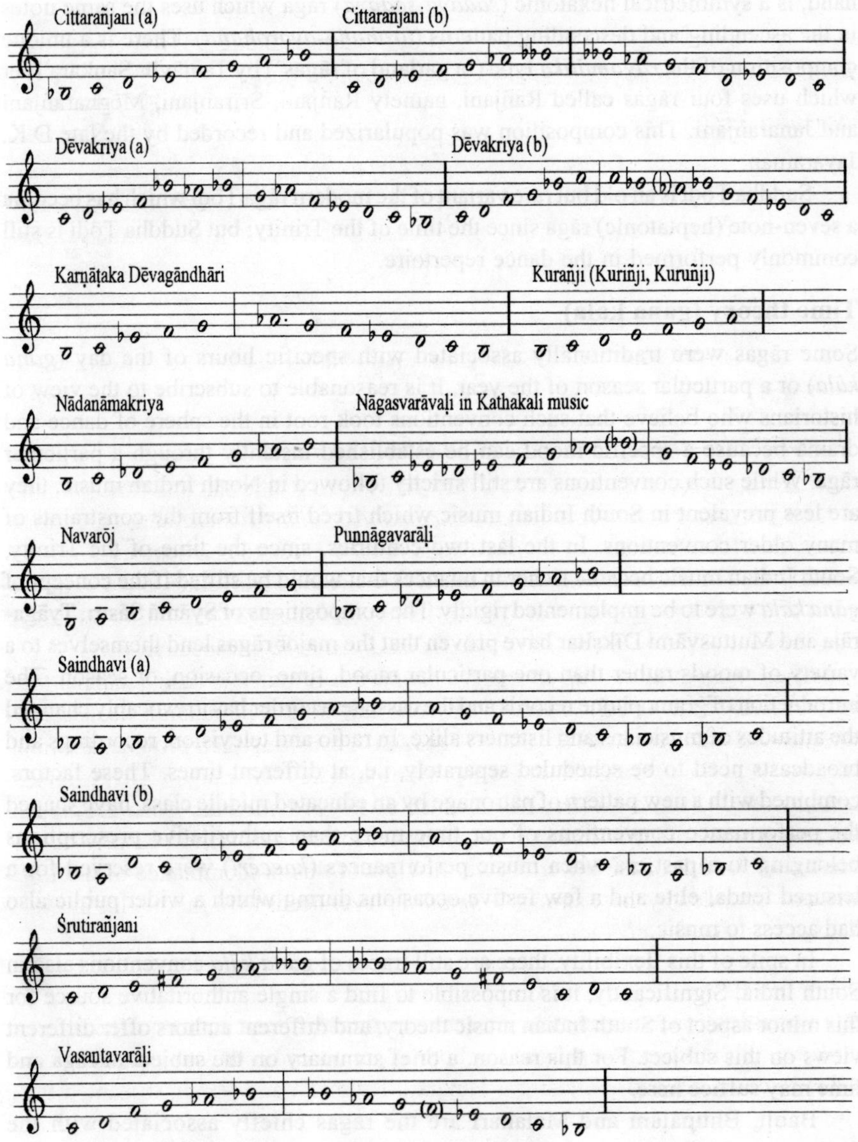

Stave 35: *Niṣādāntya, dhaivatāntya, and pañcamāntya rāgas*

Two rāgas of this type, Rañjani and Haṁsānandi, stand out and are easily identified because of a combination of two conspicuous features: both rāgas are devoid of the 5th (*pañcama*); and both have a sharp variant of the 4th (*prati madhyama*). Rañjani uses six notes found in its reference scale (*mēlakartā* 59, Dharmavati); but one combination of five notes is used in the ascent (*ārohaṇa*), and another combination of six notes in the descent (*avarohaṇa*). Haṁsānandi, on the other hand, is a symmetrical hexatonic (*ṣādava-ṣādava*) rāga which uses the same notes in the ascending and descending patterns (*ārohaṇa-avarohaṇa*). There is a unique composition of the *rāgamālikā* type ('a garland of rāgas') by Tañjāvūr Sankara Iyer which uses four rāgas called Rañjani, namely Rañjani, Śrīrañjani, Mēgharañjani and Janarañjani. This composition was popularized and recorded by the late D.K. Jayaraman.

Śuddha Tōḍi is an old but rare variant of the modern rāga Tōḍi which has become a seven-note (heptatonic) rāga since the time of the Trinity; but Śuddha Tōḍi is still commonly performed in the dance repertoire.

Time theory (gāna kāla)

Some rāgas were traditionally associated with specific hours of the day (*gāna kāla*) or a particular season of the year. It is reasonable to subscribe to the view of historians who believe that such conventions took root in the sphere of dance and drama because a specific mood can be established instantly through a particular rāga. While such conventions are still strictly followed in North Indian music, they are less prevalent in South Indian music which freed itself from the constraints of many older conventions. In the last two centuries, since the time of the Trinity, South Indian music became richer in nuances that would be stifled if the concept of *gāna kāla* were to be implemented rigidly. The compositions of Śyāmā Śāstri, Tyāgarāja and Muttusvāmi Dīkṣitar have proven that the major rāgas lend themselves to a variety of moods rather than one particular mood, time, occasion, or season. The introduction of gramophone records and the cassette recorder has irrevocably changed the attitudes of musicians and listeners alike. In radio and television, recordings and broadcasts need to be scheduled separately, i.e. at different times. These factors, combined with a new pattern of patronage by an educated middle class, have shaped the performance conventions of our time more than authoritative prescriptions belonging to a past era when music performances (*kaccēri*) were reserved for a leisured feudal elite and a few festive occasions during which a wider public also had access to music.

In spite of this flexibility, there are still traces of *gāna kāla* conventions also in South India. Significantly, it is impossible to find a single authoritative source for this minor aspect of South Indian music theory, and different authors offer different views on this subject. For this reason, a brief summary on the subject of rāga and time may suffice here.

Bauḷi, Bhūpāḷam and Malahari are the rāgas chiefly associated with the freshness and serenity experienced in the early hours of the day, before the onset of the tropical heat. In dance-dramas, these rāgas are therefore employed to evoke the mood of the early morning irrespective of the actual time of a performance. The rāgas preferred later in the morning are those evocative of vigour or valour (*vīra rasa*) such as Āsāvēri, Bilahari, Kēdāram, Malayamārutam, Māyāmāḷavagauḷa, Sāvēri, and Valaji. Midday is the time associated with rāga Dhanyāsi, Madhyamāvati, Śaṅkarābharaṇam, and Śrīrāga. Among the rāgas associated with the afternoon are Bēgaḍa, Bhairavi, Kedāragauḷa, Mukhāri, Pādi, and Rēvagupti.

Kāmbhōji, Nāṭakuranji, Pūrvīkalyāṇi, Rītigauḷa, Saurāṣṭram, and Vasanta are the rāgas sometimes associated with the evening hours. Rāgas with sharp 4th (*prati madhyama*), such as Kalyāṇi, Pūrvīkalyāṇi, Ṣaṇmukhapriya, and Siṁhēndramadhyama, are conducive to a more relaxed frame of mind and are therefore preferred in the evening hours. Tender rāgas like Āhiri and Nīlāmbari are associated with the stillness of the late evening or night hours. Some lullabies and marriage songs (*lāli*) have also been composed in rāga Nīlāmbari. *Ōmaṉa tiṅgaḷ kiḍavō* is a famous lullaby by Irayimman Tampi in this rāga (ādi tāla, *tiśra naḍai*) which was sung to Svāti Tirunāḷ when he was a child. A festive mood is invoked by the joyous rāga Vasanta. The vigorous rāga Gambhīranāṭa is associated with the *mallāri*, an instrumental piece played by a *nāgasvaram* and *tavil* ensemble (*periya mēḷam*) during temple processions.

Innovation

Tyāgarāja took delight in experimenting with the new possibilities offered by the *mēḷakartā-janya rāga* system. This system had already been envisaged by Veṅkaṭamakhi in the seventeenth century but was more successful after Govindācāri had made some improvements in the eighteenth century. Some of the rāgas created or introduced by Tyāgarāja have been adopted by other composers, while others exist only in a single composition of Tyāgarāja (*ekaika kṛti rāga*). Although many such rāgas are considered as 'minor' rāgas in view of their limited scope for rāga elaboration (*ālāpana*), there are compositions which are very popular in the repertoire: Cittarañjani ('Nādatanumaniśam', ādi tāla, see also *niṣādāntya rāgas*), Jayantaśrī ('Mārugēlarā', ādi tāla), Manōhari ('Paritāpamu', rūpaka tāla), Vijayavasanta ('Nīcittamu', ādi tāla), to name but a few. Their popularity derives from beautiful lyrics (*sāhitya*), the use of compositional devices such as variations (*saṅgati*), ornamentation (*gamaka*), and skilful placement in the tāla cycle (*graha* or *eḍuppu*). Tyāgarāja confined himself to the framework of the traditional *kīrtana* and the more advanced *kṛti* but added a new complexity and artistic quality. He also proved that the emotive power of music (*rāga bhāva*) can effectively convey the feelings that have inspired the lyrics of a piece. This achievement has contributed to the emergence of advanced instrumental music if not Karnatic concert music as we know it today.

Many other major and even minor composers added to the wealth of rāgas found in Karnatic music. In the past, innovation of this kind chiefly consisted in modifications of existing rāgas. Another easy way of obtaining a 'new' rāga was to combine two existing rāgas which is a common device also found in Hindustānī music. A typical example of this type of mixed (*miśra*) rāga is Mōhanam Kalyāṇi; it takes the ascending series of five notes from rāga Mohana, and the seven notes of rāga Kalyāṇi for the descending series. Modern composers like M. Bālamuraḷī Krishna have created new rāgas, sometimes with less than the minimum of five notes traditionally needed for defining a genuine rāga.

14

Tāla

Musical time is measured in terms of metric cycles (*tāla*). Traditional South Indian music offers a great variety of tāla formations that are associated with three contexts, modern, didactic, and scholarly:

(1) Modern: the common tāla varieties performed in a concert: ādi tāla, aṭa tāla, khaṇḍa cāpu tāla, miśra cāpu tāla, rūpaka tāla, and dēśādi tāla; some of these tālas are shortened (*cāpu*) variants of older tālas but more suitable for the requirements of modern concert and dance practice.

(2) Didactic: the tāla varieties practised as part of the elementary course followed in Karnatic music (*abhyāsa gāna*); the seven *sūḷādi tālas* of the *alaṅkāra* exercises, ascribed to Purandara Dāsa, belong to this type.

(3) Scholarly: numerous intricate tāla varieties that are of great historical interest; hundreds of tālas are listed by the authors of old music texts; many of these variants are the result of systematic permutation (*tāla prastāra*) of the elements of which a tāla is composed; tālas of this category are occasionally performed by rhythm specialists in the context of an elaborate *rāgam tānam pallavi* performance or a special percussion concert (*laya vinyāsa*).

Gestures (kriyā)

The structure of each tāla cycle can be marked by gestures which are partly audible (*saśabda kriyā*), and partly inaudible (*nihśabda kriyā*). Instrumentalists such as violin and flute players have to use their feet and heels instead of hands for obvious reasons.

In contemporary South Indian music, three different gestures (*kriyā*) are commonly used for reckoning tāla. They consist of hand and finger movements which are spaced regularly in accordance with the tempo (*kālapramāṇam*) chosen by a performer. Each gesture marks one basic time unit of a tāla.

A clap may be executed in two ways: the right palm hits the palm of the left hand from above; or—if the right hand is engaged in playing a drone (*tambūrā*)—the left palm gently hits one's left thigh. Such a clap marks either the first beat (*samam*) of a *laghu* section (e.g. symbol 'I₄'), the first beat of a *drutam* section (symbol 'O') or the beat that makes up an *anudrutam* section (symbol 'U'). In the absence of other specifications, the *laghu* section has four beats (*caturaśra*), the most common subdivision found in several tāla variants.

Fig. 28: Marking the subdivisions of musical time (*tāla*): clap.

Finger-counts consist of tapping one's thumb or left palm with the fingertips of the right hand. After the clap of the *laghu* section (first beat) is sounded, the little finger marks the second beat, the ring finger the third beat, the middle finger the fourth beat, the forefinger the fifth beat and the thumb the sixth beat. If more finger-counts are needed to complete counting a long *laghu* (e.g. in jhampa tāla), the little finger is used again, now to mark the seventh beat, and so on.

The hand that executes an audible clap also makes a waving movement to indicate the second beat of a *drutam* section. Thus, symbol 'O' stands for the combination of a clap with a turn.

Symbols

In writing, each gesture (or series of movements) is represented by a symbol. The most important symbols, I, O and U are explained in Table 12.

The pattern outlined above is also maintained whenever the melodic theme of a composition has a point of departure (*eḍuppu*) which is located before or after the starting point (*samam*) of the tāla itself.

Rhythmic syllables (jati)

An individual rhythmic syllable is called *jati* (with a short 'a') (Table 13). It is used to build, express and elaborate a particular tāla, a rhythmic pattern which may be simple or complex. The concept of tāla implies that the organization of musical time is cyclic. Tāla is equally applicable to composed and improvised music. There are three main applications for using rhythmic syllables:

Table 12: Gestures and their symbols

Gesture (kriyā)	Symbol	Section (aṅga)	Explanation
Clap	–	–	*samam*, the first beat of any tāla cycle.
Clap + counting	I4 (vertical line followed by a number)	*laghu*	stands for a variable number of beats (*kriyā*); in ādi tāla, the first 4 beats out of a total of 8 beats. (*Note*: The total number of sub-units, the clap plus fingers counted is indicated by the number.)
Clap + wave of the hand	O (full circle)	*drutam*	stands for two beats (*kriyā*); in ādi tāla, beats 5 to 8 (there are two *drutams* of 2 beats each in ādi tāla).
Clap only	U (half circle)	*anudrutam*	stands for one beat (*kriyā*); among the tāla varieties in common use, only jhampa tāla has an *anudrutam* section.

Table 13: Rhythmic syllables (*jati*)

Units	Konnakkōl syllables	Alternative syllables	Alternative syllables
Single	ta		
Two	ta ka	ki ṭa	
Three	ta ki ṭa	ta dhi mi	
Four	ta ka dhi mi	ta ka dhi na	ta ka ju nu
Five	ta dhi ki na tom	ta ka ta ki ṭa	
Six	ta dhī - ki na tom	ta ka dhi mi ṭa ka	ta ka ta ka dhi na
Seven	tā - dhī - ki na tom	ta ki ṭa ta ka dhi mi	ta ka ta dhi ki na tom
Eight	ta ka dhi mi ta ka ju nu	ta dhī - kī - nā - tom	ta jām - ta dhi ki na tom
Nine	ta ka na ka ta dhi ki na tom	tā - dhī - kī - nā - tom	
Ten	ta ki ṭa jām - ta dhi ki na tom	tā - - jām - ta dhi ki na tom	

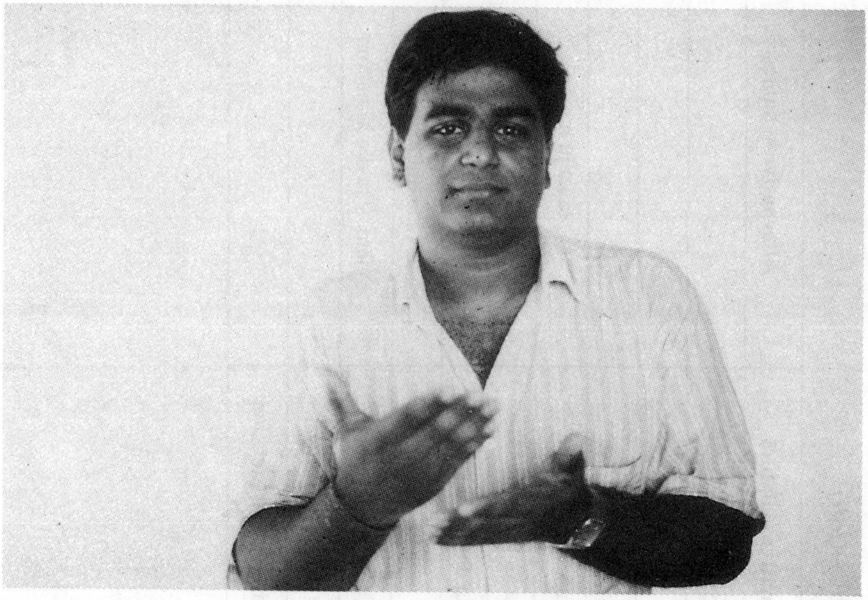

Fig. 29: Marking the subdivisions of musical time (*tāla*): a wave of the hand (the first beat of a *drutam* section).

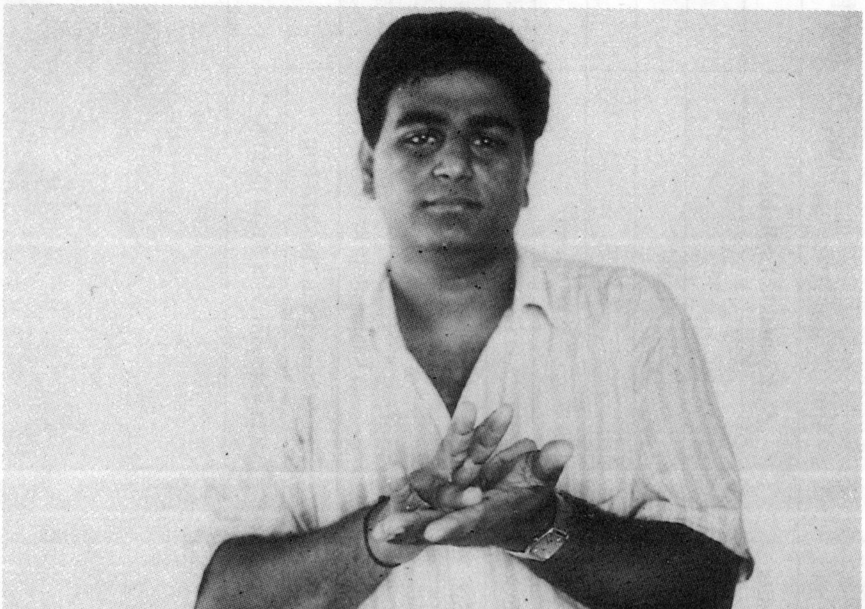

Fig. 30: Marking the subdivisions of musical time (*tāla*): finger-counts after clap (counts 2, 3, 4, etc.).

(1) *Solkaṭṭu:* to convey rhythmic ideas or to teach any type of percussion instrument;
(2) *Naṭṭuvāṅgam:* a combination of *jati* syllables and beats to accompany standard patterns of dance movements (*aḍavu*);
(3) *Konnakkōl:* rhythmic accompaniment for a singer or solo instrumentalist without actually having to use any musical instrument.

Tempo (kālapramāṇam)

A musician or dancer needs to acquire an ability to maintain an even tempo (*kālapramāṇam*) if the finer nuances of rhythm are to be mastered.

A good percussionist exercises restraint when a composition calls for a soulful approach and feeling (*bhāva*). If a musician wants to convey tranquillity (*śānta rasa*) or a romantic sentiment (*śṛṅgāra rasa*) in accordance with the lyrics (*sāhitya*), minute adjustments have to be made. This means advancing or delaying of particular notes without actually altering the tempo by way of acceleration or slowing down. The German term *Agogik* (English *agogic*) introduced by musicologist H. Riemann (1884) describes this type of minute adjustment of tempo and rhythm. It is a subtle form of *rubato* which increases the expressive quality of a performance even though it can hardly be measured or indicated in musical notation. But Indian listeners, just like their European counterparts, will describe the lack of such rhythmic manipulation in terms of having witnessed a mechanical or insensitive rendition. On the

Fig. 31: Śiva holding a *ḍamaru*, the symbol of time (*kāla*). (Drawing by V.C. Arun based on a bronze in the Tañjāvūr Museum.)

other hand, an exaggerated use of *tempo rubato* is bound to convey a sense of restlessness. In Karnatic music, such manipulations are ideally handled sparingly in order to maintain a sense of unity between text, the composer's personal style, and the circumstances in which a performance takes place.

A particular tempo, once chosen, is not changed between the beginning of a piece and its conclusion. On the contrary, it is essential that an even flow of musical time is strictly adhered to.

Compositions are mostly rendered in a medium tempo (*madhyama kāla*), or in a slow tempo (*cauka kāla*). A fast tempo (*druta kāla*) is used occasionally.

Tamil musicians often refer to a slow type of composition as being in *iraṇḍu kalai* (having two counts per *kriyā*); and to a composition in medium tempo as being in *oru kalai* (having one count per *kriyā*).

There is, of course, no universal measure for musical time in India. For practice, however, one *jati* syllable or *mātrā* can be taken as equal to one second in the first degree of speed (*prathama kāla*), half a second for the second degree of speed (*dvitīya kāla*) and a quarter of a second for the third degree of speed (*tṛtīya kāla*). In this manner, twice and four times as many syllables can be accommodated within one *kriyā* in the second and third speeds respectively compared to the first speed. Rendering a rhythm or composition in three speeds is termed *trikāla*.

Major tālas for music and dance performance

The four tālas outlined in Table 14 are the ones most widely used in South Indian music and dance performances. Two especially important tālas, ādi tāla and rūpaka tāla are modern versions of older ones that still belong to the system of *sūḷādi* tālas or *sapta tāla* (Table 15). But in the form in Table 14, they lend themselves better to practical needs.

Varieties of starting points (graha or eḍuppu)

The starting point of a song, melodic theme or rhythmic pattern is called *graha* (Sanskrit) or, more commonly, *eḍuppu* (Tamil). Shifting the *eḍuppu* from the starting point of a tāla cycle (*samam*) lends variety and liveliness to the rhythmic structure and is a common feature in Karnatic music. This means that the lyrics underlying a song (*sāhitya*) do not always begin at the point where a given tāla cycle starts.

There are three distinct starting points (*eḍuppu* or *graha*) of a theme with regard to the tāla cycle: on the first beat of the cycle (termed *sama eḍuppu* or *sama graha*); after the first beat of the cycle (termed *anāgata eḍuppu* or *anāgata graha*); and before the first beat of the cycle (termed *atīta eḍuppu* or *atīta graha*). The last variant is the least common in the concert repertoire while many compositions are either set to the first or second variant.

Starting point after the first beat

Example (1) for *anāgata eḍuppu: kṛti* 'Entarāni', rāga Harikāmbhōji, ādi tāla by Tyāgarāja. In this *kṛti*, the starting point of the theme (*araiyiḍam*, i.e. after half a beat) is maintained in all three sections of a *kṛti* (*pallavi*, *anupallavi* and *caraṇam*); in some other compositions the starting point shifts to lend emphasis to the lyrics.

Table 14: Tālas widely used in South Indian music and dance

Tāla	Technical name	Duration	Mode of reckoning
ādi	*caturaśra jāti tripuṭa tāla*	8 kriyā 4 & 2 & 2	A clap followed by three finger-counts; then twice a clap followed by a silent turn of the hand each equalling 1 *kriyā*.
cāpu	*miśra cāpu tāla*	7 kriyā 3 & 2 & 2	A clap with the back of the hand; another such clap followed by a rest; then twice a clap and a rest each equalling 1 *kriyā*.
khaṇḍa cāpu	*khaṇḍa cāpu tāla*	5 kriyā 2 & 3	A clap followed by a rest; then again two claps and a rest each equalling 1 *kriyā*.
rūpakam	*rūpaka tāla*	3 kriyā 1 & 1 & 1	A clap followed by another clap and a silent turn of the hand each equalling 1 *kriyā*.

Table 15: *Sūḷādi sapta tāla*

N.	Tāla	Technical name	Duration of one tāla cycle	Symbols
I	*dhruva*	*caturaśra jāti dhruva tāla*	14 *kriyā* (4 & 2 & 4 & 4)	I_4 O I_4 I_4
II	*maṭya*	*caturaśra jāti maṭya tāla*	10 *kriyā* (4 & 2 & 4)	I_4 O I_4
III	*rūpaka*	*caturaśra jāti rūpaka tāla*	6 *kriyā* (2 & 4)	O I_4
IV	*jhampa*	*miśra jāti jhampa tāla*	10 *kriyā* (7 & 1 & 2)	I_7 U O
V	*tripuṭa*	*tisra jāti tripuṭa tāla*	7 *kriyā* (3 & 2 & 2)	I_3 O O
VI	*aṭa*	*khaṇḍa jāti aṭa tāla*	14 *kriyā* (5 & 5 & 2 & 2)	I_5 I_5 O O
VII	*eka*	*caturaśra jāti eka tāla*	4 *kriyā* (4)	I_4

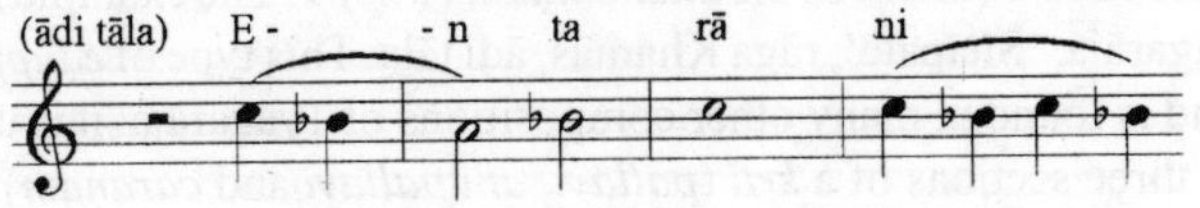

Stave 36: *Anāgata eḍuppu* (*araiyiḍam*).

Example (2) for *anāgata eḍuppu: kṛti* 'Nidhicāla', rāga Kalyāṇi, misra cāpu tāla by Tyāgarāja; starting point on the second beat out of seven beats. This starting point is found in many compositions set to miśra cāpu tāla.

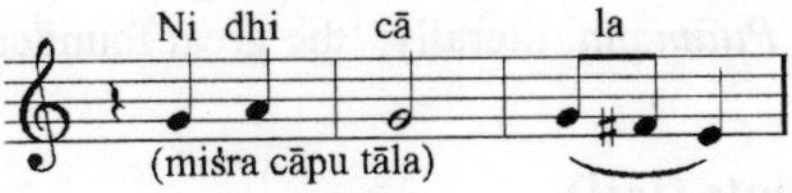

Stave 37: *Anāgata eḍuppu* (*miśra cāpu tāla*).

Starting point before the first beat

A good example for *atīta eḍuppu* is the variation (*saṅgati*) found in the opening section (*pallavi*) of a deeply moving *kṛti* by Tyāgarāja, 'Nēnenduvetukudurā' (rāga Karṇāṭaka Behāg, ādi tāla). At the beginning of this piece, the first theme (*pallavi*) is begun from the first beat (*sama eḍuppu*), and the exclamation *Hari* ('O God!') is inserted at the end of the first line so as to lead to the *samam* of the repetition of the theme ('Nēnendu . . .'). Subsequently, variations (*saṅgati*) are inserted in such a manner that *Hari* is taken from other notes (e.g. *pa dha* or 'G-A' instead of *ri ga* or 'D-E').

Stave 38: *Atīta eduppu*.

Tyāgarāja is credited with introducing a special variant of the *anāgata eḍuppu* type which is set $1^1/2$ beats (six *mātrā*) after the beginning of the tāla cycle. It can

Stave 39: *Anāgata eḍuppu* (six *mātrā* from *samam*).

also be described as a variant of the *mukkāliḍam eḍuppu*. The example is taken from a *kr̥ti* by Tyāgarāja, 'Sītāpatē', rāga Khamās, ādi tāla. This type of *eḍuppu* has a lively quality and is found in many other compositions of Tyāgarāja; it is usually maintained in all three sections of a *kr̥ti* (*pallavi*, *anupallavi* and *caraṇam*).

THE SEVEN ELEMENTARY TĀLAS (SŪḶĀDI SAPTA TĀLA)

The tālas outlined in Table 15 are termed *sūḷādi tāla* but are more commonly referred to as the seven tālas (*sapta tāla*). The *sapta tāla* form the basis of a series of musical exercises (*alaṁkāram*) which are ascribed to Purandara Dāsa (1484–1564). These exercises provide every music student with a thorough training in melodic and rhythmic structure. Purandara Dāsa, a mendicant mystic from the region of modern Karṇāṭaka, also composed countless devotional songs (*devarnāma*). He is still revered as *Karṇāṭaka Sangīta Pitāmaha*, literally, 'the great founder-father of the Karnatic music system'.

Variable tāla elements (jāti)

Among the sections (*aṅgam*) of a tāla, *laghu* alone is variable. It occurs in several tālas. A particular *laghu* variant is called *jāti* (e.g. *tisra* or *caturaśra jāti*). Table 16 will illustrate the variety of tāla patterns provided by the *laghu*.

A great number of tāla variants can be obtained by subdividing each count of a tāla (e.g. the common *caturaśra gati*). The old system of 175 tālas is based on a tabular arrangement of the seven *sūḷādi tālas* shown in Table 15. In this system, the five types of *jāti* as well as the five types of *gati* are systematically combined with one another on the basis of the seven *sūḷādi tālas* (7 *sūḷādi tālas* × 5 *jāti* × 5 *gati* = 175 tālas). This type of elaboration is, however, more of academic than of practical interest in contemporary Karnatic music, because the majority of the tāla variants obtained in this manner are only heard in special performances or within an elaborate *rāgam tānam pallavi*. Musicians of this century have focused more on permutations of rhythmic patterns (*tāla prastāra*) that are distributed over several tāla cycles (*tāla āvarta*). Such calculated arrangements play a major role in the planning of the concluding part (*kōrvai* and *muttāippu* or *muktāyi*) of a percussion solo (*tani̱yāvartta̱nam*).

Note: the terms *jāti* (long 'a') and *jati* (short 'a') pertain to two entirely different concepts. A *jati* is a rhythmic syllable used in a concert (*ko̱nnakkōl*) or a dance performance (*naṭṭuvāṅgam*).

Subdivisions (gati)

Each count (*kriyā*) of a tāla can be subdivided into several sub-units (*mātrā*, Tamil *mattirai*). A *mātrā* may consist of a musical note (*svara*), any drum-beat or rhythmic syllable (*jati*) as well as their extension (*kārvai*), or a pause (also called *kārvai*).

The grouping of sub-units is referred to as *gati* (Tamil *naḍai*): there may be three, four, five, seven or nine sub-units per beat or *kriyā* of which the division into four (*caturaśra gati* or *caturaśra naḍai*) is the most common (Table 17). Occasionally, a song is based on three sub-units per beat (*tisra gati* or *tisra naḍai*). The other subdivisions are mainly heard during a percussion solo (*tani̱yāvartta̱nam*) and in a formal improvisation of the *rāgam tānam pallavi* type.

Table 16: Variable tāla elements (*jāti*)

Jāti variant	Symbols	Number of beats (kriyā) for every laghu	Examples of common tālas
tisra jāti	I_3	3 (a clap followed by two finger-counts)	*tripuṭa tāla*
caturaśra jāti	I_4	4 (a clap followed by three finger-counts)	*dhruva*, *maṭya*, *rūpaka*, *eka* & *ādi tāla*
khaṇḍa jāti	I_5	5 (a clap followed by four finger-counts)	*aṭa tāla*
miśra jāti	I_7	7 (a clap followed by six finger-counts)	*jhampa tāla*
saṅkīrṇa jāti	I_9	9 (a clap followed by eight finger-counts)	(rarely used)

Table 17: Tāla subdivisions (*gati*)

Gati variety (subdivision)	Number of sub-units (mātrā) per beat (kriyā)
tisra gati	3
caturaśra gati	4
khaṇḍa gati	5
miśra gati	7
saṅkīrṇa gati	9

The following two examples of rhythmic permutation (*prastāra*) illustrate how the basic *gati* patterns (e.g. of four and three sub-units or *mātrā*) are temporarily re-arranged and varied in order to obtain a colourful percussive mosaic, as it were.

On account of its symmetry, ādi tāla (also called *caturaśra jāti tripuṭa tāla*) is the most flexible rhythmic cycle (8 beats of 4 *mātrā* = 32 *mātrā*). For this reason, ādi tāla is also the most preferred tāla for a *tan̲iyāvarttan̲am*, and its 32 *mātrā* (here shown as 'beads') can be re-grouped to yield new and interesting patterns. The resulting permutations (*prastāra*) can be visualized as temporary bifurcations of rhythmic patterns whereby the underlying structure of a given tāla is discretely yet carefully maintained in the background. In other words, the total amount of available counting units (*kriyā* or *akṣarakāla*) and sub-units (*mātrā*) per tāla cycle (*āvarta*) does not change here.

The same principle applies to any other tāla taken up for rhythmic elaboration. Thus a playful re-grouping of a tāla's units or sub-units, represented and practised with the help of rhythmic syllables (*jati*), temporarily produces in the listener the illusion of an altogether different rhythmic structure. While this creates additional interest by way of contrast, surprise or suspense, followed by the pleasant relief which is caused by the resolution of rhythmic tension, the performers involved must be on their guard not to slip into another tāla pattern. In order to succeed, they have to plan their return to the original rhythmic framework by way of precise calculation. While such a display of a performer's skill and imagination is desirable in the context of a rhythmic interlude (*tan̲iyāvarttan̲am*), or a group performance entirely devoted to rhythm (*laya vinyāsa*), it is rarely considered appropriate while accompanying a composition (e.g. *kṛti*).

The even flow of recurring rhythmic patterns based on a particular tāla is referred to as *sarvalaghu*. In order to keep track of the total number of syllables that need to be counted within a given tāla cycle (*āvarta*), two groups or 'strings' of four syllables can be grouped together: 'ta ka dhi mi, ta ka ju nu'. While counting the basic ādi tāla with hands and fingers (eight units or *kriyā* gestures), the available sum of sub-units (32 *mātrā* in Fig. 32, and 24 *mātrā* in Fig. 33) can be re-arranged in a variety of ways for the purpose of obtaining intricate patterns. For example, the eight groups of four

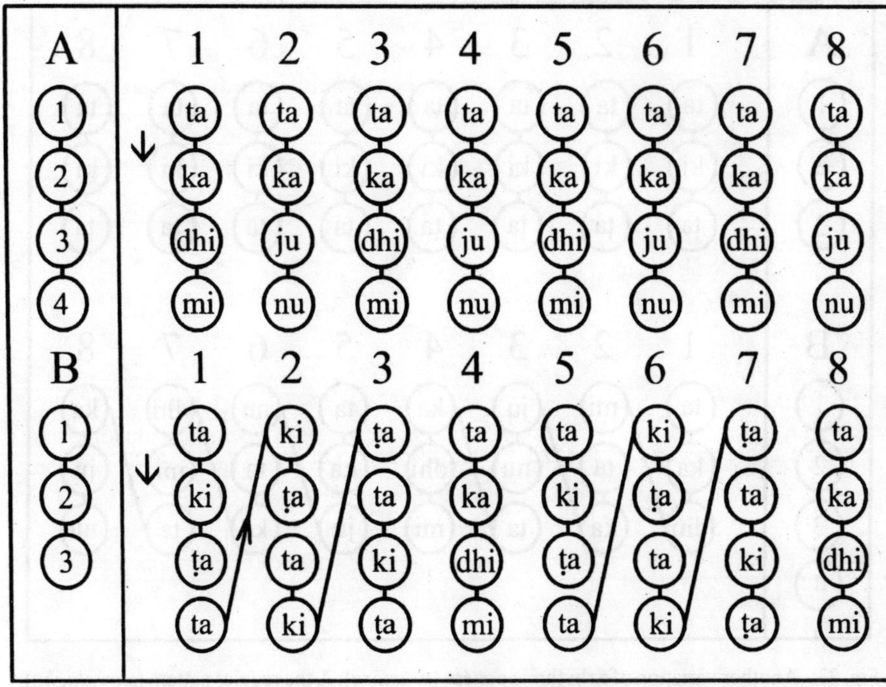

Fig. 32: Variation of a rhythmic pattern (*prastāra*): **A** the regular pattern (*sarvalaghu*) underlying ādi tāla with 32 'beads' (*caturaśra gati*); it consists of 8 'strings', each having 4 'beads'; **B** a temporary variation which consists of 10 'strings': 8 with 3 'beads' each, and 2 with 4 'beads' each.

mātrā per beat (Fig. 32 A), or three *mātrā* (Fig. 33 A), can be re-arranged in contrasting patterns. To facilitate practice, the two simple variants shown here are visualized as 'strings' on which 'beads' are strung together by the connecting lines (Fig. 32 B and 33 B).

Here one should note, however, that the variation process known as *prastāra*, which can be described as a playful variation of the number of sub-units within a given tāla, is not to be confused with the fixed tāla variants that are also based on a combination of any of the five basic *gati* patterns. For instance, composers and performers sometimes use a variant of ādi tāla which is based on triplets. This variant of ādi tāla is termed *caturaśra jāti tripuṭa tāla, tisra gati*, or simply *ādi tāla, tisra naḍai* (Fig. 33). In either context the subdivision of each beat in the form of triplets has a gentle lilt which makes it suitable for light classical forms of music (e.g. lullaby); and not surprisingly, it is also found in a popular Western dance form, the *Waltz*.

Countless other permutations of rhythmic patterns can be generated on similar lines. The following subdivisions are more widely used in a full-length percussion solo (*taṉiyāvarttaṉam* or *laya vinyāsa*) based on ādi tāla, and slowly developed in a

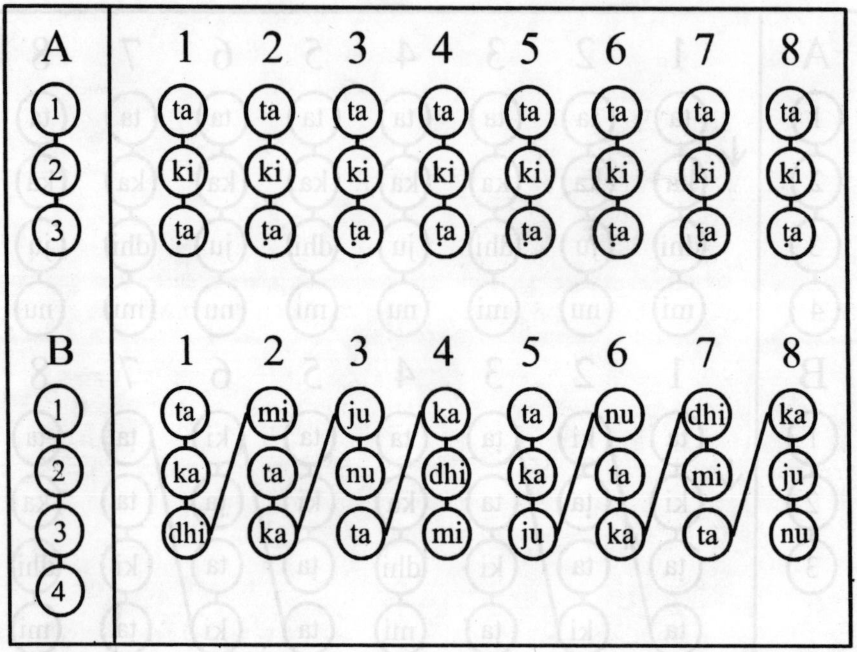

Fig. 33: Another variation of a rhythmic pattern (*prastāra*): **A** the regular pattern (*sarvalaghu*) of a common variant of ādi tāla with 24 'beads' (*tisra gati*); it consists of 8 'strings', each having 3 'beads'; **B** a temporary variation which consists of 6 'strings' with 4 'beads' each.

graded manner: five *mātrā* (known as *khaṇḍa gati* or *khaṇḍa naḍai*, 8 × 5 = 40 *mātrā*), seven *mātrā* (known as *miśra gati* or *miśra naḍai*, 8 × 7 = 56 *mātrā*), and nine *mātrā* (*saṅkīrṇa gati* or *saṅkīrṇa naḍai*, 8 × 9 = 72 *mātrā*).

SOLMIZATION OF TĀLAS (JATI)

The rhythmic patterns given in Table 19 correspond to a set of traditional melodic exercises (*alaṁkāra*) based on *svara* (musical notes) and *rāga* (pleasing combinations of notes, embellishments, and phrases).

Approximately one second (60 beats per minute) is taken as the basic time unit (*kriyā*) in the slow tempo (*vilambita kāla* or *cauka kāla*). One tāla cycle is called *āvarta*.

All exercises are performed in three speeds (*trikāla*):

(1) *Prathama kāla* ('first degree of speed'). (2) *Dvitīya kāla* ('second degree of speed'); here twice as many syllables fit into one *āvarta* compared to *prathama kāla*. (3) *Tṛtīya kāla* ('third degree of speed'); here four times as many syllables fit into one *āvarta* compared to *prathama kāla*.

While the speed of *jati* declamation (solmization) is doubled or quadrupled for the 2nd and 3rd degree of speed respectively, the hands maintain an even tempo (*kālapramāṇam*) throughout. A gradual increase or decrease of tempo is generally not admissible in South Indian music.

Table 18: Ādi tāla in three speeds (*trikāla*)

	1	2	3	4	5	6	7	8
	laghu				1st drutam		2nd drutam	
	clap	1st finger	2nd finger	3rd finger	clap	wave hand	clap	wave hand
I.	ta (-) (-) (-)	ka (-) (-) (-)	dhi (-) (-) (-)	mi (-) (-) (-)	ta (-) (-) (-)	ka (-) (-) (-)	ju (-) (-) (-)	nu (-) (-) (-)
II.	ta (-) ka (-)	dhi (-) mi (-)	ta (-) ka (-)	ju (-) nu (-)	ta (-) ka (-)	dhi (-) mi (-)	ta (-) ka (-)	ju (-) nu (-)
III.	ta ka dhi mi	ta ka ju nu	ta ka dhi mi	ta ka ju nu	ta ka dhi mi	ta ka ju nu	ta ka dhi mi	ta ka ju nu

Table 19: Rhythmic patterns for 12 sets of exercises

(1) **Dhruva tāla**: 14 units (*kriyā*) per cycle (*āvarta*)

I_4 (*caturaśra jāti* laghu)	O (drutam)	I_4 (*caturaśra jāti* laghu)	I_4 (*caturaśra jāti* laghu)
ta ka dhi mi ♩♩♩♩	**ṭa ka** ♩♩	**ta ka dhi mi** ♩♩♩♩	**ta ka ju nu** ♩♩♩♩
4 kriyā: clap and 3 finger-counts	2 kriyā: clap and wave of hand	4 kriyā: clap and 3 finger-counts	4 kriyā: clap and 3 finger-counts

(2) **Maṭya tāla**: 10 units per cycle

I_4 (*caturaśra jāti* laghu)	O (drutam)	I_4 (*caturaśra jāti* laghu)
ta ka dhi mi ♩♩♩♩	**ta ka** ♩♩	**ta ka ju nu** ♩♩♩♩
4 kriyā: clap and 3 finger-counts	2 kriyā: clap and wave of hand	4 kriyā: clap and 3 finger-counts

(*Contd.*)

(3) **Rūpaka tāla**: 6 units per cycle

O (drutam)	I_4 (*caturaśra jāti* laghu)
ta ka ♩♩ 2 kriyā: clap and wave of hand	**ta ka dhi na** ♩♩♩♩ 4 kriyā: clap and 3 finger-counts

(4) **Rūpaka tāla**: common short form

ta ♩ clap	**ki** ♩ clap	**ṭa** ♩ wave of hand

(5) **Jhampa tāla**: 10 units per cycle

I_7 (*miśra jāti* laghu)	U (anudrutam)	O (drutam)
ta ka dhi mi ta ki ṭa ♩♩♩♩♩♩♩ 7 kriyā: clap and 6 finger-counts	**ta** ♩ 1 kriyā: 1 clap	**ki ṭa** ♩♩ 2 kriyā: clap and wave of hand

(*Contd.*)

(6) **Triputa tāla**: 7 units per cycle

ta ki ṭa ♩♩♩ 3 kriyā: clap and 2 finger-counts	**ta ka** ♩♩ 2 kriyā: clap and wave of hand	**dhi mi** ♩♩ 2 kriyā: clap and wave of hand

(7) **Aṭa tāla**: 14 units per cycle

I5 (*khaṇḍa jāti* laghu) **ta ka ta ki ṭa** ♩♩♩♩♩ 5 kriyā: clap and 4 finger-counts	I5 (*khaṇḍa jāti* laghu) **ta ka ta ki ṭa** ♩♩♩♩ 5 kriyā: clap and 4 finger-counts	O (drutam) **ta ka** ♩♩ 2 kriyā: clap and wave of hand	O (drutam) **dhi mi** ♩♩ 5 kriyā: clap and wave of hand

(8) **Eka tāla**: 4 units per cycle

I4 (*caturaśra jāti* laghu) **ta ka dhi mi** ♩♩♩♩ 4 kriyā: clap and 3 finger-counts

(Contd.)

(9) **Ādi tāla**: (short name for 'caturaśra jāti triputa tāla'); 8 kriyā per cycle

I4 (*caturaśra jāti* laghu)	O (drutam)	O (drutam)
ta ka dhi mi	**ta ka**	**ju nu**
♩♩♩♩	♩♩	♩♩
4 kriyā: clap and 3 fingers-counts	2 kriyā: clap and wave of hand	2 kriyā: clap and wave of hand

(10) **Dēśādi tāla**: shortened variant of *ādi tāla*; 4 kriyā

ta	**ka**	**dhi**	**mi**
♩	♩	♩	♩
1 kriyā: clap with back of the hand	1 kriyā: clap (palms)	1 kriyā: clap (palms)	1 kriyā: clap (palms)

(11) **Miśra cāpu tāla**: 7 kriyā

ta ki ṭa	**ta ka**	**dhi mi**
♪♪♪	♪♪	♪♪
3 kriyā: two claps with back of the hand and a rest	2 kriyā: clap and a rest	2 kriyā: clap and a rest

(12) **Khaṇḍa Cāpu tāla**: 5 kriyā

ta ka	**ta ki ṭa**
♪♪	♪♪♪
2 kriyā: clap and rest	3 kriyā: two claps and a rest

The exercise for ādi tāla is given in Table 18 and practised in three speeds (*trikāla*).

I. = slow; II. = middle; and III. = fast.

Rhythmic embellishment (tīrmāṇam, aṟudi)

In concert music, the term *tīrmāṇam* refers to a short percussive phrase, and it constitutes an attractive rhythmic pattern (also known as *aṟudi*) which marks the conclusion of the sections of a composition (i.e. *pallavi*, *anupallavi*, and *caraṇam*), or of a percussion solo (*taṉiyāvarttaṉam*). In this manner, a percussionist either provides a link between these sections, or marks the final conclusion of a piece. In dance music, the term *tīrmāṇam* refers to an elaborate rhythmic pattern which is known as *kōrvai* in concert music.

A *tīrmāṇam* consists of a series of short and long syllables (*jati*), beats, or musical notes (*svara*). This pattern is always executed three times consecutively. A pattern marked by greater complexity of rhythmic elaboration is called *mōra*.

The following *tīrmāṇam* patterns comprise groups of 3, 4, 5, 6, 7, 8, 9 or 10 sub-units (*mātrā*) merging with a pause 'jam', or a heavy final syllable ('tām') (Table 20). Their appeal derives from an arrangement which leads us back to the first beat (*samam*) of a new tāla cycle (*āvarta*).

The combination of syllables set in square brackets (e.g. [ta ka ta ki ṭa]) provides a convenient filler leading to the point of departure (*eḍuppu*) for any particular *tīrmāṇam*. For the purpose of effective practice, precede every *tīrmāṇam* pattern by one round (*āvarta*) of plain 'ta ka dhi mi, ta ka ju nu'. Such a free flow of notes or rhythmic syllables is called *sarva laghu.* (4 times 'ta ka dhi mi, ta ka ju nu' = 32 *mātrā.*)

Dance syllables for ādi tāla

In Table 21—a typical series of dance syllables—the upper row represents the rhythmic syllables serving as accompaniment and embellishment (*jati*). Such syllabic accompaniment is further reinforced by corresponding sounds produced on the *mṛdaṅgam*. The lower row contains special syllables to be recited by the dancer or dance teacher (*naṭṭuvaṉar*) in the classroom. Such syllables correspond to specific dance movements (*aḍavu*) which are best memorized in this fashion. But during a performance, only the syllables seen in the upper row are meant to be pronounced, while the other syllables are not.

One series of *jati* syllables extends over one tāla cycle (*āvarta*). The first series is repeated in order to match dance movements in two directions (right and left).

Note: The following example (Table 21) is in a slow tempo (*iraṇḍu kalai*), each unit having two counts (*kriyā*) and 8 sub-units (*mātrā*). In *iraṇḍu kalai*, every beat, finger-count, and wave of ādi tāla is repeated. A *mātrā* consists either of a syllable or a pause. Underlining (e.g. kitataka) marks syllables that are rendered twice as fast as syllables that are not underlined.

Table 20: Rhythmic patterns for 8 *tīrmāṇams*

(1) **15 mātrā**	[ta ka dhi mi]	[ta ka ju nu]	[ta ka dhi mi]	[Ta ka Ta ki]	
3 × 3 + 2 × 3	[ṭa] **Din** din na	jam (-) (-) **Din**	din na jam (-)	(-) **Din** din na	**jam**
(2) **16 mātrā**	[ta ka dhi mi]	[ta ka ju nu]	[ta ka dhi mi]	[ta ka ju nu]	
3 × 4 + 2 × 2	**Ta** ka dhi na	jam (-) **Ta** ka	dhi na jam (-)	**Ta** ka dhi na	**jam**
(3) **15 mātrā** and Tām	[ta ka dhi mi]	[ta ka ju nu]	[ta ka dhi mi]	[Ta ka Ta ki]	
3 × 5	[ṭa] **Ta** dhi ki	na tom **Ta** dhi	ki na tom **Ta**	dhi ki na tom	**Tām**
(4) **18 mātrā** and Tām	[ta ka dhi mi]	[ta ka ju nu]	[ta ka dhi mi]	[Ta ka] **Ta** dhī	
3 × 6	- ki na tom	**Ta** dhī - ki	na tom **Ta** dhī	- ki na tom	**Tām**

(*Contd.*)

(5) **21 mātrā** and Tām	[ta ka dhi mi]	[ta ka ju nu]	[Ta ki ṭa] **Tā**	- dhī - ki	
3 × 7	na tom **Tā** -	dhī - ki na	tom **Tā** - dhī	- ki na tom	**Tām**
(6) **24 mātrā** and Tām	[ta ka dhi mi]	[ta ka ju nu]	**Ta** dhī - kī	- nā - tom	
3 × 8	**Ta** dhī - kī	- nā - tom	**Ta** dhī - kī	- nā - tom	**Tām**
(7) **27 mātrā** and Tām	[Ta ka Ta ki]	[ṭa] **Tā** - dhī	- kī - nā	- tom **Tā** -	
3 × 9	dhī - kī -	nā - tom **Tā**	- dhī - kī	- nā - tom	**Tām**
(8) **30 mātrā** and Tām	[Ta ka] **Ta** ki	ṭa jām - ta	dhi ki na tom	**Ta** ki ṭa jām	
3 × 10	- ta dhi ki	na tom **Ta** ki	ṭa jām - ta	dhi ki na tom	**Tām**

Note: a hyphen '-' extends the duration of the preceding syllable:

jam (-) pause of 2 *mātrā*

jam (-) (-) pause of 3 *mātrā*

Table 21: A typical series of dance syllables for *ādi tāla*

1st āvarta (to be repeated before proceeding to the 2nd āvarta)

No.				
1	tā - / tā -	ku da / tai -	na ku / tā -	ta ka / hā -
2	da na / dī -	ku gi / tai -	na ku / tā -	ta ka / hā -
3	gi na / tā -	ku ja / tai -	na ku / tā -	ta ka / hā -
4	ja na / dī -	ku di / tai -	di ku / tā -	ta ka / hā -
5	tā - / tā -	ta jām / tai -	- ta / tā -	jām - / hā -
6	tā - / tai -	- ta / tā -	rūm - / tai -	ta ka / tām -
7	tā - / - -	- ga / dī -	dīm - / tai -	ta ka / tām -
8	tai - / - -	- ta / tā -	ki ta / dī -	ta ka / tā -

(Contd.)

2nd āvarta

1				2			
tā -	ku dha	na ku	dha na	ku gi	na ku	gi na	ku ja
tai -	- tai	- -	tai -	- tai	- -	tai -	- tai

3				4			
na ku	ja na	ku di	di ku	tā -	- ta	jām -	ki ta ta ka
- -	tai -	- tai	- -	tai -	- di	tā -	tai -

5				6			
ta ri ki ta	tōm -	- -	tā -	- ta	jām -	ki ta ta ka	ta ri ki ta
di di	tai -	- -	tai -	- di	tā -	tai -	di di

7				8			
tōm -	- -	tā -	- ta	jām -	ki ta ta ka	ta ri ki ta	tōm -
tai -	- -	tai -	- di	tā -	tai -	di di	tai -

15

Concert Music

Composers of music (dhātu) and lyrics (mātu)

The person who has written both the lyrics (*sāhitya* or *mātu*) and the music of a song (Sanskrit *dhātu,* Tamil *varṇameṭṭu*) is called a *vaggēyakāra* (e.g. Tyāgarāja, Mysore Vāsudēvācāria, and Pāpanāsam Śivan̲). This does not mean, however, that composers need to re-invent every rāga employed by them. On the contrary, it is accepted practice that the musical elements of one well-made song are being re-used in another, either by the same composer, or by somebody else. For example, the musical structure (*varṇameṭṭu*) found in a song of Tyāgarāja is at times also found in a song of his junior contemporary, Muttusvāmi Dīkṣitar. This phenomenon is explainable by the fact that both composers are known to have been exposed to the musical style of their predecessor, Kṣētrajña.

A person who is recognized as being a genuine *vaggēyakāra* would have undergone training in several allied disciplines, such as music theory (*saṅgīta śāstra*), performance, poetry (*kāvya*), and often dance (*nṛtta, nṛtya*) or drama (Sanskrit *nāṭya*; Tamil *kūttu*). Given the difficulty of mastering more than one among these ancient and highly developed art forms, it is understandable that a musician who has such variegated interests and experiences is regarded as belonging to the highest class of composers.

Apart from those few composers who are thus known to be composer-poets, numerous musicians have arranged the tunes for the lyrics (*sāhitya, mātu*) written by others. The collaboration of a music expert and a poet is often concealed by the fact that only the lyricist, not the composer of the music, is acknowledged in programme notes. There are four categories of compositions where the involvement of two persons is likely: firstly, the original music for most compositions dating from a period before AD 1800 is generally thought to be lost because no system of detailed musical notation was used until then; secondly, all dance items that are based on lyrics taken from well-known works of literature are certain to have been set to music in recent times (e.g. *Gitagovinda*); thirdly, the songs of composers (*vaggēyakāra*) who are likely to have sought expert guidance for perfecting their compositions (e.g. Rāmaliṅgasvāmi, Svāti Tirunāḷ); and finally, there are many songs based on lyrics by modern authors who sought the assistance of experienced musicians and composers (e.g. Ambujam Krishna and Periasāmi Thooran̲).

The music (*dhātu*) composed by the following musicians is heard in many public concerts and dance recitals: Ālattūr Veṅkateśa Ayyar, Calcutta K.S. Krishnamūrthi, K.G. Ginde, T.K. Govinda Rao, Irayimman̲ Tampi, Kāñcīpuram Naina Piḷḷai, Kumbakōnam Viswanāthan̲, Madurai N. Krishnan̲, Mysore Vāsudēvacāria, Nēdunūri Krishnamūrthi, Nīdamaṅgaḷam Krishnamūrthy Bhāgavatar, Palghat K.V. Nārāyaṇaswāmy, Paramesvara Bhāgavatar, D. Paśupathi, S. Rājam, S. Rājāram, Rallapalli Ānanthakrishna Sarma, S.N. Ratanjankar, T.V. Śankaranārāyaṇan̲, B. Seetarāma Sarma, N. Śivarāmakrishnan̲, Dr Śrīpada Pinakapāni, the Tañjāvūr Quartette, Tiger Varadachāriar, T.M. Thiagarājan̲, Tirupāmburam N. Swāminātha Piḷḷai, Vanaja Nārāyaṇan̲, S.V. Veṅkaṭarāman̲.

A lyricist for whom one or several musicians have provided music (*dhātu*) could be referred to as a *mātu composer*.

Similarly, the description 'mātu composer' could be applied to numerous composers (*vaggēyakāra*) whose music is lost but whose lyrics have been re-composed by later musicians (e.g. Kanaka Dāsa). To this category belong most composers prior to the Trinity (late 18th century) except Paccimiriyam Āḍiappayya, and Rāmasvāmi Dīkṣitar. The original music of Subrahmaṇya Bhārati is also lost to posterity and has been replaced by musicians of our time (e.g. S.V. Veṅkaṭarāman̲) according to their individual abilities.

The following 'mātu composers' or lyricists are credited with songs that are found in today's music and dance repertoire: Acuta Dāsa, Ambujam Krishna, Harikēsanallūr Mutthiah Bhāgavatar, Karūr Dakṣiṇāmūrti, Periasāmi Thooran̲; see also Parameśvara Bhāgavatar and Svāti Tirunāḷ.

Phases of a Karnatic concert

In the absence of any fixed rules applicable to the planning of a concert, the main performer has to be prepared to make decisions regarding the course of musical events on the stage itself. A good concert is remembered for its serene listening pleasure (*saukhyam*), as well as a combination of spiritual and intellectual stimulation. Different musical items and techniques address such high expectations. At the same time, conveying a harmonious whole, along with consistent personal involvement (*sādhanā*), respect for one's tradition (*sampradāya*), and an expressive quality (*bhāva*), are achievements that are still being highly sought after.

A combination of experience and unwritten conventions develop instantaneous rapport among the performers. Obviously, spontaneous inspiration, personal feelings, preferences or idiosyncrasies, besides anxieties and organizational considerations, come into play during every performance. *Live* concerts performed without any prior rehearsals are by no means exceptional. For that matter, the musicians concerned often meet one another for the first time on the stage minutes before the start of a concert. While such a concert is likely to sacrifice some intricacies, an audience often feels compensated by ingeniously unfolding musical dialogues that can be compared to a *fugue* in the European tradition, or by a sense of excitement and novelty that also characterize a successful Jazz performance.

In a typical Karnatic concert, three phases can be distinguished: the opening phase with concise compositions that are rendered in medium and fast tempo; the middle phase characterized by its scope for slow rāga delineation and unity of mood; and the concluding phase characterized by an alternation of different moods and compositional styles.

The opening item is often a *tāṉavarṇam* or a lively piece addressing Gaṇeśa (e.g. 'Śrī Mahāganapati' by Muttusvāmi Dīkṣitar, rāga Gauḷa, miśra cāpu tāla); compositions set in rāga Haṁsadhvani, Nāṭa and *janya rāgas* derived from scale Māyāmāḷavagauḷa (*mēḷa* 15) are preferred by most musicians for the first composition (*kṛti*) that is performed after the *varṇam*. There are few if any improvised parts (brief *ālāpana* and *svara kalpana*) in this phase. Other lively rāgas and compositions are intended to establish a close rapport among musicians and audience (e.g. rāgas Bilahari, Kēdāram, and Bēgaḍa). Tyāgarāja has composed a great number of small devotional pieces which lend themselves eminently to being performed in this phase, and again immediately after the main item of a concert. Many of these lively pieces are endowed with an innovative feature introduced by Tyāgarāja, the variations known as *saṅgati* which have been imitated by later composers. A *saṅgati* provides a series of interlaced variations of a theme which stretch or emphasize certain words of the lyrics (*sāhitya*) and combine melodic variety with surprising rhythmic turns, increasing in density, intricacy and length, often within the space of a single tāla cycle (*āvarta*). Ornamental passages (*ciṭṭasvaram*) also form an attractive part of some compositions rendered in this phase.

The second phase introduces some of the major rāgas of Karnatic music, mostly belonging to a category known as *rakti rāga*, definable as a melodic entity with much potential for spontaneous creation and conducive to emotional, aesthetic, and even spiritual fulfilment. Here musicians present the most treasured compositions in their repertoire, often complemented by improvisations in the *ālāpana, niraval* and *svara kalpana* formats and of varying duration. In theory, any among the hundreds of rāgas available to Karnatic musicians can be chosen for the central part of a concert. Yet most musicians and listeners have a marked preference for one particular rāga which figures among some twenty rāgas which have been well established in the last two centuries. The main item, and the context in which it is set, aims at providing a sense of profound aesthetic satisfaction (*rasa*) and an ability to convey various emotional facets both of the rāga (*rāga bhāva*) and the lyrics (*sāhitya bhāva*) of a piece. Although the scope for creative elaboration appears to be unlimited in this phase, most critics and other discerning listeners are more impressed by musicians who pay attention to stylistic detail, maintain a chosen tempo, have a regard for the structural integrity of a piece, and integrate their improvisations with a sense of proportion. Unbridled displays of virtuosity, on the other hand, would generally be regarded as tasteless if not reckless trespasses that belong to the realm of 'light music'.

The main item, a composition and the improvised forms in which it is embedded, mostly lasts between half an hour and well over an hour depending on the occasion on which a performance takes place. Due to the preferences of organizers and audiences, an elaborate or scholarly *rāgam tānam pallavi* improvisation is heard less often than a major composition of the *kṛti* type around which improvisations are developed in a well-established format (*paddhati*). An accentuated, faster variant of rāga elaboration, known as *tāṉam*, and the 'garland' or string of several rāgas known as *rāgamālikā*, can be accommodated most satisfactorily in the central part of a concert. After the *niraval*, an extension of a musical theme as well as its lyrics, and the playful and spontaneous patterns of *svara kalpana* notes, there is almost unrestricted scope for a *taṉiyāvarttaṉam*, the rhythmic solo, which lends grandeur to the main item.

The Ālattūr Brothers popularized and refined a type of calculated rhythmic patterns (*kōrvai*) at the conclusion of the *svara kalpana* type of improvisation. Kāñcīpuram Naina Piḷḷai, an expert on all aspects of rhythm (*laya*), who is also credited with re-composing and teaching many *Tiruppugaḻ* songs, is believed to have been the first concert musician to integrate these calculated rhythmic patterns, previously confined to percussive accompaniment and the *taṉiyāvarttaṉam*, in a melodic context.

However, some musicians, including percussionist Palghat Maṇi Ayyar (*mṛdaṅgam*) and Semmaṅguḍi Śrīnivāsa Iyer (vocalist), were critical of this aspect of Karnatic music. They felt that, more often than not, indiscriminate calculation interferes with the serene listening pleasure (*saukhyam*) derived from melody based on rāga. These great performers have cautioned younger musicians against excessive indulgence in *kōrvai* patterns within a song (*kṛti*). In their opinion, rhythmic calculations belong to the domain of the percussionist. Any unwarranted introduction of such patterns by singers or other instrumentalists is bound to obliterate the emotional quality (*bhāva*) conveyed by the songs of the greatest composers such as Muttusvāmi Dīkṣitar, Tyāgarāja, and Śyāmā Śāstri. To appreciate this call for moderation, junior musicians, often easily carried away by a fascination with virtuosity and intellectual thrill, should remember that most songs of these and other composers are already rich in rhythmic subtleties and variations (*saṅgati*) which need infinite care in order to come alive.

The concluding phase focuses on a number of smaller or 'lighter' compositions some of which are known as *tukkaḍā* items. The Tamil word *tukkaḍā* is tinged by a derogatory connotation as it can also refer to something 'ordinary' if not 'inferior'. But in recent music history, musicians have striven to upgrade the quality of music rendered in the latter part of their performance. G.N. Bālasubrahmaṇyam is credited with setting new standards in this regard.

Itẹms in the concluding phase are often inspired modelled on folk tunes (*kāvaḍiccindu*), popular devotional songs from other parts of India (*bhajan*, *dēvarnāma*), love songs (Telugu *jāvaḷi,* Tamil *padam*), and dance pieces (*tillānā*). The Tamil compositions of Aruṇagirinātar (*Tiruppugaḻ*) may also find a place here on account of their attractive metres and scope for much variety and virtuosity. Some minor rāgas of great emotional appeal, notably those characterized by their limited upper range (*niṣādāntya*, *dhaivatāntya* or *pañcamāntya* rāgas), can unfold their charm in this phase of a performance. Tamil poetry (*viruttam*) and Sanskrit verse (*śloka*) are an additional attraction in an elaborate vocal concert provided the audience is receptive to poetry and subtlety of meaning. A tune akin to a lullaby (rāga Nīlāmbari) can be included towards the end of a concert. A *maṅgaḷam*, typically a quotation from a famous *kṛti by* Tyāgarāja, is regarded as an auspicious or uplifting conclusion of music performance. A brief outline of rāga Madhyamāvati is sometimes heard as a soothing relief for the minds of those listeners who have been subjected to a great diversity of emotional experiences. This pentatonic scale ('C-D-F-G-B flat') is associated with devotion (*bhakti*), stillness, and solemnity, the serene state of mind which is humble yet strong and focused, purified and therefore qualified to experience Divine Grace.

A famous composition by Tyāgarāja, 'Rāmakathāsudharasa', is set to rāga Madhyamāvati. In music and words, this *kṛti* conveys the saint's conviction that the contemplation of Rāma's virtues, described in the stories of the *Rāmāyaṇa*, will help its listener to master all challenges encountered in life and to experience the bliss which is not attainable by any other means. For Tyāgarāja, as for so many others before and after him, music and devotion were synonymous and inseparable means for the attainment of salvation (*mokṣa*). For this reason, the choice of rāga Madhyamāvati for the expression of his most cherished belief is probably not a matter of chance but a conscious decision. Similarly, the time-honoured practice of bidding one's audience farewell with the same rāga is based on experience shared by generations of musicians and listeners.

Concert format

The present concert format is said to have been introduced by musicians like Ariyakkuḍi Rāmānuja Iyeṅgār (1890–1967). Although there are no binding guidelines for concert programmes, a typical concert of our times consists of up to twelve items in the course of a two-hour concert.

Unwritten recommendations for a balanced concert format (*kaccēri dharma*) are based on the avoidance of too many rare rāgas and a careful balance of different tālas. Closely allied rāgas are not performed in succession in order to avoid the blurring of the contours of individual rāgas (*rāga rūpa*). When a rāga is introduced by way of *rāga ālāpana*, its identity is expected to be established soon rather than concealed to fellow musicians and listeners. Audience response is particularly lively in those moments when a skilled musician is able to hint at the characteristic feeling of a composition already in the *ālāpana* stage.

The South Indian concert repertoire

Thanks to the widespread use of recording technology, musicians of our times have enjoyed access to a greater number of compositions than any previous generation. For over half a century, annual music and dance conferences, seminars and workshops have been organized by the Music Academy Madras and other organizations in and outside India. The increased availability of music books, the setting up of music schools and colleges and departments of musicology in all major South Indian universities have further contributed to the dissemination of musical knowledge and exchange of ideas among musicians.

Karnatic music is literally 'learnt by heart' because first it needs to be listened to attentively, memorized faithfully, and ultimately rendered with feeling. Only then does the question of personal interpretation and elaboration (*manodharma*) by a musician even arise. The ideal listener or 'person of taste' (*rasika, sahṛdaya*), is therefore someone whose heart (*hṛt*) can attune to music before applying the critical faculty of the mind.

Compositions (kalpita saṅgīta)

South Indian music employs several forms of composition. Classifications such as devotional, folk, art or dance music are generally not very helpful. Almost each type of music has borrowed from and contributed to other branches.

Indian musicologists are generally convinced that very little music has survived the turbulent times prior to the 'golden age'. This 'classical' period of South Indian music comprising the late eighteenth and nineteenth centuries was heralded by the musical 'Trinity'. From an immensely large repertoire of songs, the original music of several thousand has found its way into the hands of the present generation of musicians. Most of the available music composed by these three poet-composers is believed to be authentic. Their compositions are mainly of the tripartite format (*kṛti*) and have served as models for many later poet-composers. Paccimiriyam Āḍiappayya, the teacher of Śyāmā Śāstri, is credited with pioneering the *kṛti* form. To the present day, a series of *kṛtis* provides the foundation of any regular concert programme.

The 'Trinity'

The 'Trinity' is an honorific which posterity has bestowed on three composers who had the greatest impact on Karnatic music, namely Tyāgarāja, Śyāmā Śāstri, and Muttusvāmi Dīkṣitar. All three composers were born in Tiruvārūr, formerly an important town in the fertile and prosperous delta of the river Kāveri. In spite of their common background and saintly disposition, each had a distinct style of his own within the framework of classical music which had evolved in the area of Tañjāvūr not long before their time. The spectacular growth and refinement of music and dance is ascribed to the enlightened royal patronage extended by the court of Tañjāvūr.

Tyāgarāja is regarded as the most accessible both musically and as a human being who speaks to each of us through his lyrics. His compositions still demonstrate how musical tradition and spontaneous creativity can ideally enhance one another.

Śyāmā Śāstri, Tyāgarāja, and Muttusvāmi Dīkṣitar, each in their own way, are credited with setting the musical and stylistic standards for all later composers. Although widely differing in their approach to composition and output, they are held in equal esteem. They are revered as accomplished artists, poets and saints at once. Legends about their lives and the miraculous effect of their music are re-told with great reverence.

Particularly noteworthy is the manner of committing their compositions to the memories of their students in order to ensure their survival for the benefit of later generations. In the absence of a detailed musical score, regarded as unsuitable for South Indian music, musical patterns were entirely based on lyrics and syllables. Tyāgarāja is known to have assigned specific portions of his songs to groups of his numerous disciples who would leave the room after hearing a particular portion in order to memorize it thoroughly. The saint later re-assembled and corrected the piece, often conceived spontaneously, in a state of mystical ecstacy, before passing it on to his students in a finished form. This method, perhaps not uncommon in earlier periods of Indian culture, would have worked only in a highly organized household of a *guru* surrounded by disciplined students.

Creative music (manodharma saṅgīta)

No two performances of Karnatic music will be identical even if a musician were to choose the same items again. During concerts and to some degree also in a dance recital, musicians are free to draw from their accumulated experience and become creative in several ways. Before, between and after a chosen composition, the musicians participating in a performance can contribute music that could be described in terms of 'structured improvisation' (*manodharma saṅgīta*). The extent of such elaboration depends on the personal preferences of a musician.

South Indian performers enjoy considerable freedom to elaborate on the chosen composition or theme in both spheres—melody (*rāga*) and rhythm (*laya*). Limits are set by the stylistic framework of a particular tradition and the expressive scope of a musician's voice or instrument. There is also an understanding that a performer should not distort the proportions or contours of the composition on which an elaboration is based.

The classical concert format provides four principal avenues for musical freedom, namely *rāga ālāpana*, *tānam*, *pallavi*, and *niraval*. These are supplemented by the stringing together of several rāgas (*rāgamālikā*), and the singing of poetry (*ślokam* and *viruttam*).

Each type of improvised music has its own function and appeal. The most important form of extemporization is an exposition of the various melodic features that make up a rāga (*rāga ālāpana*). This form flows freely, without any constraints of metre (*tāla*). The features delineated in an *ālāpana* mainly consist of permissible intervals (*svara*), range (*sthāyī*), characteristic phrases (*prayoga*), notes (*aṁśa* and *jīvasvara*), and embellishments (*gamaka*).

An optional extension of the *ālāpana* exposition also flows freely without reference to a metre (*tānam*) but involves a pulsation of phrases tied to one another on the basis of Sanskrit syllables *anaṁta* ('infinite').

The most complex form of extemporization again builds on the *rāgam* and *tāṉam* expositions. It involves a procedure that explores all the possible melodic and rhythmic variations of a chosen theme which consists of a single line of verse (*pallavi*). The playful combination of individual notes (*svara kalpana*) is performed with reference to rāga, tāla and any suitable theme. These patterns are woven, as it were, into the fabric of a composition and appeal by way of adding shape and colour to it if done with aesthetic sense.

Another important form (*niraval*) resembles the *svara kalpana* to an extent and also figures within the *rāgam tāṉam pallavi* format. The distinguishing feature of the *niraval* is its adherence to the lyrics of the chosen theme and the feeling (*bhāva*) they are intended to convey. The *niraval* form provides room for variations of the initial theme and aims at enhancing its emotional impact by transposing these phrases and ultimately carrying a theme through the entire melodic range provided by the *rāga*.

The above procedures can be supplemented by a stringing together of several rāgas to a 'musical garland' (*rāgamālikā*). Vocalists can further avail themselves of specific types of variations which are inspired by the ancient way of reciting the sacred scriptures and hymns (*ślokam* and *viruttam*).

Accompaniment

The art of accompanying the principal vocalist or instrumentalist calls for quick analysis of details, adaptability, a well-developed sense of stylistic nuances, tact, and subtlety, in order to complement rather than dominate a concert. Although a good accompanist often feels deprived of the appreciation which is commensurate with the enormous energy and perseverance required for training, there is professional scope for every good accompanist which cannot be said of most soloists.

The unwritten code of conduct requires that accompanists follow the pace and tone set by the principal soloist. Almost every improvisation by the soloist is followed by a separate solo for the accompanist who provides melodic support. Percussionists have the main rhythmic solo of a concert, known as *taṉiyāvarttaṉam*, to display their skills and ingenuity without any interference or restriction.

Percussion solo (taṉiyāvarttaṉam)

The percussion solo (*taṉiyāvarttaṉam*) is one of the highlights of every Karnatic concert. Here mathematical precision, inventiveness, and aesthetic sense combine with the sparkling displays of virtuosity. The importance assigned to rhythmic intricacies is reflected by the fact that Karnatic percussionists are free to develop their solo or ensemble improvisation at their own leisure. Both the duration and the complexity of a *taṉiyāvarttaṉam* depend on each musician's capacity and experience. Palghat Maṇi Ayyar is remembered as the master of crisp and concise statements. His play was distinguished by great poise, and his pauses were as eloquent as the variegated sounds and patterns he produced on his *mṛdaṅgam*. His is the style many percussionists of our times still seek to emulate.

Aesthetics (rasa) and philosophy of South Indian music

Since the time of the *Nāṭya Śāstra* and *Cilappatikāram*, the earliest works which contain detailed descriptions of Indian performing arts in Sanskrit and Tamil respectively, the idea has taken root that beyond temporary enjoyment, there must be another dimension to an aesthetic experience. This idea has found its expression in the simple term 'essence' (*rasa*) which also means taste.

With this background of philosophical and psychological inquiry into the nature of the arts, *Karnāṭaka Saṅgīta*, the Sanskrit expression for South Indian classical music, has become synonymous with 'tradition' although there has always been an innovative aspect to it too. Artistic accomplishments, such as personal interpretation and elaboration, are built on the foundations provided by a repertoire of compositions.

The various traditions of South Indian music agree that good music is primarily a lifelong pursuit of beauty and bliss. This pursuit, far from being hedonistic, is legitimized by the ancient doctrine that primordial sound (*nāda*) itself constitutes the means of divine Creation. Art music is thus inherently an expression of humility before all that is sacred about life. If the experience of beauty is our main motivation for enjoying music, we need not feel intimidated by the complexity resulting from factors such as the vastness of the land as well as the diversity of languages, customs and beliefs.

There is a remarkable sense of unity regarding the relationships between various elements which make up the repertoire: text and musical expression, melody and rhythm, basic note and intervals, scale and *rāga,* individual note and phrase, pitch and embellishment, theme and variation, etc. An understanding of such technicalities is by no means required for the spontaneous enjoyment of music. But conscious listening deepens the experience. A modicum of background knowledge helps to graduate from passive entertainment to an intelligent and creative pursuit of aesthetic delight (*rasa*). It is at this stage of discerning appreciation and critical faculty that a listener is referred to as a *rasika*.

Stylistic subtleties and theoretical complexities of Karnatic music constitute the most valuable assets of an ancient music system which continues to undergo an evolutionary process rather than submitting to sudden changes. The art music of South India itself is the result of conscious reflection by countless generations of musicians and theorists who applied their minds to the very nature of sound and music. At every step they sought to relate the problems of aesthetics to the inherent spiritual dimension of music. The culmination of this quest is the vast body of compositions created over a period of more than five centuries.

Lyrics (sāhitya)

Karnatic musicians have always paid much attention to the lyrics (*sāhitya*) which form an integral part of practically every type of composition. The most notable exception is a form of didactic composition (*svarajati*) which consists of a combination of musical notes (*svara*) rendered through syllables (*jati*) instead of lyrics. It is due to the devotional content that the important forms of Karnatic music (*kṛti* and the older *kīrtana*) are treated with reverence. There are forms such as the songs composed on erotic themes (*padam* and *jāvaḷi*) whose impact also depends on the subtleties of the languages used (mostly Tamil and Telugu). In Tamil radio announcements, any type of musical composition is referred to as *pāḍal* ('song').

The sole form of South Indian music which gives priority to melodic and rhythmic structure rather than lyrics is the *tānavarṇam*, an important didactic form. The lyrics of a *tillānā* are also limited to make room for abstract syllables (*jati*). Primarily a dance form, the *tillānā* is also a popular item found in the concluding phase of a music concert where it conjures the rhythmic movements of a dancer in a listener's mind.

A composer of a high order (Sanskrit *vaggēyakāra*, Tamil *iyaṟṟīyavar*) is responsible for the lyrics as well as the musical structure (*rāga* and *tāla*) to which they are set. Telugu, Sanskrit, Tamil, Kannaḍa (Canarese), and Malayālam are the languages that occur most widely in today's classical performances (see Fig. 26). In some cases composers wrote lyrics in Maṇipravāḷa, a blend of Sanskrit and Malayālam or Tamil (e.g. Irayimmaṉ Tampi and Svāti Tirunāḷ). Hindi occurs in the form of 'light' devotional songs (*bhajan*) adorning the concluding part of a concert (*tukkaḍā*).

Tyāgarāja (Telugu) and Arunagirināthar (Tamil) were among the major composers who employed a mixture of Sanskrit and their mother tongue for writing lyrics.

In cases where the lyrics have been set to music by a person other than the music composer, or even by a musician of a later period, only the name of the poet, not that of the music composer, is likely to appear in a programme note or publication.

Authenticity (sampradāya, pāṭhāntara)

Numerous composers have contributed to the repertoire performed in today's concerts in South India. Due to the absence of a detailed system of notation, the musical structure of many early compositions was lost to posterity (e.g. *kīrtana* compositions by Annamācārya). The faithful transmission of music from one generation to another (*guruśiṣya paramparā*) has been pursued very methodically from the late eighteenth century onwards.

Tyāgarāja was a pioneer in this field. He ensured that his songs were faithfully rendered by his disciples by equipping them to accurately transmit his work to their own pupils without additions or alterations of any kind.

The creative urge of a musician has its outlets in various improvisational forms known as *manodharma saṅgīta*. But in accordance with their sacred character, a musician handles the classical compositions learnt from a teacher (*guru*) with great care. Most musicians therefore strive to perform and teach such compositions as authentically in every detail as possible. Nevertheless there are different accepted versions or interpretations (*pāṭhāntara* or 'readings') of compositions by Tyāgarāja and others. These versions are associated with the major lines of disciples (*paramparā*) that trace themselves to musicians from different regions of South India who were personally trained by Tyāgarāja.

Notation

The overall picture of a rāga is exemplified by the advanced compositions learnt from an experienced teacher. A *varṇam* (literally 'colour') is a technical type of composition (*tānavarṇam)* and intended to convey the shades of a rāga through appropriate phrases (*tāna*).

Although there have been many attempts at producing authoritative manuals (*lakṣaṇagrantha*), most practising musicians regard it as meaningless, if not counterproductive, to commit their art to a detailed musical score. For this reason, every musician prides himself on the association with a master musician (*vidvān*, male form, *viduṣī*, female form). This link with a living musical tradition (*sampradāya*) is valued even if a musician chooses to define a personal style which deviates from traditional performing conventions.

Musical details are thus mainly assimilated by attentive observation, listening and faithful practice. In the past, it was even customary for a teacher to withhold theoretical knowledge from a disciple (*śiṣya*) until proficiency and artistic integrity had been evaluated with satisfactory results.

Until the early nineteenth century, notation was regarded as unnecessary because most musicians had a lifetime bond with their teachers which made them virtual members of their teachers' families (*gurukula*). Most notations of that period merely consisted of the lyrics of each song and some information about its melodic and rhythmic structure (*rāga* and *tāla*, respectively). If musical notes were written down, the notation consisted of shorthand indications such as individual letters without reference to either pitch or octave. Embellishments and microtonal adjustments for certain characteristic notes, although of prime importance for rendering a composition, were committed to memory. So far no book could replace a teacher even at a preliminary stage of learning.

The lyrics of a composition were often engraved on copper plates (especially those in Telugu) or copied onto palm-leaf bundles. As Indian society became increasingly urbanized in colonial times, new challenges and opportunities arose which also changed the nature of music education. A major encyclopedic work, *Saṅgīta Sampradāya Pradaśini* of Subbarāma Dīkṣitar (1839–1906), paved the way for publications which contain musical details such as syllabic notation for melodic and rhythmic structure, symbols for *gamaka*, as well as the lyrics. The monumental works of expert musicians like K.V. Śrīnivāsa Ayyaṅgār, R. Raṅgarāmānuja Ayyaṅgār, and Vidya Shankar, to name but a few, contain detailed information and notations of this type.

Yet in the absence of an authentic tradition or notation, much of the music which was originally composed before AD 1800 has been re-composed by eminent musicians of modern times who are, however, never listed on concert programmes or announced on the radio. Already in the late nineteenth century, Mahāvaidyanātha Śivan̲, a famous performer and composer, is said to have made several compositions of Muttusvāmi Dīkṣitar more appealing for use in public concerts by changing the slow tempo of some sections (*vilambita kāla*) to a combination of three degrees of speed (*tṛkāla*).

North and South Indian music

Unlike North Indian music (*Hindustānī Saṅgīt*), the music of South India (*Karṇāṭaka Saṅgīta*) shows a marked preference for fully-fledged compositions in concert and devotional music. Among the important forms of Karnatic music the *rāgam tān̲am pallavi* has considerable similarity with Hindustānī music.

In the nineteenth century, Karnatic composers adopted two popular types of song from Hindustānī music: *jāvaḷi* and *tillānā*, which are described in another chapter. Both forms have been adapted to the stylistic framework of South Indian music. They are considered as 'light' items (*tukkaḍā*), usually enjoyed after the main composition of a concert programme.

Tempo (kālapramāṇam)

Joint concerts of North and South Indian musicians (*jugalbandī*) are a recurring feature of many music festivals. But there remains one vital difference which inevitably makes a successful collaboration between northern and southern musicians difficult. This difference consists in the manner in which musical time is managed in the course of a performance. In Karnatic music the tempo (*kālapramāṇam*) is maintained up to the conclusion of the piece. By contrast, the most common format of Hindustānī music, *khayāl*, leads to a gradual acceleration from slow to fast, during the different stages of development that make up a North Indian concert item. The South Indian music system, on the other hand, places two different means at the disposal of musicians whose aim is variety of musical speed. One procedure can be described as a doubling or halving of the chosen tempo after which the initial tempo is resumed. The other consists of a process of permutation and combination of the basic rhythmic patterns.

Duration of a classical concert

Concerts lasting two to three hours are a relatively recent phenomenon. Until a few decades ago, it was customary for a musician to treat his audience to five or more hours. The fast-paced lifestyle of modern urban India has also changed the way in which concerts are presented. Radio and television have encouraged the more concise format which is also followed in most live concerts. A reduction of elaborate improvisations, notably the exclusion of the *rāgam tānam pallavi* format from most concerts, accounts for the greater part of time saved in shorter concerts.

Live concert and broadcast

Instead of blindly following old conventions, Ariyakuḍi Rāmānuja Iyengar (1890–1967) popularized the present performance format (*kaccēri paddhati*). It offers greater variety and flexibility than the long concerts that were heard until the 1930s with their focus on an elaborate *rāgam tāṉam pallavi* item. There are now more compositions per concert while the total duration of a performance is less due to listeners' time constraints. Broadcasts with classical music have an average duration of an hour but often less.

Their dependence on fees from broadcasts and commercial recordings rather than on live concerts has instilled a keen sense of timing in all musicians. In these changing circumstances, contemporary Karnatic musicians have sought to balance their concerts aesthetically. Rāgas and compositions are chosen with the aim of taking the audience on a musical journey with many beautiful vistas even if there is little time to linger. In spite of all outward changes, most Karnatic musicians still aspire to provide their public with a type of music which is aesthetically valid and spiritually uplifting.

Originality and spontaneity

A certain degree of originality is expected of every Karnatic musician. Frequent displays of eccentricity, on the other hand, are tolerated rather than appreciated if a rare genius offers inspired moments. Every experienced musician knows when and how to alter the course of a performance in accordance with the receptivity of an audience. No two successful concerts are therefore alike even if the same ensemble comes together. The prevailing practice of changing accompanists on almost every occasion further adds to the diversity of programmes even if a musician is a busy performer with a limited repertoire. It is not uncommon for musicians participating in a joint performance to meet one another for the first time on stage just minutes before the beginning of a concert or broadcast. Such situations call for experience and adaptability on the part of accompanists, and foresight on the part of a soloist in order to bring out the very best which every musician has to offer to his or her listeners.

Film music

Early South Indian films featured famous classical musicians, notably M.S. Subbulakshmi who won a large audience for Karnatic music by her charismatic screen presence. Several eminent Karnatic musicians have composed film music that is rooted in classical Karnatic music: M. Bālamuraḷī Krishna, S. Bālachander, Kunnakudi R. Vaidyanāthan, Madurai S. Somasundaram, Nārāyaṇa Ayyar, Pāpanāsam Śivaṉ, and Sirkazhi S. Gōvindarājaṉ. Conversely, the popular film singer and composer K.J. Jesudoss is also a classical vocalist in his own right. But in recent years, commercial film directors have taken advantage of modern sound engineering which resulted in a hybrid type of music which hardly reminds one of classical music. Contemporary film music freely combines elements from Indian and Western classical music, and devotional, dance, pop, and disco music of every description.

Communicating music

In a scenario marked by rapidly changing social and economic conditions, many musicians are keen on preserving their particular tradition (*bāṇī*). They seek to disseminate the repertoire obtained in a direct lineage of teachers and students (*guruśisya paramparā*). Contrary to earlier centuries, knowledge is now shared more freely rather than jealously guarded. Interviews, lectures, intensive courses or workshops, and publications are more frequent now. Outside India, several universities and colleges have initiated successful collaborations of this kind and even support study programmes in South India to gather first-hand experience before embarking on academic research work. Musical training is therefore easier to come by and hardly, if ever, denied due to considerations of caste or class. Classical Karnatic music, far from having lost its fascination for younger people, is increasingly patronized and studied by modern Indians with a secular rather than sectarian outlook. As the restlessness, uniformity and shallowness of modern life becomes increasingly oppressive, this art is rediscovered for its timeless beauty. If much traditional music has not been faithfully preserved in the past, this is certainly a deplorable loss. At the same time this poses a challenge to the ingenuity and creativity of new generations of musicians and listeners. This challenge has already been taken up with fervour, talent, and imagination.

16

Dance and Music; Harikathā Kālakṣepam

The historical and social context of South Indian classical dance (Bharata Nāṭyam)

South Indian temple dance can be traced back to the court of the medieval *Cōla* dynasty and beyond. The great temples of Tañjāvūr and Chidambaram are adorned by numerous sculptures and paintings depicting music and dance. Hundreds of dancers and musicians were recruited on a regular basis to serve in these temples. Already in antiquity regional dance and drama traditions had been maintained by professional actors, dancers, poets, vocalists, instrumentalists, and dance teachers. Technical treatises (e.g. the *Nāṭya Śāstra*) were written from the early centuries AD onwards to codify the various aspects of dance, drama, and music. The practice of dance and music was also described in great detail in the *Cilappatikāram,* an early work of Tamil literature which is often described as an 'epic poem'.

Dance was traditionally performed by women (Tamil *virali*, Sanskrit *dēvadāsi* or *rājādāsi*). It was common practice to dedicate or 'marry' the *dēvadāsi* ('servant of god') to the presiding deity of a temple. Their art was called *dāsi āṭṭam*. As a result of this custom neither they nor their children could ever lead a regular married life. As dancers they also received a thorough musical training imparted by musicians and dance masters (*naṭṭuvanar*), generally the male members of their community. Many a *dēvadāsi* was in fact known to be a distinguished woman of wealth and influence whose home formed the focus of cultural activities in her respective town. The participation of a *dēvadāsi* dancer during festive occasions was considered auspicious and therefore indispensable. For this reason, a *dēvadāsi* was also referred to as an ever (*nitya*)-auspicious woman (*sumaṅgaḷi*, i.e. *nitya sumaṅgaḷi*). Nevertheless many *dēvadāsis* appear to have lived their lives on the margins of society particularly in recent history. Many hereditary dancers and musicians suffered destitution when temple patronage was forcibly terminated in colonial times. Thus the prestige of the art of dancing was eroded in the late nineteenth and early twentieth centuries. The 'Devadasi Act', a law still in force today, was passed in 1947 and makes it illegal to practise any form of dance within the premises of a temple or as part of a religious procession.

Efforts aimed at 'reforming' the art of dancing coincided with the struggle for India's independence and cultural identity. The older name for dance, now obsolete, had been *sadir āṭṭam* meaning 'dance (*āṭṭam*) which is performed in the temple square (*sadir*)'. The renewed interest in dance, and the general preference for *bharata nāṭyam* as a supposedly new name for an old tradition, coincide with a period of history when patriotism was on the rise and the way for India's independence was being paved. Since the 1930s, the Music Academy Madras has played a major role in promoting dance and music. The time had arrived when Indians could again feel proud of their cultural heritage, and also of the musicians, dancers, poets, and composers who have shaped the cultural identity of southern India. The lyrics of Subrahmaṇya Bhārati (Bhāratiyar, 1882–1921), set to soulful tunes by S.V. Veṅkaṭa-rāmaṉ and other music directors associated with cinema, and the artistic choreographies created for many films of the 1940s and 1950s, served to convey the message of enlightened patriotism. On account of the popularity of films, and the dignified character of many productions of those years, the world of movies attracted leading actors, musicians such as M.S. Subbulakshmi and D.K. Paṭṭammāḷ, and dancers such as Kamalā.

Ever since that period of modern Indian history, prominent artists and intellectuals sought to support and propagate worthwhile political and social causes through indigenous art forms. The best known among them are E. Krishna Iyer, who learnt and performed *bharata nāṭyam*; Rasikamaṇi T.K. Chidambaranāda Mudalyār, remembered for being the first and foremost promoter of many artists, including T. Bālasarasvati (dancer) and Kambaṉ (Tamil poet); and Kalki Krishnamūrti, who paved the way for many exponents of *bharata nāṭyam* through his articles and reviews.

South Indian dance, then known as *sadir* and *kūttu*, had been little cared for and was even shunned by the educated elite. If it was to be patronized again, it was perceived as being in need of reformation both as an artistic heritage, and as a social phenomenon. Presentation technique was virtually absent, and some dance items were lacking in taste by modern standards. The ensuing renaissance of *bharata nāṭyam* thus coincided with the larger quest, namely the struggle for national independence of the motherland (*Bhārata Mātā*). Many Indians were determined to maintain and develop a cultural identity of their own, and the official name chosen for their land was *Bhārat*.

Contrary to popular belief, there is evidence that the expression '*bharata nāṭyam*' was not newly coined in the first half of the twentieth century. The name *bharata nāṭyam* was, of course, chosen and retrieved from obscurity with reference to the most important and ancient treatise on the performing arts (*Nāṭya Śāstra*), which tradition ascribes to Bharatamuni (between the 2nd c. BC and the 6th c. AD). But the expression *bharatam* was used to denote a male dancer like *Bharatam* Nārāyaṇasvāmi (early 20th century), an amateur for whom the art was a devotional discipline. The grandfather and father of Paṭṭaṇam Subrahmaṇya Ayyar, the famous composer, are referred to as *Bharatam* Pañcanāda Śāstrī and *Bharatam* Vaidyanātha Ayyar, respectively. The former was a court musician (*samasthāna vidvān*) of Śarabhōjī II (1798–1832) (*Great Musicians* by P. Sambamoorthy, p. 21).

Subrahmaṇya Bhārati, in a Tamil poem written prior to 1921 (the year of his demise), also employs the term *bharata nāṭyam* (*parata nāṭṭya*). He exhorts his readers to string together (*kōttiḍuvirē*) the arts of singing (*pāṭṭum*), and poetry (*kavitayum*), acting (*nāṭṭyak-*) and dancing (*-kūttiḍuvirē*):

Pāṭṭum kavitayum kōttiḍuvīrē
parata nāṭṭyakkūttiḍuvīrē
kāṭṭum vaiyapporuḷkaḻin uṇmai
kaṇḍu sāttiram sērttiḍuvīrē.

(Courtesy: Anandhi Ramachandran; quoted from
Bhāratiyar kaviraigaḷ, 3rd verse, p. 495)

Thus he eulogizes over the role of these arts not only as an integral part of India's great and ancient cultural heritage, but also their pride of place in the effort to build a modern Indian civilization. Considering the growing appreciation of traditional performing arts forms within his country, and their dissemination all over the world, it can be said that the poet's vision came true soon after he wrote these lines.

Even earlier dance was referred to as *nāṭyam* in a Tamil book entitled *Sir̲upuliyūr ulā*. This work is a typical example for a literary genre (*ulā*) in which the splendours of an annual chariot festival, as celebrated by almost every South Indian temple, are described in great detail. As indicated in its title, the setting for this work is the temple of *Sir̲upuliyūr*. The festive procession is described from the point of view of girls and women who belong to various age groups, each one responding to the appearance of the presiding deity with the type of loving feeling or attraction (*śṛṅgāra*) which is appropriate to her stage in life. Such festive processions were accompanied by female dancers (*dēvadāsi*) whose art (Tamil *kūttu*) was referred to as *nāṭyam* in the *Sir̲upuliyūr ulā*. God is having a stroll (*ulā*), as it were: the deity (*Tiru*, 'auspicious', 'prosperous', or goddess Lakṣmī) is taken out of the sanctum of the temple and carried through the streets (*Tiru-vīdi-ulā*) in an ornate chariot (*ratha*).

Another literary genre was similarly inspired by this type of festive procession, namely the *kur̲avañji*, a story which has its roots in folklore and is produced as a dance-drama. The *kur̲avañji* takes its name from the gypsy woman (*kur̲atti*) who is presented as the main character. As in the *ulā*, the subject of the *kur̲avañji* is the confluence of two primary emotional states (*bhāva*) whose inherent unity stands at the centre of a greater part of Indian literature: love (*śṛṅgāra*) and devotion (*bhakti*). The wonderful process of experiencing and sublimating human love (*nāyaka nāyikā bhāva*) is seen as a metaphor for the search of the individual soul (*jīvātmā*, depicted as 'female', the beloved or *nāyikā*) for the Supreme (*paramātmā*, depicted as 'male', the lover or *nāyaka*). This is indeed the great theme which has inspired many forms of music and dance for over twelve centuries. The most famous masterpiece based on *nāyaka nāyikā bhāva* is, of course, the *Gītagovinda*, a Sanskrit work by Jayadeva which is popular all over India. Several South Indian works were inspired by Jayadeva and have been used for dance and music productions: the compositions of Tāḷḷapāka Annamācārya, Kṣetrajñā, Muttuttāṇḍavar, Ghanam Kṛṣṇa Ayyar, Nārāyaṇa Tīrtha, Ūttukkāḍu Veṅkaṭa Subba Ayyar, Kuppusvāmi Ayyar, Vidyala Nārāyaṇasvāmi Naidu, and Vaitīśvarankoil Subbarāma Ayyar. In all works on this theme, love is seen as an integral part of devotion, to be realized and transcended in the course of one's life.

In several compositions, Tyāgarāja provides us with glimpses of this cheerful approach to self-realization, the cultivation of *bhakti*, which needs to be fuelled by intense longing for God akin to *śṛṅgāra bhāva*. The genius of Tyāgarāja finds its apt expression in colourful imagery, resonant lyrics, and carefully chosen rāgas, complemented by lively melodic patterns and variations (*saṅgati*). In his *kṛti 'Vinarādā nā manavi'* (rāga Dēvagāndhāri, ādi tāla), one among five pieces known as *Śrīraṅga pañcaratna kīrtana*, he refers to a festive procession in which Viṣṇu (Raṅga Rājā, the Lord of Śrīraṅga), is taken through the streets: 'Oh golden-hued Raṅga of Kāveri, Lord of Lakṣmī (Śrī), can't you listen (*vinarādā*) to my appeal (*nā manavi*)? When the ladies, including the royal party, so lovingly call you when you come out in procession on horse-back, why should you not respond? You are their treasure.'

(Based on the translation by C. Rāmānujāchari,
The Spiritual Heritage of Tyāgarāja).

Conventions, musical forms and themes of classical dance

From early times, South Indian dance (*nṛtta* and *nṛtya*), music (*gīta*), and drama (*nāṭya*) have been regarded as being inseparable. This integral approach to all performing arts is often explained by the meaning of three syllables, namely *bha-ra-ta*; they are said to represent the three fundamental concepts which every performer seeks to master: 'bha' for the appropriate expression of emotions (*bhāva*); 'ra' for melody (*rāga*), and 'ta' for rhythm (*tāla*).

The entire dance ensemble is referred to as 'the small ensemble' (*cinna mēḷam*). The number of accompanists can vary from performance to performance. The *cinna mēḷam* is led by a musician specialized in teaching and accompanying *bharata nāṭyam*, who is sometimes also an experienced dancer. The word *naṭṭuvāṅgam* thus refers to the function of the leading musician who conducts the performance, which consists of playing a pair of small cymbals (*tāḷam*), and singing the dance syllables (*jati* or *śolkaṭṭu*). In the past, the *naṭṭuvāṅgam* was exclusively performed by a hereditary male dance master (*naṭṭuvanar*). The decline of traditional patronage for the art now known as *bharata nāṭyam* made it possible to promote this art outside the conservative atmosphere of a temple or palace. As a result, women could choose to become professional exponents of this art. Not content with merely presenting dance as entertainment, Rukmini Devi strove to revive what she perceived to be the original sanctity and purity of temple dance, but now on the stage of a modern auditorium. In this regard, she was a pioneer who paved the way for several generations of Indian dancers.

With the notable exception of *Mōhiniyāṭṭam* and *Kathakali*, classical South Indian dance and dance-drama are normally accompanied by Karnatic music. Conversely, many compositions from the dance repertoire have also found a place in the programmes of Karnatic concert musicians on account of their immediate emotional appeal. The lyrics of these songs are often based on the *Bhāgavata Purāṇa* (*circa* 10th century), a devotional work which describes the exploits of young Kṛṣṇa. It contains many popular episodes that lend themselves to artistic treatment: the theft of butter, committed when Kṛṣṇa was still an innocent child; and the heroic deeds performed by him during adolescence, such as the slaying of the snake monster, and the lifting of the *Govardhana* mountain. Such stories are bound to evoke vivid pictures in the minds of Indian listeners. The 'lighter' (*dēśī*) songs of this category are usually heard towards the end of a classical concert where the so-called *tukkaḍā* (minor) items are performed, often in *dēśya rāgas* derived from Hindustānī music. Conversely, dancers are increasingly drawn to the musical intricacies of classical music compositions (e.g. *kṛti*) and seek to demonstrate their creative skills as choreographers and performers beyond the traditional programme pattern (*mārgam*).

The traditional sequence of a dance recital consists of seven principal dance items in the following order: *alārippu, jatisvaram, śabdam, padavarṇam, padam, jāvaḷi*, and *tillānā,* followed by a *maṅgaḷam*. This format was introduced by four brothers, commonly known as the 'Tanjore Quartette', early in the nineteenth century. In addition to these seven standard items, other forms are also included in some dance programmes, namely *kautvam, rāgamālikā, dēvarnāma, kīrtana* or *kṛti, aṣṭapadi*, and *ślokam* or *vṛttam* (*viruttam*).

HARIKATHĀ KĀLAKṢEPAM

The Sanskrit term *harikathā kālakṣepam* literally means passing time (*kālakṣepam*) with the stories (*kathā*) about God (*hari*). This composite art form is based on the major themes and characters whose stories are told in the great epics (*Rāmāyaṇa, Mahābhārata*), and in the popular legends of devotional literature such as the *Bhāgavata Purāṇa*. These exceedingly diverse elements, drawn from all parts and traditions of India, have been dramatized by learned performers (*bhāgavatar*) and interlaced with attractive songs (e.g. *kīrtana, abhaṅg, bhajan*), accompanied by the gestures (*mudrā*), facial expression (*abhinaya*), and rhythmic movements (*nṛtta*) derived from the techniques of dance and drama (*nāṭya*). A *bhāgavatar* must be a master of several languages and musical idioms. In the past, he was mostly colourfully dressed to give the performance an appealing yet dignified theatrical dimension. In a standing position, he conducted the accompanying ensemble with the help of a pair of clappers (*cipla*). Rhythmic accompaniment is coordinated by playing a pair of small cymbals (*jālrā*). Skilful drumming provides an additional dramatic dimension as well as scope for entertaining interludes. The accompanying ensemble includes two more singers (*upagāyaka*), a *tambūrā*, a violin and, more recently, often a harmonium. Rāmacandra Buva, a nineteenth-century *kīrtaṅkār* from northern Karṇāṭaka, is believed to be responsible for the enduring popularity of Marāṭhi songs in the southern *kathā* tradition.

Tañjāvūr Kṛṣṇa Bhāgavatar (1841–1903) is credited with having established the modern performance pattern (*kathā paddhati*) by fusing the two prevailing Marāṭhi *kīrtankār* traditions with the southern traditions of devotional discourse (*kālakṣepam*). Women exponents of *harikathā kālakṣepam* began to play a major role from the times of C. Sarasvatī Bai who succeeded in overcoming male prejudices on account of her personality, learning, good voice, and her exceptional competence in both the northern as well as southern traditions of music. Her tradition was carried on by C. Banni Bai, while male exponents like Bālakrishna Śāstrigaḷ have sought to revive the learned discourse based on Tamil and Sanskrit lore.

Contemporary performers have chosen to present the art of *harikathā kālakṣepam* in a seated position, resembling the arrangement for classical concerts (*kaccēri*). The modern format gives prominence to the spoken word and musical interludes based on classical and 'light classical' or devotional songs, dance pieces, and the style of musical recitation in Sanskrit and Tamil (*ślokam* or *viruttam* respectively). This style of presentation leaves, of course, no room for dance movements seen in the earlier stage of the art's development.

17

Musical Forms (Concert, Dance and Didactic Music)

aḍavu (dance)—see *alārippu*

alaṁkāram, alankāram (didactic)

The composer who is regarded as the 'father of Karnatic music', Purandara Dāsa, is credited with the series of exercises known as *alaṁkāram*. This series is designed to teach seven primary tāla patterns (*sūḷādi sapta tāla*), both simple and complex ones. Some of these tālas are often used in concert and dance music (e.g. *khaṇḍa jāti aṭa tāla*, *rūpaka tāla*), while others are less commonly used now. Most characteristically, the tonal range stays within one octave which makes the frequent practice of *alaṁkāram* exercises suited even to a beginner's voice. In the place of lyrics (*sāhitya*), each note is sung either on its corresponding syllable (*sargam*, i.e. 'sa', 'ri', 'ga', 'ma', 'pa', 'dha', 'ni'), or on a vowel (*akāram* or *akāra sādhakam*, usually 'a'). Any scale (*mēḷakartā rāga*) can be used for *alaṁkāram* practice. Most teachers insist that a pupil first masters this form in three degrees of speed while continuing to reckon the first speed (1st = *prathama kāla*, 2nd = *dvitīya kāla,* and 3rd = *tṛtīya kāla*). *See also sūḷādi.*

ālāpana, rāga ālāpana, rāgam (concert, dance)

The main branch of Indian improvisation, the exposition of a distinctive tonal pattern (*rāga*), is called *rāga ālāpana* or *ālāpana* (= ālāp in Hindustānī music). Unlike other forms of creative music (e.g. *tāṉam* and *niraval*), an *ālāpana* is characterized by the absence of a definable and recurring rhythmic pattern or metre (*tāla*). It either precedes a composition (e.g. *kṛti*), or a brief theme (*pallavi*) which stands at the centre of an elaborate musical form known as *rāgam tāṉam pallavi.* While a short rāga delineation is also a form of *ālāpana*, it is the elaborate exploration of the melodic features of a rāga which has a prominent place in a Karnatic concert. Although there are no rigid rules there is a conventional format which consists of three stages: a concise introduction (*ākṣīptika* or *āyittam*); this is followed by a detailed exposition of every characteristic feature of the rāga (*rāga vardhani*); and the conclusion which gives room for negotiating all the registers of the rāga (*sthāyī*). The last stage of a formal rāga exposition (*rāgam*) as part of the *rāgam tāṉam pallavi* format, traditionally includes *tāṉam* or *madhyama kāla*, a non-metrical but accentuated extension of an *ālāpana*.

For this purpose, a major rāga with scope for a musician's imagination is chosen. The type of rāga most suited for an elaborate *rāga ālāpana* is known as *rakti* or *naya rāga*. Sometimes other rāgas are interspersed in the form of a *rāgamālikā* which consists of a group of matching rāgas before the main rāga is resumed.

The aim of an *ālāpana* is not only to bring out the aesthetic quality (*rasa*) inherent in a rāga but also its individual character (*svarūpa*). All the characteristic intervals (*svarasthāna*), phrases (*sañcāra*), and embellishments (*gamaka*) must be combined in such a manner that not even a tinge (*chāyā*) of another rāga can be detected by a discerning listener (*rasika*). For this purpose, musicians have a ready stock of key phrases (*piḍippu*) to 'catch' the features of a rāga and to avoid slipping into another rāga with similar melodic patterns.

Different compositions (e.g. *gītam, tāṉavarṇam, kṛti*) provide a musician with suitable models for a *rāgam tāṉam pallavi* performance. These compositions contain the appropriate phrases and embellishments that convey the mood and aesthetic effect of a particular rāga. The melodic context of a note is of greater importance than the individual note itself; and the total effect of an *ālāpana* is more than the sum of its notes and phrases.

A vocalist employs a number of phrases based on the vowel 'a' and syllables such as 'ta', 'da', 'ri', na', 'nam', and 'tom'. This enables the voice to convey the emotive quality of a given rāga in a colourful and spontaneous manner. An instrumentalist always seeks to emulate the continuity and expressiveness of the voice (*gānam*, sometimes referred to as *gāyakī*, literally a 'feminine singer'). Conversely, great singers have often studied the techniques employed in instrumental music to achieve clarity and precision in their vocal rendering. The *vaiṇika* school of Vīṇā Dhanammāḷ is a case in point as it has shaped the aesthetic sensitivities of several generations of Karnatic musicians. Similarly, the music of *nāgasvaram* exponent Rājaratnam Piḷḷai and of *gōṭṭuvādyam* exponent Sakharāma Rao have enriched the stylistic and technical vocabulary underlying a *rāga ālāpana*.

A sense of anticipation is achieved by hinting at a theme or phrase which is characteristic for the composition which follows an *ālāpana*.

If followed by a *tāṉam*, as in the context of a formal *rāgam tāṉam pallavi* performance, the *rāga ālāpana* is regarded as being the slow part of the exposition (*vilambita kāla* or *cauka kāla*), and the *tāṉam* forms its extension or second part in a medium tempo (*madhyama kāla*).

In a vocal recital, there is additional scope for two forms related to the *ālāpana* exposition, namely *śloka* and *vṛttam* (*viruttam*) , the first based on Sanskrit verse, and the second on vernacular verse (Tamil or Telugu).

alārippu (dance)

The name of the opening item of a performance means 'blossoming', and it refers to a dedicatory dance form. The *alārippu* is a delineation of sequential dance movements, gestures and poses that constitute the units of dance (*aḍavu*). For musical accompaniment, rhythmical syllables (*jati* or *solkaṭṭu*) are used, but there are no lyrics (*sāhitya*). For this reason, it falls into a category of dance forms which are characterized by pure movement (*nṛtta*). The *alārippu* is mostly preceded by an offering of flowers (*puṣpāñjali*), or sometimes also by an opening item adopted from the original temple dance in praise of a particular deity (*kautvam*). An *alārippu* is traditionally followed by a *jatisvaram* (the second main item).

aṣṭapadi (dance, concert)

The songs from the *Gītagovinda* of Jayadeva (12th century AD) with lyrics in Sanskrit. As the original music was lost, it has been re-composed in modern times on the basis of South Indian rāgas.

cauka kāla varṇam (dance)—see *padavarṇam*

ciṭṭa svara (concert)

The term *ciṭṭa svara* ('set notes') refers to a short, abstract interlude without text which can be attached to a composition. It resembles the *svara kalpana* form, but has been composed rather than being improvised. When sung, the syllabic names (*sargam*) of the eligible notes are used for both forms. A *ciṭṭa svara* passage belongs to a particular composition (*kṛti*) and has either been conceived by the original composer, as in the case of Muttusvāmi Dīkṣitar and Subbarayya Śāstri, or, as in the case of Tyāgarāja, it has been added later by another musician, often anonymously. In the context of a *tāṉavarṇam*, a similar series of preset notes is known as *ettugaḍa svara*.

For both examples (Stave 40), the *rāga* is the 29th *mēḷakartā* (Dhīraśaṅkarābharaṇam), which corresponds to the major scale of Western music. The first example of a *ciṭṭa svara* was composed by Mysore Vāsudevācāriar. Except for the less common choice of tāla for the *kṛti* to which it belongs (*khaṇḍa jāti tripuṭa tāla*, 5 + 2 + 2 = 9 beats per tāla cycle), this *ciṭṭa svara* passage is quite a typical one. Normally a *ciṭṭa svara* passage follows the second and third sections (*anupallavi*, *caraṇa*).

The second example was also composed by Mysore Vāsudevācāriar, and belongs to another composition. It gives a glimpse of the lighter vein of Karnatic music, having obviously been composed with reference to a musical 'East-Western' encounter during a period of history when art-loving princes of India entertained their visitors with musical bands composed of European instruments. Many Karnatic musicians (*vidvān*), including the great Vāsudēvācāriar, were employed as court musicians (*āsthāna vidvān*). For open-minded musicians like him, the playful aspect of music was an enjoyable pastime.

In earlier times, a form called *ciṭṭa tāṉam* was committed to memory to improve one's singing of *tāṉam*.

concert items—see *ālāpana, aṣṭapadi, ciṭṭa svara, dēvarnāma, jāvaḷi, kāvaḍiccindu, kīrtana, kṛti, maṅgaḷam, niraval, padam, rāgamālikā, rāgam tāṉam pallavi, ślokam, svarajati, tāṉam, tāṉavarṇam, taniyāvarttaṉam, Tēvāram, tillānā, Tiruppugal, tukkaḍā, vṛttam* (*viruttam*)

dance items—the classical sequence of a dance programme was introduced

Stave 40: Two *ciṭṭa svaras* by Mysore Vāsudevācāriar.

by Ponnayya (Tanjore Quartette) and consists of the following seven main items: *alārippu, jatisvaram, śabdam, varṇam* (*padavarṇam*), *padam, jāvaḷi, tillānā, followed by the maṅgaḷam*; see also *ālāpana, aṣṭapadi, dēvarnāma, gītam, kautvam, kīrtana, kṛti, mallāri, rāgamālikā, ślokam, vṛttam (viruttam).*

dēvarnāma (devotional and congregational music events; concert and dance)

There are countless devotional compositions with Kannaḍa lyrics called *dēvarnāma*

The structure of the *dēvarnāma* resembles that of other devotional forms (e.g. *divyanāma kīrtana* and *kṛti*). Purandara Dāsa was the most important composer of this form, but the original tunes (*dhātu* or *varṇameṭṭu*) are lost. The lyrics ascribed to Purandara Dāsa are still held in highest regard by Karnatic musicians on account of their underlying philosophical teachings. Musicians of modern times have therefore re-composed suitable tunes in order to be able to perform these songs.

didactic forms of Karnatic music—see *alaṁkāram, gītam, sūḷādi, svarajati, tāṉavarṇam*

gītam, gīta (didactic compositions; music; *also* dance)

The *gītam* is a didactic form of music (*abhyāsa gānam*) which is rarely, if ever, heard in a public performance. In recent times, some dancers have also introduced the *gītam* in the dance repertoire, although this was not done traditionally. The function of a *gītam* is to introduce the learner to the musical rendering of lyrics (*sāhitya*) after having learnt how to render various scales and rāgas through abstract syllables (*sargam*) and vowels (*akāram*). Several common and rare tālas are applied in the *gītam* form. The two, sometimes three sections of a *gītam* are known as *khaṇḍika*. A *gītam* lacks the variations (*saṅgati*) which are characteristic of a *kṛti*. The more simple and devotional type is known as *sancāri gīta* or *sāmānya gīta*. A more complex variant, known as *lakṣaṇa gīta*, contains the name and some technical information (*lakṣaṇa*) about the rāga in which it is sung. The lyrics of a *gītam* sometimes contain meaningless syllables (e.g. *a iyam, vā iya*) which are intended to train the voice by way of stretching the words. The best-known and perhaps earliest specimen of a *gītam* is 'Śrī Gaṇanaṭha' by Purandara Dāsa (rāga Malahari, rūpaka tāla). In the nineteenth century and early in the twentieth century numerous *gītams* were composed and published.

jatisvaram (dance)

A *jatisvaram* is the second main item within the dance format introduced by the Tanjore Quartette and resembles the music form known as *svarajati*. It consists of pure movement (*nṛtta*) which takes the form of basic units of dance (*aḍavu*). The name of this item derives from the syllables (*jati*) and musical notes (*svara*), the combination of rhythm and melody. There are no lyrics in a *jatisvaram* which generally consists of three parts: opening theme (*pallavi*), middle section (*anupallavi*) and between three and five concluding lines (*caraṇa*). A *jatisvaram* is traditionally followed by a *śabdam* (the third main item).

jāvaḷi (dance and concert)

The *jāvaḷi* is the sixth main item of a dance recital. The origins of the *jāvaḷi* are not yet fully understood. In South India, the *jāvaḷi* was inspired by similar compositions belonging to Hindustānī music and introduced in the course of the nineteenth century. It is a lively form found in dance and music performances and its Telugu lyrics centre on an erotic theme (*śṛṅgāra*). Its appeal depends on the degree to which the poetic nuances of the text are brought out. The name *jāvaḷi* is said to have been chosen in order to distinguish its contents from the *padam*. The latter has a longer history, and it is performed at a slower tempo. The lyrics of both forms are often in praise of a royal patron.

The *jāvaḷi* expresses an ecstatic form of love for the Divine (*madhura bhakti*), akin to the erotic attraction between human beings (*nāyaka nāyikā bhāva*). Several major composers of the nineteenth and twentieth centuries have contributed to the repertoire of *jāvaḷis*. Both forms, *padam* and *jāvaḷi*, owe their special status to the members of the family of Vīṇā Dhanammāḷ (notably T. Bālasarasvati, T. Brinda and T. Viswanāthan̲) of the Tanjore tradition (*bāṇī*) who are reputed for their exquisite rendition. In concerts the *jāvaḷi* is usually performed in the last portion. The rāgas chosen are emotionally charged, of an immediate appeal (*rakti*), and occasionally have a tinge of folklore (*dēśī*).

From the nineteenth century to the beginning of the twentieth century, several accomplished lyricists and musicians specialized in the *jāvaḷi* form. Little biographical information is available on some of these composers who often had professions other than music. It is known that many among them drew their inspiration from the musical genius and charismatic personality of Vīṇā Dhanammāḷ, a leading vocalist and *vīṇā* exponent.

The *jāvaḷi* composers whose songs are heard in music and dance performances are: Bellary Rājā Rao, Dharmapuri Subbarāyar, Karūr Dakṣiṇāmūrti, Karūr Devuḍayya, Mutturāmaliṅga Sētupati, Paṭṭaṇam Subrahmaṇya Ayyar, Rāmnād Śrīnivāsa Ayyaṅgār, Karūr Śivarāmayya, Svāti Tirunāḷ, Taccūr Siṅgarācāryulu, Tiruppanandaḷ Paṭṭābhirāmayya, Vidyala Nārāyaṇasvāmi Naidu, and Candrasēkhara Śāstri (also known as 'Bangalore' or 'Kōlar' Chandrasēkharayya). D. Paṭṭammāḷ is a contemporary composer who has also introduced *jāvaḷi* compositions with Tamil lyrics.

Some *jāvaḷi* compositions in the dance repertoire have been ascribed to the Tañjāvūr Quartette (e.g. Cin̲n̲ayya, the eldest), but their authorship is being doubted by some dance and music historians.

kalpana svara—see *svara kalpana*

kautvam, kauthuvam, kavuthuvam (dance)

The *kautvam* is a dance which originated in South Indian temple rituals. It is in praise of different deities (*strotram* or *stuthi*), notably Vīnāyakar, Muruga, Śiva Naṭarāja, and Devī. There is a variant known as *pañcamūrti kautvam*, in 'praise of the five sacred images', to be rendered when the five main idols (*mūrti*) are placed on five separate temple chariots (*ratha*) and taken in a festive procession through the streets around the temple to which they belong. Others are in praise of great *śaivite* saints, notably Cambandhar, and Chaṇḍikeśvarar. There are other variants such as the *Navasandhi kautvam* which is in honour of the nine gods presiding over the cardinal directions of a temple. Since dance as part of temple rituals is banned under the Dēvadāsi Act of 1947, the *kautvam* cannot be seen in its original form and context any more. Some dancers like the late T. Bālasaraswati prefer not to perform *kautvam* on stage in view of this ritual context and origin in the temple dance (*dāsiyāṭṭam*), the ancient tradition from which modern *bharata nāṭyam* is derived. For this reason, the offering of flowers (*puspāñjali*) often takes the place of the *kautvam.* If included in a stage performance, *kautvam* normally precedes the dedicatory dance item (*alārippu*).

kāvaḍiccindu (concert)

Aṇṇāmalai Reḍḍiyār composed these small and lively compositions which are based on traditional Tamil pilgrim songs. They are addressed to Ṣubrahmaṇya, the popular deity of the southern hills who is also known as Muruga and Ṣanmukha.

kīrtana (devotional and congregational music; concert and dance)

Many devotional songs of this category are intended for congregational singing and therefore kept simple. The *divyanāma kīrtana* derives its name from the uttering of the sacred names of God. The opening theme (*pallavi*) is repeated as a refrain, and additional lyrics are set to a second tune (*caraṇa*). Bhadrācala Rāmadāsa and Vijayagopāla were early composers of *kīrtana*. The most popular composer of this form is Tyāgarāja whose lyrics are in Sanskrit and Telugu.

kṛti, kriti (concert and devotional music; also dance)

This is the most important and most widely used form of Karnatic music of which there are several variants. It evolved from the simple *kīrtana* and gives more scope for musical elaboration. For this reason it employs less text, and the words are generally spread over a number of notes in a theme. A typical *kṛti* has three parts: the opening *pallavi* theme in the middle range (*madhyama sthāyī*); the *pallavi* theme mostly serves as a refrain at a later stage; a second theme (*anupallavi*), which mostly reaches the upper octave (*tāra sthāyī*); the *anupallavi* is followed by a repetition of a part of the *pallavi* theme; and a concluding section (*caraṇam*). This last section of a *kṛti is* generally centred in the lower part of the middle octave and offers a rest before the *kṛti* is concluded, often with yet another rendition of the *anupallavi* tune set to new lyrics, and a repetition of the main theme of the *pallavi*. Depending on the elaboration of a *kṛti* there is a profusion of patterned variations (*saṅgati*) which were used most effectively by Tyāgarāja. Since the numerous variations composed by him also provide models for improvised music, his *kṛtis* are most suited to the needs of modern performers. (See also *rāgam tāṉam pallavi*.)

laya vinyāsa (concert)—see *taṉiyāvarttanam*

madhyama kāla, tāṉam (concert)—see *rāgam tāṉam pallavi* and *tāṉam*

maguḍi

The term *maguḍi* denotes a folk tune which is associated with the snake charmer's pipe (*maguḍi*). This bulbous instrument produces a simple melody of a few notes, produced by one of its reeds, to the accompaniment of the drone provided by a second reed. Due to the limited range of this instrument, its melody resembles rāga Punnāgavarāḷi. A *maguḍi* tune is sometimes performed by instrumentalists within the popular *tukkaḍā* group of pieces, towards the end of a concert.

mallāri (temple procession and also dance)

The *mallāri* is set to rāga Gambhīranāṭa and ādi tāla and considered a speciality of the *nāgasvaram* and *tavil* ensemble (*periya mēḷam*). The most important occasion of this type is the annual festival (*brahmōtsavam*) of a temple which lasts ten days; here the *mallāri* literally marks the 'coming out of the temple' (*kōvilpurappāḍu*) of the image of the presiding deity and is played twice daily; it thus marks the beginning of a temple procession on festive occasions.

The intricate tāla patterns of a *mallāri* involve alternating divisions of beats into four sub-units (*caturaśra jāti*) and three sub-units (*tisra jāti*); and this procedure is followed in three speeds (*trikāla*), medium tempo (*madhyama kāla*), slow tempo (*cauka kāla*), and concluded in a fast tempo (*druta kāla*). Often there are additional rhythmic complexities such as preconceived sequences (*kōrvai*) of five and seven beats, each played thrice during the concluding stage of the *mallāri*.

In a dance recital, the *mallāri* is sometimes performed as the opening item in the place of the *kautvam* (song in praise of a particular deity) or *puṣpāñjali* (flower offering).

maṅgaḷam (concert and dance)

A *maṅgaḷam*, the last item of a concert or dance recital, is set to a rāga which is regarded as being auspicious. It mostly consists of a devotional composition (*kīrtana* or *kṛti*), such as the popular *maṅgaḷam* by Tyāgarāja in rāga Saurāṣṭram ('Nīnāmarūpamulaku'). Apart from Saurāṣṭram, the most important rāgas suited to composing a *maṅgaḷam* are Madhyamāvati, Suraṭi, and Yadukulakāmbhōji (e.g. the Yadukulakāmbhōji *maṅgaḷam* by Svāti Tirunāḷ). At the very end of a concert, a brief delineation (*ālāpana*) of rāga Madhyamāvati is usually meant to induce a calm, serene state of mind after having experienced a wide range of emotions. Dhanyāsi, Ghaṇṭa, Kedāragaula, Pantuvarāḷi, Śrīrāga, and Vasanta are other rāgas that are also, but rarely, used in this context.

At the beginning and end of a dance programme or lesson, a dancer customarily performs a brief dance item known as *ādiantavandanam*. This piece which expresses respect for the earth, makes dance a form of worship, and sanctifies the dance venue which is thus converted into a temple in the minds of the performers and their audience.

niraval (concert)

The *niraval* belongs to the category of improvised music (*manodharma saṅgīta*) and its performance centres on the lyrics (*sāhitya*) of the chosen theme. This theme is often taken from the *anupallavi* section, the second theme of a *kṛti* which typically reaches from the higher notes in the middle register (*madhyama sthāyī*) to the upper register (*tāra sthāyī*). In the context of a *rāgam tāṉam pallavi* exposition, the *niraval* is the first phase of the elaboration of the chosen theme.

A *niraval* always begins with small variations which seem to be a natural extension of the original theme. Gradually the improvisation leads away from this theme. But at every given stage of a *niraval*, a musician seeks to amplify the feeling (*bhāva*) conveyed by the combination of words and rāga. This aim is reached by way of emphasis of particular syllables and by taking the original phrases into higher and lower registers. In the concluding part of a *niraval*, the density of notes is increased which gives the impression of greater speed. At the same time, notes and syllables are stretched beyond one time cycle (*āvarta*) into which the original theme was fitted. The transformation of the theme finally embraces the entire range of the chosen rāga from the highest to the lowest regions before returning to its original form.

padam, pada (devotional, dance and concert)

A *padam* is the fifth main item within the dance format introduced by the Tanjore Quartette. This form belonging to the category of narrative dance (*nṛtya*) is primarily characterized by its 'sweetness of style' (*mādhurya*). Based upon romantic themes and erotic sentiment (*śṛṅgāra*), a *padam* is rendered with simplicity of expression. The theme of a *padam* is either inspired by human love (*nāyaka nāyikā bhāva*), or in praise of a deity. In the past, the praise of a royal patron (e.g. the Nāyak kings of Tañjāvūr) was also a common theme for the lyrics of a *padam*. The *padam* resembles the *jāvaḷi* but it is an older form and should be performed in a slower tempo. Most lyrics of the later type of the *padam* are either in Tamil or Telugu. The Tamil *padam* is often addressed to Muruga (Subrahmaṇya), and its Telugu counterpart mostly to Kṛṣṇa. A *padam* is traditionally followed by a *jāvaḷi*.

The devotional songs composed by Purandara Dāsa (*dēvarnāma*) are sometimes called *pada* but do not deal with erotic themes. A number of compositions in this category deal with the childhood of Kṛṣṇa and depict motherly affection (*vātsalya*) towards the lovely and divine child in spite of his occasional mischief depicted in the popular song 'Kṛṣṇānībēganē'. The Telugu *padam* of Kṣētrajña, on the other hand, deals with the amorous episodes involving Kṛṣṇa and the cowherdesses (*gopīs*) based on the stories of the *Bhāgavata Purāṇa* (*circa* 10th c. AD).

The repertoire of the Tamil *padam* has been enriched by the following composers and lyricists (in alphabetical order): Ambujam Krishna, Irayimman Tampi, Kavikuñjara Bhārati, Mārimuttā Piḷḷai, Mūkkupullavar, Muttuttāṇḍavar, Nārāyaṇasvāmi, Pāpavināsa Mudalyār, D. Paṭṭammāḷ, Tanjore Quartette, and Vaitīśvarankoil Subbarāma Ayyar.

On similar lines, the repertoire of the Telugu *padam* has been enriched by the following composers and lyricists (in alphabetical order): Annamācārya, Ghanam Kṛṣṇa Ayyar, Kṣetrajñā, Muvvānallūr Sabhāpati Ayyar, Mysore Śeṣanna, Paccimiriyam Āḍiappayya; Subbarāmayya.

padavarṇam (dance; see also *tāṉavarṇam*)

A *padavarṇam* is the fourth main item within the dance format introduced by the Tanjore Quartette, and it treats the subject of love and devotion (*madhurabhakti* or *śṛṅgāra*) which is also the subject of the *padam* form. The *padavarṇam* is a composition mainly intended for dance, and it constitutes the most elaborate item of a dance recital. This form belongs to the category of dance items that provide scope for expression and narration (*nṛtya*). There is a similar dance *varnam* which is performed in slow tempo (*cauka kāla varṇam*). In order to give ample scope for a dancer to delineate moods through facial expression (*abhinaya*) and appropriate gestures (*mudrā*) the entire composition has lyrics (*sāhitya*). Another type of *varṇam* is mainly intended for musical purposes (*tāṉavarṇam*). A *padavarṇam* is traditionally followed by a *padam* (the fifth main item).

pallavi—see *rāgam tāṉam pallavi*

puṣpāñjali (dance)—see *kautvam, mallāri*

rāgam, rāga ālāpana—see *ālāpana*

rāgamālikā (concert and dance)

The *rāgamālikā* ('garland of rāgas') is a form of melodic variation which derives its charm from a rapid succession of rāgas within one item. It occurs in the realm of creative music (i.e. *rāga ālāpana, tāṉam, niraval, svara kalpana, ślokam, vṛttam*) and, although less commonly, in the form of a composition (e.g. *sūḷādi*). Among the two best-known *rāgamālikā* compositions are the elaborate *Mēḷarāga Mālikā Cakra* by Mahāvaidyanātha Śivan (Ayyar) and the popular *Navarāga Varṇam* ('Valaji') by Kottavāsal Veṅkaṭarāma Bhāgavatar (both 19th c.). In the field of dance music, the *śabdam* is often combined with a *rāgamālikā*.

rāgam tāṉam pallavi (concert)

A *rāgam tāṉam pallavi* performance is the most elaborate and scholarly form of creative music of South India. If rendered as a full-length concert item today, it lasts an hour or more. To some extent it resembles the North Indian *khayāl* format. The actual *pallavi* part is preceded by an elaborate *rāga ālāpana* (*rāgam*) and *tāṉam*.

The procedure of a *pallavi* can be compared to that of a *niraval*, whereas the calculations involved are more intricate and complex in a *pallavi*. Here a suitable theme is set to a line of lyrics which must be divided into two parts. The division between these parts is marked by a point (*aruḏi*) where a stressed note of the chosen rāga can be extended by a pause (*kārvai*). This theme needs to consist of a line of lyrics that can be fitted into the structure of the underlying tāla and matched with a rāga that brings out its meaning (*sāhitya bhāva*). Sometimes a *rāgamālikā* introduces several contrasting rāgas in the *tāṉam* stage, in the *niraval* stage, or both.

After the *niraval* stage, a series of abstract *svara* patterns on the lines of *svara kalpana* is performed. A process of permutations of rhythmic patterns (*tālaprastāra*) and melodic patterns (*svaraprastāra*) culminates in a conclusion where intricate strings of long and short notes (*tīrmāṇam*) are calculated and combined in such a manner that they lead back to the beginning of the original theme. The *pallavi* theme is then resumed and leads to an elaborate percussion solo (*taniyāvarttaṉam*).

The main rāga is chosen in such a manner that it evokes a feeling (*rāga bhāva*) that amplifies the meaning of the words. These words are subjected to variations in the form of shifting emphasis and lengthening. The possibilities for elaborating a *pallavi* are limitless as any rāga and tāla can be used. The choice of the point of departure within the tāla cycle (*graha* or *eḍuppu*) also gives room for a musician's imagination and ingenuity while posing a challenge to the accompanists particularly if they have not been briefed in advance. In the past, it was customary for the soloist, even an instrumentalist, to first introduce a *pallavi* by singing it before it was taken up by the ensemble. Today an advance briefing seems to be more common.

Tyāgarāja often adopted the *pallavi* technique to his *kṛti* compositions. For this purpose, he chose a short theme based on lyrics that consist of very few words in order to provide scope for variation. The opening theme of such a *kṛti*, also termed *pallavi*, is subjected to a graded series of variations (*saṅgati*) before another theme (*anupallavi*) is taken up and followed by the concluding section (*caraṇam*).

In the past, the *pallavi* was the most prominent feature of Karnatic music. Until the 1930s, a concert mainly consisted of a *rāgam tāṉam pallavi* performance preceded and followed by a few other compositions. Depending on the occasion, often a festival or marriage reception, concerts could last up to seven hours. Since several percussionists were involved, there was room for an extensive percussion solo (*taṉiyāvarttaṉam*) as part of the *rāgam tāṉam pallavi* besides one or two other solos in other parts of a performance. But eventually the *rāgam tānam pallavi* suffered a setback. Musicians specialized in this form were sometimes regarded as intellectuals, devoid of emotional sensibility (*bhāva*), and lacking in consideration for listeners who long for soulful music. Presently, thanks to serious efforts made by educational or cultural organizations like the Sruti Foundation (Chennai), there is renewed interest in scholarly performances where critics and connoisseurs (*rasika*) have the sophistication to appreciate the intricacies of a *pallavi* exposition. (See also *ālāpana, svara kalpana, taṉiyāvarttaṉam, vṛttam*.)

rāga-tāla mālikā—see *sūḷādi*

śabdam (dance)

A *śabdam* is the third main item within the dance format introduced by the Tanjore Quartette, and the first one in which the expressive aspect of dance (*abhinaya*) is introduced. Thus it falls under the category of dance with a theme or narration (*nṛtya*). The rāga of a *śabdam* is generally Kāmbhōji, sometimes followed by a series ('garland') of other rāgas (*rāgamālikā*). There are four lines of lyrics (*sāhitya*), interspersed by drum syllables (*śolkaṭṭu*). In this form, the rhythmic structure (*tāla*) comprises mostly seven beats per cycle (*miśra cāpu tāla*). A *śabdam* is traditionally followed by a *padavarṇam* (the fourth main item).

ślokam (devotional lyrics in concert, dance and drama)

The musical rendition of a Sanskrit verse (*śloka*) is referred to as *ślokam*. A similar style of singing, but based on the vernacular, is known as *vṛttam* or *viruttam* (Tamil), and *padyam* (Telugu). The *vṛttam* is believed to be the oldest form. Neither of these variants is based on any tāla cycle. The most common variant of a Sanskrit *śloka* consists of 32 syllabic instances (ceasura) in various combinations (i.e. short or long ones) which are divided into two lines of sixteen ceasuras each. Other variants comprise, for example, two or four lines of 14, 17 or 22 ceasuras, and each type is classified according to the number of syllables contained in each line (e.g. quarter).

During a musical performance, singing *ślokam* provides ample scope for melodic elaboration to highlight the appeal of both words (*sāhitya bhāva*) and melody (*rāga bhāva*); here the *ślokam* is sung in a manner that resembles the *rāga ālāpana* format. During a dance performance, on the other hand, passages resembling the *rāga ālāpana* are avoided in order to highlight the meaning of the text and its portrayal by the dancer (*abhinaya*). M.S. Subbulakshmi is credited with establishing the practice of singing a *ślokam* before taking up a composition with a related theme.

sūḷādi (didactic music)

The *sūḷādi* form is ascribed to Purandara Dāsa who developed it for the purpose of teaching difficult tāla variants. Its lyrics (*sāhitya*) consist of simple and lucid Kannaḍa verse based on episodes from popular devotional texts (*Purāṇa*). According to C.K. Shankara Narayana Rao, the Kannaḍa term *sūḷādi* denotes an 'easy way'. The original music of the *sūḷādi*, unfortunately lost and re-composed in our time by the aforementioned musician, consisted of a series of different rāgas (*rāgamālikā*) as well as different tālas (*tāla mālikā*). This musical structure is therefore referred to as *rāga-tāla mālikā*. In the *alaṁkāram*, an allied form of didactic music which is still widely used, the underlying seven tāla patterns are similarly referred to as *sūḷādi sapta tāla*.

svarajati (didactic music, concert)

This musical form resembles the dance item known as *jatisvara*. Śyāmā Śāstri has contributed some well-known pieces in this form which is otherwise less commonly heard nowadays.

svara kalpana, svaram, svara prastāra, kalpana svara (concert)

A form of improvisation, it consists of playful arrangements of notes (*svara*) which are strung together in intricate patterns (*prastāra*). The main challenge is to skilfully return to the starting note of the theme which requires that the point of departure (*eḍuppu*) of the theme must be considered within the time cycle (*tāla*). Patterns are initially short and grow into a free flow of notes (*sarva laghu*). Each round of improvisation, usually performed by soloist and accompanists in turn, leads back to the theme from which it departed. Mostly it forms part of a composition (*kṛti*) or a *pallavi* (see *rāgam tāṉam pallavi*). The *svara kalpana* also resembles a composed musical form, a playful interlude known as *ciṭṭa svara*. This resemblance is greatest if the *svara kalpana* improvisation culminates in a pre-arranged sequence (*kōrvai*), a feature popularized by Kāñcīpuram Naina Piḷḷai and refiṉed by the Ālattūr Brothers. Due to its intricacy, such a structured conclusion is also referred to as a 'crown' (*makuṭam*).

tāla mālikā—see *sūḷādi*

tāṉam (concert)

This form of improvised music (sometimes referred to as *madhyama kāla*) is characterized by its vigour and regular pulse, two features also associated with the *tānavarṇam* form. (See also *rāgam tāṉam pallavi*.)

A *tāṉam* constitutes an accentuated extension of an *ālāpana* exposition of a rāga. But on account of its increased tempo and different arrangement of musical notes, the *tāṉam* has an effect on listeners which is quite different from the *ālāpana*. While the latter can begin in a very slow tempo, a *tāṉam* exposition consists mostly of rhythmic patterns rendered in a medium tempo (*madhyama kāla*). In the past, the singing of *tāṉam* was practised with the help of systematic exercises known as *citta tāṉam*.

When sung, *tāṉam* involves the repetition of characteristic syllables (*anaṁta*, 'limitless', 'infinite'), a familiar concept in philosophy inspired by vedic tradition. Although some experts have expressed their disapproval of any deviations from the traditional *tāṉam* pattern, additional syllables have been introduced by vocalists like G.N. Bālasubrahmaṇyam (*nom ta tanana, ananda tahana tahanana*).

Syllables or instrumental phrases are separated, re-combined and accentuated before leading to a new note within the ascending or descending series prescribed for a rāga. Frequent repetition and variation of specific short phrases have the effect of an abstract *mantra* or prayer (*japam*) even when performed on an instrument.

The notes (*svara*) of a given rāga are covered systematically and in accordance with their scope for extension. Special attention is given to the *aṁśa svara*, the most dominant note characteristic of a rāga. Transient notes that require an embellishment to avoid dissonance (*vivādi*) with regard to other notes are treated differently from final notes (*nyāsa svara*). The conclusion of each phrase aims at such a final note and is characterized by a threefold repetition of a particular phrase. All the available tonal steps can be covered in both the ascending and descending orders of the rāga (*ārohaṇa-avarohaṇa*); but the ascending series of notes is treated more elaborately than the descending series.

In the past, performing *tāṉam* in an elaborate manner was a speciality of the *vīṇā* since this instrument produces relatively short notes that need to be combined into attractive patterns (*tāṉa*) in order to produce an aesthetic effect. The group of rāgas which is best suited to the *madhyama kāla* or *tāṉam* procedure is known as *ghana rāga*. A *tāṉam* produces its profound effect by way of systematic permutation (*prastāra*) and repetition of a few select notes and phrases in a manner which is reminiscent of the *ghanam* style of vedic chanting taught by a *ghanapāṭhigaḷ* (Tamil *ghanapāḍigaḷ*). This type of chanting serves the purpose of helping the student to memorize vedic texts through systematic permutations of all the syllables, words and sentences. For this purpose, the order of these syllables is re-arranged step by step without any reference to their meaning, with the result that long texts can later be recalled without fail, and recited with the right pronunciation and intonation.

tāṉavarṇam (didactic and concert)

This technical form of composition is generally performed at the beginning of a concert on account of its vigour and regular pulse, two qualities also associated with the *tāṉam* style in the *rāgam tāṉam pallavi* format. It is mostly set to either ādi tāla (8 beats per cycle) or aṭa tāla (14 beats per cycle). Each line of the composition (*varṇameṭṭu*) can be sung in three degrees of speed (*trikāla*), although one or two degrees of speed are regarded as being more conducive to listening pleasure during a performance. The Sanskrit word *varṇam* means colour, and this type of composition is primarily meant to present an exposition of all the 'colours' or melodic features of a rāga. The *varṇam* is thus a model of all that is aesthetically valid in a rāga in terms of intervals (*svarasthāna*), embellishments (*gamaka*), and phrases (*tāṉa*). Its counterpart in the field of classical dance is called *padavarṇam*. A *tāṉavarṇam* is only taught to a student after a course of preliminary exercises and small didactic songs (*gītam*) have been mastered.

Numerous composers have created pieces of this form from the eighteenth century to the present day. Its known history begins with a composition by Paccimiriyam Āḍiappayya entitled 'Viribōni' (Bhairavi rāga, aṭa tāla). In earlier times, this *varṇam* was perhaps also performed as a dance item (*padavarṇam*) on account of its romantic appeal: its lyrics speak to Rājagopāla (Kṛṣṇa), the deity of Maṉṉārguḍi whose company is being longed for by a pining, yet smiling lady. Today it is widely regarded as the best *varṇam* ever composed because it incorporates all the major features of the *varṇam* form and gives a full picture of rāga Bhairavi, its characteristic phrases (*sañcāra*), and ornamentation (*gamaka*).

Each step in a *tāṉavarṇam* also has a characteristic phrase of long and short notes by which the composer provides musicians with models which can be freely adopted in improvised variations (*ālāpana* and *svara kalpana*). The opening theme of the third part of a *varṇam* (*caraṇa*) is also called *ettugaḍa pallavi*; this theme alternates with several attractive series of individual notes (*ettugaḍa svara*) which grow longer towards the end of the *varṇam*; these special patterns can in fact be compared to *ciṭṭa svara* patterns although, in this particular form, they occur only in the *varṇam*.

taṉiyāvarttaṉam (percussion solo in a concert)

An elaborate percussion solo is performed as part of the main item of a Karnatic concert. A concert which is entirely dedicated to rhythm is sometimes referred to as *laya vinyāsa*, a term which is otherwise synonymous with *taṉiyāvarttaṉam*. Sometimes a long concert which includes *rāgam tāṉam pallavi* also provides scope for a second, shorter, *taṉiyāvarttaṉam*. Pudukōṭṭai Mānpūndia Piḷḷai (19th century) and Palghat Maṇi Ayyar (20th century) are credited with developing the potential of the *taṉiyāvarttaṉam* to its aesthetic and structural perfection.

A *taṉiyāvarttaṉam* is carefully developed on the basis of rhythmic patterns that occur in the musical theme (e.g. *pallavi* or *caraṇam*) from which it starts and is preceded by an elaboration of a line of a song (*niraval*) as well as a *svara kalpana* improvisation. In both these forms (*svara kalpana* and *niraval*), the soloist and his accompanists (e.g. a second vocalist, and a violinist) take turns. Besides the tempo of the entire composition and the mood conveyed by its lyrics, two key features are taken into account during all solo improvisations as well as a *taṉiyāvarttaṉam*. Firstly, the tāla pattern of the theme (e.g. ādi tāla); and secondly, the point of departure (*eḍuppu* or *graha*) of the theme within a tāla cycle. An ensemble of several experienced percussionists is usually led by the main drum (*mṛdaṅgam*) which lays the rhythmic foundation on which each additional percussion instrument (*upapakkavādya*) builds its own solo.

While taking turns and playing several individual solos, all percussionists consolidate their rhythmic contributions. Different gradations of tempo are achieved by an elaborate process of substituting the number of subdivisions (*gati* or *naḍai*) per beat (*akṣara*), known as *gatibhēda*. For example, if a *taniyāvartta̱nam* is played in ādi tāla, three (*tisra gati*), five (*khaṇḍa gati*) or more sub-units are temporarily played instead of the basic division into four sub-units (*caturaśra gati*). Permutations of this type require a sense of tempo (*kālapramāṇam*) in order to be pleasing. An increase of the basic tempo during a piece or *taniyāvartam*, on the other hand, is not admissible in Karnatic music. (Such an increase interferes with the finer aspects of rhythm and inhibits the perfect synchronization among performers.)

The next phase leading to the climax of the percussion solo is known as *kuṟaippu* ('reducing'). Here the duration of each musician's turn is shortened by specific increments (e.g. from four to two tāla cycles, and further to one cycle, half, and quarter of a cycle, and ultimately a single beat). In other words, the number of time units available during each turn decreases, and the available 'space' can be filled by different groups of percussive beats or *jati* syllables (e.g. 8 × 7 = 56 units for *miśra kuṟaippu* in ādi tāla, leaving two beats from the beginning or *samam* of the tāla cycle; followed by 4 × 7 = 28 units, etc.).

The phase immediately preceding the climax involves the simultaneous playing of all percussionists. At this stage, their play is synchronized in the form of a steady, pulsating flow of rhythmic patterns (*sarva laghu*) which involves a few variations and extends over a number of tāla cycles.

The climax of a fully-fledged *taṉiyāvarttaṉam* features a series of synchronized patterns (*mōrā*) and the triple 'Ta dhi ki na tom' sequence (*kōrvai*) in carefully calculated variations which lead back to the original theme and *eḍuppu* from where the soloist resumes his theme and concludes the piece.

Tēvāram (devotional, sometimes concert)

The Nāyanmār are the sixty-three Tamil saintly composers who are revered in all *śaivite* temples of South India and Sri Lanka. Their numerous hymns are based on melodic entities (*paṇ*) that can be compared to rāgas, but it should be remembered that the present concept of *janya rāga* and reference scales (*mēḷakartā rāga*, Tamil *pālai*) was introduced only about three centuries ago. Although it is not possible to reconstruct the original way in which these Tamil hymns were sung during the middle ages, there are efforts to restore their distinctiveness and sacredness as a form of temple music. Traditionally a preserve of hereditary exponents (*ōduvār*), *Tēvāram* is now also taught to candidates from other backgrounds.

tillānā (dance and concert)

A *tillānā* is the seventh main item of a dance recital within the dance format introduced by the Tanjore Quartette. This popular form of South Indian music and dance was originally inspired by the Hindustānā form known as *taranā* and is considered to be a 'semi-classical' item. Solmization of syllables (*jati*) is given more importance than lyrics. In addition to the *tillānās* composed by past masters, the Tanjore Quartette, Mysore Śeṣanna, Svāti Tirunāḷ, there are numerous modern compositions of this type in the dance and music repertoires. Several prominent musicians and composers of our time have contributed to an ever-growing *tillānā* repertoire: Calcutta K.S. Krishnamurthi, Lālguḍi Jayarāmaṉ, Bālamuraḷī Krishna, N. Ramani, and M.D. Rāmanāthaṉ. The attractive *tillāṉā* in rāga Dhanāśrī (similar to rāga Ābhēri), an item frequently included in both dance and music performances, has lyrics by Svāti Tirunāḷ and is, in its present form, set to music by Lālguḍi Jayarāmaṉ. A *tillānā* is traditionally followed by a *maṅgaḷam*.

Tiruppugaḻ (devotional and concert)

The *Tiruppugaḻ* is a form of composition introduced by Arunagirinātar (15th century). His lyrics are written in Tamil in which Sanskrit words are also frequently used. On account of its inherent charm and variety of metres (*saṉdam*, e.g. 16, 22, or 24 units per line), the *Tiruppugaḻ* is mostly presented to enliven the concluding part of a concert. Pudukōṭṭai Mānpūndia Piḷḷai is credited with collecting and codifying many *Tiruppugaḻ* compositions. Maṉṉārguḍi Pakkiri Piḷḷai is credited with having composed the music (tune and rhythmic *saṉdam* patterns) for numerous *Tiruppugaḻ* lyrics. Kāñcīpuram Naina Piḷḷai is also responsible for the music of many *Tiruppugaḻ* compositions, and S. Rājam for that of several others whose music had been lost. (See also *vṛttam*.)

tukkaḍā, 'tukkaḍā items' (concert)

The Tamil expression *tukkaḍā* refers to a category of 'minor' but attractive items performed in the latter part of a concert. Here 'light' or non-classical pieces, often in so-called *dēśya* (Hindustānī) rāgas, are enjoyed as 'musical titbits', as it were. This includes several small forms, such as the patriotic songs of Subrahmaṇya Bhārati (Bhāratiyar), pieces inspired by pilgrim songs (*kāvaḍiccindu*), devotional songs in Hindi (*bhajan*), a lullaby, and the snake charmer's tune (*maguḍi*). A lullaby may have a discernible rāga (e.g. rāga Nīlāmbari), but some pieces, such as pilgrim songs (*kāvaḍiccindu*), are based on simple folk tunes rather than classical rāgas. The same applies to pieces with quotations from Western dance music called 'Note' or 'English Note' (*nōṭṭusvaram*) and modern tunes.

Also to this category belong a number of compositions whose original tune (*varṇameṭṭu* or *dhātu*) is lost. Some lyrics of Purandara Dāsa (*dēvarnāma*) were re-composed in our times, sometimes anonymously, with the help of tunes borrowed from the classical repertoire or based on popular (*dēśī*) rāgas.

varṇam (didactic, dance and concert)—see *padavarṇam* and *tāṉavarṇam*

vṛttam, viruttam (devotional lyrics in concert, dance and drama)

In a musical recital, poetry (Tamil *viruttam*, Telugu *padyam*) can be either recited or sung. While the *ślokam*, a later addition to the repertoire of South Indian musicians, is based on Sanskrit verse (*śloka*), the *vṛttam* denotes vernacular poetry. Both variants, *vṛttam* and *ślokam*, are characterized by an appealing combination of words and melody, a free flow of lyrics which contrasts with the rhythmic structure of the other pieces, while neither is subject to a fixed rhythmic cycle (tāla). It should be noted here that *viruttam* also denotes certain complex metres that contain many syllables per line; such *viruttam* metres were employed by Arunagirinātar, except in his *Tiruppugal̲* lyrics, where he employs the so-called *san̲dam* metres.

If recited, a *vṛttam* closely follows the metre of its underlying poetry (Tamil or Malayālam). If rendered by way of singing, the syllables of a *vṛttam* can be stretched and distributed over groups of notes in a manner which is similar to *rāga ālāpana*. Either variant needs to be sung in accordance with the feeling of the poetry or the mood (*bhāva*) of a particular dramatic or poetic context.

Both *ślokam* and *vṛttam* can be performed as a 'garland' (*mālikā*) of different rāgas (*rāgamālikā*) whereby each new rāga is introduced by a brief *ālāpana* interlude (e.g. 'Navarasa', *rāgamālikā*, Sanskrit lyrics from *Rāmakarṇāmṛtam*, a purely devotional theme; recorded by Semmaṅguḍi Śrīnivāsa Iyer). The erotic connotation (*śṛṅgāra rasa*) of the lyrics tends to be more pronounced in a dance performance. In this context, the *rāga ālāpana* aspect is generally dispensed with in order to focus more on the emotional nuances of the chosen text (e.g. a passage from the *Kṛṣṇkarṇāmṛtam*); individual lines of the lyrics are therefore repeated several times to facilitate their detailed portrayal (*abhinaya*) by the dancer.

Dinḍukal Bhāvani is known to have pioneered the singing of *vṛttam* as part of a Karnatic concert (*kaccēri*). K.B. Sundarambaḷ is remembered as a celebrated exponent of this form.

18

Composers of South India

Note: The chapters on musicians and musical forms contain further explanations; *see also* Musical Signatures (section I, Mudrā index, section II, Composer index)

BIOGRAPHICAL NOTES IN ALPHABETICAL ORDER

Acuta Dāsa (1850–1902) was a musician, teacher and scholar (Sanskrit, Tamil) who gave up his original name, Abbai Naidu, and adopted the name Acuta Dāsa when he decided to devote his life entirely to *Advaita* philosophy. He wrote numerous Tamil lyrics that were published in 1929; although written as songs, his lyrics do not follow the tripartite *kṛti* format but have a continuous structure (*samaṣṭi caraṇa*). The tunes heard today were composed by his disciple Sathur Krishna Ayyaṅgār, Calcutta Krishnamūrthi, and K.R. Kumāraswāmy Ayyar. Many of his songs have the story of the saintly boy Prahlāda as their theme (*Prahlāda Bhakti Caritra*).

Āḍiappayya—*see* Paccimiriyam Āḍiappayya

Ālattūr Veṅkaṭēśa Ayyar (19th/20th century) composed the music (*dhātu*) for numerous songs in the Karnatic repertoire (e.g. Mīsu Kṛṣṇayya).

Ālvār (7th–9th centuries)—*see* Caṭakōpan̲

Ambujam Krishna (*circa* 1917–89) wrote the lyrics for over 600 devotional songs in several languages (Tamil, Telugu, Sanskrit, Kannaḍa, Hindi, Maṇipravāḷam). Tamil musicians and listeners are particularly fond of the musical and literary merits of lyrics written in Tamil, her mother tongue. She wrote her first lyrics, a Tamil song addressed to the goddess Mīnākṣi, in 1951 after visiting the memorial (*samādhi*) of Tyāgarāja in Tiruvayiāru. Over 150 of these songs (*kṛti, kīrtana, padam*), inspired by *Vaiṣṇava* philosophy, have been published in several volumes entitled *Gitamāla*. The music (Sanskrit *dhātu*, Tamil *meṭṭu*) for these poems was composed by several reputed musicians of our time: K.R. Kedarnathan, Madurai N. Krishnan, Madurai T.N. Seshagopalan, Musiri Subrahmaṇya Ayyar, S. Rāmanāthan, V.V. Saḍagōpan̲, Semmaṅgudi R. Śrīnivāsa Iyer. These compositions have been performed and recorded by many singers, often as main items of a concert, and choreographed by several renowned dancers.

Ananthakrishna Śarma—*see* Rallapalli Ananthakrishna Sarma

Annamācārya, Tāḷḷapāka Annamācārya (*circa* 1408–1503) was an early and prolific composer of Telugu songs (*kīrtana*). He studied philosophy, propagated a society free of caste divisions and belonged to a group known as *Tāḷḷapāka composers* of the region around Tirupati (Āndhra Pradesh). His compositions with erotic themes (*śṛṅgāra kīrtana*) prepared the ground for similar compositions (*padam*) by other composers like Kṣētrajña who specialized in this genre. Annamācārya is considered to be the father of the *kṛti* form which was further developed by Bhadrācala Rāmadās and Tyāgarāja. Annamācārya's lyrics are engraved in copper plates, still preserved in Tirupati. He also composed Sanskrit songs of the *padam* type. The original music of his songs is lost but has been re-composed by Rallapalli Ananthakrishna Śarma, Dr Śrīpada Pinakapāni and D. Pasupathi. His compositions always contain the name of the rāga to be used. Annamācārya used many rare rāgas (e.g. Pādi, Malahari, Nāmakriya, Sālaganāṭa, Thejjuji).

Aṇṇāmalai Reḍḍiyār (1865–91) introduced a musical form called *kāvaḍiccindu* derived from an earlier, more complex form of Tamil song called *cindu* (now out of usage). The first song of this simple but charming type of Tamil song was composed to ease his patron's strain during a pilgrimage to the temple of Muruga at Kazhugumalai (Kalugumalai). The lilting tunes are based on some rāgas but are less formal than classical music. The poet-composer wrote more than 300 verses, many among them being eulogies on his patron.

Arunācalakkavirayar, Arunācala Śāstri (1711 or 1712–88) belonged to the Tañjāvūr district and composed devotional songs (*kṛti*, *rāgamālikā*). His main work, the *Rāmanāṭakam*, is a Tamil version of the *Rāmāyaṇa* set to music (*kīrtana* form). The *Rāmanāṭakam* constitutes a type of South Indian opera or musical play. His compositions have been edited and published with the help of contemporary scholars and musicians, notably K.S. Nārāyaṇaswamy, Tiger Varadāchāriar, and Tañjāvūr Śaṅkara Iyer. Parts of the *Rāmanāṭakam* are still performed in dance and music recitals because of its high literary and musical quality.

Arunagirinātar (15th century) composed devotional songs in Tamil which are known as the *Tiruppugal̲* (*Tiruppugazh*). His biography is rich in legends but lacking in historical detail. The rhythmic intricacies of his countless songs continue to inspire today's musicians as they did earlier generations. Popular tales about the excesses of his early life are controversial and considered rather improbable. His lyrics express a total surrender to Muruga, the youthful deity of the South who is also known as Kārtikeya, Skanda and Ṣanmukha. Their language is described as a blend of Sanskrit and Tamil (Maṇipravāḷam) which was widely used in the fifteenth century.

No other poet-composer appears to have covered a wider range of metres. These include well-known as well as rare varieties of tāla. A typical metre used by Arunagirinātar, based on four to twenty-six syllables per line, is known as *canda* (Tamil *sandam*). Like other intricate verse metres, and with the exception of the *Tiruppugal̲*, this type of poetry is rendered in the *viruttam* (*vṛttam*) format.

Although many compositions have complicated tāla patterns there are many others whose simple elegance is popular with musicians and listeners alike. The authentic form of Arunagirinātar's music cannot be ascertained. The music for many *Tiruppugal̲* songs heard today was re-composed by Kāñcīpuram Naina Piḷḷai, and a few by S. Rājam.

Tiruppugal̲ compositions are mostly rendered in the latter part of a concert.

Bālamuralī Krishna, M. (b. 1930) has over 300 compositions to his credit (*kṛti, varṇam, tillānā*) and belongs to the musical lineage (*guruśisya paramparā*) of Mānambucāvaḍi Veṅkaṭa Subbayyar, a direct disciple of Tyāgarāja. He is an equally reputed vocalist and instrumentalist (violin and viola) and has introduced a number of unconventional rāgas and tālas. In addition, he has sung and composed the music of numerous films, TV and radio features.

Bālusvāmi Dīkṣitar (violin, composer; 1786–1859), a brother of Muttusvāmi Dīkṣitar, is credited with introducing the violin in Karnatic music; collaborated with Kadigai Mūkkupullavar.

Bangalore Chandrasēkharayya (Kōlar Chandrasēkharayya, Candrasēkhara Śāstri, *jāvaḷi*)—*see* jāvaḷi.

Bhadrācala Rāmadās (?1620–88; ?1622–80) (Plate 1) laid the foundation for the development of the *kṛti* form. Unlike the devotional song known as *kīrtana*, the more developed *kṛti* has an intermediate section (*anupallavi*) between the opening theme (*pallavi*) and the concluding section (*caraṇa*). Most of his lyrics, a mixture of Telugu and Sanskrit, are about Rāma, his chosen deity (*iṣṭadevatā*), besides Sītā and Kṛṣṇa. Some of his songs are of a didactic nature, others have autobiographical references. About 60 songs are available now. Tyāgarāja, the pioneer of the modern *kṛti* form, regarded Rāmadās as his chief inspiration and paid homage to him in four of his songs. According to biographers, he was a Telugu and Sanskrit scholar. His devotion to Rāma moved him to spend all his money on charitable works and even state funds of the Muslim ruler, the Nawab of Golconda (Hyderabad), for the restoration of the Rāma temple of Bhadrācalam. The story of his life abounds in miraculous events relating to the time when he suffered hardship and imprisonment. The musical authenticity of songs ascribed to Bhadrācala Rāmadās is doubtful in view of the absence of a personal tradition or detailed notation. His songs have been re-created by musicians of our time who are drawn to his lyrics.

Bhāgavatar—*see* Harikēsanallūr Mutthiah Bhāgavatar, Kōṭṭavāsal Veṅkaṭarāma Bhāgavatar, Parameśvara Bhāgavatar

Bhārati—*see* Gopālakṛṣṇa Bhārati, Kavikuñjara Bhārati, and Subrahmaṇya Bhārati

Candrasēkhara Śāstri (Kōlar Chandrasēkharayya, Bangalore Chandrasēkharayya)—*see* jāvaḷi (Musical Forms)

Caṭakōpan̲ (approximately AD 880–930) is considered to be the greatest among the twelve *Vaiṣṇava* poets remembered as Āl̲vār (literally 'those immersed in god'). He is also known as Nammāl̲vār ('our own saint') and Māran̲. Among his four works, the most important one is titled *Tiruvāymol̲i* (literally 'holy word of mouth') and consists of 1102 verses. His poetry is loved for its variety of moods, intricacy and philosophical depth. The Tamil hymns of the Āḻvār are collectively known as *Prabandham* or *Divyaprabandham*. About 4000 stanzas were composed in metres that are also found in the *Tēvāram* hymns of the *Śaivite* Nāyanmār saints, contemporaries of the Āḻvār poets. There can be no doubt that certain parts of the *Divyaprabandham* literature, known as *isaippa*, were originally meant to be sung (Tamil *isai* = music; [-p-] *-pa* for *pāṭṭu* = sing); but unlike the *Tēvāram* hymns, the *Prabandham* hymns are no longer sung to specific modes (*paṇ, rāga*) and time cycles (*tāla*), probably since troupes led by Malik Kafur raided Śrīraṅgam around AD 1327; instead of being sung, they are recited in a manner which is reminiscent of the Vedas.

A unique form of devotional dance is still being performed in Śrīraṅgam as part of the temple service and during festivals along with the traditional music that belongs to it. This dance is practised only by male dancers belonging to a hereditary tradition, and it is confined to the temple premises. Both the *Prabandham* and the ritualistic dance manifest the basic *Vaiṣṇava* precept that god (Viṣṇu) alone is to be regarded as male (*puruṣa*) while every devotee (*bhakta*), male and female alike, is seen as reaching out for *His* grace from a perspective of feminine aspiration (*strībhāva*). This relationship, described in terms of *nāyaka nāyikā bhāva*, is comparable to the love of a male lover (*nāyaka*) towards his beloved (*nāyikā*). On account of its recognition and sublimation of erotic feeling (*śṛṅgāra bhāva*), this concept has inspired poetry, sculpture, music and dance since the times when Āḻvār lyrics were first composed, collected and propagated more than a millennium ago.

Ciṉṉa Dēvuḍu Ayyar—*see* Karūr Dēvuḍayya

Ciṉṉa Siṅgarācāryulu—*see* Taccūr Siṅgarācāryulu

Ciṉṉayya, Ciṉṉiah (b. 1803) was the eldest brother of the Tañjāvūr Quartette to whom some pieces in the dance repertoire (*jāvaḷi*) are ascribed; this assumption has, however, been subjected to doubt by scholars.

Dāsa—*see* Acuta Dāsa, Haridāsa, Kanaka Dāsa, Purandara Dāsa

Dēvuḍayya or **Dēvuḍu Ayyar**—*see* Karūr Dēvuḍayya

Dharmapuri Subbarāyar (b. 1864) was a composer of *jāvaḷi*.

Dīkṣitar—*see* Muttusvāmi Dīkṣitar, Rāmasvāmi Dīkṣitar, Subbarāma Dīkṣitar

Doraisvāmi Ayyar—*see* Pallavi Doraisvāmi Ayyar

Duraisāmi Ayyar—*see* Puliyūr Duraisāmi Ayyar

Fiddle Ponnusvāmi—*see* Mutialpet Ponnusvāmi

Ghanam Kṛṣṇa Ayyar (1790–1854) was a disciple of Paccimiriyam Āḍiappayya and a musical celebrity to whom patronage was liberally extended. Under the influence of Bobbili Kēśavayya, he specialized in singing *ghanam*, a style characterized by fast *ālāpana* exposition and reminiscent of *tāṉam*. His Tamil compositions (*padam*) are still held in high esteem because of their musical quality (*bhāva*) and because they lend themselves to expressive dance (*abhinaya*). He is reputed to have handled erotic themes (*śṛṅgāra bhāva*) in a subtle manner.

Gopāla Ayyar—*see* Pallavi Gopāla Ayyar

Gopālakṛṣṇa Bhārati (1810 or 1811–81) composed the musical play *Nandanār Caritra*. This work was popularized through the *harikathā kālakṣepa* (musical discourses) of Tañjāvūr Krisna Bhāgavatar. Gopālakṛṣṇa Bhārati was a Tamil scholar who studied Hindustānī music and was acquainted with the music of the 'Trinity'. He was an associate of writer-composer Vēdanāyakam Pillai. Orphaned early in life, he first worked as a temple cook. Most of his life he spent at Māyavaram near Tañjāvūr. The temple of Chidambaram was his chief inspiration. Tiger Varadāchāriar, assisted by Tañjāvūr Śaṅkara Iyer, was responsible for preserving authentic versions of his compositions.

Govinda Rao, T.K. (b. 1929) wrote several books on music and music education. This renowned vocalist, teacher and scholar is a disciple of Musiri Subrahmaṇya Ayyar, one of the important musicians of this century. Among his many contributions to music are several compositions of his own (e.g. *tāṉavarṇam*). He also composed music for the lyrics of Periasāmi Thooraṉ.

Govindasamayya (17th century) is regarded as the earliest composer of the *tāṉavarṇam* form of South Indian music. Together with Paccimiriyam Āḍiappayya, he is referred to as the 'pathfinder' of this form (*Tāṉavarṇa Mārgadarśī*).

Gurumūrti—*see* Paidāla Gurumūrti Śāstrī

Haridāsa (15th century) denotes a movement whose members called themselves God's (*Hari*) servants (*dāsa*). They were united by the belief that a supreme God (Viṣṇu) is personally involved with mankind. As mendicant musicians they were respected for their learning, and popular for their attractive presentation of pious stories and songs. They specialized in legends of Kṛṣṇa, the embodiment of righteousness, grace, valour, and compassion which served to illustrate God's mercy. A commitment to social reforms was combined with a psychology of liberation from materialism (*saṁsāra*) and selfishness. Singing the name of the Lord (*dēvarnāma*) serves to focus the individual's mind on a higher purpose of being. A combination of song and poetry (*pada*) was therefore the chief medium for propagating their message to all sections of society. A typical saint-singer (*bhāgavatar*) wore a turban and had a pot suspended from his body for collecting food alms. With his right hand he played a small string instrument, a drone (*tambūrā*), and with his left hand a pair of wooden clappers (*cipla*) for rhythm. In this manner he could accompany his own singing and lead his followers into a state of musical and mystical intoxication.

Originating in Vijayanagar (Hampi), this *Vaiṣṇava* movement (i.e. devoted to Viṣṇu) employed the local language (Kannaḍa or Canarese) rather than 'elitist' Sanskrit. At the peak of Muslim expansion on the Indian subcontinent the Haridāsa movement represented the common ground shared by mystics belonging to Islam (*Sūfism*) and Hinduism (*Vedānta*). This dialogue had already for several centuries been maintained by wandering saints and ascetics (*sādhu, sannyāsī* and *sūfi*) who dared to question the prevailing values and beliefs of their respective societies. Purandara Dāsa, the leader of the Haridāsa movement who was a composer in his own right, facilitated the rapid spread of its ideas through music. For this purpose he developed a musical syllabus (*abhyāsa gānam*). Even after the defeat and fragmentation of the Vijayanagar empire, the Haridāsa movement continued to influence numerous composers, musicians and poets over a period of five centuries. Tyāgarāja is the best-known exponent of this tradition.

Harikēsanallūr Mutthiah Bhāgavatar (1877–1945) composed hundreds of songs (*kṛti*, *rāgamālikā*, *tānavarṇam*, *tillānā*) which are distinguished by the occurrence of rare rāgas. Sanskrit, Tamil, Telugu and Kannaḍa are the languages of his lyrics which were partly composed with the help of reputed experts in these languages. He had an impressive personal appearance and performed his musical discourses (*harikathā kālakṣepa*) in grand style. For this purpose he also composed narrative songs (*daru*). He was a singer and an accomplished instrumentalist (*gōṭṭuvādyam* and *mṛdaṅgam*). Among his patrons were the rulers of Mysore and Travancore (Kerala). Assisted by H.M. Vaidyalingam, his adopted son, he re-composed, published and taught the compositions of Svāti Tirunāḷ and Irayimman̲ Tampi. Mutthiah Bhāgavatar is believed to have endowed many compositions of both composers, including a popular lullaby (*Ōman̲a tiṅgaḷ*), with their present shape after collecting musical fragments from various local musicians.

Mutthiah Bhāgavatar was the first principal of the Trivandrum Music College and had numerous disciples who popularized his own compositions. He was associated with the music conferences organized by Abraham Paṇḍitar in Tañjāvūr and wrote a musicological work (*Saṅgīta Kālpadruma*). Budalūr Krishnamūrti Śāstrigaḷ, Madurai Maṇi Ayyar, Nārāyaṇa Ayyaṅgār, and Paṭṭamaḍai S. Krishnan̲ were among his disciples.

Irayimman̲ Tampi (1782–1856) was a scholar and poet at the court of Travancore and wrote in Sanskrit, Malayālam and Maṇipravāḷam. Like Svāti Tirunāḷ, he used the signature (*mudrā*) *Padmanābha* which makes it difficult to establish the authorship of some compositions. He composed a variety of songs (*padavarṇam*, *tānavarṇam*, *kṛti* and *padam*), often inspired by the folk music of his native Kerala where his music continues to be popular. His famous lullaby 'Ōmaṇa tiṅgaḷ kiḍavō' (rāga Nīlāmbari, *tisra naḍai* ādi tāla) was sung to Svāti Tirunāḷ when he was a child. In this song the mother compares the loveliness of her child to that of the moon, the sweet nectar of a flower, the melody sung by a cuckoo, and the grace of a peacock; she even asks herself whether the perfection of her boy could mean that he is an incarnation of Viṣṇu.

Jayacāmarājā—*see* Mysore Jayacāmarāja Wodeyar

Jayadeva (12th century) (Plate 2) inspired generations of other poets, dancers and musicians with the *Gītagovinda,* his poetic masterpiece (*mahākāvya*) written in Sanskrit. A court poet of king Lakṣmaṇa Sena, Jayadeva either hailed from a village in Bengal (Kindavila) or another one with a similar name in Orissa (Kenduli or Kindubilvam). The love of Rādhā for Kṛṣṇa is the dominant sentiment (*śṛṅgāra*) of the *Gītagovinda.* Its universal appeal derives from the congenial way Jayadeva depicts the longing of the human soul (represented by Rādhā) for the Divine (Kṛṣṇa) in terms of love (*nāyaka nāyikā bhāva*) dramatized through Rādhā's suffering in separation, and jealousy inflamed by Kṛṣṇa's involvement with the other cowherdesses (*gopī*). The erotic symbolism adopted by Jayadeva seeks to make the underlying philosophical message of *Vaiṣṇava* philosophy, the longing of the human soul (*jīvātman*) for the highest divine reality (*parabrahman*), understandable for all human beings. For this reason the theme of Rādhā and Kṛṣṇa has been adopted by many later composers (e.g. Kṣētrajña and Nārāyaṇa Tīrtha). The 24 songs of the *Gītagovinda* have 8 verses (*caraṇa*) each, hence the term *aṣṭapadi*. The *Gītagovinda* is divided into 12 sections (*sarga*). As in the case of so many medieval compositions, the original music of the *Gītagovinda* has been irretrievably lost. Composers of our times, both in North and South India, have set Jayadeva's lyrics to Karnatic rāgas which accompany dance performances in the *Odissi* and *bharata nāṭyam* styles as well as a dance-drama choreographed and performed at Kalākshētra. The *aṣṭapadi* compositions are sung as part of the indigenous temple music of Kerala (*Sōpānam*) from where they have found their way into the repertoire of Karnatic music.

Jayarāmaṉ—*see* Lālguḍi Jayarāmaṉ

Kadigai Mūkkupullavar (19th century) was an outstanding composer of Tamil songs (*padam*); along with Kadigai Nāmaśivaya, he produced pieces which have become popular as items in dance programmes; both collaborated with Bālusvāmi Dīkṣitar, the brother of Muttusvāmi Dīkṣitar and pioneer violinist.

Kadigai Nāmaśivaya—*see* Mūkkupullavar

Kanaka Dāsa (16th century) is remembered for his charming Kannaḍa songs (*pada*) which are heard in music and dance recitals (e.g. *Kṛṣṇānībegani*, Yamunā Kalyāṇi rāga, miśra cāpu tāla). He belonged to Karṇāṭaka, propagated social reforms and spent the latter part of his life in Tirupati.

Karūr Dēvuḍayya, Ciṉṉa Dēvuḍu Ayyar (1861–1901) was a composer and violinist. He wrote classical music (*kṛti*, *kīrtana* and *tāṉavarṇam*) as well as hybrid compositions ('*nōṭṭusvaram*' or 'English Note') with elements borrowed from English band music. The lyrics of his compositions were written by Karūr Dakṣiṇāmūrti Śāstrī. His teacher was Nemam Subrahmaṇya, a direct disciple of Tyāgarāja.

Kavikuñjara Bhārati (1810–96) wrote a number of Tamil songs (*kṛti*, *padam*). The major works of this reputed poet and composer are known as *Skānda Purāṇa Kīrtana*, *Perinba Kīrtanaigal* and *Aḻagar Kuravañji*. He was the grandfather of Kōtīsvara Ayyar, one of the foremost composers of the twentieth century. Kōtīsvara Bhārati was his personal name. Kavikuñjaram ('poet of elephant-like stature') is a title conferred on him which he used as his *mudrā* (signature).

Kōlar Chandrasēkharayya (Candrasēkhara Sāstri, Bangalore Chandrasēkharayya)—*see* jāvaḷi (Musical Forms)

Kōtīsvara Ayyar (1870–1936) was a disciple of Rāmnād ('Pūcci') Śrīnivāsa Ayyaṅgar, Paṭṭaṇam Subrahmaṇya Ayyar, and a grandson of Kavikuñjara Bhārati, the nineteenth-century poet and composer. Kōtīsvara Ayyar wrote a series of Tamil compositions (*kṛti*) set to the 72 scales of South Indian music (*mēlakarta rāga*) which was recorded by Karnatic vocalist S. Rājam in 1991. The only precedent for this unique achievement consists of the *rāgamālikā* by Mahāvaidyanātha Śivan which is a single long composition rather than a series of individual compositions. Many of the more than 200 pieces composed by Kōtīsvara Ayyar are popular in today's concert repertoire.

Kōṭṭavāsal Veṅkaṭarāma Bhāgavatar (19th century) wrote a number of important technical pieces (*tānavarṇam*). A *varṇam* entitled *Valaji* is his most popular composition; it presents a concise outline for nine different rāgas (*Navarāgamālikā*). As a disciple of Vīṇā Kuppayyar he belonged to the lineage (*paramparā*) of Tyāgarāja. Some of his compositions are perhaps wrongly ascribed to Paṭṭaṇam Subrahmaṇya Ayyar who also used the *mudrā* (signature) *Veṅkaṭēśa*.

Kṛṣṇa Ayyar—*see* Ambujam Krishna, Ghanam Kṛṣṇa Ayyar, Kundrakudi Kṛṣṇa Ayyar, Mīsu Kṛṣṇa Ayyar

Krishnamūrthy Bhāgavatar (Nīdamaṅgaḷam)—*see* Ūttukkāḍu Veṅkaṭa Subba Ayyar

Kṛṣṇasvāmi—*see* Wālājapet Kṛṣṇasvāmi Bhāgavatar

Kṣētrajña, Kṣētrayya (17th century) (Plate 3) restored the *padam* form, established by Annamācārya, to its former glory. His Telugu songs are of a type known as *śṛṅgāra pada,* meaning 'devotional songs based on the sentiment of love'. Through his treatment of erotic symbolism (*nāyaka nāyikā bhāva*) Kṣētrajña set the standards for songs and poetry based on *madhura bhakti*, a form of personal devotion centred upon sweet and ecstatic associations evoked by the Divine. In the absence of a direct personal tradition only his lyrics are available in their authentic form while the original music is lost. Kṣētrajña is said to have been a scholar, poet and a wandering minstrel who visited many royal courts and received lavish patronage for having composed hundreds of songs. After accepting invitations from Tirumala Nāyak, the ruler of Madurai and from Vijayarāghava Nāyak of Tañjāvūr, he moved to Golconda (Hyderabad, Āndhra Pradesh). There he was patronized by the Nawab, a Muslim ruler. He visited some twenty shrines all over South India and Sri Lanka, hence his name Kṣētrajña, literally 'one who visits holy places' (*kṣētra*). Many songs are composed in praise of the presiding deities of those places (*see also* Muttuttāṇḍavar).

Kundrakudi Kṛṣṇa Ayyar (1816–89) composed technical and dance pieces (*tāṉavarṇam* and *padavarṇam*) and is credited with introducing the *rāgamālikā*, the combinations of several rāgas, in the *pallavi* format (*rāgam tānam pallavi*). A flamboyant singer and instrumentalist (*jalataraṅgam*), he specialized in intricate expositions of a given theme (*pallavi*) which enabled him to challenge other master musicians and composers such as Mahāvaidyanātha Ayyar.

Kuñjara Bhārati—*see* Kavikuñjara Bhārati

Kuṉṉakuḍi Veṅkaṭarāma Ayyar (1909–78) was a disciple of his father, Kuṉṉakuḍi Subba Ayyar, Kāraikkuḍi Subbarāma Ayyar, and Maḻavai Subbarāma Bhāgavatar. He composed pieces for dance which are also heard in music concerts, and set several songs of Vēdanāyakam Piḷḷai to music. Rajēswari Padmanābhan̲ (*vīṇā*) has recorded his *Mōhalāhiri*, a dance piece (*padavarṇam*, Kāpi rāga, ādi tāla).

Kuppayyar—*see* Vīṇā Kuppayyar

Kuppusvāmi Ayyar (*circa* 19th century) is believed to have been a court musician during the reign of Amarasiṁha (1787–98) and that of Śarabhōjī II (Serfōjī, 1798–1832), a scholar and patron. He composed devotional songs (*kīrtana*) based on erotic symbolism (*śṛṅgāra*).

Lālguḍi Jayarāman̲ (b. 1930) composed numerous pieces which are equally popular among musicians and dancers (*jatisvaram*, *varṇam*, *kṛti*, *tillānā* and orchestral compositions). He belongs to the tradition (*paramparā*) of Tyāgarāja and has been a leading Karnatic violinist and teacher for several decades. In the concert repertoire, there are two original rāgas which were introduced by him: (1) Jayadīp, a *janya rāga* of the 14th *mēḷa* Vakulābharaṇam; its ascending order (*ārohaṇa*) is: sa, ma, pa, ni, sa; sa, ni, dha, ma, pa, ga, sa; and (2) Haṁsarūpini, a *janya rāga* of the 28th *mēḷa* Harikāmbhōji; its ascending order of notes (*ārohaṇa*) corresponds to that of rāga Mōhanam; and its descending order (*avarohaṇa*) to that of rāga Madhyamāvati.

Mahāvaidyanātha Śivan̲, Mahāvaidyanātha Ayyar (1844–93) composed the monumental *mēḷa rāga mālikā cakra*, his major contribution to Karnatic music. This composition covers all the 72 scales (*mēḷakartā*) of Karnatic music and has been recorded by eminent Karnatic vocalist M.S. Subbulakshmi. He also composed the variations (*saṅgati*) for several *kṛti* by Muttusvāmi Dīkṣitar besides contributions to the repertoire of dance music (*padavarṇam*). A vocalist, composer, and music and Sanskrit scholar, he studied under Mānambucāvaḍi Veṅkaṭa Subbayyar, a direct disciple of Tyāgarāja (*see also* Kōtīsvara Ayyar).

Mānambucāvaḍi Veṅkaṭa Subbayyar (19th century) was a reputed composer (*kṛti*, *rāgamālikā*, *tānavarṇam*), scholar of Telugu and Sanskrit, and a competent violin player. A relative and direct disciple of Tyāgarāja, he had several important musicians and composers, notably Mahāvaidyanātha Śivan and Paṭṭaṇam Subrahmaṇya Ayyar, among his disciples. His *mudrā* (signature) is *Veṅkaṭēśa*, the same as that of Paṭṭaṇam Subrahmaṇya Ayyar which has caused some confusion regarding the authorship of some compositions (*kṛti*).

Māran̲—*see* Caṭakōpan̲

Mārgadarśī Śēṣayyaṅgār, Śēṣa Ayyaṅgār (early 18th century) composed devotional songs (*kṛti*), a form which he helped to bring to perfection through his musical contribution. Only about 75 of his numerous Sanskrit compositions are believed to have survived and are used for congregational singing (*bhajana*). Two specimens of his compositions have been published in *Oriental Music in European Notation* by A.M.C. Mudalyār in 1893 ('Pāhi Śeṣa' in Ānandabhairavi rāga and tisra laghu tāla, 6 counts; and 'Śrīraṅgaṣāyinam' in Dhanyāsi rāga and jhampa tāla, 5 counts) . He was a pioneer of South Indian music whose honorific indicates that he 'paved the way' (*mārgadarśī*) for the Trinity among whom Tyāgarāja and Muttusvāmi Dīkṣitar are thought to have been influenced by his compositional techniques. Svāti Tirunāḷ is also known to have used his compositions as models. His signature (*mudrā*) is *Kosala*, derived from the ancient name of the land where Śeṣayyaṅgār had stayed and taken an interest in Hindustānī music. Ayodhya was the ancient capital of Kosala from where Rāma had ruled according to the *Rāmāyaṇa*. He was a devotee of Viṣṇu Raṅganātha of Śrīraṅgam temple where his Sanskrit compositions are sung on special occasions.

Mārimuttā Piḷḷai (1712–87) was a composer of Tamil songs (*padam*) which are famous for being at once philosophical and imaginative, devotional and even sarcastic in character; on account of their suggestiveness, they lend themselves to dance (*abhinaya*).

Mīsu Kṛṣṇa Ayyar, Kṛṣṇayyar, Krishna Iyer (1872–1940) composed the lyrics for a number of devotional songs (*kṛti*) for which tunes and solfa passages (*ciṭṭasvaram*) were provided by Ālattūr Veṅkaṭēśa Ayyar.

Mudalyār—*see* Pāpavināsa Mudalyār; *see also* Mārgadarśī Śeṣayyaṅgār and Muttusvāmi Dīkṣitar

Mūkkupullavar—*see* Kadigai Mūkkupullavar

Mūlaivīṭṭu Raṅgasvāmi, Mūlavattai Raṅgasvāmi, Raṅgasvāmi Naṭṭuvaṉar (19th century) was an outstanding musician whose prefixed name, Mūlaivīṭṭu, means 'corner-house'. He also wrote technical compositions (*tāṉavarṇam*) and dance music (*padavarṇam*). His delightful *tāṉavarṇam*, 'Cālamēla' (rāga Nāṭakurañji, ādi tāla) is a popular concert item. Another *tāṉavarṇam* by this composer, 'Vanajākśi' (rāga Kalyāṇi, aṭa tāla), is often wrongly ascribed to Pallavi Gopāla Ayyar. Further biographical details are unavailable.

Musiri Subrahmaṇya Ayyar (1889–1975) was a vocalist and teacher who composed music for the lyrics of Ambujam Krishna; *see also* T.K. Govinda Rao.

Mutialpet Ponnusvāmi (late 19th to early 20th century) was a violinist popularly referred to as *Fiddle Ponnusvāmi*. Among other compositions he authored the *tāṉa-varṇam* 'Taruni ninnubāsi' (Kāmbhōji rāga, ādi tāla). He was an associate of Tiruvōtriyūr Tyāgayyar and belonged to the circle around Vīṇā Dhanammāḷ who inspired numerous compositions.

Mutthiah Bhāgavatar—*see* Harikēsanallūr Mutthiah Bhāgavatar

Mutturāmaliṅga Sētupati (died 1873) was a ruler of Rāmanātapuram, scholar, patron of music, and a composer in Tamil and Telugu (*kṛti*, *padavarṇam*, *tillānā*, *bhajana*, *padam*, and *jāvaḷi*).

Muttusvāmi Dīkṣitar (1775–1835) (Plate 4) wrote around 400 compositions, mainly of the *kṛti* type. Besides several Telugu lyrics, he mainly used Sanskrit in his compositions. His father Rāmasvāmi Dīkṣitar was himself a distinguished musician, composer as well as administrator of music at Tiruvārūr. His teacher (*guru*) was a mystic known as Cidambaranātha Yogi who took him to Vārāṇasī (Benares). There he remained for five years and was exposed to the slow movement characteristic of the orthodox *dhrupad* (*dhrūvapada*) style of North Indian temple music. This influence is reflected in many of his slow compositions which are quite distinct from those of his contemporaries. Muttusvāmi Dīkṣitar is revered as one of the Trinity of South Indian composers but there is no evidence that Muttusvāmi Dīkṣitar and Tyāgarāja ever met one another. The music and Sanskrit poetry of Māgadarśī Śeṣayyaṅgār are also believed to have greatly influenced Muttusvāmi Dīkṣitar and his contemporaries, notably Tyāgarāja and Svāti Tirunāḷ.

The compositions of Muttusvāmi Dīkṣitar are mostly in praise of various Hindu deities whose temples he visited all over the South. A deeply religious person, he was initiated early into a cult dedicated to the feminine aspect of the Divine (*Śrīvidyā*). He was also trained as a *vīṇā* player (*vaiṇika*) and developed an original style of composition which is characterized by slow yet majestic pace and rich ornamentation tempered by a feeling of inner stillness (*śānta rasa*). His compositions thus constitute an ideal synthesis of vocal and instrumental styles and continue to inspire South India's musical minds to the present day.

Muttusvāmi Dīkṣitar had a special liking for Māḷavagauḷa rāga (i.e. the modern *mēḷakartā rāga* Māyāmāḷavagauḷa) as well as several rāgas derived from it (*janya rāga*) and composed over 40 songs in such rāgas. His first song ('Śrīnāthādiguruguho jayati', ādi tāla) is composed in Māḷavagauḷa rāga. He is perceived as a composer who revived some features of ancient music and passed them on to posterity. In this sense he was more conservative than Tyāgarāja who already followed the new scale and rāga (*mēḷa* and *janya*) system of Govindācāri. Muttusvāmi Dīkṣitar, on the other hand, retained the older nomenclature of Veṅkaṭamakhi to whose tradition he and his father Rāmasvāmi Dīkṣitar belonged. This system does not require seven notes (*sampūrṇa*) and is therefore known as *asampūrṇa paddhati*.

In many of his compositions (*kṛti*), the music (*dhātu*) is not repeated at all. The special variant of the *kṛti* form employed by him is known as *samaṣṭi caraṇa kṛti*. This variant is characterized by the absence of a middle theme (*anupallavi*), otherwise an integral part of the modern *kṛti* form. Here only two main elements occur, namely the opening theme (*pallavi*) and an 'aggregate'(*samaṣṭi*) *caraṇa* section.

In Madras, Muttusvāmi Dīkṣitar heard Western music played by the military and dance bands which inspired him to write Sanskrit lyrics, some addressed to Sarasvatī, the consort of Brahmā and goddess of wisdom, for tunes such as *God Save the King*, the English anthem. These pieces are known as *nōṭṭusvara sāhitya* or 'quasi-European airs'. Out of the 40 compositions of this type which he wrote in his youth, 36 are preserved in notation. Many of these were used as didactic pieces by music teachers of the late nineteenth and early twentieth century. Several of these and other compositions by Muttusvāmi Dīkṣitar have been published by A.M.C. Mudalyār in 1893 (*Oriental Music in European Notation*) with lyrics, transcriptions and ornamentation. This work includes a composition in 14 different rāgas (*rāgamālikā*) with an indication of each rāga in the lyrics (*raga mudrā*).

Muttusvāmi Dīkṣitar was the teacher of four brothers, known as the Tañjāvūr Quartette who spread his musical heritage all over South India. There are some rāgas which he alone has employed (e.g. Navaratnavilāsam, Mohananāṭa, Māhuri, and Kumbhakriya) although in some instances (e.g. a composition in rāga

Nāsikabhuṣani) it is presumed that he is not the real author and other composers appropriated his *mudrā* (signature) *Guruguha*. His brother Bālusvāmi Dīkṣitar was the first Karnatic musician to specialize in violin play while Vaḍivēlu of the Tañjāvūr Quartette, his disciple, is credited with gaining wide acceptance for the violin for use in classical South Indian music. (*See also* Mahāvaidyanātha Śivan, Subbarāma Dīkṣitar.)

Muttuttāṇḍavar (?16th century) belonged to a family of dancers, and *nāgasvaram* and *tavil* players (*mēḷakkārar*) at Sīrgāḷi. An exponent of *Śaiva Siddhānta* philosophy, he is said to have written several hundred compositions with Tamil lyrics on Śiva Naṭarāja of Chidambaram whose devotee he was. Some of his songs have been re-composed and popularized by Tirupāmburam N. Swāminātha Piḷḷai. The lyrics of 60 devotional songs (*kīrtana, kṛti*), inspired by puranic legends, and 25 songs with erotic lyrics (*padam*), have been published. His treatment of the theme of love (*śṛṅgāra*) is rated as being of a dignified nature (*gaurava śṛṅgāra*). Some writers even credit him with two major contributions, based on Tamil modes (*paṇ*) rather than rāga: firstly, introducing the Tamil *padam*; and secondly, pioneering the modern tripartite *kṛti* form characterized by sparse lyrics (*sāhitya*).

Muvvānallūr Sabhāpati Ayyar, Muvvalūr Sabhāpati (early 19th century) wrote Telugu songs (*padam*) which are still performed in dance recitals, and narrative songs (*nirūpaṇam*) for musical discourses (*harikathā kālakṣepa*). A dancer at the court of Tañjāvūr, he was a disciple of Muttusvāmi Dīkṣitar and an admirer of Kṣētrajña.

Mysore Jayacāmarāja Wodeyar Mahārājā (1919–74) was a patron of the arts, musician, and a composer in his own right. A disciple of Mysore Vāsudēvācāria, he wrote 94 songs, some noted for their grandeur of lyrics and melodic beauty. His choice of rāgas comprised rare and popular ones to which he added his own creations. The last ruler of Mysore State (since 1940) also attracted other leading musicians of that period to his court, namely Tiger Varadāchāriar and Ariyakkuḍi Rāmānuja Ayyaṅgār.

Mysore Sadāśiva Rao, Rāyār (19th century) composed a variety of devotional and technical pieces (*kīrtana, kṛti, svarajati, tāṉavarṇam*) and music for dance (*padavarṇam, tillānā*). He was a disciple of Wālājapet Veṅkaṭarāmaṇa Bhāgavatar and became a court musician (*samasthāna vidvān*) at Mysore. Bīḍaram Krishnappā is credited with popularizing his compositions beyond Mysore. Vīṇā (Mysore) Śeṣanna and Vīṇā Subbanna were his distinguished disciples.

Mysore Śeṣanna, Vīṇā Śeṣanna (1850–1926) wrote 53 compositions belonging to various forms (*svarajati*, *varṇam*, *kṛti*, *padam* and *tillānā*). He was a descendant of composer Paccimiriyam Ādiappayya and shaped the Mysore style of *vīṇā* play. Like his teacher, Mysore Sadāśiva Rao, he became a court musician (*vaiṇika*) attached to the royal palace of Mysore.

Mysore Vāsudēvācāria (1865–1961) composed about 200 pieces in Telugu and Sanskrit (*kṛti*), and the music for four parts out of Rukmini Devi's series of six dance-dramas on the theme of the *Rāmāyaṇa*: Sītāsvayamvaram, Rāmavanaga-manam, Pāḍukāpaṭṭābhiṣekam, and Śabarimokṣam. (*See also* S. Rājāram.) A disciple of Paṭṭaṇam Subrahmaṇya Ayyar, he is reckoned among the most influential Karnatic musicians and composers of the twentieth century. Mysore Jayacāmarāja Wodeyar, a composer in his own right, was among his prominent disciples. As principal of Kalākshētra he organized the *Saṅgīta Sirōmaṇi* course.

Nāmasivaya Pullavar—*see* Kadigai Mūkkupullavar

Nammālvār—*see* Caṭokōpan

Narasayyā—*see* Śaṭkāla Narasayyā

Narasimhacārlu—*see* Tenmaṭam Brothers

Nārāyaṇasvāmi—*see* Palghat K.V. Nārāyaṇaswāmy and Vidyala Nārāyaṇasvāmi Naidu

Nārāyaṇa Tīrtha (*circa* 1650–1750) composed Telugu songs known as *taraṅgam* (literally 'wave'). He had chosen a life of renunciation (*sannyāsī*) and presumably migrated from a place near Guntur in Āndhra Pradesh to the region of Tañjāvūr in times of political unstability. He is known for having started a tradition of pious musical congregation (*bhajana sampradāya*) in that region. His main work is *Kṛṣṇa līlā taraṅgiṇī*, a musical play with Sanskrit lyrics whose title is often translated as *River of the Sports of Śrī Kṛṣṇa*. Its description of Kṛṣṇa's life culminates with the marriage of Kṛṣṇa to Rukmini and it is inspired by legends in the *Bhāgavatam,* a popular devotional work. The *Kṛṣṇa līlā taraṅgiṇī* is a cycle of 153 songs interspersed with prose songs (*cūrṇikā*) set to Dēvagāndhāri rāga and Sanskrit verses (*śloka*). It is described as an authoritative style manual (*lakṣyagrantha*) for the 34 rāgas used in it. In the absence of an authentic tradition, some pieces are now performed with tunes that differ from the original melodic form. This work contains 10 different rhythmic cycles (*tāla*). Its 12 sections (*dvādaśa taraṅga*) are modelled on the *Gīta-govinda* of Jayadeva which has 12 cantos (*sarga*). In other aspects it differs from its model. Many songs belonging to the *Kṛṣṇa līlā taraṅgiṇī* have been re-composed by musicians of our times and are again being performed during Karnatic concerts as well as dance programmes in the *bharata nāṭyam* and *Kuchipudi* styles.

Naṭṭuvanar—*see* Mūlaivīṭṭu Raṅgasvāmi Naṭṭuvanar

Nāyanmār (7th–9th centuries) is the collective designation for sixty-three saints of the Pallava period. They composed Tamil hymns (*Tēvāram*) which are still sung by the hereditary temple musicians (*ōduvār*) attached to most Śaiva temples of Tamil Nadu. The Nāyanmār were contemporaries of the *Vaiṣṇava* poet-saints known as Ālvār.

Nīdamaṅgaḷam Krishnamūrthy Bhāgavatar—*see* Ūttukkāḍu Veṅkaṭa Subba Ayyar

Nīlakaṇṭha Śivan (1839–1900) composed numerous devotional Tamil songs (*kṛti*). His literary interest focused on the lives of the *Śaiva* saints. While many of his compositions are lost there are some which are popular with performers and have been published with notation. He was born in Padmanābhapuram, the old capital of Travancore (Kerala) and his original name was Subramaṇyaṉ. Pāpanāsam Śivaṉ was his most prominent disciple.

Oothukadu—*see* Ūttukkāḍu Veṅkaṭa Subba Ayyar

Paccimiriyam Āḍiappayya (18th century) was a court musician at Tañjāvūr. He is famous for a technical composition (*tāṉavarṇam*) entitled *Viribōni* (aṭa tāla), the sole available piece of this composer. Its enigmatic text addresses Rājāgopāla (Kṛṣṇa) as the divine lover of a lady who, though smiling, is very sad as she wants Him all to herself. Composed in 1730, this *varṇam* is an exhaustive exposition of rāga Bhairavi and set the standard by which other compositions of this type are gauged. This composition utilizes the entire range of stylistic features found in Karnatic music, notably the various types of grace notes (*gamaka*). In this manner, it brings out the grandeur and distinct emotional quality of the rāga and is therefore synonymous with Bhairavi itself. Together with Govindasamayya, Paccimiriyam Āḍiappayya is referred to as the 'path-finder' of the *varṇam* form (*Tānavarṇam Mārgadarsi*). He is also known to have composed didactic pieces for beginners (*gītam*) and pieces belonging to an ancient form no longer in use (*prabandham*). He is credited with being responsible for arranging the pattern underlying a Karnatic concert programme. The modern method of handling rāga expositions (*ālāpana* and *pallavi*) is also attributed to him. The composers known as the Trinity, Śyāmā Śāstri, Tyāgarāja, and Muttusvāmi Dīkṣitar, are said to have been influenced by him. Śyāmā Śāstri is believed to have been his foremost disciple. Pallavi Gopāla Ayyar and Ghanam Kṛṣṇayya were other prominent disciples.

Paidāla Gurumūrti Śāstrī (18th century) is said to have composed over a thousand didactic pieces (*gītam*, *sūḷādi*) some of which are still available. He is an exponent of the *lakṣaṇa gītam,* a form of composition which instructs the student about the characteristic features of a rāga through descriptive lyrics and melodic examples (*prayoga*). A rare specimen for Śahāna rāga has been re-published in *Shobhillu Saptasvara* (see Bibliography). Regarded as an important link between the tradition of Purandara Dāsa and later composers, he also composed other pieces (*kṛti*) and was active in Tañjāvūr and Madras (modern Chennai).

Palghat (Pālakkāḍu) K.V. Nārāyaṇaswāmy (b. 1923) composed music for the lyrics of Periasāmi Thooraṉ.

Pallavi Doraisvāmi Ayyar (1782–1816) is best known as the composer of technical pieces (*tāṉavarṇam*). He was born in Tiruvayiāṟu and belonged to a family of court musicians (*vaiṇika*) at Tañjāvūr. His sons were pupils of Tyāgarāja, and several of his descendants became outstanding musicians. His lyrics are in Telugu.

Pallavi Gopāla Ayyar (b. 1790) was a contemporary of Pallavi Doraisvāmi Ayyar who also composed technical pieces (*tāṉavarṇam*). He was a disciple of Paccimiriyam Āḍiappayya (*see also* Mūlaivīṭṭu Raṅgasvāmi).

Pallavi Śeṣa Ayyar (1846–1908) wrote a number of songs in Tamil (*kṛti, pada varṇa* and *tillānā*). Some of his compositions are still popular. He was a vocalist and belonged to the direct lineage (*guruśiṣya paramparā*) of Tyāgarāja. His honorific *Pallavi* derives from a specialization in the *pallavi* form (*rāgam tānam pallavi*).

Pāpanāsam Śivan (1890–1973) was a prolific and popular composer of classical Karnatic music (*kṛti*). He also wrote music for films and dance (*bharata nāṭyam*). A disciple of Nīlakaṇṭha Śivan, he employed both Tamil and Sanskrit for his lyrics and is popularly referred to as *Tamil Tyāgarāja*. At Kalākshētra he composed music for dance-dramas produced by Rukmini Devi. He is regarded as the architect of a *renaissance* of Tamil music in the twentieth century.

Pāpavināsa Mudalyār (18th century) was a composer of Tamil songs (*padam*).

Parameśvara Bhāgavatar (1815–92) left his imprint on the music of Kerala through musical discourses (*harikathā kālakṣepa*) and as a composer (*varṇam* and *kṛti*). He is credited with strengthening the indigenous style of temple music (*Sōpānam*) which also forms the musical foundation for dance (*Mōhiniyāṭṭam*) and drama (*Kathakali*). Parameśvara Bhāgavatar was a singer and teacher at the court of Travancore. Together with Vaḍivēlu (Tañjāvūr Quartette) he helped Svāti Tirunāḷ to shape his compositions. This assistance might have taken the form of setting the young king's lyrics to music or giving these compositions their final shape as songs in order to be able to teach them to other musicians. Parameśvara Bhāgavatar also played the violin, *viṇā* and the *svarabhat,* a rare bowed instrument with sympathetic strings.

Paṭṭābhirāmayya—*see* Tiruppanandāḷ Paṭṭābhirāmayya

Pattammāḷ, D. (born *circa* 1928) is a composer-poet (*vaggēyakāra*) whose songs (*kṛti, 72 kṛtimālikā, jāvaḷi*) are acclaimed by musicians and critics. All her compositions, including those of the *jāvaḷi* type (normally in Telugu), have Tamil lyrics. A namesake of senior vocalist D.K. Pattammāḷ, she was a singer in her own right before specializing in teaching and writing music. She is the author of a Tamil version of Jayadeva's *Gītagovinda* entitled *Mādhava Gītam* which was published in 1979. Together with M.N. Dhandapani she published *Ragapravaham*: *Index to Carnatic Ragas* (Madras, 1984) and also developed a new system of rāga nomenclature (discussed in *Sruti Magazine*, issue 20/20-S, December 1985).

Paṭṭaṇam Subrahmaṇya Ayyar (1845–1902) wrote about 100 songs (*padavarṇam, tānavarṇam, kṛti, jāvaḷi, tillānā*). Mānambuccāvaḍi Veṅkaṭa Subba Ayyar, a direct disciple and nephew of Tyāgarāja, was his teacher (*guru*) who also used *Veṅkaṭēśa* as his *mudrā*. There are some doubts whether some technical compositions (*tānavarṇam*) ascribed to Paṭṭaṇam Subrahmaṇya Ayyar are not in reality works of Kōṭṭavāsal Veṅkaṭarāma Bhāgavatar who also used *Veṅkaṭēśa* as his *mudrā*. The joyful rāga Kadanakutūhalam, inspired by Western tunes heard in Madras, was created by him. He was the teacher of several outstanding musicians and composers of the twentieth century: Kōtīśvara Ayyar, Rāmnād Śrīnivāsa Ayyaṅgār, Tiger Varadāchāriar, and Mysore Vāsudēvācāria.

Periasāmi Thooran, M.P. (1908–87) was a poet with several hundred Tamil songs to his credit. The musical forms to which he contributed are devotional songs (*kṛti*), popular pilgrim songs (*kāvaḍiccindu*), songs in Tamil metres (*viruttam*) and songs combining nine rāgas (*navarāgamālikā*). Many of his compositions are addressed to Muruga, others have patriotic themes inspired by Subrahmaṇya Bhārati and Mahātma Gandhi. A greater part of his songs has been set to music (*dhātu*) in collaboration with N. Śivarāmakrishnan, his music tutor at Coimbatore, and several other reputed musicians have lent their musical expertise to his compositions, namely Palghat K.V. Nārāyaṇaswāmy, T.K. Govinda Rao, T.M. Thiāgarājan, T.V. Śaṅkaranārāyaṇan, Kumbakōnam Viswanāthan, and Vanaja Nārāyaṇan. These compositions have been performed and recorded by many outstanding singers and have found equal appreciation in music and literary circles. He served on the advisory bodies of several major educational and cultural institutions of Tamil Nadu.

Piḷḷai—*see* Mārimuttā Piḷḷai, Tirupāmburam N. Swāminātha Piḷḷai, Vēdanāyakam Piḷḷai

Ponnayya—*see* Tañjāvūr Quartette

Ponnusvāmi—*see* Mutialpet Ponnusvāmi

Pūcci Śrīnivāsa Ayyaṅgār—*see* Rāmnād Śrīnivāsa Ayyaṅgār

Puliyūr Duraisāmi Ayyar (?19th century) wrote a song praising the embodiment of music and learning, the goddess Sarasvatī (*Sarasiruhāsanapriyē* in rāga Nāṭa, ādi tāla). It is the sole known composition (*kṛti*) by this composer and found in the repertoire of many musicians. No information is available about him.

Purandara Dāsa (1484–1564) (Plate 5) was a prolific composer of devotional songs (*dēvarnāma, pada*). He is regarded as the first and foremost exponent of the Haridāsa movement (see above). Born as Śrīnivāsa Naik into a rich merchant family, he renounced his wealth in order to lead a saintly life as a wandering bard and composer of sacred music. He lived in the mighty Vijayanagar empire during the reign of Kṛṣṇadevarāya and died at Hampi, its capital, shortly before it was defeated and destroyed in 1565. Many of his compositions were lost when the empire disintegrated. Vijayadāsa, himself a Haridāsa and composer, collected and popularized many of Purandara Dāsa's songs in the seventeenth century. Most musicians and scholars of Vijayanagar had emigrated to safer havens, and music began to flourish at various courts, notably Tañjāvūr, Mysore and Travancore. Purandara Dāsa continues to be revered as the *Great founder-father* (*Pitāmaha*) of Karnatic music. His charming compositions for beginners (*gitam*) are often the first musical pieces taught to a novice after following a graded course (*abhyāsa gānam*) also ascribed to him (*alaṅkāra, sūḷādi*).

As many other Karnatic composers, Tyāgarāja felt indebted to Purandara Dāsa whose songs he had heard from his mother. The lyrics of innumerable popular songs ascribed to Purandara Dāsa were re-composed by eminent musicians of the twentieth century (e.g. Rallapalli Ananthakrishna Śarma, S. Rājam). The late vocalist M.L. Vasanthakumāri and her disciples have been responsible for popularizing the compositions of Purandara Dāsa in our time.

Rājarām, S. (b. 1925) composed the music for six dance-dramas produced and choreographed by Rukmini Devi at Kalākshētra; he completed the music for the *Rāmāyaṇa* series which had been begun by his grandfather, Mysore Vāsudēvācāria; out of six dance-dramas on this theme, he composed the last two parts: Cūḍāmaṇi-pradānam and Mahāpaṭṭābhiṣekam; he also composed the music for Bhaktajayadeva, Karṇaśapatham, Siri Purandara (based on the original lyrics of Purandara Dāsa), and Śivagītimālā.

Rallapalli Ananthakrishna Śarma (1893–1979) was a vocalist, violinist and *vaiṇika* who re-composed and published the music for the Telugu lyrics of 108 compositions of Annamācārya and 40 compositions of Purandara Dāsa. He taught at Mysore and Tirupati.

Rāmadās—*see* Bhadrācala Rāmadās

Rāmaliṅgasvāmi, Vallalar Rāmaliṅga Svāmigal (1823–74) is credited with composing over six thousand Tamil songs known as *Tiru Arutpa* (first published in 1867), also known as the *Golden Book of Grace*. His musical compositions comprise various classical and popular rāgas and forms (*kīrtana, cindu, kummi*). He was an ascetic (*sannyāsī*) whose original name was Karunkuli R. Piḷḷai. His spiritual quest consisted in singing sacred music and practising *Yoga*. Denouncing ritual sacrifice, he extolled the merits of compassion, equality, non-violence (*ahiṁsā*), vegetarianism and followed the precepts of *Advaita* philosophy (non-dualism). A believer in the merit of visiting sacred places, he also initiated the construction of shrines and is remembered as an efficient organizer. Many believe that he had miraculous powers and let himself be immured alive in a room (*samādhi*) at Mottukuppam (Karunguli hamlet). He studied the Tamil classics including *Tēvāram* hymns, and his Tamil prose and poetry are rated as being of a high order. Among other works he wrote a collection of poetry which comprises a thousand verses.

Rāmasvāmi Dīkṣitar (1735–1817) was an influential composer of devotional music (*kṛti*) and the author of a piece which combines 108 (*aṣṭottaraśatta*) rāgas and tālas (i.e. a *rāga tāla mālikā*). His parents had left their native place near Kāñcīpuram (Tamil Nadu) due to political turmoil around the year 1742 and migrated southwards. Before settling in Tiruvārūr he studied Sanskrit, Telugu and music (*vīṇā*). He was guided by Muddu Veṅkaṭamakhi (Veṅkaṭa Vaidyanātha Dīkṣitar), a descendant of Veṅkaṭamakhi, the famous music theoretician. Among his responsibilities was the music performed in the temple rituals at Tiruvārūr, then a major centre of music and dance. He was the father of Muttusvāmi Dīkṣitar and is credited with introducing the rāga Haṁsadhvani which has become popular through his son's composition 'Vātāpigaṇapatim' (an invocation of Gaṇeśa, ādi tāla).

Rāmnād ('Pūcci') Śrīnivāsa Ayyaṅgār (1860–1919) was a vocalist and versatile composer trained by Paṭṭaṇam Subrahmaṇya Ayyar. His pieces (*kṛti*, *jāvaḷi*, *tillānā*, *tāṉavarṇam*) are widely performed. Kōṭīśvara Ayyar was one of his outstanding disciples.

Raṅgasvāmi Naṭṭuvaṉar—*see* Mūlaivīṭṭu Raṅgasvāmi

Reḍḍiyār—*see* Aṇṇāmalai Reḍḍiyār

Sabhāpati Ayyar—*see* Muvvānallūr Sabhāpati Ayyar

Saḍagōpan V.V. (b. 1915) founded the Tyāga Bhārati Music Education Mission (Melkote, Karnataka). A reputed vocalist, writer on music and professor at Delhi University, he also participated in Tamil films of the 1930s and composed music for the lyrics of Ambujam Krishna. In 1980 he mysteriously disappeared during a train journey from Madras to Delhi.

Saḍagōpan—*see also* Caṭakōpan

Sadāśiva Brahmendra (before 1762) was a mystic who composed songs in the *kṛti* form (in Sanskrit) besides several religious works. His place and precise date of birth are unknown but he is said to have been a contemporary of Śāhaji and Śarabhōji I. Nerūr, a village near Karūr on the banks of the river Kāveri, is the place where he lived and where his presence (*samādhi*) is still revered. The message he spread through his works and songs was that salvation is attained by liberating oneself from the process of drowning in an 'ocean of desires', that pride and selfishness should be overcome, and that anxiety can be overcome by means of self-control and by keeping the company of virtuous people. He renounced speech by taking a vow of silence for life (*mauni*). Numerous other composers (notably Tyāgarāja) regarded him as a source of inspiration. Twenty-three known songs are believed to have been preserved. S. Rājam provided the music for several songs based on his lyrics.

Sadāśiva Rao, Rāyār—*see* Mysore Sadāśiva Rao, Rāyār

Śaṅkara Ayyar—*see* Tañjāvūr Śaṅkara Iyer

Ṣaṭkāla Narasayyā (19th century) composed technical and devotional music (*tānavarṇam*, *kṛti*). He hailed from Salem in Tamil Nadu, and taught many disciples in Bangalore (Karnataka). His honorific name means 'six degrees of speed' (*ṣaṭkāla*), an indication of his extraordinary mastery of musical time (*layam*).

Seetarāma Śarma, B. (b. 1936) is a composer of dance music (*tillānā*, *jatisvaram*), vocalist and *naṭṭuvanar*. He belongs to a family of musicians and dancers of Kuchipudi village (Āndhra Pradesh). At Kalākshētra, he composed and directed the music for several dance-dramas produced by Rukmini Devi (e.g. *Mīnākṣi Kalyāṇam*, Tamil; *Kurmavatāram*, Sanskrit) besides several other Indian and international productions (e.g. *Bhagavad Gītā* by Mini Janislawski, USA; *Ritu*). He also produced musical plays for All India Radio Madras (e.g. *Tirunīlakaṇṭha Nāyanār Caritram* of Gopālakṛṣṇa Bhārati; *Sītā Kalyāṇam* from the Kamban Rāmāyaṇa).

Śeṣa Ayyar—*see* Pallavi Śeṣa Ayyar

Śeṣayyaṅgār, Śeṣa Ayyaṅgār—*see* Mārgadarśī Śeṣayyaṅgār

Śeṣanna—*see* Mysore Śeṣanna

Siṅgarācāryulu—*see* Taccūr Siṅgarācāryulu

Śivan—*see* Mahāvaidyanātha Śivan, Nīlakaṇṭha Śivan and Pāpanāsam Śivan

Plate 1: Bhadrācala Rāmadāsa.
(Copyright: S. Rājam)

Plate 2: Jayadeva.
(Copyright: S. Rājam)

Plate 3: Kṣētrajña.
(Copyright: S. Rājam)

Plate 4: Muttusvāmi Dīkṣitar.
(Copyright: S. Rājam)

Plate 5: Purandara Dāsa.
(Copyright: S. Rājam)

Plate 6: Svāti Tirunāḷ Mahārājā.
(Copyright: S. Rājam)

Plate 7: Śyāmā Śāstri.
(Copyright: S. Rājam)

Plate 8: Tyāgarāja.
(Copyright: S. Rājam)

Śivānandam—*see* Tañjāvūr Quartette

Śivarāmakrishnan, N. (b. 1913) collaborated with Periasāmi Thooran in the composition of over three hundred songs (*kṛti*).

Śrīnivāsa Ayyaṅgār, K.V. (?–1929) was an accomplished singer, dancer, musicologist and composer. At the same time, he was an educationist, and a Sanskrit, Tamil and Telugu scholar remembered for his role in founding the Music Academy Madras in 1926. He published several major music works in Tamil with notations and translations which include rāga descriptions (*lakṣaṇa*) and numerous compositions by Tyāgarāja, Paṭṭaṇam Subrahmaṇya Ayyar and others. Little is known about his life except that he had studied vedic literature and the *Divya Prabandham*. He authored the two compositions (*kṛti*) in rāga Siṁhēndramadhyama signed with the *mudrā Tyāgarāja*: 'Natajana paripāla', rūpaka tāla; and 'Nīdu caraṇamulē', miśra cāpu tāla. (There is no composition in raga Siṁhēndramadhyama by Tyāgarāja; Śrīnivāsa Ayyaṅgār also used this *mudrā* for the following pieces: 'Vinatāsuta vāhanuḍai', Harikāmbhōji rāga , ādi tāla; 'Parāmukha mēlarā Rāmayya', rāga Suraṭi, ādi tāla; and 'Abhimāna mennaḍu galgurā', rāga Vivardhini or rāga Kuñjari, ādi tāla.) His elder brothers, Tiger Varadāchāriar and Vīṇā Krishnamāchāriar, were also outstanding musicians and composers.

Śrīnivāsa Ayyaṅgār—*see also* Rāmnād Śrīnivāsa Ayyaṅgār

Subbarāma Ayyar—*see* Vaitīśvarankoil Subbarāma Ayyar

Subbarāma Dīkṣitar (1839–1906) was the grandson of Muttusvāmi Dīkṣitar and a court musician at Eṭṭayapuram (Tamil Nadu). He composed various types of music including dance music (*padavarṇam*) and is regarded as the first modern musicologist of South India. V.N. Bhāṭkhaṇḍe (1860–1936), the most influential theoris of contemporary Hindustānī music, consulted him personally in his quest for resolving the problems of divergency regarding musical theory and northern practice.

Subbarāma Dīkṣitar wrote a reference work of encyclopedic scope (*Saṅgita Sampradāya Pradaśini,* in Telugu, published in 1904). It contains the biographies of many composers and several hundred compositions in syllabic notation of which the songs of the Dīkṣitar tradition are the most important group. This work is regarded as an authoritative source of information on the compositions of Muttusvāmi Dīkṣitar and other composers. It has been translated into Tamil and published by the Music Academy Madras. Of his own compositions, only one technical piece (*tānavarṇam*), three classical songs (*kṛti*) and three narrative songs (*daru*) appear to be available now.

Subbarāmayya—*see* Vaitīśvarankoil Subbarāma Ayyar

Subbarāyar—*see* Dharmapuri Subbarāyar

Subbarāya Śāstri (1803–62) composed a number of songs (*kṛti* and *svarajati*). The second son of composer Śyāmā Śāstri, he received his musical training from his father and Tyāgarāja, both belonging to the Trinity of South Indian music. An accomplished musician (*vaiṇika*) and scholar proficient in Tamil, Telugu and Sanskrit, he is said to have been the most successful composer of *svara sāhitya,* a rare technique whereby the syllables of the lyrics are so chosen as to coincide with the solfa syllables (*svara*) of the notes. Some of his pieces are in unusual rāgas and several ones are commonly heard in concerts.

Subrahmaṇya Ayyar—*see* Musiri Subrahmaṇya Ayyar, Paṭṭaṇam Subrahmaṇya Ayyar

Subrahmaṇya Bhārati, Bhāratiyar (1882–1921) composed lyrics inspired by Nārāyaṇa Tīrtha as well as patriotic songs in which he covered traditional as well as modern themes such as the detrimental influence of the caste system. His lyrics, intended for being sung, were newly set to tunes (*varṇameṭṭu*) by S.V. Veṅkaṭarāmaṉ and other music directors of the twentieth century. The poet-musician from Eṭṭaya-puram in Tamil Nadu is revered as a *Deśiya Kavi* ('national poet') who worked for India's freedom from colonial oppression. He opposed the use of the harmonium for classical music. The style of his songs, modelled on devotional songs in the three-part *kīrtana* form, was influenced by Hindustānī as well as folk music such as *kāvaḍic-cindu* (Tamil pilgrim songs). A reputed dance and music critic, he had studied English and Sanskrit at Benares. In the absence of an authentic tradition of his songs, modern musicians are free to apply their own ingenuity in order to bring out the literary qualities and emotional depth (*bhāva*) of his lyrics.

Subramaṇyaṉ—*see* Nīlakaṇṭha Śivaṉ

Svāmināta Piḷḷai—*see* Tirupāmburam N. Swāminātha Piḷḷai

Svāti Tirunāḷ Mahārājā (1813–47) (Plate 6) is regarded as a prolific composer with over 400 pieces to his credit. Some 285 compositions are available in notation out of which 230 were published by Harikēsanallūr Mutthiah Bhāgavatar and Sem-maṅguḍi Śrīnivāsa Iyer. His style was influenced by compositions of Mārgadarśī Śeṣayyaṅgār. The South Indian forms comprise *jāvaḷi*, *kṛti*, *padavarṇam, rāgamālikā*, *svarajati*, *tillānā*, and *varṇam*. It is widely believed that Vaḍivēlu (Tañjāvūr Quartette) and Parameśvara Bhāgavatar, both court musicians and scholars, assisted him with composing the music especially for dance pieces (*padavarṇam*) to which he mainly contributed the lyrics. Both musicians also popularized these and other compositions by teaching them to their pupils.

Irayimmaṉ Tampi was another prominent poet and composer attached to the royal court. He also used *Padmanābha* as his signature (*mudrā*) which has led to confusion regarding the authorship of several pieces. Many of Svāti Tirunāḷ's compositions were collected from old musicians by Mutthiah Bhāgavatar, himself a prominent musician and composer. He published and popularized these compositions with the assistance of his son, H.M. Vaidyalingam. He also re-composed several pieces of which only the lyrics were preserved in manuscripts without any indication of either rāga or tāla. Numerous other compositions were re-composed by Semmaṅguḍi Śrīnivāsa Iyer for similar reasons. In accordance with the customs prevailing in the music world, the names of these and other musicians are never listed in concert programmes and sleeve notes.

On the basis of recent research it has become evident that it is generally difficult to ascertain the degree to which Svāti Tirunāḷ himself shaped the music of many compositions bearing his signature (*mudrā*).

Svāti Tirunāḷ also took an active interest in North Indian music (*bhajan*, *dhrupad*, *khyāl*, *tappa*, *tarāna*) and played the *svarabhat,* a bowed instrument with sympathetic strings. The music of Svāti Tirunāḷ's pieces in the Hindustānī style is ascribed to later musicians, namely K.G. Ginde and S.N. Ratanjankar.

Svāti Tirunāḷ was heir to the throne (*mahārāja*) of Travancore in southern Kerala but due to interference by the British colonial administration, little if any power remained in his hands. Remembered as a pious person (*bhakta*) devoted to Viṣṇu (*Padmanābha*), he is said to have been disposed towards reforms and charity. Known for his scholarship, he had a command of several Indian languages, notably Sanskrit, Telugu, Kannaḍa, Hindi and Maṇipravāḷam, besides his mother tongue, Malayālam, and English. Svāti Tirunāḷ extended generous and discerning patronage to classical musicians and dancers from all parts of India and even abroad.

Śyāmā Śāstri (1762 or 1763–1827) (Plate 7) was a scholarly composer who led a secure and uneventful life as hereditary priest in the temple of Baṅgāru Kāmākṣi at Tañjāvūr. Paccimiriyam Āḍiappayya was his teacher. Posterity has assigned Śyāmā Śāstri a place among the Trinity of Karnatic music together with Muttusvāmi Dīkṣitar and Tyāgarāja.

He is believed to have composed some 300 pieces (*kṛti*, *svarajati, tāṉavarṇam*) but only about 50 have been preserved. His lyrics are mainly written in Telugu but some are in Sanskrit and Tamil. Many of his songs are in praise of the feminine aspect of the Divine (Devī).

Śyāmā Śāstri created a new rāga (Ciñtāmaṇi) for which he wrote the only known *kṛti* (*Dēvibrōvasamayamidē*, ādi tāla, Telugu lyrics). Otherwise he had a preference for well-known rāgas of universal appeal, particularly those which unfold their charm at a leisurely tempo (*rakti* or *naya rāgas*). Ānandabhairavi is considered the *rakti rāga* which owes its present shape (*rāga rūpa*) to four authoritative pieces (*kṛti*) by Śyāmā Śāstri. He also established the *svarajati* in the concert repertoire through his compositions in the rāgas Bhairavi, Tōḍi and Yadukulakāmbhōji. The *svarajati* is a rare form thought to be derived from dance music (*jatisvaram*).

Śyāmā Śāstri employed an intricate compositional device known as *svarākṣara* by which a syllable that denotes a given musical note (*svara*) is made to coincide with a syllable (*akṣara*) of the lyrics. He wrote some manuscripts containing complex rhythmic patterns and used an inverted form of miśra cāpu tāla (vilōma cāpu tāla, 7 counts). His son, Subbarāya Śāstri, was a disciple of Tyāgarāja and became a reputed composer in his own right.

Taccūr Siṅgarācāryulu (1834–92) composed and taught numerous pieces for beginners (*gītam*) and other technical pieces (*tānavarṇam*). The Tenmaṭam Brothers were among his disciples. He is the author of the first printed work containing compositions in syllabic notation. Together with his brother Ciṉṉa Siṅgarācāryulu he published several works and popularized the modern rāga terminology based on the treatise *Saṁgraha-Cūḍā-Maṇi* of Gōvinda. Both brothers were held in high esteem by Subbarāma Dīkṣitar, himself a leading music expert.

Tāḷḷapāka Annamācārya—*see* Annamācārya

Tampi—*see* Irayimman Tampi

Tañjāvūr Quartette (early 19th century) is the appellation of four brothers, Cinnayya, Ponnayya, Śivānandam, and Vaḍivēlu who are reckoned among the most influential personalities to have shaped classical South Indian music and dance. They belonged to a reputed family of hereditary temple musicians (*ōduvār*) and dance teachers (*naṭṭuvanar*) attached to the *Bṛhadīśvara* temple of Tañjāvūr. Two Marāṭhā kings of Tañjāvūr, Śarabhojī II (1798–1832) and Śivājī II (1832–55), were their chief patrons. They were disciples of Muttusvāmi Dīkṣitar and their compositions include all the major forms of music and dance. Most of their work is regarded as a body of collective creations.

Cinnayya (b. 1802 or 1803), the eldest brother, was himself an accomplished dancer and dance teacher (*nāṭyācārya*). He popularized dancing among men and this prompted Śivājī to build a special dance hall for men in his palace. Cinnayya eventually became a court musician (*samasthāna vidvān*) at Mysore. He composed dance pieces (*jāvaḷi, padavarṇam, tillānā*) besides technical pieces (*tānavarṇam*) and devotional songs (*kīrtana*).

Ponnayya (b. 1804) is rated as the best composer among the four brothers. He is also credited with systematizing the sequence of items in the classical dance repertoire (*mārgam*). The aesthetically balanced performance format shaped by him is still being followed all over South India (see Chapter 17). Ponnayya composed music for each major form of dance and his descendants continued to cultivate and teach his repertoire. It reached several prominent dancers, among them Rukmini Devi, founder of Kalākshētra, through his grandson Mīnākṣisundaram Piḷḷai (1869–1954) and thus constitutes the fountainhead of classical South Indian dance (*bharata nāṭyam*) as we know it today.

Śivānandam (b. 1808) had a reputation as a *vīṇā* player (*vaiṇika*), and the Tañjāvūr style of playing the *vīṇā* was passed on to his descendants and their pupils to the present day. He was also a reputed dance teacher specialized in *abhinaya*, the expressive aspect of *bharata nāṭyam*. An ardent devotee of Śiva, he created a special repertoire of ritual dance for worship.

Svāti Tirunāḷ invited the four brothers to Travancore in 1830 when they were temporarily exiled from Tañjāvūr. Except for Vaḍivēlu, whose descendants continued to invigorate Kerala's cultural life, they returned to Tañjāvūr.

Vaḍivēlu (1810–45 or 1847) is known to have popularized the use of the European violin. It continues to be an important instrument in South Indian music whether for solo performance or accompaniment. He even accompanied his own singing during dance recitals at Travancore. Vaḍivēlu is particularly famous for dance compositions known as *padavarṇam*, the main item of any dance recital. Together with Parameśvara Bhāgavatar, his fellow court musician at Travancore, he put royal patronage to best use. The court of Travancore became a major centre of music and dance. Vaḍivēlu also contributed to the development of *Mōhiniyāṭṭam*, the feminine (*lāsya*) form of solo dance which was originally performed in the temples of Kerala.

Tañjāvūr Śaṅkara Iyer (b. 1924) is a disciple of Tiger Varadāchāriar and one of the most respected contemporary composers and music teachers. He was involved in gathering the authentic music of Gopālakṛṣṇa Bhārati and Arunācalakkavirayar. Many of his compositions (*kṛti*) are found in the repertoires of well-known musicians such as T.V. Śaṅkaranārāyaṇan and the late D.K. Jayarāman. This includes a charming composition of the *rāgamālikā* type ('a garland of rāgas') which uses all the different 'Rañjani' rāgas.

Tenmaṭam Brothers (20th century) were popular performers and teachers belonging to Āndhra Pradesh. Disciples of Taccūr Siṅgarācāryulu, they were associated with the music festivals organized by Tiruvōtriyūr Tyāgayyar in Madras and with the family of the legendary Vīṇā Dhanammāḷ. Narasiṁhācārlu, the elder, was a composer and violinist and his younger brother, Varadācārlu (d. 1952), a *vīṇā* player (*vaiṇika*). Narasiṁhācārlu wrote a number of compositions in Telugu (*gītam*, *svarajati*, *tānavarṇam*, *kīrtana*). He published many of his compositions in 1917 under the title *Saṅgītānanda Ratnākaramu*. Nine of these (*gītam*) have been re-published in *Shobhillu Saptasvara* (see Bibliography).

Thooran—*see* Periasāmi Thooran

Tiger Varadāchāriar (1876–1950) composed 70 to 80 pieces including technical pieces (*gītam*, *tānavarṇam*), a devotional piece (*kṛti*) besides dance compositions (*padavarṇam*). Three specimens (two *gītams* and one *sūḷādi*) have been re-published in *Shobhillu Saptasvara* (see Bibliography). He also wrote the music for *Kumārasambhava* (50 songs), a major dance-drama produced by Rukmini Devi which still figures prominently in the repertoire of Kalākshētra. A legendary singer already during his lifetime (hence his humorous honorific *Tiger*), he was patronized by the court of Mysore. A disciple of Paṭṭaṇam Subrahmaṇya Ayyar, he taught many eminent musicians including M.D. Rāmanāthan. Two prominent musicians, K.V. Śrīnivāsa Ayyaṅgār and Vīṇā Krishnamāchāriar, were his brothers. Together with Tañjāvūr Śaṅkara Iyer, another prominent disciple, he helped to preserve the authentic music of Arunācalakkavirayar and Gopālakṛṣṇa Bhārati. During various stages of his life he was associated with Madras University, Aṇṇāmalai University, the Music Academy Madras, and Kalākshētra.

Tīrtha—*see* Nārāyaṇa Tīrtha

Tirupāmburam N. Swāminātha Piḷḷai (1898 or 1900–1961) was a renowned flute player and educationist who is credited with having re-composed the music for the lyrics of Muttuttāṇḍavar.

Tiruppanandāḷ Paṭṭābhirāmayya (b. 1863) specialized in erotic dance songs (*jāvaḷi*) which are regarded as outstanding examples of this genre. Some of his lyrics are of a humorous nature.

Tiruvōtriyūr Tyāgayyar (1845–1917) was the son of composer Vīṇā Kuppayyar. In 1900 he published a work (*Pallavi Svara Kalpavalli*) which contained his and his father's technical compositions (*svarāvaḷi*, *gītam kṛti* and *tānavarṇam*). Twelve specimens (*gītam*) have been re-published in *Shobhillu Saptasvara* (see Bibliography).

Tyāgarāja (1767–1847) (Plate 8) is credited with perfecting the most important form of Karnatic music (*kṛti*) on the basis of traditional devotional songs (*kīrtana*). His compositions often follow a pattern of intensification, as it were, which was emulated by his pupils and later musicians. This effect is achieved by three means: (1) the upward development of melody in the second or middle part (*anupallavi*) of a *kṛti* or *kīrtana*; (2) the introduction of intricate rhythmic and melodic variations (*saṅgati*), believed to be his original contribution; and (3) the repetition of the music (*dhātu*) of the *anupallavi* as part of the concluding part (*caraṇa*); here the lyrics (*sāhitya* or *mātu*) are being continued before the first theme (*pallavi*) is taken up once again to conclude the song. The composer's signature (*mudrā*) is introduced towards the end of the lyrics (*Tyāgarāja*), and forms a part of the *caraṇa* section.

A *saṅgati* heightens the melodic and rhythmic beauty of a theme (e.g. *pallavi*) and highlights the meaning of the underlying lyrics. This intricate device enhances the depth of feeling (*bhāva*) and distinguishes art music from simple devotional songs. The *saṅgati* also helps a composer to minimize the amount of text of a song. Thereby melodic and rhythmic variety can flourish without being obstructed by too many words. A similar process, applied in an improvised manner, is known as *niraval* or *neraval*, a technique which is believed to have originated in Tyāgarāja's elaborate *saṅgati*. On the other hand, Tyāgarāja also wrote numerous simple songs that lend themselves to congregational singing (*bhajana*) by groups of devotees. These *kīrtana* have a limited tonal range which can also be negotiated by an average voice and require little musicianship.

Tyāgarāja wrote most of his lyrics in Telugu, his mother tongue which had been imported to Tañjāvūr by sixteenth-century immigrants from Vijayanagar (modern Āndhra Pradesh). In Tyāgarāja's time Telugu was still the language of the educated classes in Tañjāvūr. Tyāgarāja was the son of Rāma Brahman who specialized in discourses on the *Rāmāyaṇa* in the reign of Tulajājī II (1763–87), his patron. Śoṇṭi Veṅkaṭarāmaṇayya, a reputed court musician (*samasthāna vidvān*), accepted Tyāgarāja as his pupil (*śiṣya*) who soon acquired a reputation as a fine singer. Tyāgarāja is said to have refused to become a court musician himself in spite of lucrative offers and attempts at coercion from within his family. His inner turmoil in the face of these pressures and conflicts of conscience, perhaps aggravated by financial problems and domestic responsibilities, is reflected in many of his lyrics. But Tyāgarāja felt more than rewarded by the joys experienced during complete immersion in his self-imposed devotional regimen (*sādhanā*) which consisted of fervent prayers (*japam*), domestic worship (*pūjā*), and the participation in various festivities (*utsava*). He regarded all his mundane and spiritual activities as acts of worship directed towards Rāma, his personal God (*iṣṭadevatā*). Ecstatic outbursts often took the shape of spontaneous compositions which portray the facets of his personality in every conceivable shade. His lyrics reveal great depth of knowledge of the scriptures, epics, legends, *Purāṇa*, musical expertise, his humility as well as self-respect, introspection, and sense of humour.

His work covers about 210 rāgas many of which he introduced or invented himself (e.g. Dundhubhi, Vijayavasantam, Kokilavarāḷi, Pratāpa Varāḷi and Supradīpam). Between 700 and 1000 of his songs are estimated to be included in today's repertoire besides the countless songs by past and present composers that are intended to emulate his style, technique, themes, and format.

Tyāgarāja composed two musical narratives entitled *Prahlāda Bhakti Vijayam* ('Prahlāda's devotional victory') and *Naukā Caritram* ('Boat-story'). They differ from a stage play or dance-drama and really constitute cycles of songs (some with dialogues). These songs are interspersed by prose passages (*cūrṇikā,* traditionally set to Dēvagāndhāri rāga). Both works, together with those of Nārāyaṇa Tīrtha and Gopālakṛṣṇa Bhārati, are sometimes referred to as South Indian operas. Elements borrowed from Tyāgarāja's compositions have often been grafted onto the lyrics of other authors whose original music is either lost to posterity or whose musical expertise does not match their poetical talents. Several compositions of Tyāgarāja have been published by A.M.C. Mudalyār in 1893 whose *Oriental Music in European Notation* contains details such as lyrics, transcriptions and ornamentation.

The tradition of singing *kīrtana* in Tamil Nadu came from Mahārāṣṭra in the wake of Marāṭhā rule and patronage in Tañjāvūr, and it consists of congregational singing in accordance with certain rules (*bhajana paddhati*). This was also a period when music and dance were enriched by the devotional literature of several languages, notably Telugu, Marāṭhi, Tamil, and Sanskrit. Thus the performing arts could thrive in a cosmopolitan climate enriched by a great love of learning on the one hand and fervent devotion on the other. Marāṭhā kings ruled Tañjāvūr from the seventeenth century until 1855 when the remaining parts of the Tañjāvūr kingdom were annexed by the British. The last rulers of Tañjāvūr proved to be discerning scholars devoted to learning and the arts but were left with little political power if any. In the nineteenth century, patronage for classical music shifted to the newly emerging middle class of Madras and other centres of trade.

Tyāgarāja's devotional songs (*kīrtana*) were greatly influenced by Purandara Dāsa whose Kannaḍa songs (*dēvarnāma* or *pada*) were sung by his mother. There is a fragment of an authentic portrait of Tyāgarāja on which all portraits by later painters (notably S. Rājam) are based. He is depicted with the characteristic attributes of a traditional *bhāgavatar*, as wearing a simple dress with a turban and holding a *tambūrā* in one hand and clappers (*cipla*) in the other. This appearance conforms to the conventions of the Haridāsa movement.

In his lyrics Tyāgarāja also acknowledges the inspiration he derived from the Telugu songs (*kīrtana*) of Bhadrācala Rāmadās and the Sanskrit compositions of Sadāśiva Brahmendra. Mārgadarśī Śeṣayyaṅgār was another major composer of his time whose music and Sanskrit lyrics are believed to have influenced Tyāgarāja and his contemporaries, notably Muttusvāmi Dīkṣitar and Svāti Tirunāḷ. But the most important inspiration for his life and work was his devotion (*bhakti*) to Rāma, the righteous god-king of the *Rāmāyaṇa*, the great Sanskrit epic.

The *kīrtana* compositions of Tyāgarāja are in a festive mood because they are intended for singing during temple festivals and processions. For this reason they are also known as *utsava sampradāya kīrtana* ('festival-tradition-songs'). Many of his songs expound the religious and ethical teachings of the *Advaita* school of philosophy and therefore contain many Sanskrit words. In his lyrics, he sometimes expresses critical views about elaborate rituals and the superstitions of his time. He even denounces his fellow musicians for lowering themselves by continuing the old custom of indulging in 'ordinary men's praise' (*narastuti*) in return for patronage. Tyāgarāja preferred the principled and austere life implied by his personal name which refers to Śiva, the divinity of Tiruvārūr (the composer's native place) who is perceived as being the ruler (*rājā*) of austerities (*tyāga*). Tyāgarāja expounded and defended the path of musical worship (*nādopāsanā*) on the basis of ancient scriptures. Inspired by the custom of holy mendicancy, he and his disciples went around singing in return for food-alms (*uñchavṛtti*). Many festive occasions all over South India are accompanied by the re-enactment of this practice.

Since 1925 annual musical commemorations (*Tyāgarāja ārādhana*) are held at Tiruvayiāṟu where Tyāgarāja lived. These and similar occasions in other places in and outside India culminate in congregational singing of *divyanāma kīrtana* after singing an elaborate series of songs known as *Pañcaratna kṛti* ('five gems'). Composed in five important rāgas, namely Nāṭa, Gauḷa, Ārabhi, Varāḷi and Śrī, and set to ādi tāla, the *Pañcaratna kṛti* may originally have served the purpose of *tāṉavarṇam*, a form which provides an authoritative and aesthetic exposition of a rāga. This theory is based on the fact that, with the exception of his two musical narratives, Tyāgarāja himself did not compose music in forms other than *kṛti* and *kīrtana* but was committed to provide his disciples with a thorough musical training. One of his disciples, Wālājapet Kṛṣṇasvāmi Bhāgavatar, is presumed to have added playful interludes (*ciṭṭasvaram*) to Tyāgarāja's *kṛtis* because Tyāgarāja is known not to have composed any *ciṭṭasvaram* sequences himself.

Śyāmā Śāstri, Muttusvāmi Dīkṣitar and Tyāgarāja are revered as the Trinity of Karnatic composers. Unlike the other two, Tyāgarāja chose to follow the innovative and rational scale system of Govindācāri, the eighteenth-century theorist and author of the *Saṁgraha-Cūḍā-Maṇi*. Tyāgarāja succeeded in raising several scales (*mēḷakartā rāga*) to the status of fully-fledged rāgas through his compositions, particularly Kharaharapriya and Harikāmbhōji. Generally in the latter half of the third part of a *kṛti* (*caraṇa*), Tyāgarāja repeats the music of the second part (*anupallavi*). His rhythmic structure is lively, complex and often intended for being sung in the medium tempo. Many of his compositions in ādi tāla have a characteristic point of departure (*eḍuppu*) for all three sections (*pallavi*, *anupallavi*, and *caraṇa*) which is placed after $1^1/2$ basic counts (*akṣarakāla*) or 6 sub-units (*mātrā*) from the beginning of the time cycle (*samam*). This feature is thought to be his own original idea, perhaps inspired by devotional songs introduced from Mahārāṣṭra.

There are several exponents of the traditions that go back to Tyāgarāja in a direct lineage of disciples (*guruśiṣya paramparā*). It is only from the time of Tyāgarāja that a vast body of musical compositions has been preserved and cultivated in a systematic manner. Many of his songs give evidence of his personality and inner turmoil caused by insensitive contemporaries, pressures to conform to social conventions, and bigotry. Yet on the whole his work can be best described as a celebration of the divine purpose of all life which he believed is best realized through refined music.

Tyāgayyar—*see* Tiruvōtriyūr Tyāgayyar

Ūttukkāḍu Veṅkaṭa Subba Ayyar (1700–65) composed nearly 300 songs which were retrieved, re-composed and popularized by Nīdamaṅgaḷam Krishnamūrthy Bhāgavatar (1921–82), a descendant of Veṅkaṭa Subba Ayyar's brother. No signature (*mudrā*) was used by the composer whose lively Tamil and Sanskrit lyrics evoke the craving of the cowherdesses (*gopī*) for the youthful Kṛṣṇa, his divine dance with them (*rāsakrīda*) and his flute play. Their poetic appeal and rhythmic qualities make these songs, sometimes on erotic themes (*śṛṅgāra*), eminently suitable for dance performances. For this reason they have become popular among musicians, dancers and listeners.

Vaḍivēlu (early 19th century)—*see* Tañjāvūr Quartette

Vaidyalingam, H.M. (b. 1924)—*see* Harikēsanallūr Mutthiah Bhāgavatar

Vaitīśvarankoil Subbarāma Ayyar (19th century) composed a number of dance songs in Tamil (*padam*). He laid more stress on erotic themes (*nāyaka nāyikā bhāva*) than most other composers of this form. His songs are popular because of the choice of rāga to express a particular mood, thus providing ample scope for expressive dance (*abhinaya*). These compositions are also performed in music concerts.

Vallalar Rāmaliṅga Svāmigal—*see* Rāmalingasvāmi

Vanaja Nārāyaṇa̱n (b. 1941) composed music for the lyrics of Periasāmi Thoora̱n. She is a disciple of the late vocalist M.L. Vasanthakumāri.

Varadācārlu—*see* Tenmaṭam Brothers

Varadachariar—*see* Tiger Varadāchāriar

Vāsudevācāriar—*see* Mysore Vāsudēvācāria

Vēdanāyakam Piḷḷai, S. Vēdanāyaham Śāstriār (1824 or 1826–89) wrote the lyrics for over 100 Tamil songs (*kṛti*). Many of these pieces were set to music by Ku̱nnakuḍi Veṅkaṭarāma Ayyar, and are still being performed today. He was a Catholic Christian, had an English education and was a friend of composer Gopālakṛṣṇa Bhārati. His ardent dedication to social issues such as education for women and tolerance for all religions is expressed in his songs and Tamil novels which continue to be appreciated by members of all sections of modern society.

Veṅkaṭamakhi (17th century) composed didactic pieces (*gītam*) as well as pieces belonging to the ancient form known as *Prabandham* which is no longer in use. (A *gītam* in Rītigauḷa rāga, jhampa tāla has been published in *Shobhillu Saptasvara*; see Bibliography.) He refers to himself as the son of Govinda Dīkṣitar who was a noted music theorist holding the post of minister at the court of Raghunātha Nāyak in Tañjāvūr. Govinda Dīkṣitar is credited with having given the *viṇā* its present status and form. Like its predecessor, the open-stringed harp or lyre (Tamil *yāl*), the *viṇā* had been used since ancient times, often modified for the purpose of scientific experimentation in the study of scales and intervals described in music treatises. The best-known work of Veṅkaṭamakhi is a theoretical treatise (*Caturdaṇḍī Prakāśikā*) written around 1660. The modern system of 72 scales (*mēḷakartā*) evolved on the basis of this treatise, and the original system of Veṅkaṭamakhi, although far from being fully developed or even understood by his contemporaries, was followed by Muttusvāmi Dīkṣitar whose father had studied under Muddu Veṅkaṭamakhi (a descendant of the older Veṅkaṭamakhi). The scheme of scale patterns conceived by Veṅkaṭamakhi constitutes an irregular empiric arrangement (*asampūrṇa paddhati*). Tyāgarāja, on the other hand, adopted an improved system modified by Govindācāri whose regular and symmetrical arrangement of 72 scale patterns (*sampūrṇa paddhati*) is more consistent and therefore more challenging from the point of view of an innovative genius.

V.N. Bhāṭkhaṇḍe (1860–1936), the influential music theorist of Hindustānī music, also based his system, a simplified arrangement of 10 reference scales (*thāṭ*), on the system of 72 *mēḷakartā* scales still prevalent in South India. In our time, many leading musicians and scholars in and outside India have continued to base their studies on the *mēḷakartā rāga* system which provides the various forms of melodic music with a common denominator: the tools and techniques required for comparing and sharing musical experience beyond the ordinary boundaries of history and culture.

Veṅkaṭarāma—*see* Kōṭṭavāsal Veṅkaṭarāma Bhāgavatar, Kunnakuḍi Veṅkaṭarāma Ayyar

Veṅkaṭarāmaṇa—*see* Wālājapet Veṅkaṭarāmaṇa Bhāgavatar

Veṅkaṭa Subba Ayyar—*see* Ūttukkāḍu Veṅkaṭa Subba Ayyar

Veṅkaṭa Subbayyar—*see* Mānambucāvaḍi Veṅkaṭa Subbayyar

Veṅkaṭēśa Ayyar—*see* Ālattūr Veṅkaṭēśa Ayyar

Vidyala Nārāyaṇasvāmi Naidu (1873–1912) is best known for his erotic songs in Tamil (*jāvaḷi*) and also composed devotional pieces (*kṛti*). He belonged to Tirupati.

Vijaya Gopālasvāmi (18th century) composed devotional songs (*kīrtana*) with Telugu and Sanskrit lyrics.

Vīṇā Kuppayyar (1798–1860) composed a variety of popular pieces (*svarāvaḷi*, *gītam*, *tānavarṇam*, and *kṛti*). A direct disciple of Tyāgarāja, he was the teacher of Kōṭṭavāsal Veṅkaṭarāma Bhāgavatar. His son Tiruvōtriyūr Tyāgayyar, was also a well-known composer.

Vīṇā Śeṣanna—*see* Mysore Śeṣanna

Violin Ponnusvāmi—*see* Mutialpet Ponnusvāmi

Wālājapet Kṛṣṇasvāmi Bhāgavatar (b. 1824) was a composer (*kṛti* and *svarajati*). Like his father, Wālājapet Veṅkaṭarāmaṇa Bhāgavatar, he was a direct disciple of Tyāgarāja during the last two years of the saint's life. He contributed to the publication of *Oriental Music in European Notation* by A.M.C. Mudaliyar in 1893 which, for the first time, contains detailed notation of Karnatic compositions: *pallavis*, numerous compositions of Tyāgarāja, Muttusvāmi Dīkṣitar, and didactic music (*abhyāsa gāna*). The playful series of notes (*ciṭṭasvara*) found in many compositions of Tyāgarāja are ascribed to Wālājapet Kṛṣṇasvāmi Bhāgavatar. He wrote a biographical account covering the later part of Tyāgarāja's life.

Wālājapet Veṅkaṭarāmaṇa Bhāgavatar (1781–1874) was a direct disciple of Tyāgarāja and a renowned composer in his own right (*tāṉavarṇam, kṛti, svarajati*). Together with his son, Wālājapet Kṛṣṇasvāmi Bhāgavatar, he is credited with helping to preserve the compositions of Tyāgarāja (*kṛti*). His biographical account of the earlier part of Tyāgarāja's life was continued by his son. He performed as a vocalist. Mysore Sadāśiva Rao, a reputed composer, was his disciple.

19

Musical Signatures (Mudrā)

Most Karnatic composers weave a poetical 'signature' (*mudrā* or *aṅkitam*) into the lyrics of a song (*sāhitya*). A *mudrā* establishes the composer's identity in the absence of a written score and also serves as a safeguard against plagiarism or corruption of a composer's work. This practice has not, entirely, prevented the grafting of the *mudrā* 'Tyāgarāja' onto a composition by K.V. Śrīnivāsa Ayyaṅgār in rāga Siṁhēndramadhyama which was quite popular until the 'fraud' was discovered. To 'atone' for his sacrilege of using the great saint's signature, Śrīnivāsa Ayyaṅgār composed a second *kṛti* in the same rāga, 'Natajana', rūpaka tāla, ironically again with the same *mudrā*.

A *mudrā* is generally found in the latter portion (*caraṇam*) of most compositions except for the *varṇam*. Sometimes a *mudrā* expresses the composer's reverence for his chosen deity (*iṣṭadevatā*). In some instances it also refers to a preceptor (*guru*) as in the case of M.D. Rāmānathan.

Annāmalai Reḍḍiyār, Jayadeva, and Tyāgarāja are examples of composers who used their personal names also as signatures in their songs (*svanāma mudrākara*).

Some composers have the name of a village, town (e.g. Rāmnād) or their musical speciality (e.g. *Pallavi*) attached to their personal name. For easy reference, some composers have been given multiple entries ('Gopāla Ayyar' and 'Pallavi Gopāla Ayyar').

Some composers, including vocalist G.N. Balasubramaniam, chose not to use any *mudrā*.

The spelling of most names conforms to the transliterations prevailing in South India. The names of contemporary and living persons are not standardized. However, 'Shāstry' ('Shāstri') is uniformly spelt 'Śāstri', 'Iyer' as 'Ayyar', and Iyengar as Ayyaṅgār.

I. Mudrā index (see also II., Composer index)

Acyuta Dāsa—see Acyuta Dāsa
Ādi Veṅkaṭeśvara—see Paṭṭaṇam Subrahmaṇya Ayyar
Ambhujanābha—see Svāti Tiruṇāḷ
Annāmalai Reḍḍiyar—see Annāmalai Reḍḍiyar
Arunācala, Arunadri, Arunagiri—see Arunācala Śāstri

Bālacandra, Bālasudhakāra—see Candrasēkhara Śāstri (Bangalore Chandraśēkharayya, Kōlar Chandraśēkharayya)
Bālakṛṣṇa—see Gopālakṛṣṇa Bhārati
Bhadrādri, Bhadrāgiri, Bhadrārti, Bhadrācala, Bhadrāsaila—see Bhadrācala Rāmadās
Bṛhadēśvara—see Ci<u>nn</u>iah
Ceṅgalvarayya—see Ceyyur Ceṅgalvarayya Śāstri
dāsa—see mudrā *Gopāladāsa, Guhadāsa, Kavikuñjaradāsa, Kuñjaradāsa, Nīlakaṇṭhadāsa, Rāmadāsa, Seṣadāsa, Umādāsa, Varadadāsa*
Dharmapurīśa, Dharmapurivasa—see Dharmapuri Subbarāyar
Garbhapuriśa, Garbhapuriśadana, Garbhapurivasa, Garbhapuriyar—see Karūr Dakṣiṇāmūrti Śāstri and Karūr Devuḍayya
Gopāla—see Kṣetrajñā (Kṣētrayya)
Gopāla—see also mudrā *Gopāla, Gopāladāsa, Muvvagopāla, Rājāgopāla, Venugopāla, Vijaya Gopāla*
Gopāladāsa—see Tiruvōtriyūr Tyāgayyar and Vīṇā Kuppayyar
Gopālakṛṣṇa—see Gopālakṛṣṇa Bhārati
Guhadāsa—see Mahāvaidyanātha Śiva<u>n</u> (Ayyar), Rāmasvāmi Śiva<u>n</u>
Guruguha—see Muttusvāmi Dīkṣitar
Gurumūrti—see Paidāla Gurumūrti Śāstrī
Haṁsa, Paramahaṁsa—see Sadāśiva Brahmendra
Harikēsa, Harikēsapura—see Harikēsanallūr Mutthiah Bhāgavatar
Jayadeva—see Jayadeva
Kaginele Kēśava, Kāginele Ādikēśava—see Kanaka Dāsa
Kavikuñjara—see Kavikuñjara Bhārati
Kavikuñjaradāsa—see Kōtīsvara Ayyar
Kosala—see Mārgadarśi Śeṣa Ayyaṅgār
Kṛṣṇa—see Ku<u>n</u>ḏrakkuḍi Kṛṣṇa Ayyar
Kṛṣṇa—see also mudrā *Bālakṛṣṇa, Gopālakṛṣṇa, Mīśu Kṛṣṇa, Śyāma Kṛṣṇa, Veṅkaṭakṛṣṇa*
Kumāra—see Subbarayya Śāstri; see also mudrā *Muttukumāra*
Kumāravēle—see Arunagirināthar
Kuñjaradāsa—see Kōtīsvara Ayyar
Mīśu Kṛṣṇa—see Mīśu Kṛṣṇa Ayyar
Murali—see Balamurali Krishna
Muruga—see Ghanam Kṛṣṇayyar
Murugone—see Arunagirināthar
Muttukumāra—see Ghanam Kṛṣṇayyar, Vaitīśvarankoil Subbarāma Ayyar
Mutturāmaliṅga—see Mutturāmaliṅga Sētupati
Muvvagopāla—see Kṣetrajñā (Kṣētrayya)
Muvvapuridhamudu—see Kṣetrajñā (Kṣētrayya)
Narahari—see Tenmaṭam Narasiṁhācārlu
Narasiṁha—see Tenmaṭam Narasiṁhācārlu
Nārāyaṇa Tīrtha—see Nārāyaṇa Tīrtha
Nīlakaṇṭha, Nīlakaṇṭhadāsa—see Nīlakaṇṭha Śiva<u>n</u>

Padmanābha—see Irayimman̲ Tampi, Svāti Tirunāḷ
Padmapuri—see Vīṇā Krishnamāchāriar
Paramahaṁsa—see Sadāśiva Brahmendra
Perumale—see Arunagirināthar
Purandara Vittala—see Purandara Dāsa
Rājāgopāla—see Paccimiriyam Āḍiappayya, Taccūr Siṅgarācāryulu
Rāmadāsa—see Bhadrācala Rāmadās, Papanasam Śivan̲
Raṅgasvāmi—see Mūlaivīṭṭu Raṅgasvāmi
Sadāśiva—see Mysore Sadāśiva Rao
Sarasanārāyaṇa Tīrtha—see Nārāyaṇa Tīrtha
Śeṣa—see Pallavi Śeṣa Ayyar
Śeṣadāsa—see Mysore Śeṣanna
Siṅgarānuta—see Taccūr Siṅgarācāryulu
Śivanārāyaṇa Tīrtha—see Nārāyaṇa Tīrtha
Śivarāma—see Śivarāmayya
Śrīnivāsa—see Rāmnād ('Pūcci') Śrīnivāsa Ayyaṅgār
Śrī Rāmacandra Veṅkaṭarāmana—see Wālājapet Veṅkaṭarāmaṇa Bhāgavatar
Śrī Varada Veṅkaṭēśa—see Paṭṭaṇam Subrahmaṇya Ayyar
Śrī Vidyā—see Mysore Jayacāmarāja Wodeyar
Subbarāma—see Vaitīśvarankoil Subbarāma Ayyar
Subrahmaṇya—see Ghanam Kr̥ṣṇayyar
Śyāmā Kr̥ṣṇa—see Śyāmā Śāstri
Tālavanēśa—see Tiruppan̲andāḷ Paṭṭābhirāmayya
Tambirane—see Arunagirināthar
Tirupatipura—see Vidyala Nārāyaṇasvāmi
Tirupatīśa—see Bellary Rājā Rao, Vidyala Nārāyaṇasvāmi
Tirupati Veṅkaṭēśa—see Vidyala Nārāyaṇasvāmi Naidu
Tyāgarāja—see Tyāgarāja
Umādāsa—see Anayya
Varadadāsa—see Rāmanāthan̲, M.D.
Varada Veṅkaṭa—see Kuppusvāmi Ayyar
Varanārāyaṇa Tīrtha—see Nārāyaṇa Tīrtha
Vāsudeva—see Mysore Vāsudevācāriar
Vēdanāyaka—see Vēdanāyakam Piḷḷai
Vēlapuri Kēśava—see Kanaka Dāsa
Vēlava—see Ghanam Kr̥ṣṇayyar
Veṅkaṭa—see Pallavi Gopāla Ayyar
Veṅkaṭakr̥ṣṇa—see Rāmasvāmi Dīkṣitar
Veṅkaṭamakhi—see Veṅkaṭamakhi
Veṅkaṭēśa—see Mānambucāvaḍi Veṅkaṭa Subbayyar, Kōttavāsal Veṅkaṭarāma Bhāgavatar, Paṭṭaṇam Subrahmaṇya Ayyar, Vidyala Nārāyaṇasvāmi Naidu
Veṅkaṭēśvara—see Paṭṭaṇam Subrahmaṇya Ayyar, Śaṭkāla Narasayyā
Venugopāla—see Vīṇā Kuppayyar
Vijaya Gopāla—see Vijaya Gopālasvāmi
Yatinārāyaṇa Tīrtha—see Nārāyaṇa Tīrtha

II. Composer index (see also I., Mudrā index)

Acyuta Dāsa—mudrā: *Acyuta Dāsa*
Anayya—mudrā: *Umādāsa*
Annāmalai Reddiyar—mudrā: *Annāmalai Reddiyar*
Arunācala Śāstri (Arunācalakkavirayar)—mudrā: *Arunācala, Arunadri, Arunagiri*
Arunagirināthar—mudrā: *Kumāravēle, Murugone, Perumāle, Tambirane*
Bangalore Chandraśēkharayya (Kōlar Chandraśēkharayya, Candrasēkhara Śāstri)—mudrā: *Bālacandra, Bālasudhakāra*
Bellary Rājā Rao—mudrā: *Tirupatiśa*
Bhadrācala Rāmadāsa—mudrā: *Rāmadāsa, Bhadrādri, Bhadrāgiri, Bhadrārti, Bhadrācala, Bhadrāsaila*
Candrasēkhara Śāstri (Bangalore Chandraśēkharayya, Kōlar Chandraśēkharayya)—mudrā: *Bālacandra, Bālasudhakāra*
Ceṅgalvaraya Śāstri—mudrā: *Ceṅgalvaraya*
Cinna Devuḍu Ayyar (Karūr Devuḍayya)—mudrā: *Garbhapuriśa, Garbhapuriśadana, Garbhapurivasa, Garbhapuriyar*
Cinniah—mudrā: *Bṛhadēśvara*
Dakṣiṇāmūrti Śāstrī (Karūr)—mudrā: *Garbhapuriyar*
Devuḍayya (Karūr)—mudrā: *Garbhapuriyar*
Dharmapuri Subbarāyar—mudrā: *Dharmapuriśa, Dharmapurivasa*
Dīkṣitar, Muttusvāmi- mudrā: *Guruguha*
Dīkṣitar, Rāmasvāmi—mudrā: *Veṅkaṭakṛṣṇa*
Ghanam Kṛṣṇa Ayyar—mudrā: *Muttukumāra, Muruga, Subrahmaṇya, Vēlava*
Gopāla Ayyar (Pallavi)—mudrā: *Veṅkaṭa*
Gopālakṛṣṇa Bhārati—mudrā: *Bālakṛṣṇa, Gopālakṛṣṇa*
Gopālasvāmi (Vijaya)—mudrā: *Vijaya Gopāla*
Harikēsanallūr Mutthiah Bhāgavatar—mudrā: *Harikēsa, Harikēsapura*
Irayimmaṉ Tampi—mudrā: *Padmanābha*
Jayacāmarāja Wodeyar , Mysore—mudrā: *Śrī Vidyā*
Jayadeva—mudrā: *Jayadeva*
Kanaka Dāsa—mudrā: *Kāginele Ādikēśava, Kāginele Kēśava, Vēlapuri Kēśava*
Karūr Dakṣiṇāmūrti Śāstri and Karūr Devuḍayya—mudrā: *Garbhapuriśa, Garbhapuriśadana, Garbhapurivasa, Garbhapuriyar*
Kavikuñjara Bhārati—mudrā: *Kavikuñjara*
Kōlar Chandraśēkharayya (Bangalore Chandraśēkharayya, Candrasēkhara Śāstri)—mudrā: *Bālacandra, Bālasudhakāra*
Kōtīsvara Ayyar—mudrā: *Kavikuñjaradāsa, Kuñjaradāsa*
Kōttavāsal Veṅkaṭarāma Bhāgavatar—mudrā: *Veṅkaṭēśa*
Krishnamāchāriar (Vīṇā Krishnamāchāriar)—mudrā: *Padmapuri*
Kṛṣṇa Ayyar (Kundrakudi)—mudrā: *Kṛṣṇa*
Kṣetrajñā (Kṣētrayya)—mudrā: *Gopāla, Muvvagopāla and Muvvapuridhamudu*
Kuṉḏrakkuḍi Kṛṣṇa Ayyar—mudrā: *Kṛṣṇa*
Kuppayyar (Vīṇā Kuppayyar)—mudrā: *Venugopāla*
Kuppusvāmi Ayyar—mudrā: *Varada Veṅkaṭa*
Mahāvaidyanātha Śivaṉ (Ayyar)—mudrā: *Guhadāsa*

Mānambucāvaḍi Veṅkaṭa Subbayyar—mudrā: *Veṅkaṭēśa*
Mārgadarśi Śeṣa Ayyaṅgār (Śeṣayyaṇgār)—mudrā: *Kosala*
Mīśu Kṛṣṇa Ayyar—mudrā: *Mīśu Kṛṣṇa*
Mūlaivīṭṭu Raṅgasvāmi—mudrā: *Raṅgasvāmi*
Mutthiah Bhāgavatar (Harikēsanallūr)—mudrā: *Harikēsa, Harikēsapura*
Mutturāmaliṅga Sētupati—mudrā: *Mutturāmaliṅga*
Muttusvāmi Dīkṣitar—mudrā: *Guruguha*
Muvvagopāla—mudrā: *Kṣētrajñā*
Mysore Jayacāmarāja Wodeyar—mudrā: *Śrī Vidyā*
Mysore Sadāśiva Rao—mudrā: *Sadāśiva*
Mysore Śeṣanna—mudrā: *Śeṣadāsa*
Mysore Vāsudevācāriar—mudrā: *Vāsudeva*
Narasayyā (Śaṭkāla Narasayyā)—mudrā: *Veṅkaṭēśvara*
Narasiṁhācārlu (Tenmaṭam Brothers)—mudrā: *Narahari, Narasiṁha*
Nārāyaṇasvāmi Naidu (Vidyala)—mudrā: *Tirupatipura, Tirupati Veṅkaṭēśa*
Nārāyaṇa Tīrtha—mudrā: *Nārāyaṇa Tīrtha, Śiva-, Vara-, Yati Nārāyaṇa Tīrtha*
Nīlakaṇṭha Śivan̲—mudrā: *Nīlakaṇṭha, Nīlakaṇṭhadāsa*
Paccimiriyam Āḍiappayya—mudrā: *Rājāgopāla*
Paidāla Gurumūrti Śāstrī—mudrā: *Gurumūrti*
Pallavi Gopāla Ayyar—mudrā: *Veṅkaṭa*
Pallavi Śeṣa Ayyar—mudrā: *Śeṣa*
Papanasam Śivan̲—mudrā: *Ramadāsa*
Paṭṭābhirāmayya (Tiruppanandāḷ)—mudrā: *Tālavanēśa*
Paṭṭaṇam Subrahmaṇya Ayyar—mudrā: *Veṅkaṭēśa, Veṅkaṭēśvara, Śrī Varada Veṅkaṭēśa, Varada Veṅkaṭēśvara, Ādi Veṅkaṭēśa*
Pūcci Śrīnivāsa Ayyaṅgār—mudrā: *Śrīnivāsa*
Purandara Dāsa—mudrā: *Purandara Viṭṭala*
Rājā Rao (Bellary)—mudrā: *Tirupatīśa*
Rāmanāthan̲, M.D.—mudrā: *Varadadāsa*
Rāmasvāmi Dīkṣitar—mudrā: *Veṅkaṭakṛṣṇa*
Rāmasvāmi Śivan̲—mudrā: *Guhadāsa*
Rāmdās (Rāmadās)—*see* Bhadrācala Rāmadāsa
Rāmnād ('Pūcci') Śrīnivāsa Ayyaṅgār—mudrā: *Śrīnivāsa*
Raṅgasvāmi (Mūlaivīṭṭu)—mudrā: *Raṅgasvāmi*
Sadāśiva Brahmendra—mudrā: *Haṁsa, Paramahaṁsa*
Sadāśiva Rao—mudrā: *Sadāśiva*
Śāstri, Subbarayya—mudrā: *Kumāra*
Śāstri, Śyama—mudrā: *Śyāma Kṛṣṇa*
Śaṭkāla Narasayyā—mudrā: *Veṅkaṭēśvara*
Śeṣa Ayyar (Pallavi)—mudrā: Śeṣa
Śeṣanna (Mysore Śeṣanna, Vīṇā Śeṣanna)—mudrā: *Śeṣadāsa*
Śeṣayyaṇgār (Mārgadarśī Śeṣa Ayyaṅgār)—mudrā: *Kosala*
Siṅgarācāryulu—mudrā: *Rājagopāla, Siṅgarānuta*
Śivarāmayya—mudrā: *Śivarāma*
Śrīnivāsa Ayyaṅgār—mudrā: *Śrīnivāsa*

Subbarāma Ayyar (Vaitīśvarankoil)—mudrā: *Muttukumāra, Subbarāma*
Subbarāyar (= Dharmapuri Subbarāyar)—mudrā: *Dharmapurīśa, Dharmapurivasa*
Subbarayya Śāstri—mudrā: *Kumāra*
Subrahmaṇya Ayyar (Paṭṭaṇam)—mudrā: *Veṅkaṭēśa, Veṅkaṭēśvara*
Svāti Tirunāḷ—mudrā: *Padmanābha*; also *Abjanābha, Ambhujanābha, Jalajanābha, Pankajanābha* . . . other . . . *nābha*)
Śyāma Śāstri—mudrā: *Śyāmakṛṣṇa*
Taccūr Siṅgarācāryulu—mudrā: *Rājagopāla, Siṅgarānuta*
Tenmaṭam Narasiṁhācārlu—mudrā: *Narahari, Narasiṁha*
Thyagaraja—see Tyāgarāja
Tiruppaṉandāḷ Paṭṭābhirāmayya—see *Tālavanēśa*
Tiruvōtriyūr Tyāgayyar—mudrā: *Gopāladāsa*
Tyāgarāja—mudrā: *Tyāgarāja*
Tyāgāyya—mudrā: *Gopāladāsa*
Vaitīśvarankoil Subbarāma Ayyar—mudrā: *Muttukumāra, Subbarāma*
Vāsudevācāriar—mudrā: *Vāsudeva*
Vēdanāyakam Piḷḷai—mudrā: *Vēdanāyaka*
Veṅkaṭamakhi—mudrā: *Veṅkaṭamakhi*
Veṅkaṭa Subbayyar (Mānambucāvaḍi Veṅkaṭa Subbayyar)—mudrā: *Veṅkaṭēśa*
Vidyala Nārāyaṇasvāmi Naidu—mudrā: *Tirupatipura, Tirupati Veṅkaṭēśa*
Vijaya Gopālasvāmi—mudrā: *Vijaya Gopāla*
Vīṇā Krishnamāchāriar—mudrā: *Padmapuri*
Vīṇā Kuppayyar—mudrā: *Venugopāla, Gopāladāsa*
Wālājapet Veṅkaṭarāmaṇa Bhāgavatar—mudrā: *Śri Rāmacandra Veṅkaṭarāmana*

Biographical Notes (Musicians and Music Scholars)

The preceding chapter on composers contains more information about some musicians listed in the present chapter, and also information about several others whose compositions are found in the concert and dance repertoire, recordings, and broadcasts.

The teachers and pupils of eminent musicians and composers are listed and cross-referred as far as relevant details could be ascertained. Many exponents of the younger generation have been included because some critics regard them as the future masters of classical South Indian music. In view of the sheer number of qualified Karnatic musicians, omissions (e.g. due to a dearth of relevant information) must not be misread as judgements of merit.

For the sake of brevity, the following conventions have been adopted in the present chapter:

AIR is the official abbreviation for *All India Radio* which employs numerous Karnatic musicians as Staff Artistes, Music Directors, and Producers all over the country. In view of AIR's transfer policy, stations are only named if a long-term association has been established.

Chennai, the capital of the South Indian state of Tamil Nadu, was earlier known as *Madras*, Tañjāvūr as *Tanjore*, Palakkad as *Palghat* or *Pālakkāḍu*, Tiruvananthapuram as *Trivandrum*, and Mumbai as *Bombay*. Although the new official names have been used as consistently as possible, they may not always be applicable as in the case of names chosen by some musicians (e.g. Bombay Sisters, Palghat Maṇi Ayyar).

Harikathā refers to a musician's specialization in the composite art form known as *kālakṣepam* or *Harikathā kālakṣepam*.

Universities and **Colleges**, unless specified otherwise, refer to a person's teaching assignment in a Department of Music. The following locations are not mentioned in individual entries:

Andhra Pradesh—Shrī Veṅkaṭēśwara University (Tirupati); Telugu University (Hyderabad).

Karnataka—Mahārāṇī's Arts College (University of Mysore); Mahārāṇī's College for Women (Bangalore).

Kerala—Chembai Music College, Palakkad (Palghat, Pālakkāḍu); Rādhā Lakshmī Vilāsam (RLV) Music Academy (Tripunithura); Swāti Tirunāḷ College of Music, and S.S.T. Music College (Tiruvananthapuram).

Tamil Nadu—Aṇṇāmalai University (Chidambaram); Rājāh's College (Tiruvaiyāṟu);

Central College of Carnatic Music, Kalākshētra College of Fine Arts, Teachers' College of the Music Academy, Queen Mary's College, Stella Maris College, and Tamil Isai College (Chennai).

Many musicians have the name of their birthplace or ancestral home prefixed to their personal names (e.g. Lālguḍi Jayarāman, Palghat Maṇi Ayyar); their names are listed and cross-referred accordingly. It should be noted that these names rarely coincide with these musicians' current place of residence.

Admirers and critics often refer to popular musicians by mere initials which are mentioned in view of their honorific connotation (e.g. 'MSG' for M.S. Gōpālakrishnan).

Honorary titles, awards, and foreign concert tours have not been included for the sake of brevity; these and other details are found in the voluminous *Biographical Dictionary of Carnatic Composers and Musicians* by N. Rājagōpālan ('Garland', in four volumes). Apart from this valuable source, information has mainly been gathered from articles and interviews in *Sruti Magazine* as well as information published by the Music Academy (Journal, Souvenirs). Other sources include the *Who's Who of Indian Musicians* (Sangeet Natak Akademi), documentations, Newsletter, programme notes of *Sampradāya*, reviews, and special features in Indian periodicals (e.g. *The Hindu*, *Indian Express*, *The Illustrated Weekly of India*; for details, see Bibliography).

Many rare recordings, documents, photographs, and interviews pertaining to the different styles of Karnatic music are available for listening and research purposes in the archives of *Sampradāya*, Centre for the Music Traditions of South India (1, Musiri Subramanian Road, Chennai 600004). This collection includes a series of chamber concerts and lecture-demonstrations by senior musicians that were organized in conjunction with the Max Mueller Bhavan (German Cultural Centre), Chennai.

A wide range of recorded music from South India is in the process of being released in India and other countries, including historical 78 rpm recordings made during the first decades of this century as well as tape recordings made by AIR for broadcasting purposes. (For further details, *see* Discography.)

Abraham Pandithar, M. (musicologist, composer); 1859–1919; studied music from several teachers; is mainly remembered for organizing the first music conferences in South India (1912, 1916); strove to kindle public interest in the ancient musical heritage of the Tamils; author of the voluminous encyclopedia titled *Karuṇāmirta sāgaram*.

Adicayapuram Sītarāmayyar (*mōrsiṅg*, vocal); early 20th century; disciple of Eṭṭayapuram Rāmacandra Bhāgavatar; credited with introducing the *mōrsiṅg* as an accompaniment.

Ālandūr S. Naṭarājan̲ (violin); 1919–96; disciple of Sāttūr Krishna Ayyaṅgār, Tiger Varadāchāriar, and his brother, Dr S. Rāmanāthan̲ (vocal); disciple of Madurai Subrahmaṇya Ayyar (violin); Central College and Kalākshētra; teacher of his son and his niece, R. Lathā.

Ālattūr Śivasubrahmaṇya Ayyar ('Ālattūr Brothers', vocal); 1916–65; disciple of his father Ālattūr Veṅkaṭēśa Ayyar; the Ālattūr Brothers are credited with popularizing and refining complex rhythmic patterns (*kōrvai*) as conclusion for the melodic improvisation of the *svara kalpana* type, a feature which is believed to have been introduced by Kāñcīpuram Naina Piḷḷai; they were specialists for the *rāgam tānam pallavi* format.

Ālattūr Śrīnivāsa Ayyar ('Ālattūr Brothers', vocal); 1911–80; disciple of Ālattūr Veṅkaṭēśa Ayyar who belonged to the *guruśiṣya paramparā* of Tyāgarāja; teacher of his younger brother, Panchapakēsha Ayyar.

Alepey Veṅkaṭēśan (vocal); b. 1956; disciple of Ariyakkuḍi Rāmānuja Ayyaṅgār; President, *Sampradāya* (Centre for the Music Traditions of South India, Chennai).

Allam Durgāprasād (*gōṭṭuvādyam*); b. 1963; disciple of Nārāyaṇa Ayyar; son of Allam Kōtēśwar Rao; AIR.

Allam Kōtēśwar Rao (*gōṭṭuvādyam*); b. 1933; disciple of Nārāyaṇa Ayyar; father of Allam Durgāprasād; Kalākshētra.

Ambhi Dīkṣitar—*see* Muttusvāmi ('Ambhi') Dīkṣitar.

Ambujam Vēdāntam (vocalist, musicologist, composer); b. 1938; disciple of her mother, P. Raṅganāyaki, K.T. Śrīnivāsan, Muttunatēśa Ayyar, Kalliḍaikkuricci Rāmaliṅga Bhāgavatar, and Dr S. Rāmanāthan.

Ānandāṇkōil V. Selvaratnam Piḷḷai (*nāgasvaram*); b. 1935; disciple of his grandfather, Vīrasvāmi Piḷḷai.

Ānanḍāṇkōil V. Śivakumār (vocal); b. 1965; son and disciple of A.V. Selvaratnam, S.P. Viṣvaliṅgam, and K.J Jesudoss.

Ānanḍāṇkōil V. Sundarājan (*mṛdaṅgam, konnakkōl*); disciple of Nācciyārkōil Raghu and Trichy R. Thāyumānavan; research on *konnakkōl*.

Anantarāma Bhāgavatar—*see* Palghat Anantarāma Bhāgavatar.

Anantharāman, M.S. (violin); b. 1924; disciple of his father, violinist Pārūr Sundaram Ayyar; brother of violinist M.S. Gōpālakrishnan; father and teacher of violinists M.A. Sundarēśan and Pārūr M.A. Krishnaswāmy; Central College.

Anantharāman, R. (*mṛdaṅgam*); b.1983; grandson and disciple of Palghat Raghu.

Aṉayampaṭṭi S. Daṇḍapāṇi (*jalataraṅgam*, violin); 1926–84; disciple of his father, *jalataraṅgam* exponent Aṉayampaṭṭi Subba Ayyar, his uncle, violinist Nārāyaṇa Ayyar, violinist Bhavāni Śrīkanta Ayyar, and Peṇṇattūr Cinnasvāmi Ayyar; reputed for his renditions of those classical items that can be performed in a congenial manner on the *jalataraṅgam*; AIR.

Anilkumār, K.P. (*mṛdaṅgam*); b. 1960; learnt music first from his father, K.P. Bhaskaradas; disciple of Puducōde Krishna Ayyar and Palghat Raghu; Lecturer, Kalākshētra.

Anurādha Surēsh (vocal); b. 1968; disciple and daughter of K.V. Nārāyaṇaswāmy.

Ariparala Satyanārāyaṇa Mūrthi (violinist, scholar, composer); 1904–93; disciple of Vārāṇasī Brahmaiah Śāstrī; author of several music books.

Ariyakkuḍi Rāmānuja Ayyaṅgār (vocal); 1890–1967; disciple of several leading musicians including Nāmakkaḷ Narasiṁha Ayyaṅgār, and composer Rāmnād ('Pūcci') Srīnivāsa Ayyaṅgār; learnt compositions from Vīṇā Dhanammāḷ; developed his own style based on rendition in medium tempo (*madhyama kāla*) which was named after him (*Ariyakkuḍi bāṇi*); credited with establishing the present concert format (*kaccēri paddhati*) which continues to be followed by most leading musicians; teacher of B. Rājam Iyer, Sāvitri Satyamūrti, K.V. Nārāyaṇaswāmy, and Alepey Veṅkaṭēsan.

Arunachalam—*see* Kārukuricci P. Arunāchalam.

Aruna Sayeeram (vocal); b. 1952; disciple of T. Brinda; also renders devotional songs (*abhang*) of Hindustānī music; has studied and adapted techniques of European voice culture; collaborated with exponents of World Music.

Ashōk Ramani (vocal); b. 1962; learnt music first from his mother, Dr Rukmini Ramani, daughter of Pāpanāsam Śivan; also learnt *mṛdaṅgam* as disciple of Kumbakōnam M. Rājappa Ayyaṅgār; disciple of S. Rāmanāthan.

Atuḷ Kumār (flute); b. 1980; disciple and grandson of N. Ramani.

Āvuḍaiyārkōvil Harihara Bhāgavatar (vocal, *jalataraṅgam, gettuvādyam*); 1895–1975; disciple of his father (*gettuvādyam*), Anayampaṭṭi Subba Ayyar (*jalataraṅgam*), M. Veṅkaṭācalam Bhāgavatar (*harikathā kālakṣepam*); father and teacher of Āvuḍaiyārkōvil H. Subramaṇyam.

Āvuḍaiyārkōvil H. Subramaṇyam (*gettuvādyam*); son and disciple of Āvuḍaiyārkōvil Harihara Bhāgavatar; author of a paper on his instrument (*Tāla Vādya Seminar*) which resembles a *tambūrā* and is played with a pair of bamboo batons with brass bangles attached to both grips.

Baby—*see* E. Gāyatri and Trivandrum Baby Pārvathy.

Bakshi Subbanna (*viṇā*); 1855–1938; court musician at Mysore; teacher of V. Śrīkanta Ayyar.

Baktavatsalam—*see* Tiruvārūr Baktavatsalam.

Bāla, T.N. (vocal, *mṛdaṅgam*, *kañjīrā*, *ghaṭam*, composer); b. 1927; disciple of Madurai Maṇi Ayyar (vocal) and Śivavaḍivēlu Piḷḷai (percussion); AIR (Delhi, Chennai); lives in the USA where he worked for television.

Bālachander—*see* Tañjāvūr S. Bālachander.

Bālachander, S. (*vīṇā*); 1927–90; self-taught musician who sought to explore new realms in terms of virtuosity and expressiveness; challenged prevailing notions about traditional music; brother of S. Rājam with whom he toured India during his childhood; also worked in the field of film music; teacher of Jayanti Rādhakrishnan.

Bālāji—*see* Bombay Bālāji.

Bālāji, J. (*mṛdaṅgam*); b. 1965; disciple of Tanjore R. Rāmadoss and Rāmnād M.N Kandaswāmy.

Bālakrishna, D. (*viṇā*); son and disciple of Mysore Doreswāmy Ayyaṅgār with whom he has given numerous concerts.

Bālakrishna, D.J. (vocal); b. 1968; belongs to a family of musicians; disciple of T.V. Śaṅkaranārāyaṇan.

Bālakrishna Śāstrigaḷ, T.S. (*harikathā kālakṣepam*); b. 1918; son of violinist Samayya; disciple of Tiger Varadāchāriar and Muḍikondān Sabhāpati Ayyar.

Bālamuraḷi Krishna, M. (self-taught vocalist, composer, violinist, viola player); b. 1930; Principal of the Music Colleges of Vijayawada and Hyderabad; Producer, AIR; also worked in the field of film music.

Bālasarasvati, T. (dance, vocal); 1918–84; granddaughter of Vīṇā Dhanammāḷ; sister of Tañjāvūr Viṣwanāthan; performed and lectured all over the world; her lectures have been edited by S. Guhan and published by the Sruti Foundation (*Bāla on Dance*); she continued the old practice of singing while depicting the theme of her dance (*abhinaya*); Director, School of Dance, Music Academy.

Bālasubrahmaṇyam, B. (vocal); 1962; disciple of B. Krishnamūrthy and T. Brinda.

Bālasubrahmaṇyam, G.N. ('GNB', vocalist, composer); 1910–65; first taught by his father; disciple of Madurai Subrahmaṇya Ayyar and Tiger Varadāchāriar; also worked in the field of film music; credited with raising the aesthetic standards of the *tukkaḍā* (concluding) section of a Karnatic concert; created two rāgas (Śivaśakti and Amṛta

Behāg) and composed about 250 songs of which many were published by his disciple, Tañjāvūr S. Kalyāṇarāman; teacher of M.L. Vasanthakumāri and Trichūr V. Rāmachandran; Principal, Swāti Tirunāḷ College of Music; Producer, AIR.

Bālasubramaṇyan, K. (violin); b. 1951; disciple of his father, K.A. Kāsi Bhāgavatar (a disciple of Palghat Rāma Bhāgavatar), R.R. Śarma, K.P. Rāmakrishnan, and M. Chandraśēkharan; AIR (Coimbatore).

Bangalore G. Channamma (vocal, *vīṇā*); 1913–86; disciple of K. Ponniah Piḷḷai and Vīṇā Krishnamāchāriar; author of a textbook (*Sangeeta Bodhini*); Head of Music Department, Mahārāṇī's College, and Principal, Gānamandiram (Bangalore).

Bangalore K.S. Mañjunāthan (*ghaṭam*); 1921–89; disciple of Śrīnivāsa Ayyar and L.S. Śeṣagiri Rao; teacher of Bangalore K. Veṅkaṭarām; AIR.

Bangalore Nāgaratnammāḷ (vocal); 1878–1952; learnt violin from her uncle, Veṅkiṭasāmi Appā, and Munusvāmi Appā (a disciple of Wālājapet Kṛṣṇasvāmi Bhāgavatar); studied *bharata nāṭyam* under Bangalore Kittanna, and *abhinaya* under Madras Tiruveṅkaṭācariar; disciple of Giripatta Thimmayyah, and Bīḍaram Krishnappā; specialist for Tyāgarāja's music, and that of Purandara Dāsa (*dēvarnāma*); leading founder member of the annual Tiruvaiyāru festival (*Tyāgarāja ārādhana*); published music books in Telugu, Sanskrit, and Tamil; taught at the *Tyāga Brahmā Nilayam* in Tiruvaiyāru where she built a shrine (*samādhi*) for Tyāgarāja; her own *samādhi* is also found nearby where she is remembered and revered as an outstanding figure of Karnatic music.

Bangalore K. Veṅkaṭarām (*mṛdaṅgam*, *ghaṭam*, vocal); b. 1934; disciple of K.S. Mañjunāthan; Editor of the Proceedings, *Tāla Vādya Seminar*, teacher of B.N. Surēsh and T.S. Sathyavathy.

Banni Bai, C. (*harikathā*); b. 1912; belongs to a musical family; disciple of Bālu Piḷḷai, Nārāyaṇasvāmi Ayyar, Vīṇā Dhanammāḷ (musical repertoire), Mahādēva Ayyar (*abhinaya*, *mudrā*), Svāminātā Ayyar (Tamil, English), Mārkaṇḍēya Brahmachārya (Marāṭhi pieces), Vijaya Bhāgavatar, Kuppayya Bhāgavatar, and T.P. Kalyāṇa Śāstrigaḷ (*harikathā kālakṣepam*); regards Bangalore Nāgaratnammāḷ as her *guru*; has been portrayed in a film by Soudamini; a performance (*Rukmini Kalyāṇam*) has been presented and documented by *Sampradāya* (Chennai); teacher of Dr Premeela Gurumūrthy.

Bhāgyalekshmy, Dr S. (vocalist, scholar, dancer); belongs to a family of musicians of Tiruvananthapuram (Kerala); disciple of Dr S. Rāmanāthan and Vechoor Harihara Subramoṇia Ayyar; author of several music books in Malayālam and English (e.g. *Ragas in Carnatic Music*, *Carnatic Music Compositions: An Index*).

Bhārati—*see* Gopāla Kṛṣṇa Bhārati, Rājkumār Bhārati.

Bhāskaran, K. (flute); b. 1961; disciple of Māyavaram (Mayilāḍuturai) Saraswathi and T.R. Subrahmaṇyam; being a computer specialist by profession, he has also presented computerized music programmes for Karnatic music (e.g. *rāga ālāpana*).

Bhāskaran—*see* Sikkil R. Bhāskaran.

Bhavanārāyaṇa Rao—*see* Dwāram Bhavanārāyaṇa Rao.

Bhīmachār, L. (*mōrsiṅg*); b. 1931; disciple of H. Puttachār (*mṛdangam*).

Bīḍaram Krishnappā (vocalist, violinist, composer, *vaiṇika*); 1866–1931; studied under Tyāgarāja's own disciples, Umayāḷpuram Krishna Bhāgavatar and Sundara Bhāgavatar; learnt violin from Tirukōḍikāval Krishna Ayyar; disciple of Mysore

('Vīṇā') Śeṣanna; credited with popularizing the compositions of Mysore Sadāśiva Rao beyond Mysore; teacher of Bangalore Nāgaratnammāḷ, Titte Krishna Ayyaṅgār, Mysore T. Chowdiah, T. Puttaswāmiah, A.K. Subba Rao, and R.R. Kēśavamūrthy.

Bombay Bālāji (*mṛdaṅgam*); b. 1969; disciple of Palghat Maṇi Ayyar, Trichy Rāghava Ayyar, and Palghat Raghu.

Bombay Jayaśree (vocal); b. 1964; disciple of her mother and Lālguḍi Jayarāmaṉ.

Bombay Sisters (vocal); C. Saroja and C. Lalitha; disciples of Musiri Subrahmaṇya Ayyar and T.K. Gōvinda Rao.

Brinda, T. (vocal, *vīṇā*); 1912–96; granddaughter of Vīṇā Dhanammāḷ whose specialities (*jāvaḷi* and *pada*) she learnt from her mother, Kamākṣi Ammāḷ; some of these pieces have been published by T. Brinda; from Kāñcīpuram Naina Piḷḷai she learnt compositions of Tyāgarāja (*kṛti*); she mainly performed with her sister T. Mukta; cousin of Tañjāvūr Viṣwanāthaṉ; Central College; Visiting Professor at the Universities of California and Washington (USA); teacher of her daughter, Vegavāhini Vijayarāghavaṉ, Maitili Nāgēśwaraṉ, Sāvitri Satyamūrti, Aruna Sayeeram, B. Bālasubrahmaṇyam, Chārumathi Rāmachandraṉ, Geetha Rāja, Śakuntala Rāmaṉ, Ritha Rājāṉ, and K.N. Sashikiraṉ.

Budalūr Krishnamūrti Śāstrigaḷ (*gōṭṭuvādyam*); b. 1894; learnt music from his father, Sēthurāma Śāstrigaḷ; disciple of Konērirājāpuram Vaidyanātha and Harikēsanallūr Mutthiah Bhāgavatar; teacher of Kalpagam Swāminathaṉ; Central College; Principal, Kalākshētra; teacher of D. Kiṭṭappa, N. Narasiṁhaṉ, and Rāmā Ravi.

Calcutta K.S. Krishnamūrthi ('KSK', vocalist, composer); b. 1923; first learnt music from Maṇi Bhāgavatar; disciple of Sāttūr Krishnayyaṅgār; Senior Editor, *Sruti Magazine*; composer of *kṛti*, *tillānā*, *varṇam*, and the tunes for several devotional lyrics by Acyuta Dāsa.

Chandraśēkharaṉ, M. (violin, vocal); b. 1937; learnt music from his mother; disciple of Pallavi Narasiṁhalu Naidu, T. Jayammāḷ, and Sambaśiva Bhāgavatar; teacher of A. Kaṉyākumāri, S.D. Śrīdharaṉ, and K. Bālasubramaṇyaṉ.

Channamma—*see* Bangalore G. Channamma.

Chārumathi Rāmachandraṉ (vocal, *vīṇā*); b. 1951; learnt music first from her mother; disciple of M.L. Vasanthakumāri, Rāmnād Krishnaṉ, D.K. Jayarāmaṉ, D.K. Paṭṭammāḷ; married to vocalist Trichūr V. Rāmachandraṉ; studied *vīṇā* under T. Brinda; teacher of her daughter, Subaśree Rāmachandraṉ.

Cheluvarayaswāmy, M. (*vaiṇika*, musicologist); 1901–88; disciple of Chikka Subba Rao, M. Veṅkaṭēsa Ayyaṅgār, and Mysore V. Veṅkaṭagiriappa; teacher of his sons, notably Mysore C. Krishna Mūrthy.

Chembai Vaidyanātha Bhāgavatar (vocal, violin); 1896–1974; disciple of his father Chembai Ananta Bhāgavatar; teacher of M.R. Shaṅkaramūrthy, T.K. Gōvinda Rao, Palghat S. Krishnamoorthy, K.J. Jesudoss, V.V. Subrahmaṇyam, and Neyvēli R. Nārāyaṇan.

Chennakēśaviah, N. (vocalist, musicologist, composer); 1895–1984; disciple of Mysore Vāsudevācāriar; author of many articles and books (e.g. on the subjects of *Rāga Ālāpana* and *Tānam*, and *Compositions of Mysore Sadāśiva Rao*); teacher of Dr T. Seetha Rāmalakshmi and Maitili Nāgēśwaraṉ; his compositions comprise all the major forms of Karnatic music.

Chidambaram—*see* Sīrkāzhi Śiva Chidambaram.

Chinna—*see* Nookala Chinna Satyanārāyaṇa.

Chinna Moulana Saheb, Sheikh (*nāgasvaram*); b. 1926; belongs to a family of hereditary musicians; disciple of his father, Kasim Saheb, Cilakallūripēṭṭai Adam Sahib, and other musicians; Rājāh's College; Founder of a *nāgasvaram* school at Śrīraṅgam (*Śāradha nāgasvara saṅgīta āśram*); teacher of his sons, S. Kasim and Bābu, and of Sheikh Mehboob Subhani and Kalisabhi Mehboob.

Chintalapalli Rāmachandra Rao (vocal); 1916–85; disciple of his father, Veṅkaṭa Rao, Pālakkāḍu Sōmēśwara Bhāgavatar, and K. Ponnịah Piḷḷai; AIR Bangalore.

Chitti Babu (*viṇā*); 1936–95; disciple of Emani Śaṅkara Sastri.

Chittoor Subramaṇia Piḷḷai (vocalist, composer); b. 1898; disciple of his father, a violinist, and Kāñcīpuram Naina Piḷḷai; was famous for his mastery of rhythmic intricacies; headed the Departments of Music of Aṇṇāmalai University, Central College, Śrī Veṅkaṭēśwara University, Rājāh's College, and Rāmanāthan College, Jaffna (Sri Lanka); teacher of Madurai S. Sōmasundaram, Tadepalli Dr Lōkanādha Śarma, and others.

Chowdiah, T.—*see* Mysore T. Chowdiah.

Coimbatore G. Prakash (*mṛdaṅgam*); b. 1966; disciple of his father, Coimbatore Ganapathy.

Coimbatore N. Rāmaswāmi Piḷḷai (*mṛdaṅgam*); 1920–86; disciple of Nīḍamaṅgaḷam Mīnākṣisundaram Piḷḷai (*tavil*); adopted the style of Paḷani Subrahmaṇya Piḷḷai; AIR.

Dakṣiṇāmūrti Piḷḷai—*see* Pudukōṭṭai Dakṣiṇāmūrti Piḷḷai.

Daṇḍapāṇi—*see* Anayampaṭṭi S. Daṇḍapāṇi.

Daṇḍapāṇi Dēsikar, M.M. (vocalist, scholar, composer); 1908–72; disciple of his father and Kumbakōnam Rājamāṇikkam Piḷḷai; credited with popularizing and preserving Tamil devotional music; acted in films; Head of Department of Music, Aṇṇāmalai University; published numerous Tamil compositions from the traditional repertoire (*Tēvāram*, *Divya Prabandham*, *Tiruppugal*), and the songs of Bhārati as well as his own; teacher of Lālguḍi M. Swāmināthan and Vēdāraṇyam V. Sōmasundaram.

Deepa, S. (vocal); b. 1976; disciple of T. Rukmini and D.K. Gōvinda Rao.

Delhi Sisters—*see* K.R. Kumāraswāmy Ayyar.

Dēsamaṅgaḷam Subrahmaṇya Iyer (*viṇā*); 1899–1947; disciple of his father and his uncle; Aṇṇāmalai University; teacher of Tañjāvūr K.P. Śivānandam.

Dēvakōṭṭai A. Nārāyaṇa Ayyaṅgār (*viṇā*); 1905–87; disciple of Sakharāma Rao and Kāraikkuḍi Sambaśiva Ayyar; accompanied the latter as well as Ariyakkuḍi Rāmānuja Ayyaṅgār in concerts; Central College, Music Academy, and Bhāratīya Music College (Mumbai); teacher of Dr S. Rāmanāthan, Mokkapati Nāgēśvara Rao, Padma Veḷḷai Chandramouly, and Rājalakshmi Rāghavan.

Dhanammāḷ—*see* Vīṇā Dhanammāḷ.

Dhandapani—*see* Anayampaṭṭi S. Dhandapani.

Dorai—*see* Guruvāyūr Dorai.

Doreswāmy, R.N. (*vaiṇika*, scholar, composer); b. 1916; disciple of Salem Doreswāmy Ayyaṅgār, Chennakēsaviah, and Mysore V. Veṅkaṭagiriappa; authored *The Musical Forms of Karṇāṭaka*; Head of Music Department, Mysore University; composed and published numerous songs in four languages.

Doreswāmy Ayyaṅgār—*see* Mysore Doreswāmy Ayyaṅgār.

Durairājā—*see* Māṇguḍi R. Durairāja Ayyar.

Durgā, S.A.K., Dr (musicologist, vocalist); b. 1940; learnt music from her mother; disciple of Bālamuraḷī Krishna, Madurai Maṇi Ayyar, Mahārājāpuram Viṣwanātha Ayyar and Rāmnād Krishnan; published research on many musical subjects including voice culture and operatic forms of South Indian music; obtained her PhD at Wesleyan University (USA); post-doctoral research work at Yale University; Founder-Director of the Center for Ethnomusicology (Chennai); University of Madras/Chennai.

Durgāprasād—*see* Allam Durgāprasād.

Dwāram Bhavanārāyaṇa Rao (violin, vocal); b. 1924; son and disciple of Dwāram Veṅkaṭaswāmy Naidu; Principal, M.R. Government Music College (Vizianagaram).

Dwāram Durgaprasāda Rao (violin); son of violinist Dwāram Narasiṅga Rao; grand-nephew of Dwāram Veṅkaṭaswāmy Naidu; Principal, Government Music College (Vizianagaram).

Dwāram Mangathayaru (violin); b. 1935; daughter and disciple of Dwāram Veṅkaṭaswāmy Naidu; AIR.

Dwāram Satyanārāyaṇa (violin); son of violinist Dwāram Narasiṅga Rao; grand-nephew of Dwāram Veṅkaṭaswāmy Naidu.

Dwāram Satyanārāyaṇamūrthy (violin); son of Dwāram Veṅkaṭaswāmy Naidu; AIR.

Dwāram Veṅkaṭaswāmy Naidu (violin); 1893–1964; belonged to a family of violinists; disciple of his brother, Veṅkaṭa Krishnayya; Principal, Government Music College (Vizianagaram); teacher of his daughter, Dwāram Mangathayaru, and of his sons, Bhavanārāyaṇa Rao and Dwāram Satyanārāyaṇamūrthy; teacher of Śrīpāda Pinakapāni, Nookala Chinna Satyanārāyaṇa, Rādhā Nārāyaṇan, and P.P. Sōmayājulu.

Ellā Veṅkaṭēśwara Rao (*mṛdaṅgam*, composer); b. 1947; belongs to a family of musicians; disciple of Yellā Sōmanna; innovator in the field of ensemble music (special percussion, orchestral and ballet productions also for radio and television); wrote a book on *mṛdaṅgam* technique; conducts a charitable percussion teaching programme (*gurukulam*); music therapy; Dean, School of Fine Arts, Telugu University (Hyderabad); teacher of T.R. Sundarēśan.

Emani Śaṅkara Sastri (*vīṇā*); 1922–87; disciple of his father, *vaiṇika* Emani Achyutharāma Śāstrī; teacher of Chitti Babu; Chief Producer of Karnatic music, AIR (New Delhi), and Conductor of its National Orchestra; Producer for national television (Doordarshan).

Eswaran—*see* Mannārguḍi A. Eswaran.

Eswaran Battadiri (vocal); b. 1969; disciple of K.M Neelamana (a disciple of Chembai Vaidyanātha Bhāgavatar) and Trichūr Rāmachandran.

Eṭṭayapuram Rāmacandra Bhāgavatar (vocal); 1846–1915; specialized in the *rāgam tānam pallavi* format; teacher of Adicayapuram Sītarāmayyar and Kāñcīpuram Naina Piḷḷai.

Ganesh, K.R. (*mṛdaṅgam*); b. 1960; son and disciple of Kumbakōnam M. Rājappa Ayyar.

Ganesh and Kumāresh (violin duo); b. 1965 and 1967; disciples of their father, T.S. Rājagōpālan.

Gāyatri, E. (*vīṇā*); b. 1959; also known as 'Baby Gāyatri'; belongs to a family of musicians; disciple of T.M. Thyagarājan.

Geetha Bennett (*vīṇā*); daughter and disciple of Dr S. Rāmanāthan.

Geetha Rāja (vocal, *vīṇā*); b. 1955; disciple of T. Brinda and K.S. Nārāyaṇaswāmy; Lecturer, University of Mumbai (Bombay).

Gōpālakrishnan—*see* Narmada Gōpālakrishnan, Padma Gōpālakrishnan, Rāji Gōpālakrishnan.

Gōpālakrishnan, K.S. (flute); b. 1948; disciple of K. Śaṅkaranārāyaṇa Iyer and K. Raghava Werrier; AIR (Tiruvananthapuram).

Gōpālakrishnan, M.S. ('MSG', violin); b. 1931; belongs to a family of violinists; also a performer of Hindustānī music; brother of violinist M.S. Anantharāman; father and teacher of Narmada Gōpālakrishnan; teacher of M.A. Sundarēśan and Kāsi Viśwēśwaran.

Gōpālakrishnan, T.V. ('TVG', vocal, *mṛdaṅgam*, violin); b. 1932; disciple of his father, T.G. Viṣwanātha Bhāgavatar, and Chembai Vaidyanātha Bhāgavatar; also a vocalist in the Hindustānī style; teacher of his brother, T.V. Vāsan; versatile performer and promoter of young talent who experiments with unconventional styles.

Gōpālnath—*see* Kadri Gōpālnāth.

Gōvindarājan—*see* Sīrkāzhi S. Gōvindarājan.

Gōvindarājan, N. (*ghaṭam*); b. 1952; son of H.Y. Nārāyaṇan and Rājalakshmi Nārāyaṇan; disciple of T.R. Harihara Śarma and T.H. Vinayakram.

Gōvinda Rao, T.K. (vocalist, scholar); b. 1929; disciple of Musiri Subrahmaṇya Ayyar and Chembai Vaidyanātha; teacher of Bombay Sisters, P.R. Rāmanāthan, Dr Premeela Gurumūrthy, Dr S. Sunder, S. Deepa, and others; Chief Producer, AIR.

Gōvindasvāmi Piḷḷai—*see* Malaikōṭṭai Gōvindasvāmi Piḷḷai.

Gowri Kuppuswāmi, Dr (vocalist, musicologist); b. 1931; disciple of M.L. Vasanthakumāri, S. Kalyāṇarāman and R.K. Śrīkantan; author of numerous publications on Karnatic music; Head of Department of Music, Mysore University; teacher of Sukanya Prabhākar and Nāgamaṇi Śrīnāth.

Gowri Rāmnārayaṇan (vocalist, writer); disciple of M.S. Subbulakshmi, whom she has accompanied on many occasions.

Guruvāyūr Dorai (*mṛdaṅgam*, *kañjīrā*); b. 1935; disciple of Palghat Subba Ayyar and Palani Subrahmaṇya Piḷḷai; Visiting Professor at Washington University, Seattle (USA).

Harihara—*see* Āvuḍaiyārkōvil Harihara Bhāgavatar, Kalliḍaikkuricci S. Harihara Ayyar, Vechoor Harihara Subramoṇia Ayyar.

Harihara Subramaṇi Ayyar, N. (vocal); b. 1925; disciple of Semmaṅguḍi Śrīnivāsa Iyer; S.S.T. College of Music.

Harihara Śarma, T.R. (*mṛdaṅgam*, *mōrsiṅg*); b. 1904; father and teacher of T.H. Vinayakram and T.H. Subashchandran; author of textbooks on Karnatic percussion; founder of a renowned percussion school, Śrī Jaya Ganēsh Vidyālaya (Chennai).

Harikumār, B. (*mṛdaṅgam*); b. 1964; disciple of Māvēlikara K. Vēlukutti Nair; AIR.

Hariprasād, K. (vocal); b. 1970; disciple of Gōvinda Bhāgavatar, Salem D. Chellam Iyengar, and Vairamaṅgalam Lakshminārāyaṇan; Lecturer, Kalākshētra.

Harishankar, G. (*kañjīrā*); b. 1958; first learnt music from his father, Gōvinda Rao; disciple of Rāmnād Murugabhoopathy and Palghat Maṇi Ayyar.

Higgins, Dr Jon B. (musicologist, vocalist); 1939–84; through his own masterly rendition of Karnatic compositions he established an enduring reputation in India while he was a major promoter of Karnatic music in America; disciple of Tañjāvūr Viṣwanāthan; Professor at Wesleyan University (USA).

Hyderabad Brothers (vocal duo); born after 1950; learnt music from their father, D. Ratnamāchāriyulu; the elder brother, D. Rāghavāchary, is a disciple of Susarla Śivarām; D. Seshāchāri (AIR, Hyderabad) is a disciple of K. Sudarśanāchāriar (*mṛdaṅgam*).

Hyderabad Sisters (vocal duo); Lalitha (b. 1950) and Haripriya (b. 1952); disciples of T.G. Padmanābhan.

Jānakirāman, S.R. (vocalist, musicologist); b. 1928; disciple of Ālattūr Veṅkaṭēśa Ayyar, Tiger Varadāchāriar and others; studied musicology under P. Sambamoorthy; extensive research work; Head of Department of Musicology, Shrī Veṅkaṭēśwara University; Kalākshētra; Research Officer, Music Academy; specialist for *rāga lakṣaṇa* (theory and practice of rāga); author of a comprehensive Telugu work on Karnatic music (*Sangheetha Sastra Saramu*); produced a video demonstration on the subject of *varṇam*.

Jayalakshmi—*see* Salem S. Jayalakshmi.

Jayanth, B. (*mṛdaṅgam*); b. 1976; disciple of Palghat K. Raṅganāthan and T.K. Moorthy.

Jayanti Rādhakrishnan (*vīṇā*); niece and disciple of Padmāvathy Ananthagōpālan; disciple of S. Bālachander.

Jayarāman—*see* Lālguḍi Jayarāman, Tiruveṇkāḍu Jayarāman.

Jayarāman, D.K. (vocal); 1928–91; brother and disciple of D.K. Paṭṭammāḷ; father of J. Vaidyanāthan; learnt Tamil compositions personally from Pāpanāsam Śivan; teacher of Chārumathi Rāmachandran, Meera Śivarāmakrishnan, N. Vijay Śiva, S. Rājēśwari, and S. Sunder.

Jayaśaṅkar—*see* Tiruvizha Jayaśaṅkar.

Jayasītalakshmi, Dr S.R. (vocalist, scholar); b. 1951; disciple of B. Ponnammāḷ and Vechoor Harihara Subramoṇia Ayyar; Queen Mary's College; mother of Shankar Śrīnivās.

Jayaśree—*see* Bombay Jayaśree.

Jesudoss, K.J. (vocal); b. 1940; belongs to a musical family; disciple of Chembai Vaidyanātha Bhāgavatar and K.R. Kumāraswāmy Ayyar; mainly active in the field of film music as playback singer and composer; has established a music school in Tiruvananthapuram.

Justice T.L. Veṅkaṭarāma Ayyar (scholar, vocalist); b. 1893; related to Harikēsanallūr Mutthiah Bhāgavatar; learnt music from his mother; disciple of Muttusvāmi ('Ambhi') Dīkṣitar, a descendant of the elder Muttusvāmi Dīkṣitar; Justice, High Court (Madras) and Supreme Court; Member, Expert Committee, Music Academy; specialist for compositions of Muttusvāmi Dīkṣitar, and author of his Biography (*Life of Muttusvāmi Dīkṣitar*); teacher of Sandhyavandanam Śrīnivāsa Rao, Vidya Shankar, D.K. Paṭṭammāḷ, Kalpagam Swāmināthan, and Kaṇṇammā Sharma.

Kadri Gōpālnāth (saxophone); b. 1950; belongs to a family of *nāgasvaram* exponents; popularized the saxophone for Karnatic music; also collaborates with exponents of Jazz and World Music.

Kalārasan (violin); b. 1969; graduated from the Central College.

Kalliḍaikkuricci S. Harihara Ayyar (vocal, *harikathā*); 1912–93; disciple of Anantarāma Bhāgavatar , Śaṅkaranārāyaṇa Bhāgavatar, and Semmaṅguḍi Śrīnivāsa Ayyar;

Principal, Swāti Tirunāḷ College of Music and Rādhā Lakshmī Vilāsam Music Academy.

Kalliḍaikkuricci A. Sundaram Ayyar (*vaiṇika*, composer); 1913–74; disciple of Ambhi Dīkṣitar, the great-grandson of Muttusvāmi Dīkṣitar whose compositions he taught and published (partly in conjunction with the Music Academy); author of many music books (e.g. *Abhyāsa gānam, Śrī Muttusvāmi Dīkṣitar kīrttanaigaḷ, Tyāgarāja kīrtanamālā, Śyāmā Śāstri kīrtanamālā*); directed a *vīṇā* school in Chennai (*Karṇāṭaka vaiṇika gāna vidyālaya*).

Kalpagam Swāminātha<u>n</u> (*vīṇā* and vocal); b. 1922; disciple of Ananthakrishna Ayyar, Justice T.L. Veṅkaṭarāma Ayyar, Budalūr Krishnamūrti Śāstrī, and Musiri Subrahmaṇya Ayyar; Central College; specialist for compositions of Muttusvāmi Dīkṣitar.

Kalyāṇakrishna Bhāgavatar, M.A. (*vīṇā*); 1913–79; grandson of Kalyāṇakrishna Bhāgavatar, who is credited with evolving the Travancore style of *vīṇā* playing; son and disciple of M.K. Anantharāma Bhāgavatar; known for his masterly integration of vocal and *vīṇā* music; Swāti Tirunāḷ College of Music and Central College; Principal, Sri Rāmanātha<u>n</u> College of Music (Jaffna, Sri Lanka); Visiting Professor, Wesleyan University (USA); teacher of Mokkapati Nāgēśvara Rao, Padma Gōpālakrishna<u>n</u>, and Sulōchana Paṭṭābhirāma<u>n</u>.

Kalyāṇarāma<u>n</u>—*see* Tañjāvūr S. Kalyāṇarāma<u>n</u>.

Kāmākṣiammāḷ, T. (vocal); daughter of Vīṇā Dhanammāḷ; mother of T. Brinda and T. Mukta.

Kāñcīpuram Naina Piḷḷai (C. Subrahmaṇya Piḷḷai, vocalist, composer); 1889–1934; disciple of Eṭṭayapuram Rāmacandra Bhāgavatar; learnt compositions from Vīṇā Dhanammāḷ; known for his vast repertoire, exacting standards, uncompromising principles both as performer and as teacher; an expert for rhythmic intricacies and the *rāgam tānam pallavi* format; he is credited with introducing the calculated rhythmic concluding patterns (*kōrvai*) for the melodic improvisations of the *svara kalpana* type; re-composed the music for the *Tiruppuga<u>l</u>* songs of Arunagirinātar; teacher of Chittoor Subramaṇia Piḷḷai, N.S. Krishnaswāmy Ayyaṅgār, and T. Brinda.

Kandadevi S. A<u>l</u>agiriswāmy (violin); disciple of his grandfather, Śrīnivāsa Ayyaṅgār, Kandadevi Chellam Ayyaṅgār, and Mysore T. Chowdiah.

Kandaswāmy—*see* Rāmnād M.N. Kandaswāmy.

Kaṇṇammā Sharma (*vīṇā*, vocal); disciple of Guntur Veṅkaṭa Nārāyaṇāchāryulu (*vīṇā*), T. Jayammāḷ (daughter of Vīṇā Dhanammāḷ), Justice T.L. Veṅkaṭarāma Ayyar, and Kōṭīśvara Ayyar; AIR; lives and teaches in Ottawa (Canada).

Kaṇṇa<u>n</u>—*see* Śrīraṅgam S. Kaṇṇa<u>n</u>.

Ka<u>n</u>yakumari, A. (violin); b. 1961; disciple of M. Chandraśēkhara<u>n</u> and M.L. Vasanthakumāri, whom she accompanied on many occasions.

Kāraikkuḍi Brothers (*vīṇā*); Subbarāma Ayyar (1883–1936) and Sambaśiva Ayyar (1888–1957); belonged to a family of *vīṇā* exponents and court musicians at Kāraikkuḍi; renowned for their *tā<u>n</u>am* play, synchronization, and virtuosity, they performed mainly with Pudukōṭṭai Dakṣiṇāmūrti Piḷḷai; Subbarāma Ayyar played a *vīṇā* which was held in an upright position (Fig. 16); Sambaśiva Ayyar was the teacher of Dr Kāraikkuḍi S. Subramania<u>n</u> and Rājēśwari Padmanābha<u>n</u>; Kalākshētra.

Kāraikkuḍi R. Maṇi (*mṛdaṅgam*); b. 1945; disciple of Kāraikkuḍi Raṅgu Ayyaṅgār, T.R. Harihara Śarma and K.M. Vaidyanātha<u>n</u>; Founder-Director of the 'Sruthi Laya' ensemble which performs innovative percussive arrangements, and of the 'Sruthi Laya Seva Trust' which promotes advanced percussion training and publishes a journal on the intricacies of South Indian rhythm.

Kāraikkuḍi S. Subramaṇian, Dr (*vīṇā*, musicology); b. 1944; grandson of Vīṇā Kāraikkuḍi Subbarāmyyar; disciple and adopted son of Kāraikkuḍi Sambaśiva Ayyar; brother of Rājēśwari Padmanābhan; Founder-Director of Brhaddhvani (Research and Training Centre for Musics of the World, Chennai) where he researches new methods of teaching classical music in a contemporary, international context; holds a PhD in musicology from Wesleyan University (USA); teaches at Music Department, University, Chennai; teacher of his niece, V. Shānti.

Karthick, S. (*ghaṭam*); b. 1971; disciple of T.H. Vinayakram and T.H. Subashchandran.

Kārukuricci P. Arunachalam (*nāgasvaram*); 1921–64; belonged to a family of hereditary musicians; disciple of Kalakad Rāmanārāyaṇa Bhāgavatar and T.N. Rājaratnam Piḷḷai.

Kāsi Bhāgavatar, K.A.—*see* K. Bālasubramaṇyan.

Kāsi Viśwēśwaran, R. (violin), b. 1968; disciple of A. Nāgaratnammāḷ, Tiruvallūr V. Pārthasārathy, Pāpanāsam Bālasaraswathi, and M.S. Gōpālakrishnan; Administrative Officer, *Sampradāya* (Centre for the Music Traditions of South India, Chennai).

Kausalya, R. (vocal, *viṇā*); b. 1949; disciple of Sri Veṅkaṭasubrahmaṇyan and Chittoor Subrahmaṇya Piḷḷai (vocal); studied *viṇā* under Tañjāvūr K.P. Śivānandam and Śarada Śivānandam; Rājāh's College and Bhāratidāsan University (Trichy).

Kēdaranāthan, K.R. (vocal); 1925; brother of K.R. Kumāraswāmy Ayyar; disciple of Semmaṅguḍi Śrīnivāsa Iyer; Chembai music college (Palakkad); teacher of Seethalakshmi Veṅkaṭēśan.

Kēśavamūrthy, R.R. (violin); b. 1914; disciple of Chikka Rāma Rao and Bīḍaram Krishnappā; plays a 7-stringed violin; founded a private music college in Bangalore; disciple of his children; grandfather of Sreedhara (vocalist) and Shankar (violinist) who live in the USA; investigated the aesthetic aspect (*rasa*) of rāgas; author of many Kannaḍa works on music.

Kēsavamūrthy, R.S. (*vīṇā*, vocal); b. 1903–82; disciple of his father, R. Subba Rao, and Vīṇā Subbanna; developed a *vīṇā* with 24 strings (*Gāyatrī Vīṇā*); studied many other instruments, including piano; conducted the Mysore Palace's English Band; teacher of his 11 children and grandchildren: his sons, R.K. Śrīnivāsamūrthy, R.K. Sūryanārāyaṇa, R.K. Rāghavan, R.K. Padmanābha (*viṇā*), his granddaughter, Padmini (*viṇā*), his late son, R.K. Chandrashēkhar (violin), and his son, R.K. Prasanna Kumār (*mṛdaṅgam*); teacher of H.S. Krishnamoorthy and other leading musicians.

Kēśavulu, T. (violin); b. 1927; disciple of T. Bālasubbarayyulu; AIR.

Kiraṇāvaḷi, K.N. (vocal); b.1973; disciple of her father, N. Narasiṁhan.

Kiṭṭappa, D. (*gōṭṭuvādyam*); b. 1915; disciple of Budalūr Krishnamūrti Śāstrigaḷ.

Kiṭṭappa, K.P. (vocalist); b. 1913; son and disciple of K. Ponniah Piḷḷai; also disciple of *bharata nāṭyam* exponent, Mīnākṣisundaram Piḷḷai; brother of *vaiṇika* Tañjāvūr K.P. Śivānandam.

Kiṭṭappa, S.G. (vocal); 1906–33; husband of K.B. Sundarambaḷ; famous for his renditions of classical songs on the drama stage and on gramophone records.

Kōnērirājāpuram Vaidyanātha Ayyar (vocalist); 1878–1921; learnt to chant the *Veda*; studied rhythm (*laya*) under Pudukōṭṭai Mānpūṇḍiya Piḷḷai; teacher of Muḍikondān

C. Veṅkaṭarāma Ayyar; influential musician and teacher of liberal outlook whose qualities other musicians sought to emulate (e.g. Pāpanāsam Śivan̲); described as the last exponent of the vocal style known as *ghanam* ('weighty').

Kōtēśwar Rao—*see* Allam Kōtēśwar Rao.

Kōvilaḍi R. Mādhvaprasād (vocal, *mṛdaṅgam*); b. 1957; disciple of his father, vocalist Kōvilaḍi K. Raṅgarājan̲; and mṛdaṅgist Kān̲āḍukātān̲ Malayappa Ayyar.

Krishna, Krishnan̲, Kṛṣṇa—*see* Bālamuraḷī Krishna, Budalūr Krishnamūrti Śāstrigaḷ, Gōpālakrishnan̲, Krishnan̲, Madurai N. Krishnan̲, Nāmagiripēṭṭai Krishnan̲, Rāmnād Krishnan̲, Tañjāvūr Kṛṣṇa Bhāgavatar, Tirukōḍikāval Krishna Ayyar, Viji Krishnan̲ Naṭarājan̲.

Krishna Ayyar, C.S. (vocal); b. 1916; disciple of T.S. Sabhēśa Ayyar, K. Pon̲n̲iah Piḷḷai; Principal, Government Music Academy (Palakkad).

Krishna, T.M. (vocal); b. 1976; disciple of B. Seetarāma Śarma.

Krishnamāchār, A.V. (violinist, composer); b. 1920; disciple of Ḍakka Hanumanthāchār (vocal), Amidal Veṅkaṭa Swāmy, and B. Veṅkappa (violin); also studied Hindustānī and Western music; composed devotional and light music, and music for dance-dramas (*yakṣagāna*) by Śivarāma Kāranth.

Krishnamāchāriar—*see* Vīṇā Krishnamāchāriar.

Krishnamoorthy (Krishnamūrti)—*see* Budalūr Krishnamūrti Śāstrigaḷ, Calcutta K.S. Krishnamūrthi, Mēlakāvēri Krishnamūrthi, Nēdunūri Krishnamūrthi, T.V. Nellai Krishnamoorthy, Palghat C.S. Krishnamoorthi, Palghat S. Krishnamoorthy, Puducōde K. Krishnamūrthi, Pudukōṭṭai R. Krishnamūrthy.

Krishnamoorthy, H.S. (*vīṇā*); b. 1913; disciple of R.S. Kēśavamūrthy; College of Music and Mahārāṇī College for Women (Bangalore).

Krishnamūrthi, B. (vocalist, musicologist, composer); b. 1932; disciple of Musiri Subrahmaṇyam Ayyar, Muḍikondān̲ Veṅkaṭarāma Ayyar, Tirupāmburam N. Swāminātha Piḷḷai, and his brother, B. Rājam Ayyar; he edited numerous compositions of Tyāgarāja, Paṭṭaṇam Subrahmaṇya Ayyar and Mahāvaidyanātha Śivan̲ (Ayyar); Principal, Government Music College (Madurai); teacher of Sīrkāzhi Dr G. Śiva Chidambaram.

Krishna Mūrthy—*see* Mysore C. Krishna Mūrthy.

Krishnan̲, A.S. (*mōrsiṅg*); 1954; disciple of his father, A.K. Sundaram (*mōrsiṅg*), Mēlakāvēri Krishnamūrthy (*mṛdaṅgam*), and Man̲n̲ārguḍi A. Eswaran; brother of A.S. Muraḷī (*ghaṭam*, vocal), A.S. Reṅganāthan (*mṛdaṅgam*), and A.S. Shankar (*ghaṭam*).

Krishnan̲, G.J.R. (violinist); b. 1960; son and disciple of Lālguḍi Jayarāman̲.

Krishnan̲, T.N. (violin); b. 1928; learnt music first from his father, Nārāyaṇaswāmy Ayyar, and K. Parthasarathy Ayyaṅgār; disciple of Semmaṅguḍi Śrīnivāsa Iyer; teacher of Meera Śivarāmakrishnan̲; Principal, Central College; Head of Department of Carnatic music, University of Delhi; teacher of his daughter, Viji Krishnan̲ Naṭarājan̲.

Krishnan̲, V.R. (vocal); b. 1933; disciple of Chembai Vaidyanātha Bhāgavatar and Semmaṅguḍi Śrīnivāsa Iyer; Central College.

Krishnappā—*see* Bīḍaram Krishnappā.

Krishna Śāstrī, R. (scholar, *harikathā*); father and teacher of R.K. Śrīkantan̲; teacher of A.K. Subba Rao.

Krishnaswāmi—*see* Maṇi Krishnaswāmi, Pārūr M.A. Krishnaswāmy.

Krishnaswāmy Ayyaṅgār, N.S. (vocal); b. 1914; disciple of Kāñcīpuram Naina Piḷḷai and Tiger Varadāchāriar; teacher of D.K. Paṭṭammāḷ; Kalākshētra.

Kumār, V.L. (violin); son and disciple of V.L. Vēdagiri.

Kumāraswāmy Ayyar, K.R. (vocalist, scholar, composer); b. 1914; disciple of Mecheri Sundara Śāstrigaḷ and Semmaṅguḍi Śrīnivāsa Iyer; teacher of K.J Jesudoss and Tiruvizha Jayaśaṅkar; set several lyrics of Acuta Dāsa to music; brother of vocalist K.R. Kēdaranāthan̲; father and teacher of the Delhi Sisters; Principal, Swāti Tirunāḷ College of Music and Rādhā Lakshmī Vilāsam Music Academy.

Kumbakōnam R. Nāgarāja Rao (flute); b. 1883; encouraged by Śarabha Śāstrigaḷ; disciple of Umayāḷpuram Swāminātha Ayyar; teacher of Kumbakōnam Rājamān̲ikkam Piḷḷai.

Kumbakōnam Rājamān̲ikkam Piḷḷai (violin); 1898–1970; disciple of Nāgasvaram Kandasvāmi Piḷḷai, Pandanallūr Cinnasvāmi Piḷḷai, and Pallavi Nārāyaṇasvāmi Ayyar (vocal); and Tirukōḍikāval Krishna Ayyar (violin); also guided by Kumbakōnam R. Nāgarāja Rao and Umayāḷpuram Swāminātha Ayyar; teacher of Gōvindarāja Piḷḷai, Sāvitri Satyamūrti, Śriraṅgam R. Kaṇṇan̲, and M.M. Daṇḍapāṇi Dēsikar.

Kumbakōnam M. Rājappa Ayyar (*mṛdaṅgam*); b. 1916; disciple of Kumbakōnam Āl̲agunambi Piḷḷai and Sākkōṭṭai Raṅgu Ayyaṅgār; father and teacher of K.R. Ganesh; teacher of Umayāḷpuram K. Śivarāman̲, Śrīmuṣṇam Rāja Rao, Trichūr C. Narēndran̲, Ashōk Ramani, Sīrkāl̲i Skanda Prasād, Vijay Śiva, and Manōj Śiva.

Kumbakōnam Śrīnivāsan̲ (violin); disciple of Kumbakōnam Rājamān̲ikkam Piḷḷai; teacher of S.D. Śrīdharan̲.

Kuñjumaṇi—*see* Sikkil Sisters.

Kunnakuḍi R. Vaidyanāthan̲ (violinist, composer); b. 1935; explores the scope for innovation, virtuosity and variety in classical music; also worked in the field of film music; Chairman of the State Academy of the Performing Arts of Tamil Nadu.

Kuppuswāmi, Dr T.V. (vocalist, scholar); b. 1925; disciple of B. Krishnamūrthi, V.V. Saḍagōpan̲ and others; author of several music books (e.g. *Bhakti Mañjari*, *Carnatic Music and the Tamils*).

Kuttālam R. Viṣwanāthan̲ (*mṛdaṅgam, kañjīrā*); b. 1920; disciple of K. Ponniah Piḷḷai and Kuttālam Kuppusvāmy Piḷḷai; AIR; Dharmapuram Mutt Music College.

Lakshminārāyaṇan̲—*see* Vairamaṅgalam Lakshminārāyaṇan̲.

Lālguḍi Jayarāman̲ (violinist, vocalist, composer); b. 1930; disciple of his father V.R. Gōpāla Ayyar; brother of Padmāvathy Ananthagōpālan̲ and Śrīmathi Brahmānandam; teacher of many musicians including his son, G.J.R. Krishnan̲, his daughter J. Vijayalakshmi, T. Rukmini, Pakala Rāmdās, S.P. Rāmh, Vittal Rāmamūrthy, and Bombay Jayaśree.

Lālguḍi M. Swāmināthan̲ (vocalist); 1928–96; disciple of *Tēvāram vidvān* Tillaiyāḍi T. Sambandam Piḷḷai, Mahādēva Ayyar, and M.M. Daṇḍapāṇi Dēsikar; served as chief *ōduvār* of the Kapalīśvara temple at Mylapore (Chennai).

Lalitha, C.—*see* Bombay Sisters.

Lathā, R. (violin); disciple of her father, Dr S. Rāmanāthan̲, and her uncle, violinist Ālandūr Naṭarājan̲.

Leela Omchery (vocal); b.1932; disciple of V.V. Saḍagōpan̲ and others.

Leela, P. (vocal); b. 1934; disciple of Chembai Vaidyanātha Bhāgavatar and others.

Lōkanādha Śarma—*see* Tadepalli Dr Lōkanādha Śarma.

Mādhvaprasād—*see* Kōvilaḍi R. Mādhvaprasād.

Madurai Brothers (*nāgasvaram*); Madurai P.N. Sēthurāmaṉ (b. 1928) and Madurai P.N. Ponnuswāmy (b. 1933); leading exponents of the *nāgasvaram* tradition of temple music.

Madurai N. Krishnaṉ (vocalist, composer); b. 1928; belongs to a family of musicians and Sanskrit scholars; disciple of Ariyakkuḍi Rāmānuja Ayyaṅgār; composed and published several works with Tamil compositions (e.g. *Tiruppāvai*, Tamil poetry by Āṇḍāḷ and Divya Prabandha); produced several dance-dramas; has also contributed music to the classical dance repertoire and set the lyrics of Ambujam Krishna to music; teacher of S. Rājēśwari.

Madurai G.S. Maṇi, (vocalist, composer); b. 1934; disciple of his mother, Sampoornam Ammāḷ, Babu Ayyaṅgār and P.C. Sītarāma Ayyar; also worked in the field of film music; specialist for classical Karnatic music in films.

Madurai Maṇi Ayyar (vocal); 1912–68; disciple of Madurai Rājam Bhāgavatar and Harikēsanallūr Mutthiah Bhāgavatar; uncle and teacher of T.V. Śaṅkaranārāyaṇaṉ; teacher of S. Rājam, Tiruveṇkāḍu Jayarāmaṉ, Sāvitri Satyamūrti, T.N. Bāla, and Dr S.A.K. Durgā; developed his own style based on medium tempo; embarked on imaginative and soulful improvisations in the *svara kalpana* format for which his recordings are still popular.

Madurai S. Sōmasundaram ('Madurai Sōmu', vocalist, composer); 1919–89; belonged to a family of musicians; disciple of Chittoor Subramaṇia Piḷḷai and others; also worked in the field of film music; Head of Department of Music, Aṇṇāmalai University; Visiting Professor, Tamil University (Tañjāvūr).

Mahāliṅgam, T.R. ('Māli', flute and violin); 1926–86; original and charismatic virtuoso influenced by violinist Dwāram Veṅkaṭaswāmy Naidu; teacher of T.S. Śaṅkaran, Prapancham V. Seetharam, and N. Ramani; influenced many contemporary flute players, including Raghu and Ravi and M.S. Shashank, as *mānasa guru* (indirect teacher) through his recordings.

Mahārājāpuram Nāgarājaṉ (vocal); b. 1929; disciple of his grandfather, Nallūr Viṣwanātha Bhāgavatar and his father, Mahārājāpuram M.R. Krishnamūrthy; Principal, Sarasvatī Vidyālayam (Trichy).

Mahārājāpuram S. Rāmachandraṉ (vocal); b. 1950; disciple of his father, Mahārājāpuram Santhānam.

Mahārājāpuram Santhānam (vocal); 1928–92; disciple of Melattur Sama Dikshitar and of his father, Mahārājāpuram Viṣwanātha Ayyar; Rāmanāthaṉ College (Jaffna); father and teacher of Mahārājāpuram S. Rāmachandraṉ and Mahārājāpuram S. Śrīnivāsaṉ.

Mahārājāpuram S. Śrīnivāsaṉ (vocal); b. 1952; disciple of his father, Mahārājāpuram Santhānam.

Mahārājāpuram Viṣwanātha Ayyar (vocal); 1896–1970; disciple of Umayāḷpuram Swāminātha Ayyar and Paḻani Raṅgappier; learnt compositions (*jāvaḷi*, *padam*) from Vīṇā Dhanammāḷ; absorbed Hindustānī music techniques and styles from Bāla Gandharva during travels to North India; also worked in the field of film music; father and teacher of Mahārājāpuram Santhānam; teacher of Semmaṅguḍi Śrīnivāsa Iyer, Sandhyavandanam Śrīnivāsa Rao, S. Rājam, Dr Salem S. Jayalakshmi, and Dr S.A.K. Durgā.

Maitili Nāgēśwaran (vocal, *viṇā*); b. 1922; disciple of N. Chennakēśaviah, Tirupāmburam N. Swāminātha Piḷḷai, T. Jayammāḷ, T. Rājalakshmiammāḷ, T. Brinda, T. Mukta, T. Viṣwanāthan, and T. Śaṅkaran; specialist for the repertoire of Vīṇā Dhanammāḷ; sang for T. Bālasaraswathi's dance performances; cousin of Seetha Rājagōpāl with whom she performed often; Koḍaikanal International School and Bhāratīya Vidyā Bhavan's Vidyāshrama (Koḍaikanal).

Malaikōṭṭai Gōvindasvāmi Piḷḷai (violin); 1879–1931 (?1934); influential and versatile musician who belonged to the lineage of Bālusvāmi Dīkṣitar and Vaḍivēlu, the musicians who established the violin tradition in classical South Indian music; famous for his bowing technique; he was also an expert flute player and Tamil scholar; contributed to establishing the annual *Tyāgarāja ārādhana* Festival in Tiruvaiyāru; also sang while playing the violin (a practice adopted from traditional *vīṇā* playing); teacher of Pāpā K.S. Veṅkaṭarāmayya and Mannārguḍi Vaidyaliṅgam Piḷḷai.

Māmuṇḍiyā Piḷḷai, Mānpūṇḍiya Piḷḷai—*see* Pudukōṭṭai Mānpūṇḍiya Piḷḷai, Māmuṇḍiyā Piḷḷai.

Maṅgaḷam Shankar (vocalist); b. 1952; graduate of the Music Academy; disciple of T.M. Thyagarājan and D.K. Paṭṭammāḷ; Kalākshētra.

Mangathayaru—*see* Dwāram Mangathayaru.

Māṇguḍi R. Durairāja Ayyar (*mṛdaṅgam*); 1900–80; disciple of Tañjāvūr Vaidyanātha Ayyar; also studied drama; author of several works on Karnatic percussion; contributed music for films and dance; teacher of T.K. Rāmakrishnan.

Maṇi—*see* Kāraikkuḍi Maṇi, Madurai G.S. Maṇi, Madurai Maṇi Ayyar, Palghat Maṇi Ayyar, Trivandrum R.S. Maṇi.

Maṇi, T.A.S. (*mṛdaṅgam, ghaṭam, kañjīrā*); grandson of Palghat Anantarāma Bhāgavatar; son of T.P. Arunāchala Bhāgavatar; disciple of C.K. Aiyamaṇi Ayyar; founded a music school ('Karnataka College of Percussion'), and an ensemble ('Tāla Taraṅgiṇi'); author of a book on percussion (*Sogasuga Mridanga Taalamu*); husband of vocalist R.A. Rāmamaṇi with whom he has interacted with exponents of Jazz music; teacher of R.A. Rājagōpālan.

Maṇi Krishnaswāmi (vocalist, scholar); b. 1930; disciple of Tiger Varadāchāriar, Muḍikondān Veṅkaṭarāma Ayyar, Mysore Vāsudēvācāria, and Musiri Subrahmaṇya Ayyar.

Mañjunāthan, K.S.—*see* Bangalore K.S. Mañjunāthan.

Mannārguḍi A. Eswaran (*mṛdaṅgam*); b. 1947; disciple of Kunniseri U. Krishnaswami Ayyar; teacher of A.S. Krishnan; AIR.

Mannārguḍi Natēsa Piḷḷai (*mōrsiṅg*, *tavil*); died in 1975; began his career as a *tavil* player; remembered as a *mōrsiṅg* exponent who performed along with the leading percussionists of his time.

Mannārguḍi Pakkiri Piḷḷai (*konnakkōl*, *tavil*); 1857–1937; belonged to a family of *bharata nāṭyam* teachers (*naṭṭuvanar*); son of Cokkaliṅga Naṭṭuvanar; studied *naṭṭuvāṅgam* under his uncle, Svāmināta Naṭṭuvanar; studied vocal music under Paḷani Ghaṭam Kṛṣṇayyar, and *tavil* under Svarnam Piḷḷai; started his career as the accompanist (*tavilkārar*) of *nāgasvaram* exponent Mannārguḍi Cinna Pakkiri; credited with developing the recitation of rhythmic syllables (*jati* or *sollukkaṭṭu*), since then known as *konnakkōl*, into an art in its own right; until a few decades ago, *konnakkōl* exponents played an important role in the concerts of several leading musicians; also credited with having composed the music (i.e. the tunes and intricate tāla patterns known as *sandam*) for several hundred *Tiruppugal* lyrics; his son, Mannārguḍi Vaidyaliṅgam Piḷḷai, is said to have continued the *konnakkōl* tradition with equal competence.

Mannārguḍi Vaidyaliṅgam (Vaithiliṅgam) Piḷḷai (*konnakkōl*, vocal, *nāgasvaram*); 1900–74; disciple of his father, Mannārguḍi Pakkiri Piḷḷai, and M. Gōvindasvāmi Piḷḷai; Aṇṇāmalai University; published a book (*Tāḷamum Anubavamum*) with his father's tāla patterns (*jati*).

Manōjkumār, P. (*mṛdaṅgam*, *kañjīrā*, *mōrsiṅg*, *ghaṭam*, *maddalam*); b. 1967; disciple of T.R. Sundarēśan.

Manōj Śiva (*mṛdaṅgam*); b. 1972; disciple of Kumbakōnam M. Rājappa Ayyar and Palghat Raghu.

Mānpūṇḍiya Piḷḷai—*see* Pudukōṭṭai Māmuṇḍiyā Piḷḷai.

Mavelikara H. Rāmanāthan (vocal); b. 1922; disciple of Harihara Bhāgavatar and Semmaṅguḍi Śrīnivāsa Iyer; Professor, Rādhā Lakshmī Vilāsam (RLV) Music Academy, Tripunithura (Kerala).

Māyavaram G. Sōmasundaram, Māyuram Sōmu (*kañjīrā*); b. 1928; disciple of T. Muthuveer Piḷḷai and Kuttālam Śivavaḍivēl Piḷḷai.

Meera Sēshādri (vocal); b. 1938; learnt music and dance from her mother and Karnatic music from B.V. Rāman, and B.V. Lakshmanan; learnt *padam* and *jāvaḷi* compositions from T. Jayammāḷ; also studied Hindustānī music; taught at the Trivēni Kalā Sangham (New Delhi) before moving to Chennai where she continues to sing and teach.

Meera Śivarāmakrishnan (violin, vocal); b. 1965; disciple of her mother, violinist Rādhā Nārāyaṇan, T.N. Krishnan, and D.K. Jayarāman.

Mehboob Subhani, Sheikh and Kalisabhi Mehboob (*nāgasvaram* duo); b. 1951 and 1961 respectively; learnt music from their own parents; disciples of Chandramouli (Principal, Kurnool Music College), and Sheikh Chinna Moulana.

Mēlakāvēri Bālaji (*mṛdaṅgam*); b. 1969; disciple and son of Mēlakāvēri Krishnamūrthi.

Mēlakāvēri Krishnamūrthi (*mṛdaṅgam*); teacher of A.S. Krishnan and his son, Mēlakāvēri Bālaji.

Mīnākṣisundaram—*see* Nīḍamaṅgaḷam Mīnākṣisundaram Piḷḷai.

Mokkapati Nāgēśvara Rao (*vīṇā*); 1926–93; disciple of Behta Rājarao, M.A. Kalyāṇakrishna Bhāgavatar, and Dēvakōṭṭai A. Nārāyaṇa Ayyaṅgār; Central College; taught and performed in Japan and France; Founder of Karnatic music institutions in Paris (*Nādopāsanā, Institut de Musique Carnatique*).

Moorthy, T.K. (*mṛdaṅgam*); b. 1924; disciple of Tañjāvūr Vaidyanātha Ayyar; also accompanied leading Hindustānī musicians; teacher of J. Vaidyanāthan, K.V. Prasād, and Palghat K. Raṅganāthan.

Moulana—*see* Chinna Moulana, Sheikh.

Muḍikondān C. Veṅkaṭarāma Ayyar (vocalist, scholar); 1897–1975; disciple of Vēdāranyam Svāminātha Ayyar, Konērirājāpuram Vaidyanātha Ayyar, T. Nannusvāmi Piḷḷai, and Simiḷi Sundaram Ayyar; wrote and edited articles, and musical compositions of Rāmnād 'Pūcci' Śrīnivāsa Iyeṅgar; teacher of M.L. Vasanthakumāri, Śrīvanchiam K. Rāmachandra Ayyar, Maṇi Krishnaswāmi, D. Paśupathi, B. Krishnamūrthi, P.S. Nārāyaṇaswāmy, Premeela Gurumūrthy, and R. Vēdavaḷḷi; Kalākshētra; Principal, Teachers' College of the Music of the Music Academy.

Mukta, T. (vocal); b. 1914; granddaughter of Vīṇā Dhanammāḷ and sister of T. Brinda with whom she mainly performed; specialist for compositions of the *padam* and *jāvaḷi* types; teacher of Maitili Nāgēśwaran̲, Nāgamaṇi Śrīnāth, R. Vēdavaḷḷi, and Nirmala Pārthasārathy.

Muraḷī—*see* Trichy R.K. Muraḷī.

Muraḷī, A.S. (*ghaṭam*, vocal); b. 1970; disciple of T.V. Vāsan̲; brother of A.S. Krishnan̲ (*mōrsiṅg*), A.S. Reṅganāthan (*mṛdaṅgam*), and A.S. Shankar (*ghaṭam*).

Muraḷīdharan̲—*see* Nāgai R. Muraḷīdharan̲.

Murugabhoopathy, C.S. (*mṛdaṅgam*); b. 1914; disciple of his father, Rāmanātapuram (Rāmnād) Chitsabai Servai, and his brother, Rāmanātapuram Śaṅkara Sivan̲; teacher of G. Harishankar.

Musiri Subrahmaṇya Ayyar (vocal); 1899–1975; disciple of S. Nārāyaṇasvāmi Ayyar, violinist Karūr Cinnasvāmi Ayyar, and T.S. Sabhēśa Ayyar; also worked in the field of film music; Head of Department of Music, Aṇṇāmalai University; Principal, Central College; teacher of Kalpagam Swāminathan̲, T.K. Gōvinda Rao, Palghat S. Krishnamoorthy, B. Krishnamūrthi, Maṇi Krishnaswāmi, the Bombay Sisters, R.K. Nārāyaṇaswāmy, V.V. Subrahmaṇyam, N. Narasiṁhan̲, Padma Nārāyaṇaswāmy, Śakuntala Rāman̲, and Suguna Purushōtaman̲.

Muttusvāmi ('Ambhi') Dīkṣitar (vocalist, scholar); grandson of Bālusvāmi Dīkṣitar (1786–1859), the brother of composer Muttusvāmi Dīkṣitar; son of music scholar Subbarāma Dīkṣitar; teacher of Justice T.L. Veṅkaṭarāma Ayyar, D.K. Paṭṭammāḷ, S. Rājam, and Kalliḍaikkuricci A. Sundaram Ayyar.

Mysore T. Chowdiah (violin); 1895–1967; disciple of his uncle, Subanna, and Bīḍaram Krishnappā; brother of T. Puttaswāmiah; a popular virtuoso who used a 7-stringed violin; teacher of V. Sēthurāmiah, R.K. Veṅkaṭarāma Śāstrī, Kandadevi S. Alagiri-swāmy, Dr Salem S. Jayalakshmi, and others.

Mysore V. Doreswāmy Ayyaṅgār (*vīṇā*); 1920–97; disciple of his father, *vaiṇika* Veṅka-ṭēśa Ayyaṅgār, and Mysore V. Veṅkaṭagiriappa; Producer, AIR (Bangalore); teacher of Mysore C. Krishna Mūrthy, A.S. Padma, and his son, D. Bālakrishna.

Mysore C. Krishna Mūrthy (*viṇā*); 1934–92; disciple of his father, M. Cheluvarayaswāmy, Mysore V. Veṅkaṭagiriappa, and Mysore Doreswāmy Ayyaṅgār; AIR.

Mysore M. Nāgarāj (violin); b. 1960; son and disciple of S. Mahādēvappa; AIR.

Mysore V. ('Vīṇā') Veṅkaṭagiriappa (*vīṇā*); 1887–1952; disciple of his uncle Chikka Subba Rao, a *vaiṇika* who was also familiar with the Hindustānī system of music; together with the composer Mysore Śeṣanna ('Vīṇā Śeṣanna'), he is credited with moulding what is known as the 'Mysore style' of *vīṇā* playing; teacher of C. Raṅgaiah, M. Cheluvarayaswāmy, R.N. Doreswāmi, and Mysore V. Doreswāmy Ayyaṅgār.

Nāgabhūṣaṇam—*see* Nori Nāgabhūṣaṇam.

Nāgai R. Muraḷīdharan̲ (violin); b. 1958; disciple of his mother, Kōmaḷavalli, and R.S. Gōpālakrishnan̲; AIR.

Nāgamaṇi, N. (vocal); disciple of his father, composer Kōṭīśvara Ayyar, and Kiṭṭamaṇi Ayyar; teacher of Padmalōchani Nāgarājan̲, K.V. Krishnan̲, and Kamudi Rāmadās.

Nāgamaṇi Śrīnāth, G.N. (vocal); b. 1950; disciple of Arakere Nārāyaṇa Rao, Gowri Kuppuswami, Rāmnād Krishnan̲, T.M. Thyāgarājan̲, and T. Mukta (*padam*); studied Hindustānī music under Lalita Rāmānujam; author of several biographies of Karnatic composers (e.g. Śyāmā Śāstri, Vīṇā Kuppayyar); Head of Department of Music, Mahārāṇī's Arts College (University of Mysore).

Nāgarājan—*see* Mahārājāpuram Nāgarājan.

Nāgarājan, V. (*kañjīrā*); b. 1930; disciple of Tañjāvūr Vaidyanātha Ayyar and Palghat Maṇi Ayyar.

Nāgarāja Rao (*ghaṭam*); b. 1933; underwent traditional training (*gurukulavāsam*) under Tinniyam Veṅkaṭarāma Ayyar before becoming a professional performer.

Nāgarāja Rao, R.—*see* Kumbakōnam R. Nāgarāja Rao.

Nāgaratnammāḷ—*see* Bangalore Nāgaratnammāḷ.

Nāgavalli Nāgarāj (vocal); b. 1959; disciple of her father, violinist Anurām Krishnan.

Nāgēśvara, Nāgēśwaran,—*see* Maitili Nāgēśwaran, Mokkapati Nāgēśvara Rao.

Naina Piḷḷai—*see* Kāñcīpuram Naina Piḷḷai.

Nāmagiripēṭṭai Krishnan (*nāgasvaram*); b. 1924; belongs to a family of musicians; has also composed music for films.

Nāmakkaḷ Narasiṁha Ayyaṅgār, 'Pallavi' (vocal); 1836–1924; disciple of Mānambucāvaḍi Veṅkaṭa Subbayyar, a direct disciple of Tyāgarāja; teacher of several eminent musicians, including Turaiyūr Rājagōpāla Śarma and T.K. Raṅgachāri.

Narasiṁhāchāri (vocal); b. 1942; disciple of M.D. Rāmanāthan, S.R. Jānakirāman (vocal) and Kāraikkuḍi Krishnamūrthi (*mṛdaṅgam*).

Narasiṁhan, N. (*gōṭṭuvādyam*, vocal); b. 1943; son and disciple of K.S. Nārāyaṇa Ayyaṅgār; disciple of G.N. Bālasubrahmaṇyam, Musiri Subrahmaṇya Ayyar, Budalūr Krishnamūrti Śāstrigaḷ, and Palghat A. Rāmachandran; father and teacher of N. Ravikiran, K.N. Sashikiran, and K.N. Kiraṇāvaḷi; AIR.

Narasiṅga Rao—*see* Dwāram Durgaprasāda Rao.

Nārāyaṇa Ayyaṅgār—*see* Dēvakōṭṭai A. Nārāyaṇa Ayyaṅgār.

Nārāyaṇa Ayyaṅgār, K.S. (*gōṭṭuvādyam*); 1906–59; disciple of K.S. Subbiah Bhāgavatar, Harikēsanallūr Mutthiah Bhāgavatar, and Sakharāma Rao; learnt compositions from Vīṇā Dhanammāḷ; credited with having introduced sympathetic (resonance) strings beneath the main strings; father and teacher of N. Narasiṁhan; grandfather of N. Ravikiran.

Nārāyaṇa Ayyar, A. (*gōṭṭuvādyam*); 1911–90; disciple of Harikēsanallūr Mutthiah Bhāgavatar; teacher of Allam Koṭēśwar Rao; preferred a type of *gōṭṭuvādyam* without sympathetic (resonance) strings; worked as music director in films, and for AIR, where he prepared notations for 1000 pieces (*kṛti*), and composed music for the *Vādya Vrinda* ensemble.

Nārāyaṇa Ayyar, V. (*viṇā*); 1910; disciple of Mysore 'Vīṇā' Śeṣanna; AIR (Bangalore).

Nārāyaṇan—*see* Neyvēli R. Nārāyaṇan, Rādhā Nārāyaṇan, Rājalakshmi Nārāyaṇan, Vijayalakshmi Nārāyaṇan.

Nārāyaṇan, H.Y. (vocal); b. 1920; disciple of C.V. Krishnamūrthi Ayyar; father of Vijayalakshmi Nārāyaṇan and N. Gōvindarājan.

Nārāyaṇa Menon, Dr V.K. (*vaiṇika*, scholar); b. 1911; Director General, AIR (New Delhi); Secretary, Sangeet Natak Akademi (New Delhi); President, International Music Council; Executive Director, National Centre for the Performing Arts (Bombay).

Nārāyaṇaswāmi, Nārāyaṇaswāmy—*see* Semmaṅguḍi Nārāyaṇasvāmi Ayyar, Tañjāvūr Nārāyaṇasvāmi Appā, Umayāḷpuram K. Nārāyaṇaswāmi.

Nārāyaṇaswāmy, K.S. (*viṇā*); b. 1914; first learnt music from his brother; disciple of Ponniah Piḷḷai; contributed to the publication of the compositions of Arunācalakkavirayar, Gopāla Kṛṣṇa Bhārati, Nīlakaṇṭha Śivan and Svāti Tirunāḷ; disciple of

Dēsamaṅgaḷam Subrahmaṇya Ayyar (*viṇā*) and Ponniah Piḷḷai (*mṛdaṅgam*); Principal, Swāti Tirunāḷ College of Music; taught and performed abroad (e.g. Australia, Berlin); taught M.S. Subbulakshmi, Geetha Rāja, Pārvathy Rāman̲, Śrīrām Parasurām, and Nirmala Pārthasārathy.

Nārāyaṇaswāmy, K.V. ('KVN', vocal); b.1923; first taught by his grandfather and his father; disciple of Palghat Maṇi Ayyar and Ariyakkuḍi Rāmānuja Ayyaṅgār; taught in the USA (Wesleyan University, American Society of Eastern Arts of Berkeley and San Diego University); Central College; husband and teacher of Padma Nārāyaṇaswāmy; father and teacher of Anurādha Surēsh.

Nārāyaṇaswāmy, P.S. (vocal); b. 1934; disciple of Muḍikondān̲ Veṅkaṭarāma Ayyar, Muḍikondān̲ Maṇi Ayyar, Tirupāmburam Sōmasundaram Piḷḷai, and Semmaṅguḍi Śrīnivāsa Iyer; AIR (Chennai); teacher of Rādhā Bhāskar.

Nārāyaṇaswāmy, R.K. (vocal); b. 1916; disciple of R.K. Krishnappa and Musiri Subrahmaṇya Ayyar; brother of R.K. Śrīkantan̲; father of Dr R.N. Śrīlatha; father and teacher of the Rudrapatnam Brothers; teacher of A. Rājamma Kēśava Mūrthy.

Narēndran̲—*see* Trichūr Narēndran̲.

Narmada Gōpālakrishnan̲, Dr (violin); b. 1963; disciple of her father, M.S. Gōpālakrishnan̲, and her uncle, M.S. Anantharāman̲; AIR.

Naṭarājan̲—*see* Ālandūr Naṭarājan̲.

Naṭarājan̲, A.K.C. (clarinet); b. 1931; disciple of his father and the Ālattūr Brothers; also studied *nāgasvaram*.

Natēśa Piḷḷai—*see* Mannārguḍi Natēśa Piḷḷai.

Nēdunūri Krishnamūrthi (vocalist, violinist, composer); b. 1927; disciple of Appa Rao, Kalluri Vēnugōpāla Rao, Dwāram Narasiṅga Rao, and Dr Śrīpāda Pinakapāni; served as Principal of three music colleges.

Neeḍamaṅgaḷam—*see* Nīḍamaṅgaḷam Mīn̲ākṣisundaram Piḷḷai.

Neela—*see* Sikkil Sisters.

Nellai Krishnamoorthy, T.V. (vocal); b. 1920; disciple of L. Muthaiah Bhāgavatar; S.S.T. College of Music (Tiruvananthapuram).

Neyvēli R. Nārāyaṇan̲ (*mṛdaṅgam*); b. 1967; disciple of Tañjāvūr Upēndran̲ (*mṛdaṅgam*) and Chembai Bhāgavatar (vocal).

Neyvēli R. Santhānagōpālan̲ (vocal); b. 1963; disciple of T.N. Sēshagōpālan̲.

Neyvēli B. Veṅkaṭēsh (*mṛdaṅgam*); b. 1965; disciple of his father, A.S. Bālarāman̲, Rāmnād M.N Kandaswāmy, and Perumpallam P. Veṅkaṭēsan̲; teaches at the Cultural Department, Neyvēli Lignite Corporation.

Neyyattiṇkara Vāsudēvan̲ (vocal); disciple of Rāmnād Krishnan̲ and Semmaṅguḍi Śrīnivāsa Iyer; Rādhā Lakshmī Vilāsam (RLV) Music Academy, Tripunithura; AIR (Tiruvananthapuram).

Nīḍamaṅgaḷam Mīn̲ākṣisundaram Piḷḷai (*tavil, kañjīrā*); 1894–1949; disciple of his uncle, Gōvinda Piḷḷai, and Nāgapaṭṭin̲am Vēṇugōpāla Piḷḷai, a *nāgasvara vidvān* with whom he performed initially; is remembered for his extraordinary virtuosity, creativity, and intricacy of rhythm; father of musicologist B.M. Sundaram; teacher of his son, N.T.M. Shaṇmugha Vaḍivēl, Coimbatore N. Rāmaswāmi Piḷḷai, and others; credited with introducing the 'Special Tavil' pattern heard in contemporary performances.

Nirmala Pārthasārathy (*viṇā*, vocal); disciple of T. Mukta (vocal) and K.S. Nārāyaṇaswāmy (*viṇā*).

Nithyasree, S. (vocal); b. 1973; introduced to music by her parents, I. Śivakumār (mridangist, son of D.K. Paṭṭammāḷ), and Lalitha (vocal, daughter of Palghat Maṇi Ayyar); disciple of her grandmother, D.K. Paṭṭammāḷ.

Nookala Chinna Satyanārāyaṇa, Dr (vocal, violin); b. 1927; disciple of Maṅgaḷampalli Paṭṭābhirāmayya, Dwāram Narasiṅga Rao, Dwāram Veṅkaṭaswāmy Naidu, and Śrīpāda Pinakapāni; Principal, Government College of Music (Vijayawada, Hyderabad).

Noorani Parameśvara Bhāgavatar (vocalist, composer); 1815–92; was the chief musician at the court of Svāti Tirunāḷ; credited with systematizing the music of *Kathakali*, the dance-drama of Kerala, together with Rāmakrishna Bhāgavatar; teacher of Coimbatore Rāghava Ayyar and Palghat Anantarāma Bhāgavatar.

Nori Nāgabhūṣaṇam (vocalist, violinist, composer); 1905–84; disciple of his father, Viṣwanātha Śāstrī, and Masulipatnam Hari Nāgabhūṣaṇam; Principal, Government Music College (Secunderabad).

Padma, A.S. (*vīṇā*); b. 1929; disciple of M.J. Śrīnivāsa Ayyaṅgār and Mysore Doreswāmy Ayyaṅgār.

Padma Gōpālakrishnaṉ (vocal); b. 1929; disciple of M.A. Kalyāṇakrishna Bhāgavatar.

Padma Gurudutt (vocal); b. 1951; disciple of M.V. Veṅkaṭaramaiah, T. Puttaswāmiah, T.K. Raṅgachāri, G.R. Jaya, and K. Veṅkaṭarām.

Padma Mūrthy, Dr (music therapist, musicologist, vocalist, *vaiṇika*); b. 1932; disciple of H.S. Krishnamūrthy, R.S. Kēshavamūrthy, Mysore Vāsudevācāriar, and others; Head of Department of Dance, Drama and Music (Bangalore University); Dean and Visiting Professor, S.P. Mahila University (Tirupati); research work and papers pertaining to the psychological effect of rāgas (National Institute of Mental Health and Neuro Sciences, Bangalore); has published several books and articles on classical Karnatic music.

Padmanābha, R.K. (vocal); b. 1949; disciple of N. Nañjundaswāmi, H.R. Seetharāma Sāstry, and H.V. Krishnamūrthy; has produced several books and recordings (e.g. compositions of Mysore Vāsudevācāriar); Founder, Shārada Kalā Kēndra (Bangalore).

Padmanābha, R.K. (*vīṇā*); son and disciple of R.S. Kēśavamūrthy.

Padmanābhaṉ—*see* Rajēswari Padmanābhaṉ.

Padma Nārāyaṇaswāmy (vocal); b. 1942; disciple of Musiri Subrahmaṇya Ayyar and her husband, K.V. Nārāyaṇaswāmy.

Padma Varadaṉ (*vīṇā*); daughter and disciple of R. Raṅgarāmānuja Ayyaṅgār.

Padmāvathy Ananthagōpālaṉ (*vīṇā*); b. 1935; daughter and disciple of V.R. Gōpāla Ayyar; sister of Lālguḍi Jayarāmaṉ and Srīmathi Brahmānandam; aunt and teacher of Jayanti Rādhakrishnaṉ; has published a series of music primers; founder of a music school, 'Sadguru Saṅgīta Vidyālaya'.

Padmāvathy Nāgarājaṉ (vocal); b. 1950; daughter of H.Y. Nārāyaṇaṉ; disciple of her mother, Rājalakshmi Nārāyaṇaṉ, and Semmaṅguḍi Śrīnivāsa Ayyar.

Padma Veḷḷai Chandramouly (*vīṇā*); b. 1929; disciple of Dēvakōṭṭai A. Nārāyaṇa Ayyaṅgār.

Padmiṉi, T. (*vīṇā*); b. 1956; disciple of Ramavarapu Vijaya Lakshmi and Ramanuja Suri.

Pakala Rāmdās (violin); b. 1963; introduced to playing the violin by his father; disciple of P.P. Sōmayājulu and Lālguḍi Jayarāmaṉ; Lecturer, Kalākshētra; teacher of V. Śrīnivāsaṉ.

Pakkiri Piḷḷai—*see* Mannārguḍi Pakkiri Piḷḷai.

Pakkiri Swāmy. R.V. (*mōrsiṅg*); 1916–89; disciple of his father Vēnugōpāl Naidu, a *mṛdaṅgam* exponent and Peethambara Desai; the only percussionist who entirely specialized in this rare instrument as a career; accompanied eminent musicians like Tiger Varadāchāriar and Sīrkāzhi S. Gōvindarājan̲.

Paḻani Subrahmaṇya Piḷḷai (*mṛdaṅgam, kañjīrā*); 1909–62; disciple of his father, Paḻani Muthiah Piḷḷai, and Pudukōṭṭai Dakṣiṇāmūrti Piḷḷai; remembered for creating a subtle, aesthetic style of his own under the influence of Pudukōṭṭai Māmuṇḍiyā Piḷḷai; court musician at Travan̲core (Kerala); held posts at the Tamil Isai College and AIR; teacher of Rāmnād M.N Kandaswāmy, Tañjāvūr Raṅganāthan̲, Trichy Śaṅkaran̲, and K. Śrīvatsa.

Palghat Anantarāma Bhāgavatar (vocal, *harikathā*); 1867–1919; disciple of N. Paramēśvara Bhāgavatar and Mahāvaidyanātha Śivan̲; teacher of Palghat Rāma Bhāgavatar and T.G. Viṣwanātha Bhāgavatar; grandfather of T.A.S. Maṇi.

Palghat K. Krishnamāni (*mṛdaṅgam*); 1926–92; disciple of Pazhayannūr Krishna Ayyar.

Palghat C.S. Krishnamoorthi (*mṛdaṅgam)*; b. 1937; disciple of C.A. Subba Ayyar, Palghat Maṇi Ayyar, and Palghat Raghu; S.S.T. College of Music.

Palghat S. Krishnamoorthy (vocal); b. 1931; disciple of Chembai Vaidyanātha Bhāgavatar and Musiri Subrahmaṇya Ayyar; AIR (Tiruvananthapuram).

Palghat Maṇi Ayyar, T.S. (*mṛdaṅgam*); 1913–81; son of Śeṣan̲ Bhāgavatar; disciple of Tañjāvūr Vaidyanātha Ayyar; credited with setting the aesthetic and technical standards for Karnatic percussion in this century; father and teacher of T.R. Rājāmaṇi; teacher of Yellā Sōmanna, Palghat C.S. Krishnamoorthi, Umayāḻpuram K. Śivarāman̲, V. Nāgarājan̲, Palghat Raghu, K.V. Nārāyaṇaswāmy, J. Vaidyanāthan̲, G. Harishankar, S. Surēsh, and Bombay Bālāji; grandfather of S. Nithyasree.

Palghat Raghu (*mṛdaṅgam*); b. 1928; disciple of Tinniyam Veṅkaṭarāma Ayyar and Palghat Maṇi Ayyar; grandfather and teacher of R. Anantharāman̲ and R. Raghurām; teacher of Palghat C.S. Krishnamoorthi, Trichūr C. Narēndran̲, K.P. Anilkumār, Bombay Bālāji, and Manōj Śiva.

Palghat Rāma Bhāgavatar (vocal); 1888–1957; learnt music from his brother, Veṅkaṭakrishna Bhāgavatar, K. Rāma Bhāgavatar, and Subbarāma Bhāgavatar; disciple of Palghat Anantarāma Bhāgavatar and Umayāḻpuram Swāminātha Ayyar; teacher of Puducōde K. Krishnamūrthi and K.A. Kāsi Bhāgavatar.

Palghat K. Raṅganāthan ('Sheker'; *mṛdaṅgam*); b. 1965; disciple of Palghat Rāmanāthan̲ and T.K. Moorthy.

Palghat V.A. Sundaram (*ghaṭam*); 1929–94; disciple of Ālattūr Śrīnivāsa Ayyar and Panchapakēsha Ayyar (vocal), K.V. Rajama Ayyar (flute), his brother, Palghat V.A. Rāmachandran̲ (*mṛdaṅgam*), and K.M. Vaidyanāthan̲ (*ghaṭam*).

Pallaḍam Rājan̲ (flute); b. 1919; disciple of Pallaḍam Sanjīva Rao.

Pallaḍam Sanjīva Rao (flute); 1882–1962 disciple of Śarabha Śāstrigaḷ; was a very popular flute virtuoso; teacher of H. Rāmachandra Shāstry and Pallaḍam Rājan̲.

Panchapakēsha Ayyar, A.S. (vocal, educationist); b. 1916; brother of Ālattūr Śrīnivāsa Ayyar; learnt music from his elder brother; sang for dance performances of Rukmini Devi (the late Founder-Director of Kalākshētra); Principal of Bhāratīya Music College (Mumbai); published a series of didactic books on Karnatic music (e.g. *Keerthanamalika, Varnamalika*); teacher of Dr M.B. Vēdavaḷḷi.

Pāpā K.S. Veṅkaṭarāmayya (violin); 1901–72; disciple of Malaikōṭṭai Gōvindasvāmi Piḷḷai whose affectionate address 'child' (Tamil *pāpā*) became a permanent prefix to his name; learnt compositions from Vīṇā Dhanammāḷ; teacher and father of V. Tyāgarājan̲.

Parameśvara Bhāgavatar—*see* Noorani Parameśvara Bhāgavatar.

Pārthasārathy—*see* Nirmala Pārthasārathy.

Pārthasārathy, T.S. (scholar, critic); b. 1913; Secretary, The Music Academy (Chennai), and Editor of its Journal; Advisor to several cultural organizations, universities, and government institutions (AIR); author of essays, biographies, and translations of songs (e.g Tamil and Telugu translations of compositions of the Trinity, Tyāgarāja, Śyāmā Śāstri, and Muttusvāmi Dīkṣitar).

Pārūr M.A. Krishnaswāmy (violin); b. 1963; disciple of his grandfather, Pārūr Sundaram Ayyar, his father, M.S. Anantharāman̲ (violin), and Pathamadai Krishnan̲ (vocal); also studied Hindustānī music; AIR (Chennai).

Pārūr Sundaram Ayyar (violin); 1891–1974; disciple of Rāmasvāmi Bhāgavatar and his son, Nārāyaṇa Bhāgavatar of Tiruvananthapuram; learnt compositions from Vīṇā Dhanammāḷ; studied Hindustānī music at the Gāndharva Mahā Vidyālaya in Bombay, and also accompanied the Hindustānī vocalist Ōmkarnāth Thakūr; teacher of his sons, M.S. Anantharāman̲ and M.S. Gōpālakrishnan̲, and his grandson, Pārūr M.A. Krishnaswāmy.

Pārvathy—*see* Trivandrum Baby Pārvathy.

Pārvathy Rāman̲ (*vīṇā*, vocal); b. 1942; disciple of Semmaṅguḍi Śrīnivāsa Iyer, N.G. Seetharāma Ayyar (vocal), and K.S. Nārāyaṇaswāmy (*vīṇā*).

Paśupathi, D. (vocalist, composer); b. 1931; graduated from, and taught at, Kalākshētra; disciple of Tiger Varadāchāriar, Budalūr Krishnamūrti Śāstrigaḷ, Mysore Vāsudēvācāria, and Muḍikondān̲ Veṅkaṭarāma Ayyar; Head of Department of Music, Shrī Veṅkaṭēśwara University; re-composed about 200 pieces (*kīrtana*) of Annamācārya.

Paṭṭamaḍai S. Krishnan̲ (vocalist, composer); b. 1921; disciple of his father, K.M. Subbarāma Ayyar, and Harikēsanallūr Mutthiah Bhāgavatar; composer of *varṅam*, *kṛti*, and *tillānā* with Tamil, Telugu, and Sanskrit lyrics.

Paṭṭammāḷ, D.K. (vocal); b. 1919; acquired her repertoire from different specialists: compositions of Muttusvāmi Dīkṣitar from Ambhi Dīkṣitar and Justice T.L. Veṅkaṭarāma Ayyar; Pāpanāsam Śivan̲ (his own songs); Vīṇā Dhanammāḷ's daughter, Rājalakshmi Ammāḷ (*padam*); Vēlūr Appadurai Ācariar (*Tiruppugal*); and other specialities from V.O. Vaidyanāthan̲ (disciple of Ariyakkuḍi Rāmānuja Ayyaṅgār), N.S. Krishnaswāmy Ayyaṅgār, Kamākṣi Ammāḷ, P. Sambamūrthy; credited with pioneering the presentation of the *rāgam tānam pallavi* format by female musicians; teacher of her brother, D.K. Jayarāman̲, Chārumathi Rāmachandran̲, Maṅgaḷam Shankar, and granddaughter, S. Nithyasree.

Pichumaṇi Ayyar, R. (*vaiṇika*, composer); b. 1920; disciple of T. Kuppanna, Gōmathy Śaṅkara Ayyar, Tiger Varadāchāriar, and K.S. Nārāyaṇaswami Ayyar.

Piḷḷai—*see* Ānanḍāṇkōil V. Selvaratnam P., Chittoor Subramaṇia P., Coimbatore Ṇ. Rāmaswāmi P., Kāñcīpuram Naina P., Kumbakōnam Rājamāṇikkam P., Malaikōṭṭai Gōvindasvāmi P., Mannārguḍi Natēśa P., Mannārguḍi Pakkiri P., Mannārguḍi Vaidyaliṅgam P., Nīḍamaṅgaḷam Mīnākṣisundaram P., Palani Subrahmaṇya P., K. Ponniah P., Pudukōṭṭai Dakṣiṇāmūrti P., Pudukōṭṭai Mānpūṇḍiya P., T.N. Rājaratnam P., Semponnārkōil S.R.G. Rājānna Pillai and S.R.G. Sambandam P., Semponnārkōil Rāmaswāmi P., T.N. Sōmasundaram P., Tirupāmburam N. Swāminātha Piḷḷai.

Pinakapāni—*see* Śrīpāda Pinakapāni.

Polagam Chidambara Ayyar (*ghatam*); b. 1841; the first known *ghaṭam* exponent in classical South Indian music; little is known about this musician who is also credited with developing the playing technique of the *ghaṭam*.

Ponniah Piḷḷai, K. (vocal, *mṛdaṅgam*; dance and music scholar, composer); 1888–1945; descendant of Śivānandam (Tanjore Quartette); disciple of Pandanallūr Mīnākṣisundaram Piḷḷai (1869–1954), Palghat Anantarāma Ayyar and Tiruvōtriyūr Tyāgayyar; taught vocal and *mṛdaṅgam* at Aṇṇāmalai University; composed and published numerous dance pieces; credited with important contributions to the format and repertoire of the *bharata nāṭyam* dance style; teacher of Tañjāvūr Vaidyanātha Ayyar, Bangalore G. Channamma, Kuttālam Viṣwanāthan, C.S. Krishna Ayyar, K.S. Nārāyaṇaswāmy, Dr S. Rāmanāthan, Chintalapalli Rāmachandra Rao, O.S. Thyāgarājan; teacher of his sons, K.P. Kiṭṭappa and Tañjāvūr K.P. Śivānandam.

Ponnusvāmi—*see* Mutialpet Ponnusvāmi.

Ponnuswāmy, P.N.—*see* Madurai Brothers.

Poornapragna—*see* Sandhyavandanam Poornapragna Rao.

Prakash—*see* Coimbatur G. Prakash.

Prapancham (Prapañcam) V. Seetharam (flute); b. 1942; disciple of T.R. Mahāliṅgam; Director of Programmes, AIR (New Delhi); teacher of Tañjāvūr S. Bālachander.

Prasād, K.V. (*mṛdaṅgam*); b. 1958; disciple of T.K. Moorthy.

Prēma Hariharan (vocal); b. 1938; disciple of Akhila Natēśan, R.S. Maṇi , Tañjāvūr S. Kalyāṇarāman, and Mahārājāpuram Santhānam.

Prēma Raṅgarājan (vocal); b. 1951; disciple of Rāmabhadra Ayyaṅgār and K. Krishnamūrti (Delhi University), P. Bālakrishnan, S. Rājam, and Sulōchana Paṭṭābhirāman.

Premeela Gurumūrthy, Dr (vocal, musicology); b. 1954; disciple of T.K. Gōvinda Rao, B. Rājam Ayyar, Muḍikondān Veṅkaṭarāma Ayyar and T.M. Thyagarājan; daughter-in-law of S. Rājam; also performs Hindustāni music; obtained her PhD for research work (published) on *harikathā kālakṣepam* for which she studied several years with C. Banni Bāi; Founder-Director of Sunaada, an institution for the preservation and popularization of *harikathā*; Reader, Music Department, University of Chennai.

Pudućōde K. Krishnamūrthi (vocal); 1923–85; disciple of Palghat Rāma Bhāgavatar; Principal, Government Music Academy (Palakkad); Vice-Principal, Kalākshētra; teacher of Śakuntala Narasiṁhan and Sai Shankar.

Pudukōṭṭai Dakṣiṇāmūrti Piḷḷai (*mṛdaṅgam, ghaṭam, kañjīrā*); 1875–1936; disciple of Pudukōṭṭai Mānpūṇḍiya Piḷḷai; remembered for his sensitive and versatile play, he was the main accompanist of the famous *vīṇā* duo known as the 'Kāraikkuḍi Brothers'; also performed for drama and religious discourses (*harikathā kālakṣepam*); teacher of his son, *kañjīrā* exponent Svāminātha Piḷḷai; credited by Palghat Maṇi Ayyar, who performed along with Svāminātha Piḷḷai, with being a major influence on his style.

Pudukōṭṭai R. Krishnamūrthy (*vīṇā*); b. 1939; disciple of Gōmati Shankar Iyer and Gouri Kumāri; Shrī Veṅkaṭēśwara University.

Pudukōṭṭai Mānpūṇḍiya Piḷḷai, Māmuṇḍiyā Piḷḷai (*kañjīrā*); 1857-1922; disciple of Tirugokaranam Māriyappa Tavilkārar; influential and versatile musician credited with raising the technical and aesthetic standards of percussion in Karnatic music; believed to have introduced the sophisticated structure of a modern percussion solo (*taṉiyāvarttaṉam*) for which he composed a series of intricate patterns (*mōrā*) to conclude every stage, including the climax and conclusion of a solo (*mōrā* and *kōrvai*); these patterns are normally followed by variations of the triple 'ta dhi ki na tom' sequence which is also said to have been introduced by Mānpūṇḍiyā Piḷḷai; also credited with introducing and improving (if not inventing) the modern *kañjirā* as well as its playing technique which has since become a fully-fledged concert instrument; another valuable contribution was his collection of the available repertoire of *Tiruppugaḻ* songs which are known for their intricacy and diversity of rhythmic patterns; teacher of Pudukōṭṭai Dakṣiṇāmūrti Piḷḷai and Konērirājāpuram Vaidyanātha Ayyar.

Puttachār, H. (*mṛdaṅgam kañjirā*); teacher of his son, H.P. Rāmachār, M.S. Rāmayya, and L. Bhīmachār.

Puttaswāmiah, T. (vocal); 1910–87; disciple of Bīḍaram Krishnappā; brother of Mysore T. Chowdiah; Professor, Department of Music, University of Bangalore; teacher of Padma Gurudutt.

Rādhā Bhāskar (vocal); b. 1969; disciple of P.S. Nārāyaṇaswāmy; doctoral research (PhD) at the University of Chennai.

Rādhā Nārāyaṇaṉ (violin); b. 1937; disciple of Harihara Ayyar and Dwāram Veṅkaṭaswāmy Naidu; mother and teacher of Meera Sivarāmakrishnan.

Rādhā Veṅkaṭāchalam, Dr (vocalist); b. 1949; disciple of T.R. Subrahmaṇyam; doctorate for History of Concept of Music (Akhil Bhāratīya Gāndharva Vidyā Mandal, Deemed University, New Delhi); research on *pallavi*; Reader, Department of Music, Delhi University.

Rādhā Viṣwanāthaṉ (vocal); b. 1934; adopted daughter, disciple, and co-performer of M. S. Subbulakshmi; also learnt music from Rāmnād Krishnaṉ, Māyavaram Krishna Ayyar, and T. Brinda.

Rāghavachāry, D.—*see* Hyderabad Brothers.

Rāghavaṉ—*see* Rāmnād Rāghavan.

Rāghavaṉ, Dr V. (scholar, composer); 1908–79; Founder-Member of the Music Academy, and Editor of its Journal; author and editor of numerous music books (e.g. *Muttusvāmi Dīkṣitar*, with notations and an index of the songs of the composer, published by the National Centre for the Performing Arts), biographies, and articles (e.g. his Introductory Thesis, *The Spiritual Heritage of Tyāgarāja*); his poetry and compositions comprise several forms (e.g. *śabda*, *kīrtana*).

Raghu—*see* Palghat Raghu.

Raghu and Ravi (flute duo); b. 1954 and 1957 respectively; disciples of their father, L. Sundaram, a disciple of T.R. Mahāliṅgam.

Raghurām, R. (*mṛdaṅgam*); b.1985; grandson and disciple of Palghat Raghu.

Rājagōpāl, Rājagōpāla, Rājagōpālaṉ—*see* Turaiyūr Rājagōpāla Śarma, Raṅganāyaki Rājagōpālan, Seetha Rājagōpāl.

Rājagōpālaṉ, N. (vocal, *viṇā*); b. 1910; disciple of Nārāyaṇaswāmi Sēsha Ayyaṅgār; teacher of Dr S. Seetha.

Rājagōpālaṉ, R.A. (*mṛdaṅgam, ghaṭam*); b. 1952; son of *harikathā* exponent R.A. Krishnamāchārya; disciple of T.A.S. Maṇi; AIR (Bangalore).

Rājalakshmi Nārāyaṇaṉ (*viṇā*); b. 1928; disciple of Veṅkaṭasāmy Rāju and Dr S. Rāmanāthaṉ; Central College.

Rājalakshmi Rāghavan̲ (*viṇā*); b. 1942; disciple of Dēvakōṭṭai A. Nārāyaṇa Ayyaṅgār; Rājāh's College and Government Music College (Madurai).

Rājalakshmi Rāmānujam (vocal); b. 1931; graduated from Kalākshētra under the guidance of Tiger Varadāchāriar, Budalūr Krishnamūrti Śāstrigaḷ, and other leading musicians and dancers; also taught there; AIR; Research Assistant, Music Academy.

Rājam, S. (vocalist, scholar, painter, composer); b. 1919; first learnt music from his father, advocate U. Sundaram Ayyar; disciple of Ambhi Dīkṣitar, Ariyakkuḍi Rāmānuja Ayyaṅgār, Pāpanāsam Śivan̲, Madurai Maṇi Ayyar, and Mahārājāpuram Viṣwanātha Ayyar; brother of *vaiṇika* S. Bālachander; specialist for rare rāgas; set several lyrics of Purandara Dāsa, Sadāśiva Brahmendra, Aruṇagirinātar, and Nārāyaṇa Tīrtha to music; AIR; teacher of Vijayalakshmy Subramaṇiam, Prēma Raṅgarājan̲, and others.

Rājamaṇi, T.R. (b. 1940); son and disciple of Palghat Maṇi Ayyar; teacher of S. Surēsh.

Rājam Iyer, B. (vocalist, scholar); b. 1922; disciple of Ariyakkuḍi Rāmānuja Ayyaṅgār; a specialist in compositions of Muttusvāmi Dīkṣitar, he transcribed, edited and translated numerous collections of songs and scholarly works (e.g. *Saṅgīta Sampradāya Pradaśini* of Subbarāma Dīkṣitar); Central College; Principal of Teachers' College of the Music Academy.

Rājamma Kēśava Mūrthy, A. (vocal); b. 1929; disciple of Madurai Veṅkaṭarāma Ayyar, R.K. Śrīkantan̲, and R.K. Nārāyaṇaswāmy.

Rājan̲—*see* Palladam Rājan̲, Ritha Rājan̲.

Rājan̲, G.S. (flute); b. 1962; disciple of his father, Guruvāyūr Śrīkrishnan̲, and H. Rāmachandra Shāstry (flute); and Puducōde K. Krishnamūrthi (vocal); Programme Officer, Sangeet Natak Akademi (New Delhi).

Rājānna Pillai—*see* Sempon̲n̲ārkōil S.R.G. Rājānna Pillai and S.R.G. Sambandam Piḷḷai.

Rājappa Ayyar—*see* Kumbakōnam M. Rājappa Ayyar.

Rāja Rao—*see* Śrīmuṣṇam Rāja Rao.

Rājaratnam Piḷḷai, T.N. (*nāgasvaram*); 1898–1956; specialist for rāga Tōḍi; teacher of Kārukuricci P. Arunāchalam.

Rājēśwari, S. (vocal); b. 1946; disciple of D.K. Jayarāman̲ and Madurai N. Krishnan̲; also specialist for dance music (*naṭṭuvāṅgam*).

Rājēśwari Padmanābhan̲ (*viṇā*); b. 1939; grand-daughter of 'Vīṇā' Kāraikkuḍi Subbarāmyyar; disciple of her grand-uncle, 'Vīṇā' Sambaśiva Ayyar, and Mysore Vāsudēvācāria; noted for her refined technique and *tānam* exposition; sister and teacher of Kāraikkuḍi S. Subramaṇian̲; mother and teacher of Śrīvidya Chandramouli; teacher of her niece, V. Shānti; Lecturer, Kalākshētra.

Rājī Gōpālakrishnan̲ (vocal); disciple of T.S. Krishnaswāmy Bhāgavatar and T.R. Bālamaṇi; Bhāratīya Music College (Mumbai).

Rājkumār Bhārati, Dr (vocal); b. 1958; great-grandson of Subrahmaṇya Bhārati; disciple of his mother, Lalita Bhārati, Valliyūr Gurumūrthy, Bālamuraḷī Krishna, and T.V. Gōpālakrishnan̲.

Rāmabhadran—*see* Vellore Rāmabhadran.

Rāma Bhāgavatar—*see* Palghat Rāma Bhāgavatar.

Rāmacandra, Rāmachandra, Rāmachandran̲—*see* Chintalapalli Rāmachandra Rao, Eṭṭayapuram Rāmacandra Bhāgavatar, Mahārājāpuram S. Rāmachandran̲, Śrīvanchiam K. Rāmachandra Ayyar, Trichūr V. Rāmachandran̲.

Rāmachandra Shāstry, H. (flute); 1906–92; disciple of Palladam Sanjīva Rao; expert on *rāga lakṣaṇa*; instituted a *nāgasvaram* school at Paḻani; Veṅkaṭēśwara University and Kalākshētra; teacher of Ludwig Pesch, G.S. Rājaṉ, and T. Sashīdhar.

Rāmachandraṉ, C.K. (vocal); b. 1943; disciple of M.S. Bhāskara Menon and Semmaṅguḍi Śrīnivāsa Iyer; AIR, Kozhikode (Kerala).

Rāmachār, H.P. (*kañjīrā*, *mṛdaṅgam*); b. 1925; disciple of his father, H. Puttachār; AIR (Bangalore).

Rāmakanth, R.S. (vocal); son and disciple of R.K. Śrīkantaṉ.

Rāmakrishnaṉ, T.K. (*mṛdaṅgam*); b. 1941; disciple of Māṇguḍi R. Durairāja Ayyar and Māṇguḍi Dorairāja Ayyar (*mṛdaṅgam*); 1900–80; disciple of Tañjāvūr Vaidyanātha Ayyar; collaborated with Hindustānī musicians and contributed music to Attenborough's film 'Gandhi'; founder of Prayojana Matriculation School.

Rāmamaṇi, R.A. (vocal); disciple of M. Śeṣagiri Āchār, R.K. Śrīkantaṉ, and Aroor S. Rāmakrishna; specialist for complex rhythms (e.g. *pallavi* in dual tālas); together with her husband, T.A.S. Maṇi, she has also collaborated with Jazz musicians.

Rāmaṉ, B.V. and B.V. Lakshmanaṉ (vocal); b. 1921; disciples of Tiger Varadāchāriar and music graduates from Aṇṇāmalai University (Chidambaram); twin brothers specialized in duo performances; teachers of Meera Sēshādri.

Rāmanāthaṉ—*see* Mavelikara H. Rāmanāthaṉ.

Rāmanāthaṉ, M.D. ('MDR', vocalist, composer); 1923–84; disciple of Tiger Varadāchāriar; admired for his personal style, deep voice, and slow pace of rendition; composed songs (*kṛti* and *tillānā*) in Sanskrit, Telugu, Malayālam, and Tamil; his *mudrā* (signature) is *Varadadāsa*, a homage to his *guru*; Principal, Kalākshētra; teacher of Rāmā Ravi.

Rāmanāthaṉ, Dr N. (violin, vocal, musicology); b. 1946; disciple of Kodaganallūr Subramaṇiaṉ (violin), Pudukōṭṭai Rāmanāthaṉ (violin), and Kalliḍaikkuricci Mahādēva Bhāgavatar (vocal); authority for ancient Sanskrit texts on music (e.g. *Saṅgīta Ratnākara*); obtained his Doctorate in Musicology from Benares Hindu University; Head of Department of Music, University of Chennai.

Rāmanāthaṉ, P.R. (vocal); b. 1968; disciple of T.K. Gōvinda Rao and Chembai Kōdaṇḍa Rāma (a disciple of Chembai Vaidyanātha Bhāgavatar).

Rāmanāthaṉ , R.K. (vocalist); b. 1917; disciple of R.K. Krishnappa; brother of R.K. Śrīkantaṉ.

Rāmanāthaṉ, Dr S. (vocalist, *vaiṇika*, musicologist); 1917–85; disciple of Ponniah Piḷḷai, T.S. Sabhēsa Ayyar, Tiger Varadāchāriar (vocal), and Dēvakōṭṭai A. Nārāyaṇa Ayyaṅgār (*vīṇā*); authority on the history and performing practice of Tamil music; associated with leading organizations in this field; Principal, Śrī Sadguru Saṅgam Vidyālaya (Madurai); Central College; obtained his PhD from Wesleyan University; published his thesis (*Music in Cilappatikaaram*); Visiting Professor in the USA (Colgate, Illinois, Wesleyan, and Washington Universities); Visiting Principal, Tamiḻ Isai Saṅgam Isai Kallūri (Chennai); composed music for lyrics of Ambujam Krishna; taught his daughters, R. Lathā, Geetha Bennett and Vanathy Raghurāmaṉ; teacher of Ambujam Vēdāntam, Dr S. Bhāgyalekshmy, and S. Sowmya.

Ramani—*see* Ashōk Ramani.

Ramani, N. (flute); b. 1934; disciple of his grandfather, Azhiyur Nārāyaṇaswāmy Ayyar, and T.R. Mahāliṅgam; learnt compositions from Ālattūr Veṅkaṭēsa Ayyar and the Ālattūr Brothers; collaborated with North Indian musicians (*jugalbandī*), notably

Hariprasād Chaurāsia; founded a Flute Academy in Chennai; innovative flute virtuoso who first introduced a longer type of bamboo flute in South Indian music; teacher of many flute players, including his son, R. Tyāgarājan̲, and his daughter's son, Atuḷkumār.

Rāmānuja Ayyaṅgār—*see* Ariyakkuḍi Rāmānuja Ayyaṅgār, Raṅgarāmānuja Ayyaṅgār.

Rāmānuja Chārilu (violin); b. 1960; disciple of his father and N.C.H. Krishnamāchārlu; AIR.

Rāmā Ravi (vocal); b. 1943; disciple of T.K. Rāmasvāmi Ayyaṅgār, Budalūr Krishnamūrti Śāstrigaḷ, M.D. Rāmanāthan̲, and T. Viṣwanāthan̲.

Rāmaswāmi—*see* Coimbatore Rāmaswāmi Piḷḷai, Sempon̲n̲ārkōil Rāmaswāmi Piḷḷai.

Rāmayya, M.S. (*mr̥daṅgam*, *tablā*, vocal); b. 1922; disciple of his father, Subbanna, and Jan Saheb (*tablā*), Muttusvāmi Dēvar, Veṅkaṭēśa Dēvar, H. Puttachār, and Śrīnivāsulu Naidu (*mr̥daṅgam*), and B. Devendrappah (vocal); AIR (Bangalore).

Rāmdās—*see* Pakala Rāmdās.

Ramesh, R. (*mr̥daṅgam*); b. 1959; disciple of his father, K.R. Rādhakrishnan̲, and Kāraikkuḍi Maṇi.

Rameshbabu, K.P. (*mr̥daṅgam*); b. 1970; disciple of his father, K.P. Bhaskaradas, Puducōde Krishna Ayyar, and Kāraikkuḍi Maṇi.

Rāmh, S.P. (vocal); b. 1970; disciple of Lālguḍi Jayarāman̲.

Rāmnād M.N. Kandaswāmy (*mr̥daṅgam*, *kañjīrā*); b. 1926; disciple of Paḻani Subrahmaṇya Piḷḷai; teacher of Neyvēli B. Veṅkaṭēsh and J. Bālāji; AIR.

Rāmnād Krishnan̲ (vocal); 1918–73; learnt music from his elder brother, Lakshminārāyaṇan̲; disciple of Subrahmaṇya Ayyar, Sōmu Bhāgavatar and Rāmnād C.S. Śaṅkara Śivan̲; Central College; Visiting Professor, Wesleyan University (USA); teacher of his brother, Rāmnād Rāghavan̲, Dr S.A.K. Durgā, Chārumathi Rāmachandran̲, Neyyattiṇkara Vāsudēvan̲, Rādhā Viṣwanāthan̲, G.N. Nāgamaṇi Śrīnāth, Vēgavāhini Vijayarāghavan̲, and Dr Ritha Rājan̲.

Rāmnād Rāghavan̲ (*mr̥daṅgam*); b. 1927; disciple of his brother, Rāmnād Krishnan̲, and Rāmnād Śaṅkara Śivam.

Raṅgachāri, T.K. (vocal); 1912–79; disciple of Nāmakkaḷ Narasiṁha Ayyaṅgār, K.S. Subbiah Bhāgavatar, and Sabhēśa Ayyar; Aṇṇāmalai University; Central College; teacher of Vairamaṅgalam Lakshminārāyaṇan̲, and Padma Gurudutt.

Raṅgaiah, C. (vocalist, scholar, composer); 1895–1984; disciple of Śivarāmaiah, Chikka Subba Rao, Mysore V. Veṅkaṭagiriappa, and Mysore Vāsudevācāriar; author of several works on music; his 500 compositions in Sanskrit and Kannaḍa have been published; these comprise all the major forms and many rare rāgas of Karnatic music; teacher of his sons, notably C.R. Laxminārāyaṇa, Dr K. Varadarājan̲, and Rājēśwari Pandit.

Raṅganāthan̲—*see* Tañjāvūr Raṅganāthan̲.

Raṅganāyaki Rājagōpālan̲ (*viṇā*); b. 1932; disciple of Kāraikkuḍi Sambaśiva Ayyar with whom she performed regularly; Music Academy.

Raṅgarāmānuja Ayyaṅgār, R. (*vaiṇika*, scholar); 1901–80; professed his indebtedness to Viṇā Dhanammāḷ, her music, style and values; stressed the need for a scientific approach to music history, musicology and education; published several works (e.g. *History of South Indian Music*) and brought out the largest collection of notations covering 1500 pieces of several composers (*Kritimanilai*, in Tamil); teacher of Śrīpāda Pinakapāni and Professor Harold S. Powers; held guest lectures at several universities in the USA; father and teacher of Padma Varadan̲.

Rathnamāla Prakāsh, R.S. (vocal); daughter and disciple of R.K. Śrīkantan̲; specialized in light music for ballet, film, radio and television productions.

Ravi, B. (*ghaṭam*); b. 1979; disciple of Palghat K. Raṅganāthan and T.K. Moorthy.

Ravi, V.V. (violin); b. 1957; belongs to a family of musicians and is a disciple of his brother, V.V. Subramaṇiam; AIR.

Ravikiran̲, N. (*citravīṇā* or *gōṭṭuvādyam*); b. 1967; grandson of Nārāyaṇa Ayyaṅgār; was taught by his father, N. Narasiṁhan̲; prefers the name *citravīṇā* for the instrument widely known as *gōṭṭuvādyam* ('stick-played instrument'); has also collaborated with exponents of Jazz and World Music; brother of K.N. Sashikiran̲ and K.N. Kiraṇāvaḷi.

Ravindran̲, S. (*vīṇā*); b. 1933; disciple of his mother, Lalitha Bai Shamanna, who was a versatile musician, teacher, and founder of several institutions for music education; influenced by the style of *vaiṇika* S. Bālachander; taught *vīṇā* at the Teachers' College, Music Academy Madras.

Reṅganāthan, A.S. (*mṛdaṅgam*); b. 1961; disciple of Mēlakāvēri Krishnamūrthy and Tiruvārūr Baktavatsalam; brother of A.S. Krishnan̲ (*mōrsiṅg*), A.S. Shankar (*ghaṭam*), and A.S. Muraḷī (*ghaṭam*, vocal).

Ritha Rājan̲, Dr (vocalist, scholar); b. 1948; disciple of Rāmnād Krishnan̲ and T. Brinda; PhD thesis on the stylistic differences (*pāṭhāntara*) of different traditions (*guruśiṣya paramparā*) of the Trinity; Queen Mary's College.

Rudrapatnam Brothers (vocal duo)—*see* R.N. Thyāgarājan̲ and Dr R.N. Taranath.

Rukmini, T. (violin, vocal); b. 1936; disciple of Lālguḍi Jayarāman̲ and Semmaṅguḍi Śrīnivāsa Iyer.

Sabhāpati—*see* Bālakrishna Śāstrigaḷ, T.S. Sabhēśa Ayyar, Vidya Shankar.

Sabhēśa Ayyar, T.S. (vocal, violin); 1872–1948; son of violinist Sambaśiva Ayyar; grandson of Sabhāpati Śivan̲, and grand-nephew of Gōvinda Śivan̲, both disciples of Tyāgarāja; disciple of Mahāvaidyanātha Śivan̲ Ayyar; was the first Principal of the Department of Music, Aṇṇāmalai University; teacher of Vidya Shankar, K.S. Nārāyaṇaswāmy, Musiri Subrahmaṇya Ayyar, Dr S. Rāmanāthan̲, T.K. Raṅgachāri, and Sathūr Subramaṇiam.

Sai Shankar (vocal); b. 1961; disciple of Puducōde K. Krishnamūrthi and Vairamaṅgalam Lakshminārāyaṇan̲; Lecturer, Kalākshētra.

Sakharāma Rao, T. (*gōṭṭuvādyam*); died 1930; disciple of Mutthiah Bhāgavatar; first reputed musician to specialize in playing the modern *gōṭṭuvādyam* which his father, Śrīnivāsa Rao, had introduced as a fretless variant of the *vīṇā*; like Vīṇā Dhanammāḷ, he preferred to perform without any percussion support; teacher of Nārāyaṇa Ayyaṅgār and Semmaṅguḍi Śrīnivāsa Iyer.

Śakuntala Narasiṁhan̲ (vocal); b. 1940; disciple of Puducōde K. Krishnamūrthi and several other eminent *vidvāns*; studied Hindustānī music under Ahmed Khan.

Śakuntala Rāman̲ (vocal); b. 1939; disciple of T. Brinda, Musiri Subrahmaṇya Ayyar, and others.

Salem S. Jayalakshmi, Dr (vocal); b. 1932; disciple of Mahārājāpuram Viṣwanātha Ayyar, T. Chowdiah, and others; particularly involved in propagating Tamil music; Founder, International Music Trust, and Cultural Centre of Performing Arts (Chennai).

Sambamoorthy Ayyar, Prof. P. (musicologist); 1901–73; disciple of Maṇattaṭṭai Duraisāmi Ayyar (1865–1926) and Wālājapet K.K. Rāmasvāmi Ayyar; studied comparative musicology at Munich (Germany); author of numerous textbooks and reference works in Tamil and English (e.g. *South Indian Music* in six volumes, *Dictionary* *of South Indian Music and Musicians*, *Great Composers*, *Great Musicians*); experimented with novel methods to make music education more accessible and interesting; first lecturer of music, Queen Mary's College; Head of Department of Music, University of Chennai; Professor of Musicology, Śrī Veṅkaṭēśwara University; instituted the Development Centre for Musical Instruments (*Saṅgīta Vādyalaya*), an institution devoted to research and innovative designs (Chennai); teacher of S.R. Jānakirāmaṉ, D.K. Paṭṭammāḷ, and Dr T. Seetha Rāmalakshmi.

Sambandam Pillai—*see* Semponnārkōil S.R.G. Rājānna Pillai and S.R.G. Sambandam Piḷḷai.

Sambaśiva Ayyar—*see* Kāraikkuḍi Brothers.

Sandhyavandanam Poornapragna Rao (vocalist); b. 1959; son and disciple of Sandhyavandanam Śrīnivāsa Rao.

Sandhyavandanam Śrīnivāsa Rao (vocalist, scholar); 1918–94; disciple of Pakka Hanumantāchārya, Chilarmattur Rāmayya, Justice T.L. Veṅkaṭarāma Ayyar, and Mahārājāpuram Viṣwanātha Ayyar; authority on the music of Purandara Dāsa and the questions regarding authenticity in Karnatic music; Principal, Central College and Teachers' College of the Music Academy; AIR; father and teacher of Sandhyavandanam Poornapragna Rao.

Sanjay Subramaṇiam (vocal); b. 1968; studied violin before specializing in singing under the guidance of Rukmini Rājagōpālan and Calcutta Krishnamūrthi.

Sanjīva Rao—*see* Palladam Sanjīva Rao.

Śaṅkaraṉ—*see* Trichy Śaṅkaraṉ; *see also* Shankar.

Śaṅkaraṉ, T. (vocalist, scholar); b. 1906; grandson of Vīṇā Dhanammāḷ; son and disciple of her daughter, Lakshmirathnam; absorbed music from other family members, and taught by violinist Mecheri Sundara Śāstrī (disciple of Kāñcīpuram Naina Piḷḷai); AIR; taught special compositions to noted musicians like Pāpā K.S. Veṅkaṭarāmayya, D.K. Paṭṭammāḷ, and M.S. Subbulakshmi; Director, Tamiḻ Isai Saṅgam Isai Kallūri (Chennai); published numerous articles; Contributing Editor, *Śruti Magazine*.

Śaṅkaraṉ, T.S. (flute); 1932; disciple of his father, T.N. Sambaśivam, and T.R. Mahāliṅgam; teacher of Śrīrām Gaṇgādharan and Sunilkumār.

Śaṅkaranārāyaṇaṉ, T.V. ('TVS', vocal); b. 1945; disciple and nephew of Madurai Maṇi Ayyar; teacher of D.J. Bālakrishna.

Santhānagōpālaṉ—*see* Neyvēli R. Santhānagōpālaṉ.

Santhānam—*see* Mahārājāpuram Santhānam.

Śarabha Śāstrigaḷ (flautist, composer); 1872–1904; disciple of Mānambucāvaḍi Veṅkaṭa Subbayyar (nephew and disciple of Tyāgarāja); a blind musical genius who is credited with being the first to have raised the standard of flute playing to the level of refined classical music suited for concerts (*kaccēri*); composed music for the stories of the 63 Tamil saints (Nāyanmār); teacher of Palladam Sanjīva Rao.

Śārada Śivānandam (*vīṇā*); b. 1927; disciple and wife of Tañjāvūr K.P. Śivānandam; Rājāh's College and Central College; teacher of R. Kausalya.

Sarasvatī Bai, C. (*harikathā*); 1894–1974; disciple of Tiruvaiyāṟu Kṛṣṇācār, a Sanskrit scholar and associate of Tañjāvūr Kṛṣṇa Bhāgavatar whose format (*kathā paddhati*) was followed by Sarasvatī Bai; scholar of several languages (Sanskrit, Kannaḍa, Tamil, Telugu, Marāṭhi); particularly famous for her presentations on the themes of *Nandanār caritram* and *Bhadrācala Rāmdās*.

Saravanaṉ, L. (flute); b. 1969; disciple of K.S. Nārāyaṇaṉ, V. Sundarēsaṉ, Nāgai R. Muraḷīdharaṉ, and N. Ramani.

Saroja, C.—*see* Bombay Sisters.

Sashīdhar, T. (flute); b. 1964; disciple of H. Rāmachandra Shāstry (flute), Pucucōde K. Krishnamūrthi, and Vairamaṅgalam Lakshminārāyaṇan̲ (vocal); Lecturer, Kalākshētra.

Sashikiran̲, K.N. (vocal); b. 1970; disciple of his father, N. Narasiṁhan̲, T. Brinda, and Tañjāvūr Viṣwanāthan̲; studied *mṛdaṅgam* with Palghat V.A. Sundaram.

Sathyavathy, Dr T.S. (vocal, *mṛdaṅgam*, musicologist); disciple of her sister, Vasantha Mādhavi (vocal), Bangalore K. Veṅkaṭarām (*mṛdaṅgam*), and R.K. Śrīkantan̲ (vocal); specialist for the rhythmic aspect of *pallavi* singing.

Satyanārāyaṇa, Satyanārāyaṇamūrthy—*see* Ariparala Satyanārāyaṇa, Dwāram Satyanārāyaṇa, Dwāram Satyanārāyaṇamūrthy, Nookala Chinna Satyanārāyaṇa.

Satyanārāyaṇa, Dr R. (musicologist, composer); b. 1929; disciple of his mother, Varalakshmi Rāmiah, and his brother, R. Chandraśēkhariah; author of many articles and books (e.g. *The Kuḍumiyāmalai Inscription On Music*, *Studies in Indian Dance*); Director, Regional Centre for Research and Development, and Director, Sangeetha Nritya Academy (Mysore).

Sāvithri Rājan̲ (*vaiṇika*, scholar); 1908–91; disciple of Tiger Varadāchāriar and Vīṇā Dhanammāḷ; expert on various traditional forms of didactic music (*abhyāsa gānam*); published a book on the didactic repertoire of South Indian music titled *Shobhillu Saptasvara* with introduction, Sanskrit *ślokas* and syllabic transcriptions (with Michael Nixon, in English and Tamil); advisor to many performers and music teachers, recorded a representative selection of her *vīṇā* repertoire; featured in *The Flying Bird*, a documentary film by C.S. Lakshmi and Vishnu Mathur.

Sāvitri Satyamūrti (violin); b. 1930; disciple of Madurai Subramaṇya Ayyar, Erode Viṣwanātha Ayyar, Rājamānikkam Piḷḷai (violin), Ariyakkuḍi Rāmānuja Ayyaṅgār, Madurai Maṇi Ayyar, and T. Brinda (vocal); teacher of R.K. Śrīrām Kumār.

Sayeeram—*see* Aruna Sayeeram.

Seetha, Dr S. (*vaiṇika*, vocalist, musicologist); b. 1931; disciple of her mother and N. Rājagōpālan̲; Head of Department of Music, University of Chennai; author of several books and papers (e.g. *Tanjore as a Seat of Music*, and *Subrahmaṇya Bhārati's Compositions*); teacher of Dr M.B. Vēdavaḷḷi.

Seethalakshmi, G. (vocal); disciple of Semmaṅguḍi Śrīnivāsa Iyer; Swāti Tirunāḷ College of Music.

Seethalakshmi Veṅkaṭēśan̲ (vocal); b. 1926; disciple of Palghat Vaidyanātha Ayyar, Tañjāvūr Śaṅkara Ayyar, K.S. Kēdaranāthan̲, and Semmaṅguḍi Śrīnivāsa Iyer.

Seetha Rājagopāl (vocal); disciple of T. Kamākṣiammāḷ and her daughter, T. Mukta; cousin of Maitili Nāgēswaran̲ with whom she often performed.

Seetha Rāmalakshmi, Dr T. (musicologist, vocalist, violinist); disciple of Prof. P. Sambamoorthy and N. Chennakēśaviah; author of *References to Music in Non-Saṅgīta Literature*, and *A Study of the Compositions of Purandara Dāsa and Tyāgarāja*; taught at the Directorate of Higher Education (Hyderabad), and Department of Performing Arts, Bangalore University.

Selvaratnam Piḷḷai—*see* Ānanḍāṅkōil A.V. Selvaratnam Piḷḷai.

Semmaṅguḍi Nārāyaṇasvāmi Ayyar (violin, vocal); 1889–1944; nephew and disciple of Tirukōḍikāval Krishna Ayyar; teacher of Semmaṅguḍi Śrīnivāsa Iyer.

Semmaṅguḍi Śrīnivāsa Iyer (vocalist, composer); b. 1908; belongs to a family of musicians; disciple of Semmaṅguḍi Nārāyaṇasvāmi Ayyar, *gōṭṭuvādyam* exponent Sakharāma Rao, Mahārājāpuram Viṣwanātha Ayyar, and Umayāḷpuram Swāminātha

Ayyar; began to perform in 1926; specialist for the music traditions associated with Svāti Tirunāḷ; credited with re-composing the music (*dhātu*) for many lyrics of Svāti Tirunāḷ; Principal, Swāti Tirunāḷ College of Music; Chief Producer, AIR; teacher of T.M. Thyagarājan̲, M.S. Subbulakshmi, Harihara Subramaṇi Ayyar, Kalliḍaikkuricci S. Harihara Ayyar, Mavelikara H. Rāmanāthan̲, P.S. Nārāyaṇaswāmy, K.R. Kumāraswāmy Ayyar, Trivandrum R.S. Maṇi, V.R. Krishnan̲, T.N. Krishnan̲, Seethalakshmi Veṅkaṭēsan̲, T. Rukmini, C.K. Rāmachandran̲, N. Vijayalakshmi Nārāyaṇan̲, Sujātha Vijayarāghavan̲, Pārvathy Rāman̲, and K.R. Kēdaranāthan̲.

Semponn̲ārkōil S.R.G. Rājānna Piḷḷai and S.R.G. Sambandam Piḷḷai (*nāgasvaram* duo); b. 1928 and 1931 respectively; grandsons of Semponn̲ārkōil Rāmaswāmi Piḷḷai; disciples of their father, Gōvindaswāmi Piḷḷai, and their uncle, Dakṣiṇāmūrti Piḷḷai.

Semponn̲ārkōil Rāmaswāmi Piḷḷai (*nāgasvaram*); 1861–1923; grandfather of *nāgasvaram* duo Semponn̲ārkōil S.R.G. Rājānna Pillai and S.R.G. Sambandam Piḷḷai.

Sēshāchāry, D.—*see* Hyderabad Brothers.

Sēshagiri Dās, S. (*kañjīrā*); disciple of T.M. Veṅkaṭesha Dēvaru; AIR (Mysore).

Sēshagōpālan̲, T.N. (vocal, *vīṇā*); b. 1948; disciple of Rāmanātapuram Śaṅkara Śivam; taught vocal music and *vīṇā* at Madurai University; teacher of Neyvēli R. Santhānagōpālan̲.

Sēthurāman̲, P.N.—*see* Madurai Brothers.

Shankar—*see* Harishankar, Maṅgaḷam Shankar, Sai Shankar, Vidya Shankar; *see also* Śaṅkaran̲.

Shankar, A.S. (*ghaṭam*); b. 1964; disciple of T.V. Vāsan̲; brother of A.S. Krishnan̲ (*mōrsiṅg*), A.S. Reṅganāthan (*mṛdaṅgam*), and A.S. Muraḷī (*ghaṭam*, vocal).

Shankar, Dr L. (violinist); disciple of his father, V. Lakshminārāyaṇa; active in Jazz Fusion music.

Shankar, S. (vocal); b. 1950; disciple of his mother, Rājamma (Śāstrī), and Vallabham Kalyāṇasundaram.

Shaṅkaramūrthy, M.R. (vocalist, scholar); 1922–93; disciple of Chembai Vaidyanātha Bhāgavatar and R.R. Kēsavamūrthy; author of many books on music.

Shaṅkaran̲ Namboodiri (vocal); b. 1972; disciple of his uncle, Nārāyaṇa Namboodiri, and T.V. Gōpālakrishnan̲.

Shankar Śrīnivās (vocal); b. 1974; son of Dr S.R. Jayasītalakshmi.

Shaṇmuga Vaḍivu (*vīṇā*, vocal); b. 1889; disciple of Karūr Veṅkaṭarāma Bhāgavatar; mother and teacher of M.S. Subbulakshmi.

Shaṇmugha Vaḍivēl, N.T.M. (*tavil*); son and disciple of Nīḍamaṅgaḷam Mīn̲ākṣisundaram Piḷḷai.

Shānti, Dr V. (*vīṇā*, vocal); b. 1967; disciple of her grandmother, Kāraikkuḍi Vīṇā Lakshmi Ammāḷ, her uncle, Kāraikkuḍi S. Subramaṇian̲, and her aunt, Rājēswari Padmanābhan̲.

Shashank, M.S. (flute); b. 1978; disciple of R.K. Śrīkantan̲ and K.V. Nārāyaṇaswāmy.

Sheela, M.S. (vocal); disciple of her mother, M.N. Ratna, and R.K. Śrīkantan̲; Visiting Lecturer, Department of Music, Bangalore University.

Sheikh—*see* Chinna Moulana, Mehboob Subhani, Sheikh and Kalisabhi Mehboob.

Shyāmāsundar, C.K. (*kañjīrā*, *mṛdaṅgam*, vocal); b. 1939; disciple of Tanjore Rāma Doss Rao.

Shyāmsundar, T. (*mṛdaṅgam*); b. 1955; disciple of T.R. Harihara Śarma, T.H. Vinayakram, and Kāraikkuḍi R. Maṇi.

Sikkil R. Bhāskaran̲ (violinist); b. 1936; belongs to a family of musicians and dancers;

disciple of Māyavaram (Mayilāḍuturai) Gōvindarāja Piḷḷai and Rājamānikkam Piḷḷai; AIR.

Sikkil Sisters (flute duo); Sikkil Kuñjumaṇi (b. 1930) learnt to play the flute from her uncle and taught her younger sister, Neela (b. 1940).

Sīrkāzhi (Sīrkāḻi) S. Gōvindarājan̲ (vocal); 1933–88; disciple of Tirupāmburam N. Swāminātha Piḷḷai; Head of Music Department, Aṇṇāmalai University; also worked in the field of film music; father of Sīrkāzhi Dr G. Śiva Chidambaram.

Sīrkāzhi Dr G. Śiva Chidambaram (vocal) b. 1959; son of Sīrkāzhi (Sīrkāḻi) S. Gōvindarājan̲; a medical doctor by profession, he is a disciple of B. Krishnamūrthi (vocal) and R. Pichumaṇi (*vīṇā*).

Sītarāmayyar—*see* Adicayapuram Sītarāmayyar.

Śiva—*see* N. Vijay Śiva.

Śiva Chidambaram—*see* Sīrkāzhi Śiva Chidambaram.

Śivakumār, A.V.—*see* Ānanḍāṇkōil V. Śivakumār.

Śivānandam—*see* Tañjāvūr K.P. Śivānandam.

Śivarāman̲—*see* Umayāḷpuram K. Śivarāman̲.

Sōmanna—*see* Yellā Sōmanna.

Sōmasundaram—*see* Madurai S. Sōmasundaram, Māyavaram G. Sōmasundaram, Vēdāraṇyam V. Sōmasundaram.

Sōmasundaram Piḷḷai, T.N. (*nāgasvaram*); b. 1912; disciple of Naṭarājasundaram Piḷḷai; Principal of the *nāgasvara* school at Paḻani, Nāgasvara Kallūri.

Sōmayajulu, P.P. (violin); b. 1930; disciple of Dwāram Veṅkaṭaswāmy Naidu; AIR; Shrī Veṅkaṭēśwara University.

Soolamaṅgaḷam Sisters (vocal); R. Jayalakshmi (b. 1937) and R. Rājalakshmi (1940–92); popular exponents of devotional and national songs as well as film music.

Sowmya, S. (vocal); b. 1968; disciple of S. Rāmanāthan̲.

Śrīdharan̲, S.D. (violin); b. 1948; disciple of Kumbakōnam Śrīnivāsan̲ and M. Chandraśēkharan̲.

Śrīkanta Ayyar, V. (*vīṇā*); b. 1920; grandson of Vīṇā Śeṣanna; disciple of Bakshi Subbanna; Bangalore University.

Śrīkantan̲, R.K. (vocalist, scholar, composer); b. 1920; disciple of his father, R. Krishna Śāstrī, and his brother, R.K. Veṅkaṭarāma Śāstrī; credited with preserving and popularizing many songs of the Haridāsa composers by way of restoring their musical structure in an aesthetic fashion suited to modern concerts; Producer, AIR; Visiting Professor, Department of Oriental Music, York University (Toronto); teacher of his son, R.S. Rāmakanth, A. Rājamma Kēśava Mūrthy, Gowri Kuppuswami, R.A. Rāmamaṇi, M.S. Sheela, T.S. Sathyavathy, and M.S. Shashank.

Śrīlatha, Dr R.N. (vocalist, musicologist); daughter and disciple of R.K. Nārāyaṇaswāmy; research and publication on the music traditions of Karṇāṭaka; University of Mysore.

Śrīmathi Brahmānandam (violin); b. 1941; daughter of V.R. Gōpāla Ayyar; disciple of her brother, Lālguḍi Jayarāman̲, and Pallavi Rāmayyar; sister of Padmāvathy Ananthagōpālan̲.

Śrīmuṣṇam Rāja Rao (*mṛdaṅgam*); b. 1955; disciple of his father and Kumbakōnam M. Rājappa Ayyar.

Śrīnivās, U. (mandolin); b. 1970; belongs to a family of musicians; introduced the electric mandolin in classical South Indian music; has collaborated with Jazz musicians.

Śrīnivāsan̲—*see* Kumbakōnam Śrīnivāsan̲, Mahārājāpuram S. Śrīnivāsan̲.

Śrīnivāsan, V. (violin); b. 1967; disciple of Pakala Rāmdās.

Śrīpāda Pinakapāni, Dr (vocalist, scholar, composer); b. 1913; medical doctor, disciple of Mysore B. Lakshmana Rao and Raṅgarāmānuja Ayyaṅgār; guided by Dwāram Veṅkaṭaswāmy Naidu; emulates the *vaiṇika* style (*bāṇī*) of Vīṇā Dhanammāḷ whose Friday concerts he attended in the late 1930s; noted for his ability to bring out the *bhāva* of a rāga in a slow tempo with emphasis on *gamaka* and *anusvara*; teacher of Nēdunūri Krishnamūrthi, Śrīraṅgam Gōpālaratnam, Nookala Chinna Satyanārāyaṇa, and Vōleti Veṅkaṭēśwārulu; has published a work on the improvised forms of South Indian music (*Manodharma Saṅgītam*).

Śrīrām Gaṇgādharan (vocal); b. 1969; disciple of T.S. Śaṅkaran and Rukmani Rājagōpālan.

Śrīrām Kumār, R.K. (violin); b. 1966; disciple of his grandfather, R.K. Veṅkaṭarāma Śāstrī, Sāvitri Satyamūrti, and V.V. Subramaṇiam.

Śrīrām Parasurām (vocal, violin); b. 1964; disciple of his mother, Parvathy Parasurām, Rāmakrishna Śarma, Pudukōṭṭai V. Krishnamūrthy Bhāgavatar, Vaidyanātha Bhāgavatar, K.S. Nārāyaṇaswāmy, and Tañjāvūr Viṣwanāthan; learnt Hindustānī music from C.R. Vyas; studied Western violin at the University of Akron, Ohio (USA); also performed with and composed for Jazz ensembles.

Śrīraṅgam Gōpālaratnam (vocalist, composer); 1939(?)–93; disciple of K. Jogarao, Śrīpāda Pinakapāni, and Vōleti Veṅkaṭēśwārulu; AIR; Principal, Music College, and Professor of Music Department, Telugu University (Hyderabad); specialist for the music traditions of Āndhra Pradesh (e.g. Annamācārya's compositions, *Kuchipudi, jāvaḷi*).

Śrīraṅgam R. Kaṇṇan (vocalist, scholar); 1924–88; disciple of Rājāmaṇi Rao, Veṅgarai Rājam Ayyaṅgār, Valadi Krishna Ayyar, Kālidās N. Nīlakantha Ayyar, and Kumbakōnam Rājamāṇikkam Piḷḷai; published Karnatic compositions by Tyāgarāja and Muttusvāmi Dīkṣitar (Sanskrit with Hindi translation); Benares Hindu University.

Śrīraṅgam S. Kaṇṇan (*mōrsiṅg*); b. 1952; disciple of K.M. Rājarām (*mṛdaṅgam*) and Pudukōṭṭai S. Mahādēvan (*mōrsiṅg*).

Śrīraṅgam R. Raṅganāthan (vocal); b. 1924; disciple of Tiger Varadāchāriar, Sathūr Krishna Ayyaṅgār, and T.K. Raṅgachāri; AIR (Pondicherry).

Śrīvanchiam K. Rāmachandra Ayyar (vocal); b. 1917; disciple of his father, S. Krishnamūrthi, *nāgasvaram* exponent Ramiah Piḷḷai, Muḍikondān C. Veṅkaṭarāma Ayyar, and Kāraikkuḍi Sambaśiva Ayyar; edited music manuscripts at the Saraswathi Mahal Library (Tañjāvūr); Rājāh's Music College.

Śrīvatsa, K. (*mṛdaṅgam*); b. 1948; disciple of Paḷani Subrahmaṇya Piḷḷai and P.A. Veṅkaṭarāman; AIR.

Śrīvidya Chandramouli (*vīṇā*); b. 1965; daughter and disciple of Rājēśwari Padmanābhan.

Subashchandran, T.H. (*mṛdaṅgam*, *ghaṭam*, *kañjīrā*, *mōrsiṅg*, *konnakkōl*); b. 1946; son and disciple of T.R. Harihara Śarma; disciple of Palghat Rāmachandra Ayyar and K.M. Vaidyanāthan; brother of T.H. Vinayakram; taught at the California Institute of Fine Arts.

Subaśree Rāmachandran (vocal); b. 1977; disciple of her parents, Chārumathi Rāmachandran and Trichūr V. Rāmachandran.

Subbanna—*see* Bakshi Subbanna.

Subbarāma Ayyar—*see* Kāraikkuḍi Brothers.

Subba Rao, A.K. (scholar, flautist); disciple of his father, Krishnappa, R. Krishna Śāstrī, and Bīḍaram Krishnappā.

Subba Rao, B. (vocal, *viṇā*, *gōṭṭuvādyam*, violin, musicology); 1894–1975; disciple of Viṣwanātha Śāstrī (vocal); also studied Hindustānī music; author of an important reference work on the rāgas of both music systems of India (*Rāga Nidhi*); teacher of Vanaja A. Iyeṅgār.

Subbiah Bhāgavatar, K.S.—*see* T.K. Raṅgachāri and K.S. Nārāyaṇa Ayyaṅgār.

Subbulakshmi, M.S. ('MS', vocal); b. 1916; disciple of Shaṇmuga Vaḍivu (her mother), Semmaṅguḍi Śrīnivāsa Iyer, and K.S. Nārāyaṇaswāmy; also learnt songs (*padam*) from T. Brinda; her interpretation emphasizes the devotional aspect of Karnatic music and has defined the aesthetic standards which most women singers seek to emulate; performed at the United Nations and at Carnegie Hall (New York); sang and acted in several films including 'Mīrā' and 'Śakuntalā'; teacher of her adopted daughter, Rādhā Viṣwanāthan̲.

Subrahmaṇya, Subramaṇian̲—*see* Kāñcīpuram Naina Piḷḷai, Kāraikkuḍi S. Subramaṇian̲, Palani Subrahmaṇya Piḷḷai, Valayapatti A.R. Subrahmaṇya, and Vijayalakshmy Subramaṇiam.

Subrahmaṇyam, T.R. ('TRS', vocalist; composer); b. 1929; disciple of Māyavaram Śivarāma Ayyar, G. Sitarāma Bhāgavatar and D.S. Maṇi Bhāgavatar; Central College; Reader, Music Department, Delhi University; Honorary Director, Gandharva Mahā Vidyālaya (New Delhi); teacher of Rādhā Veṅkaṭāchalam, K. Bhāskaran̲, and Vijayalakshmy Subramaṇiam.

Subrahmaṇyam, V.V. (violinist, composer); b. 1944; belongs to a family of musicians; disciple of Chembai Vaidyanātha Bhāgavatar and Musiri Subrahmaṇya Ayyar; teacher of his brother V.V. Ravi; Government Music College (Madurai).

Subramaṇia Ayyar , C.—*see* Vidya Shankar.

Subramaṇiam, Dr L. (violinist, composer); disciple of his father, V. Lakshminārāyaṇa; has collaborated with exponents of Jazz and World Music.

Subramaṇian̲, E.M. (*ghaṭam*); b. 1947; son and disciple of Elapalli Mahādēva Ayyar.

Sudha Raghunāthan̲ (vocal); b. 1956; disciple of M.L. Vasanthakumāri.

Suguna Purushōtaman̲ (vocal); b. 1941; disciple of Musiri Subrahmaṇya Ayyar.

Suguna Varadachāri (vocalist and musicologist); b. 1945; disciple of Musiri Subrahmaṇya Ayyar.

Sujātha Vijayarāghavan̲ (vocalist, scholar); b. 1947; disciple of her mother, Anantalakshmi Saḍagōpan̲, and Semmaṅguḍi Śrīnivāsa Iyer.

Sukan̲ya Prabhākar (vocal); b. 1952; disciple of V. Rāmaratnam, Gowri Kuppuswami, and Nāgaratna Sadāśiva.

Sukan̲ya Rāmgōpal (*ghaṭam*, *mṛdaṅgam*); great-granddaughter of scholar Dr U.V. Swāminātha Ayyar; disciple of T.H. Vinayakram.

Sulōchana Paṭṭābhirāman̲ (vocal); b. 1931; disciple of M.A. Kalyāṇakrishna Bhāgavatar, Sāttūr A.G. Subrahmaṇiam, and Semmaṅguḍi Śrīnivāsa Iyer; teacher of Prēma Raṅgarājan̲.

Sundarājan̲, A.V.—*see* Ānanḍāṇkōil V. Sundarājan̲.

Sundaram—*see* Kalliḍaikkuricci A. Sundaram Ayyar, Palghat V.A. Sundaram, Pārūr Sundaram Ayyar.

Sundarambal, K.B. (vocal); 1907–80; wife of S.G. Kiṭṭappa; popular classical singer who also had a successful career in films; most famous exponent of the *viruttam* form (Tamil lyrics); learnt compositions from Vīṇā Dhanammāḷ.

Sundarēśan̲, M.A. (violin); b. 1959; disciple of his father, M.S. Anantharāman̲, and his uncle, M.S. Gōpālakrishnan̲; also trained in the Hindustānī style of violin play; AIR.

Sundarēśan̲, T.R. (*mr̥daṅgam, ghaṭam, kañjīrā, mōrsiṅg, kon̲nakkōl*); b. 1963; learnt music from his father; disciple of Ellā Veṅkaṭēśwara Rao; co-author of *Eloquent Percussion: A Guide to South Indian Rhythm*; Lecturer, Kalākshētra.

Sunder, Dr S. (vocal); b. 1960 disciple of Trichy Swāminātha Ayyar, D.K. Jayarāman̲, and T.K. Gōvinda Rao; a regular performer and broadcasting musician, he is a medical doctor by profession.

Sunilkumār (flute); b. 1965; disciple of T.S. Śaṅkaran̲.

Surēsh, B.N. (flute); 1946–90; disciple of Shivarāmiah and Bangalore K. Veṅkaṭarāma.

Surēsh, S. (*mr̥daṅgam*); b. 1961; disciple of Palghat Maṇi Ayyar and his son, T.R. Rājāmaṇi.

Sūryanārāyaṇa, R.K. (*vaiṇika*, composer); b. 1926; disciple of his father, R.S. Kēśavamūrthy; inherited and played a rare *vīṇā* with 23 strings (i.e. having sympathetic strings to give a rich sound); composed over 400 songs in five languages.

Sūryanārāyaṇa Mūrthy (clarinet); b. 1931; disciple of S. Nāganna; AIR (Vijayawada).

Swāminātha̲n̲—*see* Kalpagam Swāminātha̲n̲, Lālguḍi M. Swāminātha̲n̲, Umayāḷpuram Swāminātha Ayyar.

Swāminātha Piḷḷai—*see* Tirupāmburam N. Swāminātha Piḷḷai.

Tadepalli Lōkanādha Śarma, Dr (vocal); b. 1945; disciple of his father, Veṅkaṭa Subramaṇya Śāstry, and Chittoor Subramaṇia Piḷḷai; specialist for musical instruments as described in Sanskrit literature; Director, Development Centre for Musical Instruments (*Saṅgīta Vādyalaya*, Chennai).

Tañjāvūr S. Bālachander (flute); b. 1961; disciple of his mother, Tañjāvūr V. Prēma, Nāgaratna Ammāl, Pōḻakuḍi Gaṇeśa Ayyar, Prapancham V. Seetharam, and N. Ramani; AIR.

Tañjāvūr S. Kalyāṇarāman̲ (vocal); 1930–94; belongs to a family of musicians; disciple of G.N. Bālasubrahmaṇyam; published his *guru's* compositions.

Tañjāvūr Kr̥ṣṇa Bhāgavatar (*harikathā*, composer); 1841–1903; disciple of two exponents of the northern *kirtaṅkār* tradition patronized by Śivājī II at Tañjāvūr, Morkar (Morgaumkar) Bhāvā, a Marāṭhā scholar (died 1904), and Viṣṇu Bhāvā; apart from the northern musical elements, he included devotional compositions by Tyāgarāja, Muvvānallūr Sabhāpati Ayyar, Gopālakr̥ṣṇa Bhārati's popular music play, the *Nandanār Caritra*, and also composed his own music; multifaceted singer and instrumentalist (violin, *svarabhat*, *mr̥daṅgam*); scholar of several major languages (Tamil, Sanskrit, Hindi, Telugu, Kannaḍa, Marāṭhi); credited with establishing the southern format of *harikathā kālakṣepam* which was also adopted by lady *bhāgavatars*, Sarasvatī Bai and Banni Bai.

Tañjāvūr Nārāyaṇasvāmi Appā (*mr̥daṅgam*, vocal); 19th century; disciple of Morkar Bhāvā and ŚivasāmiAppā; counted among the prominent exponents of the Marāṭhi music tradition (*kīrtaṅkār*) who were patronized at the court of Tañjāvūr and influenced the musical style and technique of the southern type of *harikathā kālakṣepam*; accompanied his own singing on the *mr̥daṅgam;* conducted congregational singing (*bhajana*) which resulted in the characteristic blending of northern and southern styles of devotional music still heard in South India; developed the complex patterns (Urdu *faran*) from which the modern playing technique of the *mṛdaṅgam* has evolved; accompanied prominent musicians like Mysore ('Vīṇā') Śeṣanna and Mahāvaidyanātha Ayyar.

Tañjāvūr Prapancham S. Ravīndran̲ (*mṛdaṅgam*); b. 1960; disciple of Venugōpāl Naidu and Tañjāvūr Bālakrishnan̲.

Tañjāvūr V. Prēma (vocal); b. 1935; disciple of Pōl̲akuḍi Gaṇeśa Ayyar (a disciple of Tiger Varadāchāriar); mother and teacher of Tañjāvūr S. Bālachander.

Tañjāvūr Raṅganāthan̲ (*mṛdaṅgam*); 1925–87; grandson of Vīṇā Dhanammāḷ; disciple of Pal̲ani Subrahmaṇya Piḷḷai; brother of Tañjāvūr Viṣwanāthan̲ with whom he taught at the California Institute of the Arts (Valencia), and at Wesleyan University (USA).

Tañjāvūr K.P. Śivānandam (*vaiṇika*, vocalist, scholar); b. 1917; descendant of the Tanjore (Tañjāvūr) Quartette; grandson and disciple of Mīn̲ākṣisundaram Piḷḷai (music, dance); son and disciple of K. Pon̲n̲iah Piḷḷai; studied *vīṇā* under Dēsamaṅgaḷam Subrahmaṇya Iyer and Gōmati Shankar Iyer; Head of Department of Music, Aṇṇāmalai University; Central College; with his elder brother, K.P. Kiṭṭappa, he edited several works on the music tradition of his ancestors; performed with his wife and disciple, Śārada Śivānandam; teacher of R. Kausalya and Mokkapati Nāgēśvara Rao.

Tañjāvūr Upēndran (*mṛdaṅgam*); 1934–91; belonged to a family devoted to music and dance; teacher of Neyvēli R. Nārāyaṇan.

Tañjāvūr Vaidyanātha Ayyar (*mṛdaṅgam*); 1894–1947; disciple of Kaṇṇusvāmi Naṭṭuvan̲ar, and his son K. Pon̲n̲iah Piḷḷai; belonged to the family of Mahāvaidyanātha Ayyar; *guru* of Palghat Maṇi Ayyar and T.K. Moorthy.

Tañjāvūr Viṣwanāthan̲, Dr (flautist, vocalist, musicologist); b. 1926; belongs to a family of musicians and dancers; grandson of Vīṇā Dhanammāḷ; disciple of his mother, Jayammāḷ, his sister, T. Bālasaraswathi, and Tirupāmburam N. Swāminātha Piḷḷai; brother of Tañjāvūr Raṅganāthan̲; Head of Music Department, University of Madras (Chennai); taught at several American universities, namely the University of California (Los Angeles), the California Institute of the Arts (Valencia), and at Wesleyan University (USA) where he obtained his PhD; teacher of Maitili Nāgēśwaran̲, Jon Higgins, Dr M.B. Vēdavaḷḷi, and Rāmā Ravi.

Taranath, Dr R.N. (vocal); b. 1948; son and disciple of R.K. Nārāyaṇaswāmy, and disciple of his uncle, R.K. Veṅkaṭarāma Śāstrī; performs with his brother, R.N. Thyāgarājan̲ ('Rudrapatnam Brothers').

Thāyumānavan̲—*see* Trichy R. Thāyumānavan̲.

Thyāgarājan̲, O.S. (vocal); b. 1947; disciple of Tiger Varadāchāriar, Pon̲n̲iah Piḷḷai, and Lālguḍi Jayarāman̲.

Thyāgarājan̲, R.N. (vocal); b. 1945; son and disciple of R.K. Nārāyaṇaswāmy, and disciple of his uncle, R.K. Veṅkaṭarāma Śāstrī; performs with his brother, Dr R.N. Taranath ('Rudrapatnam Brothers'); AIR; Assistant Director, Doordarshan Kendra (Chennai).

Thyāgarājan̲, T.M. ('TMT'; vocalist, composer); b. 1923; learnt music first from his father, *mṛdaṅga vidvān* Mahāliṅgam Piḷḷai; disciple of Semmaṅguḍi Śrīnivāsa Iyer;

Principal, Central College and Music Academy; teacher of Nāgamaṇi Śrīnāth, E. Gāyatri, and Maṅgaḷam Shankar.

Thyāgarājan—*see also* Tyāgarājan.

Tinniyam Veṅkaṭarāma Ayyar (*mṛdaṅgam*, vocal); b. 1900; disciple of Tinniyam Sēthurāma Ayyar; author of *The Art of Playing Mridangam* and *Pallavi Ratnamāla*; teacher of Palghat Raghu and Nāgarāja Rao.

Tirukōḍikāval Krishna Ayyar (violin); 1857–1913; disciple of his father, Kuppusvāmi Ayyar, a scholar and exponent of *harikathā kālakṣepam*, and composer Kōṭṭavāsal Veṅkaṭarāma Bhāgavatar; learnt violin under Satanūr Pañcanātha Ayyar and 'Fiddle' Subbarayar; teacher of his nephew, Semmaṅguḍi Nārāyaṇasvāmi, Kumbakōnam Rājamāṉikkam Piḷḷai, Tirukōḍikāval Rāmasvāmi Ayyar, and Bīḍaram Krishnappā.

Tirupāmburam N. Swāminātha Piḷḷai (flute, vocal); 1900–61; disciple of his father; Head of Department of Music, Aṇṇāmalai University; Central College; teacher of Tañjāvūr Viṣwanāthaṉ, B. Krishnamūrthi, Maitili Nāgēśwaraṉ, and Sīrkāzhi S. Gōvindarājaṉ.

Tiruppāṟkaḍal S. Veerarāghavaṉ (violin); b. 1930; disciple of his father Śrīnivāsa Ayyaṅgār.

Tiruvārūr Baktavatsalam (*mṛdaṅgam*); b. 1956; disciple of Tiruvārūr Krishnamūrthyi.

Tiruveṇkāḍu Jayarāmaṉ (vocal); disciple of Svāmināta Dīkṣitar, T.S. Vēmbu Ayyar, and Madurai Maṇi Ayyar.

Tiruvizha (Tiruviḷa) Jayaśaṅkar (*nāgasvaram*); b. 1937; disciple of his father, Thiruvizha Rāghava Panicker, K.R. Kumāraswāmy Ayyar, and influenced by T.N. Rājaratnam Piḷḷai; has been experimenting with unconventional ensembles (e.g. violin accompaniment); also played for films; AIR.

Titte Krishna Ayyaṅgār (vocalist, scholar); 1902–97; disciple of his father, Titte Nārāyaṇa Ayyaṅgār, Bīḍaram Krishnappā, Vīṇā Sēshanna, and Tiger Varadāchāriar; author of several books on Karnatic music; Head of the Department of Music, Mahārāṇī's College (Mysore); expert on *rāga ālāpana*, *svara kalpana*, and *tāṉam*; teacher of R. Vēdavaḷḷi.

Trichūr R. Mōhaṉ (*mṛdaṅgam*); disciple of Umayāḷpuram K. Śivarāmaṉ; founder-director of a music school at Thrissur (Kerala).

Trichūr C. Narēndraṉ (*mṛdaṅgam*); b. 1951; disciple of Kumbakōnam Rājappa Ayyar, Umayāḷpuram Śivarāmaṉ, and Palghat Raghu; taught at the San Diego State University.

Trichūr V. Rāmachandraṉ (vocal). b. 1940; disciple of G.N. Bālasubrahmaṇyam and M.L. Vasanthakumāri; husband of Chārumathi Rāmachandraṉ; teacher of Eswaran Battadiri, his daughter Subaśree Rāmachandraṉ, and others.

Trichy R.K. Muraḷī (*ghaṭam*); b. 1966; disciple of Trichy R. Thāyumānavaṉ.

Trichy Śaṅkaraṉ (*mṛdaṅgam*); b. 1942; belongs to a musical family; disciple of Paḻani Subrahmaṇya Piḷḷai; taught at Toronto University (Canada).

Trichy R. Thāyumānavaṉ (*mṛdaṅgam, kañjirā, konnakkōl*); b. 1935; disciple of M.V. Dakshinamoorthy and Kumbakōnam M. Rājappa Ayyar; Founder of a percussion school (Gurupriya Laya Vidyālaya); teacher of Valaṇkaimāṉ K. Tyāgarājaṉ, Trichy R.K. Muraḷī, and Ānanḍāṇkōil V. Sundarājaṉ.

Trivandrum Baby Pārvathy (vocalist, composer); b. 1972; disciple of Ananthalakshmi Veṅkaṭarāmaṉ and T.M. Thyāgarājaṉ.

Trivandrum R.S. Maṇi (vocal); 1926–88; disciple of C.S. Krishna Ayyar, Kumāraswāmy Ayyar, Kēśava Bhāgavatar, and Semmaṅguḍi Śrīnivāsa Iyer; teacher of several musicians, including his daughter, S. Visalakshi.

Turaiyūr Rājagōpāla Śarma (vocalist, scholar, composer); 1905–87; disciple of Nāmakkaḷ Narasiṁha Ayyaṅgār and Tiger Varadāchāriar; also contributed to the fields of gramophone recording and film music; taught and composed music at Kalākshētra; author of works on *harikathā kālakṣepam* (musical discourse) of which he, like his father, was an exponent; published articles on 400 classical compositions (*kṛti*).

Tyāgarājaṉ, R. (flute); b. 1962; son and disciple of N. Ramani.

Tyāgarājaṉ, V. (violin); b. 1927; son and disciple of Pāpā K.S. Veṅkaṭarāmayya; Visiting Professor at Wesleyan University (USA); AIR.

Tyāgarājaṉ—*see* Valaṇkaimāṉ K. Tyāgarājaṉ

Uma Mahēshwari, D. (*harikathā kālakṣepam*); b. 1960; disciple of her grandfather and father, both *nāgasvaram* exponents; studied Āndhra dance under Naṭarāja Rāmakrishna, and *harikathā* at the Sri Sarvaraya Harikathā Pāṭhaśālā (Kapileswarapuram) which she now directs.

Umayāḷpuram Māli (*mṛdaṅgam*); b. 1959; disciple of Umayāḷpuram K. Śivarāmaṉ.

Umayāḷpuram K. Nārāyaṇaswāmi (*ghaṭam*); b. 1929; disciple of his father, Umayāḷpuram Kōdaṇḍarāma Ayyar; AIR.

Umayāḷpuram K. Śivarāmaṉ (*mṛdaṅgam*); b. 1935; disciple of Kumbakōnam M. Rājappa Ayyar and Palghat Maṇi Ayyar; teacher of Trichūr C. Narēndraṉ and Umayāḷpuram Māli.

Umayāḷpuram Swāminātha Ayyar (vocal); b. 1867; studied under Tyāgarāja's own disciples, Umayāḷpuram Krishna Bhāgavatar and Sundara Bhāgavatar; and under Mahāvaidyanātha Ayyar; teacher of R. Nāgarāja Rao, Kumbakōnam Rājamāṉikkam Piḷḷai, Semmaṅguḍi Śrīnivāsa Iyer, and Mahārājāpuram Viṣwanātha Ayyar.

Unnikrishnaṉ, P. (vocal); b. 1966; disciple of S. Rāmanāthaṉ, Sāvithri Sathyamūrthy, and Calcutta K.S. Krishnamūrthi; has also sung music for films.

Upēndraṉ—*see* Tañjāvūr Upēndraṉ.

Vaidyanātha(n)—*see* Konērirājāpuram Vaidyanātha Ayyar, Kunnakuḍi R. Vaidyanāthaṉ, Tañjāvūr Vaidyanātha Ayyar.

Vaidyanātha Bhāgavatar—*see* Chembai Vaidyanātha Bhāgavatar.

Vaidyanāthaṉ, J. (*mṛdaṅgam*); b. 1965; son of D.K. Jayarāmaṉ, disciple of Palghat Maṇi Ayyar and T.K. Moorthy.

Vaidyanāthaṉ, L. (violinist, composer); b. 1942; disciple of his father, V. Lakshminārāyaṇa; active in film music.

Vairamaṅgalam Lakshminārāyaṇaṉ (vocal); b. 1928; disciple of T.K. Raṅgachāri; Lecturer, Kalākshētra.

Valaṇkaimāṉ K. Tyāgarājaṉ (*mṛdaṅgam*); b. 1966; disciple of Trichy R. Tāyumānavaṉ.

Valayapatti A.R. Subrahmaṇyam (*tavil*); b. 1940; disciple of his father, *nāgasvaram* exponent, Arumugam Piḷḷai, his brother, Palanivēl Piḷḷai, and Maṉṉārguḍi Rājagōpāl Piḷḷai.

Vanaja A. Iyeṅgār (violin, *vicitra vīṇā*); b. 1935; disciple of B. Subba Rao (Karnatic music) and Namdeobuwa Warekar (Hindustānī music).

Vanathy Raghurāmaṉ (vocal); b. 1968; daughter and disciple of Dr S. Rāmanāthaṉ.

Vāsan, T.V. (*ghaṭam*); b. 1949; disciple of his father, T.G. Viśwanātha Bhāgavatar (vocal), Veludaya Nair, and his brother, T.V. Gōpālakrishnan; teacher of A.S. Shankar and A.S. Muraḷī; AIR.

Vasanthakumāri, M.L. ('MLV', vocal); 1928–90; disciple of both her parents, of G.N. Bālasubrahmaṇyam and Muḍikondān Veṅkaṭarāma Ayyar; sang classical music in films early in her career; taught at J. Krishnamūrti's Rishi Valley School; teacher of A. Kanyākumāri and Chārumathi Rāmachandran.

Vāsudēvan—*see* Neyyattiṅkarai Vāsudēvan.

Vasundara Rājagōpālan (vocal); b. 1952; disciple of Delhi Gōpāla Ayyar and T.R. Subrahmaṇyam.

Vechoor Harihara Subramoṇia Ayyar (vocal); 1915–94; Rādhā Lakshmī Vilāsam (RLV) Music Academy, Tripunithura; Principal, Swāti Tirunāḷ Saṅgīta Sabhā Music College, Tiruvananthapuram; teacher of Dr S. Bhāgyalekshmy and Dr S.R. Jayasītalakshmi.

Vēdagiri, V.L. (violin); b. 1929; disciple of Vallampati Lakshmīnārāyaṇa Ayyar; father and teacher of V.L. Kumār; AIR.

Vēdakrishnan (*mṛdaṅgam*); b. 1967; belongs to a family of musicians.

Vēdāntam—*see* Ambujam Vēdāntam.

Vēdāraṇyam V. Sōmasundaram (vocalist, scholar); b. 1919; disciple of M.M. Daṇḍapāṇi Dēsikar; exponent of *Tēvāram* hymns (*ōduvār*); author of a book on Tamil music (*Tirumurai Isai Amudam*); Tamil Isai Music College.

Vēdavaḷḷi, Dr M.B. (vocalist, *vaiṇika*; scholar, composer); b. 1935; disciple of Titte Krishna Ayyaṅgār, Mysore M.A. Narasiṁhachar, A.S. Panchapakēsha Ayyar, Muḍikondān Veṅkaṭarāma Ayyar, Tañjāvūr Viśwanāthan, S. Seetha, and others; author of several scholarly works (e.g. *Mysore as a Seat of Music, Karṇāṭaka Saṅgīta Sudha,* and *Rāgam Tānam Pallavi: Their Evolution, Structure and Exposition*); has provided the music for Kannaḍa devotional lyrics by V. Śrīnivāsa Rao (*Kīrtanāñjaḷi*); Stella Maris College; Head of Department of Music, Seethalakshmi Rāmaswāmy College (Trichy); Head of Department of Music, University of Madras/Chennai.

Vēdavaḷḷi, R. (vocalist, scholar); b. 1935; disciple of Śrīraṅgam Ayyaṅgār, Muḍikondān Veṅkaṭarāma Ayyar, and T. Mukta; Music Academy.

Vēdavaḷḷi, Rāmaswāmy (violin); b. 1925; disciple of Madurai Subramaṇia Ayyar and Varāhūr Muttusvāmi Ayyar.

Veerarāghavan—*see* Tiruppārkaḍal Veerarāghavan.

Vēgavāhini Vijayarāghavan (vocal); b. 1947; daughter and disciple of T. Brinda and Rāmnād Krishnan.

Vellore Rāmabhadran (*mṛdaṅgam*); b. 1929; disciple of his father, Vellore Gōpālāchāri.

Veṅkaṭagiriappa—*see* Mysore V. Veṅkaṭagiriappa.

Veṅkaṭarāma—*see* Bangalore K. Veṅkaṭarām, Justice T.L. Veṅkaṭarāma Ayyar, Muḍikondān C. Veṅkaṭarāma Ayyar, Pāpā K.S. Veṅkaṭarāmayya, Tinniyam Veṅkaṭarāma Ayyar.

Veṅkaṭarāma Śāstrī, R.K. (violin); 1910–93; disciple of Mysore Vāsudēvācāria and T. Chowdiah; brother and teacher of R.K. Śrīkantan; grandfather and teacher of R.K. Śrīrām Kumār; AIR.

Veṅkaṭēśwarulu—*see* Vōleti Veṅkaṭēśwārulu.

Veṅkaṭēśwara Rao—*see* Ellā Veṅkaṭēśwara Rao.

Veṅkitasubramoṇia Iyer, Dr S. (vocalist, musicologist); 1919–84; disciple of Palghat Veṅkaṭadri Bhāgavatar and Attuṅgal Padmanābha Bhāgavatar; author of articles and books on the music traḏitions of Kerala (e.g. *Swati Tirunal and his Music* and *Sangitasastra Pravesika*); Head of Department of Sanskrit, University of Tiruvananthapuram (Kerala).

Vidya Shankar (*vaiṇika*, vocalist, musicologist); b.1919; daughter of violinist and musicologist C. Subramaṇia Ayyar (1885–1960); studied *vīṇā* and vocal music from T.S. Sabhēśa Ayyar; also disciple of Sabhāpati Ayyar, Justice T.L. Veṅkaṭarāma Ayyar, and Śyāmā Śāstrī (i.e. the great-grandson of the elder Śyāmā Śāstrī, whose compositions she published with notations); collaborated with V. Rāghavaṉ, the noted Sanskrit scholar, in his musical research; author of a biography of Śyāmā Śāstrī and *The Art and Science of Carnatic Music* (published by the Music Academy); taught *vīṇā*, vocal music, mathematics, and Sanskrit at Kalākshētra; Central College and Vidyā Mandir (Chennai).

Vijayalakshmi, J. (violin) b. 1966; daughter and disciple of Lālguḍi Jayarāmaṉ.

Vijayalakshmi Nārāyaṇaṉ, N. (*vīṇā*); b. 1962; daughter of H.Y. Nārāyaṇaṉ; disciple of her mother, Rājalakshmi Nārāyaṇaṉ, Kalpagam Swāmināthaṉ, and Semmaṅguḍi Śrīnivāsa Ayyar.

Vijayalakshmy Subramaṇiam (vocal); b. 1962; disciple of S. Rājam, T.R. Subrahmaṇyam, and V.R. Krishnaṉ; Programme Executive, AIR (Chennai, Pondicherry).

Vijay Śiva, N. (vocal); b. 1967; disciple of D.K. Jayarāmaṉ.

Viji Krishnaṉ Naṭarājaṉ (violin); b. 1963; daughter and disciple of T.N. Krishnaṉ.

Vilvadri Ayyar (*ghaṭam*); 1901–71; belonged to a family of percussionists; initially he also played *mṛdaṅgam* for drama and *harikathā kālakṣepam*.

Vīṇā Dhanammāḷ (*vīṇā*, vocal); 1868–1938; belonged to an old family tradition of musicians and dancers; disciple of Satanūr Pañcanātha Ayyar and Wālājapet Bālakṛṣṇa Dās ('Padam Bāldās'), a *vaiṇika* and specialist in the *padam* form; regarding the *vīṇā* as a *sarva vādya* (an instrument complete and perfect in itself), she played it without plectrum, and often accompanied by her own singing; her music is documented in a set of historical recordings; her personal style, known as the *Vīṇā Dhanammāḷ bāṇī*, is still regarded as a yardstick in terms of adherence to traditional values (*sampradāya*) and profundity of musical expression (*rāga bhāva*); musicians, critics and composers attended her private recitals in Chennai; her continuing impact is ascribed to the scope of her repertoire, knowledge and refinement; many songs by leading composers like Narasiṁhācārlu, Mutialpet Ponnusvāmi, Tiruvōtriyūr Tyāgayyar, and especially Dharmapuri Subbarāyar (*jāvaḷi*) were composed for, or inspired by, Dhanammāḷ; these compositions (mainly *jāvaḷi* and *padam*) have been preserved, taught, and published by her grandchildren, T. Śaṅkaraṉ, dancer T. Bālasaraswati, T. Mukta, T. Brinda, and Tañjāvūr Viṣwanāthaṉ.

Vīṇā Krishnamāchāriar (*vaiṇika*, vocalist, composer); died 1947; son of *harikathā* exponent Rāmānujachāriar; brother of Tiger Varadāchāriar; disciple of P. Nīlakaṇṭha Śāstrī and Taccūr Siṅgarācāryulu; his compositions encompass different forms (*var-ṇam, kṛti, jāvaḷi, tillānā*) as well as a Kalākshētra dance drama (*Kutrāla Kuravañji*), and have been published by Kalākshētra (*Gāna Mañjari*); teacher of Bangalore G. Channamma.

Vinayakram, T.H. ('Vikku', *ghaṭam*); b. 1942; son and disciple of T.R. Harihara Śarma; Principal of a school for Karnatic percussion (Śrī Jaya Ganēsh Vidyālaya, Chennai);

taught in the USA and has collaborated with exponents of Jazz and World Music; teacher of N. Gōvindarājan, Sukanya Rāmgōpāl, T. Shyāmsundar, and S. Karthick.

Viṣwanātha(n)—*see* Kuttālam Viṣwanāthan, Mahārājāpuram Viṣwanātha Ayyar, Tañjāvūr Viṣwanāthan.

Viṣwanātha Bhāgavatar, T.G. (vocal); 1902(?)–85; disciple of his father, violinst Gōpālakrishna Bhāgavatar, and Palghat Anantarāma Bhāgavatar; introduced songs from Kerala's *Kathakali* repertoire (dance-drama) and *sōpānam saṅgita* (temple hymns) in Karnatic music concerts; father and teacher of T.V. Gōpālakrishnan and T.V. Vāsan.

Viśwēśwaran, R. (*vaiṇika*, vocalist, composer); b. 1931; self-taught *vaiṇika*; performed with his three brothers ('Mysore Quartette'); composed in Telugu, Kannaḍa, and Sanskrit; Professor and Head of Music Department, Mysore University.

Vittal Rāmamūrthy (violin); disciple of T. Rukmini and Lālguḍi Jayarāman.

Vōleti Veṅkaṭēśwārulu (vocal, educationist); 1928–89; disciple of Śrīpāda Pinakapāni and other noted teachers; Music Producer, AIR (Vijayawada); influenced many musicians; produced a series of educational broadcasts; explored the common ground of Hindustānī and Karnatic music; teacher of Srīraṅgam Gōpālaratnam.

Yellā Sōmanna (*mṛdaṅgam*); b. 1918; disciple of Palghat Maṇi Ayyar; teacher of Ellā Veṅkaṭēśwara Rao; AIR (Vijayawada).

Bibliography

A handwritten copy of an old Lakshana Grantha. H. Ramachandra Shastry; unpublished (courtesy: R. Vaidyanathan).

Abhijñana- Sakuntalam of Kālidāsa edited with an Exhaustive Introduction, Translation and Critical and Explanatory Notes by C.R. Devadhar and N.G. Suru. Motilal Banarsidass, Delhi, 1934 (rpt 1991).

Alvars of South India by K.C. Varadachari Bharatiya, Vidya Bhavan, Bombay, 1970.

Analysis of Beauty (with the rejected passages from the manuscript drafts and autobiographical notes) by William Hogarth; edited with an introduction by Joseph Burke. Oxford at the Clarendon Press, London, 1955.

Archeology of Indian Musical Instruments by K. Krishna Murthy, Sundeep Prakashan, Delhi, 1985.

Art and Architecture of the Indian Subcontinent by J.C. Harle, Penguin Books, 1990 (1986).

Art and Architecture of Indian Temples (vol. I) by S.K. Ramachandra Rao, Kalpatharu Research Academy, Bangalore, 1993.

Art and Science of Carnatic Music by Vidya Shankar, The Music Academy Madras (Chennai), 1983.

Art of the Mridhangam by T.R. Harihara Sarma, Chennai/Madras, 1969.

Art, The Integral Vision: A Volume of Essay in Felicitation of Kapila Vatsyayan by B.N. Saraswati, S.C. Malik and Madhu Khanna (eds), D.K. Printworld, New Delhi, 1994.

Bala on Bharata Natyam. Compiled and translated by S Guhan, The Sruti Foundation, Chennai/Madras, 1991.

Be As You Are: The Teachings of Sri Ramana Maharshi. David Godman (ed.), Penguin, New Delhi, 1992.

Bharata Natyam: The Tamil Heritage by Lakshmi Viswanythan, published by the author, Chennai/Madras, 1991.

Bharatiya Sangeet Raganidhi by B. Subba Rao, The Music Academy Chennai/Madras, 1980 (4 vols; the edns of 1980, 1982, 1984 and 1985 respectively).

Carnatic Music and the Tamils by T.V. Kuppuswami, Kalinga Publications, Delhi, 1992.

Carnatic Music Composers: A Collection of Biographical Essays by B. Dayananda Rao (ed.), Triveni Foundation, Hyderabad, 1994.

Cilappatikaram by V. R. Ramachandra Dikshitar (Appendix III, on music with P. Sambamoorthy), The South India Saiva Siddhanta Works Publishing Society, Chennai/Madras, 1939 (1978).

Comparative Study of Some of the Leading Music Systems of the 15th, 16th, 17th and 18th Centuries by V. N. Bhatkhande, Low Price Publications, Delhi (rpt 1990).

Comparative Study of Thaalas in Hindustani and Karnatak System: Palghat Mani Lecture by T.V. Gopalkrishnan, Percussive Arts Centre, Bangalore, 1991.

Compositions of Tyāgarāja by T.K. Govinda Rao, Ganamandir Publications, Chennai/Madras, 1995.

Conference of the Birds by Farid Ud-Din Attar, translated with an Introduction by Afkham Darbandi and Dick Davis, Penguin Books, 1984.

Dictionary of Bharata Natya by U.S. Krishna Rao, Orient Longman, Chennai/Madras, 1990.

Dictionary of Contemporary Tamil (Tamil-Tamil-English), published by Cre-A, Madras, 1994.

Dictionary of South Indian Music and Musicians by P. Sambamoorthy, The Indian Music Publishing House, Chennai/Madras, 1984 (3 vols; the edns of 1984, 1959 and 1971 respectively; vol. IV is yet to appear posthumously).

Ekaika kṛti rāgas: Documentation for a Lecture by S.R. Janakiraman, The Music Academy Chennai/Madras, 1996.

Eloquent Percussion: A Guide to South Indian Rhythm by Ludwig Pesch and T.R. Sundaresan, Eka.Grata Publications, Amsterdam, 1996.

Encyclopedia of Tamil Literature by Shu Hikosaka and G. John Samuel (chief eds) and M. Shanmugam Pillai, Institute of Asian Studies, Institute of Asian Studies, Madras, 1990 (vol. 1) and 1992 (vol. 2).

Essays in Musicology by R. C. Mehta (ed.), Indian Musicological Society, Bombay and Baroda, 1983 (rpt 1989).

Flute by P. Sambamoorthy: The Indian Music Publishing House, Chennai/Madras, 1982 (4th edn).

Fundamentals of Ancient Indian Music and Dance by Sures Chandra Banerji, L.D. Series 57, L.D. Institute of Indology, Ahmedabad, 1976.

Garland . . . Biographical Dictionary of Carnatic Composers and Musicians (Book I, *A Garland*; Book II, *Another Garland*; Book III, *Yet Another Garland*; Book IV, *The Fragrant Garland*) by N. Rajagopalan, published by the author (Chennai/Madras), 1990/1993/1994/1996.

Glossary of Sanskrit: From the Spiritual Tradition of India by Diana Morrison, Nilgiri Press, Blue Mountain Center of Meditation, Berkeley, 1970/1977.

GNB: A Biography by T.S. Vedagiri, K.S. Muthuraman and K.S. Mahadevan, published by G.B. Duraiswamy, Chennai/Madras, 1985.

Great Composers by P. Sambamoorthy, The Indian Music Publishing House, Chennai/Madras, vol. I, 3rd edn (1978); vol. II, 2nd edn (1970).

Great Integrators: The Saint-Singers of India by V. Raghavan, Publications Division, New Delhi, 1979.

The Hindu (English Daily), Chennai/Madras.

Hindu Art by T. Richard Blurton, British Museum Press, London, 1994.

Hindu World: An Encyclopedic Survey of Hinduism by Benjamin Walker, Munshiram Manoharlal, New Delhi, 1983 (two vols).

A Historical Study of Indian Music by Swami Prajnananda, New Delhi, 1981 (2nd edn).

History of India by Romila Thapar, Penguin, 1966 (1984).

History of Indian Music by P. Sambamoorthy, The Indian Music Publishing House, 1982 (2nd edn).

History of South India by Nilakanta Sastri, Oxford University Press, Chennai/Madras, 1966 (1987).

History of South Indian (Carnatic) Music by R. Rangaramanuja Ayyangar, published by the author, Chennai/Madras, 1972.

History of Tamil Literature by C. Jesudasan and Hephzibah Jesudasan, The Heritage of India Series, YMCA Publishing House, Calcutta, 1961.

History of the Tamils from the Earliest Times to AD 600 by P.T. Srinivasa Iyengar, reprinted by Asian Educational Services, New Delhi, 1989.

How to Know God: The Yoga Aphorisms of Patanjali, translated with a New Commentary by Swami Prabhavananda and Christopher Isherwood, New American Library, New York, 1969.

Hymns for the Drowning: Poems for Visnu by Nammalvar, translated by A.K. Ramanujam, Penguin (India), New Delhi, 1993.

Index for Bharatanatyam Compositions by T.S. Parthasarathy and A.M. Sundaram, Fine Arts Foundation—India, Chennai/Madras (year not stated).

Index of Songs in South Indian music by Gauri Kuppuswamy and M. Hari Haran, B.R. Publishing Corporation, Delhi, 1981.

India: Art and Architecture in Ancient and Medieval Periods by P. N. Chopra (ed.), Publications Division New Delhi, 1981 (1991).

Indian Aesthetics: Music and Dance by K.S. Ramaswami Sastri, Sri Venkateswara University, Tirupati, 1966.

Indian Dance (collection of articles written for *The Hindu*) by C.R. Srinivasa Ayyangar, Chennai/Madras, 1948.

Indian Express (English daily), Chennai/Madras.

Indian Horizons: Vol. XXXIV, nos 3–4, *Bankim Chandra Chatterji: His Life Work and Influence* by V.S. Naravane, Indian Council for Cultural Relations, New Delhi, 1985.

Inscriptions on Music from South India by K.V. Ramesh (manuscript provided by the author in 1988), Dept. of Epigraphy, Government of India, Mysore (undated).

Intonation in North Indian Music by Mark Levy, Biblia Impex, New Delhi, 1982.

Journal of the Indian Musicological Society, vol. 27, Special Issue on Music: Intercultural Aspects, S.A.K. Durga (guest ed.), Baroda, 1996.

Journal of the Music Academy Madras (Chennai).

Kalakshetra Quarterly, Chennai/Madras.

Kalakshetra, Rukmini Devi: Reminiscences by S. Sarada, Kala Mandir Trust, Madras, 1985.

Kathakalaksepa: A Study by Premeela Gurumurthy, International Society for the Investigation of Ancient Civilizations, Chennai/Madras, 1994.

Kudumiyanmalai Inscriptions on Music by Dr V Premalatha (published by the author), Madurai, 1986.

Layamani Layam: A Magazine from Sruthi Laya Seva Trust of Karaikudi R. Mani, Chennai.

Mamallapuram and the Pallavas by Michael Lockwood, The Christian Literature Society, Chennai/Madras, 1982.

Music and Dance in Rabindranath Tagore's Education Philosophy by Santidev Ghose, Sangeet Natak Akademi, New Delhi, 1978.

Musical Instruments in Indian Sculpture by G.H. Tarlekar and Nalini Tarlekar, Pune Vidyarthi Griha Prakashan, Poona, 1972.

Music Composers of India by T.S. Parthasarathy, Chennai/Madras, 1982.

Music Cultures of the Pacific, the Near East, and Asia by William P. Malm, Prentice-Hall, New Jersey, 1967.

Music in Cilappatikaaram by S. Ramanathan, Kamaraj University, Madurai, 1979.

Music in India: The Classical Traditions by Bonnie C. Wade, Manohar, New Delhi, 1979/1991.

The Music of Early Minnesang by James V. McMahon, Camden House, Columbia, South Carolina, 1990.

Musik für Vina: English and German Commentary by Pia Srinivasan-Buonomo, Musikethnologische Abteilung, Museum für Völkerkunde, Artur Simon (ed.), Berlin, 1980.

Musings of a Musician: Recent Trends in Carnatic Music by R. Rangaramanuja Ayyangar, Wilco, Bombay, 1977.

Muttuswami Dikshitar by V. Raghavan (articles on various subjects; Index to the Songs of Sri Muttuswami Dikshitar; Discography), National Centre for the Performing Arts, Bombay, 1975.

Myths and Symbols in Indian Art and Civilization by Heinrich Zimmer, Joseph Campbell (ed.), Bollingen Series VI, Princeton University Press (C) 1946, Princeton, New Jersey, 1972.

Nārada-Purāṇa: Ancient Indian Traditions and Mythology Series, vols 15 and 16, translated and annotated by Ganesh Vasudeo Tagare, New Delhi, 1981.

Natyasastra: English Translation with Critical Notes by Adya Rangacharya, IBH Prakashana, Bangalore, 1986.

Nāṭyaśāstra: A Treatise on Ancient Indian Dramaturgy and Histrionics Ascribed to Bharata-Muni, translated and edited by Manomohan Ghosh, 2 vols, published by Manisha, Calcutta, 1995 (1951) (3rd revised edn).

New Dictionary of Music by Arthur Jacobs, Penguin Books, 3rd edn, 1976.

New Grove Dictionary of Music and Musicians (chapters on Indian music) by Nazir A. Jairazbhoy and Harold S. Powers, Macmillan Publishers Ltd., London, 1980.

New Oxford Companion to Music by Denis Arnold (gen. ed.), Oxford University Press, London, 1983.

Nityasumaṅgalī: Devadasi Tradition in South India by Saskia C. Kersenboom-Story, Motilal Banarsidass, Delhi, 1987.

Oriental Music in European Notation by A.M.C. Mudaliyar, originally published in 1893, Cosmo Publications, New Delhi, 1982.

Penguin Dictionary of Indian Classical Music by Raghava R. Menon, Penguin Books India, New Delhi, 1995.

Permutative Genius in Tala (-Prastara) in Indian Music by Akella Mallikarjuna Sharma, Telugu University, Hyderabad, 1992.

Persian Records: Information pertaining to the migration of Indian musicians to Iran under the Sāsānid dynasty, personal communication by Feridun Rahimi-Laridjani, Chennai, 1997.

The Poems of Ancient Tamil by George L. Hart III, University of California Press, Berkeley and Los Angeles, 1975.

Practical Sanskrit Dictionary by Arthur Anthony Macdonnell, Oxford University Press, London, 1924 (1976).

Puranic Encyclopaedia by Vettam Mani, Motilal Banarsidass, Delhi, 1975 (rpt 1993).

Ragadhana: An Alpha-Numerical Directory of Ragas by Ludwig Pesch, Irinjalakuda, 1993.

Raga Lakshana: Summary of the Raga Lakshana Discussions of the 25 Conferences of the Experts' Committee of the Music Academy Madras, The Music Academy Chennai/Madras, 1980.

Ragas in Carnatic Music by S. Bhagyalekshmy, CBH Publications, Trivandrum, 1990.

Ragas of Karnatak Music by T.S. Parthasarathy, The Journal of the Music Academy Chennai/Madras (vol. LII), 1981.

Ragas of North India by Walter Kaufmann, Oxford & IBH Publishing Co., New Delhi (1968) 1993.

Ragas of South India by Walter Kaufmann, Oxford & IBH Publishing Co., New Delhi, 1976.

Reflections on the Art of Living: A Joseph Campbell Companion by Diane K. Osbon (ed.), Harper Collins, New York, 1991.

Research Methodology for Music by S.A.K. Durga, Center for Ethnomusicology, Chennai/Madras, 1991.

Sacred and Profane Dimensions of Love in Indian Traditions as exemplified in the *Gītagovinda* of Jayadeva by Lee Siegel, Oxford University Press, New Delhi, 1992.

The Sacred and the Secular in India's Performing Arts: Ananda K. Coomaraswamy Centenary Essays, V. Subramaniam (ed.), Ashish Publishing House, New Delhi, 1980.

Samgraha-Cuda-Mani by S. Subrahmanya Sastri, Pandit (ed.), Introduction by Srinivasa Ayyangar, The Adyar Library, Chennai/Madras, 1938.

Sangeet Natak: Silver Jubilee Volume by H.K. Ranganath (ed.), Sangeet Natak Akademi, New Delhi, 1981.

Science of Music by K. Vasudeva Sastri, Research Publications, Tanjore, 1954.

Semmangudi: A Music Portrait by N. Pattabhi Raman, Sruti Foundation, Madras, 1993.

Shobhillu Saptasvara: Svaravali, Gitam, Prabandham, Suladi by Savithri Rajan and Michael Nixon, published by the authors, Chennai/Madras, 1982.

Short Historical Survey of the Music of Upper India by V. N. Bhatkhande, Indian Musicological Society, Baroda, 1916 (rpt 1985).

Sogasuga Mridanga Taalamu: A Reference Book on South Indian Percussion (2 vols) by T.A.S. Mani, KCP Publications, Bangalore (date not given).

Some Thoughts on Indian Aesthetics and Literary Criticism by K. Krishnamoorthy, University of Mysore, 1968.

Sources of Indian Tradition (Introduction to Oriental Civilizations, 2 vols) by W.M. Theodore de Bary (gen. ed.), compiled by Stephen Hay and I.H. Qureshi, Columbia University Press, New York, 1958.

South Indian Music by P. Sambamoorthy, The Indian Music Publishing House (6 vols; the edns of 1972, 1976, 1973, 1975, 1977 and 1969 respectively).

Spiritual Heritage of Tyagaraja by C. Ramanujachari and V. Raghavan, 3rd impression, Sri Ramakrishna Math, Chennai/Madras, 1981.

Sruti Magazine for Indian Music and Dance, published by the Sruti Foundation, Chennai/Madras (monthly).

Student's Sanskrit–English Dictionary by Vaman Shivram Apte, Poona, 1890, reprinted by Motilal Banarsidass, New Delhi, 1988.

Subbaraya Sastry's and Annaswamy Sastry's Compositions: text, translation transliteration and notation with gamaka-signs by Vidya Shankar, Parampara, Chennai/Madras, 1995.

The Sufis by Idries Shah, Doubleday, New York, 1964.

The Sword and the Flute: Kali and Krsna (Dark Visions of the Terrible and the Sublime in Hindu Mythology) by David R. Kinsley, University of California Press, London, 1975/1977.

Syama Sastry's Compositions: text, translation transliteration and notation with gamaka-signs by Vidya Shankar, Parampara, 3rd edn, Chennai/Madras, 1989 (1947).

Talavadya Seminar: Proceedings of the Talavadya Seminar Nos 1, 2 and 3, compiled and edited by Bangalore K. Venkataram, published by Karnataka Sangeetha Nrithya Academy, Bangalore (3 vols), 1994, 1996 and 1996.

Tamil Culture and Civilization (Readings: The Classical Period) by X.S. Thani Nayagam, Asia Publishing House, Bombay, 1970.

Tamil Literature by M. S. Purnalingam Pillai, reprint by Asian Educational Services (first published 1929), New Delhi/Chennai/Madras, 1994.

Tanjore as a Seat of Music by S. Seetha, University of Chennai/Madras, 1989.

Tyagaraja: Life and Lyrics by William J Jackson, Oxford University Press, Chennai/Madras, 1991.

Varnam: A Special Form in Karnatic Music by Lalitha Ramakrishna, Harman Publishing House, New Delhi, 1991.

Varnamanjari by T.K. Govinda Rao, Ganamandir Publications, Chennai/Madras, 1979.

Voice Culture by S.A.K. Durga, Indian Musicological Society, Baroda, 1978.

Voice Culture and Singing by Friedrich Brückner-Rüggeberg and Ludwig Pesch, Kalakshetra Quarterly, vol. V, no. 3, Kalakshetra, Chennai/Madras, 1983.

The Way of the Sufi by Idries Shah, Dutton Paperback, New York, 1970 (1968).

Who's Who of Indian Musicians: Sangeet Natak Akademi, New Delhi, 2nd edn, 1984.

The Wonder That Was India: A survey of the history and culture of the Indian subcontinent before the coming of the Muslims by A.L. Basham, Rupa & Co., New Delhi, 1992 (1954).

The Wonder That Was India (vol. II) by S.A.A. Rizvi, Sidgwick and Jackson, London, 1987.

Discography

Note: The following selection contains recordings on compact disc (CD), pre-recorded cassettes and long-play records (LP); thus it reflects the general availability of South Indian music at the time of publication; numerous new titles appear on the market every month.

Spellings of names reflect prevailing usage on commercially released recordings; other variants are also used by various companies.

Some older recordings in the long-play record format (LP) are of outstanding musical and documentary value (e.g. Museum Collection Berlin, UNESCO Collection). Most of these records can be found in the archives of educational institutions and museums.

Throughout India, pre-recorded cassettes still play a major role in making even rare recordings accessible to music lovers and students alike; not all recordings of musical and historical interest are likely to be released on CD also.

Recording companies and labels

Entries for artists and titles refer to the company code listed below:

1. CHHANDA DHARA (Germany)
2. EMI/RPG/HMV (The Gramophone Co. of India)
3. ETHNIC AUDIVIS (France)
4. INRECO (USA)
5. JVC (Japan)
6. MUSIC OF THE WORLD (USA)
7. MUSIC TODAY (India)
8. NIMBUS
9. OCORA/RADIO FRANCE (France)
10. OMI MUSIC (Canada)/MAGNASOUND (India)
11. ORIENTAL RECORDS (USA)
12. SANGEETHA (India), KOEL
13. SILVER DISC (Singapore)
14. WATER LILY (USA)
15. WELTMUSIK/WERGO (Germany)
16. HARMONIA MUNDI; Le chant du monde (France)/Musêe de l'homme (France)
17. LIBERTY MUSIC (Singapore)

18. AVM Audio (India)
19. LICHTHAUS MUSIK (Germany)
20. MUSEUM COLLECTION BERLIN, Museum für Völkerkunde (Germany)

Vocal (female voice)

Aruna Sayeeram (2, 3, 18, 19)
Bombay Sisters (12)
Charumati Ramachandran (11)
S. Jayashri (10)
S. Nithyashree (2)
D.K. Pattammal (2, 11)
Priya Sisters (V. Shanmuga Priya and V. Haripriya, 2)
Radha Jayalakshmi (2)
S. Rajeswari (2)
C. Saroja and C. Lalitha (11)
S. Sowmya (2)
M.S. Subbulakshmi (2); see also *mēḷa rāga mālikā cakra* (Compilations, below)
Sudha Raghunathan (2, 4, 7, 10, 11)
M.L. Vasanthakumari ('MLV',2, 10, 11)

Vocal (male voice)

Alathur Brothers (2)
Ariyakudi Ramanuja Iyengar (2)
Balamurali Krishna (1, 2, 7 and 11)
Balasubramaniam ('GNB', 2, 4)
Chembai Vaidyanatha Bhagavatar (2)
Jon B. Higgins (2)
Hyderabad Brothers (D. Seshachari and D. Raghavachary, 2, 7)
D.K. Jayaraman (2, 10, 11)
K.J. Jesudas (17)
T.M. Krishna (2)
Madurai Mani Iyer (2)
Madurai Somasundaram (2)
Maharajapuram Santhanam (2, 3, 7, 11)
K.V. Narayanaswamy (2, 11)
B. Rajam Iyer (11)
M.D. Ramanathan (2)
K. Rama Rao (*naṭṭuvāṅgam*, see dance music, 1)
Ramnad Krishnan (2; double LP, Nonesuch Records New York)
Sankaran Namboodri (2)
T.V. Sankaranarayanan (2)
Semmangudi Srinivasa Iyer (2, 11, 18)
T.N. Seshagopalan (2, 11)
R.K. Srikantan (11)
O.S. Thyagarajan (2)
Trichur Ramachandran (2, 11)
Vijay Siva (2)
M.S. Viswanathan (2)

Pullāṅkuḻal (bamboo flute)

B.V. Balasai (2)
K. Bhaskaran (CBS India)
K.S. Gopalakrishnan (15)
Mali (T.R. Mahalingam, 2, 11)
C.T. Raghavaraman (see dance music, 1)
N. Ramani (2, 10, 11)
Sikkil Sisters (2, 10, 12)
T. Viswanathan

Vīṇā (fretted lute)

S. Balachander (2, 5, 11)
Chitti Babu (2)
Emani Sankara Sastri (9)
E. Gayathri (2, 10)
Karaikudi S. Subramanian (double LP with English and German commentary, 20)
K.S. Narayanaswamy (11)
Mysore Doreswamy Iyengar (2, 7)
Rajeswari Padmanabhan (2, 5 and double LP with English and German comentary, 20)

Goṭṭuvādyam, citravīṇā (fretless lute)

A. Durga Prasad (2)
N. Ravikiran (1, 2, 7, 10, 12, 14)

Nāgasvaram, nādasvaram (double-reed instrument)

Karakurichi P. Arunachalam (2)

Madurai Sethuraman and Ponnuswamy (2)
Namagiripettai Krishnan (2, 10, 11)
T.N. Rajaratnam Pillai (2)
Sheikh Chinna Moulana (2, 11, 15)
Thiruvizha Jayashankar (2)

Violin (solo and accompaniment)

M.S. Anantharaman (11)
Bangalore Thyagarajan (17)
Dwaram Mangathayaru (11)
Dwaram Venkataswamy Naidu (2)
Ganesh and Kumaresh (10)
M.S. Gopalakrishnan (2)
A. Kanyakumari (6, 10, 12)
G.J. R. Krishnan (10, 11)
T.N. Krishnan (solo violin, 2, 7, 10)
Kunnakudi R. Vaidyanathan (2, 10, 12, 13)
Lalgudi G. Jayaraman (2, 10, 11)
Madurai S. Balasubramaniam (11)
Mysore M. Nagaraj (2)
V.V. Ravi (10, 11)
T. Rukmini (11)
R.K. Sriramkumar (11)
L. Subramaniam (9, 11, 14)
V.V. Subrahmanyam (2)
M.A. Sundaresan (11)
Tirupparkadal Veeraraghavan (11)
Usha Rajagopalan (11)
Venkitachalam (15)
Viji Jayaraman (11)
The Violin Trio (2)
Vittal Ramamurthy (10)

Mandolin (electric mandolin)

U. Srinivas (1, 2, 7, 10, 11)

Harmonium

Palladam S. Venkataramana Rao (10)

Jalatarangam (musical water bowls)

Anayampatti S. Dhandapani (10)

Clarinet

A.K.C. Natarajan (2)

Saxophone

Kadri Gopalnath (10, 11 and 12)

Mṛdaṅgam (double-faced drum)

T.V. Gopalakrishnan (11)
K. Gopinath (see dance music, 1)
Guruvaiyur Dorai (7, 11)
Karaikudi R. Mani (see also Sruthi Laya Ensemble, 2 and 11)
Madurai Srinivasan (11)
Mannargudi Eswaran (10)
Mavelikara Krishnankutty Nair (17)
T.K. Moorthy (2)
Neyveli R. Narayanan (10)
Palghat Mani Iyer (2, 11 and violin Subramaniam, 9)
T. Ramdos (11)
R. Ramesh (11)
T. Shyamsundar (11)
Srimushnam Raja Rao (10, 11)
V. Suresh (11)
Tanjore Upendran (20)
Thiruvarur Bhaktavatsalam (10, 11)
Trichur Mohan (1, 10)
Trichur Narendran (11 and *vīṇā* Narayanaswamy, 11)
Trichy Sankaran (*mṛdaṅgam* solo, 6 and violin Lalgudi Jayaraman, 10)
Trivandrum Surendran (15)
J. Vaidyanathan (10, 11)
Vellore Ramabhadran (2, 11)

Various percussion instruments

Chitambaranath (*kañjīrā*, 17)
Gopalkrishnan (*ghaṭam*, 7, 17)
Gurumurthy (*ghaṭam*, 11)
G. Harishankar (*kañjīrā*, 2, 11, 10)
S. Karthick (*ghaṭam*, 2)
Nagaraja Rao (*ghaṭam*, 10)
V. Nagarajan (*kañjīrā*, 2)
Pakkiri Swamy (*morsing*, 17)
K. Rama Rao (*naṭṭuvāṅgam*, see dance music, 1)
A.S. Shankar (*ghaṭam*, 10)
Sruthi Laya Ensemble (Karaikudi Mani, 2)

T.H. Subashchandran (1)
E.M. Subramaniam (*ghaṭam*, 10)
Udipi Sreedhar (*ghaṭam*, 15)
T.V. Vasan (*ghaṭam*, 11)
Valayapatti A.R. Subramaniam (*tavil*, 2)
T.H. Vinayakaram (*ghaṭam*, 2, 11)

Dance music

An Evening of Bharata Natyam (2)
Music for Bharata Natyam (11)
Odissi Dance Music (Guru Kelucharan Mohapatra and Bhubaneswara Misra, 5)
Traditional Indian Dance Music: Bharata Natyam (1)

Compilations (various artists, special and historical recordings)

Festival of India: Masters of Music, The Great Tradition (sampler of recordings; past and present musicians of North and South India, 2)
Gems from the Carnatic Classicals (2)
Inde du sud: Kerala (Ritual Music and Theatre of Kerala); Collection CNRS Musēe de l'Homme (16)
Instrumental Marvels: Carnatic Classical (2)
Mēla Rāga Mālikā Cakra of Mahāvaidyanātha Śivan (exposition of all the 72 scales of Karnatic music) sung by M.S. Subbulakshmi (2)
Rare Gems (11)
Swara Bhushani/Great Masters (11)
UNESCO Anthology of Indian music LP in 2 parts recorded by Alain Daniēlou, 1955); Lyrichord LLST 7350
UNESCO COLLECTION: A Musical Anthology of the Orient, India IV (recordings and commentary by John Levy); 1. Semmangudi Srinivasa Aiyar (vocal) accompanied by K.S. Narayanaswami (*vīṇā*); 2. *vīṇā* solo by K.S. Narayanaswami accompanied by Palghat Raghu (*mṛdaṅgam*); 3. Semmangudi Srinivasa Aiyar (vocal solo)—Navarasa; rāga mālikā (Nādanāmakriya, Śahāna, Ānandabhairavi, Pūrvīkalyāṇi and Kānaḍa); 4. *vīṇā* by K.S. Narayanaswami accompanied by Palghat Raghu (*mṛdaṅgam*); 5. tuning of the *vīṇā*
Various artists (12)

Combinations (non-traditional and unconventional ensembles)

Aruna: Thousand Names of the Divine Mother Aruna Sayeeram, Michael Reimann and Christian Bollmann (vocal, overtone singing, organ, didgeridoo and various other instruments, 19)
Jugalbandi and rāgam-tānam-pallavi (T.N. Krishnan, South Indian violin and N. Rajam, North Indian violin with Zakir Hussain, tabla and T.V. Gopalakrishnan, *mṛdaṅgam*, 11)
Pushkaram (B.V. Balasai, flute; A. Durga Prasad, *gōṭṭuvādyam;* Karaikudi R. Mani, *mṛdaṅgam*; G. Harishankar, *kañjīrā*, 2)
South Indian ensemble (Kanyakumari, *violin* with *tavil*, etc. accompaniment 6)
Vocal—South Indian style (Balamurali Krishna)—accompanied by tabla (1)

Alphabetical Index of Rāgas and Scales

The *mēḷakartā rāgas* and *janya rāgas* listed here are also rendered in staff notation (*see* staves 17–26 and 28–35), and each is allocated a place in accordance with the conventional categories explained below (i.e. *auḍava, ṣāḍava, ghana rāga, rakti rāga*, etc.). A few rāgas are traditionally assigned to more than one category (e.g. Saurāṣṭram, 17; Hindustānī dēśya, rakti), but outlined only once in staff notation. The remaining *janya rāgas*, those which cannot be assigned to any conventional category, form another large group which, although outwardly inconspicuous, plays an important part in the concert and dance music repertoire.

In the Index, the 72 Karnatic reference scales (*mēḷakartā rāgas*) are cross-referred with the ten reference scales of Hindustānī music (*thāṭ*) for the purpose of comparative studies. This is useful in view of the fact that the northern *thāṭ* system, introduced by Paṇḍit V.N. Bhāṭkhaṇḍe (1860–1936), is based on the southern *mēḷakartā* scheme. The scales and church modes of Western classical music are also listed and cross-referred to facilitate intercultural communication. Syllabic notation (*sargam*) and other technical details (e.g. sources, cross-reference with the rāgas of Hindustānī music) are given in *Ragadhana: An Alpha-Numerical Index of Ragas*.

A *mēḷakartā rāga* is identified by the word 'mēḷa' followed by its *mēḷakartā rāga* number, e.g. 'Dhīrasaṅkarābharaṇam, mēḷa 29'. Similarly, every *janya rāga* is listed along with the number of the *mēḷakartā rāga* from which all or most of its tonal steps (*svarasthāna*) are derived. For example, the entry 'Kiraṇāvaḷi, 21—*stave 23*' informs us that the 21st *mēḷakartā rāga* (i.e. Kīravāṇi) is the reference scale of rāga Kiraṇāvaḷi. Any additional notes (*anyasvara*), and those notes which must be avoided (*varja*), are thus viewed, at least for the purpose of reference, as characteristic modifications of the reference scale.

In staff notation, all *mēḷakartā rāgas* are placed in numerical order (1–36, 37–72), and next to their 'twin scales' from which they are distinguished only by the use of the natural fourth (left columns) or the sharp fourth (right columns), termed *śuddha madhyama* and *prati madhyama* respectively. The first *mēḷakartā rāga* ('Kanakāṅgi, mēḷa 1') is therefore placed next to the 37th *mēḷakartā rāga* ('Sālagam, mēḷa 37'), and the 36th *mēḷakartā rāga* ('Calanāṭa, mēḷa 36') next to the 72nd *mēḷakartā rāga* ('Rasikapriya, mēḷa 72'). Some *janya rāgas*, on the other hand, are placed in alphabetical order among other rāgas which share a particular feature or restriction (e.g. *auḍava, ṣāḍava, niṣādāntya*), while others are placed in the order supplied by their usual context (i.e. *dēśya rāga, ghana rāga pañcaka*).

The selection given here represents all the major rāgas found in South Indian classical music. In order to cover the repertoire heard today to the greatest possible extent, whether performed by concert musicians or preserved through recordings of historical value, many popular, rare and 'mixed' rāgas are also covered here. The latter were mostly adopted from North Indian (Hindustānī) music, modified and popularized by composers of the past like Muttusvāmi Dīkṣitar and Tyāgarāja, or more recently by performing musicians and composers like Harikēsanallūr Mutthiah Bhāgavatar and Lālguḍi Jayarāmaṉ. Many of these *dēśya rāgas* have been assimilated to such a degree that their 'foreign' origins, although still discernible to music scholars, are immaterial to the minds of South Indian musicians who are proud of their tradition of open-mindedness towards other cultures.

Certain rāgas have to be grouped together in order to appreciate their aesthetic value or traditional significance (e.g. the group known as *ghana rāga*). There are also other factors that define modern usage of many rāgas, for instance the standardization brought about by curricula followed in educational institutions, the findings of musicologists, changing performance conventions, the tastes fostered by the electronic media, the wide dissemination of old and new recordings, and the feedback received in the process of intercultural exchange programmes. This means that the study of rāgas needs also to be approachable from different backgrounds and points of view. Traditional systems of rāga classification are now being viewed by many musicians and listeners as being either too vague (e.g. *ghana—naya—dēśya*), or too rigid (e.g. *mēḷakartā—janya*). Nevertheless, a Karnatic concert can be said to 'feel incomplete' if wholly devoid of a rāga which is associated with the traditional, albeit vague *rakti* category, be it in the form of an introductory *tāṉavarṇam*, or an elaborate *rāga ālāpana* for the main item.

Until recently, historical factors could be blamed for having prevented the formulation of a wholly consistent system of rāga classification. But with numerous published sources at their disposal, modern musicians and scholars have to be on their guard—what appears to be one and the same rāga, merely going by its name, may in fact denote two or more distinct melodic entities, just as most personal names apply to more than one person. This applies particularly to the differences which remain between several North and South Indian rāgas bearing the same name, irrespective of their common roots (i.e. the North Indian origins implied by the South Indian *dēśya* category). As a case in point, the name Dēvakriya refers to two distinct rāgas, not merely variants of the same rāga.

Some *janya rāgas* are listed under more than one *mēḷakartā* number in different sources in accordance with different expert opinions or traditions. Some alternative versions of *janya rāgas* are specifically associated with the tradition of Muttusvāmi Dīkṣitar (e.g. Dēvakriya, Dhanyāsi) who adhered to a nomenclature which deviates from that followed by most other traditions, notably that of Tyāgarāja.

Abbreviations, descriptive terms and categories pertaining to the rāgas listed in the rāga index and the corresponding transcriptions in staff notation (staves):

auḍava—*auḍava rāga* (*see* Stave 28); a rāga based on five notes (pentatonic), provided it takes the same notes (*svarasthāna*) in the ascending (*ārohaṇa*) and descending (*avarohaṇa*) course; the latter, being a 'mirror image', as it were, of the former is not shown in staff notation. The following rāgas belong to the *auḍava* category:
Amṛtavarṣiṇi, Bhūpāḷam, Dēvakriya, Dēvarañji (Dēvarañjini), Gambhīranāṭa,

Haṁsadhvani, Hindōḷam, Karṇāṭaka Śuddha Sāvēri, Madhyamāvati, Mēgharañjani, Mōhanam, Nāgasvarāvaḷi, Rēvagupti (Rēgupti), Rēvati, Śuddha Dhanyāsi, Śuddha Sāvēri, Udayaravicandrika, Valaji.

dēśya—*dēśya rāga* (*see* Staves 33 and 34); some rāgas are directly adopted from Hindustānī music (Hindustānī dēśya), and these are mostly associated with devotional and popular forms of music (e.g. Byāg); others have been fully assimilated for a long time (e.g. Saurāṣṭram).

dhaivatāntya—*dhaivatāntya rāga* (*see* Stave 35); a rāga in which no note higher than dhaivata should be touched.

Dīkṣ.-ēkaika—a rāga which is defined by a single composition (*ēkaika kṛti rāga*) by Muttusvāmi Dīkṣitar. Such *janya rāgas* are found in various categories (e.g. Dēvarañji, *auḍava*, *see* Stave 28). The following rāgas of this category have been included: Dēvarañji (*Namaste paradevate*, tisra ēka tāla), Jīvantika (*Bṛhadīśa kaṭākṣeṇa*, rūpaka tāla), Mādhavamanōhari (*Mahālakṣmī*, ādi tāla), Māhuri (*Māmava raghurāma*, miśra cāpu tāla), Pūrṇapañcamam (*Sādhujanacitta*, tripuṭa tāla), Śuddha Taraṅgiṇi (*Māye tvaṁ yāhi*, ādi tāla).

ghana—*ghana rāga* (*see* Stave 30); a rāga either belonging to the group of five *ghana rāgas* known as the *ghana rāga pañcaka*, or a secondary group known as the *dvitīya ghana rāga pañcaka*.

mēḷa—*mēḷakartā rāga* (*see* Staves 17 to 19); a reference scale which may also appear in other categories such as *rakti rāga* (e.g. Tōḍi = Hanumatōḍi).

niṣādāntya—*niṣādāntya rāga* (*see* Stave 35); a rāga in which no note higher than niṣāda should be touched: Cittarañjani, Dēvakriya, Nādanāmakriya, Nāgasvarāvaḷi in Kathakali music, Punnāgavarāḷi, Saindhavi, Śrutirañjani, Vasantavarāḷi.

pañcamāntya—*pañcamāntya rāga* (*see* Stave 35); a rāga in which no note higher than pañcama should be touched. Only one rāga of this type, namely Navarōj, is commonly heard.

pañcama varja—*pañcama varja rāga*; a rāga in which pañcama, the 5th note, must be avoided altogether. The following rāgas of this type are heard in the music and dance repertoire: Ābhōgi, Haṁsānandi, Hindōḷam, Jayamanohari, Lalita, Mēgharañjani, Rañjani, Ravicandrika, Śrīrañjani, Śuddha Tōḍi, Vasanta.

rakti—*rakti rāga* (*see* Staves 31 and 32); a rāga soliciting depth of feeling (*bhāva*), to be brought out by subtle phrases, and having scope for creative elaboration (*manodharma*).

ṣāḍava—*ṣāḍava-ṣāḍava rāga* (*see* Stave 29); a rāga based on six notes (hexatonic), provided it takes the same notes (*svarasthāna*) in the ascending and descending course; wherever the latter constitutes a mere reversal ('mirror image') of the former, it is not shown in staff notation.

Śāstri-ēkaika—a rāga which is defined by a single composition (*ēkaika kṛti rāga*) by Śyāmā Śāstri; Ciñtāmaṇi (*Dēvi brōva samayamidē*, ādi tāla) is the most prominent representative of this category (*see* Stave 21).

Tyāg.-ēkaika—a rāga which is defined by a single composition (*ēkaika kṛti rāga*) by Tyāgarāja; such *janya rāgas* are found in various categories (e.g. Candrajyōti, *ṣāḍava*, see Stave 29). The following rāgas belong to this category: Bhinnaṣaḍjam (*Sarivārilōna*, ādi tāla), Bindumāliṇi (*Entamuddō*, ādi tāla), Cittarañjani (*Nādatanumaniśam Śaṅkara*, ādi tāla), Dīpakam (*Kalalanērccina*, ādi tāla), Kaikavaśi (*Vācāmagōcaramē*, ādi tāla), Kalakaṇṭhi (*Śrījanaka tanayē*, ādi tāla), Kalānidhi (*Cinnanāḍēnācēyi,* ādi tāla), Kōkilavarāḷi (*Samukhāna nilva*, ādi tāla), Mañjari (*Paṭṭi viḍuvarādu*, ādi tāla), Nādacintāmaṇi (*Evarani nirṇayiñcirirā*, ādi tāla), Naḷinākānti (*Manavinālakiñca*, ādi tāla), Siddhasēna (*Evaraina lērā*, ādi tāla), Srutirañjani (*Ēdāri saṁcarimturā*, ādi tāla), Supradīpam (*Varaśikhi vāhana*, ādi tāla), Vasantavarāḷi (*Pāhi rāmadūta*, rūpaka tāla).

Tyāg.—a rāga either introduced or popularized by Tyāgarāja. The following rāgas belong to this category which also includes several *mēlakartā rāgas*: Candrajyōti, Ceñcukāmbhōji, Chāyānāṭa, Dēvakriya, Dhēnuka, Gaurīmanōhari, Harikāmbhōji, Jayantaśrī, Jiṅgla, Kalyāṇavasanta, Kāntāmaṇi, Kāpinārāyaṇi, Karṇāṭaka Behāg, Kharaharapriya, Kōkilapriya, Kuntaḷavarāḷi, Mānavati, Manōhari, Mārarañjani, Nāgānandini, Navarasa Kannaḍa, Rāmapriya, Ṛṣabhapriya, Sālagabhairavi, Sāramati, Sarasāṅgi, Sarasvati Manōhari, Siṁhavāhini, Śūlini, Sūryakāntam, Vācaspati, Vāgadhīśvari, Vakulābharaṇam, Vanaspati, Vijayaśrī, Vijayavasanta.

Note: Page numbers for text references and/or staves are given in brackets; bold page numbers refer to the (main) stave.

Ābhēri (= Bhimpalāsī, Bimplās; *see also* Karṇāṭaka Dēvagāndhāri), 22; Hindustānī dēśya*; stave 33* (116, **122**)

Ābhōgi, 22; auḍava, pañcama varja*; stave 28* (110, **114**, 116, 124)

Aeolian church mode, mēḷa 20*; stave 18* (**104**)

Āhiri, 8, 14; rakti*; stave 31* (**120**, 127)

Amṛtavarṣiṇi, 66; auḍava; *stave 28* (101, **114**)

Ānandabhairavi, 22, 20; rakti*; stave 31* (113, **120**, 124)

Āndhāḷi, 28*; stave 20* (**107**)

Āndōḷika, 28, 22*; stave 20* (**107**)

Ārabhi (*see* ghana rāga pañcaka), 29*; stave 30* (117, **118**)

Āsāvarī *ṭhāṭ* of Hindustānī music, mēḷa 20*; stave 18* (**104**)

Āsāvēri (Asāvēri), 8*; stave 20* (**107**, 126)

Aṭāṇa, 29; rakti*; stave 31* (89, **120**)

Bāgēśrī, 22; Hindustānī dēśya*; stave 33* (121, **122**)

Bahudāri, 28*; stave 20* (**107**, 116)

Balahaṁsa, 28*; stave 20* (**107**)

Baṅgāḷa (*see also* Śuddha Baṅgāḷa), 28, 29*; stave 20* (**107**)

Bauḷi (*see* dvitīya ghana rāga pañcaka), 15*; stave 30* (117, **118** 126)

Bēgaḍa (Byāgaḍā), 29; rakti*; stave 31* (77, **120**, 124, 126, 155)

Behāg *see* Byāg; *see also* Karṇāṭaka Behāg)

Bhairav *ṭhāṭ* of Hindustānī music, mēḷa 15*; stave 18* (**104**)

Bhairavam, 17*; stave 20* (**107**)

Bhairavī *ṭhāṭ* of Hindustānī music, mēḷa 8*; stave 17* (**103**)

Bhairavi, 20; rakti*; stave 31* (74, 75, 108, 114, **120**, 124, 126)

Bhairavi *see also* Ānandabhairavi, Naṭhabhairavi, Sālagabhairavi, Sindhubhairavi, Vasantabhairavi

Bhāṣāṅga Brindāvana Sāraṅga *see* Brindāvana Sāraṅga (Vṛndāvana Sāraṅga)

Bhāṣāṅga Kāpi *see* Hindustāni Kāpi

Bhavāni, 44; ṣāḍava*; stave 29* (**115**)

Bhavapriya, mēḷa 44*; stave 17* (**103**)

Bhimpalāsī (Bimplās) *see* Ābhēri

Bhinnaṣaḍjam, 9; Tyāg.-ēkaika*; stave 20* (**107**)

Bhūpāḷam, 15; auḍava*; stave 28* (**114**, 126)

Bhūṣāvaḷi, 64*; stave 20* (**107**)

Bhūṣāvati (= mēḷa 64 in the tradition of Muttusvāmi Dīkṣitar; in practice = Vācaspati), mēḷa 64; *stave 19* (**105**)

Bilahari, 29; rakti*; stave 31* (116, **120** 124, 126, 155)

Bilāval *ṭhāṭ* of Hindustānī music, mēḷa 29*; stave 19* (**105**)

Bimplās (Bhimpalāsī) *see* Ābhēri*; stave 33* (**122**)

Bindumāliṇi, 16; Tyāg.-ēkaika*; stave 20* (**107**)

Brindāvana Sāraṅga (= *Bhāṣāṅga* Brindāvana Sāraṅga, Vṛndāvana Sāraṅga; *see also* Karṇāṭaka Brindāvana Sāraṅga),

Glossary-cum-Index

English headwords and supplementary glossary entries are provided and cross-referred for the benefit of readers keen on appreciating the aesthetic, psychophysiological, religious, and metaphysical context to which many poet-composers have alluded in their lyrics. For the greatest among them, like Purandara Dāsa and Tyāgarāja, their insights and beliefs bestowed an ultimate purpose to their art: not merely to mitigate their listeners' sorrows by way of distraction, but to increase the very joy and dignity of human existence. In short, they sought to inspire all of us to get immersed in the study and practice of divine music. (See also dedication page). This ideal furthers, to the present day, a unique artistic project: the continuance of an ancient tradition of artistic excellence which boldly asserts itself in the *Nāṭya Śāstra* by redefining and sanctifying the arts as a 'fifth *Veda*', namely wisdom that is accessible to all of mankind.

Historical orientation is facilitated by a special glossary entry ('history of Karnatic music'); it connects the subjects and names covered in various other contexts—hence spread over many chapters, sections and alphabetical entries of this book (including the Glossary-cum-Index). This immense subject is expounded in some of the books, journals and periodicals listed in the Bibliography.

The following five sections of this book contain more information, arranged alphabetically, with further cross-references, and hence not covered again in the Glossary-cum-Index in order to avoid duplication:

Musical Forms (Concert, Dance and Didactic Music)—Chapter 17
Composers of South India—Chapter 18
Musical Signatures (*Mudrā*)—Chapter 19
Biographical Notes (Musicians and Music Scholars)
Alphabetical Index of Rāgas and Scales

Note: Chapter numbers (e.g. Ch. 10) indicate that a given topic or name either figures in the heading of a chapter or section, or provides the headword of an alphabetical entry in the aforementioned sections. (See also *List of Figures, Tables and Staves*). Individual page numbers are given immediately after the headword of an entry.

Long vowels 'e' and 'o' are generally not diacriticized in Sanskrit words as there are no short variants (see also *Guide to Pronunciation and Transliteration*); to facilitate correct pronunciation of all glossary entries, a few exceptions are made for those words and names that refer to a purely South Indian context (e.g. *Sōpānam*, *vāggēyakāra*).

abhaṅg 170
kīrtana with Marāṭhi lyrics (e.g. by Tukārām); introduced during Marāṭhā rule at Tañjāvūr; also sung by *bhajana* groups

Abhijñāna Śākuntalam (Sanskrit) 68
drama by Kālidāsa having Śakuntalā as its heroine; as the author's other works, it contains references to the feelings and emotional states (*bhāva*) evoked by music

Abhinavagupta
literary and aesthetic theorist (10th–11th *c*.); exponent of *Tantra* philosophy; commentator on the *Nāṭya Śāstra*; advocated the acceptance of *śānta rasa* as the ninth sentiment, and *bhakti rasa* as its accessory sentiment

abhinaya (Sanskrit) 170
facial and corporal expression of a sentiment in dance and drama (= Tamil *avinayanam*); mime based on the lyrics of a particular composition (e.g. a *padam*); the four conventional branches of *abhinaya* are (1) *āngika*, (2) *vācika*, (3) *āhārya*, and (4) *sātvika*
see also *jāvaḷi*, *pada*, *sañcāribhāva*

abhyāsa gāna (Sanskrit) 71, 81, Ch. 10
comprises graded music lessons (e.g. *alaṁkāram*, *saraḷi variśa*) and didactic compositions (e.g. *gītam*, *sulādi*, *svarajati*, *tānavarṇam*)
see *abhyāsa gānam*, Kuḍumiyāmalai, *mōrā*, *nōṭṭusvara sāhitya*, solfa
see also Purandara Dāsa, Wālājapet Kṛṣṇasvāmi Bhāgavatar

absolute
see *Brahman*, *dharma*, *mantra*, *Parabrahman*, *śruti*

abstract
see *gāyaki*, *viśeṣa prayoga*

ācārya (Sanskrit)
lit. a 'teacher, spiritual guide'; learned person or master
see also *guru*, *maṭha*, *Śaṅkarācārya*, teacher

accāmaram (Tamil)
dark, hard wood used for making the *nāgasvaram*

accent 78

accidental note
see *anyasvara*

accompaniment, accompanist 36, 41, 42, 47, 60, 160, Ch. 5, 15
see *pakkavādya*
see also drone, *eḍakka*, *kaccēri dharma*, *konnakkōl*, *kōvilpurappāḍu*, *mōrā*, *Sāmaveda*, *sarva vādya*, solo, *svara kalpana*, Vijayarāghava Nāyaka, *yālpāṇar*

acoustics 93

acting, mime
see *abhinaya*, *āhārya*, *āṭṭam*, *avinayanam*, dance, *harikathā kālakṣepam*, *nāṭya*, *nṛtya*, *sthānaprāpti*

aḍavu (Tamil) 43, 53, 133, 148, Ch. 17
basic unit of dance; a term probably derived from the Telugu word for 'feet'; comparable to a letter of the alphabet
see also *karaṇa*, *kōrvai*, *nṛtta*, *tīrmāṇam*

adbhuta (Sanskrit)
sentiment (*rasa*) associated with wonder
see also *navarasa*

ādhāra ṣaḍja (Sanskrit) 25, 38, 51, 54, 55, 70
any suitable pitch chosen by a musician as a basic note (tonic); by definition, it is always present, and in any rāga, but can be shifted temporarily to a higher pitch (i.e. *madhyama śruti*)
see also *avikṛta*, *śruti*

ādi (Sanskrit)
lit. 'first, primary, pre-eminent'

ādiantavandanam (Sanskrit)
brief dance item expressing respect for the earth (i.e. to sanctify the dance venue, convert it into a temple; make one's dance a form of worship)

Adicayapuram Sitarāmayyar 52

Ādi Śaṅkara (Śaṅkara, *Śaṅkarācārya*) 15
South Indian philosopher (AD 788–820/838?) and ascetic (*saṁnyāsin*) from Kālaḍī in central Kerala; his teachings and terminology continue to inform some of the more orthodox sections of South Indian society, notably many composers, musicians, and their audiences; revered as author of commentaries (*bhāṣyam*) on the *Bhagavad Gītā*, *Vedānta* and the

scriptures (*śruti*, i.e. the *Veda*); his influence is also felt on account of several popular works believed to have been inspired by him (e.g. *Bhāgavata Purāṇa*); the philosophical framework underlying this tradition is known as monism (*Advaita*) and partly based on the *Upaniṣad*; he and his followers further combined *Śaiva* traditions with other cults while advocating simplified rituals and certain reforms; challenged both Buddhism and the excesses then associated with some Hindu sects (e.g. *śākta*, *Tantra*, *kāpālika* worship); an ardent pilgrim of holy places (*kṣētra*, *tīrtha*), he established the spiritual centres (*maṭha*) at Badrināth (Himālaya), Purī (Orissa), Dvārakā (Gujarāt), and Śṛṅgēri (Karṇāṭaka); his 'illusion-doctrine' (*māyāvāda*) recognizes but one ultimate Reality who transcends all attributes (*Brahman*); only as far as involved in the phenomenal world, *Brahman* is perceived as the supreme God (Īśvara) who creates the universe in a playful manner (*līlā*), as a self-conscious yet desireless supreme being; the individualized 'soul' (*jīvātman*) realizes its true nature, namely its ultimate identity with *Brahman*, once it rises above all outward differences: 'one essence and no other' (*ekam evādvitīyam*); the remedy to the maladies that prevent the required realization, namely delusion (*māyā*) and ignorance (*avidyā*), is thus twofold: 'ordinary' understanding (*apara vidyā*) pertaining to the illusory nature of the world; and by transcending the bondage or limitations of our senses and reason, we can aspire towards the 'higher' knowledge (*para vidyā*) of *Brahman*

see also *bhakti*, *saṁsāra*, Śaṅkarācārya

ādi tāla 140, Fig. 32, 33, Tables 18, 20, 21, Staves 36, 38, 39

the most flexible and hence important tāla of Karnatic music (= *caturaśra jāti tripuṭa tāla*)

see also *oṉṟarai eḍuppu*

Aḍiyārkunallār, Aṭiyārkkunallār

chief commentator on the *Cilappatikāram*; expounds the intricacies of ancient Tamil music and dance

āḍu kaḷa makaḷ (Tamil)

female dancer; lit. 'daughter (*makaḷ*) of the dance (*āḍu*) platform (*kaḷa*)'

Advaita (Sanskrit) 72

philosophic concept of non-duality propagated by Ādi Śaṅkara and others see *Bhāgavata purāṇa*, *bhakti*

see also Acuta Dāsa, Rāmaliṅgasvāmi, Tyāgarāja, Vidyāraṇya

aerophones

wind instruments

see *vādya*

aesthetics 17, 22, 30, 31, 33, 36, 40, 47, 50, 59, 93, 101, 155, 160, 161, 164, Ch. 15

see also Abhinavagupta, *ālaṅkārika*, appreciation, *navarasa*, *rasa*

Africa 93

āgama 69

agattiyam, Agattiyar, Agastya 47

Agni purāṇa

see *Purāṇa*

agogic 133

by definition, the adjective 'agogic' refers to a barely measurable form of heightening the expressive quality in music; a subtle form of phrasing and accentuation achieved by delaying a note; features as part of a characteristic phrase (*sañcāra*) and some types of embellishment (*gamaka*); entails the conscious and temporary deviation from a chosen tempo (*kālapramāṇam*) or rhythmic pattern

see also *odukkal*, rubato

āhārya abhinaya (Sanskrit)

in drama, the expression (*abhinaya*) of a person's characteristics, or those of any other being (divine, demonic, or animal) by outward means, such as costume, make-up, hairstyle, accessories, and jewellery

āhata (Sanskrit)

an embellishment (*gamaka*) listed among the *daśavidha gamaka*; consists of pairs of two adjacent notes in an

ascending series (e.g. *sa-ri, ri-ga, ga-ma, ma-pa*)
see also *tripuccha*
āhata nāda (Sanskrit)
sound which is 'struck' (i.e. audible, as in music)
see *nāda*
see also *anāhata nāda*
ahiṁsā (Sanskrit)
lit. 'harmlessness'; the principle of non-violence advocated by most Indian philosophers and all saints
see also Rāmaliṅgasvāmi
AIR 79, 224
'All India Radio', the national radio corporation of India
aja (Sanskrit)
lit. 'goat'
see *gāndhāra* (*ga*)
see also animal imagery
ājñā (Sanskrit) Fig. 25
sixth *cakra* between the eyebrows ('third eye'); visualized as having bright white colour and a lotus with a thousand petals
Akalanka 96
author of the *Saṅgītasāra Saṁgraha*; advocated 24 micro-intervals (*śruti*)
akāra, *akāra sādhakam* (Sanskrit)
vocal exercises based on vowel '*a*' rather than syllables or words; can also be varied by substituting '*a*' with the other vowels (*i, u, e, o, m,* hence *ikāram, ukāram* etc.)
see also *briga*, *mantra*
ākāśa (Sanskrit)
lit. 'sky, ether, space, quality of sound, Brahmā'; the substance permeating the universe; the first element; associated with hearing
see also *mahābhūta*, *nāda*, Naṭarāja, sound
akṣara (Sanskrit)
lit. 'syllable'; (1) unit of a tāla; every count, 'beat' or basic unit (= *akṣara kāla*) to be reckoned for a *tāla* (= *kriyā*); the total number of *akṣara* per tāla cycle (*āvarta*) is defined by the divisions of a tāla (*aṅga*) as well as its *jāti* variety (e.g. *miśra jāti jhampa tāla* = 10 *akṣarakāla*); can be sub-divided into five different *gati* varieties (= *naḍai*); (2) not to be confused with the usage found in older texts where *akṣara* refers to a *gati* variety or *naḍai* (e.g. *caturaśra gati* = four *akṣara* per *mātrā*); (3) a combination of letters (*saṁkhyākṣara*); used in the *kaṭapayādi sūtra*; serves to memorize the serial number of a *mēḷakartā rāga*; this also reveals its position and tonal structure
see *jati, kriyā, mātrā, naḍai, sūḷādi sapta tāla, svarākṣara*
see also *gatibheda, mantra, svarākṣara*
akṣara kāla (Sanskrit) 140
long or short duration of a count or time-unit (*akṣara*); determines the speed or tempo (*kāla*) of music
see also *kriyā*
ākṣiptika, *āyittam* (Sanskrit)
introductory part of a rāga *ālāpana*
alagu (Tamil)
lit. '(minimum) unit of measurement'; a microtonal step (= *māttirai, śruti*)
alaṁkāram, *alaṅkāra* (Sanskrit) 71, 73, 80, 128, 138, 142, 172, Ch. 17, Staves 8, 9–15
set of seven melodic exercises set to seven different tālas (*sūḷādi saptatāla*)
see *abhyāsa gāna*
see also *dhaivata* (*dha*)
ālaṅkārika (Sanskrit)
literary scholar
see *navarasa*
ālāpana (Sanskrit) 13, 37, 77, 80, 113, 117, 119, 127, 155, 157, 159, 172, Ch. 17
exposition of a particular rāga (= *rāga ālāpana*, *rāgam*); based on familiar combinations of phrases (*sañcāra*); often modelled on ideas developed in a composition such as a *tānavarṇam*
see also *gāyaki, ghana rāga, makariṇi, muktāyi, patyam*
alārippu (Tamil) 173, Ch. 17
lit. 'blossoming'; the opening item of a *Bharata nāṭyam* performance
see also *nṛtta*
Ālattūr Brothers 156
Alexander the Great 12
alien notes
see *anyasvara*

alpatva, alpa (Sanskrit) 114, 124
lit. 'a note (*svara*) applied sparingly' (e.g. a note described as *vivādī*)
see also *bahutva*
alphabet (Sanskrit) Tables 1, 11
alphabet (Tamil, Grantha) Table 2
alpha-numerical mnemonics 97, Ch. 12
see also *kaṭapayādi sūtra*, mnemonics, mnemonic svara syllables
Ālvār 14, 27, 34
Tamil poets and mystics
see also *Pallava*
Amarasiṁha
Marāṭhā ruler at Tañjāvūr (1787–98); composer of Marāṭhi songs; after his stepbrother, Śarabhōjī II, ascended the throne, Amarasiṁha established his court at Tiruvidaimarudur; spent liberally on the arts despite objections from a dominant East India Company; associated with renowned musicians and composers like Ghanam Kṛṣṇayya and Gopālakṛṣṇa Bhārati
Ambujam Krishna 153
Amir Khusro 14
amplification, loudness 20, 55, 60, 77
aṁśa svara (Sanskrit) 77, 159
lit. 'share, part, portion, inheritance; partial incarnation (*aṁśa avatāra*)'; refers to the most prominent note among the *jīva svaras* of a rāga; the note on which a soloist can linger to bring out its unique beauty (*rāga rūpa*) or pause (e.g. during a *rāga ālāpana, niraval*)
see also *bahutva*
anāgata eḍuppu, anāgata graha 134, 137, Staves 36, 37, 39
refers to the starting point of a theme at a particular point (*iḍam*), namely after beginning of the tāla cycle (*samam*); the four common varieties are (1), a 'a quarter' (*kāliḍam*), (2), 'half' (*araiyiḍam* = two quarters), (3), 'three quarters' (*mukkāliḍam*), (4) '1½' counting units (*onṟarai eḍuppu* = six quarters)
see also *atīta eḍuppu, sama eḍuppu*
anāhata (Sanskrit)
lit. 'unbeaten, new, unbleached'
anāhata cakra (Sanskrit) Fig. 25
fourth *cakra* near the heart; visualized as having grey colour and a lotus with twelve petals
see also *hṛd*
anāhata nāda (Sanskrit)
lit. 'unstruck' (i.e. 'inaudible sound'); the cosmic music associated with the *anāhata cakra*; believed to be perceived by an accomplished *yogī*
see also *āhata nāda*
see nāda
anala (Sanskrit) 23
lit. 'fire'
Analysis of Beauty
see William Hogarth
anaṁta (Sanskrit) 118, 159
lit. 'infinite, boundless'; (1) epithet of Parabrahma, Śiva, Kṛṣṇa, Viṣṇu and the serpent Śeṣa on which he rests; (2) the syllables sung and re-arranged during *tāṉam*
ānanda (Sanskrit) 87
lit. 'happiness, joy, delight, pleasure; God, Supreme Spirit (= *Brahman*, Śiva)'
anatomy
see human anatomy
Aṉayampaṭṭi S. Daṇḍapāṇi 19, 55
ancient
see antiquity
Āṇḍāḷ
young authoress of a collection of Tamil poetry (*Tiruppāvai*); hails the concept of *madhurabhakti*
Andhra Pradesh [Āndhra Pradēsh] 11, 18, 224, Fig. 26
South Indian state where Telugu is spoken
see also Bhadrācala Rāmdās
āndoḷa, āndoḷita (Sanskrit)
an embellishment (*gamaka*) listed among the *daśavidha gamaka*; consists of a 'swinging' between two notes (i.e. from an extended basic note, there is a glide to a higher note, and an oscillation between both notes)
see also *Sōpānam*
aṅga, aṅgam (Sanskrit) 50, 138
lit. 'limb, part'; (1) the section of a composition (i.e. *pallavi, anupallavi, caraṇam*); (2) a part of a musical instrument (e.g. resonator); (3) the section of a tāla (*jāti*, i.e. *drutam*,

anudrutam, laghu); (4) one among the ten features of tāla (*tāla daśa prāṇa*)
see also *prabandha*, *sūḷādi sapta tāla*

āṅgika abhinaya (Sanskrit)
dramatic expression (*abhinaya*), by way of gestures, movements of body or limbs, to represent a character

animal imagery 56, 60, Ch. 6, Fig. 24, Tables 6, 8
see also *Bhāgavata purāṇa*, chimera, *Daśāvatārā*, *Nārada purāṇa*
see also *aja*, *aśva*, *aṁśa*, birds, *paśu*, *yāḷi*

āñjali
gesture (*mudrā*) used in greeting
see also *namaskāra*

Āñjaneya (Sanskrit)
see Hanūmān

aṅkitam (Sanskrit)
lit. 'marked' (*aṅkita*)
see *mudrā*

Annamācārya 162

anonymous
see Nārada, *Nāṭya Śāstra*

antarā (Sanskrit)
second section in *dhrupad* music

antara gāndhāra (Sanskrit)
highest variant of the third scale degree (= *tīvra ga*); mnemonic syllable '*gu*'

antara mārga (Sanskrit)
hinting of another rāga by way of adding an unusual note (*anyasvara*); one among the thirteen ancient rāga features (*trayodaśa lakṣaṇa lakṣaṇa*)
see also *viśeṣa prayoga*

antiquity, ancient civilization 12, 14, 15, 33, 46, 58, 60, 67, 68, 71, 88, 93, 94, 119, 166
see also archaeology, China, Dattilam, epigraphy, Roman, *Hellenism*, *ṛṣi*, *śruti* , *Veda*

anudātta (Sanskrit) 119
lowest of three notes used in vedic chanting

anudrutam (Sanskrit) 128, Table 12
an element or 'limb' (*aṅga*); a fixed section (*aṅga*) of some tālas (i.e. mainly *miśra jāti jhampa tāla*); comprises one counting unit (*akṣarakāla*, *kriyā*); indicated by a clap; represented by symbol 'U'

anumandra sthāyī (Sanskrit) 61
lowest register (octave) below *mandra sthāyī*; written with two dots below each *svara* letter
see also *tristhāyī*

anupallavi (Sanskrit)
middle section (i.e. second theme) of a composition (e.g. *kṛti*, *varṇam*); followed by a *caraṇam*
see also *aṟudi*, *rāgam tānam pallavi*, *saṅgati*

anusāraṇi (Tamil)
(1) the third out of four strings of a *tambūrā*; mostly tuned to the tonic or basic note (*ādhāra ṣaḍja*) as the second string (*sāraṇi*); (2) the upper secondary string (*pakka sāraṇi*) of a *vīṇā*
see also *madhyama śruti*

anusvara (Sanskrit)· 74, 77, 78, 96, Ch. 1, Stave 28
an auxiliary note attached to a principal note (*svara*); a combination of several auxiliary notes is also the basis for some types of embellishments (*gamaka*)

anuvādi (Sanskrit)
an assonant note; the notes of a rāga that are neither classified as *vādī*, *saṁvādi* nor *vivādī*
see also *saṁvādi*, *vādī*, *vivādī*

anya (Sanskrit)
lit. 'different, extraordinary, strange'

anya rāga kāku, *anya rāgaja*
see *kāku*

anyasvara (Sanskrit) 106, 108, 110. 113, 114, 124, Ch. 1
an 'alien' or accidental note found in the *bhāṣāṅga* type of rāga
see also *antara mārga*, *viśeṣa*

āpas (Sanskrit)
lit. 'water, sin'
see *mahābhūta*

Appar (Appar Svāmigaḷ)
Tamil *Śaiva* saint; one of the three authors referred to as 'Trinity' (*mūvar*) of the *Tēvāram* hymns (approx. 7th *c.* AD); also known as Vāgīśa and Tirunāvukkarasar (Nāvukkarasar means 'king of bards' or 'king of tongues'); an elder contemporary of Tiruñāṉa Saṁbandar

appeal 10
see emotion, *rasa*
appreciation 22, 69
see *rasika*, *sahṛdaya*
see also aesthetics, patrons, psyche
apsara (Sanskrit) 87
female divine being, nymph
apūrva sañcāra (Sanskrit)
lit. a 'rare (*apūrva*) phrase (*sañcāra*)' which is characteristic of a particular rāga
see also *alpatva*, *kaṭakam*, *tāna pustaka*, *viśeṣa prayoga*
Arabs 10, 14
see also *sūfi*
ārādhana (Sanskrit)
lit. 'adoration; honoring, pleasing'
see Tiruvaiyāru, *uñchavṛtti*
araiyiḍam (Tamil) 134, Stave 36
starting the theme at a point which is set two quarters or 'half' (*arai*) a beat or two *mātrā* after the start of the tāla cycle (*samam*); *a* variant of *anāgata eḍuppu*
see also *eḍuppu*, *iḍam*
araṅgēṟṟam (Tamil) 80
first public music or dance performance (debut)
āratī (Sanskrit)
see *pūjā*
archaeology 10, 11, 14
see also Wheeler, Sir Mortimer
architecture 69
ardhamaṇḍalī Fig. 8
basic posture of a *Bharata nāṭyam* dancer (from Sanskrit *ardha*, 'half, i.e. half seated)
see also *aḍavu*, *maṇḍala*
Arikkamēṭṭu 11
an ancient Roman settlement near Pondicherry
Ariyakkuḍi Ramanuja Ayyangar 157, 164
āroha (Sanskrit)
an embellishing phrase (*gamaka*) which takes the form of an ascending series of notes
see *daśavidha gamaka*
see also *avaroha*
ārohaṇa (Sanskrit) 71
ascending series of notes within a scale or rāga
see also *avarohaṇa*, chromatic scale
ārohaṇa-avarohaṇa (Sanskrit) 73, 77, 96, 118, 126
an ascending and descending series of notes used to characterize a particular rāga
see also *ālāpana*, *rāga rūpa*, *vakra rāga*, *viśeṣa prayoga*
art, artists 29, Ch. 3
see *kalā*
see also *aṟubattu nāṉgu kalaigaḷ*, *catuṣṣaṣṭi kalā*, *gāndharva*, *isai*, Kalākshētra, *Mōkṣamu galadā*, *rasika*, *sahṛdaya*, *saṅgīta*, synaesthesia
artha (Sanskrit)
see *puruṣārtha*
aṟubattu nāṉgu kalaigaḷ (Tamil) 35
the 64 arts listed in Tamil and Sanskrit literature, which include dance, vocal, and instrumental music
see also *catuṣṣaṣṭi kalā*
aṟudi (Tamil) 148, Ch. 14, Table 20
lit. 'final'; a stop (1) a rhythmic conclusion or ending phrase (= *tīrmāṇam*); played by a percussionist (e.g. *mṛdaṅgam*); concludes one section of a composition and leads to the next (e.g. from *pallavi* to *anupallavi*); (2) the pivotal note (= *padagarbha*) which is elongated (*kārvai*) and corresponds to a stressed text syllable; required for the theme of a *pallavi*
see also *uttarāṅga*
Aruṇagirināthar 162
asaṁpūrṇa rāga (Sanskrit) 95, 99, 123
lit. 'not complete'; a scale or, in most cases, a *janya rāga* with less than seven notes in either ascending order (*ārohaṇa*), descending order (*avarohaṇa*), or both (*ārohaṇa-avarohaṇa*)
see also *rāgāṅga rāga*
asaṁpūrṇa paddhati (Sanskrit)
system of scales based on *asaṁpūrṇa mēḷa rāgas* which was established by Veṅkaṭamakhi and followed by Muttusvāmi Dīkṣitar and his tradition; based on the concept of *asaṁpūrṇa paddhati*, whereas Tyāgarāja followed the so-called *saṁpūrṇa paddhati*

see Gōvinda
see also Dhautapañcama, Phenadyuti
āsanam (Sanskrit)
lit. 'seat, posture'
see *yoga*
ascending
see *āhata*, *āroha*, *ārohaṇa*, *asaṁpūrṇa*, *krama*, *saṁpūrṇa*, *tripuccha*
Asia 12, 14, 16, 93
see also China, history of Karnatic music
āśrama (Sanskrit)
one of the four stages in the life (*caturāśramam*) of a religious citizen according to ancient Hindu authorities: (1) student (*brahmacārī*); disciple of a spiritual teacher (*guru*); (2) householder; head of the family (*gṛhastha*); (3) hermit dwelling in the forest (*vānaprastha*); (4) homeless mendicant (*saṁnyāsin*) preparing for the final goal of existence (*mokṣa*); as other orthodox beliefs and customs, the *caturāśramam* system has been declared redundant for a person who has control over his mind, by Tyāgarāja (e.g. in his *kṛti*, Manasusvādhīnamaina), and Ramana Maharshi
assonant note
see *anuvādī*
aṣṭapadi (Sanskrit) 174, Ch. 17
lit. 'eight padas' (verses); the *Gītagovinda* consists of 24 *aṣṭapadi* (i.e. songs with eight verses each)
see also Jayadeva, *meṭṭu*, D. Pattammal, *śṛṅgāra*
āsthāna vidvān (Sanskrit)
lit. a learned musician (*vidvān*); attached to a 'place' (*sthāna*) or 'assembly' (*āsthāna*, hence also *samasthāna vidvān*); (1) formerly a court musician (e.g. the late *vaiṇika* M.A. Kalyāṇakrishna Bhāgavatar is referred to as *Āsthāna Vidvān* of Travancore Palace); (2) a title bestowed by a religious centre (*maṭha*) or organization (e.g. Semmaṅguḍi Śrīnivāsa Iyer, '*Āsthāna Vidvān* and *Saptagiri Saṅgīta Vidvān Maṇi* of the Tirumalai Tirupathi Devastanams')
see also Mysore Sadāśiva Rao, Tañjāvūr Quartette
aṣṭottaraśatta (Sanskrit)
108 rāgas and tālas, a *rāga tāla mālikā* of Rāmasvāmi Dīkṣitar
asura (Sanskrit) 87
demon or evil character, often endowed with supernatural powers and defeated by the divine incarnations of Viṣṇu and the heroes whose deeds are described in the epics (*Rāmāyaṇa*, *Mahābhārata*), religious lore (*Purāṇa*), and compositions (e.g. the *kṛti* songs of Tyāgarāja)
see also *daśāvatārā*, *deva*
aśva (Sanskrit)
horse; symbolizes a king's sovereign power
see *dhaivata* (*dha*)
see also animal imagery
aṭa tāla Stave 14; Table 19
see *khaṇḍa jāti aṭa tāla*
see also *tāṉavarṇam*
aṭa tāla varṇam
see *tāṉavarṇam*
see also Mysore Śēṣanna, Paccimiriyam Āḍiappayya
Atharvaveda (Sanskrit)
see *Veda*
atīta eḍuppu, *atīta graha* 134, 137, Stave 38
refers to the starting point of a theme at a particular point (*iḍam*), namely before beginning of the tāla cycle (*samam*)
see also *sama eḍuppu*, *anāgata eḍuppu*
ati tāra sthāyī (Sanskrit) 61
register (octave) above *tāra sthāyī*; written with two dots above each *svara* letter
see also *tristhāyī*
ātman (Sanskrit)
lit. 'individual soul, Self, *Brahman*, supreme spirit; essence, nature'; the 'true self' of many Indian doctrines; attained by way of self-realization; the purpose of religious practice (*sādhanā*, *yoga*); hence described as being eternal, immortal, distinct from the appearance or transitory nature of body and senses (*saṁsāra*)
see also *jīvātman*, *Parabrahman*

āṭṭam (Tamil) 166
lit. 'dance'; also dance-drama (e.g. *Mōhiniyāṭṭam*)
see *sadir āṭṭam*
Attar, Farid Ud-Din 24
sūfī poet (b. 1120); author of The *Conference of the Birds*
auḍava-auḍava rāga 95, 109, 117, 120, 123, Stave 28
rāga based on five notes
see also *sampūrṇa*
audible
see *āhata nāda, saśabda kriyā*
see also *anāhata nāda*
audience, listening 20, 22, 23, 36, 52, 60, 65, 72, 80, 110, 116, 117, 119, 133, 155, 156, 157, 158, 164, 165
see also ear, *rasika, sahṛdaya*
augmented notes Table 10
auspiciousness 12, 29, 116, 168
see also *maṅgaḷam, maṅgaḷa vādya, nitya sumaṅgaḷi, Tiru*
authenticity 10, 158, 162, Ch. 15
see also *bāṇī, pāṭhāntara, sampradāya*
author
see commentaries, composers, *lakṣaṇakāra*, poets, theorists
avanaddha vādya (Sanskrit) 36
membranophone or drum
see *vādya*
avaroha (Sanskrit)
an embellishing phrase (*gamaka*) which takes the form of a descending series of note
see *daśavidha gamaka*
see also *āroha*
avarohaṇa (Sanskrit) 71
descending series of notes within a scale or rāga
see also *ārohaṇa*, chromatic scale
āvarta, tāla āvartana (Sanskrit) 53, 138, 140, 148, 155
one complete cycle of a tāla; comprises all its divisions (*aṅga*, e.g. *laghu, drutam*); calculated in terms of basic units, counts or beats (*akṣarakāla, kriyā*) as well as subdivisions of these units (*gati, mātrā*)
avatāra (Sanskrit)
lit. 'descent'; an incarnation of the supreme godhead; Rāma and Kṛṣṇa are the most important among the ten *avatāras* of Viṣṇu whose divine interventions form the basis of numerous songs and dance compositions
see *Daśāvatārā*
avidyā (Sanskrit) 27
lit. 'illusion, (spiritual) ignorance, folly'
see also *māyā, vidyā*, Śaṅkara
avikṛta (Sanskrit) 71
lit. 'not changed'; the immutability of two notes, namely *ṣaḍja* and *pañcama*, is a basic convention of the modern *mēḷakartā rāga* system; in a *janya rāga*, *pañcama* can be deleted but not modified
see also *ādhāra ṣaḍja, vikṛta svara*
avinayanam (Tamil)
mime
see *abhinaya*
Āvuḍaiyārkōvil (Āvuḍaiyārkoil)
temple famous for its musical tradition
Āvuḍaiyārkōvil Harihara Bhāgavatar (*gettuvādyam, jalataraṅgam*) 19
Ayōdhya
capital of Rāma
see also Mārgadarśī Śēṣayyaṅgār
ayurveda 59
indigenous tradition of medicine and healing methods cultivated in India and Sri Lanka
Ayyaṅgār (= Iyengar)
an honorific added to the names of some (male) *Vaiṣṇava* brahmins
Ayyar (= Iyer)
an honorific added to the names of some (male) brahmins.
bagpipe (*turutti*)
see *cinna mēḷam*
bahutva (Sanskrit) 124
lit. 'a note (*svara*) applied abundantly (*bahu*)'; e.g. an *amśa svara*
see also *alpa*
Bālachander, S. 165
Bālagōpāl, C.K. Fig. 11, 13
Bālakrishna Śāstrigaḷ 170
Bālamuraḷī Krishna 35, 61, 127, 165
Bālasarasvati, T. 167
Bālasubrahmaṇyam, G.N. 156
Bālusvāmi Dīkṣitar 53

to one of the eight terrifying forms of Śiva (Bhairava)
see also *śakti*

bhajan, bhajana (Sanskrit) 53, 156, 161, 170, Fig. 6
lit. 'adoration, sharing, service'; (1) the practice of congregational singing as member of a regular group (*goṣṭhi*); also a tradition (*bhajana paddhati*) associated with composers like Mārgadarśī Śēṣayyaṅgār, Nārāyaṇa Tīrtha, Pāpanāsam Śivan, and Tyāgarāja; (2) simple devotional songs with Hindi lyrics; similar to the South Indian *kīrtana* (e.g. *abhaṅg*); often set to the popular tunes (*varṇameṭṭu*) associated with some rāgas; many are also set to *dēśya* rāgas

bhakta (Sanskrit)
lit. 'devotee, votary'; Rāma is worshipped by a Rāma *bhakta* (e.g. Tyāgarāja); this relationship is often expressed by the suffix '*-dāsa*' (e.g. Bhadrācala Rāmadāsa, Purandara Dāsa)
see also *bhāgavata mēḷam, iṣṭadevatā, pūjā*

bhakti (Sanskrit) 14, 16, 24, 31, 58, 60, 64, 72, 157, 168
lit. 'devotion'; from *bhaj* ('to grant, cultivate, serve, adore'); (1) combined with the erotic sentiment (*śṛṅgāra*), *bhakti* or longing for the Divine, forms the main theme of lyrics in Karnatic music (*nāyaka nāyikā bhāva* or *madhurabhakti*); (2) an accessory sentiment (*rasa*) in aesthetic theory (e.g. Abhinavagupta); (3) the medieval movement of mystics traced back to the Ālvār (*Vaiṣṇava* poets) and Nāyanmār (*Śaiva* poets) of Tamil Nadu, and continued by the Haridāsa movement of Karnataka; mainly due to the popularity and charm of the stories about Kṛṣṇa's childhood and youth as narrated in the *Bhāgavata purāṇa*, the concept of *bhakti* spread all over and beyond India
see also Āṇḍāḷ, history of Karnatic music, *jīvātman*, Kṣētrajña, *līlā*, Māṇikkavācakar, *navarasa*, *Paripāḍal*, *Prahlāda Bhakti Vijayam*, *sūfi*, Tyāgarāja, *Vaiṣṇava*, *yoga*

bhakti rasa (Sanskrit)
tenth sentiment (*rasa*) associated with devotion
see also *navarasa*

Bhāṇḍīra
colloquial Sanskrit (*Prākrit*) used in some devotional songs to describe the flute of Kṛṣṇa and the *rāsakrīḍā* dance of the *gopīs*

Bhārat 167
official name for the modern Indian state

bha-ra-ta 169
statement (of uncertain origin), now often used to define and recall the three primary aspects of dance and music (hence '*Bharata nāṭyam*')

Bharata, Bharata Muni 167, Fig. 2
lit. 'actor'; also a personal name (e.g. a brother of Rāma); the author(s) to whom the *Nāṭya Śāstra* is ascribed

Bharatam 167

Bharata nāṭyam 43, 47, 166–70, Ch. 16, Fig. 8
principal form of classical South Indian dance; many of its poses (*karaṇa*) are seen in, or inspired by *Cōla* iconography
see also *Bṛhadīśvara*, *mārgam*, *sadir*

Bhārati, Bhāratiyar Ch. 16, 18
see Subrahmaṇya Bhārati

bhāṣāṅga rāga (Sanskrit) 95, 110, 124, Ch. 13
a type of *janya rāga*; has an additional or 'alien' note (*anyasvara*) which does not belong to its parental scale (*mēḷakartā rāga*)
see also mnemonic svara syllables, *upāṅga rāga*

bhaṣyam (Sanskrit)
lit. 'speaking, exposition, explanation'; a commentary on religious texts (e.g. Ādi Śaṅkara on the *Bhagavad Gītā*) or technical subjects (by Patañjali on Pāṇini's *sūtras*)
see also commentaries

Bhāṭkhaṇḍe, V.N.
North Indian musicologist and theorist, educationist, reformer (1860–1936) credited with shaping Hindustānī music as it is known today through his theoretical and historical studies,

criticism, text books, institutional syllabi); consolidated Hindustānī music theory (e.g. *ṭhāṭ*) on the basis of his studies of the *mēḷakartā rāga* (*mēḷa-janya rāga*) system during travels to the South
see also *Hindustānī saṅgīt*, History of Karnatic music, *rāga rāgiṇī*

bhāva (Sanskrit) 10, 33, 37, 59, 60, 65, 89, 133, 154, 156, 168, 169
lit. 'feeling, emotion, sentiment, sincerity, devotion, love'; (1) a particular emotion underlying a *rāga* (*rāga bhāva*), drama and dance (*sthāyibhāva*), song and poetry (*sāhitya bhāva*); (2) the quality of expressiveness displayed during a music or dance performance
see also *gāna kāla*, *gāyaki*, *kāku*, *navarasa*, *nāyaka nāyikā bhāva*, *rasa*, Subrahmaṇya Bhārati, Tyāgarāja, *vibhāva*, voice culture, *vyabhicāribhāva*

bhayānaka (Sanskrit)
sentiment (*rasa*) associated with fear
see also *navarasa*

bheda (Sanskrit)
literally, 'change, difference, variety'; (1) *gatibheda*, the substitution of one type of rhythmic subdivision (*gati* or *naḍai*) for another; (2) *graha bheda*, *śruti bheda* and *svara bheda* denote a shift of the first note or tonic to another scale degree (e.g. *ṛṣabha* becomes *ṣaḍja*); in earlier times of history, a method for arriving at new musical modes (*mūrchanā*); in modern practice, applied sparingly to surprise listeners within a given rāga by creating the fleeting impression of another rāga; achieved by way of shifting the underlying scale patterns

bībhatsa (Sanskrit)
sentiment (*rasa*) associated with disgust
see also *navarasa*

bifurcation
see *komal-tīvra*, *Saṅgīta Ratnākara*

bijākṣara (Sanskrit)
monosyllabic *mantra*; mystical 'seed' sound
see also *akṣara*

bird 34, 61
in mythology, birds are divine messengers and know secrets rarely revealed to man
see also animal imagery, *haṁsa*, cuckoo, heron, peacock

birkā
see *briga*

black
see colour
see also *karaṇai*

bliss 160
see *mokṣa*, *mūlādhāra*, *nirvāṇa*, *yoga*
see also joy

book, manual, manuscript, publication 157, 163, 165
see history of Karnatic music, *kaṭakam*, *khaṇḍa*, Sarasvatī Mahāl Library, *tāna pustaka*, theorist, treatise

bowed, bowing
see *svarabhat*, *svaravil*

Brahmā (Sanskrit) 29, 64
Creator personified and represented in iconography and literature (hence masculine); springs from the lotus in the navel of Viṣṇu (= *Padmanābha*); his consort is Sarasvatī
see also *Nādabrahmā*
see also *ākāśa*, *Brahman*, Īśvara

brahmacārī (Sanskrit)
first stage in the life (student)
see *āśrama*

Brahman (Sanskrit) 30, 72
lit. 'Supreme Spirit' (= *ānanda*, *paramātman*); the transcendent and immanent Absolute without attribute (hence neuter)
see also Ādi Śaṅkara, *ātman*, Īśvara, *jīvātman*, *mokṣa*, *Parabrahman*

brāhmaṇa (Sanskrit)
brahmin; a member of a priestly class

Brahmā purāṇa
see *guṇa*, *Purāṇa*

brahmotsavam (Sanskrit) 35, 44
main annual festival (*utsava*) of a temple (*kōvil*)
see also *kōvilpurappāḍu*, *mēḷam*, *pañcavādya*

breath, breath control 65, 66
see *prāṇa*, *prāṇāyāma*

see also diaphragm, *mokṣa*, *maṇipūra*, *nābhi*, *nāda*, *Tantra*, voice culture
Bṛhaddeśī 11, 88, 91
work by Mataṅga (5th c. AD); the first treatise to employ the word *rāga* as a musical term (*rañjayate iti rāgaha*, 'that which delights')
see also *rāga*
Bṛhaddhvani (Sanskrit)
lit. 'large, broad or extensive (*bṛhat*) sound (*dhvani*)'; the *Research and Training Centre for Musics of the World* founded by Dr Kāraikkuḍi S. Subramaṇian in Chennai
see also history
Bṛhadīśvara (Sanskrit)
the great Śiva temple at Tañjāvūr; famous for its grandeur and the quality of its paintings; during the *Cōḻa* period, a major centre of dance; the dance style now known as *Bharata nāṭyam* is said to have evolved and flourished in it until the early colonial period; previously endowed with several hundred resident dancers (*dēvadāsi*, *rājādāsi*)
see also Rājārājā I
bridge
see *meṭṭu*, *vīṇā*
brief
see short
briga, *birkā* 37, 54
rapid passages of notes (*svara*, *sañcāra*); possibly derived from the Sanskrit root *bhrig* (lit. 'crackling sound of fire, flame glittering, shining'; mostly in the form of vowels (*akāram*); often rendered during the concluding phase of an *ālāpana*
Brindavan (Vṛndāvana)
town in North Indian associated with the *Vaiṣṇava* cult of Kṛṣṇa and Rādhā
British 10
broadcast 18, 126, 161, 163, 164, Ch. 15
see also AIR, Doordarshan
Brōvabhāramā 116
Budalūr Krishnamūrti Śāstrigaḷ 43
Buddha *avatāra* (Sanskrit)
Buddha being regarded as the ninth incarnation of Viṣṇu
see *Daśāvatārā*
Buddhism 11, 12, 67
see also China, Śaṅkara, history of Karnatic music, *Maṇimēgalai*
bull
see *go*
cakra (Sanskrit) 65, 95, Fig. 25
lit. 'wheel, discus' (i.e. the weapon in depictions of Viṣṇu); (1) a group of six out of 72 scales (*mēḷakartā rāga*); all 72 are included in the composition known as *mēḷa rāga mālikā cakra*; (2) in the *Śaivite* tradition of *Tantra*, the psychophysiological conception of the human body refers to seven energy centres or *cakras*, namely *mūlādhāra* (the lowest), *svādiṣṭhāna*, *maṇipūra*, *anāhata*, *viśuddha*, *ājñā*, and *sahasrāra* (the highest); each *cakra* is visualized as having a particular colour, and as a lotus with a specific number of petals
see also *Kuṇḍalinī*, voice
Cālamēla 116
calculation 49, 70, 71, 72, 140
see *āvarta*, *kuraippu*, microtone, *miśra*, *prastāra*
calm, quiet 66
see *guṇa*, *navarasa*
Cāḷukya 69
Campbell, Joseph 22
American writer on mythology (1904–88; *The Hero with a Thousand Faces*; *The Masks of God*); translated and edited the *Upaniṣads* and *The Gospel of Sri Ramakrishna* with Swami Nikhilananda; published the works of Heinrich Zimmer, the German-born indologist (e.g *Philosophies of India*, *The Art of Indian Asia*)
canda
see *sandam*
Candra Gupta II 67
caṅgam
see *śaṅgam*
cāpu tāla
see *miśra cāpu tāla*, *khaṇḍa cāpu tāla*
caraṇa, *caraṇam* (Sanskrit)
lit. 'the single line of a stanza; foot, support, accomplishment'; the concluding section of a composition (e.g. *kṛti*, *varṇam*); always preceded by

a *pallavi*, and mostly by an *anupallavi* (except for a simple *kīrtana*)
see also *pallavi*, *samaṣṭi caraṇa*, *saṅgati*

caritra (Sanskrit)
lit. 'biography, performance, behaviour'; a musical play or South Indian opera
see *Nandanār Caritra*, *Naukā Caritram*
see also *Prahlāda Bhakti Vijayam*

Carnatic
see Karnatic music

catuḥśruti dhaivata (*dhi*)
the middle variant of the sixth scale degree (= *tīvra dha*); the major sixth
see also *śuddha niṣāda*; mnemonic syllable '*dhi*'

catuḥśruti ṛṣabha (*ri*)
the middle variant of the second scale degree (= *tīvra ri*); the major second
see also *śuddha gāndhāra*; mnemonic syllable '*ri*'

caturaśra gati (Sanskrit) 128, Fig. 32
see also *caturaśra naḍai*

caturaśra jāti (Sanskrit)
symbol 'I4'
laghu section with four beats

caturaśra jāti dhruva tāla
first of the *sūḷādi sapta tāla* (14 *akṣara*)

caturaśra jāti ēka tāla
last of the *sūḷādi sapta tāla* (4 *akṣara*)

caturaśra jāti maṭhya tāla
second of the *sūḷādi sapta tāla* (10 *akṣara*)

caturaśra jāti rūpaka tāla
third of the *sūḷādi sapta tāla* (6 *akṣara*)

caturāśramam (Sanskrit)
lit. 'the four (*catur-*) stages (*āśrama*)'; formerly prescribed for the religious life of an individual; an archaic concept, hence regarded as being incompatible with the needs of modern society (e.g. by Ramana Maharshi)

caturaśra naḍai
subdivision of a tāla (= *gati*) with four *mātrā* per beat (*kriyā*)
see also *prastāra*

Caturdaṇḍī Prakāśikā 40, 94, 97
see Veṅkaṭamakhi

catuṣṣaṣṭi kalā (Sanskrit) 35
proverbial 64 arts which include music and dance
see also *aṟubattu nāṉgu kalaigaḷ*

cauka kāla (Sanskrit) 78, 134
slow tempo (= *vilambita kāla*)

ceṇḍa (Malayālam) Fig. 4
large cylindrical drum used mainly used in the *Kathakali* dance-drama of Kerala; suspended vertically from the shoulder; played with the fingers of one hand, and a bent stick in the other hand

ceṅgilam, *ceṅgala* (Malayālam)
large circular disc which is mainly used to keep time in *Kathakali* dance-drama; made of bell-metal, it is played with a stick

centre(s)
see Bṛhaddhvani, *Bṛhadīśvara*, Kalākshētra, *Kāñcīpuram*, Maṉṉārguḍi, Music Academy Madras, Pālakkāḍu, Paḷani, Sampradāya, Śāntinikētan, Śarabhōjī II, Śrīraṅgam, Tañjāvūr
see also *cakra*, history of Karnatic music, *kṣetra*, *samasthāna vidvān*, *tīrtha*

Cētulāra śṛṅgāramu 64
kṛti by Tyāgarāja which describes the composer's deep emotional involvement in his worship (*pūjā*) of Rāma, his favoured form of godhead (*iṣṭadevatā*)
see also *bhakta*

change 161
see *bheda*, *kāku*
see also variation

chant
see *gātravati*, *Sāmaveda*, *Veda*, vedic chanting

charm, charming
see *bhakti*, *rakti*, *rakti rāga*, *rasa*, *Tantra*, *Veda*, *viśeṣa prayoga*
see also beauty

chāyā (Sanskrit) 75, 78, 111
lit. 'shade, tinge'; (1) the most characteristic notes of a rāga (= *jīva svara*); (2) also refers to a phrase or embellishment (*gamaka*) which is reminiscent of another rāga; occurs in a *chāyālaga rāga*, also referred to as 'mixed' (*miśra rāga*)
see also *kāku*, *rāga rūpa*, *svarūpa*, *viśeṣa prayoga*

Chennai 29, 224, Fig. 26

see also Harikēsanallūr Muthiah Bhāgavatar, Subbarāma Dīkṣitar
dāsa (Sanskrit)
lit. 'servant, slave'; a votary of the highest godhead (*Hari*, *Īśvara*), or a particular deity (e.g. Bhadrācala Rāmadāsa)
see also *bhakta*
daśa prāṇa
see *tāla daśa prāṇa*
Daśāvatār, *Daśāvatārā* (Sanskrit)
ten incarnations (*avatār*) of Viṣṇu, namely (1) Matsya, (2) Kūrma, (3) Varāha, (4) Narasiṁha, (5) Vāmana, (6) Paraśurāma, (7) Rāma, (8) Kṛṣṇa, (9) Buddha, (10) Kalki; an important subject of religious lore (*Purāṇa*) and iconography; often alluded to in the lyrics of devotional songs and poetry (e.g. *Gītagovinda*)
daśavidha gamaka (Sanskrit) 73, 74
the proverbial ten (*daśa*) types of embellishment (*gamaka*); also mentioned in Mīṉākṣime, a *kṛti* by Muttusvāmi Dīkṣitar; figure in *Vīribōni*, the famous aṭa tāla *varṇam*; some of these (e.g. *āroha*, *avaroha*, *mūrcchanā*) were absorbed in the stylistic framework of Karnatic music but are not termed *gamaka* any longer see (1) *āroha*, (2) *avaroha*, (3) *ḍhālu*, (4) *sphurita*, (5) *kampita*, (6) *āhata*, (7) *pratyāhata*, (8) *tripuccha*, (9) *āndoḷa*, (10) *mūrcchanā*
dāsiyāṭṭam (Tamil) 166
dance (*āṭṭam*) performed by a female temple dancer (*dēvadāsi*) or court dancer (*rājādāsi*)
see also *Mōhiniyāṭṭam*
Dattilam 119
musical treatise ascribed to *Dattila*, an ancient authority on music which is quoted by many later authors.
debut
see *araṅgēṟṟam*
deflection
see *nokku*, *vaḷi*
degree of speed
see *prathama kāla*, *dvitīya kāla*, *tṛtīya kāla*
delay
see agogic, *odukkal*
delight 34, 102
see *ānanda*, *saukhyam*
see also *Bṛhaddeśī*, *citta*, *ciṭṭasvaram*, emotion, *Kumārasaṁbhava*, *rāga*, *rakti*, *rañjana*, *rasa*
dēśa (Sanskrit) 119
lit. 'place, region, country, province'
see *dēśī*
dēśādi tāla (Sanskrit) Table 19
shortened variant of *ādi tāla* (four beats)
deśa kāku, *deśī*; *deśyam* (Sanskrit)
see *kāku*
descending, descent
see *asaṁpūrṇa*, *avaroha*, *avarohaṇa*, *avatāra*, *krama*, *pratyāhata*, *saṁpūrṇa*
deśī, *deśīya* (Sanskrit) 91, 170
lit. 'provincial, dialect (*deśī*)'; 'native, inhabiting (*deśīya*)'; a style or convention which is not in conformity with fixed rules or classical conventions (*mārga*)
deśī rāga, *deśī saṅgīta* (Sanskrit) 119
rāga or type of music associated with a particular region (*deśa*); also refers to 'light' or 'folk' forms of music or dance
see also *deśya rāga*, *mārga rāga*, *tukkaḍā*
destruction, destructive 23
see also *Purāṇa*, Śiva
deśya rāga (Sanskrit) 110, 115, 120, 124, 170, Ch. 13, Staves 33, 34
of South Indian origin 121
of North Indian origin 121–2
see also *bhajan*, *kāvaḍiccindu*
deva (Sanskrit) 87
(male) celestial being, deity
dēvadāsi (Tamil) 166
female dancer attached to a temple in former times
see also *nitya sumaṅgaḷi*, *rājādāsi*
deva gāndharva (Sanskrit)
celestial musician
see Tumburu
Devanāgarī (Sanskrit)
modern script used to write Sanskrit and Hindi
dēvarnāma 138, 156, 175, Ch. 17
devotional song in Kannaḍa
see also *meṭṭu*, Purandara Dāsa

Devī (Sanskrit)
lit. 'goddess'; often revered as divine mother
see also Durgā, Kamākṣi, Lakṣmī, Pārvatī, Śrī, *Tantra*, *vidyā*

devotion, devotional music 64, 121, 158, 163, 168
see *bhakti*, *bhakti rasa*, *madhurabhakti*
see also Ādi Śaṅkara, *Bhāgavata purāṇa*, *bhajan*, Bhāṇḍīra, *bhāva*, *dēvarnāma*, *divyanāma kīrtana*, *ekasthāyī rāga*, *goṣṭhi*, Haridāsa, *harikīrtan*, history of Karnatic music, *kīrtana*, *kīrttanaigaḷ*, *mokṣa*, *nāda yoga*, *navarasa*, *nindāstsuti*, *pada*, *Prahlāda Bhakti Vijayam*, *Sirupuliyūr ulā*, *sūfism*, *Vaiṣṇava*, *yoga*

dha Table 10
(1) the abbreviation for any variant of *dhaivata*; (2) the mnemonic svara syllable for *śuddha dhaivata*
dha-dhi-dhu see mnemonic svára syllables
dha-na see *uttarāṅga*

dhaivata (*dha*)
sixth scale degree; traditionally associated with the horse; mostly pronounced '*da*' when sung (i.e. *saraḷi variśai*, *alaṁkāram*, *svara kalpana*)
see also enharmonic scale degrees

dhaivatāntya rāga 124, 156, Ch. 13, Stave 35
rāga in which no note higher than *dhaivata* should be touched
see also *madhyama śruti*

ḍhālu
(1) the 'sparkling' embellishment (*gamaka*); an embellishment consisting of several upward glides taken from the basic note *ṣaḍja* (e.g. *sa-pa*, *sa-ma*, *sa-ga*, *sa-ri*); (2) pulling a *vīṇā* string in order to take a higher note
see also *daśavidha gamaka*

dhara, *dhāra* (Sanskrit)
lit. 'holding, wearing, endowed with'
see *mūlādhāra*, Muraḷī, Śiva

dhāraṇā (Sanskrit)
lit. 'memory, intellect, keeping the mind collected'; the practice of fixed attention (e.g. through *yoga*)

dharma (Sanskrit)
lit. 'universal or absolute law, custom, justice, merit, character, soul'; *svadharma* denotes individual duty or social function
see also *puruṣārtha*

dhātu (Sanskrit) 153, Ch. 15
lit. 'essential element, soul'; the musical structure of a composition (= *varṇameṭṭu*)
list of contemporary composers 154
see also *dhātu*, *mātu*, *sama eḍuppu*, *vāggēyakāra*

Dhautapañcama 99
69th *mēḷakartā* rāga used by Muttusvāmi Dīkṣitar; resembles Dhātuvardhani
see *asampūrṇa paddhati*

dhi Table 10
see mnemonic svara syllables
see also *catuḥśruti dhaivata*

dhīm
jati syllable

dhin, *din*
(1) a *jati* syllable; (2) an 'open' *mṛdaṅgam* stroke of the right forefinger whereby the ringfinger touches the edge of the black spot; produces a musical note which corresponds to the tonic (*ṣaḍja*)

dhrupad (Sanskrit)
from *dhruvapada*, lit. 'fixed, firm (*dhruva*), refrain, stanza (*pada*)'; a formal, austere, mostly slow-paced (*vilambit*) type of music; most often a male vocal style; believed to have influenced Muttusvāmi Dīkṣitar while in Benāres; consists of four sections or stages (i.e. *ąstāi*, *antarā*, *sañcāri*, and *ābhōg*); a major branch of *Hindustānī* music since it was patronized by Rājā Man Singh (about AD 1500); largely superseded by the *khyāl* style since the early 19th *c*.
see also *sūfi*, Svāti Tirunāḷ

dhruvā (Sanskrit)
song used in drama; already mentioned in the *Nāṭya Śāstra*

dhruva tāla Stave 9; Table 19
tāla with four sections (*aṅga*), namely *laghu*, *drutam*, *laghu*, *laghu*
see *caturaśra jāti dhruva tāla*, *sūḷādi sapta tāla*

dhu Table 10
see mnemonic svara syllables
see also enharmonic scale degrees, *kaiśikī ni*, *ṣaṭśruti dhaivata*

dhvani (Sanskrit) 88
lit. 'sound, echo'; applies to poetry (*kāvya*) where *dhvani* refers to the device of 'suggested sense' which overrides the sense expressed by the words used
see also Bṛhaddhvani

dhyāna (Sanskrit) 31, 91, 92
lit. 'meditation, reflection, contemplation.'
see also *pūjā*, *rāga rāgiṇī*, *yoga*

diaphragm 58, 65
muscle in the abdominal region (solar plexus); regulates breathing; concentrating on the region near the navel (*nābhi*, *maṇipūra*) helps a singer to activate the diaphragm (a precondition for voice culture)

diatonic 106
any major or minor scale in Western music (opposite of chromatic)

didactic 128, Ch. 10, 17
see also *abhyāsa gānam*, *jati*, *Purāṇa*, solfa, *śolkaṭṭu*

dīm
mṛdaṅgam stroke; played with four fingers of the right hand; produces a musical note which corresponds to the major second (*catuḥśruti ri*)

diminished notes Table 10

din see *dhin*

dīrgha (Sanskrit)
long, extended (e.g. a syllable)
see also *hṛsva*, *kārvai*

dīrgha svara (Sanskrit)
long or extended note
see also *arudi*, *kārvai*

discourse
see Rāma Brahmā

dissonance, dissonant 72, 106, Ch. 1
see also *vivādī*

divinity, divine music 24, 31, 34, 61, 87
see also *bhakti*, *nāda*, *Nādabrahmā*, *nādopāsanā*, *praṇava*, *upaveda*

divyanāma kīrtana (Sanskrit)
simple devotional song intended for congregational singing

Divya Prabandham
an important collection of *Vaiṣṇava* hymns; often referred to as the 'Tamil Veda'
see *madhurabhakti*, prabandham, Śrīraṅgam
see also Caṭakōpan̠, K.V. Śrīnivāsa Ayyaṅgār

dōlak 50
drum used in Hindustānī music

Doordarshan 79
the national television corporation of India

drama, dramaturgy 12, 58, 59, 93, 126
see *kāvya*, *kūttu*, *nāṭya*
see also *Abhijñāna Śākuntalam*, acting, *āhārya abhinaya*, *āṅgika abhinaya*, *āṭṭam*, *bhāgavata mēḷam*, *ceṇḍa*, *ceṅgila*, *caritra*, *cūrṇikā*, dance, *daru*, *Daśāvatārā*, *dhruvā*, *guṇa*, *kāku*, Kālidāsa, *karuṇa*, *Kathakali*, *kuratti*, *kuravan̠*, *kuravañji*, *līlā*, mime, *navarasa*, *nāgasvaram*, Narasiṁha, *Nāṭya Śāstra*, opera, *patyam*, Śakuntalā, Sanskrit, *sāttvika abhinaya*, *sāttvika bhāva*, *śiras*, *Sōpānam*, *sthāyibhāva*, *vācika abhinaya*, *vibhāva*, *vyabhicāribhāva*, *Yakṣagāna*

drone 15, 26, 40, 43, 44
reference pitch (*ādhāra ṣadja*); the continuous background sound or base note provided by any type of instrument (e.g. *tambūrā*), or part of an instrument (e.g. the secondary strings of a *vīṇā*)
see also *cinna mēḷam*, *eḍakka*, *ēktār*, *madhyama śruti*, *nāgasvaram*, *pakka sāraṇi*, *śruti box*

dṛṣṭi (Sanskrit)
eye movement in dance
see also *nṛtya*

drum, drummer
see rhythm instruments
see also *kiṇaiyan̠*, *vādya*

druta, *drutam* (Sanskrit)
lit. 'quickly, swiftly, immediately'

druta kāla (*durita kāla*) 134
fast tempo

drutam 128, Table 12
an element or 'limb' (*aṅga*) of some tālas; a fixed section (*aṅga*) of some tālas

(e.g. ādi tāla, aṭa tāla, tripuṭa tāla); comprises two counting units (*akṣarakāla*, *kriyā*); indicated by a clap and a wave of the hand (*visarjita*); represented by symbol 'O'

dur (German)
major scale in Western music (from Latin 'hard')
see also *tīvra*

duration of a concert Ch. 15

Durgā
see *vidyā*
see also Devī, *śakti*

duritam (Tamil)
lit. 'quick pace' (= *durita kāla*)
see *druta kāla*

dvitīya (Sanskrit)
lit. second

dvitīya ghana rāga pañcaka (Sanskrit) 78, 117, Stave 30
'secondary' group of five rāgas
see also *ghana rāga pañcaka*

dvitīya kāla (Sanskrit) 134, 142
second (*dvitīya*) degree of speed (*kāla*) which is twice as fast as the first degree (*prathama kāla*)
see also *kalai*, *trikāla*, *tṛtīya kāla*

dvitīyāṅga (Sanskrit)
second (*dvitīya*) part (= *uttarāṅga*) of the *rāgam tānam pallavi* format
see also *prathamāṅga*

Dwāram Veṅkataswāmy Naidu 18

ear, hearing, listener 21, 23, 38, 78, 79
see *śruti*
see also *ākāśa*, *anāhata nāda*, audience, *bheda*, *harikathā kālakṣepam*, *karṇa paraṁpara*, *mahābhūta*, sound

eclecticism 10, 15
see also hybrid styles, *jugalbandī*

eccu (Tamil)
see *heccu*

eḍakka, *iḍaikka* (Malayālam, Tamil)
small hour-glass shaped drum characteristic of the *Sōpānam* style of music in Kerala; used in temple, drama and dance music (e.g. to accompany female characters), and in folk arts (e.g. puppetry); its tonal range is more than one octave; serves as percussion, drone and melody instrument, all at once; the tension (i.e. pitch) of the membranes, made from a cow's stomach, are controlled with strings held in the player's left hand; the right hand uses a thin stick
see also *uḍukkai*

Edārisañcarinturā 96
a kṛti by Tyāgarāja

education 79, Ch. 4, 10
see also Montessori

eḍuppu (Tamil) 85, 129, 134, 148, Staves 36–9
starting point (= *graha*)
see also *anāgata eḍuppu*, *araiyiḍam*, *graha*, *iḍam*, *kāliḍam*, *kuraippu*, *mātrā*, *mukkāliḍam*, *odukkal*, *onṟarai eḍuppu*, *sama eḍuppu*, *samam*, *tīrmāṇam*

ekāgratā (Sanskrit) 26
lit. 'one-pointedness, single-mindedness'; concentration
see also *yoga*

ekaika kṛti rāga (Sanskrit) 96, 127, 278
a rāga newly created to compose a particular song (*eka* = one); in many cases, no other compositions have since been added

ekasthāyī rāga (Sanskrit) 124
a rāga whose tonal range is limited to one octave (*sthāyī*); some rāgas of this category are derived from popular music or devotional music such as *Tēvāram* hymns, e.g. Jhinjōṭī (Jañjhūṭi), Kurañji, Nādanāmakriya

eka tāla (Sanskrit) Stave 15; Table 19
tāla variant having only one section (i.e *laghu*)
see *caturaśra jāti eka tāla*

Ekōji I (Veṅkhāji, 1676–83)
first Marāṭhā ruler of Tañjāvūr; Telugu continued to be used as the court languagc cven after the fall of the Telugu Nāyak dynasty, which was achieved with the help of the Sultan of Bijapur; followed by Śahajī
see also Vijayarāghava Nāyak

Ekōji II
Marāṭhā ruler of Tañjāvūr (1736–39); son of Tulajājī I; a patron and composer of pieces in Sanskrit and Telugu; succeeded by Pratāpasiṁha

flat notes Table 10
see *komal*
see also enharmonic scale degrees, *tīvra*
flautist
see flute
flow
see *sarvalaghu*
flower 34
see lotus, *pūjā*
flute 43, 45, 46, Ch. 5, Fig. 5, 20 ,
Sanskrit *muraḷī*, *vaṁśa*, *veṇu*; Tamil *pullāṅkul̲al*; Telugu *pillanagrōvi*, Kannaḍa *pillanaṅgrōvi*; a wind instrument (*suṣira vādya*); the transverse (side-blown) flute is preferred in Indian classical music and generally made from bamboo (*vaṁśa*)
see also *Bhāgavata purāṇa*, Bhāṇḍīra, *gāyaki*, *heccu śruti*, Kṛṣṇa, *kul̲al*, *mukharandhra*, Muraḷī, *svaranāḍi*, *taggu śruti*, *tutukāram*, *vādya trayam*, *vaiṇuka*, Veṇugopāla
flute-player, flautist 36
see Kṛṣṇa, Muraḷīdharan̲, *vaiṇuka*, *veṇuvāda*, *veṇuvādaka*
folk music, dance 158
see *kuravañji*, light music
foot, feet 16, 54
see *caraṇa*, *pada*
see also *aḍavu*, *karaṇa*, *maṇḍala*
foreign
see *anyasvara*, history of Karnatic music, *yavana*
format
see *kaccēri paddhati*
forms (music and dance) Ch. 17
formula
see *kaṭapayādi sūtra*, *sūtra*
see also *mārga saṅgīta*, *sādhanā*
fourth scale degree (*svara*)
see *ma*, *madhyama*
frets 11, 40, 42, 94
see also *mēḷam*, *meṭṭu vīṇā*
full bench 36

ga Table 10
(1) the abbreviation for any variant of *gāndhāra*; (2) the mnemonic svara syllable for *śuddha gāndhāra*
see also enharmonic scale degrees
ga-gi-gu see mnemonic svara syllables

gait
see *gati*, *naḍai*
gamaka (Sanskrit) 13, 18, 35, 42, 43, 54, 71, 72, 77, 79, 89, 95, 96, 117, 119, 159, 163, Ch. 9, Stave 7
lit. 'suggestive, convincing, proof'; refers to various types of embellishment; either based on individual notes (*svara*) or formed by groups of notes
see *āhata*, *jāru*, *kampita*, *khaṇḍippu*, *līnam*, *mūrcchanā*, *nokku*, *odukkal*, *orikkai*, *pratyāhata*, *ravai*, *sphurita*, *tripuccha*, *vaḷi*
see also agogic, *anusvara*, enharmonic scale degrees, *ēr̲ra jāru*, *daśavidha gamaka*, *gumki*, Haripāla Deva Kallinātha, *janta svara*, *kāku*, microtone, *paṇ*
gāna (Sanskrit)
lit. 'music'
see also *abhyāsa gāna*, *gāna rasa*, *sāmagāna*, *Yakṣagāna*
gāna kāla (Sanskrit) 126, Ch. 13
lit. 'singing time'; refers to the 'time theory' which prescribes specific hours of the day or a season for certain rāgas or types of music; many or most South Indian rāgas are now termed *sārvakālika rāga*
see also *bhāva*, *navarasa*, *rasa*
gānam (Sanskrit) 35
lit. 'singing, a song'; also an instrumental style meant to emulate the expressive power of the human voice with regard to feeling (*bhāva*) and continuity
see also *gāyaki*
Gaṇapati
see Gaṇeśa
gāna rasa (Sanskrit)
pure aesthetic enjoyment in music; besides the common types of *rasa*, *gāna rasa*
see also *navarasa*, *rasa*
gāndhāra (*ga*)
third scale degree; traditionally associated with the goat
see also enharmonic scale degrees
gāndharva (Sanskrit) 87, 119
lit. 'male (celestial) singer' (e.g. Tumburu; female = *gāndharvī*); pertaining to the art of vocal and instrumental music

(*gāndharva saṅgīta*) if conforming with classical conventions (*mārga*); also a subordinate *Veda* (*upaveda*)

Gaṇeśa (Gaṇapati) 116, 155
son of Śiva and Pārvatī and brother of Subrahmaṇya; remover of obstacles; depicted as elephant-headed, anthropomorphic image with a large belly, hence also addressed as *lambodara* (e.g. in the Sanskrit lyrics of a *gītam*, Śrī Gaṇanaṭha)
see also *kautvam*, Muruga, *Vātāpigaṇapatim*

Gaṅgā (Sanskrit)
the most sacred river of North India; also known as Ganges

garbhagṛha (Sanskrit)
lit. 'womb-house', the sanctum of a Hindu temple
see also *Sōpānam*

garland 34
see *mālikā*, *rāgamālikā*

Garuḍa
mythological, divine bird; the mount of Viṣṇu

gati (Sanskrit) 138, 140, 141, Ch. 14, Table 17
lit. 'gait, motion, turn' (= Tamil *naḍai*); pulsation caused by the regular subdivision of each beat (*akṣara*) in a given tāla (3, 4, 5, 7, or 9 sub-units; i.e. *tisra gati*, *caturaśra gati*, *khaṇḍa gati*, *miśra gati*, *saṅkīrṇa gati*)
see also *āvarta*, *jāti*, *tāla daśa prāṇa*, *yati*

gatibheda (Sanskrit)
substituting the number of sub-units (*gati*) per counting unit or beat (*akṣarakāla*, *kriyā*); involves, for instance, three sub-units (*tisra gati*) or five sub-units (*khaṇḍa gati*) in the place of four (*caturaśra gati*), which is the most common subdivision

gati variants
five customary *gati* variants can be combined with the scheme of 35 tālas (i.e. five *jāti* combinations of the seven *sūḷādi sapta tāla*) which results in the scheme of 175 tāla variants, most of which are less commonly heard; typically performed in the context of the *rāgam tānam pallavi* and *tāla vādya kaccēri* formats (e.g. *khaṇḍa jāti khaṇḍa gati tripuṭa tāla* = 9 *kriyā*, 45 *mātrā*)

gātravatī, *gātra vīṇā* (Sanskrit) 61
'human lute' (*vīṇā*) used in singing *sāman* chant (*Sāmaveda*); referred to by the *Nārada purāṇa* along with the *dāravī*, the 'wooden lute'

gāyaka (Sanskrit)
male singer

gāyaki, *gāyakī* (Sanskrit) 35, 73, 89, 96
lit. 'a female singer' (*gāyakī*); (1) in *Hindustānī* music, the term refers to a type of instrumental style endowed with 'vocal qualities' (e.g. *khayāl gāyakī*); (2) in Karnatic music, the term now refers to the ability of an instrumentalist to maintain the integrity of meaning and feeling in a composition based on lyrics (e.g. *kṛti*, *pallavi* or *jāvaḷi*); accordingly, phrasing must emulate the distribution of the underlying text syllables by way of plucking (*miṭṭu*), violin bowing (*svaravil*), or tongueing (*tutukāram* for flautists, *tatakāram* for *nāgasvaram* players); ideally this vocal quality (*gānaṃ*) is also transferred to an *ālāpana* and other 'abstract' items with scope for creativity and spontaneity (*manodharma saṅgīta*)
see also *rāga bhāva*, *sāhitya bhāva*

gender
see feminine, male

gestures Table 12, Fig. 28–30
see *kriyā*

gettuvādyam
percussive string instrument (drone-cum-rhythm); played with two flat bamboo sticks to which metal bells are attached for rhythmic accents; resembles a *tambūrā*
see also Āvuḍaiyārkōvil

ghanam, *ghana* (Tamil) 78, 117, 119, 121, Ch. 13
lit. 'heavy, respectable'
see *kramam*, *mūlamantram*

Ghanam Kṛṣnayya
see Amarasiṃha

ghanapāḍigal, *ghanapāṭhigaḷ* (Tamil) 119
person trained to recite vedic texts

ghana rāga (Sanskrit) 115
(1) a rāga with ample scope for *ālāpana*, *tānam* and *rāgamālikā*; (2) a rāga which retains its charm also in a faster tempo, hence with reduced ornamentation (*gamaka*)
see also *ghanam*, *naya*

ghana rāga pañcaka (Sanskrit) 78, 117, Stave 30
primary set of five *ghana rāgas*
see also *dvitīya ghana rāga pañcaka*, *pañcaratna kṛti*

ghana vādya (Sanskrit) 36
an idiophone; a solid percussion or rhythm instrument without membrane (i.e. made of bell-metal)
see *ceṅgila*, *jālrā*, *mōrsiṅg*, *tāḷam*

ghaṇṭā (Sanskrit)
bell rung during worship (*pūjā*)

gharānā
musical lineage in North Indian music
see also *bāṇī*, *karṇa paraṁpara*, *paraṁpara*, *saṁpradāya*

ghāta (Sanskrit)
'beat' for reckoning tāla
see *kriyā*

ghaṭam 51, Ch. 5, Fig. 22
claypot
see also *upapakkavādyam*

ghazal 19
see *sūfī*

ghī, ghee
clarified, molten butter
see *pūjā*

gi Table 10
mnemonic svara syllable for *sādhāraṇa gāndhāra*

gīta, *gītam* (Sanskrit) 47, 62, 71, 85, 169, 176, Ch. 17
(1) song in general; (2) a type of didactic song in South Indian music (*gītam*)
see *abhyāsa gāna*, *saṅgīta*, *lakṣaṇa gīta*
see also Paccimiriyam Āḍiappayya, Paidāla Gurumūrti Śāstrī, Purandara Dāsa, Taccūr Siṅgarācāryulu, Tenmaṭam Brothers, Tiger Varadāchāriar, Tiruvōtriyūr Tyāgayyar, Veṅkaṭamakhi, Vīṇā Kuppayyar

Gītagovinda (Sanskrit) 14, 153, 168
dramatic poem (*kāvya*) by Jayadeva; opens with an invocation to the ten incarnations of Viṣṇu (*Daśāvatārā*); inspired by the *Bhāgavata purāṇa*; a cycle of songs (*aṣṭapadi*) which deal with the love of Kṛṣṇa and Rādhā and describe the irresistible effect of Kṛṣṇa's flute play; regarded as the masterpiece of religious eroticism (*madhurabhakti*, *śṛṅgāra*)
see also Nārāyaṇa Tīrtha, D. Pattammal

gītavāditra (Sanskrit)
lit. 'song (*gīta*) and instrumental music (*vāditra*, *vādya*)'

glamour 23

glide, slide, glissando
see *āndoḷa*, *ḍhālu*, *jāru*, *mīnd*, *svarita*

gloom
see *tamas*

go (Sanskrit)
lit. 'cattle, cow'; the bull or mount of Śiva
see also animal imagery, *ṛsabha*

goal
see *mokṣa*, *saṁsāra*

goat 61
see *aja*

God, godhead 16, 64
see Hari, *iṣṭadevatā*, Īśvara

Golden Age 158
see Tulajājī II

Goleman, Daniel 33

golu
see *kolu*

Gopāla (Sanskrit)
see Kṛṣṇa

Gōpālakṛṣṇa Bhārati
see also Amarasiṁha

gopī (Sanskrit) 31
cowherdess associated with Kṛṣṇa
see also *Bhāgavata purāṇa*, *jīvātman*, Rādhā, *rāsakrīḍā*

gopuccha yati (Sanskrit)
see yati

goṣṭhi, *goṣṭhī* (Sanskrit)
lit. 'assembly, discourse, society, relatives'; a group of like-minded musicians and amateurs who meet to sing and learn devotional songs (*bhajana*)

gōṭṭuvādyam 37, 40, 42, Ch. 5, Fig. 17
first reference (*gōṭivādya*) by Raghunātha Nāyaka I; some instruments have sympathetic strings

see also *citrāviṇā*, Harikēsanallūr Mutthiah Bhāgavatar, *kuḍam*, *miṭṭu*, *sarva vādya*

Gōvinda, Govindācāri 40, 127
South Indian music theorist and author of the *Saṁgraha-Cūḍā-Maṇi*; introduced the concept of *saṁpūrṇa paddhati* for scales (*mēḷakartā rāga*) which has been adopted by most composers since Tyāgarāja; contributed to the establishment of Vijayanagar culture in the court of Tañjāvūr
see also *lakṣaṇa gīta*

Gōvinda Dīkṣitar 39, 40, 94
music scholar and minister of the late 16th and early 17th centuries who served three Nāyak rulers of Vijayanagar and Tañjāvūr; author of a music treatise, *Saṅgīta Sudhā*, which has also been ascribed to his patron and disciple, Raghunātha Nāyak; credited with the development of the modern south Indian *vīṇā* (*Sarasvatī vīṇā*, named *Raghunātha mēḷa vīṇā* after his royal patron); father of Veṅkaṭamakhi
see *tāna pustaka*

grace, graceful 23, 24, 76
see *lāsya*
see also *gamaka*, *tribhaṅga*

grace notes
see *gamaka*

graha (Sanskrit) 13, 134, Staves 36–9
lit. 'to seize, to assume'; (1) the starting point of a theme (*iḍam*) within the tāla cycle; (= Tamil *eḍuppu*); (2) starting note of a rāga (= *graha svara*)
see also *bheda*, *makuṭam*, *nyāsa*, *sama eḍuppu*

grail, the holy grail 24
symbol for divine wisdom of compassion and voluntary sacrifice (the crucification in the Christian tradition); represented as the cup of the Last Supper

grāma, *svaragrāma* (Sanskrit)
literally, 'collection, village'; a scale employed in ancient music; two out of three conceivable types (i.e. *ma grāma* and *sa grāma*) were described by most writers as being useful
see also *mūrcchanā*, Rāmāmātya

gramophone 126
see history of Karnatic music

grantha (Sanskrit)
South Indian script having characters to represent Sanskrit words; based on Tamil
see also Kuḍumiyāmalai, *lakṣaṇagrantha*

Greek, Greece 10, 11, 12, 24, 93
see *Hellenism*, *yavana*

gṛhastha (Sanskrit)
lit. 'householder'; the second stage (*āśrama*) in life

gu Table 10
mnemonic svara syllable for *antara gāndhāra*

Guido d'Arezzo Table 3
Italian monk and musical theorist (997–1050); introduced the first European system of solmization as a didactic method
see also *solfa*

gumki (*gumuki*, *gumiki*) 50, 52
sound modulation akin to a *gamaka* which is applied in percussive music (e.g. *mṛdaṅgam*, *kañjīrā*); a speciality of the *eḍakka* drum which can reproduce melodic patterns in the *Sōpānam* style

guṇa (Sanskrit)
lit. 'quality' referred to in philosophical texts (e.g. *Bhagavad Gītā*) and personal teachings (e.g. Ramana Maharshi about '*sattvic* food'); also applied in dramaturgy; any one of three principal attributes or *guṇas* can characterize a personality at the expense of the other two: (1) *sattva* ('purity', e.g. a quiet, or saintly disposition); (2) *rajas* ('passion', e.g. an overactive or violent disposition); (3) *tamas* ('gloom', e.g. an apathetic or indecisive disposition); each *guṇa* is also associated with six of the 18 major *Purāṇas*, namely *Viṣṇu purāṇa* (*sattva guṇa*), *Brahmā purāṇa* (*rajas guṇa*), and *Śiva purāṇa* (*tamas guṇa*)
see also *rajas*, *sattvam*, *tamas*

Gupta 67

guru (Sanskrit) 79, 159, Ch. 4
lit. 'heavy, great, dear'; a respected teacher, preceptor, or spiritual guide; an authority on any subject

see also *karṇa paraṁpara*, *mānasa guru*, *mānasika guru*, *paraṁpara*, *śiṣya*
gurudakṣiṇa (Sanskrit) 28
parting gift (*dakṣiṇa*) to one's preceptor (*guru*)
Guruguha
see Muruga, Subrahmaṇya
gurukula (Sanskrit) 28, 79, 162
teacher's household
gurukulavāsa (Sanskrit) Ch. 10
traditional method of studying a subject or skill; a personalized apprenticeship (i.e. belonging to one's teacher's household)
see also *mānasika guru*
guruśiṣya paraṁparā (Sanskrit) 162, 165, Ch. 15
see *bāṇī*, *paraṁpara*, *saṁpradāya*
gypsy
see *kuratti*, *kuravaṉ*, *kuravañji*

haṁsa (Sanskrit)
legendary bird which symbolizes the faculty of discrimination
see also birds
hand 53, Fig. 11, Table 12
see dhīm, *drutam*, *kañjīrā*, *karaṇa*, *kriyā*, *mudrā*
Hanūmān (Āñjaneya) 88
loyal and selfless devotee of Rāma who helped him to rescue Sītā; he is depicted as a monkey; in mythology, a master singer and rival of Nārada; his name is associated with traditional musicology
see also *kaṭakam*, *Rāmāyaṇa*
happiness
see *ānanda*
see also joy
Hara (Sanskrit)
see Śiva
Hari (Sanskrit) 16, 137, 170
God; often synonymous with Viṣṇu
see bhakta, dāsa
Haridāsa 15, 53, 67, Ch. 18
lit. 'God's servant'; devotees of Kṛṣṇa or Rāma whom they regard as the incarnations of righteousness, grace and compassion
see Purandara Dāsa, Tyāgarāja
harikathā (Sanskrit)
stories (*kathā*) about God (*Hari*); a religious discourse which later developed into the musical discourse known as *harikathā kālakṣepam*
harikathā kālakṣepam (Sanskrit) 16, 36, 53, 170, Ch. 16
lit. 'passing (*kṣepam*) time (*kāla*) by listening to divine stories (*harikathā*)'; a musical discourse on a religious theme
see *kīrtana*, Maṇipravāḷam, *upagāyaka*
see also Gōpālakṛṣṇa Bhārati, Harikēsanallūr Mutthiah Bhāgavatar, Kundrakudi Kṛṣṇa Ayyar, Muvvalūr Sabhāpati Ayyar, Paramēśvara Bhāgavatar, Rāma Brahmā, Tañjāvūr Kṛṣṇa Bhāgavatar
harikīrtan
lit. 'devotional singing in praise of Viṣṇu (= Hari)'
Haripāla Deva Kallinātha
music theorist (14th *c.*?); the author of the Sanskrit treatises titled *Kalānidhi* and *Saṅgīta Sudhākara*; the latter deals with the subject of embellishments (i.e. seven *gamaka*); known as the first (North Indian) writer to distinguish between *Karṇāṭaka saṅgīta* and *Hindustāni saṅgīt*
see also *Karṇāṭaka deśa*
Hariprasād, K. Fig. 14
harmonics 38, 55
harmonium 18, 19, 44, 170, Fig. 1, 6
portable keyboard instrument (reed-organ); operated with bellows; originated in Europe; now mainly popular in Hindustānī music
see also *śruti box*
harp 91, 93, Fig. 27
see *yāḻ*
see also Samudragupta, Tirunīlakaṇṭha Nāyaṉār
hāsya, *hāsyam* (Sanskrit)
lit. 'ridicule, laughter, joke'; the comic sentiment, laughter
see also *navarasa*, ridiculous
head
see *śiras*
see also *āśrama*, *kāku*, *karaṇa*, *sahasrāra*, Śaṅkarācārya, *sthānaprāpti*, *tribhaṅga*
healing, medicine 23, 59

hearing, listener
see ear, *rasika*, sound
heart 65, Fig. 25
see *hṛd*
see also *anāhata cakra*, chest, lotus, *manas*, *sahṛdaya*, *uras*
heat
see *nāda*
heavy 61, 117
see *ghanam*, *guru*, *śyāmā*
heccu kaṭṭai (= *eccu kaṭṭai*, Tamil)
small (i.e.high-pitched) *mṛdaṅgam*
heccu sāraṇi (= *eccu sāraṇi*, Tamil)
the highest of the three secondary strings (*pakka sāraṇi*) of a *vīṇā;* tuned to the upper octave of the basic note, *tāra sthāyī ṣaḍja* (Sanskrit *tīvra sāraṇi*)
heccu śruti (Tamil *eccu śruti*)
high pitch of a small instrument (e.g. *mṛdaṅgam*, flute, *tambūrā*); corresponds to the range of a female voice (i.e. 4 to 5 '*śruti*')
see also *taggu śruti*
heccu sthāyī (Tamil *heccu sthāyī*) Staves 1, 2
upper octave of the vocal range (= *tāra sthāyī*)
Hellenism 10
heptatonic
scale pattern based on seven notes (*saptasvara*)
see *asaṁpūrṇa*, *saṁpūrṇa*
see also hexatonic scale, *janaka rāga*, *mēḷakartā rāga*, pentatonic scale, *varja*
hereditary practice 12, 58, 67
see *iṣṭadevatā*, *naṭṭuvanar*, *ōduvār*, *Sōpānam*, *Tēvāram*, *veḷḷāḷar*, *Yakṣagāna*
heritage
see culture
heron 61
see *krauñca*
Hesse, Hermann 24
German-born poet, novelist and pacifist (1877–1962); profoundly influenced by Indian philosophy as seen in *Siddharta* (1922), *Journey to the East* (1932), and his Utopian novel *Magister Ludi* (*The Glass Bead Game*, 1943), Nobel-Prize for Literature in 1946; his works convey the message that music, science, spirituality and social commitment must be re-integrated within each individual if civilization is to flourish
hexatonic
scale pattern based on six notes
see *ṣāḍava rāga*
see also *asaṁpūrṇa paddhati*, heptatonic scale, pentatonic scale, *varja*
high, upper 60
āndoḷa, *antara gāndhāra*, *dhaivatāntya rāga*, *ḍhālu*, *ēṟṟa jāru*, *heccu kaṭṭai*, *heccu sāraṇi*, *heccu śruti*, *kākalī niṣāda*, *khaṇḍippu*, *komal-tīvra*, *līna*, mnemonic svara syllables, *niṣādāntya rāga*, *orikkai*, *pañcamāntya rāga*, *prati madhyama*, *sadir*, *ṣaṭśruti dhaivata*, *ṣaṭśruti ṛṣabha*, *śiras*, *timiri*, *tīvra*, *udātta*, *uttarāṅga*
Hindi 161
since India's independence, the official indigenous language of the Indian State; written in *Devanāgarī* script; used alongside English and several major regional languages (e.g. Tamil, Malayālam, Kannaḍa, Telugu); in South Indian music, Hindi lyrics are sung by *bhajan* groups and also found in the 'light classical' repertoire (*tukkaḍā*)
see also Ambujam Krishna, Svāti Tirunāḷ
Hinduism, Hindu 11, 15, 26
Hindustānī
pertaining to India, either as a whole, or its northern regions (*Hindustān*)
Hindustānī saṅgīt 15, 18, 19, 72, 89, 119, 121, 126, 163
the modern music system of North India; has a distinct identity since the bifurcation of Indian classical music into North and South Indian branches (first mentioned in the *Saṅgīta Sudhākara* of Haripāla Deva Kallinātha); comprises several distinct styles (e.g. *Dhrupad*, *Khyāl*) as well as regional schools and traditions (*gharānā*); its theoretical foundations were renewed and systematized by V.N. Bhāṭkhaṇḍe (e.g. the *ṭhāṭ* system)
see *deśya rāga*, *dhrupad*, *gāyaki*, history of Karnatic music, *Karṇāṭaka saṅgīta*,

mīnd, *pakaḍ*, *rāga-rāgiṇī*, Śivājī II, *tambūrā*, *tīvra*
see also Mārgadarśī Śēṣayyaṅgār, Muttusvāmi Dīkṣitar, Subrahmaṇya Bhārati, Svāti Tirunāḷ

Hiraṇyakaśipu
demonic character (lit. 'golden garment')
see *Mēlaṭṭūr bhāgavata mēḷam*

history of Karnatic music
the theoretical foundations of the present system of classical South Indian music are traceable to Rāmāmātya (Vijayanagar, 16th *c.* AD); countless other personages have shaped its characteristic forms, motifs, themes, conventions, instruments, techniques, and styles from early times (as seen in the Kuḍumiyāmalai inscription), and to the present day; exponents, scholars and their patrons were informed by a variety of factors such as prevailing beliefs, traditions, opportunities, and political circumstances: (1) regional music traditions (*dēśī saṅgīta*); often described in texts other than music treatises (e.g. *Cilappatikāram, Purāṇa*); still traceable in the temple music of Kerala (*Sōpānam*) and Tamil Nadu (*Tēvāram*); (2) regional styles (*deśī*) of dance (*nṛtya*) and drama (*kūttu*); (3) vēdic traditions (*sāmagāna*) and religious works (e.g. *Upaniṣad*); (4) ancient styles (*gāndharva*) and conventions (*mārga*); numerous treatises and commentaries on the subject of *saṅgīta* (e.g. *Dattilam*, *Nāṭya Śāstra*, *Saṅgīta Ratnākara*); some of these were emulated and adapted by the music scholars of Vijayanagar (notably Gōvinda Dīkṣitar and Rāmāmātya) and their successors at Tañjāvūr; the introduction of the *mēḷa-janya rāga* system by Veṅkaṭamakhi and its propagation by Gōvinda constitute one of the most significant developments; the contributions by the Nāyak and Marāṭhi dynasties (as patrons, scholars and composers) are also regarded as important by historians; (5) Hindu and Jain metaphysics concerned with the nature and value of music (*nāda*); the emergence of psychological and physiological concepts based on sources like *Yoga* and *Tantra* (e.g. *cakra*); (6) devotional fervour and ideals expressed by the poets and composers of the *bhakti* movement (e.g. Āḻvār, Nāyaṉmār, Haridāsa); (7) exchanges with neighbouring cultures in the course of trade relations (Middle East, Central Asia, Persia, South East Asia), and pilgrimage (Buddhist visitors from China and delegations sent from India); Indian expansion (e.g. the impact of *Cōḻa* rule in South East Asia); (8) studies by South Indians in the North (e.g. Muttusvāmi Dīkṣitar, Subrahmaṇya Bhārati), and vice versa; (9) contacts with the culture of Islām, notably its unorthodox branches (i.e. *sūfism*), and its indigenous variants during Moghul (Mughal) rule (16th to early 19th *c.*); (10) the establishment of European colonies; interest in Western music among regional rulers (e.g. Tañjāvūr, Travancore, Mysore, Eṭṭayapuram); the consequent introduction of the violin, printing of music books, and exploration of novel didactic methods (e.g. *nōṭṭusvara sāhitya*); (11) since the late 19th *c.*, new professional opportunities in modern cities, esp. Chennai (Madras); (12) the rapid spread of gramophone records, radio, film, television; (13) social reforms; (14) repeated attempts to consolidate the theory of North and South Indian music (e.g. by V.N. Bhāṭkhaṇḍe); (15) institutional music education, research, documentation, and publications (e.g. University and Music Academy Madras, Kalākshētra, modern centres like Bṛhaddhvani and Sampradāya); (16) international exchange programmes (concert tours, intercultural studies, Ethnomusicology, Comparative Musicology); (17) academic interest in Karnatic music in other parts of India and abroad; (18) patronage by an informed lay public since the

instrumental music, instruments 29, 102, 116, 127, Ch. 5
classification 36
see *aṅga*, *arubattu nāngu kalaigaḷ*, *Cilappatikāram*, *ēktār*, *gānam*, *gāndharva*, *gāyaki*, *gettuvādyam*, *gītavāditra*, *heccu śruti*, *jalataraṅgam*, *kiṇaiyan*, *kuḷal*, *maguḍi*, *maṅgaḷa vādya*, *mēḷakkārar*, *mēḷam*, *meṭṭu*, musician, *nāgasvaram*, *pakkavādya*, *pañcavādya*, *Pattupāṭṭu*, rhythm instruments, *saṅgīta*, *Sarasvatī Vīṇā*, *Sōpānam*, *taggu śruti*, *tāla vādya kaccēri*, *tavilkārar*, *tristhāyī*, *vāditra*, *vādya*, *vādya trayam*, *vaiṇika*, *vaiṇuka*, *veṇuvāda*, *vīṇā*, *vīṇāvāda*, *yālpāṇar*

Intakanna yānanda mēmi
see dedication page

intermediate notes
see *anusvara*, *gamaka*, *janta svara*, *sphurita*

interpretation 157, 160
see *bāṇī*, *lakṣya*, *pāṭhāntara*

interval, intonation 71, 93, 95, Ch. 8, Tables 6–8
see also *bheda*, *laya*, *rāga-rāgiṇī*, *svarasthāna*, *śruti*

invocation
see *pūjā*

irakka jāru 75

Iran
see Sāsānian

iraṇḍu kalai (Tamil) 134, 148
lit. 'phase (*kalai*) two (*iraṇḍu*)'; denotes a variation of a particular tāla whereby twin counts are used for a very slow tempo or pace; each count of a tāla (*kriyā*) is executed twice (e.g. 16 *kriyā* and 64 *mātrā* for ādi tāla); thus one *tāla āvarta* has twice the duration of medium tempo (*madhyama kāla*); preferable for applying and appreciating complex rhythmic patterns in the concluding stages of *svara kalpana* and *taniyāvarttanam* variations
see also *kāla*, *muktāyi*, *oru kalai*

Irayimman Tampi 127, 161

irregular, extraordinary
see *anyasvara*, *bhāṣāṅga rāga*, *tāna pustaka*, *viśeṣa sañcāra*, *yati*

isai, *iśai* (Tamil)
union of music and dance
see *Muttamil*

isaippa (Tamil)
part of the *Divyaprabandham* literature; originally intended to be sung; Tamil *isai* = music; [-p-] *pa* for *pāṭṭu* = sing
see also Caṭakōpan

isai veḷḷāḷar (Tamil)
'cultivator' (*veḷḷāḷar*) of 'music' (*isai*)
see *veḷḷāḷar*

Islām, Muslim 15, 53
see *sūfi*, history of Karnatic music, Śaṅkara

iṣṭadevatā (Sanskrit) 64
lit. the 'favourite, most revered (*iṣṭa*) aspect or form of god (*devatā*)'; mostly regular worship maintained as a family tradition (e.g. Devī or Kamākṣi for Śyāmā Śāstri, Rāma for Tyāgarāja)
see also *Cētulāra śṛṅgāramu*

Īśvara (Sanskrit)
supreme godhead and Creator of the universe, Lord
see also Ādi Śaṅkara, *bhakta*, *Brahman*, *dāsa*

iyal
see *Muttamil*

iyarrīyavar (Tamil) 161
composer

Iyeṅgār
see Ayyaṅgār

Iyer
see Ayyar

jackwood
see *palāmaram*

Jagannātha (Sanskrit)
'Lord of the Universe' (i.e. Kṛṣṇa)

jagat (Sanskrit)
lit. 'world, universe; the ever-changing'

Jainism 67
see history of Karnatic music

jalataraṅgam (Sanskrit) 19, 55, Ch. 5
an instrument which consists of a set of porcelain bowls filled with water
see also Kundrakudi Kṛṣṇa Ayyar

jālrā 16, 52, 53, 170, Ch. 5, Fig. 6
pair of small cymbals used in *harikathā kālakṣepam* and *bhajana* singing; classified as *ghana vādya*

see also *Tantra*, World Music
Jesudoss, K.J. 165
Jew's harp 52
see *mōrsing*
jhampa tāla Table 19, Stave 12
tāla which consists of three sections (*aṅga*), namely *laghu*, *anudrutam*, *drutam*
see *miśra jāti jhampa tāla*, *sūḷādi sapta tāla*
jīva (Sanskrit)
lit. 'living, creature, principle of life, personal soul'
see also *mókṣa*
jīvā, *jīvāḷi* (Tamil)
thread inserted between the bridge and each string of a *tambūrā*; usually a piece of cotton (rarely silk or wool); causes the characteristic bright tonal quality ('buzz')
jīva svara (Sanskrit) 75, 159
lit. 'soul-note'; a characteristic note (= *chāyā svara*)
see also *aṁśa svara*, *vādi*
jivātma, *jīvātman* (Sanskrit) 30, 72, 168
lit. 'individual soul'; in *bhakti* literature, dance and music lyrics, equated with the devotee ('female' or beloved) who longs for the Absolute (*Brahman*)
see *madhura bhakti*
see also Ādi Śaṅkara, *ātman*, *Bhāgavata purāṇa*, Īśvara, *śṛṅgāra*
joy, enjoyment, happiness 31, 34
see *ānanda*, *Bhāgavata purāṇa*, *bhakti*, bliss, *gāna rasa*, *jana rañjaka rāga*, *lālitam*, *maṅgaḷam*, *rasa*, *rasika*, *sahṛdaya*, Śaṅkara, *saukhyam*, sweet
jugalbandī 20, 163
(1) an interaction between musicians having different backgrounds or specializations (e.g. instruments); (2) a joint performance of North and South Indian musicians

kaccēri 37, 47, 115, 126, 171
lit. a 'court (of law)'; denotes an assembly, concert or other public performance
see also *layavinyāsa*, *tāla vādya kaccēri*
kaccēri dharma 36, 157
etiquette guiding the roles of soloist and accompanists during a performance
kaccēri paddhati 36, 115, 159, 164
format or plan underlying a typical concert programme
Kadri Gōpālnāth 17, 55
kaiśikī niṣāda
the middle variant of the seventh scale degree (*ni*; = *komal ni*); mnemonic syllable '*ni*'
kākalī niṣāda
the highest variant of the seventh scale degree (*ni*; = *tīvra ni*); mnemonic syllable '*nu*'
kāku (Sanskrit) 70, 72
(1) modifications of musical notes that affect their pitch or tonal quality (*svarakāku*); (2) melodic figures that reveal the characteristic quality and *bhāva* of a rāga; (3) introducing elements associated with local or regional idioms (*deśa kāku*, *deśī*; *deśyam*); (4) introducing shades (*chāyā*) or elements belonging to another rāga (*anya rāga kāku*; *anya rāgaja*); (5) in dramaturgy, the change of voice which express emotions; (6) in vocal music produced from chest, neck and head respectively
see also microtone, *navarasa*, *śruti*
kalā (Sanskrit) 29
lit. 'art, skill, small part, bit'; (1) any art; ancient texts list 64 arts and skills including music and dance (Sanskrit *catuṣṣaṣṭi kalā*, Tamil *aṟubattu nāṅgu kalaigaḷ*); (2) in earlier times, the number of minor time units (= *kalai*) into which each count (*kriyā*) of a tāla is subdivided (e.g. one, two, four *akṣara* per *kriyā*); one of the ten features of tāla (*tāla daśa prāṇa*)
kāla (Sanskrit) Fig. 31
lit. 'measure of time, fate, black, weather'; (= Tamil *kalai*) (1) speed, tempo (e.g. *prathama kāla*); Tamil *kalái* (i.e. *iraṇḍu kalai*, *oru kalai*); (2) in archaic usage, *kāla* denotes 'duration'; one of the ten features of tāla (*tāla daśa prāṇa*); (3) the principle of maintaining or changing time underlying the performing arts; (4) the cyclic,

transient, impermanent, or dynamic aspect in Indian philosophy
see also *akṣarakāla*, *gāna kāla*, *kālapramāṇam*, *laya*, *mahākāla*, *tāla daśa prāṇa*

kalai (Tamil)
see *iraṇḍu kalai*, *kalā*, *oru kalai*

kālakṣepam (Sanskrit) 16
see *harikathā kālakṣepam*

Kalākshētra, *Kalākṣetra* (Sanskrit) 29, 31, Fig. 9
lit. 'a centre (*kṣetra*) for arts (*kāla*)'; founded by Rukmini Devi-Arundale at Chennai in 1936 on similar lines as Śāntinikētan
see also history of Karnatic music, Jayadēva, Mysore Vāsudēvācāria, Pāpanāsam Śivan̲, Pasupathi, Rājaram, M.D. Rāmanāthan̲, Tañjāvūr Quartette, Tiger Varadāchāriar

Kalānidhi
Sanskrit commentary on the *Saṅgīta Ratnākara* by Haripāla Deva Kallinātha
see also *Saṅgīta Sudhā*

kālapramāṇam (Sanskrit) 78, 128, 133, 142, 163, Ch. 14, 15
lit. 'a tempo (*kāla*) which is correct or standardized (*pramāṇam*)'
see also agogic

kāliḍam (Tamil)
starting the theme at a point which is set 'a quarter' (*kāl*) of a beat or one *mātrā* after the start of the tāla cycle (*samam*); *a* variant of *anāgata eḍuppu*
see also *eḍuppu*, *iḍam*

Kālidāsa 67, 68
ancient author of poetry and plays (approx. 4th–5th *c.* AD); in *Abhijñāna Śākuntalam*, *Kumārasaṁbhava* and *Meghadūta* he describes the emotions evoked by music and nature's sounds
see also *kīcaka*

Kalki, Kalkin (Sanskrit)
tenth and last incarnation (*avatāra*) of Viṣṇu who is yet to come; mounted on a white horse and holding a flaming sword
see *Daśāvatārā*

Kalki 167
pseudonym of R. Krishnamūrti (1899–1954); Tamil novelist, journalist, publisher, and freedom-fighter

Kallinātha
see Haripāla Deva Kallinātha

kalpana (Sanskrit)
lit. 'arranging, imagination; anything placed for decoration'
see also *svara kalpana*

kalpita saṅgīta (Sanskrit) 13, 85, 158, Ch. 15
see also *manodharma saṅgīta*

kāma (Sanskrit)
lit. 'desire, wish, affection, love, object of desire, lust'; one of the four ends of life
see also *puruṣārtha*

Kāmakoṭi Maṭh (Sanskrit)
religious centre (*maṭha*, Anglicized '*Mutt*') at *Kāñcīpuram*; its Sanskrit name is explained as denoting the 'farthest boundary line' (*koṭi*); has a large following among South Indian musicians; headed by the *Paramācārya* who is seniormost among three residing ascetics (*saṁnyāsin*), each belonging to a different generation

Kāmākṣi
divine mother (Bāṅgāru Kāmākṣi, Devī); inspired many compositions by Śyāmā Śāstri
see *iṣṭadevatā*

Kamalā 167

Kamban̲ 167

kaṁpita (Sanskrit) 75, Stave 7
an embellishment (*gamaka*); a shake or an oscillation
see also *daśavidha gamaka*, *nokku*

Kanaka Dāsa 154

Kanchipuram [*Kāñcīpuram*] 67, 69
town in Tamil Nadu; capital of the ancient *Pallava* dynasty; an important religious centre with numerous ancient temples; seat of the spiritual authority known as *Śaṅkarācārya*
see also *Kāmakoṭi Maṭh*, Mahābalipuram, *maṭha*

Kāñcīpuram Naina Piḷḷai 36, 156

kañjīrā 47, Ch. 5, Fig. 5
hand-held drum (tambourine)
see also *gumki*, *upapakkavādyam*

Kannaḍa Fig. 26

language mainly spoken in the modern state of Karnataka
see also Ambujam Krishna, Harikēsanallūr Mutthiah Bhāgavatar, Kanaka Dāsa, Svāti Tirunāḷ

kaṇṭha (Sanskrit) 66, Fig. 25
lit. 'throat, neck, voice'; according to the *Nāṭya Śāstra*, to be used by actors for calling when neither very near nor very far from one another
see Sōbhillusaptasvara, *sthānaprāpti*

Kanyākumāri
English 'Cape Comorin'; the southern tip of the Indian peninsula; a place of pilgrimage

Karaikudi brothers 40

karaṇa (Sanskrit)
term used for 108 classical combinations of poses and movements of the hands, feet, head, and eyes (= Tamil *aḍavu*)
see also *Cōḻa*

karaṇai (Tamil) 51
raised black disc or 'spot' on the right membrane of a *mṛdaṅgam;* applied to produce a distinct basic pitch, *ṣaḍja* when the open '*dhin*' is played by the forefinger while pressing the ringfinger to its edge

karṇa paraṁpara (Sanskrit) 79
lit. 'ear-based' lineage or succession
see also *paraṁpara*

Karnataka [Karṇāṭaka] 11, 16, 49, 69, 170, 224, Fig. 26
South Indian state where Kannaḍa is mainly spoken
see also Śaṅkara, *Yakṣagāna*

Karṇāṭaka deśa (Sanskrit)
South Indian regions where an indigenous music system, known as *Karṇāṭaka saṅgīta*, is primarily practised (i.e. Andhra Pradesh, Karnataka, Kerala, Tamil Nadu); first referred to by Haripāla Deva Kallinātha as 'the country between the *Kāveri* and *Kṛṣṇa* rivers'

Karṇāṭaka Pitāmaha
see *Pitāmaha*

Karṇāṭaka saṅgīta (Sanskrit) 119, 160, 163
the classical music system of South India (Tamil *saṅgīdam*); its most conspicuous features are the 72 fundamental scales (*mēḷakartā rāga*) as well as the intricate *tāla* system with its scope for infinite variation of rhythmic patterns (*prastāra*)
see also Gōvinda, Gōvinda Dīkṣitar, Haripāla Deva Kallinātha, *Hindustāni saṅgīt*, history of Karnatic music, *Sōpānam*, *Tēvāram*

Karnatic (Carnatic) music
Anglicized word for *Karṇāṭaka saṅgīta*
see also history of Karnatic music

karuṇa (Sanskrit) 60, 64
sentiment (*rasa*) associated with compassion and pathos; one of the nine sentiments (*navarasa*); the rāgas regarded as being most suitable for evoking *karuṇa* rasa (e.g. compassion or sadness) in dance-drama are Āhiri, Naṭhabhairavi (= Jaunpuri), Rañjani, Śubhapantuvarāḷi, Tōḍi

kārvai (Tamil) 138
(1) extending the duration of a note by one or several basic units of time (*mātrā*); (2) a pause inserted between two notes or drum beats
see also *aruḏi*, *ciṭṭasvaram*, *kōrvai*

Kāśī (Vārāṇasī, Benāres)
city believed to be sacred to Śiva; situated on the river Ganges
see also Muttusvāmi Dīkṣitar, Subrahmaṇya Bhārati

kaṭakam (Tamil)
music compendium (e.g. *Hanūmān kaṭakam*)
see also *tāna pustaka*

kaṭapayādi sūtra (Sanskrit) 97, 99, Table 11
lit. 'formula (*sūtra*) based on numbers (*saṁkhyā*)'; a mnemonic aid whereby each letter (syllable) of a Sanskrit word corresponds to a number (1 to 9 or 0); in Karnatic music, two syllables are prefixed to the names of the 72 scales (*mēḷakartā rāga*, e.g. 'Dhī-ra'—Śaṅkarābharaṇam, reversed 'ra' = 2, and 'dhi' = 9, 29th position)

kathā kālakṣepam (Sanskrit)
see *harikathā kālakṣepam*

Kathakali 169
most popular form of dance-drama in Kerala; based on Malayālam lyrics
see also *Sōpānam*

kaṭṭai (Tamil)
'wood'; refers to a *mṛdaṅgam*
see also *heccu kaṭṭai*, *taggu kaṭṭai*
kautvam (*kauthuvam*, *kavuthuvam*) 177, Ch. 17
form of dance
kāvaḍiccindu (Tamil) 156, 178, Ch. 17
compositions by Aṇṇāmalai Reḍḍiyār based on popular pilgrims's songs about Muruga; often set to *dēśya* rāgas
see also Pēriasāmi Thooran, Subrahmaṇya Bhārati
Kāveri [Kāvēri] 158, 169
sacred river of South India on which Tiruvaiyāṟu is located
see also *Karṇāṭaka deśa*, Tiruvaiyāṟu
kavitayum (Tamil) 167
kāvya, *kāvyam* (Sanskrit) 153
poetical work or text of a play (*nāṭya*); its aim is to delight and educate through aesthetic experience (*rasa*)
see also *Gītagovinda*, *kūttu*, *sāhitya*, Sanskrit
Kerala [Kērala] 11, 12, 224, Fig. 4, 26
South Indian state where Malayālam is mainly spoken
see Ādi Śaṅkara, *cenda*, *eḍakka*, *Kathakali*, *kombu*, *kuḻal*, *mēḷam*, *Mōhiniyāṭṭam*, *Pālakkāḍu*, *pañcavādya*, Paraśurāma, percussion, *Sōpānam*, *utsava*
see also Irayimman Tampi, Jayadēva, Paramēśvara Bhāgavatar, Tañjāvūr Quartette, Svāti Tirunāḷ
keyboard instruments 17, 70, Fig. 1
see also harmonium, *śruti*
khaṇḍa (Sanskrit)
lit. 'chapter, book'
see *Bhāgavata Purāṇa*
khaṇḍa cāpu tāla Table 19
short tāla marked by two claps, the first having two counts (*mātrā*), and the second three counts (2 + 3; rarely also 3 + 2)
khaṇḍa gati (*khaṇḍa naḍai*)
see *khaṇḍa naḍai*
see also *gati*, *gati variants*
khaṇḍa jāti (Sanskrit)
symbol 'I_5'
laghu section with five beats
khaṇḍa jāti aṭa tāla
the sixth of the seven tālas known as *sūḷādi sapta tāla*; 5 + 5 + 2 + 2 = 14 counting units (*akṣara*)
see also *aṅga*, *drutam*, *laghu*
khaṇḍa naḍai
subdivision of a tāla (Sanskrit *khaṇḍa gati*) having five *mātrā* per beat (*kriyā*)
khaṇḍika (Sanskrit)
section of a *gīta* composition
khaṇḍippu (Tamil) 76, Stave 7
Khwaja Salahudin 16
khyāl, *khayāl* 163
lit. 'idea, imagination'; the style and format preferred in contemporary *Hindustāni Saṅgīt*; provides more scope for virtuosity and improvisation than the *dhrupad* style preferred earlier; the South Indian *rāgam tānam pallavi* format is characterized by similar scope for elaboration although it plays a less dominant role in concerts today
see also Svāti Tirunāḷ
kīcaka (Sanskrit)
type of bamboo mentioned by Kālidāsa
see also bamboo, flute
kiṇaiyaṉ (Sanskrit) 12
player of the *kiṇai* drum used by the ancient Tamils
kīrtana 19, 49, 96, 127, 161, 162, 170, 178, Ch. 17
from Sanskrit *kīrti* ('fame, glory'); a devotional song; a form from which the classical *kṛti* and the *harikathā kālakṣepam* form evolved
see *abhaṅg*, *mokṣa* , Pratāpasiṃha, *yoga*
see also Ambujam Krishna, Annamācārya, Arunācalakkavirayar, Bhadrācala Rāmadās, Haridāsa, Māргadarśi Śēṣayyaṅgār, Muttuttāṇḍavar, Mysore Sadāśiva Rao, Nīlakaṇṭha Śivaṉ, Rāmaliṅgasvāmi, Svāti Tirunāḷ, Subrahmaṇya Bhārati, Tenmaṭam Brothers, Tyāgarāja, Vijaya Gōpālasvāmi
kīrtaṅkār 50, 170
an exponent of the *kīrtana*
see also *bhāgavatar*
kīrttanaigaḷ (Tamil)
simple songs (= *kīrtana*) based on devotional lyrics

kokila (Sanskrit)
Indian cuckoo; associated with *pañcama* (the fifth tonal step) and the spring season (*vasanta*)
see also animal imagery, birds, *rāsakrīḍā*
kolu, *golu* (Tamil) 29, Fig. 10
festive display of sacred and beautiful objects on the occasion of *Sarasvatī pūjā*
komal, *komala* (Sanskrit)
lit. 'tender, agreeable, beautiful'; the lower variant of the second, third, fourth, sixth, and seventh scale degrees; *komal gāndhāra*, *dhaivata* and *niṣāda* correspond to the 'flat' notes found in Western minor scales (= German 'moll', lit. 'soft'); *komal ri* = *śuddha ṛṣabha*, *komal ga* = *sādhāraṇa gāndhāra* (= *ṣaṭśruti ṛṣabha*); *komal ma* = *śuddha madhyama*; *komal dha* = *śuddha dhaivata*; *komal ni* = *kaiśikī niṣāda* (= *ṣaṭśruti dhaivata*)
see also enharmonic scale degrees, *tīvra*
komal-tīvra
process of assigning each among the five variable scale degrees (*vikṛta svara*) two variants, a lower (*komal*) and a higher (*tīvra*) variant; this results in twelve common *svara* variants (*svarasthāna*) from which most of the popular *janya rāgas* of Karnatic music are formed; not applicable to a several important rāgas (e.g. Nāṭa and Varāḷi) which contain a third variant (i.e. neither *kōmal* nor *tīvra*)
see also enharmonic scale degrees
kombu (Tamil)
bow-shaped brass horn used in Kerala during temple festivals (*utsava*)
see also *pañcavādya*
Konērirājapuram Vaidyanātha Ayyar 79
konnakkōl, *konugōl* (Tamil) 36, 47, 133, 138, Ch. 5
accompaniment in the form of rhythmic syllables (*jati*)
see also *tāla vādya kaccēri*
kōrvai (Tamil) 37, 85, 138, 148, 156
lit. 'contrasting or concluding pattern'; explained by practitioners in terms of 'stringing together of rhythmic patterns (e.g. *faran*, *yati*) in an aesthetic manner'; (1) a preset string of syllables (e.g. a variations of the triple 'Ta dhi ki na tom' sequence); marks the conclusion (*muktāyi*) of a rhythmic improvisation (e.g. *taniyāvarttanam*); (2) the pre-arranged conclusion (*makuṭam*) of a melodic improvisation (*svara kalpana*); (3) an elaborate combination of dance movements (*aḍavu*)
see also *kārvai*, *mōrā*, *pūrvāṅga*, *uttarāṅga*
Kōṭīśvara Ayyar 101
kōvil, *-koil* (Tamil)
temple
kōvilpurappāḍu (Tamil)
emergence of the image of the presiding deity of the temple (*kōvil*) during a major festival (*brahmotsavam*); the accompanying *periya mēḷam* ensemble plays a special piece (*mallāri*) for this occasion
krama, *krama rāga* (Sanskrit) 95
lit. 'course, step, order'; a regular (e.g. straight) series of notes; a melodic pattern (*krama sañcāra*) which coincides with the ascending (*ārohaṇa*) or descending (*avarohaṇa*) order of a particular rāga; also a type of *janya rāga*
see also *tāna pustaka*, *vakra*, *viśeṣa prayoga*
kramam (Sanskrit) 119
arrangement of words in the *ghanam* style of vedic recitation
krauñca (Sanskrit)
bird (heron) associated with *madhyama* (the fourth tonal step) and conjugal fidelity
see also animal imagery, birds, *madhyama* (*ma*)
Krishna
see Kṛṣṇa
Krishna Iyer, E. 167
Krishnamūrti, Jiddu 28
influential Indian-born philospher and educationist (1895–1986); his work aims at liberating the individual from external and internal conditioning

kriyā (Sanskrit) 128, 138, 140, Ch. 14, Table 12
lit. 'act, execution' (e.g. in rituals); a gesture used to reckon musical time (*tāla*); marks the total number of counting units (= *akṣara*) as well as the *tāla* divisions (*aṅga*) of a particular tāla; a *kriyā* is executed either (1) audibly (*saśabda kriyā*), such as a 'beat' (*ghāta*, Tamil *taṭṭu*); or (2) inaudibly (*niḥśabda kriyā*), namely by a wave of the hand, or by finger counts
see also *gati variants*, *ghāta*, *iraṇḍu kalai*, *laya*, *mātrā*, *mudrā*, *tāla daśa prāṇa*

Kṛṣṇa (Sanskrit) 16, 31, 47, 169
worshipped as the eighth incarnation of Viṣṇu (Kṛṣṇa *avatāra*); popularly depicted as a cowherd (Gopāla) of dark complexion (*śyāmā*); in early Tamil literature known as Tirumāl (e.g. *Paripāḍal*); in Sanskrit literature celebrated as Veṇugopāla, the divine player of the flute (*veṇu*), or Muraḷī, Muraḷīdharan̲ (*muraḷī* = flute); in his *kṛti Prāṇanātha*, Tyāgarāja refers to the irresistible music (*venugāna*) of Kṛṣṇa's flute
see *anaṁta*, *Bhagavad Gītā*, *Bhāgavata Purāṇa*, *bhakti*, Bhāṇḍīra, Brindavan, *cūrṇikā*, *Daśāvatārā*, *Gītagovinda*, *gopī*, Haridāsa, Jagannātha, *Kṛṣṇa līlā taraṅgiṇī*, *līlā*, *nāyaka nāyikā bhāva*, Rādhā, Rājagopāla, *rāsakrīḍā*, *śṛṅgāra*, Vṛndāvan
see also Bhadrācala Rāmadās, Jayadēva, Nārāyaṇa Tīrtha, Paccimiriyam Āḍiappayya, Ūttukkāḍu Veṅkaṭa Subba Ayyar

Kṛṣṇa līlā taraṅgiṇī
translated as 'River of the Sports of Śrī Kṛṣṇa'; a work by the South Indian composer Nārāyaṇa Tīrtha; inspired by Jayadeva's *Gītagovinda*
see also *cūrṇikā*

kṛti (Sanskrit) 19, 96, 127, 140, 158, 178, Ch. 17
lit. 'creation, work, composition; enchantment'; the most important form of South Indian music
see *anupallavi*, *caraṇa*, *kīrtana*, *mokṣa*, *pallavi*, *prabandha*, *samaṣṭi caraṇa*, *saṅgati*, *yati*

kṣetra, *kṣetram* (Sanskrit) 29
lit. 'field, sacred place, centre of pilgrimage'
see also Ādi Śaṅkara, Kalākshētra, Kṣētrayya, *tīrtha*

Kṣētrayya, Kṣētrajña 153

kuḍam (Tamil)
lit. 'pot'; the wooden resonator of a *viṇā* (*vīṇaikkuḍam*), *tambūrā* and *gōṭṭuvādyam*; made of *palāmaram*

Kuḍumiyāmalai
rock inscription in ornate Grantha script at a temple near Pudukōṭṭai; ascribed to Mahendravarman Pallava I who was personally involved in music; a series of exercises (*abhyāsa gānam*) in seven sections, each divided into fifteen groups of four musical notes; probably intended for practising an early type of a stringed instrument (*vīṇā*)

kuḻal (Tamil, Malayālam) 12, Fig. 4
lit. 'pipe'; a short double-reed instrument of Kerala; similar to a *mukhavīṇā*, *nāgasvaram* or *shenai*
see also *pullāṅkuḻal*

Kumāra (Sanskrit)
lit. 'youth, son, boy'
see Muruga, Subrahmaṇya

Kumārasaṁbhava (Sanskrit) 68
work of poetry (*kāvya*) by Kālidāsa which contains references to the delights and power of nature' s own music (e.g. the wind filling the holes of the *kīcaka* bamboo)

Kuṇaṅkuṭi Mastān̲ 15

kuṇḍalinī (Sanskrit) 23
lit. 'circular, spiral, winding, coiling as a serpent (*kuṇḍalin*)'; refers to the dynamic aspect ('serpent power') of the *cakra* concept of human psychology and physiology

Kunnakuḍi R. Vaidyanāthan̲ 165

kuraippu (Tamil)
lit. 'reducing'; calculated patterns within a *svara svara kalpana* improvisation; based on a particular target note (*svara*) within the tāla cycle (*eḍuppu*); shortened in specific increments (i.e. half, quarter etc.)

see also *uttarāṅga*
kuratti (Tamil) 168
female gypsy; a folk character in dance-dramas
kuravan̲ (Tamil)
male gypsy; a folk character in dance-dramas
kuravañji (Tamil) 168
dance-drama inspired by folk themes; has gypsies for its central characters
see also Rukmini Devi-Arundale
Kūrma *avatāra* (Sanskrit)
lit. 'tortoise'; the second incarnation of Viṣṇu
see *Daśāvatārā*
Kurukṣetra (Sanskrit)
location of a great battle in the *Mahābhārata* epic
kūttan̲ (Tamil)
male dancer
kūttapirān̲ (Tamil)
name of Śiva, the divine dancer (= Naṭarāja)
kūttu (Tamil) 19, 47, 153, 168
any type of folk play or drama; often based on the epics or *Purāṇa*
see dance-drama, *nāṭya*
see also *Muttamil̲*

laghu (Sanskrit) 128, 138, Tables 12, 16
the variable section (*aṅga*) of some tālas (e.g. ādi tāla, aṭa tāla); comprises between 3 and 9 counting units (*akṣarakāla*, *kriyā*)
see also *jāti*, I3, I4, I5, I7, I9
lakṣaṇa (Sanskrit) 70
lit. 'description, definition, scope'; the characteristic features of a rāga (*rāga lakṣaṇa*, *rāga rūpa*); both the *Saṅgīta Ratnākara* and the *Saṅgīta Sudhā* mention thirteen *lakṣaṇa* (*trayodaśa lakṣaṇa*); of these, Veṅkaṭamakhi deleted those three which he regarded as separate types of *janya rāgas*, namely *ṣāḍava*, *auḍava* and *antara mārga*; the songs (*kṛti*) of the 19th *c.* Trinity of Karnatic composers are now referred to as authoritative models; they also define the form (*rāga rūpa*) of several rāgas which only recently gained sufficient status to be considered for creative exploration (*manodharma*)
see also *lakṣaṇakāra*, *lakṣya*, *Svara Mēḷa Kalānidhi*
lakṣaṇa gīta (Sanskrit)
didactic composition which illustrates and explains the special features (*lakṣaṇa*) of a rāga; Gōvinda's *lakṣaṇa gītas* cover the 72 *mēḷakartā rāgas* explained in his *Saṁgraha-Cūḍā-Maṇi*, and 294 others to illustrate the *janya rāgas* known in his time
lakṣaṇagrantha (Sanskrit) 95, 97, 162
technical manual; a work on music
see treatise
see also Nārāyaṇa Tīrtha
lakṣaṇakāra (Sanskrit)
music theorist, author of a treatise
Lakṣmī (Śrī) 168
consort (*śakti*) of Viṣṇu; a goddess associated with beauty and prosperity
lakṣya (Sanskrit) 70
lit. 'perceptible, expressed, example'; denotes the acceptance or validity of a particular interpretation of a rāga; sanctioned with reference to the phrases (*prayoga*, *viśeṣa sañcāra*) found in well-known compositions (e.g. *gītam*, *kṛti*, *tānavarṇam*); may involve a degree of deviation from theoretical guidelines (*lakṣaṇa*) whereby experts tend to confine their approval to a particular instrumental or vocal style (*bāṇī*), or a particular variant of interpretation (*pāṭhāntara*)
see also *Svara Mēḷa Kalānidhi*
lāli 127
marriage song; often in rāga Nīlāmbari
lālita (Sanskrit)
lit. 'loved, desired' (*lālitam*, lit. 'pleasure, love, joy')
language 33, 34, 160, 161, 170
see Bhāṇḍīra, Hindi, Kannaḍa, Malayālam, Maṇipravāḷam, Marāṭhi, Sanskrit, Tamil, Telugu
see also Ekōji I, *jāvaḷi*, *Muttamil̲*, Raghunātha Nāyaka
lāsya (Sanskrit) Fig. 7, 8
graceful, feminine manner of dancing
see *Mōhiniyāṭṭam*, *tribhaṅga*

see also Tañjāvūr Quartette
laughter 65
see also *hāsya*
laya, layam (Sanskrit) 8, 36, 64, 156
(1) the rhythmic aspect of Indian music; musical time (i.e. the modern concept of *tāla*); the proverbial 'father' (*pitā*) of music; (2) degree of speed; i.e. the time interval between two counting units of a tāla (*kriyā*)
see *layavinyāsa, śruti, tāla daśa prāṇa, tāla vādya kaccēri*, tempo
see also Ṣaṭkāla Narasayyā
layavādyakāra (Sanskrit) 50
percussionist
layavinyāsa (Sanskrit) 47, 128, 140, Ch. 17
systematic exposition (*vinyāsa*) of rhythmic intricacies (*laya*); mostly in the form of a special ensemble performance devoted to a particular *tāla*
see also *prastāra, tāla vādya kaccēri, yati*
letters (Sanskrit) Table 11
see *kaṭapayādi sūtra, saṁkhyākṣara*
liberation 64
see *mokṣa*
see also Krishnamūrti, *mantra, sādhanā, sahasrāra, saṁsāra*
light and folk music 61, 121, 155, 170
see *dēśī, dēśya rāga, mellisai, rāga-rāgiṇī, tukkaḍā*
life 27, 30, 31, 34, 112, 161, 164
see also *āśrama, Bhagavad Gītā, caturāśramam, jīva, kāma, mokṣa, prāṇa, saṁsāra, saṁskāra, sattvam*
līlā (Sanskrit)
lit. 'play, diversion, sport, pleasure'; in philosophy and mythology, the 'playful' activity of the supreme Creator (e.g. envisaged as Viṣṇu or Kṛṣṇa); a metaphor for 'semblance' or reality on a cosmic or superhuman scale which can neither be perceived by the sensory apparatus nor comprehended by way of reasoning; *bhakti* poetry gave this abstract conception a more popular form which highlights the amorous connotation of *līlā*; Kṛṣṇa (God) and Rādhā (the human soul) have since been visualized as lovers (*madhurabhakti, nāyaka nāyikā bhāva*)
see also Ādi Śaṅkara, *cūrṇikā, Kṛṣṇa līlā taraṅgiṇī, māyā*
līna, līnam (Sanskrit) Stave 7
lit. 'concealed, dissolved, vanished'; an embellishment (*gamaka*); a brief higher note departing from a long note
see also *orikkai*
lineage, tradition
see Āvuḍaiyārkōvil, *bāṇī, gharānā, gurukulavāsa, guruśiṣya paramparā*, Hanūmān, *Hindustānī saṅgīt, iṣṭadevatā, karṇa paraṁpara, Karṇāṭaka saṅgīta, mārga, mārgam, mēḷakkārar, nāḍī, Nārada purāṇa*, Pālakkāḍu, *paraṁpara, ṛṣi, saṁpradāya, saṅgīta*, Vijayanagar
listener, hearing
see audience, ear, *mānasa guru*
literary works, literature, letters 10, 29
Abhijñāna Śākuntalam, aṣṭapadi, Bhāgavata Purāṇa, Cilappatikāram, Divya Prabandham, Gītagovinda, Kumārasaṁbhava, Maṇimēgalai, Paripāḍal, Pattupāṭṭu, Purāṇa, śāstra, Sirupuliyūr ulā, Tantra, Tēvāram, Tiruppugal, Tirumurai, Tiruppāvai, Veda
see also drama, poetry, poets, treatises
live concert 80, 154, 164, Ch. 15
long
see elongation
lotus
symbol of divine beauty, perfection and purity, and of the human heart (Sanskrit *padmam, kamalam* etc.); many deities (e.g. Lakṣmī) are depicted as being seated on a lotus
see *cakra, Padmanābha*
love, lover, erotic sentiment 31, 64
see *madhurabhakti, śṛṅgāra*
see also *Bhāgavata purāṇa, bhāva, Gītagovinda, jāvaḷi, kāma, lālita, līlā*, Māṇikkavācakar, Muruga, *navarasa, puruṣārtha*, Rādhā, *rakti*, Tirumāl, *vātsalya rasa*
low, lower
see *anudātta, anumandra sthāyī, bāri, irakka jāru, janta svara, komal, komal-tīvra, mandra sthāyī*, mnemonic svara

syllables, *odukkal*, *pūrvāṅga*, *sphurita*, *śuddha dhaivata*, *śuddha gāndhāra*, *śuddha madhyama*, *śuddha niṣāda*, *śuddha ṛṣabha*, *taggu kaṭṭai*, *taggu śruti*, *tripuccha*, *tristhāyī*

lullaby 127, 141, 156
  see Nīlāmbari rāga, *Ōmana tiṅgaḷ kiḍavō*
  see also Irayimman Tampi

lute 91, 94
  see *dāravī*, *gōṭṭuvādyam*, *tambūrā*, *vīṇā*
  see also *daṇḍi*, *gātravatī*, Nārada, *vādya trayam*, *vaiṇuka*

lyre, *lyra* 93

lyrics 10, 31, 58, 153, 154
  see *mātu*, *sāhitya*
  see also *abhinaya*, *aṅkitam*, *bhakti*, Gaṇeśa, *gāyaki*, *jīvātman*, languages, *līlā*, literary works, Maṇipravāḷam, *māyā*, *meṭṭu*, *mudrā*, *muktāyi*, *narastuti*, *navarasa*, *nindāstsuti*, *nōṭṭusvara pāṭṭu*, poetry, *rasika*, *sama eḍuppu*, *saṁsāra*, *svarākṣara*, *Tantra*, *tutukāram*, *vāggēyakāra*, *Vedānta*, *viruttam*, *yoga*

ma Table 10
  (1) the abbreviation for both variants of *madhyama* (i.e. *śuddha madhyama* and *prati madhyama*); (2) the mnemonic svara syllable for *śuddha madhyama*

ma-mi see mnemonic svara syllables

madhurabhakti (Sanskrit)
  'sweet' (*madhura*) or 'agreeable' form of devotion (*bhakti*); refers to the concept of sanctified love (*nāyaka nāyikā bhāva*) which is widely found in Indian literature (e.g. *Bhāgavata Purāṇa*, *Gītagovinda*, *Tirukkōvai*); expressed by profound love and longing (*śṛṅgāra bhāva*) for the Divine; the devotee regards him- or herself as the 'female'. beloved (*nāyikā*, i.e. the 'soul') and always addresses God (*paramātma*) as the 'male' lover (*nāyaka*)
  see *Divya Prabandhami*, *padam*
  see also Āṇḍāḷ, Kṣētrajña, Māṇikkavācakar

mādhurya (Sanskrit)
  sweetness of style (e.g. that of a padam)

madhyama (*ma*)
  the fourth scale degree (*svara*); traditionally associated with the heron
  see also *ma*, *mi*

madhyama kāla (Sanskrit) 78, 134
  (1) the second or medium degree of speed; (2) a moderate tempo; (3) sometimes used as synonym for the *tānam*
  see also *dvitīya kāla*, *iraṇḍu kalai*, *makariṇi*, *trikāla*

madhyama śruti (Sanskrit) 39
  tuning system applicable to rāgas with a limited range (i.e. *dhaivatāntya*, *niṣādāntya* and *pañcamāntya* rāgas)

madhya sthāyī (Sanskrit) 62, 80, Fig. 25; Staves 1, 2, 5
  the middle octave
  see *tristhāyī*, *svarāvaḷi*

Madras
  see Chennai

Madurai Fig. 26
  city in Tamil Nadu; capital of the *Pāṇḍya* dynasty; associated with early Tamil literature (*Saṅgam*, *Cilappatikāram*)

Madurai S. Sōmasundaram 165

ma grāma (Sanskrit)
  ancient scale; built on the fourth note (*madhyama*) instead of the first note (i.e. *sa grāma*)

maguḍi (Tamil) 178, Ch. 17
  (1) the snake charmer's bulbous reed-pipe; (2) a folk tune, similar to rāga Punnāgavarāḷi, which is associated with the instrument

Mahābalipuram
  see Māmallapuram

Mahābhārata (Sanskrit) 16, 30, 69, 170
  one of the two great epics of India
  see also *Bhagavad Gītā*, *Kurukṣetra*, *Rāmāyaṇa*

mahābhūta (Sanskrit)
  the five primary substances of the world; perceived by corresponding senses, namely (1) ether (*ākāśa*, hearing), (2) wind (*vāyu*, touch), (3) fire (*tejas*, sight), (4) water (*āpas*, taste), (5) earth (*pṛthvī*, smell)

mahākāla (Sanskrit)
  lit. 'great (*mahā*) destiny or time (*kāla*)'; the principle of time (*kāla*) associated with death or dissolution; embodied by Śiva
  see also Naṭarāja

mahānāṭakam
Telugu play
see also *Prahlāda Mahānāṭakam*, Vijayarāghava
mahārājā (Sanskrit)
king
see also *samasthāna vidvān*
mahārāṇī (Sanskrit)
queen
Maharashtra [Mahārāṣṭra] 19, 49, 50 Fig. 26
state of the Indian union where the Marāṭhi language is mainly spoken
see also Marāṭhā, *sūfi*, *harikathā kālakṣepam*
Mahāvaidyanātha Śivan 62, 101, 121, 163
Mahēndravarman I
Pallava ruler (600–30); believed to be the author of an important musical inscription at the Kuḍumiyāmalai temple
major scale 106, Table 10
makariṇi (Sanskrit)
concluding part of an elaborate *rāga ālāpana* (= *tāṉam*, *madhyama kāla*)
see also *muktāyi*, *sthāyi*
makuṭam (Sanskrit)
lit. 'crown'; a conclusion for a *ciṭṭasvara* or *svara kalpana* passage (= *kōrvai*, *muktāyi*); mostly a familiar pattern, namely a variation corresponding to the five *jati* syllables '*Ta dhi*(*n*) *ki na tom*'; a matching sequence of notes (*svara*) is rendered thrice in succession and thereby leads back to the starting point of a chosen theme (e.g. *pallavi* of a *kṛti*)
Malayālam
language mainly spoken in Kerala
see *Kathakali*, Maṇipravāḷam
see also M.D. Rāmanāthaṉ, Svāti Tirunāḷ
male 31, 170
see *deva*, *dhrupad*, *gāndharva*, *madhurabhakti*, Naṭarāja, *naṭṭuvanar*, *rāga-rāgiṇī*
mālikā (Sanskrit)
lit. 'garland, series, string'
see *rāgamālikā*
Malik Kafur 15
see Caṭakōpaṉ
mallāri (Sanskrit) 35, 179, Ch. 17
from *malla* 'a strong, excellent god or man'; a piece in rāga Gambhīranāṭa; played by *nāgasvaram* and *tavil* ensemble (*mēḷam*) during festive temple processions (*utsvam*)
see also *kōvilpurappāḍu*
Māmallapuram (Mahābalipuram) 69, Fig. 2, 26
ancient port city of the *Pallava* dynasty which had its capital at *Kāñcīpuram*; famous for its monuments, sculptures and friezes depicting several stages in the development of early temple architecture and iconography
manas (Sanskrit)
lit. 'mind, heart, intelligence, imagination, wish'
mānasa guru, *mānasika guru* (Sanskrit) 79
an 'imagined' teacher; the inspiring master whose style or technique is sought to be emulated by way of listening (i.e. in the absence of personal contact)
see also *guru*, *gurukulavāsa*
Manasusvādhīnamaina
see *āśrama*
maṇḍala (Sanskrit) 41
(1) lit. 'round, circular' (e.g. diagram); (2) 'collection, division'; (3) a position of the feet
see also *ardhamaṇḍalī*
mandolin 17, 55
mandra sthāyī (Sanskrit) 54, 62, 76, Fig. 25; Staves 1, 2, 5
the lower register (octave)
see also *anumandra sthāyī tristhāyī*
maṅgaḷam (Sanskrit) 156, 179, Ch. 17
lit. 'auspiciousness, fortitude, blessing, happiness, festival, ceremony, marriage'; a composition performed as a joyous conclusion of a dance or music performance
see also *nitya sumaṅgaḷi*
maṅgaḷa vādya (Sanskrit) 43
an 'auspicious instrument' (notably *nāgasvaram*); required for celebrating a festival (*brahmotsavam*) or marriage
Māṇikkavācakar
Tamil *Śaiva* poet whose name means 'utterer of gems'; his work is collectively referred to as *Tiruvācakam* ('sacred utterings'); a minister of a

Pāṇḍya king of Madurai in the 9th *c.* (dates between the 3rd and the 7th *c.* are also given); in *Tirukkōvai*, he hails the concept of *madhurabhakti* (sanctified love) as a path towards salvation; his music has traditionally been recited, and also sung to rāga Mōhanam; in modern times, rāgas Ārabhi and Kāmbhōji are also employed for some of his hymns

Maṇimēgalai (Tamil) 67
work written during the Buddhist period of South India; its theme is connected with that of the *Cilappatikāram*

Maṇipravāḷam (Sanskrit) 91, Fig. 26
lit. 'diamond (*maṇi*) and coral' (*pravāḷa*); a mixture of two languages, namely Sanskrit (= *maṇi*), and vernacular (= *pravāḷa*, i.e. Tamil or Malayālam); employed for the lyrics of many compositions as well as in *harikathā kālakṣepam*
see also Ambujam Krishna, Irayimman Tampi, Svāti Tirunāḷ

maṇipūra (Sanskrit) Fig. 25
lit. 'gem-site'; the third *cakra* near the navel (solar plexus); visualized as having red colour and a lotus with ten petals
see also diaphragm, *nābhi*

Mannārguḍi
formerly an important religious and musical centre of Tamil Nadu; also referred to as *Dakṣina Dvāraka*
see Rājagopāla

Mannārguḍi Pakkiri Piḷḷai 47

manodharma (Sanskrit) 49
lit. 'mental quality'; here imagination, spontaneity

manodharma saṅgīta (Sanskrit) 13, 36, 85, 157, 159, 162, Ch. 15
the creative (improvised) branch of South Indian music; inherent in forms and techniques such as *ālāpana*, *kalpita saṅgīta*, *niraval*, *rāgam tānam pallavi*, *taniyāvartanam*
see also *gāyaki*, imagination, *kalpita saṅgīta*, *lakṣaṇa*

mantra (Sanskrit) 64
lit. 'incantation, vedic hymn, prayer, sacred text, charm, spell'; the term applies to the prose formula of the *Yajurveda* as well as the magic formula in the tradition of *Tantra*; comprises one or several syllables; the effective use of the monosyllabic '*om*' (*bījākṣara*) is believed to depend on frequent repetition with full concentration; unlike a *śloka*, an individual *mantra* conveys no specific meaning; if bestowed by an accomplished sprititual preceptor (*guru*), it is believed to help an individual to achieve absolute self-control, the requirement for self-realization and ultimate liberation (*mokṣa*)
see also *mūlamantram*, *praṇava*, *pūjā*, *Veda*, *yoga*

manual
see *tāna pustaka*
see also commentaries, *śāstra*, treatise

manuscript
see book

Map of South India Fig. 26

Marāṭhā 49, 92
lit. 'a person hailing from Mahārāṣṭra'; a dynasty of rulers, patrons and scholars who made Tañjāvūr the cultural capital of South India from the late 17th to the early 19th *c.* (in chronological order): Ekōji I (Veṅkhāji), Śahajī II, Śarabhōjī I, Tulajājī I (Tukkojī), Ekōji II, Pratāpasiṁha, Tulajājī II, Amarasiṁha, Śarabhōjī II (Serfōjī), Śivājī II
see also *abhaṅg*, Nāyaka

Marāṭhi 170, Fig. 26
language of Mahārāṣṭra

mārga (Sanskrit) 91, 170
lit. 'path'; (1) an archaic concept which defines religious or artistic practices; implies adherence to the rules of an established tradition (e.g. *gāndharva*); hence any unorthodox practice is labelled regional or provincial (*deśī*), just like a dialect; (2) one of the ten features of tāla listed in the old system of music (*tāla daśa prāṇa*); pertains to compositions (i.e. duration per count)
see also *lakṣaṇa*, *lakṣya*, *pāṭhāntara*, *sādhanā*, *tāla daśa prāṇa*

mārgadarśī (Sanskrit)
lit. 'one who shows the path (*mārga*)'; refers to a musical 'pioneer' (e.g. Mārgadarśī Śeṣa Iyeṅgār)
see Paccimiriyam Āḍiappayya

mārgam
the traditional format or sequence of dance items in *Bharata nāṭyam*, namely *alārippu, jatisvaram, śabdam, padavarṇam, padam, jāvaḷi, tillānā, maṅgaḷam*
see also *paddhati*

mārga rāga
term applied to an obsolete category of standardized rāgas which is mentioned in ancient treatises
see also *deśya rāga*

mārga saṅgīta (Sanskrit) 119
the sacred, formalized type of music believed to be in accordance with primordial teachings (e.g. *Veda, Upaniṣad*)

marriage 12, 36, 44, 166
see *lāli, maṅgaḷam, maṅgaḷa vādya*

Marugēlarā 97, 127
a *kṛti* by Tyāgarāja

master 47, 88, 162
in South India, the word 'Master' is often prefixed to the name of a male child prodigy
see also *ācārya, bhāgavatar, mānasa guru, paṇḍita, viduṣī, vidvān*

mātā (Sanskrit)
lit. 'mother'
see also *śruti*

Mataṅga
see *Bṛhaddeśī*

maternal
see mother

maṭha, maṭh (Sanskrit)
lit. 'place of learning, monastery' (= Mutt); many musicians are affiliated to a *maṭha* in the honorary capacity known as *āsthāna vidvān* (e.g. the *maṭha* of the *Śaṅkarācārya* of *Kāñcīpuram*)
see also Ādi Śaṅkara

maṭhya tāla, maṭya tāla Table 19, Stave 10
tāla with three sections (*aṅga*), namely *laghu, drutam, laghu*
see *caturaśra jāti maṭhya tāla, sūḷādi sapta tāla*

mātrā (Sanskrit), *māttirai* (Tamil) 134, 138, 140, 141, Table 17
lit. 'unit of measurement, metre, standard, moment, element, particle'; (1) sub-unit or fraction of a basic counting unit (*akṣara, kriyā*); (2) measure for the duration of a note (*svara*), rhythmic syllable (*jati*), pause (*kārvai*) or point of departure (*graha, eḍuppu*); a number given with reference to a particular *tāla* structure (e.g. six *mātrā* for *oṉrarai eḍuppu*)
see also *akṣara kāla, āvarta, gati, gati variants, iraṇḍu kalai*

Matsya *avatāra* (Sanskrit)
lit. 'fish'; the first incarnation of Viṣṇu
see *Daśāvatārā*

māttirai (Tamil)
lit. 'the time taken for batting one's eyes or snapping one's fingers'; (1) unit of time (= *mātrā*); (2) measure for microtonal steps (= *śruti*)
see also *alagu, mātrā*

mātu (Sanskrit) 153, Ch. 15
the lyrics (= *sāhitya*) of a composition
see also *dhātu, meṭṭu*; *vāggēyakāra*

māyā (Sanskrit) 27, 30
lit. 'illusion, deceit' (e.g. as to the nature of the 'Self' in relation to God and the universe); the subject of many lyrics in Karnatic music (e.g. those by Muttusvāmi Dīkṣitar and Tyāgarāja)
see also Ādi Śaṅkara, *avidyā, ātman, līlā, saṁsāra*

Māye tvam yāhī (Sanskrit)
see *yati*

mayūra (Sanskrit)
peacock; the bird associated with *ṣaḍja* (the first tonal step); often found in pictures of Kṛṣṇa and Sarasvatī; the mount of Muruga
see also animal imagery, *ṣaḍja* (*sa*)

media
see AIR, history of Karnatic music

meditation 26
see *dhyāna, pūjā, samādhi, yantra, yoga*

medium
see middle

Meghadūta (Sanskrit) 68
work by Kālidāsa; refers to a concert for Śiva produced by wind that fills the bamboo, a chorus of the wives of celestial beings, and thunder resounding in the caves
mēḷa, *meḷakartā rāga* (Sanskrit) 40, 70, 74, 84, 94, 95, 106, 120, Ch. 12, Table 10, Staves 17–19
reference scale (= *janaka rāga*)
see *kaṭapayādi sūtra*, *lakṣaṇa gīta*, *pūrvāṅga*, *rāgāṅga rāga*, Rāmāmātya, *Saṁgraha-Cūḍā-Maṇi*, *ṭhāṭ*, *uttarāṅga*
see also Kōṭīsvara Ayyar, Mahāvaidyanātha Śivan, D. Pattammal, Tyāgarāja
mēḷa-janya rāga system Ch. 12, 13
Karnatic music is based on a system of 72 scales; hundreds of old and new rāgas can either be derived from (= *janya rāga*), or allocated to, a particular scale; a classification first mentioned in the *Saṅgita Sāra* of Vidyāraṇya, and established by Rāmāmātya; developed further by Veṅkaṭamakhi and Gōvinda
see also Bhāṭkhaṇḍe, *ṭhāṭ*
mēḷakkārar (Tamil)
male musician; traditionally someone belonging to a family of dancers, *nāgasvaram* and *tavil* players
see also *tavilkārar*
mēḷam (Tamil) 94
lit 'ensemble' (1) a dance ensemble (*cinna mēḷam*); (2) a drama ensemble (*nāṭya mēḷam*); (3) an ensemble of temple musicians (*periya mēḷam*); (4) during a temple festival (*utsavam*) of Kerala, an ensemble of five types of instruments (*pañcavādya*); (5) the assembly of metal frets of a *vīṇā* on a base of wax
see also *mallāri*
mēḷa paddhati, *mēḷakartā paddhati* (Sanskrit) 95
system of 72 reference scales
see Rāmāmātya, *paddhati*
mēḷa rāga mālikā cakra (Sanskrit)
composition by Mahāvaidyanātha Śivan; covers all the 72 scales of Karnatic music in the systematic order of the *mēḷakartā* system
Mēlaṭṭūr bhāgavata mēḷam
Telugu dance-drama; devoted entirely to enacting *Prahlāda Caritram* at Mēlaṭṭūr village near Tañjāvūr; during an annual drama festival, it celebrates the victory of Narasiṁha *avatāra* (Viṣṇu) over Hiraṇyakaśipu, demonic father of Prahlāda, a saintly young devotee (*bhakta*) of Viṣṇu; influenced by the Telugu plays (*mahānāṭakam*) which were written and patronized by the rulers of Tañjāvūr (notably Śāhajī and Vijayarāghava)
see also *nāṭya mēḷam*, *Prahlāda Bhakti Vijayam*, Tulajājī II, Veṅkaṭarāma Śāstrī
mellisai (Tamil)
light music
melody, melodious 31, 38, 76, 138, 156, 159, 161
see *alaṁkāram*, *bha-ra-ta*, *bheda*, *eḍakka*, *gumki*, *jāti*, *kāku*, *krama*, *meṭṭu*, *paṇ*, *prayoga*, *rāga*, *Sāmaveda*, *sañcāra*, *saṅgati*, *saukhyam*, *ślokam*, *svara prastāra*, *tāna pustaka*, *viśeṣa prayoga*
membrane 45, 51, 52
see *avanaddha vādya*
memory, memorization 33, 47, 60, 80, 85, 157, 158, 163
see mnemonics
see also *saṁskāra*, *smṛti*, *tāla*
metaphysics
of sound 92
see also history of Karnatic music, *nāda*
metre 78
see *mātrā*, *sandam*, *viruttam*
meṭṭu (Tamil)
(1) the musical structure of a song (= *varṇameṭṭu*, Sanskrit *dhātu*); complemented by the lyrics (*sāhitya*, *mātu*); *meṭṭu amai* refers to 'setting' the lyrics of another composer or poet to music; re-composing a song whose original music was lost (e.g. *aṣṭapadi*, *dēvarnāma*); (2) the bridge and frets of a string instrument (*vīṇā*)
see also *mēḷam*, *pāṭṭu*, *viruttam*
mi Table 10
the mnemonic svara syllable for *prati madhyama*
microtone, smallest intervals 42, 46, 55, 58, 70, 96, 106, 163, Ch. 8

any interval which is smaller than a semitone step (*svarasthāna*); 22 are generally accepted and referred to as *śruti*; most microtones of Indian music are of a transitory nature and occur as part of the embellishments (*gamaka*) and phrases (*sañcāra*) to reinforce the expressive quality of a rāga; a favourite subject of writers on Indian music whose calculations are, however, rarely used by performing musicians except for experimental purposes
see Akalanka, *alagu*, *kāku*, *śruti*

middle, medium
see *anupallavi*, *a͟rudi*, *catuḥśruti dhaivata*, *catuḥśruti ṛṣabha*, *kaiśikī niṣāda*, *madhyama kāla*, *madhya sthāyī*, mnemonic svara syllables, *padagarbha*, *sādhāraṇa gāndhāra*, *svarāvaḷi*, *svarita*, *tristhāyī*, *trikāla*, *uttarāṅga*

Milton, John 21
English poet and writer (1608–74); author of *Paradise Lost*; his works extol the wonder of creation, moral passion, human dignity, and free will

mime
see *abhinaya*
see also acting

Mīnākṣi
presiding deity in the great temple of Madurai

Mīn͟ākṣime (Sanskrit) 74
kṛti by Muttusvāmi Dīkṣitar (rāga Pūrvīkalyāṇi, ādi tāla) in which ten kinds of embellishments (*daśavidha gamaka*) are mentioned as being pleasing to goddess Mīn͟ākṣi

mind 27, 38, 158
see also *āśrama*, *ātmān*, *ekāgratā*, *hṛd*, *manas*, psychology, *saṁsāra*, *saṁskāra*, *Tantra*, *yoga*

mīnd
embellishment (*gamaka*) found in *Hindustānī* music (= glide)

Minnesang 13

minor rāgas 116, 127
see *ēkaika kṛti rāga*, *dēśya rāga*, *tukkaḍā*

miśra (Sanskrit)
lit. 'mixed, diverse'; in the context of rhythmic calculation, a division or subdivision into seven units
see *gati*, *jāti*, *laghu*, *mātrā*
see also *saṅkīrṇa*

miśra cāpu tāla Table 19, Stave 37
short tāla of seven units (3 + 2 + 2 = 7 *mātrā*)

miśra gati (Sanskrit)
see *miśra naḍai*

miśra jāti (Sanskrit)
symbol 'I7'
laghu section with seven beats

miśra jāti jhampa tāla
the fourth of seven basic tālas (*sūḷādi sapta tāla*); 7 + 1 + 2 = 10 counting units (*akṣara*)
see also *aṅga*, *anudrutam*, *drutam*, *laghu*

miśra naḍai
subdivision of a tāla (Sanskrit *miśra gati*); seven *mātrā* per beat (*kriyā*)

miśra rāga 111, 127
lit. 'mixed'; a rāga which borrows melodic elements from another rāga; also referred to as 'tinged' rāga (*chāyālaga*)

mīṭṭu (Tamil)
lit. 'plucking' a string (e.g. *gōṭṭuvādyam*, *vīṇā*)
see also *gāyaki*

mixed, mixture
see *chāyā*, *karaṇai*, Maṇipravāḷam, *miśra*, *saṅkīrṇa*, *svarita*

mnemonics 88, 99 Ch. 12, Table 10
see *akṣara*, alpha-numerical mnemonics, *bha-ra-ta*, *kaṭapayādi*, *piḍippu*, *rāga rāgiṇī*, *saṁkhyā*, *sūtra*

mnemonic svara syllables Table 10
a method based on three pairs of vowels (i.e. '*a-a*', '*i-i*', '*u-u*'); these are combined with two pairs of notes (i.e. *ri-ga*, and *dha-ni*); the resulting six vowel-combinations help to remember six corresponding pairs of musical notes: '*ra-ga*', '*ra-gi*', '*ra-gu*', '*ri-gi*', '*ri-gu*', '*gu-gu*'; each svara-combination constitutes a semitonal interval-pattern; this method provides the structure of the modern system of 72 reference scales of Veṅkaṭamakhi (*mēḷakartā rāga*); *mēḷakartā rāgas* 1 to 6 (the first '*cakra*') all contain the same combination, namely '*ra-ga-ma*'; *mēḷa* 1 = '*dha-na*', *mēḷa* 2 = '*dha-ni*' etc.);

'*a*' = lowest, '*i*' = middle, and '*u*' = highest variant (*ga-gi-gu*); only one variant applies in any given *mēḷakartā rāga* (e.g. *gi* in *mēḷa* 22), but two or more variants can occur in a *janya rāga* (i.e. a *bhāṣāṅga rāga*, such as Hindustāni Kāpi and Sindhubhairavi); unlike the proverbial seven syllables (*saptasvara*, i.e. *sa*, *ri*, *ga*, *ma*, *pa*, *dha*, *ni*), these mnemonic syllable variants are not used in singing
see also enharmonic scale degrees, memory, *pūrvāṅga*, *uttarāṅga*, *svarasthāna*

modal shift, modes 94, Stave 16

modern, modernity 22, 128

modification, modulation 66
see *chāyā*, *gumki*, *kāku*; *mūrcchanā*, *sthāna*
see also permutation

Moghul, Mughal 10, 92
Muslim dynasty of North India
see history of Karnatic music, *sūfi*

mōharā
see *mōrā*

Mōhiniyāṭṭam (Malayālam) 169
a graceful, feminine (*lāsya*) dance style; originally the temple dance (*āṭṭam*) of Kerala
see also Tañjāvūr Quartette

mokṣa (Sanskrit) 23, 24, 157
literally, 'liberation, release, delivery'; in *Vedānta* philosophy, the merging of the *jīvātman* (individual soul) with the *Brahman* (Absolute); salvation through spiritual knowledge (*vidyā*); like many of his predecessors and successors, Tyāgarāja describes devotional music (*kīrtana*, *kṛti*) as the ideal and easiest path towards this ultimate goal in life, notably in his *kṛti Mōkṣamu galadā* (rāga Sāramati)
see also *mantra*, *mūlādhāra*, *nāda yoga*, *puruṣārtha*, *samādhi*

Mōkṣamu galadā 23

moll (German)
minor scale in Western music (from Latin 'soft')
see *kōmal*, *naya rāga*, *tīvra*

monism
see Ādi Śaṅkara

Montessori, Dr Maria 33
Italian-born medical doctor and educationist (1870–1952); lived and taught in India during World War II
see also Rukmini Devi-Arundale

mood 38, 60, 88, 96, 126
see *bhāva*, *rasa*

mōrā, *mōharā* 148
(1) refers to a curriculum of numerous, often complex rhythmic lessons (e.g. including a *yati* pattern); composed to practise different tālas and the correct finger strokes that produce the characteristic cross-rhythms of Karnatic music; also meant to prepare the player of a percussion instrument (e.g. *mṛdaṅgam*) for the complexities of concert music, namely the accompaniment of classical compositions (e.g. *kṛti*) and improvised solo-play (i.e. *taniyāvarttaṉam*); (2) pre-arranged and elaborate percussive patterns which can include intricate *yati* patterns and extend over four or more tāla cycles; most commonly a *kōrvai* pattern played thrice; performed in the concluding part of a *taniyāvarttaṉam* (e.g. cadential *mōrā*); followed by a *tīrmāṇam* and the final pattern (*muktāyippu*)
see also *faran*, *makuṭam*, *muktāyi*

mōrsiṅg 52, Ch. 5, Fig. 5
small rhythm instrument made of steel; an idiophone ('Jew's harp')
see *vādya*)

mother 31
see Devī, feminine, Kāmākṣi, *mātā*, *śakti*, *śruti*, *vātsalya rasa*

mouth- or blowing-hole 46
see *mukharandhra*

mṛdaṅgam (Sanskrit) 12, 43, 49, 50, 85, 148, 160, Ch. 5, Fig. 5, 21
double-faced drum with a body made of *palāmaram*
see also *ciṉṉa mēḷam*, *dhin*, *dīm*, *gumki*, *jati*, *heccu kaṭṭai*, *karaṇai*, *mulavu*, *pakkavādya*, *taggu kaṭṭai*, *tablā*, *taggu śruti*, *vādya trayam*

mṛdaṅga yati (Sanskrit)
see yati

mudal nūl (Tamil) 47

mudrā (Sanskrit) 170, 218, Ch. 19, Fig. 11, 12
lit. 'seal, stamp, impression'; (1) a mark (*aṅkitam*) or signature woven into the lyrics (*sāhitya*) of a song (*vāggēyakāra mudrā* or *aṅkitam*); reveals a composer's identity and discourages alterations by other musicians; (2) the mentioning of the rāga's name in the lyrics (*rāga mudrā*), a common feature of compositions by Muttusvāmi Dīkṣitar; (3) a hand gesture in dance and drama
see also *kriyā*, *svanāma mudrākara*

Müller, Max 26

mukharandhra (Sanskrit)
mouth- or blowing-hole of the flute

mukhavīṇā 19, 44
see *nāgasvaram*

mukkāliḍam eḍuppu (Tamil) 138
starting the theme at a point which is set 'three quarters' (*mukkāl*) of a beat or three *mātrā* after the start of the tāla cycle (*samam*); a variant of *anāgata eḍuppu*
see also *eḍuppu*, *iḍam*

muktāyi (Telugu) 47, 138
precise conclusion of an improvisation or section of a composition (= Tamil *muttāippu*); (1) the conclusion of a *rāga ālāpana* exposition; (2) Tamil *muktāyippu* or *muttāyippu* (lit. 'effective or precise end'); either the conclusion of a *svara kalpana* interlude (*makuṭam*); or a complex rhythmic pattern, the climax of a *taṉiyāvarttaṉam*; (3) the solfa syllables (*muktāyi svara*) following the *anupallavi* section of a *tānavarṇam* (= *ciṭṭasvara*); (4) a concluding part of the *anupallavi* section of a *padavarṇam* which also has lyrics (*sāhitya*)
see also *iraṇḍu kalai*, *kōrvai*, *mōṟā*, *pūrvāṅga*, *uttarāṅga*

mūlādhāra (Sanskrit) 63, 64, 65, Fig. 25
lit. the 'bearing (*dhāra*) the root or base (*mūlam*)'; the first or lowest *cakra* (i.e. near the lower end of the spine and genitals); the location where *nāda* and the bliss resulting from it are believed to originate; visualized as having yellow colour and a lotus with four petals; referred to in *Svararāgasudhā*, a *kṛti* by Tyāgarāja (*mūlādhāraja nādameruguṭa / mudamagu mokṣa murā*)

Mūlaivīṭṭu Raṅgasvāmi 116

mūlamantram (Sanskrit) 119
statement or group of words taken up in the *ghanam* style of vedic recitation

mulavu (Tamil) 12
an ancient drum; possibly a precursor of the *mṛdaṅgam*
see also *paṟaiyaṉ*, *tuṭiyaṉ*

muracu 12
an ancient drum

muraḷī (Sanskrit)
flute
see also Kṛṣṇa

Muraḷī
Kṛṣṇa envisaged as divine flute player (Muraḷīdharaṉ, lit. 'holding a flute')

mūrcchanā (Sanskrit) 93
literally, 'fainting, modulation of sounds'; (1) a mode, scale pattern or rāga resulting from the re-distribution of the intervals belonging to a basic scale (*grāma*); (2) one among the ten types of embellishment (*daśavidha gamaka*); consists of a series of fast upward phrases, each ending on a long note (e.g. *s r g m p d N*, *r g m p d n S* etc.)
see also *bheda*, Rāmāmātya

mūrti (Sanskrit)
lit. 'manifestation, image'; the idol of a deity in a temple or domestic shrine
see also *pūjā*

Muruga (Ṣaṇmukha, Vēlaṉ)
Tamil god associated with beauty, love and war; also identified with Subrahmaṇya; described as a dancer in ancient Tamil literature; depicted as mounted on a peacock, holding a spear (*vēl*); several main shrines are located on hilltops (e.g. Paḻani) or an artificial mound (e.g. Svāmimalai)
see *kautvam*, *kāvaḍiccindu*, *Paripāḍal*
see also Aṇṇāmalai Reḍḍiyār, Aruṇagirināthar

music
see *gāṇa*, *gīta*, *isai*, Hindustānī music, Karnatic music, *Muttamil*, *saṅgīta*

sound 'heard' only by a select few (e.g. *yogin*); this involves two types of energy, symbolized by wind and fire; their corresponding syllables are '*na*' for air (i.e. breath), and '*da*' for fire or heat (e.g. of the body)
see also *āhata nāda*, *anāhata nāda*, history of Karnatic music, *nādopāsanā*, *prāṇāyāma*, *Tantra*

Nādabrahmā (Sanskrit)
music (*nāda*) perceived as a manifestation of divinity (*Brahmā*)

naḍai (Tamil) 138, 141, Table 9
lit. 'gait, walk'; (1) subdivision of a tāla cycle (= Sanskrit *gati*); applicable to each count or 'beat' (*kriyā*); (2) a rhythmic composition belonging to a particular tāla; serves to practise variation patterns (*prastāra*) applicable in a *taṉiyāvarttaṉam*
see *tisra naḍai*, *caturaśra naḍai*, *khaṇḍa naḍai*, *miśra naḍai*, *saṅkīrṇa naḍai*

nādasvaram (Tamil) 44
see *nāgasvaram*

Nādatanumaniśam Śaṅkaram 97, 127
a *kṛti* by Tyāgarāja

nāda yoga (Sanskrit) 64
musical knowledge and practice pursued as a yogic discipline (*sādhanā*); believed to be accessible to any person; simple devotional songs (e.g. *kīrtana*) have been composed and taught for this purpose for many generations (e.g. Purandara Dāsa, Sadāśiva Brahmendra, Tyāgarāja), and in our times (e.g. Pāpanāsam Śivaṉ)
see also *mokṣa*, *nādopāsanā*, *Tantra*, *yoga*

nāḍi (Sanskrit)
lit. 'tubular or hollow plant, stalk; flute'
see also *svaranāḍi*

nāḍī (Sanskrit)
channels of the subtle body in the tradition of *Tantra*

nādopāsanā (Sanskrit) 64
worship (*upasāna*) through music (*nāda*)
see also *bhakta*, *nāda yoga*, *yoga*

nādopāsanācē 64
kṛti by Tyāgarāja

nāgasvaram (Sanskrit) 12, 19, 35, 43, 127, Ch. 5, Fig. 18
Tamilized *nādasvaram*; a family of double-reed instruments used on auspicous occasions (hence *maṅgaḷa vādya*); (1) the longer, more common *bāri*; (2) the shorter, high-pitched *timiri*; (3) another short type known as *mukhavīṇā*, mostly used in popular drama (*kūttu*); (4) the drone variety (*ottu*), now practically obsolete
see also *āccāmaram*, *ciṉṉa mēḷam*, *gāyaki*, *mallāri*, *mēḷam*, *suṣira vādya*, *tatakāram*, *tutukāram*

namaskāra, *namaste* (Sanskrit)
lit. 'salutation, obeisance'; a respectful greeting extended to God (*Īśvara*) or a person; consists of holding the hands together (*āñjali*) while saying 'namastē'
see also *pūjā*

Nandanār Caritra
musical play by Gopālakṛṣṇa Bhārati
see also *caritra*

Nārada 87, 88
(1) the divine, albeit troublesome, messenger and ardent devotee of Viṣṇu according to popular mythology; described as a great musician and also known as 'the lute player' (*Vīṇāsya*); (2) the person to whom several (anonymous?) musical treatises are ascribed
see also Hanūmān, *Svarārṇavam*

Nārada Purāṇa 56, 58, 61, Ch. 6
10th c. religious text (*Purāṇa*) of some 3000 stanzas wherein Nārada, the divine messenger, defines the duties of a human being; one of the six *Viṣṇu purāṇas*; also refers to the animals associated with the seven notes (*saptasvara*)
see also animal imagery, *dāravī*, *gātravatī*, *Purāṇa*, *saptasvara*

Narasiṁha
lit. 'man-lion'; the fourth incarnation (*avatāra*) of Viṣṇu; slays Hiraṇyakaśipu, the subject of a dramatic scene which provides the highlight in dance-drama (notably *Kathakali* and *Mēlaṭṭūr bhāgavata mēḷam*)
see also *Daśāvatārā*

Narasiṁha Varman II
 Pallava ruler (700–28); Fig. 2
narastuti (Sanskrit) 67
 singing in praise (*stuti*) of a person (*nara*); in poetry such as the lyrics of a *kṛti* (*Nidhicāla sukhamā*, rāga Kalyāṇi, miśra cāpu tāla), such eulogizing was strongly denounced by Tyāgarāja as being undignified of a musician
 see also *nindāstsuti*
Nārāyaṇa
 see Viṣṇu
Nārāyaṇa Ayyaṅgār 43
Nārāyaṇa Ayyar 43, 165
Nārāyaṇa Tīrtha Ch. 18, 19
 see also *cūrṇikā*, *Kṛṣṇa līlā taraṅgiṇī*, *rāsakrīḍā*, *tīrtha*
nāsā (Sanskrit) 66, Fig. 25
 lit. 'nose'
 see Śōbhillusaptasvara
nāṭakam (Tamil) 47
 see dance, dance-drama
 see also *Muttamil̲*
Naṭarāja (Sanskrit)
 lit. the 'king among dancers'; Śiva as divine or cosmic dancer; the presiding deity of the great temple at Chidambaram; as embodiment of dance (*nṛtyamūrti*), his vigorous dance movement (*tāṇḍava*) symbolizes eternal energy causing the evolution, maintenance, and dissolution of the world (*mahākāla*); integrates the opposites (terrific and auspicious); an image perfected in the iconography of Cōl̲a bronzes (since the 10th *c.*), ideally revealing several or most of the nine sentiments (*navarasa*); the upper right hand carries a small drum (*damaru*), representing at once sound and ether (*ākāśa*), the first of the five elements which stands for divine truth (i.e. medium of revelation, speech, tradition); from this most subtle divine substance of creation, the others evolve to form and dissolve the universe: air, fire (annihilation, held in the palm of the upper left hand), water, and earth
 see also *kūttapirān̲*, *tāṇḍava*
Naṭarājan̲, A.K.C. 55
naṭṭuvanar (Tamil) 43, 50, 52, 148, 166, 169
 (1) the director of a dance ensemble (*cinn̲a mēḷam*); (2) a professional (male) dance teacher; formerly a hereditary profession
naṭṭuvāṅgam (Tamil) 43, 47, 133, 138
 rhythmic coordination of dance movements with the help of a cymbals (*tāḷam*) and special rhythmic syllables (*jati*)
nature, natural 29, 60, 68, 87
 see also *Bhagavad Gītā*, human nature, *Kumārasaṁbhava*
nāṭṭya (Tamil) 167
nāṭya, *nāṭyam* (Sanskrit) 47, 153, 168, 170
 lit. 'a complete theatrical performance (drama, dance and music)'
 see *kāvya*, *kūttu*, *Nāṭya Śāstra*, *saṅgīta*
nāṭyācārya (Sanskrit)
 lit. 'dance master'
 see *naṭṭuvan̲ar*
 see also Tañjāvūr Quartette
nāṭya mēḷam (Sanskrit)
 (1) an ensemble (*mēḷam*) which performs dance-dramas (*nāṭya*); (2) an ensemble consisting of male brahmins who perform the *Mēlaṭṭūr bhāgavata mēḷam* since its inception by Veṅkaṭarāma Śāstrī
Nāṭya Śāstra 40, 47, 73, 88, 91, 160, 166, 167
 the earliest and best known Sanskrit treatise (*śāstra*) on the subject of drama, including dance, music, and other allied subjects (e.g. *bhāva* and *rasa*, theatre architecture); ascribed to Bharata Muni (between 2nd *c.* BC and 2nd *c.* AD); defines *nāṭya* as being an imitation of the actions of the whole world, and as a fifth *Veda* from which to derive knowledge by way of delightful aesthetic experience (*rasa*); a major influence on later theorists (e.g. Śārṅgadēva)
 see also Abhinavagupta, *bha-ra-ta*, *dhruvā*, *jāti*, *kaṇṭha*, *navarasa*, *śiras*, *sthānaprāpti*
Naukā Caritram
 'Boat-Story'; the title of a musical play by Tyāgarāja
nautch
 see *nāc*

navarasa (Sanskrit)
lit. the concept of 'nine (*nava*) principal sentiments (*rasa*)'; a theory based on literary and dramaturgical conventions; the eight original *rasas* of the *Nāṭya Śāstra* comprise *śṛṅgāra* (erotic), *vīra* (courage), *karuṇa* (compassion), *hāsya* (amusement), *adbhuta* (wonder), *raudra* (anger), *bhayānaka* (fear), *bībhatsa* (disgust); the present concept of *navarasa* dates from the period between the 6th and 10th *c.* AD when *śānta rasa* (quietude) was finally accepted by literary scholars (*ālaṅkārika*); a tenth *rasa*, *bhakti* (devotion), was added after Abhinavagupta proposed it as an important accessory sentiment of *śānta rasa*; some *rasas* (i.e. *śṛṅgāra*, *bhakti*, *karuṇa*, *vīra*) are common in classical music; guided by his acquaintance with musical, literary and aesthetic theory as well as religious and philosophical conventions, Tyāgarāja explored the gamut of all nine sentiments in his music and lyrics
see also *gāna rasa*, *kāku*, Naṭarāja, *rasa*, *sthāyibhāva*, *Tantra*

navel
see diaphragm, *nābhi*, *maṇipūra*, Śōbhillusaptasvara

naya, *nayam* (Tamil) 77, 112, 114, 119, 120, 121, Ch. 13
lit. 'soft, subtle, new'; (1) a rāga with scope for slow and detailed *ālāpana* elaboration (*naya rāga*); a category broadly identical with *rakti rāga*; (2) *nayam* denotes a quality associated with a particular style of singing
see *ghana rāga*, moll
see also Śyāmā Śāstri

Nāyaka, Nāyak 92
dynasty of Tañjāvūr founded by Śevappa; the main patrons of the arts in the 17th *c.*
see Raghunātha Nāyak, Vijayarāghava Nāyaka)
see also Gōvinda Dīkṣitar, Marāṭhā, Veṅkaṭamakhi

nāyaka nāyikā bhāva (Sanskrit) 72, 168
see *madhurabhakti*, *līlā*, *padam*, *śṛṅgāra*
see also Caṭakōpan̲, Jayadēva, Kṣētrajña, Vaitīśvarankoil Subbarāma Ayyar

Nāyanmār, Nāyan̲ār 14, 93
collective name for the highly revered 63 Tamil poets and *Śaiva* mystics
see also *mūvar*, Tirunīlakaṇṭha Nāyan̲ār

neck 58, 66
see *daṇḍi*, *kāku*, *kaṇṭha*, Śōbhillusaptasvara, *vīṇādaṇḍa*, *viśuddha*

Nēnendu vetukudurā 137, Stave 38

new, New Age 20
see also innovation

ni Table 10
(1) the abbreviation for any variant of *niṣāda*; (2) the mnemonic svara syllable for *kaiśikī niṣāda*

Nīcittamu 127

Nidhicāla sukhamā 137, Stave 37
see also *narastuti*

nihśabda kriyā (Sanskrit) 128
silent gesture for reckoning musical time (*tāla*)
see also *kriyā*

nindāstsuti (Sanskrit)
literally, 'covert praise' (from '*nind*, to censure, to ridicule'); a literary device in devotional literature; in order to remind God of His devotee's plight, the poet-composer mockingly assumes a reproachful attitude; this contrast serves to highlight a basic attitude of total surrender to a merciful God; expressed in the lyrics of Karnatic composers (e.g. Tyāgarāja)
see *Paridānam' iccitē*
see also *narastuti*

Ninnuvinā nāmadēndu 35
kṛti by Tyāgarāja

niraval 37, 119, 155, 156, 159, 179, Ch. 17
variations of notes based on the rhythmic as well as the syllabic structure of a chosen theme (e.g. *anupallavi*)

nirūpaṇam (Sanskrit)
lit. 'seeing, form, ascertaining'; a narrative song
see Muvvalūr Sabhāpati Ayyar

nirvāṇa (Sanskrit) 24
concept of death or dissolution as prerequisites for 'eternal bliss, highest felicity'

see also *mokṣa*

niṣāda (*ni*)
the seventh scale degree (*svara*); traditionally associated with the elephant
see also enharmonic scale degrees, mnemonic svara syllable, *ni*

niṣādāntya rāga (Sanskrit) 120, 124, 156, Ch. 13, Stave 35
rāga in which no note higher than niṣāda should be touched
see also *madhyama śruti*

nitya (Sanskrit)
continual, constant, regular, fixed, necessary, ordinary

nitya sumaṅgaḷi (Sanskrit)
an 'ever (*nitya*) auspicious woman'; the social role formerly assigned to a *dēvadāsi* dancer
see also *maṅgaḷam*

nokku 76, Stave 7

North Indian music and culture 69, Ch. 15
see *Hindustāni Saṅgīt*, *jugalbandī*
see also Karnatic music

nose 66
see *nāsā*

notation 77, 133, 153, 162, 163, Ch. 1, 15
see also *anumandra sthāyī*, *ati tāra sthāyī*, *mandra sthāyī*, *mātrā*, *Rāga Vibodha*, *sargam*, solfa notation

note, notes 26, 38, 60, Ch. 1, 6
see *saptasvara*, *sargam*, *svara*, *vādī*
see also *ādhāra ṣadja*, agogic, *āhata*, *aṁśa svara*, *āndoḷa*, *anudātta*, *anusāraṇi*, *anusvara*, *anyasvara*, *āroha*, *ārohaṇa-avarohaṇa*, *avaroha*, *auḍava*, *avikṛta*, *bhāṣāṅga*, *bheda*, *briga*, *chāyā*, *dhaivatāntya*, *ḍhālu*, *dhin*, *dīm*, *dīrgha*, *gamaka*, *heccu sāraṇi*, heptatonic, hexatonic, *janta svara*, *jāru*, *jīva svara*, *kāku*, *kaṁpita*, *kārvai*, *komal-tīvra*, Kuḍumiyāmalai, *kuraippu*, *ma grāma*, *mūrcchanā*, *Nārada purāṇa*, *niraval*, *niṣādāntya*, *nōṭṭusvara*, *nyāsa*, *odukkal*, *ottu*, *padagarbha*, *pañcamāntya*, *pañcama varja*, pentatonic, *pratyāhata*, *rāga*, *ravai*, *Ṛgveda*, *ṣāḍava*, *sampūrṇa*, *sāraṇi*, *sarvalaghu*, *Sōpānam*, *śruti*, *sthāna*, *svara prastāra*, *Svarārṇavam*, *svarita*, *tāṉam*, *tāṉavarṇam*, tonic, *tripuccha*, *udātta*, *upāṅga*, *uttarāṅga*, *vaḷi*, *varja*, *viśēṣa*, *viśrānti*

nōṭṭusvara sāhitya 35
Tamilized 'note' (*nōṭṭu*); English or 'Western' tunes adapted by Muttusvāmi Dīkṣitar and combined with Sanskrit lyrics (*sāhitya*); intended as entertaining lessons for beginners (*abhyāsa gāna*)
see also history

nṛtta (Sanskrit) 170, Ch. 16
an aspect of Indian dance consisting of 'pure dance' movements and poses (i.e. without any particular theme or expression)
see *aḍavu*, *alārippu*, *jatisvaram*, *nṛtya*, *saṅgati*, *saṅgīta*, *tīrmāṇam*

nṛtya, *nṛtyam* (Sanskrit) 47, Ch. 16
an aspect of Indian dance having a particular theme or expression (mime)
see *abhinaya*, *bhāva*, *dṛṣṭi*, Naṭarāja, *navarasa*, *nṛtta*

nu Table 10
the mnemonic svara syllable for *kākalī niṣāda*

numbers
see *akṣara kāla*, *cakra*, *gatibheda*, *gati variants*, *kaṭapayādi sūtra*, *kriyā*, *rāga rāgiṇī*, *saṁkhyā*, *yantra*, *yati*

nyāsa, *nyāsa svara* (Sanskrit) 13, 106
those notes of a rāga on which phrases (*sañcāra*) can end
see also *graha*

O
the symbol for *drutam*

octaves 37, 40, 81
see range

odukkal (Tamil) 76, Stave 7
lit. 'pushed aside'; (1) a type of embellishment (*gamaka*); (2) delaying a note briefly with reference to the starting point (*eḍuppu*, *graha*) of a tāla cycle
see also agogic

ōduvār (Tamil) 58, 67
hereditary temple musicians of Tamil Nadu; specialized in singing *Tēvāram* hymns
see Tulajāji II
see also Tañjāvūr Quartette

O Jagadambā 113
Om, *Oṁkāra* (Sanskrit) 23
sacred syllable (*praṇava*); believed to be the source of all sound; the *Chāndogya Upaniṣad* declares *Oṁkāra* to be the essence of music and an esoteric means of realization (*udgīta vidyā*) in worship
see also *mantra*, *mokṣa*, *nāda*
Ōmana tiṅgaḷ kiḍavō 127
lullaby by Irayimman Tampi
onṟarai eḍuppu (Tamil) Stave 39
starting the theme at a point which is '1 1/2' beats (*onṟarai*) or six *mātrā* after the start of the tāla cycle (*samam*); a popular variant of *anāgata eḍuppu*; characteristic of many ādi tāla compositions (i.e. *kṛti*, *kīrtana*) by Tyāgarāja and later composers
see also iḍam
opera 59
see musical play
organizer 155
see *sabhā*
originality 164, Ch. 15
see also authenticity, style
orikkai (Tamil) 76, Stave 7
Orissa 14, Fig. 26
ornamentation, oscillation
see *gamaka*
oru kalai 134
medium tempo
see also *iraṇḍu kalai*, *kāla*
ottu (Tamil) 44
see *nāgasvaram*
overtones 61, Stave 4
see *tambūrā*

pa
abbreviation for *pañcama*; a mnemonic svara syllable
Paccimiriyam Āḍiappayya 154, 158, Ch. 18
see also *daśavidha gamaka*, Tulajājī II
pada, *padam* (Sanskrit) 72, 156, 180, Ch. 17
lit. 'stanza, verse; foot, division'; (1) initially, any devotional song (e.g. by Purandara Dāsa); (2) a form of dance music with ample scope for expression (*abhinaya*); also referred to as *śṛṅgāra prabandha*; flourished at Tañjāvūr during the reign of Vijayarāghava Nāyaka, himself a *pada* composer; its prevalent theme is *madhurabhakti* (*nāyaka nāyikā bhāva*)
see Kṣētrayya, Muttuttāṇḍavar
see also *dhrupad*
pāḍal (Tamil; plural *pāḍalkaḷ*) 161
any song or composition
padagarbha (Sanskrit)
the pivotal, elongated, or stressed note of a *pallavi* (= Tamil *aruḏi*); placed between the first part (*prathamāṅga*) and the second part (*dvitīyāṅga*) of a *pallavi*; provides a point of rest or pause (*viśrānti*)
see also *rāgam tānam pallavi*
pāḍam (Tamil)
lit. 'singing'
see also *pada*
padavarṇam 180, Ch. 17
varṇam primarily intended for dance
see Pratāpasiṁha, *tīrmāṇam*
see also Ambujam Krishna, Irayimman Tampi, Kundrakudi Kṛṣṇa Ayyar, Kunnakuḍi Veṅkaṭarāma Ayyar, Mysore Sadāśiva Rao, Paṭṭaṇam Subrahmaṇya Ayyar, Mūlaivīṭṭu Raṅgasvāmi, Subbarāma Dīkṣitar, Svāti Tirunāḷ, Tañjāvūr Quartette
paddhati (Sanskrit) 13, 155
lit. 'way, road'; a customary pattern or method; the typical sequence of items followed in a concert
see also *asaṁpūrṇa paddhati*, *bhajan*, *kaccēri paddhati*, *mārgam*, *mēḷa paddhati*, Rāmāmātya, *saṁpūrṇa paddhati*
Padmanābha (Sanskrit)
lit. 'lotus-navel'; an epithet of the reposing Viṣṇu
see also Brahmā
pāḍu (Tamil)
to sing
painting 14, 29, 47
see also iconography
pakaḍ
key phrase in *Hindustānī* music
see also *piḍippu*
pakka sāraṇi 40, 43
the three secondary strings of a *vīṇā* (*śruti*-cum-*tāla*)
see *anusāraṇi*, *heccu sāraṇi*, *sāraṇi*

pakkavādya 36, Ch. 5
category of instruments mainly used for concert accompaniment, namely violin and *mṛdaṅgam* (sometimes also *vīṇā* or *gōṭṭuvādyam*)
see also *upapakkavādyam*

Pālakkāḍu, Palakkaḍ Fig. 26
new official name for the centre of a district in Kerala (Anglicized Palghat); famous for its traditions of music, dance and drama

palāmaram (Tamil) 39, 40, 50
jackwood (*artocarpus integrifolia*); the preferred wood for the resonating parts of several South Indian instruments (e.g. *mṛdaṅgam*, *tambūrā*, *vīṇā*)
see also *daṇḍi*, *kuḍam*

Paḻani
major temple town dedicated to Murugaṉ and pilgrim centre in Tamil Nadu

palate 66

Palghat
see Pālakkāḍu

Palghat Maṇi Ayyar 47, 156, 160

Pallaḍam Sanjīva Rao

Pallava 19, 69, Fig. 2
dynasty that dominated South India from the end of the 6th *c.* to the end of the 9th *c.* with *Kāñcīpuram* as capital and Māmallapuram as main port; converted from Buddhism to the cult of Śiva under Mahēndravarman I; best known for its patronage of architecture and sculpture; the *Śaiva* hymns of the Nāyaṉmār, and the *Vaiṣṇava* hymns of the Āḻvār mystics were composed in the *Pallava* period; superseded by a dynasty of *Cōḻa* kings, their former vassals
see also Kuḍumiyāmalai, Narasiṁha Varman II, *yāḷi*

pallavi
(1) the opening section or first theme of a composition (e.g. *kṛti*, *varṇam*); usually followed by either an *anupallavi* section, a *caraṇam* section, or both; (2) the sole theme of a *rāgam tānam pallavi* elaboration
see *araiyiḍam*, *aṟudi*, *dvitīyāṅga*, *padagarbha*, *prathamāṅga*, *saṅgati*

see also Annamācārya, Bhadrācala Rāmadās, Kundrakudi Kṛṣṇa Ayyar, Paccimiriyam Āḍiappayya, Pallavi Śēṣa Ayyar, Tyāgarāja

paṇ 12
(1) a melodic entity of ancient Tamil music which was based on a number of different *paṇs*; the precursor of a modern rāga; more suitable for bardic lore than today's art music which greatly relies on ornamentation (*gamaka*); hence largely abandoned except for several popular rāgas that are believed to correspond to certain *paṇs* (e.g. Nīlāmbari); (2) *Tēvāram paṇ*; the modes of the Tamil hymns (*Tēvāram*); sung in *Śaiva* temples of Tamil Nadu
see also *Sōpānam*, *yāḻmuṟi paṇ*

pāṇaṉ, *pāṇar* (Tamil) 12, 67
singer, bard or panegyrist of ancient times
see also *yāḻpāṇar*

pañcama (*pa*)
the fifth scale degree; traditionally associated with the cuckoo
see also *avikṛta svara*, *madhyama śruti*

pañcamāntya rāga (Sanskrit) 124, 156, Ch. 13, Stave 35
rāga in which no note higher than pañcama should be touched (i.e, Navarōj)
see also *madhyama śruti*

pañcama varja rāga (Sanskrit) Ch. 13
rāga without the 5th scale degree (*pañcama*)

pañcaratna kṛti
lit. the 'five gems'; a famous series of elaborate songs by Tyāgarāja; all set to ādi tāla; a systematic exposition of the five *ghana* rāgas (i.e. Nāṭa, Gauḷa, Ārabhi, Śrī and Varāḷi); five other *kṛtis* are known as the *Śrīraṅga pañcaratna kīrtana*
see also *ghana rāga pañcaka*

pañcavādya (Sanskrit) 12, Fig. 4
lit. 'five instruments'; a characteristic music ensemble of Kerala, namely *ceṅgila*, *eḍakka*, *cenda*, *kombu*, and *kuḻal*
see also *mēḷam*

samasthāna vidvān, Śarabhōjī II, Svāti Tirunāḷ Mahārājā, Tulajājī II, Veṅkaṭamakhi, Vijayarāghava Nāyak
Paṭṭammāḷ, D. 101
Paṭṭammāḷ, D.K. 167
Paṭṭaṇam Subrahmaṇya Ayyar 167
patterns
see *Karṇāṭaka saṅgīta*, *krama*, *kuraippu*, mnemonic svara syllables, *mōrā*, *mūrcchanā*, *paddhati*, *sarvalaghu*, *svara prastāra*, *tāla prastāra*, *tāna pustaka*, *tīrmāṇam*, *vakra prayoga*, *viśēṣa prayoga*, *yati*
pāṭṭu (Tamil) 167
(1) a poem; (2) the text or lyrics of a song
see *kāvya*, *meṭṭu*, *sāhitya*
Pattupāṭṭu (Tamil)
lit. 'ten songs', included in the *Śaiva* canon *Tirumuṟai*; an early work referring to musical instruments
patyam (Telugu)
poetry sung in the manner of a *rāga ālāpana* in dance and drama performances; mostly set to a popular form of rāga Mōhanam reminiscent of rāga Harikāmbhoji
see also term *viruttam*
pause 160
see *aṁśa svara*, *kārvai*, *padagarbha*, *viśrāma*, *viśrānti*, *yati*
peacock 60, 61
see *mayūra*
pentatonic 110, 157
scale pattern based on five notes
see *auḍava rāga*
see also *asaṁpūrṇa paddhati*, heptatonic, hexatonic, *varja*
percussion
see *avanaddha vādya*, drum, *ghana vādya*, rhythm, rhythm instruments, *vādya*
performance, performer
see concert, musician
periya mēḷam (Tamil) 43, 44, 45, 127, Ch. 5, Fig. 18, 19
'large (*periya*) ensemble (*mēḷam*)'; mainly heard in temples, during street processions and marriages
see also *cinna mēḷam*, *nāgasvaram*, *tavil*, *śruti peṭṭi*, *tāḷam*
Periyasāmi Thooran 153
permutation 117
see *prastāra*, *svara prastāra*, *tāla prastāra*
see also enharmonic scale degrees, mnemonic svara syllables, variation
Persia 12, 15
see Sāsānian
Phenadyuti 99
2nd *mēḷakartā* rāga used by Muttusvāmi Dīkṣitar; resembles Ratnāṅgi
see *asaṁpūrṇa paddhati*
philosophy 15, 26, 31
see Ādi Śaṅkara, *ahiṁsā*, *Bhagavad Gītā*, *kāla*, *saṁsāra*, *saṁskāra*, *Tantra*, *Vedānta*, *vidyā*
phrase 78
see *apūrva sañcāra*, *āroha*, *aṟudi*, *avaroha*, *briga*, *chāyā*, enharmonic scale degrees, *janta*, *lakṣya*, *mūrcchanā*, *nyāsa*, *pakaḍ*, *piḍippu*, *prayoga*, *sañcāra*, *svara prastāra*, *tānam*, *tāna pustaka*, *tutukāram*, *vakra prayoga*, *viśeṣa prayoga*
physiology 58, 59, 65, 78, Fig. 25
see *cakra*, *kuṇḍalinī*, Śōbhillusaptasvara, voice
piḍil (Tamil) 53
see violin
piḍippu (Tamil)
key phrase to remember or identify a rāga; corresponds to *pakaḍ* of *Hindustānī* music
pilgrimage, pilgrim songs
see also Ādi Śaṅkara, history of Karnatic music, *kāvaḍiccindu*, *kṣetra*, Paḻani, *tīrtha*
pillanagrōvi, *pillanaṅgrōvi*
flute in Telugu and Kannaḍa respectively (*krōvi* = pipe)
pitā (Sanskrit)
father
see *laya*
Pitāmaha (Sanskrit) 138
the great (*mahā*) father (*pitā*) of Karnatic music (*Karṇāṭaka Pitāmaha*); an epithet bestowed on Purandara Dāsa by posterity
pitch 39, 42, 43, 44, 54, 71, 77, 101, Ch. 1, Fig. 1
see also *ādhāra ṣaḍja*, *eḍakka*, frets, *heccu kaṭṭai*, *heccu śruti*, *janta svara*,

Prahlāda Mahānāṭakam
Telugu play by Vijayarāghava; inspired numerous dramas, musical plays, and dance dramas (e.g. *Prahlāda Caritram*)
see also *bhāgavata mēḷam*
praise, eulogy 67
see *stuti*, *narastuti*, *nindāstsuti*
see also *harikīrtan*
Prākrit
see Bhāṇḍīra
see also Maṇipravāḷam
prāṇa (Sanskrit)
lit. 'breath, vitality, essence, inspiration, principle of life'
see *tāla daśa prāṇa*
see also *nāda*
Prāṇanātha 96
kṛti by Tyāgarāja
Praṇatārtiharaprabho (Sanskrit) 101
the first *rāgamālikā* to use all the 72 *mēḷakartā rāgas*, and in a systematic manner
praṇava (Sanskrit)
the mystic syllable *Om* (*Oṁkāra*)
see also *mokṣa*
prāṇāyāma (Sanskrit) 23, 59
breath control as part of a religious discipline and *yoga*
see also *nāda*, *yantra*
Prānēsh Fig. 11, 12
prastāra (Sanskrit) 49, 128, 140, 141, Fig. 32, 33
lit. 'spreading out'; a permutation or variation of tāla
see *svara prastāra*, *tāla prastāra*
see also *caturaśra naḍai*, *tāla daśa prāṇa*, *tisra naḍai*, *yati*
Pratāpasiṁha
Marāṭhā ruler of Tañjāvūr (1739–63); son of Tulajājī I; father of Tulajājī II; during his reign, several music and dance forms (*kīrtana*, *svarajati*, *padavarṇam*), evolved or flourished; credited with twelve dramas written in Marāṭhi
prathama kāla (Sanskrit) 134, 142
lit. 'the first degree of speed'; denotes a tempo which is doubled for the second degree, and quadrupled for the third degree
see also *trikāla*
prathamāṅga (Sanskrit)
lit. 'first part, section' (= *pūrvāṅga*)
see *pūrvāṅga*
prati madhyama (Sanskrit) 101, 102, 125, 127
the higher (lit. 'opposite') variant of the fourth scale degree; mnemonic syllable '*mi*'
see also *śuddha madhyama*
pratyāhata (Sanskrit) 75, Stave 7
lit. 'withholding, retreat (*pratyāhāra*)'; (1) an embellishment (*gamaka*); (2) also a figure pairs of descending notes (e.g. *sa-ni*, *ni-dha*, *dha-pa*, *pa-ma*)
see also *daśavidha gamaka*
prayer 29
see *japa*, *mantra*, *pūjā*, *sandhyā vandanam*
prayoga (Sanskrit) 13, 71, 77, 159
lit. 'usual form, practice'; refers to a characteristic melodic phrase of a rāga
see also *briga*, enharmonic scale degrees, *lakṣya*, *sañcāra*
precision
see *muktāyi*
precursor
ēktār, *mulavu*, *paṇ*, violin, *yāḻ*
Prem Latha Sharma 92
Pritvija Fig. 12
procession 168
see *mallāri*, *periya mēḷam*, *ulā*, *uñchavṛtti*
programme note 153
pronunciation Tables 1, 2
see Guide to Pronunciation and Transliteration
prose
see *cūrṇikā*, *mantra*, *Veda*, *Yakṣagāna*
see also literary works
prostate plexus
see *svādiṣṭhāna*
pṛthvī, *Pṛthvī* (Sanskrit)
lit. 'earth'; the goddess of earth
see *mahābhūta*
psyche, psychology, intelligence 22, 26, 27, 33 58, 59, 65, 78, 88, 89
see also *cakra*, *kuṇḍalinī*, mind
publication
see book
Pudukōṭṭai Mānpūṇḍiya Piḷḷai 47, 51

pūjā (Sanskrit) 29, 34
an elaborate form of regular worship (*upāsana*); consists of prayers, repetition (*japa*) of a sacred syllables (*mantra*), meditation (*dhyāna*) and various other activities such as invocations (*āvāhana*, *havana*), ringing a bell (*ghaṇṭā*), ritual offering of flowers, waving (*āratī*) of a lighted lamp (*dīpa*), offering special food (*prasāda*), salutation (*namaskāra*), and various substances (e.g. milk, *ghī*, saffron-water, sandalwood paste) to a divine image or idol (*mūrti*); at home, it is mainly dedicated to a family or personal deity (*iṣṭadevatā*)
see also *Cētulāra śṛṅgāramu*

pullāṅkuḻal (Tamil) 43, 45, 46, Fig. 5, 20
transverse bamboo flute of South India (= *pillāṅkuḻal*); mostly played with seven fingers
see also flute, *kuḻal*

Purāṇa (Sanskrit) 16, 24, 31, 69, 87
lit. 'ancient, legendary'; a vast body of sacred Sanskrit literature (*smṛti*) of varying importance; written in verse; compiled between the 6th and the 16th c. AD; a variety of subjects is covered by texts of different length: encyclopedic compilations from other works (e.g. *Agni purāṇa*, one of the six *Śiva purāṇas*); elucidations of scriptures and religious lore (e.g. mythical accounts of the creation of mankind, the origin and destruction of the world); genealogies of gods, saints and sages (*ṛṣi*), and dynasties; the history of sacred places; didactic material (including music); each of the great 18 *Purāṇas* (*Mahāpurāṇa*) is dedicated to a particular deity; six *Purāṇas* are devoted to each, Viṣṇu (e.g. *Bhāgavata Purāṇa*, *Nārada Purāṇa*), Śiva, and Brahmā; minor texts of this type (*upapurāṇa*) have been composed even in the more recent past
see also *asura*, *dāravī*, *Daśāvatārā*, *Daśāvatār*, *gātravatī*, *Gītagovinda*, *guṇa*, history of Karnatic music, *kūttu*

Purandara Dāsa 16, 81, 128, 138, Ch. 18

puruṣa (Sanskrit)
lit. 'man'; a human or cosmic being
see Caṭakōpan

puruṣārtha (Sanskrit)
fourfold aim of human existence comprising *artha* (wealth), *kāma* (love), *dharma* (righteousness), and *mokṣa* (salvation through spiritual knowledge, regarded as the highest aim)

pūrva (Sanskrit)
lit. 'first, foremost'

pūrvāṅga (Sanskrit) 101
lit 'the first part (*aṅga*, *prathamāṅga*)'; (1) the first four notes in a scale (tetrachord), namely *sa*, *ri*, *ga*, *ma*; (2) any of the six combinations of the lower four notes within the middle octave that underly the formation of the 72 reference scales of Karnatic music (*mēḷakartā rāga*); each combination has a mnemonic pair of syllables, not considering *ṣaḍja* and *pañcama* (i.e. *ra-ga*, *ra-gi*, *ra-gu*, *ri-gi*, *ri-gu*, *ru-gu*); (3) the first part (*aṅga*) of a composition or complex rhythmic pattern (i.e. *kōrvai* or *muktāyi*); (4) the first part of the theme (*pallavi*) within a *rāgam tānam pallavi* exposition; always followed by a long pivotal note (*aṟudi* or *padagarbha*) and a second part (*uttarāṅga*)
see also *dvitīyāṅga*, *saṁvādi*

puṣpāñjali Ch. 17

quarter-tone
see *śruti*

ra Table 10
see also mnemonic svara syllables, *ri*, *śuddha ṛṣabha*

ra-ga see *pūrvāṅga*

ra-ri-ru see mnemonic svara syllables

rabāb
see violin

Rabīndranāth Tagore 28, 33
Anglicized name of Rabīndranāth Ṭhākur (1861–1941); educationist and poet of Bengal (Nobel-Prize for Literature in 1913); founded Viśva Bhāratī and Śāntinikētan

Rādhā
the favourite *gopī* of Kṛṣṇa, her lover, in

status as court language during his
reign; himself a *vaiṇika* and composer
of *prabandha*; regarded as the most
important Telugu, Sanskrit and music
scholar of his dynasty; author of a
Telugu work, *Śṛṅgāra Sāvitrī*, wherein
the *gōṭṭuvādyam* is mentioned for the
first time (i.e. the '*gōṭivādya*', played
by Tumburu, the celestial musician); his
name is closely associated with his
teacher, Gōvinda Dīkṣitar, and his
influential music treatise (*Saṅgīta
Sudha*); patron of Veṅkaṭamakhi
see also Nāyaka, Vijayarāghava Nāyak
Raghunātha vīṇā
    modern Tañjāvūr *vīṇā* (Sarasvatī *vīṇā*),
    said to be created by Gōvinda Dīkṣitar,
    and named in honour of his patron,
    Raghunātha Nāyak
Raghuvaṁśa 97, 116
    lit. 'the dynasty of *Raghu*' (i.e. Rāma); a
    popular *kṛti* by Paṭṭaṇam Subrahmaṇya
    Ayyar
rāgiṇī (Sanskrit) 88
    female counterpart or 'spouse' of a rāga
    see *rāga rāgiṇī*
rājā (Sanskrit)
    lit. 'king'
rājādāsi (Sanskrit) 166
    female court dancer
    see also *dāsiyāṭṭam, dēvadāsi*
Rājagopāla (Sanskrit)
    lit. 'royal Gopāla' (= Kṛṣṇa); the presiding
    deity at the temple of Dakṣiṇa Dvāraka
    (i.e. Mannārguḍi); revered by the
    Nāyak kings (notably Vijayarāghava
    Nāyaka); addressed in the *Viribōni*
    varnam
Rājārājā I
    Cōla ruler (985–1014)
Rājaratnam Piḷḷai
    see *timiri*
rajas (Sanskrit)
    lit. 'excessive activity, passion, power,
    dirt'; in philosophy, *rajas guṇa* denotes
    human preoccupations and obsessions
    at the expense of spiritual fulfilment
    and peace
    see *guṇa, sattvam, tamas*
    see also *Brahmā purāṇa, Purāṇa*, Ramana
    Maharshi

Rājēśwari Padmanābhan 35
rākṣasa (Sanskrit)
    male demon (e.g. in the *Rāmāyaṇa*
    epic)
rakti (Sanskrit) 117
    lit. 'pleasingness, loveliness, charm'
rakti rāga Ch. 13, Staves 31, 32, 113, 114,
    115, 116, 119, 120, 155
    see emotion, *naya rāga, rāga*
    see also Śyāmā Śāstri
Rāma (Rāmacandra, Raghu) 16, 64, 157
    prince of Ayodhya; worshipped as the
    seventh incarnation of Viṣṇu (Rāma
    avatāra); invoked by poets and
    composers as perfect embodiment of
    righteousness, fortitude and
    compassion; the personal deity
    (*iṣṭadevatā*) of Tyāgarāja
    see also *Cētulāra śṛṅgāramu, Daśāvatārā,
    Rāmāyaṇa,* Sītā
Rāma Brahmā
    father of Tyāgarāja; held musical
    discourses on the *Rāmāyaṇa* at the
    court of Tulajājī II
Rāmacandra Buva 170
Rāmachandra Shāstry, H. Fig. 5
Rāmakathāsudharasa 157
Rāmaliṅgasvāmi 153
Rāmāmātya
    minister of Rāma Rājā (16th *c.*); the last
    ruler of Vijayanagar; author of *Svara
    Meḷa Kalānidhi*, the treatise which
    marks the beginning of a distinct South
    Indian music system; sought to resolve
    the discrepancies between ancient
    music theory (*grāma-mūrcchanā-jāti-
    paddhati*) and contemporary south
    Indian practice by introducing a new
    mēḷa paddhati; combined four
    enharmonic svara variants with twelve
    semitones (*vikṛta* and *śuddha svara*);
    thereby he established the theoretical
    basis for the modern South Indian
    mēḷa-janya rāga system
Ramana Maharshi
    influential ascetic and spiritual teacher of
    Tiruvaṇṇāmalai, Tamil Nadu (1879–
    1950); sought to transmit primordial
    wisdom mainly through a silent
    process; also referred to the scriptures
    (e.g. *Upaniṣad*) while expounding the

ru Table 10
the mnemonic svara syllable for *ṣaṭśruti ṛṣabha*
rubato (Italian) 133
lit. 'robbed'; adjustment of time for the purpose of musical expression
see agogic
Rukmini Devi-Arundale 28, 29, 33, 169
educationist, theosophist and dancer (1904–86); produced and choreographed many dance-dramas based on the epics (e.g. *Rāmāyaṇa*), mythological and folk themes (e.g. *kuravañji*); Founder-Director of Kalākshētra; associated with Dr Maria Montessori
rūpa (Sanskrit) 62, 70
lit. 'form'; the distinct identity of a rāga (*rāga rūpa*)
rūpaka tāla Tables 9, 19, Stave 11
(1) a less common, older variant belonging to the *sūḷādi sapta tāla* group; comprises two parts (*aṅga*), namely a *drutam* followed by a *laghu* (i.e. *caturaśra jāti rūpaka tāla*); (2) a more common, shortened variant comprising three counting units (*kriyā* or *akṣara*); subdivided into four *mātrā* per unit (*caturaśra gati* rūpaka tāla = 12 *mātrā*)

sa
abbreviation for *ṣaḍja*; a mnemonic svara syllable
sa grāma see *ma grāma*
śabdam (Sanskrit) 182, Ch. 17
from *śabda* (lit. 'sound, significant word, epithet'); an expressive dance item
see also Tañjāvūr Quartette
sabhā (Sanskrit) 36
lit. 'assembly, council, audience'; (1) a venue for performing music and dance; (2) in the 20th *c.*, a cultural association, institution, or music club
see also *sadir*
sacred music, sanctity of arts 161, 162, 169
see *upaveda*
see also *mārga saṅgīta*, *nāda*, *nādopāsanā*, *sādhanā*, *Sāmaveda*, Sanskrit, *Sōpānam*, *Tēvāram*
ṣāḍava-ṣāḍava rāga (Sanskrit) 95, 109, 120, 123, Stave 29
rāga based on six notes
see also *sampūrṇa*
sādhanā (Sanskrit) 60, 154
lit. 'accomplishment, means, instrument'; the pursuit of religious and other knowledge or an art (e.g. dance, music) as a means of self-realization; believed to lead to liberation (*mokṣa*)
see also *ātman*, *nāda yoga*
sādhāraṇa gāndhāra
the middle variant of the third scale degree; mnemonic syllable '*gi*'
see also *komal ga*, *ṣaṭśruti ṛṣabha*
sādhu (Sanskrit)
holy man; a mendicant devoted to a religious cult or discipline (*sādhanā*)
see also Haridāsa
sadir, *sadir āṭṭam* 166–7
(1) denotes the highest court of law in several North Indian languages, namely Bengali, Hindi, Marāṭhi Urdu; (2) in South India, the term denoted classical dance (*āṭṭam*) before it became commonly known *Bharata nāṭyam*; originally performed in a temple square (*sadir*, i.e. *sadir āṭṭam*); (3) possibly a corruption of the Telugu word *caduru* ('a *sabhā*, dance')
see also *nāc*
ṣaḍja (*sa*) 72
the first scale degree (tonic); traditionally associated with the peacock
see also *ādhāra ṣaḍja*, *dhin*
Śāhajī II
second Marāṭhā ruler of Tañjāvūr (1684–1712); elder brother of Tulajājī I; succeeded by Śarabhōjī I
see also *Mēlaṭṭūr bhāgavata mēḷam*, Śarabhōjī I, *Yakṣagāna*
sahasrāra (Sanskrit) 66, Fig. 25
from *sahas*, lit. 'strength, victory, lustre, brightness'; and related to '*sahasrin*' lit. 'commanding a thousand'; hence the cakra known as the 'lotus of a thousand petals'; the seventh *cakra* visualized as being near or above the crown of the head; associated with ultimate liberation and self-realization

sāhitya (Sanskrit) 127, 133, 134, 153, 155, 161, Ch. 15
lyrics (= *mātu*) of a music or dance composition
see also Ādi Śaṅkara, *cittasvaram, pāṭṭu, patyam*, poetry, *varṇameṭṭu*
sāhitya bhāva (Sanskrit) 155
expressive quality of poetry or lyrics
see also *bhāva, gāyaki, rāga bhāva*
sahṛdaya (Sanskrit) 67, 89, 157
lit. 'good-hearted, kind, compassionate, sincere'; a person of artistic and aesthetic sensibilities, taste, critical faculty; appreciator of art and literature
see also audience, *rasa, rasika*
saint, saintly 158
see *ahiṁsā, guṇa, Purāṇa, samādhi, Tēvāram, Tiru, vairāgyam, yogin*
Śaiva, Śaivite
religion whose followers regard Śiva as the supreme godhead
see also Ādi Śaṅkara, Appar, *çakra*, Māṇikkavācakar, *mūvar*, Nāyaṉmār, *Pallava, paṇ, Pattupāṭṭu, Tantra, Tēvāram, Tirumuṟai*, Tiruñāṉa Saṁbandar, *Vaiṣṇava*
Śaiva Siddhānta
see Muttuttāṇḍavar
Sakharāma Rao 43
śākta (Sanskrit)
see Ādi Śaṅkara
śakti (Sanskrit) 87
lit. 'energy'; the maternal aspect of the Divine; the power symbolized by the female consorts of several gods like Śiva (Pārvatī), Viṣṇu (Lakṣmī), and Brahmā (Sarasvatī); the terrifying (*bhairava*) aspect of such energy is personified by Kālī and Durgā
see also mother, *Tantra*
Śakuntalā
heroine of the best known drama by Kālidāsa, *Abhijñāna Śākuntalam*
salvation
see Haridāsa, *mokṣa, puruṣārtha, samādhi*
sama, samam (Sanskrit) 128, 134
lit. 'same, equal, straight'; the beginning of a tāla cycle
see also *sama eḍuppu*
samādhi (Sanskrit)
(1) lit. 'deep meditation, silence, absorption'; (2); the final resting place where a saint is buried (rather than cremated) and revered (e.g. the *samādhi* of Tyāgarāja at Tiruvaiyāṟu)
see also *yoga*
sama eḍuppu 134
a variant of starting point (*eḍuppu, graha*) whereby the composition (*dkātu*) and the lyrics (*sāhitya, mātu*) coincide with the first beat of the tāla cycle (*samam*); by contrast, *atīta eḍuppu* and *anāgata eḍuppu* constitute an earlier or later starting point respectively
see also *samam*
sāmagāna (Sanskrit)
see *Sāmaveda*
samasthāna vidvān (Sanskrit)
see *āsthāna vidvān*
samaṣṭi caraṇa (Sanskrit)
lit. 'same (*sama*) kernel or seed (*aṣṭi*)'; a type of *kṛti* without *anupallavi* used by Muttusvāmi Dīkṣitar; its themes are continuously interwoven with the *pallavi*
see also *ettugaḍa pallavi*
Sāmaveda (Sanskrit) 63, 87, 119
lit. 'wisdom of melody or chant'; a text book for priests; pertains to knowledge of melodies; regarded by some theorists as the original source of India's classical music; comprises 1549 verses intended for singing; all but 75 verses are based on the *Ṛgveda*; contains the chants accompanying the *soma* sacrifice
see also *gātravatī, Veda*
sama yati (Sanskrit)
see yati
Saṁgraha-Cūḍā-Maṇi 40, 97
an important treatise by Gōvinda; known to Tyāgarāja; prepared the ground for the modern *mēḷakartā rāga* system
saṁkhyā (Sanskrit)
lit. 'number, reason, manner'
see *kaṭapayādi sūtra*
saṁkhyākṣara (Sanskrit) 99
a letter combination which corresponds to a specific serial number
saṁnyāsin/*sannyāsi* (Sanskrit)
(1) fourth stage in the life (*āśrama*); (2) an

ascetic; one who renounces the world (i.e. a celibate); a holy man
see *Kāmakoṭi*, Ādi Śaṅkara
see also Haridāsa, Nārāyaṇa Tīrtha, Rāmaliṅgasvāmi

sampradāya, Sampradāya 74, 154, Ch. 15
lit. 'tradition, custom, usage'; (1) doctrine or knowledge; (2); traditional handing down of knowledge; (3) within a given school of music, the word refers to a practitioner's adherence to an authentic style of rendering rāgas and compositions as well as commitment to musical continuity for future generations; (4) Sampradāya Centre for South Indian Music Traditions at Chennai (founded by Michael Nixon and Ludwig Pesch in 1980)
see also *bāṇī*, *gharānā*, *guruśiṣya paramparā*, history of Karnatic music, *karṇa parampara*, *parampara*

sampūrṇa (Sanskrit) 95, 96, 99, 106, 109, 123, Ch. 12, 13
lit. 'all, filled, whole'; a complete (i.e. heptatonic) scale (*janaka rāga*, *mēḷakartā rāga*); any rāga (*janya rāga*) or scale pattern comprising all the seven scale degrees (*saptasvara*) either in the ascending order (*ārohaṇa*), descending order (*avarohaṇa*), or both (*ārohaṇa-avarohaṇa*)
see also *auḍava rāga*, *ṣāḍava rāga*

sampūrṇa paddhati (Sanskrit) 100
system (*paddhati*) of scales based on *sampūrṇa mēḷa rāgas* (i.e. scales having the same seven notes or *saptasvara* both in the ascending order and the descending order (*ārohaṇa-avarohaṇa*)); the music of Tyāgarāja is based on the concept of *sampūrṇa paddhati* (introduced by Gōvinda), whereas Veṅkaṭamakhi and Muttusvāmi Dīkṣitar followed the so-called *asampūrṇa paddhati*

samsāra (Sanskrit) 27
lit. 'course, passage'; in philosophical texts (1) mundane existence, the world, worldly illusion (*māyā*); (2) transmigration of souls, the cycle of rebirth; both themes occur in the lyrics of Tyāgarāja and other composers who reiterate that excessive attachment to worldly possession and desire for pleasure (*kāma*) obliterate the innate sense of spiritual fulfilment which obstruct a person's progress towards liberation, the ultimate goal (*mokṣa*)
see also Ādi Śaṅkara, *ātman*

saṁskāra (Sanskrit)
lit. 'refining, making perfect; merit of action; training of the mind, capacity, embellishment, memory'; in religious and philosophical literature the word applies to (1) past experiences underlying a mental pattern, notion, recollection; (2) one of the 40 Hindu rites and sacraments that traditionally marked a person's entire life

Saṁskṛta
see Sanskrit

saṁsthāna vidvān (Sanskrit)
court musician
see also *āsthāna vidvān*

Samudragupta 67

saṁvādi (Sanskrit)
(1) a consonant note; usually a pure fifth interval (= *sa-pa*) from another note (e.g. *vādi*); (2) the second most important note of a rāga; in Hindustānī music to be found in the *uttarāṅga* if the *vādi* belongs to the *pūrvāṅga*, and vice versa
see also *anuvādī*, *vādi*, *vivādī*

sañcāra (Sanskrit) 37, 71, 76, 89
phrase or pleasing combination of phrases; the melodic material for a *rāga ālāpana* (*rāgam*)
see also agogic, *lakṣya*, *prayoga*, *rāga rūpa*, *tāṉavarṇam*

sañcāri (Sanskrit)
see *dhrupad*

sañcāribhāva (Sanskrit)
refers to the scope for bringing out the meaning of a dance song through *abhinaya*; hence the chosen passage is repeated several times
see also *vyabhicāribhāva*

saṉdam (Tamil)
complex metres (= *canda*) found in the Tamil compositions of Arunagirinātar

sandhyā vandanam (Sanskrit)
prayer recited during sunset

śaṅgam, caṅgam, saṅgam (Tamil) 67
(1) the proverbial early 'assemblies' of Tamil poets; believed to have taken place before or until the early centuries AD; (2) the early historical period of Tamil literature (i.e. early first millennium AD)
see also *Cilappatikāram*

saṅgati (Sanskrit) 35, 127, 137, 155, 156
melodic and rhythmic variations on a theme; an integral element of many compositions; Tyāgarāja is credited with having introduced (or perfected) the *kṛti* form with elaborate series of *saṅgati* (e.g. in the *pallavi, anupallavi,* or *caraṇam*)
see also Mahāvaidyanātha Śivan

saṅgīta (Sanskrit) 47, 88
originally, the combination of three art forms, namely (1) vocal music (*gīta*), (2) instrumental music (*vāditra*), and (3) dance (*nṛtta*)
see also *Muttamiḻ*, Sarasvatī Mahāl Library

Saṅgītadarpaṇa (Sanskrit)
lit. 'mirror of music' (17th *c.* AD?); a treatise in which the older North Indian rāga system based on the *rāga rāgiṇī* classification is described

Saṅgīta Ratnākara (Sanskrit) 23, 44, 91, 119
treatise on music and dance by Śārṅgadeva (13th *c.* AD); precedes the bifurcation of Indian music into *Karṇāṭaka saṅgīta* and *Hindustāni saṅgīt*; believed to have influenced the theoretical foundations of both systems to some extent
see also *Kalānidhi, lakṣaṇa*

Saṅgīta Saṁpradāya Pradaśini 163
musicological work by Subbarāma Dīkṣitar

Saṅgīta Sāra (Sanskrit)
music treatise by Vidyāraṇya (14th *c.*, now lost); the first work to suggest the *mēḷa-janya rāga* classification; mentions 15 *mēḷakartā* (i.e. *asaṁpūrṇa mēḷa*) and 50 *janya* rāgas; its contents were quoted by Gōvinda Dīkṣitar and elaborated upon by other theorists

Saṅgīta Sārāmṛta (Sanskrit)
music treatise (1735) by Tulajājī I
see also *Karṇāṭaka deśa*

Saṅgītasāra Saṁgraha (Sanskrit) 96
music treatise by Akalanka; known to Tyāgarāja

saṅgīta śāstra (Sanskrit) 153
lit. 'musical science (*śāstra*)'; theory

Saṅgīta Sudhā (Sanskrit) 39
treatise by Gōvinda Dīkṣitar; believed to have been inspired by several early works on music, notably the *Saṅgīta Ratnākara*, and its commentary by Kallinātha (*Kalānidhi*), as well as the *Saṅgīta Sāra* of Vidyāraṇya; elaborates on all important topics of music (e.g. *śruti, svara, rāga, prabandha, tāla, vādya*), as well as dance
see also Raghunātha Nāyaka, *lakṣaṇa*

Śaṅkara
from Sanskrit *śaṁ*, lit. 'joy'; (1) a name of Śiva; (2) the philosopher also known as Ādi Śaṅkara and Śaṅkarācarya

Śaṅkarācārya (Sanskrit)
lit. 'Śaṅkara the preceptor (*ācārya*)'; (1) Ādi Śaṅkara, the *Advaita* philosopher; (2) the spiritual head of the *Kāñcī Kāmakoṭi Maṭh* (often Anglicized as 'Pontiff')

saṅkīrṇa (Sanskrit)
lit. 'mixed'; (1) dividing the variable tāla division known as *laghu* into seven counts (*saṅkīrṇa jāti*); (2) subdividing each tāla count into seven units (*saṅkīrṇa gati, saṅkīrṇa naḍai*); (3) some 'mixed' or ambivalent rāgas (e.g. Dvijāvanti and Ghaṇṭā) are also referred to as *saṅkīrṇa* rāgas (= *chāyā laga rāga, miśra*)

saṅkīrṇa gati (Sanskrit)
see *saṅkīrṇa naḍai*

saṅkīrṇa jāti (Sanskrit)
symbol 'I9'
laghu section with nine beats

saṅkīrṇa naḍai
subdivision of a tāla (Sanskrit *saṅkīrṇa gati*) having nine *mātrā* per beat (*kriyā*)

Ṣaṇmukha (Sanskrit)
'six-faced' god, namely Muruga or Subrahmaṇya

(1) metric pattern (= *tāla*); (2) a pair of cymbals used in a *Bharata nāṭyam* ensemble (*cinna mēḷam*) and temple music (*periya mēḷam*); classified as *ghana vādya*
see also *jālrā*
tāla mālikā (Sanskrit) Ch. 17; a sequence of different rāgas
tāla prastāra (Sanskrit) 47, 138
permutation of rhythmic patterns; particularly the re-grouping of sub-units (*gati*) during a *taniyāvarttanam*
see also *prastāra*, *svara prastāra*
tāla strings of the *vīṇā*
see *pakka sāraṇi*
tāla vādya kaccēri
performance (*kaccēri*) entirely dedicated to the rhythmic aspect of music (*laya*); presented by several percussion instruments (*tāla vādya*), including the *upapakkavādya* instruments; sometimes complemented by *konnakkōl*
see also *gati variants*; *layavinyāsa*
tāla variants
see *gati*, *jāti*
see also Arunagirinātar
tām
rhythmic syllable
tamas (Sanskrit) 26
lit. 'darkness'; in philosophy, *tamas guṇa* denotes gloom or sluggishness
see *guṇa*, *rajas*, *sattvam*
see also *Purāṇa*, Ramana Maharshi, *Śiva purāṇa*
tambourine 52
see *kañjīrā*
tambūrā (Sanskrit) 26, 35, 37, 43, 53, 55, 61, 124, 128, 170, Ch. 5, Fig. 5, 9, 14, Stave 4
long-necked, four-stringed and fretless lute; serves as drone; acquired prominence during the rule of Vijayarāghava Nāyaka; known as *tānpurā* in *Hindustānī* music
see also *anusāraṇi*, *cinna mēḷam*, *daṇḍi*, *ēktār*, *gettuvādyam*, *heccu śruti*, *jīvā*, *kuḍam*, *sāraṇi*, *taggu śruti*
Tamil, Tamil 10, 12, 14, 88, 161, Fig. 26, Table 2
language mainly spoken in Tamil Nadu
see also *abhinaya*, Aḍiyārkunallār, alphabet, *arubattu nāngu kalaigal*, *grantha*, literary works, poetry, poets, *śuddha mēḷa*, *veḷḷāḷar*
Tamil lyrics 171
see *pāṭṭu*
see also literary works, *meṭṭu*, poetry, *varṇameṭṭu*
Tamil Nadu [Tamil Nāḍu] 11, 224, Fig. 26
(1) the region (*nāḍu*) where Tamil literature first flourished; (2) the modern South Indian state where Tamil is the main language
see also *bhakti*, *Cōla*, *Karṇāṭaka deśa*, *ōduvār*, *Pallava*, *paṇ*, *Pāṇḍya*
tāna, *tānam* (Sanskrit) 78, 117, 118, 156, 159, Ch. 17
lit. 'protracted tone, keynote'; the pulsating, albeit non-metrical, grouping of notes and phrases; also termed *makariṇi* in the concluding part of an elaborate rāga *ālāpana* of which it can be an extension
see *anamta*, *ghana rāga*, *madhyama kāla*, *rāgam tānam pallavi*
tāna pustaka (Sanskrit)
music manual (e.g. of Gōvinda Dīkṣitar; = Tamil *kaṭakam*); contains the characteristic and admissible melodic patterns (*tāna*) for different rāgas; this covers regular phrases (*krama sañcāra*), irregular ones (*viśeṣa sañcāra*), and rare ones (*apūrva sañcāra*)
tānavarṇam (Sanskrit) 85, 154, 161, 162, 184, Ch. 17
musical form which gives a summary of the characteristic features (*sañcāra*) and peculiar phrases (*viśeṣa prayoga*) of a rāga (i.e. *rāga rūpa*)
see also *abhyāsa gāna*, *ālāpana*, *aṭa tāla varṇam*, *ciṭṭasvara*, *ettugaḍa svara*, *lakṣya*, *muktāyi*, Paccimiriyam Āḍiappayya, *padavarṇam*, *rāga rūpa*, *svarākṣara*
tāṇḍava (Sanskrit) Fig. 8
vigorous or male aspect of dance
see also Naṭarāja
taniyāvarttanam, *tani* (Tamil) 37, 47, 85,

Tirumurai
Tamil *Śaiva* canon
see *Pattupāṭṭu*
Tiruñāṉa Sambandar
Tamil poet and *Śaiva* saint; one of the three principal authors (*mūvar*) of the *Tēvāram* hymns (approx. 7th c. AD); a younger contemporary of Appar
Tirunāvukkarasar, Tirunāvukkarasu
see Appar
Tirunīlakaṇṭha Nāyaṉār, Sambandar 89, Fig. 27
famous *yāḻ* player (*yālpāṇar*)
see also *yāḻmuri paṇ*
Tirupati
important temple town and centre of pilgrimage in southern Andhra Pradesh; associated with Annamācārya, Kanaka Dāsa, Vidyala Nārāyaṇasvāmi Naidu
Tiruppāvai (Tamil)
collection of poetry by Āṇḍāḷ
Tiruppugaḻ (Tamil) 156, 187, Ch. 17
compositions of Aruṇagirinātar
see also *sanḏam*
Tiruvācakam (Tamil)
see Māṇikkavācakar
Tiruvaiyāru Fig. 26
town near Tañjāvūr where Tyāgarāja lived and his *samādhi* is located on the banks of the Kāvēri river; the venue of an annual festival in his honour (*Tyāgarāja ārādhana*)
see also *uñchavṛtti*
Tiruvārūr 158, Fig. 26
major temple town in Tamil Nadu; the birthplace of Tyāgarāja, Śyāmā Śāstri and Muttusvāmi Dīkṣitar
Tiruvāymōli (Tamil)
the most important work by Caṭakōpaṉ
tisra gati (Sanskrit) Fig. 33
see *tisra naḍai*
tisra jāti (Sanskrit)
symbol 'I_3'
laghu section with three beats
tisra jāti tripuṭa tāla (Sanskrit)
the fifth of the seven tālas known as *sūḷādi sapta tāla*; 3 + 2 + 2 = 7 counting units (*akṣara*)
see also ādi tāla, *aṅga*, *caturaśra jāti tripuṭa tāla*, *drutam*, *laghu*
tisra naḍai
subdivision of a beat into three units (*mātrā*) per beat (*kriyā*)
see also *prastāra*, *tisra gati*
tīvra (Sanskrit)
lit. 'severe, violent, sharp, excessive' (cf. German 'dur', lit. 'hard'); (1) the higher variant of the second, third, fourth, sixth, and seventh scale degrees (*ri*, *ga*, *ma*, *dha*, *ni*); the *tīvra svaras* of Karnatic music furnish the 65th *mēḷakartā rāga* (= Mēcakalyāṇi); (2) in *Hindustānī* music, *tīvra* applies only only to *madhyama* (= *prati madhyama*); the other variable scale degrees (*ri*, *ga*, *dha*, *ni*) are either defined as *kōmal* (flat) or *śuddha* (natural, e.g. Bilāval *ṭhāṭ*)
see also enharmonic scale degrees, *kōmal-tīvra*, Mēcakalyāṇi
tīvra dha
see *catuḥśruti dhaivata*
tīvra ga
see *antara gāndhāra*
tīvra ma
see *prati madhyama*
tīvra ni
see *kākalī niṣāda*
tīvra ri
see *catuḥśruti ṛṣabha*
tīvra sāraṇi
see *heccu sāraṇi*
tōm
jati syllable; corresponds to a stroke on the *mṛdaṅgam*
tone
see microtone, modification, place, semitone, Śōbhillusaptasvara, *śruti*, *sthāna*, *svarita*, *tāṉa*, voice culture, *yāḻmuri paṇ*
tongue 66
see *rasanā*
tongueing
tutukāram (flute), *tatakāram* (*nāgasvaram*)
see also *gāyaki*
tonic, basic note 46, 61
see *ādhāra ṣaḍja*, *sa*, *ṣaḍja*
tonic solfa
see solfa, solmization
tradition 31, 33, 69, 87, 116, 160, 165

authorship of *Saṅgīta Sārāmṛta* which is regarded as the last great Sanskrit classic dealing with South Indian music theory
see also *Yakṣagāna*
Tulajājī II
Marāṭhā ruler of Tañjāvūr (1763–87); scholar and patron of the arts; credited with creating the conditions for a 'Golden Age' of Karnatic music during which the so-called 'Trinity' of composers could flourish; son and successor of Pratāpasiṁha; played the *vīṇā*, his favourite instrument; among the leading musicians at his court were Soṇṭi Veṅkaṭarāmaṇayya (*guru* of of Tyāgarāja, a *vaiṇika*), Rāma Brahmā (father of Tyāgarāja), Rāmasvāmi Dīkṣitar (father of Muttusvāmi Dīkṣitar), Subbarāyar Ōduvār (father of the Tañjāvūr Quartette), and Paccimiriyam Āḍiappayya (believed to be the guru of Śyāmā Śāstri); helped to popularize the performance of the *Mēlaṭṭūr bhāgavata mēḷam* dramas; father of Śarabhōjī II
Tumburu (Sanskrit)
celestial musician (*deva gāndharva*); depicted as playing the *gōṭṭuvādyam* in a Telugu work by Raghunātha Nāyaka (*Śṛṅgāra Sāvitrī*)
turutti, *tutti* (Tamil)
lit. 'bellows'; a bagpipe
see also *cinna mēḷam*
tuṭiyaṉ (Tamil)
drummer in ancient Tamil literature
see also *mulavu*, *paṟaiyaṉ*
tutukāram
tongueing (flute); articulating the letter '*t*' to produce a separate note or to begin a musical phrase; also used to emulate the text syllable as part of the lyrics (*sāhitya*) of a song (e.g. *kṛti*)
see also *gāyaki*, *tatakāram*
Tyāgarāja 19, 23, 49, 62, 63, 67, 88, 96, 127, 153, 155, 156, 157, 162, 169, 278, 279
see ādi tāla, *āśrama*, *asura*, *cūrṇikā*, enharmonic scale degrees, Gōvinda, *kīrtana*, *kṛti*, *māyā*, *narastuti*, *navarasa*, *Naukā Caritram*, *nindāstsuti*, *onṟarai* *eḍuppu*, *pañcaratna kṛti*, *Prahlāda Bhakti Vijayam*, Rāma, Rāma Brahmā, *Saṁgraha-Cūḍā-Maṇi*, *saṁpūrṇa paddhati*, *saṁsāra*, *saṅgati*, Śōbhillusaptasvara, *Svarārṇavam*, Tiruvaiyāru, Tiruvārūr, Trinity, Tulajājī II, *uñchavṛtti*, *Vedānta*, Veṅkaṭarāma Śāstrī, *yoga*
Tyāgarāja ārādhana
see Tiruvaiyāru, *uñchavṛtti*

U
the symbol for *anudrutam*
udātta (Sanskrit) 119
the highest of three notes used in vedic chanting
udgīta vidyā (Sanskrit)
see *Om*
uḍukkai (Tamil)
drum in (ancient) Tamil music
see also *eḍakka*
ulā (Tamil) 168
lit. a 'stroll' taken by deity through the streets (*Tiru vīdi ulā*) during a temple procession; a popular literary and musical motif
see also *Sirupuliyūr ulā*
uñchavṛtti (Sanskrit)
collecting (food) alms during a procession; a practice associated with Tyāgarāja and his disciples; re-enacted symbolically during some music festivals in his honour (*Tyāgarāja ārādhana*)
unison, unisono 37, 80
unit
see *aḍavu*, *akṣara*, *akṣara kāla*, *alagu*, *anudrutam*, *drutam*, *gati*, *jāti*, *kārvai*, *kriyā*, *laya*, *mātrā*, *māttirai*, *tāla prastāra*, *śruti*
unity 161
see Ādi Śaṅkara, *Advaita*, *Conference of the Birds*, *yoga*
universe 31
see also Ādi Śaṅkara, *ākāśa*, *Īśvara*, Jagannātha, *jagat*, *māyā*, Naṭarāja
University
see history of Karnatic music
upagāyaka (Sanskrit) 170
assistant singer in a musical discourse (*harikathā kālakṣepam*)

upāṅga rāga (Sanskrit) 95
lit. 'supplement'; a type of *janya rāga*; based on notes exclusively derived from its *mēḷakartā rāga* (i.e. devoid of *anyasvara*)
see also *bhāṣāṅga rāga*, *viśeṣa prayoga*
Upaniṣad (Sanskrit)
large body of religious texts based on *Veda*
see also Campbell, *Om*, Ādi Śaṅkara
upapakkavādyam (Sanskrit) 36, 52
secondary percussion insturment (e.g. *ghaṭam* , *kañjīrā*, *mōrsiṅg*)
upapurāṇa (Sanskrit)
see *Purāṇa*
upāsana (Sanskrit)
any form of ritual or contemplative worship
see *nādopāsanā*, *pūjā*
upaveda (Sanskrit)
sacred music being considered as an extension of the *Veda* (*i.e. gāndharva veda*)
see also *mārga saṅgīta*, *nāda*, *Nāṭya Śāstra*, vedic chanting
upper
see high
uras (Sanskrit)
lit. 'chest, breast, bosom'
see also heart
utsava, *utsavam* (Sanskrit) 12
temple festival
see also *brahmotsavam*, *ciṉṉa mēḷam*, Kerala, *mallāri*, *mēḷam*, *pañcavādya*
uttarāṅga (Sanskrit) 101
(1) the upper or second set of four notes (tetrachord) in a scale, namely middle *pa*, *dha*, and *ni*, and upper *sa* (*tāra sthāyī ṣaḍja*); (2) any of the six combinations of the higher four notes within the middle octave that underly the formation of the 72 reference scales of Karnatic music (*mēḷakartā rāga*); each combination has a mnemonic pair of syllables, not considering *pañcama* and *ṣaḍja* (i.e. *dha-na*, *dha-ni*, *dha-nu*, *dhi-ni*, *dhi-nu*, *dhu-nu*); (3) the second part (= *dvitīyāṅga*) of a complex rhythmic pattern (i.e. *kōrvai* or *muktāyi*), often slightly longer than the preceding *pūrvāṅga* (e.g. 62 + 66 *mātrā* for two *āvarta* of ādi tāla in slow tempo, instead of 64 + 64 = 128 *mātrā*); may also comprise a 'reduction' pattern (*kuraippu*); (4) the second half of the theme (*pallavi*) within a *rāgam tānam pallavi* exposition; typically shorter than the *pūrvāṅga*, namely according to the duration occupied by the elongated pivotal note (*aṟudi* or *padagarbha*)
see also *saṁvādi*

vācika abhinaya (Sanskrit)
the mode of expression (*abhinaya*) in dance and drama which involves the spoken word (*vāc*)
vādi, *vādin* (Sanskrit)
lit. 'asserting, speaking (*vādin*)'; (1) the most important note of a particular rāga (= *jīva svara*); (2) also referred to as 'sonant note' when assessing the degree of consonance (*saṁvādi*) or dissonance (*vivādī*) produced by the other notes or intervals
see also *anuvādī*
vāditra (Sanskrit)
lit. 'instrumental music'
see also *gītavāditra*, *saṅgīta*
Vaḍivēlu 53
vādya (Sanskrit) 91, Ch. 5
ancient classification of musical instruments: (1) stringed instruments or cordophones (*tata vādya*); (2) idiophones (*ghana vādya*); (3) membranophones (*avanaddha vādya*, i.e. drums); (4) wind instruments (*suṣira vādya*)
see also *Saṅgīta Sudhā*, *vāditra*, *vīṇā*
vādya trayam (Sanskrit)
three instruments (*vādya*) combined in ancient music (*vīṇā*, *veṇu*, *mṛdaṅga*)
vāggēyakāra (Sanskrit) 63, 153, 154
lit. 'word (*vāc*) singer (*geya*)'; the composer responsible for a song's musical structure (*varṇameṭṭu* or *dhātu*) as well as its lyrics (*sāhitya* or *mātu*)
see also *meṭṭu*
vāggēyakāra mudrā (Sanskrit)
composer's signature which figures in the lyrics of a song
see also *aṅkitam*, *mudrā*

Vāgīśa
see Appar
Vande Mātaram 17
vaiṇika (Sanskrit) 35, 40, 91
player of a *vīṇā*; a lutanist
see also Raghunātha Nāyaka, *vīṇāvāda*, *viṇāvādaka*
vaiṇuka (Sanskrit)
player of a flute (*veṇu*); a flautist
vairāgyam (Sanskrit)
absence of worldly desires; regarded as an indispensible virtue by many Indian philosphers, saints, and composers
Vaiṣṇava
religion based on devotion (*bhakti*) to Viṣṇu (= Kṛṣṇa, Rāma)
see Ayyaṅgār, *Bhāgavata purāṇa*, Brindavan, *Divya Prabandham*, Hari, Nārada, Nārāyaṇa, *Pallava*, Rādhā, *Śaiva*, Śrīraṅgam, *Yakṣagāna*
see also Āḻvār, Ambujam Krishna, Caṭakōpan̲, Haridāsa, Jayadēva, Mārgadarśī Śēṣayyaṅgār, Svāti Tirunāḷ
vakra prayoga (Sanskrit) 77
lit. 'bent, winding, indirect'; a melodic pattern (*prayoga*) going 'zigzag' rather than taking a regular or straight course (*krama*); extraordinary phrase (*viśeṣa prayoga*) permitted in some other rāgas
vakra rāga (Sanskrit) 95, 124, Ch. 13
type of rāga which has a *vakra prayoga* incorporated in its *ārohaṇa-avarohaṇa*
vaḷi (Tamil)
lit. 'air, wind'; an embellishment (*gamaka*); consists of the deflection of pitch applied to an individual note (Tamil *vaḷai* = bend, curve)
Vālmīki
author of the best known version of the *Rāmāyaṇa* (Sanskrit epic)
Vāmana *avatāra* (Sanskrit)
lit. 'dwarf'; the fifth incarnation of Viṣṇu
see *Daśāvatārā*
vaṁśa (Sanskrit)
(1) lit. 'reed, pipe, bamboo' (from *va* = 'air, wind'); a flute; (2) 'family, race, dynasty'
vānaprastha (Sanskrit)
third stage in life (i.e. hermit)
see *āśrama*
Varāha *avatāra* (Sanskrit)
lit. 'boar, hog'; the third incarnation of Viṣṇu
see *Daśāvatārā*
Vārāṇasī (Sanskrit) 19
holy city on the Ganges also known as Benāres and Kāśī
see also Muttusvāmi Dīkṣitar
variable, variety
see *vikṛta*
see also *avikṛta*, enharmonic scale degrees, *laghu*, *rāgamālikā*
variation, variety 21, 22, 155, 164
see also *bheda*, *kāku*, *layavinyāsa*, *manodharma saṅgīta*, *naḍai*, *niraval*, *prastāra*, *saṅgati*, *svara kalpana*, *yati*
varja rāga, *varjya svara* 95 (Sanskrit) 8
process of 'excepting' (Sanskrit *varjam*) one or several notes or scale degrees (*svara*) with reference to a heptatonic scale (*mēḷakartā rāga*); results in a hexatonic or heptatonic scale patterns
varṇam (Sanskrit) 162, Ch. 17
from Sanskrit *varṇa* (lit. 'colour, hue, quality, class, race'); (1) a musical piece composed for the purpose of demonstrating the characteristics of a rāga (*tān̲avarṇam*); (2) a type of dance music (*padavarṇam*)
see also *abhyāsa gāna*, *anupallavi*, *aṭa tāla varṇam*, *daśavidha gamaka*, *ettugaḍa pallavi*, *mārgam*, *muktāyi*, *rāga*
see also Paccimiriyam Āḍiappayya
varṇameṭṭu (Tamil) 153
(1) the characteristic tune for a popular rāga to which various lyrics (*sāhitya*) can be sung (e.g. *bhajana*); (2) the musical structure of any composition (= *dhātu*)
see also *meṭṭu*, *vāggēyakāra*
vasanta (Sanskrit)
spring
see also cuckoo
vāstu (Sanskrit) 69
Vātāpigaṇapatim (Sanskrit) 116
vātsalya rasa (Sanskrit)
sentiment which is evocative of motherly love
vāyu (Sanskrit)
wind

vr̥ttam (Sanskrit) 187, Ch. 17
see *viruttam*
vyabhicāribhāva (Sanskrit)
ever-changing or minor collateral feelings expressed in dance and drama (= *sañcāribhāva*)

wave, waving 22
of the hand Fig. 29, Table 12
see also *drutam*, *kriyā*, *visarjita*
Western music, culture 24, 59, 70, 80, 95, 141, 165, Ch. 6
see also *dur*, Europe, history of Karnatic music, *komal*, moll, *nōṭṭusvara sāhitya*, rondo, Śarabhōjī II, Śivājī II, *śruti*, *tīvra*, violin, World Music, *yavana*
see also Muttusvāmi Dīkṣitar, Paṭṭaṇam Subrahmaṇya Ayyar
Wheeler, Sir Mortimer 11, 20
wind, wind instruments 12, 68
see *suṣira vādya*
see also bagpipe, flute, *Kumārasaṁbhava*, *Meghadūta*, *nāda*, *nāgasvaram*, *vādya*, *vaṁśa*
wonder 34
see also *adbhuta*
wood 39, 40, 43, 45, 53
see *āccāmaram*, *artocarpus integrifolia* (jackwood), *dāravī*, *kaṭṭai*, *palāmaram*, *taṭṭukal̲i*, *taṭṭuppalakai*
World, World Music 10, 13, 17, 65, 96, 168
the modern conception of music which implies that all indigenous traditions or music systems, anywhere in the world and from any period of history, offer valuable contributions to the future music of mankind; it took roots in the 1970's and largely superceded an earlier, predominantly Western or Eurocentric, orientation of music education and musicology
see also Br̥haddhvani, Jazz, *Tantra*
worship
see *ādiantavandanam*, *bhakta*, *bhakti*, *Cētulāra śr̥ṅgāramu*, *dāsa*, *iṣṭadevatā*, *nādopāsanā*, *Om*, *pūjā*

Yajurveda
see *Veda*
Yakṣagāna
(1) the Telugu plays written by or for the rulers of Tañjāvūr (e.g. Śāhajī, Tulajājī I, Vijayarāghava Nāyaka);
(2) the popular dance-drama of Karnataka; its episodes are traditionally based on *Vaiṣṇava* themes; prose texts and dialogues are often improvised by actors whose profession was originally hereditary (known as *yakṣa*)
see also *gāna*
yāl̲ (Tamil) 10, 15, 67, 89, 93, Fig. 27
ancient harp of the Tamils; a precursor of the modern *vīṇā*; played by a *yālpāṇar* (e.g. Tirunīlakaṇṭha Nāyan̲ār)
yāḷi (Sanskrit) 41, Fig. 2
mythical animal; found as decoration in temples (e.g. *Pallava* iconography) and on instruments (e.g. *vīṇā*)
yālmuri̲ paṇ (Tamil) 89, Fig. 27
archaic tune or mode (*paṇ*); believed to correspond to modern rāga Nīlāmbari which is also characterized by its need for intricate intonation; Tamil music tradition regards the advent of *yālmuri̲ paṇ* as the catalyst for the disappearance of the harp (*yāl̲*), in exchange for the more malleable technique and tone of the lute (*vīṇā*)
yālpāṇar (Tamil)
player of the *yāl̲*
see also *pāṇar*, Tirunīlakaṇṭha Nāyan̲ār
yantra (Sanskrit) 64
lit. 'instrument'; in the tradition of *Tantra*, a real or imagined linear diagram which facilitates deep medition (*dhyāna*) and concentration (e.g. a hexagram formed by two interlocking triangles); the numbers underlying each design symbolize certain divine entities, or their attributes on which to dwell (e.g. nine triangles for Śrīdevī); associated with special breathing exercises (*prāṇāyāma*)
yati (Sanskrit)
lit. 'check, stopping, guidance, pause, caesura'; a figurative arrangement; applies to groups of musical notes (*svara*), rhythmic patterns (*gati*), and text syllables (*sāhitya*); listed among the traditional 'ten features of tāla' (*tāla daśa prāṇa*); played during the concluding phase (*mōrā*, *kōrvai*) of a

rhythmic expositions (*layavinyāsa*, *taniyāvarttanam*); can also be woven into a composition (e.g. *Māye tvam yāhī*, a *kṛti* by Muttusvāmi Dīkṣitar), and also into the conclusion of a *ciṭṭasvaram* or *svara kalpana* sequence; five common *yati* varieties are derived from 'graphic' number-patterns: (1) decreasing 'like a cow's tail' (*gopuccha yati*), (2) increasing or broadening 'like a river' (*strotovaha yati*), (3) of uniform length (*sama yati*), (4) first increasing, then decreasing like the contours of a *mṛdaṅgam* (*mṛdaṅga yati*), (5) first decreasing, then increasing like the contours of a *ḍamaru* (*ḍamaru yati*); less discernible patterns are termed *viṣama yati* (lit. 'irregular, rugged')

yavana (Sanskrit) 10
lit. 'European, foreigner'; derived from 'Ionian' (i.e. Greek)

yazh see *yāḻ*

yoga (Sanskrit) 23, 26, 59, 62, 63
lit. 'yoke, union' (from *yuj*, 'to unite, harness, concentrate'); refers to a system of philosophy as well as several methods for self-development such as fixed attention (*dhāraṇā*), contemplation (*dhyāna*), deep meditation (*samādhi*), postures (*āsanam*), and breath-control (*prāṇāyāma*); expounded in the *Yoga Sūtra* of Patañjali as aiming at the 'control of the activity of one's mind'; Tyāgarāja and other major composers have pursued *yoga* through suitable music (*nāda yoga*); their aim is to combine devotion (*bhakti*) with the practice of sacred music (*nādopāsanā*), which is intended to be blissful and accessible to all; the system of modern and scientifically oriented *yoga* techniques is referred to as *hathayoga*
see also *ekāgratā*, history of Karnatic music, *mokṣa*, *mūlādhāra*, Rāmaliṅgasvāmi, *sādhanā*, *Tantra*

yogin (male), *yoginī* (female) (Sanskrit)
lit. 'ascetic, saint, magician'; a follower of *yoga* philosophy, or practitioner of a particular discipline based on it
see also *nāda*

zigzag pattern 8
see *vakra prayoga*